Treaty Series

Treaties and international agreements registered or filed and recorded with the Secretariat of the United Nations

VOLUME 3201

Recueil des Traités

Traités et accords internationaux enregistrés ou classés et inscrits au répertoire au Secrétariat de l'Organisation des Nations Unies

United Nations • Nations Unies
New York, 2025

Print ISBN: 978-92-1-003302-2
e-ISBN: 978-92-1-106846-7
ISSN: 0379-8267
e-ISSN: 2412-1495

TABLE OF CONTENTS

I

Treaties and international agreements
registered in August 2017
Nos. 54669 to 54671

ANNEX A

Ratifications, accessions, subsequent agreements, etc.,
concerning treaties and international agreements
registered in August 2017 with the Secretariat of the United Nations

TABLE DES MATIÈRES

I

Traités et accords internationaux
enregistrés en août 2017
N°s 54669 à 54671

ANNEXE A

Ratifications, adhésions, accords ultérieurs, etc.,
concernant des traités et accords internationaux
enregistrés en août 2017 au Secrétariat de l'Organisation des Nations Unies

NOTE BY THE SECRETARIAT

Under Article 102 of the Charter of the United Nations, every treaty and every international agreement entered into by any Member of the United Nations after the coming into force of the Charter shall, as soon as possible, be registered with the Secretariat and published by it. Furthermore, no party to a treaty or international agreement subject to registration which has not been registered may invoke that treaty or agreement before any organ of the United Nations. The General Assembly, by resolution 97 (I), established regulations to give effect to Article 102 of the Charter (see text of the regulations, vol. 859, p. VIII; https://treaties.un.org/Pages/Resource.aspx?path=Publication/Regulation/Page1_en.xml).

The terms "treaty" and "international agreement" have not been defined either in the Charter or in the regulations, and the Secretariat follows the principle that it acts in accordance with the position of the Member State submitting an instrument for registration that, so far as that party is concerned, the instrument is a treaty or an international agreement within the meaning of Article 102. Registration of an instrument submitted by a Member State, therefore, does not imply a judgement by the Secretariat on the nature of the instrument, the status of a party or any similar question. It is the understanding of the Secretariat that its acceptance for registration of an instrument does not confer on the instrument the status of a treaty or an international agreement if it does not already have that status, and does not confer upon a party a status which it would not otherwise have.

*

* *

NOTE DU SECRÉTARIAT

Aux termes de l'Article 102 de la Charte des Nations Unies, tout traité ou accord international conclu par un Membre des Nations Unies après l'entrée en vigueur de la Charte sera, le plus tôt possible, enregistré au Secrétariat et publié par lui. De plus, aucune partie à un traité ou accord international qui aurait dû être enregistré mais ne l'a pas été ne pourra invoquer ledit traité ou accord devant un organe de l'Organisation des Nations Unies. Par sa résolution 97 (I), l'Assemblée générale a adopté un règlement destiné à mettre en application l'Article 102 de la Charte (voir texte du règlement, vol. 859, p. IX; https://treaties.un.org/Pages/Resource.aspx?path=Publication/Regulation/Page1_fr.xml).

Les termes « traité » et « accord international » n'ont été définis ni dans la Charte ni dans le règlement, et le Secrétariat a pris comme principe de s'en tenir à la position adoptée à cet égard par l'État Membre qui a présenté l'instrument à l'enregistrement, à savoir que, en ce qui concerne cette partie, l'instrument constitue un traité ou un accord international au sens de l'Article 102. Il s'ensuit que l'enregistrement d'un instrument présenté par un État Membre n'implique, de la part du Secrétariat, aucun jugement sur la nature de l'instrument, le statut d'une partie ou toute autre question similaire. Le Secrétariat considère donc que son acceptation pour enregistrement d'un instrument ne confère pas audit instrument la qualité de traité ou d'accord international si ce dernier ne l'a pas déjà, et qu'il ne confère pas à une partie un statut que, par ailleurs, elle ne posséderait pas.

*

* *

I

Treaties and international agreements

registered in

August 2017

Nos. 54669 to 54671

Traités et accords internationaux

enregistrés en

août 2017

N°s 54669 à 54671

No. 54669

Multilateral

Minamata Convention on Mercury. Kumamoto, 10 October 2013

Entry into force: *16 August 2017, in accordance with article 31(1) , the Convention shall enter into force on the ninetieth day after the date of deposit of the fiftieth instrument of ratification, acceptance, approval or accession. For each State or regional economic integration organization that ratifies, accepts or approves this Convention or accedes thereto after the deposit of the fiftieth instrument of ratification, acceptance, approval or accession, the Convention shall enter into force on the ninetieth day after the date of deposit by such State or regional economic integration organization of its instrument of ratification, acceptance, approval or accession. Any instrument deposited by a regional economic integration organization shall not be counted as additional to those deposited by member States of that organization*

Authentic texts: *Arabic, Chinese, English, French, Russian and Spanish*

Registration with the Secretariat of the United Nations: *ex officio, 16 August 2017*

Multilatéral

Convention de Minamata sur le mercure. Kumamoto, 10 octobre 2013

Entrée en vigueur : *16 août 2017, conformément au paragraphe 1 de l'article 31, la Convention entre en vigueur le quatre-vingt-dixième jour suivant la date du dépôt du cinquantième instrument de ratification, d'acceptation, d'approbation ou d'adhésion. Pour chaque État ou organisation régionale d'intégration économique qui ratifie, accepte ou approuve la Convention, ou y adhère, après le dépôt du cinquantième instrument de ratification, d'acceptation, d'approbation ou d'adhésion, la Convention entre en vigueur le quatre vingt dixième jour suivant la date du dépôt, par cet État ou cette organisation, de son instrument de ratification, d'acceptation, d'approbation ou d'adhésion. Tout instrument déposé par une organisation régionale d'intégration économique n'est pas considéré comme venant s'ajouter aux instruments déjà déposés par les États membres de cette organisation*

Textes authentiques : *arabe, chinois, anglais, français, russe et espagnol*

Enregistrement auprès du Secrétariat de l'Organisation des Nations Unies : *d'office, 16 août 2017*

Participant	Ratification, Accession (a), Acceptance (A) and Approval (AA)		
Afghanistan	2 May	2017	a
Antigua and Barbuda	23 Sep	2016	a
Benin	7 Nov	2016	
Bolivia (Plurinational State of)	26 Jan	2016	
Botswana	3 Jun	2016	a
Bulgaria	18 May	2017	
Burkina Faso	10 Apr	2017	
Canada (with declaration)	7 Apr	2017	
Chad	24 Sep	2015	
China (with declaration)	31 Aug	2016	
Costa Rica	19 Jan	2017	
Denmark	18 May	2017	AA
Djibouti	23 Sep	2014	
Ecuador	29 Jul	2016	
European Union (with declaration)	18 May	2017	AA
Gabon	24 Sep	2014	A
Gambia	7 Nov	2016	
Ghana	23 Mar	2017	
Guinea	21 Oct	2014	
Guyana	24 Sep	2014	
Honduras	22 Mar	2017	
Hungary	18 May	2017	
Japan	2 Feb	2016	A
Jordan	12 Nov	2015	
Kuwait	3 Dec	2015	
Lesotho	12 Nov	2014	a
Liechtenstein	1 Feb	2017	a
Madagascar	13 May	2015	
Mali	27 May	2016	
Malta	18 May	2017	
Mauritania	18 Aug	2015	
Mexico	29 Sep	2015	

Participant	Ratification, Accession (a), Acceptance (A) and Approval (AA)		
Monaco	24 Sep	2014	
Mongolia	28 Sep	2015	
Netherlands (with declaration)	18 May	2017	A
Nicaragua	29 Oct	2014	
Norway (with declaration)	12 May	2017	
Panama	29 Sep	2015	
Peru (with declarations)	21 Jan	2016	
Romania	18 May	2017	
Samoa	24 Sep	2015	
Senegal	3 Mar	2016	
Seychelles (with declaration)	13 Jan	2015	
Sierra Leone	1 Nov	2016	
Swaziland	21 Sep	2016	a
Sweden	18 May	2017	
Switzerland	25 May	2016	
Togo	3 Feb	2017	
United Arab Emirates	27 Apr	2015	
United States of America (with declaration)	6 Nov	2013	A
Uruguay	24 Sep	2014	
Zambia	11 Mar	2016	

Note: The texts of the declarations and reservations are published after the list of Parties -- Les textes des déclarations et réserves sont reproduits après la liste des Parties.

Participant	Ratification, Adhésion (a), Acceptation (A) et Approbation (AA)		
Afghanistan	2 mai	2017	a
Antigua-et-Barbuda	23 sept	2016	a
Bénin	7 nov	2016	
Bolivie (État plurinational de)	26 janv	2016	
Botswana	3 juin	2016	a
Bulgarie	18 mai	2017	
Burkina Faso	10 avr	2017	
Canada (avec déclaration)	7 avr	2017	
Chine (avec déclaration)	31 août	2016	
Costa Rica	19 janv	2017	
Danemark	18 mai	2017	AA
Djibouti	23 sept	2014	
Émirats arabes unis	27 avr	2015	
Équateur	29 juil	2016	
États-Unis d'Amérique (avec déclaration)	6 nov	2013	A
Gabon	24 sept	2014	A
Gambie	7 nov	2016	
Ghana	23 mars	2017	
Guinée	21 oct	2014	
Guyana	24 sept	2014	
Honduras	22 mars	2017	
Hongrie	18 mai	2017	
Japon	2 févr	2016	A
Jordanie	12 nov	2015	
Koweït	3 déc	2015	
Lesotho	12 nov	2014	a
Liechtenstein	1er févr	2017	a
Madagascar	13 mai	2015	
Mali	27 mai	2016	
Malte	18 mai	2017	
Mauritanie	18 août	2015	
Mexique	29 sept	2015	

Participant	Ratification, Adhésion (a), Acceptation (A) et Approbation (AA)		
Monaco	24 sept	2014	
Mongolie	28 sept	2015	
Nicaragua	29 oct	2014	
Norvège (avec déclaration)	12 mai	2017	
Panama	29 sept	2015	
Pays-Bas (avec déclaration)	18 mai	2017	A
Pérou (avec déclarations)	21 janv	2016	
Roumanie	18 mai	2017	
Samoa	24 sept	2015	
Sénégal	3 mars	2016	
Seychelles (avec déclaration)	13 janv	2015	
Sierra Leone	1er nov	2016	
Suède	18 mai	2017	
Suisse	25 mai	2016	
Swaziland	21 sept	2016	a
Tchad	24 sept	2015	
Togo	3 févr	2017	
Union européenne (avec déclaration)	18 mai	2017	AA
Uruguay	24 sept	2014	
Zambie	11 mars	2016	

Declaration made upon Ratification

Déclaration faite lors de la Ratification

CANADA

CANADA

[TEXT IN ENGLISH – TEXTE EN ANGLAIS]

"Pursuant to Article 30 (5) of the Convention, Canada declares that any amendment to an annex to the Convention shall enter into force for Canada only upon the deposition of its instrument of ratification, acceptance, approval, or accession with respect thereto."

[TEXT IN FRENCH – TEXTE EN FRANÇAIS]

« En vertu de l'article 30 (5) de la Convention, le Canada déclare que tout amendement à une annexe n'entre en vigueur à son égard qu'après le dépôt de son instrument de ratification, d'acceptation ou d'approbation dudit amendement ou d'adhésion à celui-ci. »

Declaration made upon Ratification *Déclaration faite lors de la Ratification*

CHINA **CHINE**

[TEXT IN CHINESE – TEXTE EN CHINOIS]

根据《中华人民共和国香港特别行政区基本法》和《中华人民共和国澳门特别行政区基本法》，中华人民共和国政府决定本公约适用于中华人民共和国香港特别行政区和澳门特别行政区。

[TRANSLATION – TRADUCTION][1]

In accordance with the Basic Law of the Hong Kong Special Administrative Region of the People's Republic of China and the Basic Law of the Macao Special Administrative Region of the People's Republic of China, the Government of the People's Republic of China decides that the Convention applies to the Hong Kong Special Administrative Region and the Macao Special Administrative Region of the People's Republic of China.

[TRANSLATION – TRADUCTION]

Conformément aux dispositions de la Loi fondamentale de la Région administrative spéciale de Hong Kong (République populaire de Chine) et de la Loi fondamentale de la Région administrative spéciale de Macao (République populaire de Chine), le Gouvernement de la République populaire de Chine décide que la Convention s'applique à la Région administrative spéciale de Hong Kong et à la Région administrative spéciale de Macao de la République populaire de Chine.

[1] Translation provided by the Government of China – Traduction fournie par le Gouvernement de la Chine.

Declaration made upon Approval

EUROPEAN UNION

Déclaration faite lors de l'Approbation

UNION EUROPÉENNE

[TEXT IN ENGLISH – TEXTE EN ANGLAIS]

"Declaration of Competence by the European Union in accordance with Article 30 (3) of the Minamata Convention on Mercury

The following States are at present Members of the European Union: the Kingdom of Belgium, the Republic of Bulgaria, the Czech Republic, the Kingdom of Denmark, the Federal Republic of Germany, the Republic of Estonia, Ireland, the Hellenic Republic, the Kingdom of Spain, the French Republic, the Republic of Croatia, the Italian Republic, the Republic of Cyprus, the Republic of Latvia, the Republic of Lithuania, the Grand Duchy of Luxembourg, Hungary, the Republic of Malta, the Kingdom of the Netherlands, the Republic of Austria, the Republic of Poland, the Portuguese Republic, Romania, the Republic of Slovenia, the Slovak Republic, the Republic of Finland, the Kingdom of Sweden, the United Kingdom of Great Britain and Northern Ireland.

Article 30 (3) of the Minamata Convention provides: *'3. In its instrument of ratification, acceptance, approval or accession, a regional economic integration organization shall declare the extent of its competence in respect of the matters governed by this Convention. Any such organization shall also inform the Depositary, who shall in turn inform the Parties, of any relevant modification of the extent of its competence.'*

The European Union declares that, in accordance with the Treaty on the Functioning of the European Union, and in particular Article 192 (1) thereof, it is competent for entering into international agreements, and for implementing the obligations resulting therefrom, which contribute to the pursuit of the following objectives:

- preserving, protecting and improving the quality of the environment;
- protecting human health;
- prudent and rational utilisation of natural resources;
- promoting measures at international level to deal with regional or worldwide environmental problems, including climate change.

The following list of legal instruments of the Union illustrates the extent to which the Union has exercised its internal competence, in accordance with the Treaty on the Functioning of the European Union, regarding matters governed by the Minamata Convention. The Union is competent for the performance of those obligations from the Minamata Convention on Mercury regarding which the provisions of Union legal instruments, in particular those listed below, establish common rules and insofar as these common rules are affected or altered in scope by the provisions of the Minamata Convention or an act adopted in implementation thereof.

- Regulation (EU) of the European Parliament and the Council of 17 May 2017 on mercury, and repealing Regulation (EC) No 1102/2008,
- Directive 2011/65/EU of the European Parliament and the Council of 8 June 2011 on the restriction of the use of certain hazardous substances in electrical and electronic equipment (OJ L 174, 1.7.2011, p. 88),
- Directive 2006/66/EC of the European Parliament and the Council of 6 September 2006 on batteries and accumulators and waste batteries and accumulators and repealing Directive 91/157/EEC (OJ L 266, 26.9.2006, p. 1),
- Directive 2000/53/EC of the European Parliament and the Council of 18 September 2000 on end-of-life vehicles (OJ L 269, 21.10.2000, p. 34),
- Regulation (EC) 1223/2009 of the European Parliament and of the Council of 30 November 2009 on cosmetic products (OJ L 342, 22.12.2009, p. 59),
- Regulation (EC) 1907/2006 of the European Parliament and of the Council of 18 December 2006 concerning the Registration, Evaluation, Authorisation and Restriction of Chemicals (REACH), establishing a European Chemicals Agency, amending Directive 1999/45/EC and repealing Council Regulation (EEC) No 793/93 and Commission Regulation (EC) No 1488/94 as well as Council Directive 76/769/EEC and Commission Directives 91/155/EEC, 93/67/EEC, 93/105/EC and 2000/21/EC (OJ L 396, 30.12.2006, p. 1),
- Regulation (EU) 528/2012 of the European Parliament and of the Council of 22 May 2012 concerning the making available on the market and use of biocidal products (OJ L 167, 27.6.2012, p. 1),
- Regulation (EC) 1107/2009 of 21 October 2009 concerning the placing of plant protection products on the market and repealing Council Directives 79/117/EEC and 91/414/EEC (OJ L 309, 24.11.2009, p. 1),

- Council Directive 93/42/EC of 14 June 1993 concerning medical devices (OJ L 169, 12.7.1993, p. 1),
- Directive 2010/75/EU of the European Parliament and of the Council of 24 November 2010 on industrial emissions (integrated pollution prevention and control) (OJ L 334, 17.12.2010, p. 17),
- Directive 2012/18/EU of the European Parliament and of the Council of 4 July 2012 on the control of major-accident hazards involving dangerous substances, amending and subsequently repealing Council Directive 96/82/EC (OJ L 197, 24.7.2012, p. 1),
- Regulation (EC) No 166/2006 of the European Parliament and of the Council of 18 January 2006 concerning the establishment of a European Pollutant Release and Transfer Register and amending Council Directives 91/689/EEC and 96/61/EC (OJ L 33, 4.2.2006, p. 1),
- Directive 2004/107/EC of the European Parliament and of the Council of 15 December 2004 relating to arsenic, cadmium, mercury, nickel and polycyclic aromatic hydrocarbons in ambient air (OJ L 23, 26.1.2005, p. 3),
- Directive 2000/60/EC of the European Parliament and of the Council of 23 October 2000 establishing a framework for Community action in the field of water policy (OJ L 327, 22.12.2000, p. 1),
- Directive 2008/98/EC of the European Parliament and of the Council of 19 November 2008 on waste and repealing certain Directives (OJ L 312, 22.11.2008, p. 3),
- Council Directive 1999/31/EC of 26 April1999 on the landfill of waste (OJ L 182, 16.7.1999, p. 1),
- Regulation (EC) No 1013/2006 of the European Parliament and of the Council of 14 June 2006 on shipments of waste (OJ L 190, 12.7.2006, p. 1).

The exercise of competences which Member States of the European Union have transferred to the European Union pursuant to the Treaties is, by its nature, subject to continuous development. The Union therefore reserves the right to adjust this Declaration."

[TEXT IN FRENCH – TEXTE EN FRANÇAIS]

« Déclaration de compétences de l'Union européenne conformément à l'article 30, paragraphe 3, de la convention de Minamata sur le mercure

Les États membres de l'Union européenne sont actuellement: le Royaume de Belgique, la République de Bulgarie, la République tchèque, le Royaume de Danemark, la République fédérale d'Allemagne, la République d'Estonie, l'Irlande, la République hellénique, le Royaume d'Espagne, la République française, la République de Croatie, la République italienne, la République de Chypre, la République de Lettonie, la République de Lituanie, le Grand-Duché de Luxembourg, la Hongrie, la République de Malte, le Royaume des Pays-Bas, la République d'Autriche, la République de Pologne, la République portugaise, la Roumanie, la République de Slovénie, la République slovaque, la République de Finlande, le Royaume de Suède et le Royaume-Uni de Grande-Bretagne et d'Irlande du Nord.

L'article 30, paragraphe 3, de la convention de Minamata dispose: *« 3. Dans leurs instruments de ratification, d'acceptation, d'approbation ou d'adhésion, les organisations régionales d'intégration économique indiquent l'étendue de leur compétence à l'égard des questions régies par la présente Convention. En outre, ces organisations informent le Dépositaire, qui en informe à son tour les Parties, de toute modification pertinente de l'étendue de leur compétence ».*

L'Union européenne déclare que, conformément au traité sur le fonctionnement de l'Union européenne, et notamment son article 192, paragraphe 1, elle est compétente pour conclure des accords internationaux et pour faire respecter les obligations qui en découlent, en vue d'atteindre les objectifs suivants:

- la préservation, la protection et l'amélioration de la qualité de l'environnement,

- la protection de la santé des personnes,
- l'utilisation prudente et rationnelle des ressources naturelles,
- la promotion, sur le plan international, de mesures destinées à faire face aux problèmes régionaux ou planétaires de l'environnement, et en particulier la lutte contre le changement climatique.

La liste des instruments juridiques de l'Union qui figure ci-après montre dans quelle mesure l'Union a exercé sa compétence interne dans les matières régies par la convention de Minamata, conformément au traité sur le fonctionnement de l'Union européenne. L'Union est compétente pour l'exécution des obligations découlant de la convention de Minamata sur le mercure pour lesquelles des dispositions d'instruments juridiques de l'Union, notamment de ceux qui sont énumérés ci-dessous, établissent des règles communes et dans la mesure où ces règles communes pourraient être affectées ou voir leur portée altérée par les dispositions de la convention de Minamata ou par un acte adopté en application de celle-ci.

- Règlement (UE) du Parlement européen et du Conseil du 17 mai 2017 relatif au mercure et abrogeant le règlement (CE) n° 1102/2008
- Directive 2011/65/UE du Parlement européen et du Conseil du 8 juin 2011 relative à la limitation de l'utilisation de certaines substances dangereuses dans les équipements électriques et électroniques (JO L 174 du 1.7.2011, p. 88)
- Directive 2006/66/CE du Parlement européen et du Conseil du 6 septembre 2006 relative aux piles et accumulateurs ainsi qu'aux déchets de piles et d'accumulateurs et abrogeant la directive 91/157/CEE (JO L 266 du 26.9.2006, p. 1)
- Directive 2000/53/CE du Parlement européen et du Conseil du 18 septembre 2000 relative aux véhicules hors d'usage (JO L 269 du 21.10.2000, p. 34)
- Règlement (CE) n° 1223/2009 du Parlement européen et du Conseil du 30 novembre 2009 relatif aux produits cosmétiques (JO L 342 du 22.12.2009, p. 59)
- Règlement (CE) n° 1907/2006 du Parlement européen et du Conseil du 18 décembre 2006 concernant l'enregistrement, l'évaluation et l'autorisation des substances chimiques, ainsi que les restrictions applicables à ces substances (REACH), instituant une agence européenne des produits chimiques, modifiant la directive 1999/45/CE et abrogeant le règlement (CEE) n° 793/93 du Conseil et le règlement (CE) n° 1488/94 de la Commission ainsi que la directive 76/769/CEE du Conseil et les directives 91/155/CEE, 93/67/CEE, 93/105/CE et 2000/21/CE de la Commission (JO L 396 du 30.12.2006, p. 1)
- Règlement (UE) n° 528/2012 du Parlement européen et du Conseil du 22 mai 2012 concernant la mise à disposition sur le marché et l'utilisation des produits biocides (JO L 167 du 27.6.2012, p. 1)

- Règlement (CE) n° 1107/2009 du Parlement européen et du Conseil du 21 octobre 2009 concernant la mise sur le marché des produits phytopharmaceutiques et abrogeant les directives 79/117/CEE et 91/414/CEE du Conseil (JO L 309 du 24.11.2009, p. 1)

- Directive 93/42/CEE du Conseil du 14 juin 1993 relative aux dispositifs médicaux (JO L 169 du 12.7.1993, p. 1)

- Directive 2010/75/UE du Parlement européen et du Conseil du 24 novembre 2010 relative aux émissions industrielles (prévention et réduction intégrées de la pollution) (JO L 334 du 17.12.2010, p. 17)

- Directive 2012/18/UE du Parlement européen et du Conseil du 4 juillet 2012 concernant la maîtrise des dangers liés aux accidents majeurs impliquant des substances dangereuses, modifiant puis abrogeant la directive 96/82/CE du Conseil (JO L 197 du 24.7.2012, p. 1)

- Règlement (CE) n° 166/2006 du Parlement européen et du Conseil du 18 janvier 2006 concernant la création d'un registre européen des rejets et transferts de polluants et modifiant les directives 91/689/CEE et 96/61/CE du Conseil (JO L 33 du 4.2.2006, p. 1)

- Directive 2004/107/CE du Parlement européen et du Conseil du 15 décembre 2004 concernant l'arsenic, le cadmium, le mercure, le nickel et les hydrocarbures aromatiques polycycliques dans l'air ambiant (JO L 23 du 26.1.2005, p. 3)

- Directive 2000/60/CE du Parlement européen et du Conseil du 23 octobre 2000 établissant un cadre pour une politique communautaire dans le domaine de l'eau (JO L 327 du 22.12.2000, p. 1)

- Directive 2008/98/CE du Parlement européen et du Conseil du 19 novembre 2008 relative aux déchets et abrogeant certaines directives (JO L 312 du 22.11.2008, p. 3)

- Directive 1999/31/CE du Conseil du 26 avril 1999 concernant la mise en décharge des déchets (JO L 182 du 16.7.1999, p. 1)

- Règlement (CE) n° 1013/2006 du Parlement européen et du Conseil du 14 juin 2006 concernant les transferts de déchets (JO L 190 du 12.7.2006, p. 1).

L'exercice des compétences transférées à l'Union européenne par ses États membres en vertu des traités est, par nature, appelé à évoluer constamment. L'Union se réserve donc le droit d'adapter la présente déclaration. »

[TEXT IN SPANISH – TEXTE EN ESPAGNOL]

Declaración de competencia de la Unión Europea de conformidad con lo dispuesto en el artículo 30, párrafo 3, del Convenio de Minamata sobre el Mercurio

En la actualidad son miembros de la Unión Europea los Estados siguientes: el Reino de Bélgica, la República de Bulgaria, la República Checa, el Reino de Dinamarca, la República Federal de Alemania, la República de Estonia, Irlanda, la República Helénica, el Reino de España, la República Francesa, la República de Croacia, la República Italiana, la República de Chipre, la República de Letonia, la República de Lituania, el Gran Ducado de Luxemburgo, Hungría, la República de Malta, el Reino de los Países Bajos, la República de Austria, la República de Polonia, la República Portuguesa, Rumanía, la República de Eslovenia, la República Eslovaca, la República de Finlandia, el Reino de Suecia y el Reino Unido de Gran Bretaña e Irlanda del Norte.

El artículo 30, párrafo 3, del Convenio de Minamata dispone lo siguiente: *«3. En sus instrumentos de ratificación, aceptación, aprobación o adhesión, las organizaciones de integración económica regional declararán el ámbito de su competencia en relación con los asuntos regidos por el presente Convenio. Esas organizaciones también informarán al Depositario sobre cualquier modificación importante de su ámbito de competencia y este, a su vez, informará de ello a las Partes.»*

La Unión Europea declara que, en virtud del Tratado de Funcionamiento de la Unión Europea y, en particular, de su artículo 192, apartado 1, es competente para concluir acuerdos internacionales y llevar a la práctica las obligaciones que de ellos se deriven y que contribuyan a alcanzar los siguientes objetivos:

— la conservación, la protección y la mejora de la calidad del medio ambiente,

— la protección de la salud de las personas,

— la utilización prudente y racional de los recursos naturales,

— el fomento de medidas a escala internacional destinadas a hacer frente a los problemas regionales o mundiales del medio ambiente, y en particular a luchar contra el cambio climático.

La siguiente lista de instrumentos jurídicos de la Unión muestra en qué medida la Unión ha ejercido su competencia interna, de conformidad con el Tratado de Funcionamiento de la Unión Europea, en relación con las materias reguladas por el Convenio de Minamata. La Unión es competente para la ejecución de las obligaciones del Convenio de Minamata sobre el Mercurio respecto de las cuales establecen normas comunes las disposiciones de instrumentos jurídicos de la Unión, en particular los que se enumeran a continuación, y en la medida en que dichas normas comunes se ven afectadas o alteradas en su ámbito de aplicación por las disposiciones del Convenio de Minamata o de un acto adoptado en aplicación del mismo.

— Reglamento (UE) del Parlamento Europeo y del Consejo de 17 de mayo de 2017 sobre el mercurio y por el que se deroga el Reglamento (CE) n.° 1102/2008,

— Directiva 2011/65/UE del Parlamento Europeo y del Consejo, de 8 de junio de 2011, sobre restricciones a la utilización de determinadas sustancias peligrosas en aparatos eléctricos y electrónicos (DO L 174 de 1.7.2011, p. 88),

— Directiva 2006/66/CE del Parlamento Europeo y del Consejo, de 6 de septiembre de 2006, relativa a las pilas y acumuladores y a los residuos de pilas y acumuladores y por la que se deroga la Directiva 91/157/CEE (DO L 266 de 26.9.2006, p. 1),

— Directiva 2000/53/CE del Parlamento Europeo y del Consejo, de 18 de septiembre de 2000, relativa a los vehículos al final de su vida útil (DO L 269 de 21.10.2000, p. 34),

— Reglamento (CE) n.° 1223/2009 del Parlamento Europeo y del Consejo, de 30 de noviembre de 2009, sobre los productos cosméticos (DO L 342 de 22.12.2009, p. 59),

— Reglamento (CE) n.° 1907/2006 del Parlamento Europeo y del Consejo, de 18 de diciembre de 2006, relativo al registro, la evaluación, la autorización y la restricción de las sustancias y mezclas químicas (REACH), por el que se crea la Agencia Europea de Sustancias y Mezclas Químicas, se modifica la Directiva 1999/45/CE y se derogan el Reglamento (CEE) n.° 793/93 del Consejo y el Reglamento (CE) n.° 1488/94 de la Comisión, así como la Directiva 76/769/CEE del Consejo y las Directivas 91/155/CEE, 93/67/CEE, 93/105/CE y 2000/21/CE de la Comisión (DO L 396 de 30.12.2006, p. 1).

— Reglamento (UE) n.º 528/2012 del Parlamento Europeo y del Consejo, de 22 de mayo de 2012, relativo a la comercialización y el uso de los biocidas (DO L 167 de 27.6.2012, p. 1),

— Reglamento (CE) n.º 1107/2009 del Parlamento Europeo y del Consejo, de 21 de octubre de 2009, relativo a la comercialización de productos fitosanitarios y por el que se derogan las Directivas 79/117/CEE y 91/414/CEE del Consejo (DO L 309 de 24.11.2009, p. 1),

— Directiva 93/42/CEE del Consejo, de 14 de junio de 1993, relativa a los productos sanitarios (DO L 169 de 12.7.1993, p. 1),

— Directiva 2010/75/UE del Parlamento Europeo y del Consejo, de 24 de noviembre de 2010, sobre las emisiones industriales (prevención y control integrados de la contaminación) (DO L 334 de 17.12.2010, p. 17),

— Directiva 2012/18/UE del Parlamento Europeo y del Consejo, de 4 de julio de 2012, relativa al control de los riesgos inherentes a los accidentes graves en los que intervengan sustancias peligrosas y por la que se modifica y ulteriormente deroga la Directiva 96/82/CE (DO L 197 de 24.7.2012, p. 1),

— Reglamento (CE) n.º 166/2006 del Parlamento Europeo y del Consejo, de 18 de enero de 2006, relativo al establecimiento de un registro europeo de emisiones y transferencias de contaminantes y por el que se modifican las Directivas 91/689/CEE y 96/61/CE del Consejo (DO L 33 de 4.2.2006, p. 1),

— Directiva 2004/107/CE del Parlamento Europeo y del Consejo, de 15 de diciembre de 2004, relativa al arsénico, el cadmio, el mercurio, el níquel y los hidrocarburos aromáticos policíclicos en el aire ambiente (DO L 23 de 26.1.2005, p. 3),

— Directiva 2000/60/CE del Parlamento Europeo y del Consejo, de 23 de octubre de 2000, por la que se establece un marco comunitario de actuación en el ámbito de la política de aguas (DO L 327 de 22.12.2000, p. 1),

— Directiva 2008/98/CE del Parlamento Europeo y del Consejo, de 19 de noviembre de 2008, sobre los residuos y por la que se derogan determinadas Directivas (DO L 312 de 22.11.2008, p. 3),

— Directiva 1999/31/CE del Consejo, de 26 de abril de 1999, relativa al vertido de residuos (DO L 182 de 16.7.1999, p. 1),

— Reglamento (CE) n.° 1013/2006 del Parlamento Europeo y del Consejo, de 14 de junio de 2006, relativo a los traslados de residuos (DO L 190 de 12.7.2006, p. 1).

El ejercicio de las competencias transferidas a la Unión Europea por sus Estados miembros en virtud de los Tratados está sujeto, por su propia naturaleza, a continua evolución. Por consiguiente, la Unión Europea se reserva el derecho de adaptar la presente declaración.

Declaration made upon Acceptance *Déclaration faite lors de l'Acceptation*

NETHERLANDS **PAYS-BAS**

[TEXT IN ENGLISH – TEXTE EN ANGLAIS]

"The Kingdom of the Netherlands declares, in accordance with Article 25, paragraph 2, of the Minamata Convention on Mercury, that it accepts both means of dispute settlement referred to in that paragraph as compulsory in relation to any Party accepting one or both means of dispute settlement."

[TRANSLATION – TRADUCTION]

Le Royaume des Pays-Bas déclare, conformément au paragraphe 2 de l'article 25 de la Convention de Minamata sur le mercure, qu'il accepte comme obligatoires les deux moyens de règlement des différends visés à ce paragraphe, à l'égard de toute Partie acceptant l'un des deux ou les deux moyens de règlement des différends.

Declaration made upon Ratification *Déclaration faite lors de la Ratification*

NORWAY **NORVÈGE**

[TEXT IN ENGLISH – TEXTE EN ANGLAIS]

"In accordance with Article 25, paragraph 2 of the Convention, Norway hereby declares (b) Submission of the dispute to the International Court of Justice."

[TRANSLATION – TRADUCTION]

Conformément au paragraphe 2 de l'article 25 de la Convention, la Norvège déclare par la présente (b) La saisine de la Cour internationale de Justice.

Declarations made upon Ratification | *Déclarations faites lors de la Ratification*

PERU | **PÉROU**

[TEXT IN SPANISH – TEXTE EN ESPAGNOL]

"En ejercicio del derecho a formular declaraciones o comunicaciones permitidas por el Convenio y en relación con lo dispuesto en el artículo 25°, numeral 2, la República del Perú desea poner en conocimiento de las Partes la Declaración que formulara en fecha 7 de julio de 2003, la misma que se transcribe a continuación, efectuada bajo el párrafo 2 del artículo 36° del Estatuto de la Corte Internacional de Justicia, según la cual se reconoce como obligatoria ipso facto, sin necesidad de un convenio especial y respecto a cualquier otra Parte que acepte la misma obligación, sujeto a la condición de reciprocidad: la jurisdicción de la Corte Internacional de Justicia en todas las controversias de orden jurídico.

Dicha Declaración, no obsta la posibilidad de recurrir al mecanismo arbitral o de conciliación previstos en el Convenio (Anexo E), para el asunto controvertido, si con la otra (s) parte (s) en la controversia así se conviniera por escrito.

Lo señalado en la presente Declaración no impide a las Partes resolver la controversia mediante negociación directa o cualquier otro medio de solución de controversias reconocido por el presente Convenio".

"En ejercicio del derecho a formular declaraciones o comunicaciones permitidas por el Convenio y en relación con lo dispuesto en el artículo 30°, numeral 5, la República del Perú declara que con respecto a ella, una enmienda de un anexo sólo entrará en vigor una vez que haya depositado su instrumento de ratificación, aceptación, aprobación o adhesión con respecto a dicha enmienda".

[TRANSLATION – TRADUCTION]

- Declaration under article 25 (2)

In exercise of the right to make the declarations or communications permitted under the Convention and in relation to article 25, paragraph 2, the Republic of Peru wishes to bring to the attention of the parties the declaration that it made on 7 July 2003 [...] which was made under Article 36, paragraph 2, of the Statute of the International Court of Justice, pursuant to which the Republic of Peru recognizes as compulsory ipso facto and without special agreement, in relation to any other party accepting the same obligation, subject to the condition of reciprocity, the jurisdiction of the International Court of Justice in all legal disputes.

Such declaration does not preclude the possibility of recourse to the arbitration and conciliation procedures established in the Convention (annex E) for the matter disputed if the other party or parties to the dispute agree to such in writing.

The present declaration does not prevent the parties from settling the dispute through direct negotiation or any other means of settlement recognized by the Convention.

- Declaration under article 30 (5)

In exercise of the right to make the declarations or communications permitted under the Convention and in relation to article 30, paragraph 5, the Republic of Peru declares that, with regard to it, any amendment to an annex shall enter into force only upon the deposit of its instrument of ratification, acceptance, approval or accession with respect thereto.

[TRANSLATION – TRADUCTION]

- Déclaration conformément au paragraphe 2 de l'article 25

Dans l'exercice de son droit de faire des déclarations ou communications autorisées par la Convention et en application des dispositions du paragraphe 2 de l'article 25 de ladite Convention, la République du Pérou souhaite porter à la connaissance des Parties la déclaration [...] qu'elle a faite le 7 juillet 2003 en vertu du paragraphe 2 de l'article 36 du Statut de la Cour internationale de Justice et dans laquelle elle a reconnu comme obligatoire de plein droit et sans convention spéciale, à l'égard de tout autre État acceptant la même obligation, c'est-à-dire sous condition de réciprocité, la juridiction de la Cour internationale de Justice pour la résolution de tous les différends d'ordre juridique.

Ladite déclaration n'empêche pas le recours aux procédures d'arbitrage et de conciliation prévues par la Convention (Annexe E) en cas de différend, pourvu qu'il en soit ainsi convenu par écrit avec l'autre partie ou les autres parties au différend.

La teneur de la présente déclaration n'empêche pas les parties de régler un différend par voie de négociation directe ou par tout autre moyen de règlement des différends reconnu par la Convention.

- Déclaration conformément au paragraphe 5 de l'article 30

Dans l'exercice de son droit de faire des déclarations ou communications autorisées par la Convention et en application des dispositions du paragraphe 5 de l'article 30 de ladite Convention, la République du Pérou déclare que tout amendement à une annexe n'entre en vigueur à son égard qu'après le dépôt de son instrument de ratification, d'acceptation ou d'approbation dudit amendement ou d'adhésion à celui-ci.

Declaration made upon Ratification

SEYCHELLES

Déclaration faite lors de la Ratification

SEYCHELLES

[TEXT IN ENGLISH – TEXTE EN ANGLAIS]

"... in accordance with Article 30 (5) of the Convention, [...] any amendment to an annex to the Convention shall enter into force for the Republic of Seychelles only upon the deposit of its instrument of ratifications, acceptance, approval, or accession with respect thereto."

[TRANSLATION – TRADUCTION]

... conformément au paragraphe 5 de l'article 30 de la Convention, [...] tout amendement à une annexe à la Convention n'entrera en vigueur pour la République des Seychelles qu'après le dépôt de son instrument de ratification, d'acceptation d'approbation ou d'adhésion à celui-ci.

Declaration made upon Acceptance

UNITED STATES OF AMERICA

Déclaration faite lors de l'Acceptation

ÉTATS-UNIS D'AMÉRIQUE

[TEXT IN ENGLISH – TEXTE EN ANGLAIS]

"The United States hereby declares, pursuant to Article 30, paragraph 5, that any amendment to an annex to the Convention shall enter into force for the United States only upon the deposit of its instrument of ratification, acceptance, approval, or accession with respect thereto."

[TRANSLATION – TRADUCTION]

Conformément au paragraphe 5 de l'article 30, les États-Unis déclarent, par la présente, que tout amendement à une annexe à la Convention n'entrera en vigueur pour les États-Unis qu'après le dépôt de son instrument de ratification, d'acceptation ou d'approbation dudit amendement ou d'adhésion à celui-ci.

المادة ٦

١ - يجوز لهيئة التوفيق أن تدير إجراءات التوفيق بالطريقة التي تراها مناسبة، واضعة في الاعتبار على نحو كامل ظروف القضية والآراء التي قد يعرب عنها طرفا المنازعة، بما في ذلك أي طلب لتسوية سريعة. ويجوز لها أن تعتمد نظامها الداخلي حسب الضرورة، ما لم يتفق الطرفان على خلاف ذلك.

٢ - يجوز لهيئة التوفيق، في أي وقت أثناء الإجراءات، أن تطرح مقترحات أو توصيات لتسوية المنازعة.

المادة ٧

يتعاون طرفا المنازعة مع هيئة التوفيق. ويسعيا بوجه خاص إلى الامتثال لطلبات الهيئة تقديم مواد خطية، وتقديم الأدلة، وحضور الاجتماعات. وعلى الطرفين وأعضاء هيئة التوفيق الالتزام بحماية سرية أي معلومات أو مستندات يحصلون عليها بشكل سري أثناء إجراءات الهيئة.

المادة ٨

تتخذ هيئة التوفيق قراراتها بأغلبية أصوات أعضائها.

المادة ٩

تقدم هيئة التوفيق تقريراً يتضمن توصيات لتسوية المنازعة في موعد أقصاه اثني عشر شهراً من اكتمال إنشائها، وينظر فيه طرفا المنازعة بحسن نية، ما لم تكن المنازعة قد تمت تسويتها بالفعل.

المادة ١٠

تبت هيئة التحكيم في أي خلاف بشأن ما إذا كان لديها اختصاص النظر في مسألة أحيلت إليها.

المادة ١١

يتحمل طرفا المنازعة بالتساوي تكاليف هيئة التحكيم، ما لم يتفقا على خلاف ذلك. وتحتفظ الهيئة بسجل بجميع تكاليفها وتقدم إقراراً نهائياً بشأن تلك التكاليف إلى الطرفين.

الجزء الثاني: إجراءات التوفيق

تكون إجراءات التوفيق لأغراض الفقرة ٦ من المادة ٢٥ من الاتفاقية على النحو التالي:

المادة ١

يوجّه أي طرف في منازعة طلباً خطياً إلى الأمانة لإنشاء هيئة توفيق عملاً بالفقرة ٦ من المادة ٢٥ من هذه الاتفاقية، وتوجه نسخة منه إلى الطرف الآخر أو الأطراف الأخرى في المنازعة. وتبلغ الأمانة عندئذ جميع الأطراف بذلك.

المادة ٢

١ - تتألف هيئة التوفيق من ثلاثة أعضاء، ما لم يتفق طرفا المنازعة على خلاف ذلك، ويعين كل طرف معني أحدهم، ويعين رئيس للهيئة يختاره هذان العضوان بصورة مشتركة.

٢ - في المنازعات التي تنشأ بين أكثر من طرفين، تعيّن الأطراف التي لها نفس المصلحة عضوها في الهيئة بصورة مشتركة وبالاتفاق فيما بينها.

المادة ٣

إذا لم تتم أي تعيينات من قِبَل الطرفين في غضون شهرين من تاريخ استلام الأمانة الطلب الخطي المشار إليه في المادة ١ أعلاه، يجري الأمين العام للأمم المتحدة، بناء على طلب أي طرف، تلك التعيينات في غضون فترة إضافية مدتها شهران.

المادة ٤

إذا لم يتم اختيار رئيس هيئة التوفيق في غضون شهرين من تعيين العضو الثاني في الهيئة، يعيّن الأمين العام للأمم المتحدة الرئيس، بناء على طلب أي طرف في المنازعة، في غضون فترة إضافية مدتها شهران.

المادة ٥

تساعد هيئة التوفيق طرفي المنازعة بطريقة مستقلة ومحايدة في محاولاتهما التوصل إلى تسوية ودية للمنازعة.

٢ - يجب على هيئة التحكيم، قبل إصدار قرارها النهائي، أن تتأكد من أن للادعاء سنداً راسخاً من حيث الواقع والقانون.

المادة ١٤

تصدر المحكمة قرارها النهائي في غضون خمسة أشهر من التاريخ الذي تشكلت فيه بالكامل ما لم تجد أن من الضروري تمديد تلك المهلة الزمنية لفترة ينبغي ألا تتجاوز خمسة أشهر إضافية.

المادة ١٥

يقتصر القرار النهائي لهيئة التحكيم على موضوع المنازعة ويذكر الأسباب التي استند إليها. ويتضمن أسماء الأعضاء الذين شاركوا وتاريخ القرار النهائي. ويجوز لأي عضو من أعضاء الهيئة أن يلحق بالقرار النهائي رأياً مستقلاً أو مخالفاً.

المادة ١٦

يكون القرار ملزماً لطرفي المنازعة. ويكون تفسير الاتفاقية الوارد في القرار النهائي ملزماً أيضاً للطرف الذي يتدخل بموجب المادة ١٠ أعلاه بقدر ما يتعلق بالأمور التي تدخّل ذلك الطرف بشأنها. ويكون القرار النهائي غير قابل للاستئناف إلا إذا اتفق طرفا المنازعة مسبقاً على إجراء استئنافي.

المادة ١٧

أي خلاف قد ينشأ بين الملزمين بالقرار النهائي وفقاً للمادة ١٦ أعلاه، بشأن تفسير ذلك القرار أو طريقة تنفيذه، يجوز أن يعرضه أي منهم على هيئة التحكيم التي أصدرته لكي تبت فيه.

المادة ٨

يقع على طرفي المنازعة وعلى المحكّمين الالتزام بحماية سرية أي معلومات أو مستندات يحصلون عليها بشكل سري أثناء إجراءات هيئة التحكيم.

المادة ٩

يتحمل طرفا المنازعة بحصتين متساويتين تكاليف هيئة التحكيم، ما لم تقرر الهيئة خلاف ذلك بسبب الظروف الخاصة للقضية. وتحتفظ الهيئة بسجل لجميع تكاليفها وتقدم إقراراً نهائياً بشأنها إلى الطرفين.

المادة ١٠

يجوز لطرف له مصلحة ذات طابع قانوني في موضوع المنازعة قد تتأثر بالقرار الذي يُتخذ في القضية أن يتدخل في الإجراءات بموافقة هيئة التحكيم.

المادة ١١

يجوز لهيئة التحكيم أن تستمع إلى ادعاءات مضادة ناشئة مباشرة عن موضوع المنازعة وأن تبت فيها.

المادة ١٢

تُتخذ قرارات هيئة التحكيم بشأن كل من الإجراءات والمضمون بأغلبية أصوات أعضائها.

المادة ١٣

١ - إذا لم يمثُل أحد طرفي المنازعة أمام هيئة التحكيم أو لم يدافع عن قضيته يجوز للطرف الآخر أن يطلب من الهيئة أن تواصل الإجراءات وأن تصدر قرارها. ولا يشكل غياب طرف أو عدم دفاع طرف عن قضيته عائقاً أمام الإجراءات.

المادة ٣

١ - إذا لم يعيّن أحد طرفي المنازعة محكّماً في غضون شهرين من التاريخ الذي يتلقى فيه الطرف المدعى عليه إخطار التحكيم، يجوز للطرف الآخر أن يُخطر الأمين العام للأمم المتحدة، الذي يجب عليه أن يقوم بعملية التعيين في غضون فترة إضافية مدتها شهران.

٢ - إذا لم يعيّن رئيس هيئة التحكيم في غضون شهرين من تاريخ تعيين المحكّم الثاني، يقوم الأمين العام للأمم المتحدة، بناء على طلب أحد الطرفين، بتعيين الرئيس في غضون فترة إضافية مدتها شهران.

المادة ٤

تصدر هيئة التحكيم قراراتها وفقاً لأحكام هذه الاتفاقية والقانون الدولي.

المادة ٥

تقرر هيئة التحكيم نظامها الداخلي، ما لم يقرر طرفا المنازعة خلاف ذلك.

المادة ٦

يجوز لهيئة التحكيم، بناء على طلب أحد الطرفين، أن توصي بتدابير مؤقتة أساسية للحماية.

المادة ٧

ييسر طرفا المنازعة عمل هيئة التحكيم ويقومان، بوجه خاص، وباستخدام جميع الوسائل الموجودة تحت تصرفهما، بما يلي:

(أ) تزويدها بجميع المستندات والمعلومات والتسهيلات ذات الصلة؛

(ب) تمكينها، عند الاقتضاء، من استدعاء شهود أو خبراء وتلقي أدلتهم.

المرفق هاء

إجراءات التحكيم والتوفيق

الجزء الأول: إجراءات التحكيم

تكون إجراءات التحكيم لأغراض الفقرة ٢ (أ) من المادة ٢٥ من الاتفاقية على النحو التالي:

المادة ١

١ - يجوز لأي طرف أن يشرع في اللجوء إلى التحكيم وفقاً للمادة ٢٥ من هذه الاتفاقية بتوجيه إخطار خطي إلى الطرف الآخر أو الأطراف الأخرى في المنازعة. ويكون الإخطار مشفوعاً ببيان الادعاء، إلى جانب أي مستندات داعمة، ويذكر الإخطار موضوع التحكيم ويشمل، بوجه خاص، مواد الاتفاقية المتنازع على تفسيرها أو تطبيقها.

٢ - يُخطر الطرف المدعي الأمانة بأنه يحيل منازعة للتحكيم عملاً بالمادة ٢٥ من هذه الاتفاقية. ويكون الإخطار مشفوعاً بالإخطار الخطي المقدم من الطرف المدعي، وبيان الادعاء، والمستندات الداعمة المشار إليها في الفقرة ١ أعلاه. وتحيل الأمانة المعلومات التي تتلقاها بذلك إلى جميع الأطراف.

المادة ٢

١ - إذا أحيلت منازعة للتحكيم وفقاً للمادة ١ أعلاه، تُنشأ هيئة تحكيم. وتتألف الهيئة من ثلاثة أعضاء.

٢ - يعين كل طرف في المنازعة محكّماً ويعيّن المحكمّان اللذان يتم تعيينهما على هذا النحو وبالاتفاق المشترك بينهما المحكّم الثالث، الذي يصبح رئيس هيئة التحكيم. وفي المنازعات بين أكثر من طرفين، تعين الأطراف التي لها نفس المصلحة محكّماً واحداً بصورة مشتركة بالاتفاق فيما بينها. ولا يكون رئيس هيئة التحكيم من مواطني أي من أطراف المنازعة، ولا يكون محل إقامته المعتاد على أراضي أي من هذه الأطراف، ولا يعمل لدى أي منها، ولا يكون قد نظر في القضية بأي صفة أخرى.

٣ - يُملأ أي شاغر على النحو الموصوف للتعيين الأولي.

المرفق دال

قائمة بالمصادر الثابتة لانبعاثات الزئبق ومركباته في الغلاف الجوي

فئة المصادر الثابتة:

محطات توليد الطاقة التي تعمل بالفحم الحجري؛

المراجل الصناعية التي تعمل بالفحم الحجري؛

عمليات الصهر والشوي المستخدمة في إنتاج المعادن غير الحديدية[1]؛

مرافق ترميد النفايات؛

مرافق إنتاج خبث الإسمنت.

(١) لأغراض هذا المرفق، تشير ''المعادن غير الحديدية'' إلى الرصاص والزنك والنحاس والذهب الصناعي.

(ح) استراتيجية للصحة العامة بشأن تعرض الحرفيين والمشتغلين بتعدين الذهب الضيق النطاق ومجتمعاتهم المحلية للزئبق. وينبغي أن تتضمن هذه الاستراتيجية جملة أمور، من بينها جمع البيانات الصحية، وتدريب المشتغلين بالرعاية الصحية، والتوعية من خلال المرافق الصحية؛

(ط) استراتيجيات لمنع تعرض الفئات السكانية الضعيفة للزئبق المستخدم في تعدين الذهب الحرفي والضيق النطاق، لا سيما الأطفال والنساء في سن الإنجاب، وبخاصة النساء الحوامل؛

(ي) استراتيجيات لتوفير المعلومات للحرفيين والمشتغلين بتعدين الذهب الضيق النطاق والمجتمعات المحلية المتضررة؛

(ك) جدول زمني لتنفيذ خطة العمل الوطنية.

٢ - يجوز لكل طرف أن يدرج في خطة عمله الوطنية استراتيجيات إضافية لتحقيق أهدافه، منها استخدام أو تطبيق معايير لتعدين الذهب الحرفي والضيق النطاق دون استخدام الزئبق، وآليات قائمة على الأسواق، أو أدوات للتسويق.

المرفق جيم

تعدين الذهب الحرفي والضيق النطاق

خطط العمل الوطنية

١ - يدرج كل طرف يخضع لأحكام الفقرة ٣ من المادة ٧ في خطة عمله الوطنية ما يلي:

(أ) أهداف وطنية ونسب تخفيض مستهدفة؛

(ب) إجراءات لإنهاء:

'١' ملغمة الركاز الكاملة؛

'٢' الحرق المكشوف للملغم أو للملغم المعالج؛

'٣' حرق الملغم في مناطق سكنية؛

'٤' رشح السيانيد في الرواسب أو الركاز أو النفايات التي أضيف لها الزئبق دون إزالة الزئبق أولاً؛

(ج) خطوات تيّسر إضفاء طابع رسمي على قطاع تعدين الذهب الحرفي والضيق النطاق أو تنظيمه؛

(د) تقديرات أساسية لكميات الزئبق المستخدمة وللممارسات المستخدمة في تعدين وتصنيع الذهب الحرفي والضيق النطاق على أراضيه؛

(هـ) استراتيجيات لتشجيع الحد من انبعاثات وإطلاقات الزئبق، والتعرض له، في تعدين وتصنيع الذهب الحرفيين والضيقي النطاق، بما في ذلك الطرائق التي لا تستخدم الزئبق؛

(و) استراتيجيات لإدارة التجارة ومنع تحويل وجهة الزئبق ومركبات الزئبق القادمة من مصادر خارجية ومحلية لاستخدامها في تعدين وتصنيع الذهب الحرفيين والضيقي النطاق؛

(ز) استراتيجيات لإشراك أصحاب المصلحة في تنفيذ خطة العمل الوطنية ومواصلة تطويرها؛

عملية التصنيع باستخدام الزئبق	الأحكام
ميثلات أو إيثيلات الصوديوم أو البوتاسيوم	تتخذ الأطراف تدابير تشمل على نحو غير حصري ما يلي: '١' تدابير لخفض استخدام الزئبق بهدف التخلص التدريجي من هذا الاستخدام بأسرع وقت ممكن وخلال ١٠ سنوات من دخول الاتفاقية حيِّز النفاذ؛ '٢' خفض الانبعاثات والإطلاقات من حيث إنتاج الوحدة بنسبة ٥٠ في المائة بحلول عام ٢٠٢٠ مقارَنة بعام ٢٠١٠؛ '٣' حظر استخدام الزئبق الخام من التعدين الأوّلي؛ '٤' دعم البحث والتطوير فيما يتعلق بالعمليات الخالية من الزئبق؛ '٥' عدم السماح باستخدام الزئبق بعد خمس سنوات من التاريخ الذي يتحقق فيه مؤتمر الأطراف من أن العمليات الخالية من الزئبق أصبحت مجدية من الناحيتين الاقتصادية والتقنية؛ '٦' إبلاغ مؤتمر الأطراف بالجهود المبذولة لتطوير و/أو تحديد بدائل والتخلص التدريجي من استخدام الزئبق عملاً بالمادة ٢١.
إنتاج البوليوريثان باستخدام محفزات تحتوي على الزئبق	تتخذ الأطراف تدابير تشمل على نحو غير حصري ما يلي: '١' اتخاذ تدابير للحدّ من استخدام الزئبق، بهدف التخلّص التدريجي من هذا الاستخدام في أسرع وقت ممكن، وخلال ١٠ سنوات من دخول الاتفاقية حيِّز النفاذ؛ '٢' اتخاذ تدابير للحد من الاعتماد على الزئبق الناتج عن تعدين الزئبق الأوّلي؛ '٣' اتخاذ تدابير للحدّ من انبعاثات وإطلاقات الزئبق في البيئة؛ '٤' تشجيع البحث والتطوير فيما يتعلّق بالمحفِّزات والعمليات الخالية من الزئبق؛ '٥' إبلاغ مؤتمر الأطراف بالجهود المبذولة لتطوير و/أو تحديد بدائل والتخلّص التدريجي من استخدام الزئبق عملاً بالمادة ٢١. لا تنطبق الفقرة ٦ من المادة ٥ على عملية التصنيع هذه.

المرفق باء

عمليات التصنيع التي يستخدم فيها الزئبق أو مركبات الزئبق

الجزء الأول: العمليات الخاضعة للفقرة ٢ من المادة ٥

عمليات التصنيع التي يُستخدم فيها الزئبق أو مركّبات الزئبق	تاريخ التخلُّص
إنتاج الكلور والقلويات	٢٠٢٥
إنتاج الأسيتالدهيد الذي يُستخدم فيه الزئبق أو مركبات الزئبق كمحفز	٢٠١٨

الجزء الثاني: العمليات الخاضعة للفقرة ٣ من المادة ٥

عملية التصنيع باستخدام الزئبق	الأحكام
إنتاج مونومر كلوريد الفينيل	تتخذ الأطراف تدابير تشمل على نحو غير حصري ما يلي: '١' خفض استخدام الزئبق من حيث إنتاج الوحدة بنسبة ٥٠ في المائة بحلول عام ٢٠٢٠ مقارنة باستخدام عام ٢٠١٠؛ '٢' تعزيز التدابير الرامية إلى الحد من الاعتماد على الزئبق المنتج من عمليات التعدين الأولي؛ '٣' اتخاذ تدابير للحدّ من انبعاثات وإطلاقات الزئبق في البيئة؛ '٤' دعم البحث والتطوير فيما يتعلق بالمواد الحافزة والعمليات الخالية من الزئبق؛ '٥' عدم السماح باستخدام الزئبق بعد خمس سنوات من التاريخ الذي يتحقق فيه مؤتمر الأطراف من أن المحفّزات الخالية من الزئبق استناداً إلى العمليات القائمة قد أصبحت مجدية من الناحيتين الاقتصادية والتقنية؛ '٦' إبلاغ مؤتمر الأطراف بشأن جهوده لتطوير و/أو تحديد بدائل والتخلص التدريجي من استخدام الزئبق عملاً بالمادة ٢١.

الجزء الثاني: المنتجات الخاضعة للفقرة ٣ من المادة ٤

المنتجات المضاف إليها الزئبق	الأحكام
ملاغم الأسنان	تراعي التدابير التي يتخذها الطرف للتخلص التدريجي من استعمال ملاغم الأسنان الظروف الداخلية للطرف المعني والتوجيهات الدولية ذات الصلة، وتشمل تدبيرين اثنين أو أكثر من التدابير المدرجة في القائمة التالية: '١' وضع أهداف وطنية ترمي إلى الجمع بين الوقاية من تسوُّس الأسنان وتعزيز الصحة، وبذلك تقلل الحاجة إلى تصليح الأسنان؛ '٢' وضع أهداف وطنية ترمي إلى تقليل استعمالها؛ '٣' تشجيع استعمال بدائل خالية من الزئبق فعّالة من حيث التكلفة وفعّالة إكلينيكياً لتصليح الأسنان؛ '٤' تشجيع البحث والتطوير للمواد الجيدة الخالية من الزئبق المستخدمة في تصليح الأسنان؛ '٥' تشجيع المنظمات المهنية التمثيلية ومدارس طب الأسنان على تعليم وتدريب المهنيين والطلاب في طب الأسنان على استعمال بدائل خالية من الزئبق لتصليح الأسنان، وتشجيع أفضل الممارسات الإدارية؛ '٦' عدم تشجيع بوالص وبرامج التأمين التي تفضل استعمال الملاغم لتصليح الأسنان بدلاً من استعمال مواد خالية من الزئبق؛ '٧' تشجيع بوالص وبرامج التأمين التي تفضل استعمال بدائل جيدة للملاغم في تصليح الأسنان؛ '٨' حصر استعمال الملاغم على شكلها الحويصلي؛ '٩' تشجيع استعمال أفضل الممارسات البيئية في مرافق طب الأسنان للحد من إطلاقات الزئبق ومركّبات الزئبق في المياه والأراضي.

المنتجات المضاف إليها الزئبق	التاريخ الذي لن يُسمح بعده بتصنيع المنتج أو استيراده أو تصديره (تاريخ التخلص)
مصابيح الفلورسنت الأفقية لأغراض الإنارة العامة: (أ) مصابيح الفلورسنت الثلاثية الشريط < ٦٠ واط ويزيد ما تحتوي عليه من الزئبق عن ٥ ملغ لكل مصباح (ب) مصابيح فوسفور الهالوفوسفات ≤ ٤٠ واط وما تحتويه من الزئبق يزيد عن ١٠ ملغ لكل مصباح	٢٠٢٠
المصابيح التي تعمل بالضغط المرتفع لبخار الزئبق وتُستعمل لأغراض الإنارة الشاملة	٢٠٢٠
الزئبق في مصابيح الفلورسنت ذات المهبط البارد للوحات العرض الإلكترونية: (أ) القصيرة (≤ ٥٠٠ ملم) ويزيد ما تحتوي عليه من الزئبق عن ٣،٥ ملغ لكل مصباح (ب) المتوسطة الطول (> ٥٠٠ ملم و ≤ ١٥٠٠ ملم) ويزيد ما تحتوي عليه من الزئبق عن ٥ ملغ لكل مصباح (ج) الطويلة (> ١٥٠٠ ملم) ويزيد ما تحتوي عليه من الزئبق عن ١٣ ملغ لكل مصباح	٢٠٢٠
مواد التجميل (ويزيد ما تحتوي عليه من الزئبق عن جزء واحد بالمليون)، بما في ذلك الصابون والكريم لتفتيح البشرة، ويستثنى منها مواد تجميل منطقة العين حيث يستخدم الزئبق كمادة حافظة ولا يوجد لها بديل فعّال ومأمون[1]	٢٠٢٠
مبيدات الآفات، والمبيدات الأحيائية، ومواد تطهير الجروح	٢٠٢٠
أجهزة القياس غير الإلكترونية التالية، ما عدا أجهزة القياس غير الإلكترونية المركّبة في المعدات الكبيرة أو المستخدمة في القياس العالي الدقة والتي لا يوجد لها بديل خالٍ من الزئبق: (أ) البارومترات؛ (ب) أجهزة قياس الرطوبة؛ (ج) مقاييس الضغط؛ (د) مقاييس الحرارة؛ (هـ) مقاييس ضغط الدم	

(١) ليس القصد إدراج مواد التجميل أو الصابون أو الكريم المحتوية على ملوثات نزرة من الزئبق.

المرفق ألف

المنتجات المضاف إليها الزئبق

تُستثنى المنتجات التالية من هذا المرفق:

(أ) المنتجات الأساسية للدفاع المدني وللاستخدامات العسكرية؛

(ب) منتجات لأغراض البحث، ومعايرة أجهزة القياس، وللاستخدام كمعيار مرجعي؛

(ج) القواطع والمرحِّلات، ومصابيح الفلورسنت ذات المهبط البارد، ومصابيح الفلورسنت ذات الإلكترود الخارجي للوحات العرض الإلكترونية وأجهزة القياس، إذا لم يوجد بديل خالٍ من الزئبق مناسب للاستعاضة به؛

(د) المنتجات المستعملة في الممارسات التقليدية أو الدينية؛

(هـ) أمصال التطعيم التي تحتوي على الثيوميرسال كمادة حافظة.

الجزء الأول: المنتجات الخاضعة للفقرة ١ من المادة ٤

المنتجات المضاف إليها الزئبق	التاريخ الذي لن يُسمح بعده بتصنيع المنتج أو استيراده أو تصديره (تاريخ التخلص)
البطاريات، ما عدا البطاريات الزرّية المصنوعة من أكسيدي الزنك والفضة التي تحتوي على الزئبق بنسبة < ٢٪ والبطاريات الزرّية الهوائية المصنوعة من الزنك والمحتوية على الزئبق بنسبة < ٢٪	٢٠٢٠
القواطع والمرحلات، ما عدا قناطر قياس السعة أو الفقد العالية الدقة والقواطع والمرحلات اللاسلكية ذات الذبذبة العالية، وأجهزة المراقبة والتحكُّم، على ألا يزيد ما تحتوي عليه من الزئبق عن ٢٠ ملغ لكل قنطرة أو مفتاح أو مرحِّل	٢٠٢٠
مصابيح الفلورسنت الصغيرة لأغراض الإنارة العامة ≤ ٣٠ واط ويزيد ما تحتوي عليه من الزئبق عن ٥ ملغ لكل مشعلة مصباح	٢٠٢٠

المادة ٣٣

الانسحاب

١ - يجوز لأي طرف أن ينسحب من الاتفاقية في أي وقت بعد مضي ثلاث سنوات من تاريخ بدء نفاذها بالنسبة لذلك الطرف، وذلك بتوجيه إخطار خطّي إلى الوديع.

٢ - يكون أي انسحاب من هذا القبيل نافذاً بانقضاء سنة واحدة على تاريخ تسلُّم الوديع إخطار الانسحاب أو في تاريخ لاحق حسبما يتحدَّد في إخطار الانسحاب.

المادة ٣٤

الوديع

يكون الأمين العام للأمم المتحدة هو الوديع لهذه الاتفاقية.

المادة ٣٥

حجّية النصوص

يودَع أصل هذه الاتفاقية، الذي تتساوى نصوصه الإسبانية والإنكليزية والروسية والصينية والعربية والفرنسية في الحجّية لدى الوديع.

وإثباتاً لما تقدَّم، قام الموقّعون أدناه، المخوَّلون حسب الأصول، بالتوقيع على هذه الاتفاقية.

في كوماموتو، اليابان، في اليوم العاشر من شهر تشرين الأول/أكتوبر من عام ألفين وثلاثة عشر.

٣ - تُعلن أي منظمة إقليمية للتكامل الاقتصادي في صكوك تصديقها أو قبولها أو إقرارها أو انضمامها مدى اختصاصها بالمسائل التي تنظمها هذه الاتفاقية. وتُخطر أي منظمة من هذا القبيل أيضاً الوديع، الذي يخطِر بدوره الأطراف، بأي تعديل ذي صلة يطرأ على نطاق اختصاصها.

٤ - تُشَجَّع كل دولة أو منظمة إقليمية للتكامل الاقتصادي على أن تحيل إلى الأمانة وقت تصديقها أو قبولها أو إقرارها أو انضمامها للاتفاقية معلومات عن تدابيرها لتنفيذ الاتفاقية.

٥ - يجوز لأي طرف أن يُعلن في صك تصديقه أو قبوله أو إقراره أو انضمامه أن أي تعديل لمرفق ما لا يدخل حيز النفاذ بالنسبة له إلا عند إيداع صك تصديقه أو قبوله أو إقراره أو انضمامه المتعلق بذلك التعديل.

المادة ٣١

بدء النفاذ

١ - يبدأ نفاذ هذه الاتفاقية في اليوم التسعين بعد تاريخ إيداع الصك الخمسين من صكوك التصديق أو القبول أو الإقرار أو الانضمام.

٢ - يبدأ نفاذ الاتفاقية بالنسبة لأي دولة أو منظمة إقليمية للتكامل الاقتصادي تصدّق على هذه الاتفاقية أو تقبلها أو تقرها أو تنضم إليها بعد إيداع الصك الخمسين من صكوك التصديق أو القبول أو الإقرار أو الانضمام في اليوم التسعين بعد تاريخ إيداع هذه الدولة أو المنظمة الإقليمية للتكامل الاقتصادي صك تصديقها أو إقرارها أو قبولها أو انضمامها.

٣ - لأغراض الفقرتين ١ و٢ لا يُعتبر أي صك مودَع من قبِل أي منظمة إقليمية للتكامل الاقتصادي صكاً إضافياً للصكوك التي أودعتها الدول الأعضاء في تلك المنظمة.

المادة ٣٢

التحفُّظات

لا يجوز إبداء أي تحفُّظات على هذه الاتفاقية.

المادة ٢٨

حق التصويت

١ - يكون لكل طرف في هذه الاتفاقية صوت واحد، فيما عدا ما هو منصوص عليه في الفقرة ٢.

٢ - تمارِس أي منظمة إقليمية للتكامل الاقتصادي حقها في التصويت بشأن المسائل التي تدخل في نطاق اختصاصها، بإدلائها بعدد من الأصوات مساوٍ لعدد الدول الأعضاء فيها التي تكون أطرافاً في الاتفاقية. ولا تمارِس هذه المنظمة حقها في التصويت إذا كانت أي دولة من دولها الأعضاء تمارِس حقها في التصويت، والعكس بالعكس.

المادة ٢٩

التوقيع

يُفتَح باب التوقيع على هذه الاتفاقية في كوماموتو، اليابان لجميع الدول والمنظمات الإقليمية للتكامل الاقتصادي بتاريخ ١٠ و١١ تشرين الأول/أكتوبر ٢٠١٣، وبعد ذلك في مقر الأمم المتحدة في نيويورك حتى تاريخ ٩ تشرين الأول/أكتوبر ٢٠١٤.

المادة ٣٠

التصديق أو القبول أو الإقرار أو الانضمام

١ - تخضع هذه الاتفاقية للتصديق أو القبول أو الإقرار من جانب الدول والمنظمات الإقليمية للتكامل الاقتصادي. ويُفتح باب الانضمام إلى الاتفاقية للدول والمنظمات الإقليمية للتكامل الاقتصادي اعتباراً من اليوم التالي لتاريخ إقفال باب التوقيع عليها. وتودع صكوك التصديق أو القبول أو الإقرار أو الانضمام لدى الوديع.

٢ - تكون أي منظمة إقليمية للتكامل الاقتصادي تصبح طرفاً في هذه الاتفاقية، بدون أن يكون أي من الدول الأعضاء فيها طرفاً فيها، ملزمة بجميع الالتزامات الناشئة عن الاتفاقية. وفي حالة المنظمات التي تكون واحدة أو أكثر من الدول الأعضاء فيها طرفاً في هذه الاتفاقية، تتولى المنظمة ودولها الأعضاء البت في مسؤولية كل منها عن الوفاء بالتزاماتها بموجب الاتفاقية. وفي هذه الحالات، لا يجوز للمنظمة والدول الأعضاء فيها أن تمارس معاً وفي الوقت ذاته الحقوق الناشئة عن الاتفاقية.

المادة ٢٧

اعتماد المرفقات وتعديلها

١ - تشكل مرفقات هذه الاتفاقية جزءاً لا يتجزأ منها، وما لم يُنص صراحة على خلاف ذلك، تشكل أية إشارة إلى هذه الاتفاقية إشارة في الوقت ذاته إلى أي مرفقات لها.

٢ - تقتصر أي مرفقات إضافية تُعتمد بعد بدء نفاذ هذه الاتفاقية على المسائل الإجرائية أو العلمية أو التقنية أو الإدارية.

٣ - ينطبق الإجراء التالي على اقتراح واعتماد ونفاذ أي مرفقات إضافية لهذه الاتفاقية:

(أ) تُقترح مرفقات إضافية لهذه الاتفاقية وتُعتمد طبقاً للإجراء المنصوص عليه في الفقرات ١ إلى ٣ من المادة ٢٦؛

(ب) يقوم أي طرف لا يستطيع قبول أي مرفق إضافي بإخطار الوديع كتابةً بذلك في غضون سنة من تاريخ قيام الوديع بإبلاغه باعتماد ذلك المرفق. ويبلِّغ الوديع، دون تأخير، جميع الأطراف بأي إخطار يتلقاه. ويجوز لأي طرف في أي وقت أن يُخطر الوديع، خطياً، بأنه يسحب إخطاره السابق بعدم قبول أي مرفق إضافي، وعند ذلك يبدأ نفاذ المرفق بالنسبة لهذا الطرف وفقاً للفقرة الفرعية (ج)؛

(ج) عند انقضاء سنة واحدة من تاريخ تعميم الوديع للتبليغ باعتماد أي مرفق إضافي، يصبح المرفق نافذاً بالنسبة لجميع الأطراف التي لم تقدم إخطاراً بعدم القبول وفقاً لأحكام الفقرة الفرعية (ب).

٤ - يخضع اقتراح واعتماد وبدء نفاذ أي تعديلات لمرفقات هذه الاتفاقية لنفس الإجراءات المتبعة في اقتراح واعتماد وبدء نفاذ أي مرفقات إضافية لهذه الاتفاقية، باستثناء أن أي تعديل لمرفق ما لا يبدأ نفاذه بالنسبة لأي طرف يكون قد قدم إعلاناً بشأن تعديل المرفقات وفقاً للفقرة ٥ من المادة ٣٠، وفي هذه الحالة يبدأ نفاذ هذا التعديل بالنسبة لهذا الطرف في اليوم التسعين بعد التاريخ الذي أودع فيه لدى الوديع صك تصديقه أو قبوله أو إقراره أو انضمامه فيما يتعلق بهذا التعديل.

٥ - إذا اتصل مرفق إضافي أو تعديل على مرفق بتعديل لهذه الاتفاقية، لا يدخل المرفق الإضافي أو التعديل حيِّز النفاذ إلى أن يدخل تعديل الاتفاقية حيِّز النفاذ.

٥ - لا يؤثّر انقضاء سريان أي إعلان أو تقديم إشعار إلغاء أو إعلان جديد بأي وسيلة من الوسائل في الإجراءات التي قد تكون قيد النظر أمام أي هيئة تحكيم أو محكمة العدل الدولية ما لم يتفق الطرفان في المنازعة على خلاف ذلك.

٦ - إذا لم يقبل طرفا المنازعة نفس وسيلة تسوية المنازعة عملاً بالفقرة ٢ أو الفقرة ٣، وإذا لم يتمكّنا من تسوية منازعتهما عن طريق الوسائل المذكورة في الفقرة ١ خلال مدة اثني عشر شهراً بعد قيام أحد الطرفين بإخطار الطرف الآخر بوجود منازعة بينهما، تحال المنازعة إلى لجنة توفيق بناءً على طلب أي من طرفي المنازعة. وتنطبق الإجراءات الواردة في الجزء الثاني من المرفق هاء على التوفيق بموجب هذه المادة.

المادة ٢٦

تعديلات الاتفاقية

١ - يجوز لأي طرف أن يقترح تعديلات لهذه الاتفاقية.

٢ - تُعتمد تعديلات هذه الاتفاقية في اجتماع لمؤتمر الأطراف. وتُبلّغ الأمانة نص أي تعديل مقترح لهذه الاتفاقية إلى الأطراف قبل موعد الاجتماع الذي سيُقترح فيه اعتماده بستة أشهر على الأقل. وتُبلّغ الأمانة أيضاً الموقعين على هذه الاتفاقية بالتعديلات المقترحة وتبلّغ بها كذلك الوديع، للعِلْم.

٣ - تبذل الأطراف قصارى جهدها للتوصل إلى اتفاق على أي تعديل مقترح لهذه الاتفاقية بتوافق الآراء. وإذا استُنفدت جميع الجهود الرامية إلى التوصل إلى توافق في الآراء، دون التوصل إلى اتفاق، يُعتمد التعديل، كحل أخير، بأغلبية ثلاثة أرباع أصوات الأطراف الحاضرة والمصوّتة في الاجتماع.

٤ - يُرسل الوديع التعديل المعتمد إلى جميع الأطراف للتصديق عليه أو قبوله أو إقراره.

٥ - يتم إخطار الوديع كتابةً بالتصديق على أي تعديل أو قبوله أو إقراره. ويبدأ نفاذ أي تعديل يعتمد وفقاً للفقرة ٣ بالنسبة للأطراف التي قبلت الالتزام به اعتباراً من اليوم التسعين بعد تاريخ إيداع صكوك التصديق عليه أو قبوله أو إقراره من قِبَل ثلاثة أرباع الأطراف على الأقل التي كانت أطرافاً وقت اعتماد التعديل. ويبدأ نفاذ التعديل بعد ذلك بالنسبة لأي طرف آخر في اليوم التسعين بعد تاريخ إيداع ذلك الطرف وثيقة تصديقه على هذا التعديل أو قبوله أو إقراره.

(و) الدخول، بتوجيه عام من مؤتمر الأطراف، في ما قد يكون لازماً من الترتيبات الإدارية والتعاقدية لأداء وظائفها بفعالية؛

(ز) أداء وظائف الأمانة الأخرى المحددة في هذه الاتفاقية، وغيرها من الوظائف التي يقررها مؤتمر الأطراف.

٣ - يؤدي المدير التنفيذي لبرنامج الأمم المتحدة للبيئة وظائف الأمانة لهذه الاتفاقية، ما لم يقرر مؤتمر الأطراف، بأغلبية ثلاثة أرباع عدد الأطراف الحاضرة والمصوّتة، أن يوكِل وظائف الأمانة إلى واحدة أو أكثر من المنظمات الدولية الأخرى.

٤ - يجوز لمؤتمر الأطراف، بالتشاور مع الهيئات الدولية المختصة، العمل على تعزيز التعاون والتنسيق بين الأمانة وأمانات الاتفاقيات الأخرى المتعلقة بالمواد الكيميائية والنفايات. ويجوز لمؤتمر الأطراف، بالتشاور مع الهيئات الدولية المختصة، أن يقدِّم توجيهات إضافية بشأن هذه المسألة.

المادة ٢٥

تسوية المنازعات

١ - تسعى الأطراف إلى تسوية أي منازعة بينها فيما يتعلّق بتفسير أو تطبيق هذه الاتفاقية عن طريق التفاوض أو أي طرق سلمية أخرى تختارها بنفسها.

٢ - عند التصديق على هذه الاتفاقية أو قبولها أو إقرارها أو الانضمام إليها، أو في أي وقت لاحق، يجوز لأي طرف ليس منظمة إقليمية للتكامل الاقتصادي أن يعلن، في صك خطّي يُقدَّم للوديع فيما يخص أي منازعة تتعلّق بتفسير أو تطبيق الاتفاقية، عن اعترافه بإحدى الوسيلتين التاليتين أو كلتيهما على سبيل الإلزام لتسوية المنازعات إزاء أي طرف يقبل نفس الالتزام:

(أ) التحكيم وفقاً للإجراءات المبيَّنة في الجزء الأول من المرفق هاء؛

(ب) عرض المنازعة على محكمة العدل الدولية.

٣ - يجوز لأي طرف من المنظمات الإقليمية للتكامل الاقتصادي أن يُصدِر إعلاناً له نفس الأثر فيما يتعلق بالتحكيم وذلك وفقاً للفقرة ٢.

٤ - يظل الإعلان الصادر عملاً بالفقرة ٢ أو ٣ سارياً إلى أن تنقضي فترة سريانه وفقاً لأحكامه أو لحين انقضاء ثلاثة أشهر بعد إيداع إشعار خطّي بإلغائه لدى الوديع.

(ج) الاستعراض المنتظم لجميع المعلومات التي تتاح له وللأمانة عملاً بالمادة ٢١؛

(د) النظر في أي توصيات تقدّم إليه من قِبَل لجنة التنفيذ والامتثال؛

(هـ) بحث واتخاذ أي إجراء إضافي يراه ضرورياً لتحقيق أهداف هذه الاتفاقية؛

(و) استعراض المرفقين ألف وباء عملاً بالمادة ٤ والمادة ٥.

٦ - يجوز للأمم المتحدة ووكالاتها المتخصصة والوكالة الدولية للطاقة الذرية، وكذلك أي دولة ليست طرفاً في هذه الاتفاقية، أن تكون ممثّلة في اجتماعات مؤتمر الأطراف بصفة مراقب. ويجوز قبول أي هيئة أو وكالة، سواء كانت وطنية أو دولية أو حكومية أو غير حكومية ذات اختصاص في المسائل التي تشملها هذه الاتفاقية وأبلغت الأمانة برغبتها في أن تكون ممثلة في اجتماع لمؤتمر الأطراف بصفة مراقب، ما لم يعترض على ذلك ثلث الأطراف الحاضرة على الأقل. ويخضع قبول المراقبين ومشاركتهم للنظام الداخلي الذي يعتمده مؤتمر الأطراف.

المادة ٢٤

الأمانة

١ - تُنشأ بموجب هذا النص أمانة.

٢ - تضطلع الأمانة بالوظائف التالية:

(أ) وضع الترتيبات لاجتماعات مؤتمر الأطراف وهيئاته الفرعية وتزويدها بالخدمات وفقاً للمقتضى؛

(ب) تيسير تقديم المساعدة إلى الأطراف، ولا سيما الأطراف من البلدان النامية والأطراف التي تمر اقتصاداتها بمرحلة انتقال، في تنفيذ هذه الاتفاقية، بناء على طلبها؛

(ج) التنسيق، وفقاً للمقتضى، مع أمانات الهيئات الدولية ذات الصلة، ولا سيما الاتفاقيات الأخرى المتعلقة بالمواد الكيميائية والنفايات؛

(د) مساعدة الأطراف في تبادل المعلومات المتصلة بتنفيذ هذه الاتفاقية؛

(هـ) إعداد تقارير دورية استناداً إلى المعلومات الواردة عملاً بالمادتين ١٥ و ٢١ وغيرها من المعلومات المتاحة، وإتاحتها للأطراف؛

٣ - يُجرى التقييم على أساس المعلومات العلمية والبيئية والتقنية والمالية والاقتصادية المتاحة، بما في ذلك:

(أ) التقارير ومعلومات الرصد الأخرى المقدّمة إلى مؤتمر الأطراف عملاً بالفقرة ٢؛

(ب) التقارير المقدمة عملاً بالمادة ٢١؛

(ج) المعلومات والتوصيات المقدَّمة عملاً بالمادة ١٥؛

(د) التقارير والمعلومات الأخرى ذات الصلة بشأن سير الترتيبات القائمة بمقتضى هذه الاتفاقية والمتعلقة بالمساعدات المالية ونقل التكنولوجيا وبناء القدرات.

المادة ٢٣

مؤتمر الأطراف

١ - يُنشأ بموجب هذا النص مؤتمر للأطراف.

٢ - ينعقد الاجتماع الأول لمؤتمر الأطراف بدعوة من المدير التنفيذي لبرنامج الأمم المتحدة للبيئة في موعد لا يتجاوز سنة واحدة بعد تاريخ دخول هذه الاتفاقية حيِّز النفاذ. وبعد ذلك تُعقد الاجتماعات العادية لمؤتمر الأطراف على فترات منتظمة يقررها المؤتمر.

٣ - تُعقد اجتماعات استثنائية لمؤتمر الأطراف في أوقات أخرى حسبما يراها المؤتمر ضرورية، أو بناءً على طلب خطّي من أي طرف، بشرط أن يؤيده ثلث عدد الأطراف على الأقل، في غضون ستة أشهر بعد أن تبلغ الأمانة الأطراف بهذا الطلب.

٤ - يوافق مؤتمر الأطراف بتوافق الآراء في أول اجتماع له على نظام داخلي وقواعد مالية، له أو لأي من هيئاته الفرعية، إضافة إلى الأحكام المالية التي تنظم سير عمل الأمانة، ويعتمد تلك النصوص.

٥ - يُبقي مؤتمر الأطراف تنفيذ هذه الاتفاقية قيد الاستعراض والتقييم المستمرين. ويؤدي المؤتمر المهام الموكلة إليه بموجب هذه الاتفاقية. وتحقيقاً لهذه الغاية يقوم مؤتمر الأطراف بما يلي:

(أ) إنشاء الهيئات الفرعية التي يراها ضرورية لتنفيذ هذه الاتفاقية؛

(ب) التعاون، عند الاقتضاء، مع المنظمات الدولية المختصة والهيئات الحكومية الدولية والمنظمات غير الحكومية؛

٣ - يتعيَّن على الأطراف، لدى اضطلاعها بالأعمال الواردة في الفقرتين ١ و٢، أن تستشير أصحاب المصلحة الوطنيين لتيسير وضع خططها للتنفيذ وتنفيذها واستعراضها وتحديثها.

٤ - للأطراف أيضاً أن تقوم بالتنسيق فيما بينها بشأن الخطط الإقليمية الرامية إلى تيسير تنفيذ هذه الاتفاقية.

المادة ٢١

الإبلاغ

١ - يقدِّم كل طرف، عن طريق الأمانة، إلى مؤتمر الأطراف تقارير عن التدابير التي اتخذها لتنفيذ أحكام هذه الاتفاقية وعن مدى فعالية تلك التدابير والتحديات المحتملة التي قد تواجهه في تحقيق أهداف الاتفاقية.

٢ - يُدرِج كل طرف في تقاريره المعلومات على النحو المطلوب في المواد ٣ و ٥ و ٧ و ٨ و ٩ من هذه الاتفاقية.

٣ - يبتّ مؤتمر الأطراف إبان اجتماعه الأول في مسألة توقيت وشكل الإبلاغ الذي يجب أن تتبعه الأطراف، مع مراعاة استصواب تنسيق الإبلاغ مع الاتفاقيات الأخرى ذات الصلة المتعلقة بالمواد الكيميائية والنفايات.

المادة ٢٢

تقييمات الفعالية

١ - يقيِّم مؤتمر الأطراف مدى فعالية هذه الاتفاقية، ابتداءً من فترة لا تزيد عن ستة أعوام بعد تاريخ دخول الاتفاقية حيِّز النفاذ وبشكل دوري بعد ذلك على فترات يقررها مؤتمر الأطراف.

٢ - ولتيسير التقييم، يبدأ مؤتمر الأطراف، إبان اجتماعه الأول، بوضع الترتيبات لتزويده ببيانات رصد مقارنة عن وجود الزئبق ومركبات الزئبق وانتقالها في البيئة، وكذلك الاتجاهات في مستويات الزئبق ومركّبات الزئبق الملاحَظة في الأوساط الأحيائية والفئات السكانية الضعيفة.

والثدييات البحرية والسلاحف البحرية والطيور، وكذلك التعاون على صعيد جمع وتبادل العينات الملائمة ذات الصلة؛

(ج) تقييمات آثار الزئبق ومركباته على صحة الإنسان والبيئة، إضافة إلى الآثار الاجتماعية والاقتصادية والثقافية، ولا سيما فيما يتعلق بالفئات السكانية الضعيفة؛

(د) المنهجيات المنسقة للأنشطة المضطلع بها بموجب الفقرات الفرعية (أ) و (ب) و (ج)؛

(هـ) المعلومات عن الدورة البيئية للزئبق ومركباته وانتقالها، (بما في ذلك الانتقال البعيد المدى والتراكم)، وتحول ومصير الزئبق ومركباته في مجموعة من النظم الإيكولوجية، وإيلاء الاعتبار المناسب للتمييز بين الانبعاثات والإطلاقات البشرية المنشأ والإطلاقات الطبيعية للزئبق، وإعادة الزئبق لدورته البيئية من ترسباته القديمة؛

(و) المعلومات المتعلقة بالتجارة في الزئبق ومركبات الزئبق والمنتجات المضاف إليها الزئبق؛

(ز) والمعلومات والبحوث بشأن التوافر التقني والاقتصادي للمنتجات والعمليات الخالية من الزئبق، وأفضل التقنيات المتاحة وأفضل الممارسات البيئية لخفض انبعاثات وإطلاقات الزئبق ومركباته ورصدها.

٢ - ينبغي للأطراف، وفقاً للمقتضى، أن تعتمد على شبكات الرصد وبرامج البحوث القائمة عند اضطلاعها بالأنشطة المحددة في الفقرة ١.

المادة ٢٠

خطط التنفيذ

١ - يجوز لكل طرف، عقب إجراء تقييم أوّلي، أن يضع ويُطبِّق خطة تنفيذ تراعي ظروفه المحلية، للوفاء بالالتزامات بموجب هذه الاتفاقية. ويتعيَّن إحالة أي خطة من هذا النوع إلى الأمانة في أسرع وقت بعد إعدادها.

٢ - يجوز لكل طرف أن يستعرض خطته الخاصة بالتنفيذ وأن يحدّثها مراعياً في ذلك ظروفه المحلية وبالرجوع إلى التوجيهات الصادرة عن مؤتمر الأطراف وغير ذلك من التوجيهات ذات الصلة.

المادة ١٨

إعلام الجمهور وتوعيته وتثقيفه

١ - يقوم كل طرف، في حدود إمكانياته، بتعزيز وتيسير ما يلي:

(أ) تزويد الجمهور بالمعلومات المتاحة عن:

'١' الآثار الصحية والبيئية للزئبق ومركباته؛

'٢' بدائل الزئبق ومركباته؛

'٣' المواضيع المحددة في الفقرة ١ من المادة ١٧؛

'٤' نتائج أنشطته في مجالات البحوث والتطوير والرصد بموجب المادة ١٩؛

'٥' أنشطته الرامية إلى الوفاء بالتزاماته بموجب هذه الاتفاقية؛

(ب) التثقيف والتدريب وتوعية الجمهور فيما يتعلق بأثر التعرض للزئبق ومركباته على صحة الإنسان والبيئة، بالتعاون مع المنظمات الحكومية الدولية والمنظمات غير الحكومية ذات الصلة والفئات السكانية الضعيفة، وفقاً للمقتضى.

٢ - يستخدم كل طرف الآليات الموجودة أو يولي الاعتبار لوضع آليات، مثل سجلات إطلاق ونقل الملوثات، وفقاً للمقتضى، لجمع ونشر المعلومات عن تقديرات كمياته السنوية من الزئبق ومركباته التي يتم انبعاثها أو إطلاقها أو التخلص منها من خلال الأنشطة البشرية.

المادة ١٩

البحوث والتطوير والرصد

١ - تسعى الأطراف، مع مراعاة ظروفها وقدراتها، إلى إعداد وتحسين ما يلي:

(أ) قوائم جرد لاستخدام واستهلاك الزئبق ومركباته وانبعاثاتها البشرية المنشأ إلى الجو وإطلاقاتها في المياه والأراضي؛

(ب) نماذج رصد تمثيلي للمناطق الجغرافية لمستويات الزئبق ومركبات الزئبق لدى الفئات السكانية الضعيفة وفي الأوساط البيئية، بما في ذلك الأوساط الحيوية مثل الأسماك

(ب) المعلومات عن خفض أو إنهاء إنتاج الزئبق ومركباته واستخدامها أو التجارة فيها، وانبعاثاتها واطلاقتها؛

(ج) المعلومات عن البدائل المجدية تقنياً واقتصادياً لما يلي:

'١' المنتجات المضاف إليها الزئبق؛

'٢' عمليات التصنيع التي يُستخدم فيها الزئبق أو مركّبات الزئبق؛

'٣' الأنشطة وعمليات التصنيع التي ينتج عنها انبعاث أو إطلاق الزئبق أو مركباته؛

بما في ذلك المعلومات عن المخاطر الصحية والبيئية والتكاليف والفوائد الاقتصادية والاجتماعية لهذه البدائل؛

(د) المعلومات الوبائية المتعلقة بالآثار الصحية المرتبطة بالتعرض للزئبق ومركباته، وذلك بالتعاون الوثيق مع منظمة الصحة العالمية والمنظمات الأخرى ذات الصلة، وفقاً للمقتضى.

٢ - يجوز للأطراف أن تتبادل المعلومات المشار إليها في الفقرة ١ بشكل مباشر، أو عبر الأمانة، أو بالتعاون مع المنظمات الأخرى ذات الصلة، بما فيها أمانات الاتفاقيات المتعلقة بالمواد الكيميائية والنفايات، وفقاً للمقتضى.

٣ - تيسر الأمانة التعاون على صعيد تبادل المعلومات المشار إليها في هذه المادة، وكذلك مع المنظمات ذات الصلة، بما فيها أمانات الاتفاقات البيئية المتعددة الأطراف والمبادرات الدولية الأخرى. وإضافة إلى المعلومات الواردة من الأطراف، فإن هذه المعلومات تشمل المعلومات المقدمة من المنظمات الحكومية الدولية والمنظمات غير الحكومية التي لديها خبرة في مجال الزئبق، ومن المؤسسات الوطنية والدولية التي تتمتع بتلك الخبرة.

٤ - يعين كل طرف نقطة اتصال وطنية لتبادل المعلومات في إطار هذه الاتفاقية، بما في ذلك ما يتعلق بموافقة الأطراف المستوردة بموجب المادة ٣.

٥ - لأغراض هذه الاتفاقية، لا تعتبر المعلومات الخاصة بصحة وسلامة الإنسان والبيئة معلومات سرية. وتقوم الأطراف التي تتبادل المعلومات الأخرى عملاً بهذه الاتفاقية بحماية أي معلومات سرية وفق ما هو متفق عليه بصورة متبادلة.

المادة ١٦

الجوانب الصحية

١ - تشجع الأطراف على ما يلي:

(أ) التشجيع على وضع وتنفيذ استراتيجيات وبرامج ترمي إلى تحديد وحماية المجموعات السكانية المعرضة للخطر، لا سيما فئات السكان الضعيفة، ويمكن أن تشمل اعتماد مبادئ توجيهية صحية تستند إلى حقائق علمية وتتعلق بالتعرض للزئبق ومركبات الزئبق، ووضع أهداف للحد من التعرض للزئبق، حيثما يقتضي الأمر ذلك، وتثقيف الجمهور، بمشاركة قطاع الصحة العامة والقطاعات الأخرى المشاركة؛

(ب) التشجيع على وضع وتنفيذ برامج تثقيفية ووقائية قائمة على حقائق علمية وتتعلق بالتعرض المهني للزئبق ولمركبات الزئبق؛

(ج) تعزيز خدمات الرعاية الصحية الملائمة لوقاية الفئات السكانية المتضررة جراء التعرض للزئبق أو لمركبات الزئبق وعلاجها ورعايتها؛

(د) تكوين وتعزيز القدرات المؤسسية والمهنية الصحية للوقاية من الأخطار الصحية الناجمة عن التعرض للزئبق ومركبات الزئبق وتشخيصها وعلاجها ورصدها.

٢ - ينبغي لمؤتمر الأطراف، في معرض بحثه للقضايا أو الأنشطة المتعلقة بالصحة، أن يقوم بما يلي:

(أ) التشاور والتعاون مع منظمة الصحة العالمية، ومنظمة العمل الدولية، وسائر المنظمات الدولية ذات الصلة، وفقاً للمقتضى؛

(ب) تعزيز التعاون وتبادل المعلومات مع منظمة الصحة العالمية ومنظمة العمل الدولية وسائر المنظمات الحكومية الدولية ذات الصلة، وفقاً للمقتضى.

المادة ١٧

تبادل المعلومات

١ - يعمل كل طرف على تيسير تبادل ما يلي:

(أ) المعلومات العلمية والتقنية والاقتصادية والقانونية المتعلقة بالزئبق ومركباته، بما في ذلك المعلومات عن السمية والسمية الإيكولوجية والسلامة؛

٥ - يقدم مؤتمر الأطراف توصيات بشأن كيفية زيادة تعزيز المساعدة على بناء القدرات والمساعدة التقنية ونقل التكنولوجيا بموجب هذه المادة.

المادة ١٥

لجنة التنفيذ والامتثال

١ - تُنشأ بهذا النص آلية تشمل لجنة بصفة هيئة فرعية تابعة لمؤتمر الأطراف، لتعزيز تنفيذ واستعراض الامتثال لجميع أحكام هذه الاتفاقية. وتتسم الآلية، بما في ذلك اللجنة، بطابع تيسيري وتولي اهتماماً خاصاً للقدرات والظروف الوطنية للأطراف.

٢ - تعمل اللجنة على تعزيز تنفيذ جميع أحكام هذه الاتفاقية واستعراض الامتثال لها. وتتدارس اللجنة قضايا التنفيذ والامتثال الفردية والعامة معاً وتقدم توصيات، وفقاً للمقتضى، إلى مؤتمر الأطراف.

٣ - تتألّف اللجنة من ١٥ عضواً، ترشحهم الأطراف وينتخبهم مؤتمر الأطراف مع إيلاء المراعاة الواجبة للتمثيل الجغرافي العادل استناداً إلى المناطق الخمس للأمم المتحدة؛ ويُنتَخَب الأعضاء الأوائل في الاجتماع الأول لمؤتمر الأطراف وبعد ذلك وفقاً للنظام الداخلي الذي يقره مؤتمر الأطراف عملاً بالفقرة ٥؛ ويكون لأعضاء اللجنة اختصاص في ميدان ذي صلة بهذه الاتفاقية ويعكس توازناً مناسباً في الخبرات.

٤ - ويجوز أن تدرس اللجنة مسائل على أساس ما يلي:

(أ) تقارير مقدمة كتابياً من أي طرف فيما يخص امتثاله؛

(ب) تقارير وطنية وفقاً للمادة ٢١؛

(ج) طلبات من مؤتمر الأطراف.

٥ - تصوغ اللجنة نظامها الداخلي الذي يُعرَض على مؤتمر الأطراف للموافقة عليه في اجتماعه الثاني؛ ويجوز لمؤتمر الأطراف أن يعتمد اختصاصات أخرى للجنة.

٦ - تبذل اللجنة كل جهد لاعتماد توصياتها بتوافق الآراء. وإذا استُنفِدَت جميع الجهود الرامية إلى التوصُّل إلى توافق الآراء ولم يتم التوصُّل إليه، تعتمد هذه التوصيات كملاذ أخير بأغلبية ثلاثة أرباع أصوات الأعضاء الحاضرين والمصوِّتين، على أساس اكتمال نصاب قانوني وهو ثلثا عدد الأعضاء.

المادة ١٤
بناء القدرات والمساعدة التقنية ونقل التكنولوجيا

١ - تتعاون الأطراف لتقدم، في حدود إمكانيات كل منها، مساعدة لبناء القدرات ومساعدة تقنية ملائمة وفي الوقت المناسب، إلى الأطراف من البلدان النامية، لا سيما الأطراف من أقل البلدان نمواً أو الدول الجزرية الصغيرة النامية، والأطراف التي تمر اقتصاداتها بمرحلة انتقال، لمساعدتها على الوفاء بالتزاماتها بموجب هذه الاتفاقية.

٢ - يجوز تقديم المساعدة لبناء القدرات والمساعدة التقنية عملاً بالفقرة ١ والمادة ١٣، من خلال الترتيبات الإقليمية ودون الإقليمية والوطنية، بما في ذلك المراكز الإقليمية ودون الإقليمية القائمة، ومن خلال الوسائل المتعددة الأطراف والوسائل الثنائية الأخرى، ومن خلال الشراكات، بما فيها الشراكات التي تشمل القطاع الخاص. وينبغي السعي للتعاون والتنسيق مع الاتفاقات البيئية الأخرى المتعددة الأطراف في مجال المواد الكيميائية والنفايات من أجل زيادة فعالية المساعدة التقنية وتقديمها.

٣ - تُشجع الأطراف من البلدان المتقدمة، والأطراف الأخرى وتُيَسِّرُ في حدود قدرات كل منها، وبدعم من القطاع الخاص وأصحاب المصلحة الآخرين ذوي الصلة، وفقاً للمقتضى، تطوير التكنولوجيات البديلة ونقلها ونشرها والحصول على أحدث التكنولوجيات البديلة السليمة بيئياً، للأطراف من البلدان النامية، لا سيما أقل البلدان نمواً والدول الجزرية الصغيرة النامية، والأطراف التي تمر اقتصاداتها بمرحلة انتقال، لتعزيز قدراتها على تنفيذ هذه الاتفاقية تنفيذاً فعّالاً.

٤ - يقوم مؤتمر الأطراف، بحلول موعد اجتماعه الثاني وما بعده، على أساس منتظم، آخذاً في الاعتبار العروض والتقارير المقدمة من الأطراف، بما في ذلك المنصوص عليها في المادة ٢١، والمعلومات المقدمة من أصحاب المصلحة الآخرين، بما يلي:

(أ) النظر في المعلومات عن المبادرات القائمة والتقدم المحرز فيما يتعلق بالتكنولوجيات البديلة؛

(ب) النظر في احتياجات الأطراف من التكنولوجيات البديلة، لا سيما الأطراف من البلدان النامية؛

(ج) تحديد التحديات التي تواجهها الأطراف في نقل التكنولوجيا، لا سيما الأطراف من البلدان النامية.

(ب) برنامج دولي محدَّد لدعم بناء القدرات والمساعدة التقنية.

٧ - يوفِّر الصندوق الاستئماني التابع لمرفق البيئة العالمية موارد مالية جديدة كافية يمكن التنبؤ بها وتتاح في الوقت المناسب للوفاء بالتكاليف دعماً لتنفيذ هذه الاتفاقية على النحو الذي يوافق عليه مؤتمر الأطراف. ولأغراض هذه الاتفاقية، يتم تشغيل الصندوق الاستئماني التابع لمرفق البيئة العالمية بتوجيهات من مؤتمر الأطراف ويُعتَبر الصندوق مسؤولاً أمامه. ويقدم مؤتمر الأطراف توجيهات بشأن الاستراتيجيات العامة والسياسات وأولويات البرنامج وأهلية الحصول على الموارد المالية واستخدامها. وإضافة إلى ذلك، يقدِّم مؤتمر الأطراف توجيهات لوضع قائمة إرشادية بفئات الأنشطة التي يمكن أن تتلقّى الدعم من الصندوق الاستئماني التابع لمرفق البيئة العالمية. ويوفِّر الصندوق الاستئماني موارد للوفاء بالتكاليف الإضافية المتفق عليها للمنافع البيئية العالمية والتكاليف الكاملة المتفق عليها لبعض أنشطة التمكين.

٨ - ينبغي للصندوق الاستئماني التابع لمرفق البيئة العالمية، أن يأخذ في الاعتبار تخفيضات الزئبق المحتملة لأي نشاط مقترح بالنسبة لتكاليفه لدى توفير الموارد من أجل نشاط ما.

٩ - وتحقيقاً لأغراض هذه الاتفاقية، سيتم تشغيل البرنامج المشار إليه في الفقرة ٦ (ب) بتوجيه من مؤتمر الأطراف ويكون البرنامج مسؤولاً أمامه. ويبتّ مؤتمر الأطراف في اجتماعه الأول بشأن المؤسسة المضيفة للبرنامج، التي تكون كياناً قائماً، ويقدم التوجيه لها، بما في ذلك عن فترة البرنامج. ويدعى جميع الأطراف وسائر أصحاب المصلحة من ذي الصلة إلى توفير الموارد المالية للبرنامج على أساس طوعي.

١٠ - يتفق مؤتمر الأطراف والكيانات التي تؤلِّف الآلية في الاجتماع الأول لمؤتمر الأطراف، على ترتيبات لتنفيذ الفقرات سالفة الذكر.

١١ - يقوم مؤتمر الأطراف باستعراض، مستوى التمويل، والتوجيهات المقدَّمة من مؤتمر الأطراف إلى الكيانات المكلَّفة بتشغيل الآلية المنشأة بموجب هذه المادة ومدى فاعليتها وقدرتها على معالجة الاحتياجات المتغيِّرة للبلدان النامية الأطراف والأطراف التي تمر اقتصاداتها بمرحلة انتقال وذلك في موعد لا يتجاوز انعقاد اجتماعه الثالث، وبعد ذلك على أساس منتظم. واستناداً إلى هذا الاستعراض، يتخذ مؤتمر الأطراف الإجراء المناسب لتحسين فعالية الآلية.

١٢ - تدعى جميع الأطراف إلى المساهمة في الآلية، في حدود قدراتها. وتشجِّع الآلية توفير الموارد من مصادر أخرى، من بينها القطاع الخاص، وأن تسعى إلى حشد هذه الموارد من أجل الأنشطة التي تدعمها.

(د) خيارات لإدارة الأخطار التي تشكّلها المواقع الملوّثة؛

(هـ) تقييم الفوائد والتكاليف؛

(و) التحقّق من صحة النتائج.

٤ - تشجِّع الأطراف على التعاون في وضع استراتيجيات وتنفيذ أنشطة لتحديد المواقع الملوَّثة بالزئبق وتقييمها وتحديد أولوياتها وإدارتها والقيام، وفقاً للمقتضى، بتطهيرها.

المادة ١٣

الموارد والآلية المالية

١ - يضطلع كل طرف بتوفير، موارد تتعلّق بالأنشطة الوطنية التي ترمي إلى تنفيذ هذه الاتفاقية، في حدود إمكاناته، ووفقاً لسياساته وأولوياته وخططه وبرامجه الوطنية، ويجوز أن تشتمل هذه الموارد على تمويل محلي من خلال السياسات والاستراتيجيات الإنمائية والميزانيات الوطنية ذات الصلة، ومن خلال تمويل ثنائي ومتعدد الأطراف إلى جانب إشراك القطاع الخاص.

٢ - ترتبط الفعالية العامة لتنفيذ هذه الاتفاقية من جانب البلدان النامية الأطراف بالتنفيذ الفعال لهذه المادة.

٣ - تشجِّع المصادر المتعددة الأطراف والإقليمية والثنائية للمساعدة المالية والتقنية ولبناء القدرات ونقل التكنولوجيا، بصفة عاجلة، على تعزيز وزيادة أنشطتها بشأن الزئبق دعماً للأطراف من البلدان النامية في تنفيذ هذه الاتفاقية فيما يتصل بالموارد المالية والمساعدة التقنية ونقل التكنولوجيا.

٤ - تراعي الأطراف مراعاة تامة، في إجراءاتها المتعلقة بالتمويل، الحاجات المحدَّدة والظروف الخاصة للأطراف من الدول الجزرية الصغيرة النامية أو من أقل البلدان نمواً.

٥ - يحدد هذا النص آلية لتوفير موارد مالية كافية يمكن التنبؤ بها وتتاح في الوقت المناسب. والهدف من هذه الآلية هو دعم الأطراف من البلدان النامية والأطراف التي تمر اقتصاداتها بمرحلة انتقال في تنفيذ التزاماتها بموجب هذه الاتفاقية.

٦ - تشتمل الآلية على ما يلي:

(أ) الصندوق الاستئماني التابع لمرفق البيئة العالمية؛

(ب) عدم استرجاعها أو إعادة تدويرها أو استعادتها أو إعادة استخدامها مباشرةً إلا من أجل استخدام مسموح به للطرف بموجب هذه الاتفاقية أو للتخلص السليم بيئياً منها عملاً بالفقرة ٣ (أ)؛

(ج) بالنسبة للأطراف في اتفاقية بازل، عدم نقلها عبر الحدود الدولية إلا لغرض التخلص السليم بيئياً منها طبقاً لأحكام هذه المادة، وتلك الاتفاقية. وفي الظروف التي لا تنطبق فيها اتفاقية بازل على النقل عبر الحدود الدولية، يسمح الطرف بالنقل فقط بعد أن تؤخَذ في الاعتبار القواعد والمعايير والتوجيهات الدولية ذات الصلة.

٤ - يسعى مؤتمر الأطراف للتعاون عن كثب مع الهيئات ذات الصلة في اتفاقية بازل على صعيد استعراض واستكمال المبادئ التوجيهية المشار إليها في الفقرة ٣ (أ)، وفقاً للمقتضى.

٥ - تُشجَّع الأطراف على التعاون مع بعضها البعض ومع المنظمات الحكومية الدولية المختصة والكيانات الأخرى، وفقاً للمقتضى، لتنمية القدرات العالمية والإقليمية والوطنية على الإدارة السليمة بيئياً لنفايات الزئبق، والحفاظ عليها.

المادة ١٢

المواقع الملوّثة بالزئبق

١ - يسعى كل طرف إلى وضع استراتيجيات مناسبة لتحديد وتقييم المواقع الملوَّثة بالزئبق أو مركّبات الزئبق.

٢ - تُتخَذ أي إجراءات للحد من المخاطر التي تشكّلها هذه المواقع بطريقة سليمة بيئياً تشمل، حيثما كان ذلك مناسباً، تقييماً للمخاطر بالنسبة لصحة الإنسان وللبيئة الناجمة عن الزئبق أو مركّبات الزئبق التي تحتوي عليها.

٣ - يعتمد مؤتمر الأطراف توجيهات بشأن إدارة المواقع الملوّثة يمكن أن تشمل طرائق ومناهج من أجل:

(أ) تحديد المواقع وسيماتها؛

(ب) إشراك الجمهور؛

(ج) تقييمات الأخطار على صحة الإنسان والبيئة؛

٤ – تتعاون الأطراف، وفقاً للمقتضى، مع بعضها البعض ومع المنظمات الحكومية الدولية المختصة والكيانات الأخرى، لتعزيز بناء القدرات من أجل التخزين المؤقّت السليم بيئياً للزئبق ومركّبات الزئبق.

المادة ١١

نفايات الزئبق

١ – تنطبق التعاريف ذات الصلة الواردة في اتفاقية بازل بشأن التحكم في نقل النفايات الخطرة والتخلص منها عبر الحدود، على النفايات التي تشملها هذه الاتفاقية بالنسبة للأطراف في اتفاقية بازل. وتستخدم الأطراف في هذه الاتفاقية التي ليست أطرافاً في اتفاقية بازل تلك التعاريف للاسترشاد بها فيما يتعلق بالنفايات الخاضعة لهذه الاتفاقية.

٢ – تحقيقاً لأغراض هذه الاتفاقية، تعني نفايات الزئبق المواد أو الأشياء:

(أ) المكونة من الزئبق أو مركبات الزئبق؛

(ب) المحتوية على الزئبق أو مركبات الزئبق؛

(ج) الملوثة بالزئبق أو بمركبات الزئبق.

بكمية تزيد عن المستويات الحدّية ذات الصلة التي يحدِّدها مؤتمر الأطراف، بالتعاون مع الهيئات ذات الصلة في اتفاقية بازل وبطريقة متسقة، والتي يجري التخلص منها أو المزمع التخلص منها أو المطلوب التخلص منها بموجب أحكام القانون الوطني أو هذه الاتفاقية. ويستثنى من هذا التعريف الغطاء الصخري أو الترابي الذي يغطي المعدن الخام أو نفايات الصخور أو نفايات الخام، ويستثنى من ذلك بالتعدين الأولي للزئبق، إلا إذا كانت تحتوي على زئبق أو مركبات زئبق تزيد كميتها عن المستويات الحدية التي يحددها مؤتمر الأطراف.

٣ – يتخذ كل طرف التدابير الملائمة للقيام بما يلي بخصوص نفايات الزئبق:

(أ) إدارة هذه النفايات بطريقة سليمة بيئياً، على أن تؤخذ في الاعتبار المبادئ التوجيهية الموضوعة بموجب اتفاقية بازل ووفقاً للاشتراطات التي يعتمدها مؤتمر الأطراف في مرفق إضافي وفقاً لما تنص عليه المادة ٢٧. ويراعي مؤتمر الأطراف، عند وضعه الاشتراطات، أنظمة وبرامج إدارة النفايات السارية لدى الأطراف؛

(ج) استراتيجية للتحكُّم في ملوّثات متعددة من شأنها تحقيق منافع مشتركة لضبط إطلاقات الزئبق؛

(د) تدابير بديلة لخفض الإطلاقات من المصادر ذات الصلة.

٦ - يضع كل طرف قائمة جرد للإطلاقات من المصادر ذات الصلة، وذلك في غضون خمسة أعوام بعد تاريخ دخول الاتفاقية حيِّز النفاذ بالنسبة له، وأن يحتفظ بها بعد ذلك.

٧ - يعتمد مؤتمر الأطراف، في أقرب وقت من الناحية العملية، توجيهات بشأن ما يلي:

(أ) أفضل التقنيات المتاحة وأفضل الممارسات البيئية، آخذاً في الاعتبار أي فرق بين المصادر الجديدة والقائمة، والحاجة إلى تقليل الآثار الشاملة لعدة أوساط إلى أدنى حدّ؛

(ب) منهجية لإعداد قوائم جرد الإطلاقات.

٨ - يجب على كل طرف أن يدرج في تقاريره المقدَّمة عملاً بالمادة ٢١ معلومات عن تنفيذه لهذه المادة، وبخاصة معلومات بشأن التدابير التي اتخذها وفقاً للفقرات ٣ إلى ٦ ومدى فعالية التدابير.

المادة ١٠

التخزين المؤقت السليم بيئياً للزئبق، بخلاف نفايات الزئبق

١ - تنطبق هذه المادة على التخزين المؤقت للزئبق ولمركبات الزئبق على النحو المُعرَّف في المادة ٣ والذي لا يندرج في معنى تعريف نفايات الزئبق الوارد في المادة ١١.

٢ - يتخذ كل طرف تدابير لكفالة الاضطلاع بالتخزين المؤقّت للزئبق ومركبات الزئبق المخصصة لاستخدام مسموح به لطرف ما بموجب هذه الاتفاقية بطريقة سليمة بيئياً، آخذاً في الاعتبار أي مبادئ توجيهية ووفقاً لأي اشتراطات اعتمدت عملاً بالفقرة ٣.

٣ - يعتمد مؤتمر الأطراف مبادئ توجيهية بشأن التخزين المؤقت السليم بيئياً للزئبق ومركّبات الزئبق، آخذاً في الاعتبار أي مبادئ توجيهية ذات صلة توضَع بموجب اتفاقية بازل بشأن التحكُّم في نقل النفايات الخطرة والتخلّص منها عبر الحدود وأي توجيه آخر ذي صلة. ويجوز لمؤتمر الأطراف أن يعتمد اشتراطات للتخزين المؤقت تُدرَج في مرفق إضافي لهذه الاتفاقية وفقاً للمادة ٢٧.

٢ - ولأغراض هذه المادة:

(أ) ''الإطلاقات'' تعني إطلاقات الزئبق أو مركّبات الزئبق في الأراضي أو المياه؛

(ب) ''المصدر ذو الصلة'' يعني أي مصدر ثابت هام بشري المنشأ للإطلاق يحدّده طرف على أنه لم يعالج في أحكام أخرى من هذه الاتفاقية؛

(ج) ''المصدر الجديد'' يعني أي مصدر ذي صلة بدأ بناؤه أو إجراء تعديلات كبيرة عليه قبل سنة واحدة على الأقل من تاريخ دخول هذه الاتفاقية حيّز النفاذ بالنسبة للطرف المعني؛

(د) ''تعديل كبير'' يعني إجراء تعديل على مصدر ذي صلة ينجم عنه زيادة هامة في الإطلاقات، باستثناء أي تغيير في الإطلاقات الناجمة عن استرداد مُنتَج فرعي، ويترك للطرف أمر البت فيما إذا كان التعديل كبيراً أو لا؛

(هـ) ''المصدر القائم'' يعني أي مصدر ذي صلة ليس مصدراً جديداً؛

(و) ''القيمة الحدّية للإطلاقات'' تعني وضع حد لتركيزات أو كتلة الزئبق أو مركّبات الزئبق الناجمة عن مصدر ثابت للإطلاقات، وكثيراً ما يشار إليها بعبارة ''الزئبق الكلي''.

٣ - يحدد كل طرف فئات المصادر الثابتة ذات الصلة، في موعد أقصاه ثلاثة أعوام من تاريخ دخول الاتفاقية حيّز النفاذ بالنسبة له، وبعد ذلك على نحو منتظم.

٤ - يتخذ أي طرف لديه مصادر ذات صلة تدابير لضبط الإطلاقات، ويجوز له أن يُعد خطة وطنية تحدّد التدابير التي ستتخذ لضبط الإطلاقات وأهدافها وغاياتها والنتائج المتوخّاة منها. وتُعرض أية خطة على مؤتمر الأطراف خلال أربعة أعوام من تاريخ دخول الاتفاقية حيِّز النفاذ بالنسبة لذلك الطرف. وإذا وضع طرف خطة تنفيذ وفقاً للمادة ٢٠، يجوز له أن يدرج فيها الخطة المعدّة عملاً بهذه الفقرة.

٥ - تتضمّن الخطة واحداً أو أكثر من التدابير التالية، وفقاً للمقتضى:

(أ) وضع قِيَم حدّية لضبط، وحيثما أمكن، لخفض الإطلاقات من المصادر ذات الصلة؛

(ب) استخدام أفضل التقنيات المتاحة وأفضل الممارسات البيئية لضبط الإطلاقات من المصادر ذات الصلة؛

٧ - يضع كل طرف، في أقرب وقت من الناحية العملية وفي موعد لا يتجاوز خمسة أعوام بعد تاريخ دخول الاتفاقية حيِّز النفاذ بالنسبة له، قائمة جرد للانبعاثات من المصادر ذات الصلة، ويحتفظ بها بعد ذلك.

٨ - يعتمد مؤتمر الأطراف في اجتماعه الأول توجيهات بشأن ما يلي:

(أ) أفضل التقنيات المتاحة وأفضل الممارسات البيئية آخذاً في الاعتبار أي فرق بين المصادر الجديدة والمصادر القائمة، وضرورة تقليل الآثار الشاملة لعدة أوساط إلى أدنى حدّ؛

(ب) دعم الأطراف لتنفيذ التدابير الواردة في الفقرة ٥، وبخاصة تحديد الأهداف ووضع القِيَم الحدّية للانبعاثات.

٩ - ينبغي أن يعتمد مؤتمر الأطراف، في أقرب وقت من الناحية العملية، توجيهات بشأن:

(أ) معايير يمكن أن تضعها الأطراف عملاً بالفقرة ٢ (ب)؛

(ب) منهجية لإعداد قوائم جرد الانبعاثات.

١٠ - يبقي مؤتمر الأطراف التوجيهات التي وُضعَت عملاً بالفقرتين ٨ و٩ قيد الاستعراض، ويستكملها وفقاً للمقتضى، وتأخذ الأطراف التوجيهات في الاعتبار عند تنفيذ الأحكام ذات الصلة من هذه المادة.

١١ - يدرج كل طرف معلومات بشأن تنفيذه هذه المادة في تقاريره المقدَّمة عملاً بالمادة ٢١، وخصوصاً المعلومات بشأن التدابير التي اتخذها وفقاً للفقرات ٤ إلى ٧ وبشأن فعالية التدابير.

المادة ٩

الإطلاقات

١ - تُعنى هذه المادة بضبط، وحيثما أمكن، بخفض إطلاقات الزئبق أو مركّبات الزئبق المشار إليها غالباً بعبارة "الزئبق الكلي"، في الأراضي والمياه، من مصادر ثابتة ذات صلة لا تتناولها أحكام أخرى من هذه الاتفاقية.

٣ - يتخذ أي طرف لديه مصادر ذات صلة تدابير لضبط الانبعاثات ويجوز له أن يقوم بإعداد خطة وطنية تحدد التدابير التي ستتخذ لضبط الانبعاثات والغايات والأهداف والنتائج المتوخاة منها. وتُعرض أية خطة على مؤتمر الأطراف في غضون ٤ سنوات من تاريخ دخول الاتفاقية حيز النفاذ بالنسبة لذلك الطرف. وإذا وَضع طرف خطة تنفيذ عملاً بالمادة ٢٠، يجوز للطرف أن يضمّنها الخطة المعدّة عملاً بهذه الفقرة.

٤ - فيما يتعلق بالمصادر الجديدة لكل طرف، يشترط الطرف استخدام أفضل التقنيات المتاحة وأفضل الممارسات البيئية لضبط الانبعاثات وتخفيضها، وحيثما أمكن، في أقرب وقت ممكن من الناحية العملية، بحيث لا يتجاوز خمسة أعوام من تاريخ دخول الاتفاقية حيز النفاذ بالنسبة لذلك الطرف. ويجوز للطرف أن يستخدم قِيَماً حدّية للانبعاثات تتسق وتطبيق أفضل التقنيات المتاحة.

٥ - يدرج كل طرف، فيما يتعلق بمصادره القائمة، في أي خطة وطنية تدبيراً أو أكثر من التدابير التالية وأن ينفّذ ما يلي، مراعياً في ذلك ظروفه الوطنية والجدوى الاقتصادية والتقنية للتدابير وملاءمة تكاليفها، وذلك في أقرب وقت ممكن من الناحية العملية، ولكن في موعد أقصاه عشرة أعوام بعد تاريخ دخول الاتفاقية حيِّز النفاذ بالنسبة له:

(أ) هدف كمّي لضبط، وحيثما أمكن، لخفض الانبعاثات من المصادر ذات الصلة؛

(ب) القِيَم الحدّيّة للانبعاثات بغية ضبط، وحيثما أمكن، خفض الانبعاثات من المصادر ذات الصلة؛

(ج) استخدام أفضل التقنيات المتاحة وأفضل الممارسات البيئية لضبط الانبعاثات من المصادر ذات الصلة؛

(د) استراتيجية لضبط الملوّثات المتعددة يمكن أن توفر منافع مشتركة لضبط انبعاثات الزئبق؛

(هـ) تدابير بديلة لخفض الانبعاثات من المصادر ذات الصلة.

٦ - يجوز للأطراف أن تُطَبق نفس التدابير على جميع المصادر القائمة ذات الصلة، أو يجوز لها أن تعتمد تدابير مختلفة وفقاً لفئات المصادر المختلفة. ويكون الهدف من تلك التدابير المطبّقة من جانب الطرف إحراز تقدُّم معقول في خفض الانبعاثات مع مرور الوقت.

(و) استخدام آليات تبادل المعلومات القائمة لتعزيز المعرفة، وتشجيع أفضل الممارسات البيئية، والتكنولوجيات البديلة الصالحة بيئياً وتقنياً واجتماعياً واقتصادياً.

المادة ٨

الانبعاثات

١ - تُعنى هذه المادة بالضبط والتخفيض، حيثما أمكن، لانبعاثات الزئبق أو مركبات الزئبق المشار إليها غالباً بعبارة ''الزئبق الكلي''، في الغلاف الجوي، من خلال تدابير تهدف إلى ضبط الانبعاثات من المصادر الثابتة التي تندرج في فئات المصادر الواردة في المرفق دال.

٢ - لأغراض هذه المادة:

(أ) ''الانبعاثات'' تعني انبعاثات الزئبق ومركبات الزئبق في الغلاف الجوي؛

(ب) ''المصدر ذو الصلة'' يعني مصدراً يندرِج في فئة من فئات المصادر الواردة في المرفق دال، ويجوز لأي طرف إذا ما اختار ذلك، أن يضع معايير لتحديد المصادر المشمولة بفئة للمصادر مدرجة في المرفق دال طالما اشتملت المعايير المتعلقة بأي فئة على نسبة ٧٥ في المائة على الأقل من الانبعاثات الصادرة من تلك الفئة؛

(ج) ''المصدر الجديد'' يعني أي مصدر ذي صلة يندرج في فئة واردة في المرفق دال، بدأ بناؤه أو إجراء تعديلات كبيرة عليه قبل سنة واحدة على الأقل من تاريخ:

'١' دخول هذه الاتفاقية حيِّز النفاذ بالنسبة للطرف المعني؛ أو

'٢' دخول تعديل على المرفق دال حيِّز النفاذ بالنسبة للطرف المعني ليصبح المصدَر خاضعاً لأحكام هذه الاتفاقية بمقتضى ذلك التعديل لا غير؛

(د) ''تعديل كبير'' يعني إجراء تعديل على مصدر ذي صلة تنتج عنه زيادة كبيرة في الانبعاثات، باستثناء أي تغيير في الانبعاثات الناجمة عن استرداد مُنتَج فرعي. ويترك للطرف أمر البت فيما إذا كان التعديل كبيراً أو لا؛

(هـ) ''المصدر القائم'' يعني أي مصدر ذي صلة لا يُعتبر مصدراً جديداً؛

(و) ''القيمة الحدية للانبعاثات'' تعني وضع حدّ لتركيزات الزئبق أو مركبات الزئبق أو كتلتها أو معدل انبعاثاتها الناجمة عن مصدر ثابت للانبعاثات، والمعبر عنها غالباً بعبارة ''الزئبق الكلي''.

المادة ٧

تعدين الذهب الحرفي والضيِّق النطاق

١ - تنطبق التدابير الواردة في هذه المادة والمرفق جيم على تعدين وتصنيع الذهب الحرفي والضيق النطاق التي تُستخدم فيه ملغمة الزئبق لاستخراج الذهب من الركاز.

٢ - يتخذ كل طرف، تجري في أراضيه عملية تعدين أو تصنيع حرفي وضيق النطاق للذهب، خاضعة لهذه المادة، خطوات للحد من استخدام الزئبق ومركبات الزئبق، والتخلص منه حيثما أمكن، في هذا التعدين والتصنيع، ومنع انبعاثات وإطلاقات الزئبق من هذا التعدين والتصنيع في البيئة.

٣ - يخطر كل طرف الأمانة إذا كان قد قرر، في أي وقت كان، أن تعدين وتصنيع الذهب الحرفي والضيق النطاق في أراضيه هو أكثر من كونه عديم الأهمية. ويقوم الطرف، إذا قرر ذلك، بما يلي:

(أ) وضع وتنفيذ خطة عمل وطنية وفقاً للمرفق جيم؛

(ب) تقديم خطة عمله الوطنية إلى الأمانة في موعد لا يتجاوز ثلاث سنوات بعد بدء نفاذ الاتفاقية بالنسبة له أو بعد ثلاث سنوات من إرسال الإخطار إلى الأمانة، أيهما أبعد؛

(ج) القيام بعد ذلك بتقديم استعراض كل ثلاث سنوات للتقدم المحرز في الوفاء بالتزاماته بموجب هذه المادة وإدراج هذه الاستعراضات في تقاريره المقدمة عملاً بالمادة ٢١.

٤ - يجوز للأطراف أن تتعاون مع بعضها البعض ومع المنظمات الحكومية الدولية المختصة والكيانات الأخرى، وفقاً للمقتضى، لتحقيق أهداف هذه المادة. ويجوز أن يشمل هذا التعاون ما يلي:

(أ) وضع استراتيجيات لمنع تحويل وجهة الزئبق أو مركبات الزئبق لاستخدامها في تعدين وتصنيع الذهب الحرفي والضيق النطاق؛

(ب) مبادرات التثقيف والتوعية وبناء القدرات؛

(ج) تشجيع إجراء بحوث بشأن الممارسات المستدامة لبدائل غير الزئبق؛

(د) تقديم المساعدة التقنية والمالية؛

(هـ) إقامة شراكات للمساعدة في تنفيذ التزاماتها بموجب هذه المادة؛

٥ - ينقضي أجل جميع الإعفاءات عملاً بالفقرة ١، بعد انقضاء خمس سنوات من تاريخ الإنهاء التدريجي المعني المُدرَج في المرفق ألف أو باء، ما لم يُشر طرف ما في السجل إلى فترة زمنية أقصر.

٦ - يجوز لمؤتمر الأطراف، بناءً على طلب من أحد الأطراف، أن يقرر تمديد فترة الإعفاء حتى خمس سنوات، ما لم يطلب الطرف فترة زمنية أقصر. وعند اتخاذ القرار، يراعي مؤتمر الأطراف على النحو الواجب ما يلي:

(أ) تقرير من الطرف يبرِّر فيه الحاجة إلى تمديد الإعفاء ويعرض الأنشطة التي تم الاضطلاع بها أو المزمع الاضطلاع بها لإنهاء الحاجة إلى الإعفاء في أقرب وقت ممكن عملياً؛

(ب) المعلومات المتاحة، بما في ذلك توافر منتجات وعمليات بديلة خالية من الزئبق أو تنطوي على استهلاك كمية أقل من الزئبق مقارنة بالاستخدام المُعفى؛

(ج) الأنشطة المزمعة أو المضطلع بها لتوفير تخزين سليم بيئياً للزئبق وللتخلّص من نفايات الزئبق.

ولا يجوز تمديد أي إعفاء إلاّ مرة واحدة لكل مُنتَج حُدِّد له موعد إنهاء تدريجي.

٧ - يجوز لأي طرف في أي وقت أن يسحب الإعفاء بناءً على إخطار خطّي يقدّمه إلى الأمانة. ويسري سحب الإعفاء اعتباراً من التاريخ المحدَّد في الإخطار.

٨ - بصرف النظر عمّا جاء في الفقرة ١، لا يجوز لأي دولة أو منظمة إقليمية للتكامل الاقتصادي أن تسجِّل نفسها للحصول على إعفاء بعد خمس سنوات من تاريخ الإنهاء التدريجي فيما يتعلق بالمُنتَج المعني المُدرَج أو العملية المعنية المدرجة في المرفق ألف أو المرفق باء، ما لم يظل طرف أو أكثر من طرف مسجَّلين للحصول على إعفاء لذلك المُنتَج أو لتلك العملية، بعد حصولهم على تمديد عملاً بالفقرة ٦. وفي تلك الحالة، يجوز لأي دولة أو منظمة إقليمية للتكامل الاقتصادي، في الأوقات المحدَّدة في الفقرتين ١ (أ) و(ب)، التسجيل للحصول على إعفاء من أجل ذلك المُنتَج أو تلك العملية، الذي سينقضي بعد مرور عشر سنوات من تاريخ الإنهاء التدريجي ذي الصلة.

٩ - لا يجوز لأي طرف التمتُّع فعلاً بإعفاء في أي وقت بعد مرور عشرة أعوام من تاريخ الإنهاء التدريجي لمُنتَج مُدرَج أو عملية مُدرَجة في المرفق ألف أو المرفق باء.

١١ - وعند أي استعراض للمرفق باء عملاً بالفقرة ١٠، يراعي مؤتمر الأطراف، على الأقل، ما يلي:

(أ) أي مقترح مقدَّم بموجب الفقرة ٩؛

(ب) المعلومات المتاحة بمقتضى الفقرة ٤؛

(ج) توافر بدائل خالية من الزئبق للأطراف، تتسم بجدواها التقنية والاقتصادية، مع مراعاة مخاطرها وفوائدها للبيئة والصحة.

المادة ٦

الإعفاءات المتاحة للطرف عند الطلب

١ - يجوز لأي دولة أو منظمة إقليمية للتكامل الاقتصادي أن تسجِّل نفسها للحصول على واحدٍ أو أكثر من الإعفاءات من تواريخ الإنهاء التدريجي المدرجة في المرفق ألف والمرفق باء، والمشار إليها فيما بعد بكلمة "إعفاء"، وذلك بإخطار الأمانة خطّياً:

(أ) بأنها أصبحت طرفاً في الاتفاقية؛ أو

(ب) في حالة أي مُنتَج مضاف إليه الزئبق يضاف إلى المرفق ألف بموجب تعديل أو أي عملية تصنيع يُستخدَم فيها الزئبق تضاف إلى المرفق باء بموجب تعديل، في موعد لا يتجاوز تاريخ بدء نفاذ التعديل المطبّق بالنسبة للطرف.

ويكون أي تسجيل من هذا القبيل مشفوعاً ببيان يعلّل حاجة الطرف إلى الإعفاء.

٢ - ويمكن تسجيل إعفاء، إما فيما يتعلق بفئة مُدرجة في المرفق ألف أو باء أو فيما يتعلق بفئة فرعية تحدّدها أي دولة أو منظمة إقليمية للتكامل الاقتصادي.

٣ - يجب أن يُحَدَّد في سجلّ كل طرف حصل على إعفاء أو أكثر. وتُنشئ الأمانة السجل وتحتفظ به وتتيحه للجمهور.

٤ - يشتمل السجل على ما يلي:

(أ) قائمة بالأطراف التي حصلت على إعفاء أو أكثر؛

(ب) الإعفاء أو الإعفاءات المسجلة لكل طرف؛

(ج) تاريخ انقضاء كل إعفاء.

(ب) إدراج المعلومات عن التدابير المتخذة عملاً بهذه الفقرة في التقارير المقدّمة منه عملاً بالمادة ٢١؛

(ج) السعي إلى تحديد المرافق الموجودة داخل أراضيه التي تستخدم الزئبق أو مركبات الزئبق في العمليات المدرجة في المرفق باء وموافاة الأمانة، في غضون فترة لا تتعدّى ثلاث سنوات بعد تاريخ دخول الاتفاقية حيِّز النفاذ بالنسبة للطرف، بمعلومات عن عدد وأنواع هذه المرافق وبتقدير للكمية السنوية المستخدمة من الزئبق أو مركبات الزئبق المستخدمة في تلك المرافق. وتقوم الأمانة بإتاحة هذه المعلومات للجمهور.

٦ - لا يسمح أي طرف باستخدام الزئبق أو مركّبات الزئبق في مرفق لم يكن موجوداً قبل تاريخ دخول الاتفاقية حيِّز النفاذ بالنسبة له، في عمليات التصنيع الواردة في المرفق باء. ولا تسري أية إعفاءات على هذه المرافق.

٧ - يحول كل طرف دون تطوير أي مرفق يستخدِم أي عملية تصنيع أخرى يُستخدَم فيها الزئبق أو مركّبات الزئبق عن عمد و لم يكن موجوداً قبل تاريخ دخول الاتفاقية حيِّز النفاذ، باستثناء الحالات التي يستطيع فيها الطرف أن يبيِّن ما يُقنع مؤتمر الأطراف بأن عملية التصنيع توفر منافع بيئية وصحية هامة، وأنه لا تواجد بدائل متاحة خالية من الزئبق ومجدية تقنياً واقتصادياً توفر هذه المنافع.

٨ - تُشجّع الأطراف على تبادل المعلومات بشأن التطوّرات التكنولوجية الجديدة ذات الصلة والبدائل الخالية من الزئبق المجدية اقتصادياً وتقنياً، والتدابير والتقنيات الممكنة لخفض، وحيثما أمكن، لإنهاء استخدام الزئبق ومركّبات الزئبق في عمليات التصنيع المُدرجة في المرفق باء والقضاء على انبعاثات وإطلاقات الزئبق ومركبات الزئبق الناجمة عنها.

٩ - يجوز لأي طرف أن يقدِّم اقتراحاً لتعديل المرفق باء بغية إدراج عملية تصنيع يُستخدَم فيها الزئبق أو مركّبات الزئبق. ويتضمن الاقتراح معلومات تتصل بتوافر بدائل من غير الزئبق للعملية و جدواها التقنية والاقتصادية والمخاطر والفوائد البيئية والصحية.

١٠ - يقوم مؤتمر الأطراف باستعراض المرفق باء، في موعد لا يتجاوز خمس سنوات بعد تاريخ دخول الاتفاقية حيِّز النفاذ، ويجوز له أن ينظر في إدخال تعديلات على هذا المرفق وفقاً للمادة ٢٧.

٩ - عند استعراض المرفق ألف عملاً بالفقرة ٨، يراعي مؤتمر الأطراف، على الأقل، ما يلي:

(أ) أي مقترح مقدَّم بموجب الفقرة ٧؛

(ب) المعلومات المتاحة عملاً بالفقرة ٤؛

(ج) توافر بدائل خالية من الزئبق للأطراف تتسم بجدواها التقنية والاقتصادية، مع مراعاة مخاطرها وفوائدها للبيئة وصحة الإنسان.

المادة ٥

عمليات التصنيع التي يُستخدَم فيها الزئبق أو مركّبات الزئبق

١ - لأغراض هذه المادة والمرفق باء، لا تشمل عمليات التصنيع التي يُستخدَم فيها الزئبق أو مركّبات الزئبق العمليات التي تستخدِم المنتجات المضاف إليها الزئبق أو عمليات تصنيع المواد المضاف إليها الزئبق أو العمليات المستخدَمة في معالجة النفايات المحتوية على الزئبق.

٢ - لا يسمح أي طرف، من خلال اتخاذ تدابير مناسبة، باستخدام الزئبق أو مركّبات الزئبق في عمليات التصنيع المدرجة في الجزء الأول من المرفق باء بعد انقضاء موعد الإنهاء التدريجي المحدَّد في ذلك المرفق لفرادى العمليات، إلاّ إذا كان لدى الطرف إعفاء مسجّل عملاً بالمادة ٦.

٣ - يتخذ كل طرف تدابير لتقييد استخدام الزئبق أو مركّبات الزئبق في العمليات المدرجة في الجزء الثاني من المرفق باء، وفقاً للأحكام المحدّدة فيه.

٤ - تقوم الأمانة، استناداً إلى المعلومات المقدمة من الأطراف، بجمع وحفظ المعلومات عن العمليات التي تستخدم الزئبق أو مركّبات الزئبق وبدائلهم، وتجعل هذه المعلومات متاحة للجمهور. ويجوز أن تقدِّم الأطراف معلومات أخرى ذات صلة وأن تقوم الأمانة بإتاحتها للجمهور.

٥ - على كل طرف لديه مرفق واحد أو أكثر يستخدِم الزئبق أو مركّبات الزئبق في عمليات التصنيع المدرجة في المرفق باء أن يقوم بما يلي:

(أ) اتخاذ تدابير للتعامل مع انبعاثات الزئبق أو مركبات الزئبق وإطلاقاتها من تلك المرافق؛

(د) لا يكون مؤهّلاً للمطالبة بإعفاءات عملاً بالمادة ٦ فيما يتعلق بأي فئة منتجات يتم من أجلها اختيار هذا البديل.

يقوم مؤتمر الأطراف، في موعد لا يتجاوز خمس سنوات من تاريخ دخول الاتفاقية حيِّز النفاذ، وكجزء من عملية الاستعراض بموجب الفقرة ٨، باستعراض التقدُّم المحرز وفعالية التدابير المتخذة بموجب هذه الفقرة.

٣ - يتخذ كل طرف تدابير بشأن المنتجات المضاف إليها الزئبق، المُدرجَة في الجزء الثاني من المرفق ألف وفقاً للأحكام المبيَّنة في ذلك الجزء.

٤ - تقوم الأمانة، بناءً على معلومات تقدّمها الأطراف، بجمع معلومات عن المنتجات المضاف إليها الزئبق وبدائلها، وأن تحتفظ بهذه المعلومات، وتجعلها متاحة للجمهور. ويجب على الأمانة أيضاً أن تتيح للجمهور أي معلومات أخرى ذات صلة تقدمها الأطراف.

٥ - يتخذ كل طرف تدابير لمنع إدخال منتجات مضاف إليها الزئبق لا يُسمَح بتصنيعها أو استيرادها أو تصديرها بموجب هذه المادة، في منتجات مجمَّعة.

٦ - يثني كل طرف عن التصنيع أو التوزيع التجاري لمنتجات مضاف إليها الزئبق غير مشمولة بأي استعمال معروف للمنتجات المضاف إليها الزئبق قبل تاريخ دخول هذه الاتفاقية حيِّز النفاذ بالنسبة لذلك الطرف، إلاّ إذا أظهر تقييم لمخاطر وفوائد هذا المُنتَج أن له فوائد تعود على البيئة أو صحة الإنسان. ويقدم الطرف إلى الأمانة، وفقاً للمقتضى، معلومات عن أي مُنتَج من هذا القبيل، بما في ذلك أي معلومات عن مخاطر هذا المُنتَج وفوائده للبيئة وصحة الإنسان. ويجب على الأمانة أن تجعل هذه المعلومات متاحة للجمهور.

٧ - يجوز لأي طرف أن يقدِّم مقترحاً إلى الأمانة بإدراج مُنتَج مضاف إليه الزئبق في المرفق ألف، ويشمل الاقتراح معلومات تتصل بمدى توافر بدائل لهذا المُنتَج خالية من الزئبق والجدوى التقنية والاقتصادية لها، ومخاطرها وفوائدها للبيئة وصحة الإنسان، مع مراعاة المعلومات المتاحة عملاً بالفقرة ٤.

٨ - يقوم مؤتمر الأطراف باستعراض المرفق ألف، في موعد لا يتجاوز خمس سنوات بعد تاريخ دخول الاتفاقية حيِّز النفاذ، ويجوز له أن ينظر في إدخال تعديلات على هذا المرفق وفقاً للمادة ٢٧.

١٢ - يقدِّم مؤتمر الأطراف في اجتماعه الأول مزيداً من التوجيهات فيما يتعلق بهذه المادة، وخصوصاً فيما يتعلق بالفقرة ٥ (أ)، والفقرتين ٦ و٨ ويضع ويعتمد مضمون الشهادة المطلوب المشار إليه في الفقرتين ٦ (ب) و٨.

١٣ - يقيِّم مؤتمر الأطراف ما إذا كانت التجارة في مركّبات زئبق محدّدة تخلّ بهدف هذه الاتفاقية، وينظر فيما إذا كان ينبغي إخضاع مركّبات زئبق محدَّدة للفقرتين ٦ و ٨، من خلال إدراجها في مرفق إضافي يُعتَمد وفقاً للمادة ٢٧.

المادة ٤

المنتجات المضاف إليها الزئبق

١ - لا يسمح أي طرف، من خلال اتخاذه تدابير مناسبة، بتصنيع أو استيراد أو تصدير المنتجات المضاف إليها الزئبق المُدرجة في الجزء الأول من المرفق ألف بعد انقضاء موعد الإنهاء التدريجي المحدَّد لتلك المنتجات، إلاّ إذا حُدِّد إعفاء في المرفق ألف أو كان لدى الطرف إعفاء مسجّل عملاً بالمادة ٦.

٢ - كبديل عن الفقرة ١، يجوز للطرف أن يشير وقت التصديق أو لدى دخول التعديل على المرفق ألف حيِّز النفاذ بالنسبة له، إلى أنه سينفِّذ تدابير أو استراتيجيات مختلفة للتعامل مع المنتجات المُدرجة في الجزء الأول من المرفق ألف. ولا يجوز للطرف أن يختار هذا البديل إلا إذا أمكنه أن يثبت أنه قلّل فعلاً إلى الحدّ الأدنى تصنيع واستيراد وتصدير الغالبية الكبرى من المنتجات المُدرجة في الجزء الأول من المرفق ألف وأنه قد نفّذ تدابير أو استراتيجيات لخفض استخدام الزئبق في منتجات إضافية ليست مدرجة في الجزء الأول من المرفق ألف وقت إخطاره الأمانة بقراره باستخدام هذا البديل. وإضافة إلى ذلك، يقوم الطرف الذي يختار هذا البديل بما يلي:

(أ) يقدِّم تقريراً في أول فرصة إلى مؤتمر الأطراف يصف فيه التدابير أو الاستراتيجيات المنفّذة، بما في ذلك تقدير كمّي للتخفيضات المُنجَزة؛

(ب) ينفِّذ تدابير أو استراتيجيات لخفض استخدام الزئبق في أي منتجات مُدرجَة في الجزء الأول من المرفق ألف لم تحدد قيمة حدّها الأدنى بعد؛

(ج) ينظر في تدابير إضافية لتحقيق تخفيضات أخرى؛

'١' لدى غير الطرف تدابير تكفل حماية صحة الإنسان والبيئة وتكفل امتثاله لأحكام المادتين ١٠ و ١١؛

'٢' وأن هذا الزئبق سوف يُستخدَم فقط استخداماً مسموحاً به لطرف بموجب هذه الاتفاقية أو من أجل التخزين المؤقت السليم بيئياً على النحو المبيَّن في المادة ١٠.

٧ - يجوز للطرف المُصَدِّر أن يعتمد على إخطار عام مقدَّم إلى الأمانة من الطرف المستورد أو من الدولة غير الطرف باعتبار ذلك الموافقة الخطّية المطلوبة بمقتضى الفقرة ٦. ويوضِّح هذا الإخطار العام أي شروط وأحكام يقدِّم الطرف المستورِد أو غير الطرف بمقتضاها موافقته. ويجوز لذلك الطرف أو غير الطرف في أي وقت إلغاء هذا الإخطار. وعلى الأمانة أن تحتفظ بسجل عام لجميع الإخطارات من هذا النوع.

٨ - لا يسمح أي طرف باستيراد الزئبق من غير طرف سيقدِّم له موافقته الخطّية ما لم يكن غير الطرف قد قدَّم شهادة بأن ذلك الزئبق ليس من مصادر محدَّدة على الها مصادر غير مسموح بها بموجب الفقرة ٣ أو الفقرة ٥ (ب).

٩ - يجوز للطرف الذي يُقدِّم إخطاراً عاماً بالموافقة بموجب الفقرة ٧ أن يقرِّر عدم تطبيق الفقرة ٨، شريطة أن يواصل تطبيق قيود شاملة على تصدير الزئبق وأن يتخذ تدابير محلية لكفالة أن يدار هذا الزئبق المستورد بطريقة سليمة بيئياً. ويقدِّم الطرف إخطاراً بهذا القرار إلى الأمانة، يتضمن معلومات تصف قيوده على الصادرات والتدابير التنظيمية المحلية، فضلاً عن معلومات عن كميات الزئبق وبلدان منشأ الزئبق المستورد من غير الأطراف. وتحتفظ الأمانة بسجل عام لجميع الإخطارات من هذا النوع. وتقوم لجنة التنفيذ والامتثال باستعراض وتقييم أي إخطارات ومعلومات داعمة عملاً بالمادة ١٥ ويجوز أن تقدم توصيات، وفقاً للمقتضى، إلى مؤتمر الأطراف.

١٠ - يظل الإجراء المبيَّن في الفقرة ٩ متاحاً لحين اختتام الاجتماع الثاني لمؤتمر الأطراف. ولا يتاح بعد ذلك الوقت، ما لم يقرِّر مؤتمر الأطراف خلاف ذلك بأغلبية بسيطة من الأطراف الحاضرين المصوِّتين، باستثناء ما يتعلق بطرف قدَّم إخطاراً بموجب الفقرة ٩ قبل نهاية الاجتماع الثاني لمؤتمر الأطراف.

١١ - يُدرِج كل طرف أن في تقاريره المقدَّمة عملاً بالمادة ٢١ معلومات تبيِّن استيفاء الاشتراطات الواردة في هذه المادة.

(ب) الكمّيات النـزرة من الزئبق أو مركّبات الزئبق الموجودة بطبيعتها في المنتجات المعدنية مثل الفلزّات أو الخامات أو المنتجات المعدنية غير المحتوية على الزئبق، بما في ذلك الفحم أو المنتجات المشتقة من هذه المواد، والكميات النـزرة غير المقصودة في المنتجات الكيميائية؛ أو

(ج) المنتجات المضاف إليها الزئبق.

٣ - لا يسمح أي طرف بتعدين الزئبق الأوّلي الذي لم يكن يجري على أراضيه في تاريخ دخول الاتفاقية حيّز النفاذ بالنسبة له.

٤ - لا يسمح أي طرف إلاّ بتعدين الزئبق الأوّلي الذي كان يجري على أراضيه في تاريخ دخول الاتفاقية حيّز النفاذ بالنسبة له لفترة تصل إلى خمسة عشر عاماً بعد ذلك التاريخ. وخلال هذه الفترة لا يُستخدَم الزئبق الناتج عن عملية التعدين هذه إلاّ في صناعة المنتجات المضاف إليها الزئبق عملاً بالمادة ٤، أو في عمليات التصنيع وفقاً للمادة ٥ أو يتم التخلّص منه عملاً بالمادة ١١، باستخدام عمليات لا تؤدّي إلى استرداد أو إعادة تدوير أو استخلاص أو إعادة الاستخدام المباشر أو الاستخدامات البديلة.

٥ - يقوم كل طرف بما يلي:

(أ) يسعى إلى تحديد كل كمية على حِدة من مخزونات الزئبق أو مركّبات الزئبق التي تزيد على ٥٠ طناً مترياً بالإضافة إلى مصادر الإمداد بالزئبق التي تتولّد عنها مخزونات تزيد عن ١٠ أطنان مترية سنوياً والموجودة على أراضيه؛

(ب) يتخذ تدابير تكفُل، إذا ما قرَّر الطرف توافر فائض الزئبق نتيجة وقف تشغيل مرافق إنتاج الكلور والقلويات، التخلُّص من هذا الزئبق وفقاً للمبادئ التوجيهية للإدارة السليمة بيئياً المشار إليها في الفقرة ٣ (أ) من المادة ١١، باستخدام عمليات لا تؤدّي إلى استرداد أو إعادة تدوير أو استخلاص أو الاستخدام المباشر أو الاستخدامات البديلة.

٦ - لا يسمح أي طرف بتصدير الزئبق إلاّ:

(أ) إلى طرف زوّد الطرف المُصَدِّر بموافقته الخطّية، وليس لأي غرض سوى:

'١' استخدام يسمح به للطرف المستورد بموجب هذه الاتفاقية؛ أو

'٢' لغرض التخزين المؤقت السليم بيئياً على النحو المبيَّن في المادة ١٠؛ أو

(ب) إلى غير طرف زوّد الطرف المُصَدِّر بموافقته الخطّية، بما فيها شهادة تثبت أن:

(ز) ''الطرف'' يعني دولة أو منظمة إقليمية للتكامل الاقتصادي توافق على الالتزام بهذه الاتفاقية وتكون الاتفاقية سارية المفعول بالنسبة لها؛

(ح) ''الأطراف الحاضرة والمصوّتة'' تعني الأطراف الحاضرة والتي تدلي بأصواتها إيجاباً أو سلباً في اجتماع الأطراف؛

(ط) ''التعديل الأوّلي للزئبق'' يعني التعديل الذي تكون المادة الرئيسية المقصودة فيه هي الزئبق؛

(ي) ''المنظمة الإقليمية للتكامل الاقتصادي'' تعني منظمة أنشأتها دول ذات سيادة في منطقة معيّنة تنقل إليها الدول الأعضاء فيها الاختصاص فيما يتعلق بالمسائل التي تحكمها هذه الاتفاقية، وتخوّلها، حسب الأصول، وفقاً لإجراءاتها الداخلية، التوقيع على هذه الاتفاقية أو التصديق عليها أو قبولها أو إقرارها أو الانضمام إليها؛

(ك) ''الاستخدام المسموح به'' يعني أي استخدام من طرف ما للزئبق أو مركّباته يتسق مع هذه الاتفاقية، بما في ذلك الاستخدامات المتسقة مع المواد ٣ و ٤ و ٥ و ٦ و ٧، دون أن يقتصر عليها.

المادة ٣

مصادر الإمداد بالزئبق والتجارة فيه

١ - لأغراض هذه المادة:

(أ) تشمل الإشارات إلى ''الزئبق'' خلائط الزئبق مع مواد أخرى، بما في ذلك سبائك الزئبق التي لا يقل تركيز الزئبق فيها عن ٩٥ في المائة من وزنها؛

(ب) ''مركّبات الزئبق'' وتعني (أول) كلوريد الزئبق (المعروف أيضاً باسم الكالوميل)، و (ثاني) أكسيد الزئبقيك، و (ثاني) كبريتات الزئبقيك، وثاني نترات الزئبقيك، وفلز الزنجفر، وسلفيد الزئبق.

٢ - ولا تُطَبّق أحكام هذه المادة على ما يلي:

(أ) كمّيات الزئبق أو مركبات الزئبق التي ستُستخدَم في البحوث على نطاق مختبري أو كمعيار مرجعي؛ أو

المادة ٢

التعاريف

لأغراض هذه الاتفاقية:

(أ) ''تعدين الذهب الحرفي والضيِّق النطاق يعني تعدين الذهب من قِبَل عمال مناجم أفراد أو شركات صغيرة باستثمار رأسمالي وإنتاج محدودين؛

(ب) ''أفضل التقنيات المتاحة'' تعني التقنيات الأكثر فعالية في منع، وحيثما يكون ذلك غير عملي، في الحد من انبعاثات وإطلاقات الزئبق في الهواء والماء والأراضي وأثر تلك الإطلاقات والانبعاثات على البيئة ككل، مع مراعاة الاعتبارات الاقتصادية والتقنية لطرف ما أو لمرفق ما موجود على أراضي ذلك الطرف. وفي هذا السياق:

'١' ''أفضل'' يعني الأكثر فعالية في تحقيق مستوى عام مرتفع من حماية البيئة ككل؛

'٢' ''التقنيات المتاحة''، فيما يتعلق بطرف معين ومرفق معين على أراضي ذلك الطرف، تعني التقنيات التي تُستحدث على نطاق يمكّن من التنفيذ في قطاع صناعي ذي صلة في ظل ظروف صالحة اقتصادياً وتقنياً، مع أخذ التكاليف والفوائد في الاعتبار، سواء استُخدمت تلك التقنيات أو تم استحداثها، أو لم تُستخدم أو تستحدث، على أراضي الطرف المعني، بشرط أن تكون متاحة لمشغّل المرفق، وفقاً لما يحدده ذلك الطرف؛

'٣' ''التقنيات'' تعني التكنولوجيات المستخدمة والممارسات التشغيلية والطرائق التي تصمم بها المنشآت وتُبنى وتصان ويجري تشغيلها وإخراجها من الخدمة؛

(ج) ''أفضل الممارسات البيئية'' تعني تطبيق أنسب خليط من تدابير واستراتيجيات التحكم البيئي؛

(د) ''الزئبق'' يعني عنصر الزئبق الأولي (Hg(0), CAS No. 7439-97-6)؛

(هـ) ''مركب الزئبق'' يعني أي مادة تتكون من ذرات من الزئبق ومن ذرة أو أكثر من عناصر كيميائية أخرى لا يمكن فصلها إلى مركبات مختلفة إلا من خلال تفاعلات كيميائية؛

(و) ''المُنتج المضاف إليه الزئبق'' يعني المُنتج أو مكوِّن المُنتج الذي يحتوي على الزئبق أو مركّب زئبق أُضيف عمداً؛

وإذ تشدِّد على أهمية الدعم المالي والتقني والتكنولوجي ودعم بناء القدرات، وبخاصة للبلدان النامية والبلدان التي تمر اقتصاداتها بمرحلة انتقال، بغية تعزيز القدرات الوطنية من أجل إدارة الزئبق وتشجيع التنفيذ الفعَّال للاتفاقية،

وإذ تُقِرّ أيضاً بأنشطة منظمة الصحة العالمية لحماية صحة الإنسان فيما يتصل بالزئبق وبأدوار الاتفاقات البيئية المتعددة الأطراف ذات الصلة، لا سيما اتفاقية بازل بشأن التحكُّم في نقل النفايات الخطرة والتخلُّص منها عبر الحدود واتفاقية روتردام لتطبيق إجراء الموافقة المسبقة عن علم على مواد كيميائية ومبيدات آفات معيَّنة خطرة متداولة في التجارة الدولية،

وإذ تُقرّ بأن هذه الاتفاقية وسائر الاتفاقات الدولية في مجال البيئة والتجارة هي اتفاقات مساندة لبعضها البعض،

وإذ تشدِّد على أنه ليس في هذه الاتفاقية ما يرمي إلى التأثير على حقوق أي طرف وعلى التزاماته الناشئة عن أي اتفاق دولي قائم،

وإذ تُدرك أن السرد الوارد أعلاه لا يرمي إلى إقامة ترتيب هرمي بين هذه الاتفاقية والصكوك الدولية الأخرى،

وإذ تشير إلى أنه لا يوجد في هذه الاتفاقية ما يمنع أي طرف من اتخاذ تدابير محلية إضافية تتسق وأحكام هذه الاتفاقية سعياً إلى حماية صحة الإنسان والبيئة من التعرُّض للزئبق وفقاً للالتزامات الأخرى المترتبة على الطرف بموجب القانون الدولي الساري،

قد اتفقَت على ما يلي:

المادة ١

الهدف

الهدف من هذه الاتفاقية هو حماية صحة الإنسان والبيئة من الانبعاثات والإطلاقات البشرية المنشأ للزئبق ومركّبات الزئبق.

[TEXT IN ARABIC – TEXTE EN ARABE]

اتفاقية ميناماتا بشأن الزئبق

إن الأطراف في هذه الاتفاقية،

إذ تقر بأن الزئبق مادة كيميائية تثير انشغالاً عالمياً بسبب انتقالها البعيد المدى في الجو، وثباتها في البيئة بمجرد دخولها إليها بوسائط بشرية المنشأ، وقدرتها على التراكم بيئياً في النظم الإيكولوجية، وآثارها السلبية الكبيرة على صحة الإنسان والبيئة،

وإذ تشير إلى المقرر ٢٥/٥ المؤرخ ٢٠ شباط/فبراير ٢٠٠٩ الذي اتخذه مجلس إدارة برنامج الأمم المتحدة للبيئة للبدء باتخاذ إجراءات دولية لإدارة الزئبق على نحو يتسم بالكفاءة والفعالية والاتساق،

وإذ تشير إلى الفقرة ٢٢١ من الوثيقة الختامية الصادرة عن مؤتمر الأمم المتحدة للتنمية المستدامة بعنوان ''المستقبل الذي نصبو إليه'' التي تدعو إلى خاتمة موفّقة للمفاوضات بشأن صكّ عالمي مُلزِم قانوناً بشأن الزئبق لمعالجة الأخطار التي تهدّد صحة الإنسان والبيئة،

وإذ تشير إلى أن مؤتمر الأمم المتحدة للتنمية المستدامة أعاد التأكيد على مبادئ إعلان ريو بشأن البيئة والتنمية، ومنها ضمن أمور أخرى، المسؤوليات المشتركة والمتباينة، وإذ تسلّم بالظروف الخاصة بالبلدان وقدراتها والحاجة إلى اتخاذ إجراء عالمي،

وإدراكاً منها للشواغل الصحية، خصوصاً في البلدان النامية، الناجمة عن التعرُّض للزئبق، بالنسبة للفئات السكانية الضعيفة، وخصوصاً الأطفال والنساء، ومن خلالهم الأجيال القادمة،

وإذ تلاحظ مظاهر ضَعف النُظم الإيكولوجية ومجتمعات الشعوب الأصلية بوجه خاص في المنطقة المتجمّدة الشمالية بسبب تعرّضها للتضخّم الأحيائي للزئبق وتلوُّث الأغذية التقليدية، وإذ تشعر بالقلق إزاء مجتمعات الشعوب الأصلية بوجه أعمّ فيما يخص آثار الزئبق،

وإذ تُدرك الدروس الهامة المستخلصة من مرض ميناماتا وبخاصة الآثار الصحية والبيئية الخطيرة الناجمة عن التلوُّث بالزئبق والحاجة إلى كفالة إدارة سليمة للزئبق ومنع وقوع أحداث مماثلة في المستقبل،

[TEXT IN CHINESE – TEXTE EN CHINOIS]

关于汞的水俣公约

本公约缔约方，

认识到鉴于汞可在大气中作远距离迁移、亦可在人为排入环境后持久存在、同时有能力在各种生态系统中进行生物累积、而且还可对人体健康和环境产生重大不利影响，此种化学品已成为全球性关注问题，

回顾联合国环境规划署理事会在其 2009 年 2 月 20 日第 25/5 号决定中要求各方着手采取国际行动，对汞实行高效率的、有成效的和连贯一致的管理，

回顾标题为《我们希望的未来》的联合国可持续发展大会成果文件第二百二十一段，其中呼吁各方成功地完成为拟定一项具有法律约束力的全球性汞文书进行的谈判工作，以期应对汞对人体健康和环境构成的风险，

回顾联合国可持续发展大会重申了《里约环境与发展宣言》中所阐明的各项原则，其中除其他外包括共同但有区别的责任的原则，并确认各国各自的国情和能力彼此不同，同时亦确认需要在全球范围内采取应对行动，

意识到特别是在发展中国家，因人口中的脆弱群体接触汞而引发的各种健康问题，尤其是对妇女和儿童以及通过她们给子孙后代造成的健康问题，

注意到北极地区的生态系统和当地土著社区因汞的生物放大作用及其传统食物被污染而尤其处于特别脆弱的境地，并对这些土著社区普遍更易受到汞的影响表示关注，

认识到在水俣病方面所汲取的各种重大教训，特别是因汞污染而对健康和环境产生的严重影响，并认识到需要确保对汞实行妥善的管理，防止此类事件未来再度发生，

强调提供财政、工艺和技术、以及能力建设诸方面的支持十分重要，特别是应向发展中国家和经济转型国家提供此种支持，以便增强对汞实行管理的国家能力并促进有效地执行本公约，

还认识到世界卫生组织为保护人体健康免受汞相关影响而开展的各项活动、以及各项相关的多边环境协定在此方面发挥的作用，特别是其中的《控制危险废物越境转移及其处置巴塞尔公约》和《关于在国际贸易中对某些危险化学品和农药采用事先知情同意程序的鹿特丹公约》，

认识到本公约同环境与贸易领域内的其他国际公约彼此相辅相成，

强调本公约的任何条文均非意在妨碍任何缔约方依照任何现行国际协定享受其权利和承担其义务，

理解以上所列举的内容并非意在在本公约与其他国际文书之间建立一种等级制度，

注意到本公约不得阻止缔约方根据其在适用的国际法下所承担的其他义务，采取符合本公约条文的额外国内措施，以努力保护人体健康和环境免受汞接触影响，

兹协议如下：

第一条

目标

本公约的目标是保护人体健康和环境免受汞和汞化合物人为排放和释放的危害。

第二条

定义

就本公约而言：

(一)“手工和小规模采金业”系指由个体采金工人或资本投资和产量有限的小型企业进行的金矿开采；

(二)“最佳可得技术”系指在考虑到某一特定缔约方或该缔约方领土范围内某一特定设施的经济和技术因素的情况下，在防止并在无法防止的情况下减少汞向空气、水和土地的排放与释放以及此类排放与释放给整个环境造成的影响方面最为有效的技术。在这一语境下：

1. “最佳”系指在实现对整个环境的高水平全面保护方面最为有效；

2. “可得”技术，就某一特定缔约方和该缔约方领土范围内某一特定设施而言，系指其开发规模使之可以在经济上和技术上切实可行的条件下，在考虑到成本与惠益的情况下，应用于相关工业部门的技术——无论上述技术是否应用或开发于该缔约方领土范围内，只要该缔约方所确定的设施运营商可以获得上述技术；以及

3. "技术"系指所采用的技术、操作实践，以及设备装置的设计、建造、维护、运行和退役方式。

(三) "最佳环境实践"系指采用最适宜的环境控制措施与战略的组合;

(四) "汞"系指元素汞(Hg(0)，化学文摘社编号：7439-97-6);

(五) "汞化合物"系指由汞原子和其他化学元素的一个或多个原子构成、且只有通过化学反应才能分解为不同成分的任何物质;

(六) "添汞产品"系指含有有意添加的汞或某种汞化合物的产品或产品组件;

(七) "缔约方"系指同意受本公约约束，且本公约已对其生效的国家或区域经济一体化组织;

(八) "出席会议并参加表决的缔约方"系指出席缔约方会议并投出赞成票或反对票的缔约方;

(九) "原生汞矿开采"系指以汞为主要获取材料的开采活动;

(十) "区域经济一体化组织"系指由某一特定区域的主权国家组成的组织，其成员国已将本公约所辖事项的处理权限让渡于它，且它已按照其内部程序正式获得签署、批准、接受、核准或加入本公约的授权；以及

(十一) "允许用途"系指缔约方任何符合本公约规定的汞或汞化合物用途，其中包括但不限于那些符合第三、四、五、六和七条规定的用途。

第三条

汞的供应来源和贸易

一、就本条文而言:

(一) "汞"包含汞含量按重量计至少占95%的汞与其他物质的混合物，其中包括汞的合金；以及

(二) "汞化合物"系指氯化亚汞(I)(亦称甘汞)、氧化汞(II)、硫酸汞(II)、硝酸汞(II)、朱砂矿石和硫化汞。

二、本条文之规定不得适用于:

(一) 拟用于实验室规模的研究活动或用作参考标准的汞或汞化合物用量；或

(二) 在诸如非汞金属、非汞矿石、或包括煤炭在内的非汞矿产品、或从此类材料中衍生出来的产品中存在的、属于自然生成的痕量汞或汞化合物、以及在化学产品中无意生成的痕量汞；或

(三) 添汞产品。

三、每一缔约方均不得允许进行本公约对其生效之际未在其领土范围内进行的原生汞矿开采活动。

四、每一缔约方应只允许本公约对其生效之际业已在其领土范围内进行的原生汞矿开采活动自本公约对其生效之日后继续进行最多 15 年。在此期间，源自此种开采活动的汞应当仅用于依照第四条生产添汞产品、依照第五条采用的生产工艺、或依照第十一条对汞进行的处置，而且所采用的作业方式不得导致汞的回收、再循环、再生、直接再使用或用于其他替代用途；

五、各缔约方均应当：

(一) 努力逐个查明位于其领土范围内的 50 公吨以上的汞或汞化合物库存、以及那些每年出产 10 公吨以上库存的汞供应来源；

(二) 采取各种措施，确保只要缔约方查明氯碱设施的退役过程中出现过量的汞，便应当依照第十一条第三款第一项中所阐明的环境无害化管理准则对之加以处置，而且所采用的处置方式不得导致汞的回收、再循环、再生、直接再使用或用于其他替代用途；

六、任何缔约方均不得允许汞的出口，除非：

(一) 出口至某一业已向出口缔约方出具书面同意的缔约方，而且仅应用于以下目的：

1. 进口缔约方在本公约下获准的某种允许用途；或

2. 依照第十条的规定进行环境无害化临时储存；或

(二) 出口至某一业已向出口缔约方出具书面同意、包括以下情况证明的非缔约方：

1. 该非缔约方已采取了确保人体健康和环境得到保护、而且确保第十条和第十一条的规定得到遵守的措施；以及

2. 此种汞将仅用于本公约允许缔约方使用的用途，或用于依照第十条的规定进行环境无害化的临时储存。

七、出口缔约方可凭借进口缔约方或非缔约方向秘书处发出的一般性通知作为第六款所规定的书面同意。此种一般性通知中应当列明进口缔约方或非缔约方表明其同意进口的任何条款和条件。该缔约方或非缔约方可随时撤消这一通知。秘书处应当保存一份记录此种通知书的公共登记簿。

八、任何缔约方均不得允许从它将提供书面同意的非缔约方进口汞，除非该非缔约方已提供了证书，表明所涉及的汞并非来自第三款或第五款第二项规定不允许使用的来源。

九、依照第七款发出一般性同意通知的缔约方可决定不适用第八款的规定，但条件是该缔约方对汞的出口实行一系列综合限制措施、而且亦在其本国内采取措施，确保对所进口的汞实行环境无害化的管理。所涉缔约方应当向秘书处提供一份此种决定的通知，其中列出介绍说明其所实行的出口限制措施和国内管制措施的信息、以及它从非缔约方进口的汞的数量及来源国的信息。秘书处应当保存一份记录此种通知书的公共登记簿。履行和遵约委员会应当依照第十五条审查和评价此种通知书及其证明资料，并可酌情就此向缔约方大会提出建议。

十、第九款中所列相关程序应当在缔约方大会第二次会议结束之前提供各缔约方使用。其后，这一程序将不再可用，除非缔约方大会以出席会议并参加表决的缔约方用简单多数方式另外作出决定。缔约方在缔约方大会第二次会议结束之前依照第九款提供了一份说明者不在此列。

十一、每一缔约方均应在其依照第二十一条提交的报告中提供表明其已遵守本条文的各项规定的信息。

十二、缔约方大会应当在其第一次会议上就本条文、特别是其中第五条第一款、第六和第八款提供进一步指导，并应确定并通过第六条第二款和第八款所述证明书应列明的相关内容。

十三、缔约方大会应当对贸易中的具体汞化合物是否已损及本公约目标进行评价，并应当审议应否把相关汞化合物列入依照第二十七条所通过的补充附件，从而将之纳入第六和第八款规定的适用范围。

第四条

添汞产品

一、每一缔约方均应采取适当措施，不允许在针对附件 A 第一部分所列添汞产品明确规定的淘汰日期过后生产、进口或出口此类产品，除非已在附件 A 中具体规定了例外情况，或所涉缔约方已依照第六条登记了某项豁免。

二、作为第一款的替代办法，缔约方可在批准附件 A 的某一修正案，或其对之生效时表明它将采取不同的措施或战略来处理附件 A 第一部分中所列产品。缔约方只有在能够证明它业已把附件 A 第一部分所列绝大多数产品的生产、进口和出口数量降到最低限度的情况下，方可选择采用这一替代办法，而且还需能够在它向秘书处通知其决定使用这一替代办法时证明它已采取措施或战略来减少未列入附件 A 第一部分的其他产品中的汞的数量。此外，选择采用这一替代办法的缔约方还应当:

(一) 在第一时间向缔约方大会汇报和说明其所采用的措施或战略的情况，包括所减少的具体数量;

(二) 采取措施或战略，减少附件 A 第一部分中所列、尚未达到最低限值的任何产品中的汞的使用数量;

(三) 考虑采取补充措施来实现进一步的减少；以及

(四) 对于那些业已选择这一替代办法的任何产品类别而言，不具备依照第六条申请豁免的资格。

自本公约开始生效之日起 5 年之内，缔约方大会应当作为第八款所规定的审查程序的一部分，审查依照本款采取的措施的进展情况及其成效。

三、各缔约方均应按照附件 A 第二部分中所列规定针对该附件中所列添汞产品采取相关措施。

四、秘书处应根据缔约方所提供的信息，收集和保存有关添汞产品及其替代品的信息，并应向公众提供此种信息。秘书处还应将缔约方提交的任何其他相关信息公之于众。

五、各缔约方均应采取措施，防止将本条所规定的不得生产、进口和出口的添汞产品纳入组装产品。

六、各缔约方均应不鼓励在本公约对其生效之前为用于任何已知用途之外的用途而生产和商业分销添汞产品，除非所涉产品的风险和效益评估结果表明其对环境或人体健康有益。缔约方应当酌情向秘书处提供关于任何此种产品的信息，其中包括所涉产品的环境和人体健康风险及惠益方面的信息。秘书处应当把此种信息公之于众。

七、任何缔约方均可向秘书处提交关于将某种添汞产品列入附件 A 的提议，其中应列有与该产品无汞替代品的可得性、技术和经济可行性以及环境与健康风险和惠益相关的信息，同时亦应考虑到依照第四款应提供的信息。

八、自本公约生效之日起 5 年之内，缔约方大会应对附件 A 进行审查并可考虑根据第二十七条对该附件进行修正。

九、在依照本条第八款对附件 A 进行的任何审查过程中，缔约方大会至少应考虑到以下事项:

(一) 依照第七款提交的任何提议;

(二) 依照第四款中提供的信息；以及

(三) 缔约方获得在经济上和技术上均为可行的无汞替代品的情况，同时亦考虑到其所涉环境和人体健康风险和惠益。

第五条

使用汞或汞化合物的生产工艺

一、就本条文和附件 B 而言，“使用汞或汞化合物的生产工艺”不得包括使用添汞产品的工艺、添汞产品的生产工艺、以及处理含汞废物的工艺。

二、各缔约方均应采取适当措施，不得允许在附件 B 第一部分中针对所列各种生产工艺明确规定的淘汰日期过后，在上述工艺中使用汞或汞化合物，除非该缔约方依照第六条登记了某项豁免。

三、各缔约方均应按照附件 B 第二部分的规定，采取措施限制在其中所列生产工艺中使用汞或汞化合物。

四、秘书处应当在缔约方所提供的信息的基础上收集并保存关于使用汞或汞化合物及其替代品的工艺方面的信息，缔约方亦可提供其他相关的信息，并应由秘书处将这些信息公之于众。

五、拥有一处或多处在附件 B 所列生产工艺中使用汞或汞化合物的设施的各缔约方均应：

(一) 采取措施解决源自上述设施的汞或汞化合物的排放和释放问题；

(二) 在其依照第二十一条提交的报告当中，纳入依照本款规定所采取措施的相关信息；且

(三) 努力查明其领土范围内将汞或汞化合物用于附件 B 所列工艺的设施，并自本公约对其生效之日起 3 年之内向秘书处提交此类设施数量和类型的相关信息，以及上述设施内汞或汞化合物的估计年用量。秘书处应将上述信息公布于众。

六、每一缔约方均不得在本公约生效之日前不存在的使用附件 B 所列生产工艺的设施中使用汞或汞化合物。此种设施不得适用任何豁免。

七、每一缔约方均不鼓励本公约对其生效之前尚不存在的设施采用任何其他有意添加汞或汞化合物的生产工艺，除非缔约方能够以缔约方大会满意的方式表明所涉生产工艺能够提供重大环境和健康惠益，而且没有任何在技术上和经济上均为可行的无汞替代工艺能够提供此种惠益。

八、鼓励缔约方相互交流以下诸方面的信息：相关的新技术的开发、经济上和技术上可行的无汞替代工艺、以及旨在减少并在可行情况下消除附件 B 所列生产工艺中汞和汞化合物的使用以及源自上述工艺的汞和汞化合物的排放和释放的可能性措施和技术。

九、任何缔约方均可对附件 B 提出修正提案，以期把使用汞或汞化合物的生产工艺列入其中。修正提案中应当包括关于无汞替代工艺的可得情况、技术和经济上的可行性、以及环境与健康风险与惠益诸方面的信息。

十、自本公约生效之日起 5 年之内，缔约方大会应对附件 B 进行审查，并可考虑根据第二十七条中所规定的程序对该附件进行修正。

十一、在依照第十款审查附件 B 时，缔约方大会至少应考虑到以下事项：

(一) 依照第九款提交的任何提案；

(二) 根据第四款提供的信息；以及

(三) 相关缔约方在技术上和经济上均为可行的无汞替代工艺的可获得情况，同时亦考虑到所涉环境与健康风险和惠益。

第六条

缔约方提出要求后可以享受的豁免

一、任何国家或区域经济一体化组织均可采用书面通知秘书处的方式，登记一项或多项针对附件 A 或附件 B 所列淘汰日期的豁免，以下称为“豁免”：

(一) 成为本公约缔约方之际；或者

(二) 若有任何添汞产品以修正形式增列入附件 A，或有任何使用汞的生产工艺以修正形式增列入附件 B，则应当在不迟于相关修正对缔约方生效之日提出。

任何此种登记均应随附一份解释所涉缔约方为何需要享受该项豁免的说明。

二、可针对附件 A 或附件 B 所列某一类别登记一项豁免、或可针对由任何国家或区域经济一体化组织所确定的其中某一分类别登记一项豁免。

三、应当在一份登记簿中列明享有一项或多项豁免的每一缔约方。秘书处应负责建立和保管登记簿并向公众开放。

四、登记簿应包括下列内容：

(一) 享有一项或多项豁免的缔约方清单；

(二) 每一缔约方所登记的一项或多项豁免；以及

(三) 每项豁免的失效日期。

五、除非缔约方在登记簿中注明了一个更短的有效期，否则依照第一款确定的豁免应当于附件 A 或附件 B 中所规定的相关淘汰日期 5 年后失效。

六、缔约方大会可应缔约方的要求，决定将某项豁免的有效期延长 5 年，除非所涉缔约方要求的是一个较此更短的豁免时期。在作出决定时，缔约方大会应充分考虑到以下情形：

(一) 缔约方阐述延长豁免有效期的必要性，并概述已经开展和计划开展的、旨在可行情况下尽快消除实行该项豁免之必要性的各项活动的报告；

(二) 可得信息，包括不含汞或汞用量低于豁免用途的替代产品和工艺的可得性方面的信息；以及

(三) 计划开展的或正在开展的旨在对汞进行环境无害化储存、并对汞废物进行环境无害化处置的各项活动。

某项豁免按产品和淘汰日期计算只可延期一次。

七、缔约方可随时书面通知秘书处，撤消某项豁免。豁免的撤消应自相关通知内注明的日期开始生效。

八、尽管有第一款的规定，任何国家或区域经济一体化组织均不得在附件 A 或附件 B 中所列相关产品或工艺的淘汰日期到期后 5 年之后登记注册任何豁免，除非一个或多个缔约方就该产品或工艺一直享有业经登记的豁免，而且业已依照第六款的规定获准延期。在此种情形中，一国或一经济一体化组织可按第一条第一款和第二款中所给出的时间段就该产品或工艺登记某项豁免。此种豁免应当自相关的淘汰日期起 10 年后失效。

九、任何缔约方均不得自附件 A 或附件 B 中所列产品或工艺的淘汰日期起 10 年后的任何时候针对这些产品或工艺享有任何豁免。

第七条

手工和小规模采金业

一、本条文以及附件 C 中所规定的措施适用于采用汞齐法从矿石当中提取黄金的手工和小规模采金与加工活动。

二、其领土范围内存在适用本条文的手工和小规模采金与加工活动的每一缔约方均应采取措施，减少并在可行情况下消除此类开采与加工活动中汞和汞化合物的使用及其汞向环境中的排放和释放。

三、每一缔约方若在任何时候确定其领土范围内的手工和小规模采金与加工活动已超过微不足道的水平，均应就此通知秘书处。若缔约方已作出此种确认，则应：

(一) 根据附件 C 制订并实施一项国家行动计划；

(二) 在本公约对其生效后 3 年之内，或在通知秘书处后 3 年之内——二者之间以较迟者为准，将其国家行动计划提交秘书处；且

(三) 其后，每 3 年对其在履行本条文规定的各项义务方面所取得的进展进行一次审查，并将上述审查结果纳入依照第二十一条提交的报告。

四、缔约方可酌情开展彼此之间以及与相关政府间组织及其他实体之间的合作，以实现本条文之目标。上述合作可包括：

(一) 制定战略，以防止将汞或汞化合物挪用于手工和小规模采金与加工活动；

(二) 教育、推广以及能力建设举措；

(三) 推动研究可持续的无汞替代方法；

(四) 提供技术援助和财政援助；

(五) 旨在协助履行其在本条文下的各项承诺的合作伙伴关系；以及

(六) 利用现行的信息交流机制推广知识、最佳环境实践以及在环境上、技术上、社会上和经济上切实可行的替代技术。

第八条

排放

一、本条文适用于通过对属于附件 D 中所列来源类别的范围的点源的排放采取措施，以控制、并于可行时减少通常表述为“总汞”的汞和汞化合物向大气中的排放问题。

二、对于本条文而言：

(一) “排放”系指汞或汞化合物向大气中的排放；

(二) “相关来源”是指属于附件 D 中所列来源类别范围的某种来源。缔约方可选择确立相关标准，用以确定附件 D 中所列某一来源类别内所涵盖的相关来源，只要关于其中任何来源的标准中包括来自所涉类别的排放量至少为 75%即可；

(三) “新来源”是指属于附件 D 中所列类别的、且其建造或重大改造工程始于自以下日期起至少 1 年以后的任何相关来源：

1. 本公约对所涉缔约方开始生效之日；或

2. 对附件 D 的某一修正案对所涉缔约方开始生效之日——该来源系完全因为上述修正案才开始适用本公约之各项规定；

(四) “重大改造”是指对可导致排放量大幅增加的相关来源的重大改造工程，其中不包括因对副产品的回收而导致的排放量的任何变化。应当由所涉缔约方决定某一改造是否属于重大改造；

(五) “现有来源”系指不属于新来源的任何相关来源；

(六) “排放限值”系指对源自排放点源的汞或汞化合物的浓度、质量或排放率实行的限值，通常表述为某种来自某一点源的“总汞”；

三、拥有相关来源的缔约方应当采取措施，控制汞的排放，并可制订一项国家计划，设定为控制排放而采取的各项措施及其预计指标、目标和成果。任何计划均应自本公约开始对所涉缔约方生效之日起 4 年内提交缔约方大会。如果缔约方选择依照第二十条制订一项国家实施计划，则该缔约方可把本款所规定的计划纳入其中。

四、对于新来源而言，每一缔约方均应要求在实际情况允许时尽快、但最迟应自本公约开始对其生效之日起 5 年内使用最佳可得技术和最佳环境实践，以控制并于可行时减少排放。缔约方可采用符合最佳可得技术的排放限值。

五、对于现有来源而言，每一缔约方均应在在实际情况允许时尽快、但不迟于自本公约开始对其生效之日起 10 年内，在其国家计划中列入并实施下列一种或多种措施，同时考虑到其国家的具体国情、以及这些措施在经济和技术上的可行性及其可负担性；

(一) 控制并于可行时减少源自相关来源的排放的量化目标；

(二) 采用控制并于可行时减少来自相关来源的排放限值；

(三) 采用最佳可得技术和最佳环境实践来控制源自相关来源的排放；

(四) 采用针对多种污染物的控制战略，从而取得控制汞排放的协同效益；

(五) 减少源自相关来源的排放的替代性措施。

六、缔约方既可对所有相关的现有来源采取同样的措施，亦可针对不同来源类别采取不同的措施。目标是使其所采取的措施得以随着时间的推移在减少排放方面取得合理的进展。

七、每一缔约方均应在实际情况允许时尽快，且自本公约开始对之生效之日起 5 年内建立、并于嗣后保存一份关于相关来源的排放情况的清单。

八、缔约方大会应当在其第一次会议上针对下列事项通过指导意见:

(一) 最佳可得技术和最佳环境实践，同时亦考虑到新来源与现有来源之间的任何差异，并就尽最大限度减少跨介质影响的必要性提供指导意见； 以及

(二) 为缔约方实施本条第五款中所规定的措施提供支持，特别是在确立国家目标和订立排放限值方面提供支持。

九、缔约方大会应当在实际情况允许时尽快就下列事项通过指导意见:

(一) 缔约方可依照第二条第二款制定的标准；

(二) 用于拟定排放清单的方法学。

十、缔约方大会应当定期审查并酌情更新依照第八和第九款提出的指导意见。缔约方应当在执行本条各相关条款时考虑到这些指导意见。

十一、每一缔约方均应在其依照第二十一条提交的报告中列入关于其实施本条条款情况的信息，特别是关于其依照第四至第七款所采取的措施、以及关于这些措施的实际成效的信息。

第九条

释放

一、本条文适用于控制，以及于可行时，减少来自那些未在本公约的其他条款中涉及的相关点源向土地和水中释放通常表述为“总汞”的汞和汞化合物。

二、就本条文而言：

(一) “释放”是指汞或汞化合物向土地或水中的释放；

(二) “相关来源”是指那些由缔约方所确定的、未在公约其他条款中涉及的任何重大人为释放点源；

(三) “新来源”是指任何相关的来源，此种来源的建造或重大改造系自本公约开始对所涉缔约方生效之日起至少 1 年之后启动；

(四) “重大改造”是指对某一相关来源进行的、导致其排放量大幅增加的改造，其中不包括因对其副产品进行的回收而导致的释放量的任何改变。应当由所涉缔约方认定所涉改造是否属于重大改造；

(五) “现有来源”是指任何不属于新的来源的相关来源；

(六) “释放限值”是指针对源自某一点源所释放的、通常表述为“总汞”的汞或汞化合物的浓度或质量确定的一种限值。

三、每一缔约方均应不迟于本公约对其开始生效之日起 3 年内、并于其后定期查明相关的点源类别。

四、那些拥有相关来源的缔约方应采取各种措施控制其释放，并可制定一项国家计划，列明为控制释放而采取的各种措施及其预计指标、目标和成果。任何计划均应自本公约对所涉缔约方开始生效之日起 4 年内提交缔约方大会。如果缔约方依照第二十条制定了一项实施计划，则所涉缔约方可把依照本款制定的计划列入这一执行计划之中。

五、相关措施应当酌情包括下列一种或多种措施：

(一) 采用释放限值，以控制并于可行时减少来自相关来源的释放；

(二) 采用各种最佳可得技术和最佳环境实践，以控制来自各类相关来源的释放；

(三) 订立一项同时对多种污染物实行控制的战略，以期在控制释放方面取得协同效益；

(四) 采取旨在减少来自相关来源的释放的其他措施。

六、在实际情况允许时尽快、且不迟于自本公约对其开始生效之日起 5 年内建立、并于嗣后保持一份关于各相关来源的释放情况的清单。

七、缔约方大会应在实际情况允许时尽快通过关于下列事项的指导意见：

(一) 最佳可得技术和最佳环境实践，同时亦考虑到新的来源与现有来源之间的任何区别、以及尽最大限度减少跨媒介影响的必要性；

(二) 用于拟定释放清单的方法学。

八、每一缔约方均应在其依照第二十一条提交的报告中提供关于本条执行情况的信息，特别是关于其依照第三至第六款所采取的措施及其成效方面的信息。

第十条

汞废物以外的汞环境无害化临时储存

一、本条文适用于第三条中所界定的、不属于第十一条中所列汞废物定义涵盖范围之内的汞和汞化合物的临时储存问题。

二、每一缔约方均应采取措施，顾及本条第三款通过的任何指导准则，遵照依本条第三款通过的任何要求，确保使拟用于缔约方在本公约下获准的允许用途的此类汞和汞化合物的临时储存以环境无害化的方式进行。

三、缔约方大会应在顾及《控制危险废物越境转移及其处置巴塞尔公约》下制定的任何相关指导准则、以及其他相关指导意见的情况下，针对此类汞和汞化合物的环境无害化临时储存问题制定指导准则。缔约方大会可依照第二十七条以本公约增列附件的形式通过关于临时储存问题的各项规定。

四、缔约方应酌情相互合作，并与相关政府间组织及其他实体合作，以加强各方在此类汞和汞化合物的环境无害化临时储存问题上的能力建设。

第十一条

汞废物

一、就《控制危险废物越境转移及其处置巴塞尔公约》缔约方而言，《巴塞尔公约》的相关定义适用于本公约所涵盖的废物。对于那些不属于《巴塞尔公约》缔约方的本公约缔约方而言，则应以这些定义为指导，用于本公约所涵盖的废物。

二、就本公约而言，汞废物系指汞含量超过缔约方大会经与《巴塞尔公约》各相关机构协调后统一规定的阈值，按照国家法律或本公约之规定予以处置或准备予以处置或必须加以处置的下列物质或物品：

(一) 由汞或汞化合物构成；

(二) 含有汞或汞化合物；或者

(三) 受到汞或汞化合物污染。

这一定义不涵盖源自除原生汞矿开采以外的采矿作业中的表层土、废岩石和尾矿石，除非其中含有超出缔约方大会所界定的阈值量的汞或汞化合物。

三、每一缔约方均应采取适当措施，以使汞废物：

(一) 得以在虑及在《控制危险废物越境转移及其处置巴塞尔公约》下制定的指导准则、并遵照缔约方大会将依照第二十七条以增列附件的形式通过的各项要求的情况下，以环境无害化的方式得到管理。缔约方大会在拟订这些要求时应虑及缔约方的废物管理规定和方案；

(二) 仅为缔约方在本公约下获准的某种允许用途、或为依照第三条第一款进行环境无害化处置而得到回收、再循环、再生或直接再使用；

(三) 《巴塞尔公约》缔约方不得进行跨越国际边境的运输，除非以遵照本条以及《巴塞尔公约》的条款进行环境无害化处置为目的。在《巴塞尔公约》对跨越国际边境的运输不适用情况下，缔约方只有在虑及相关国际规则、标准和准则后，才得允许进行此类运输。

四、在酌情审查和更新第三条第一款所述及的指导准则时，缔约方大会应寻求与《巴塞尔公约》的相关机构密切合作。

五、鼓励缔约方酌情相互合作，并与相关政府间组织及其他实体合作，开发并保持全球、区域和国家对汞废物实行环境无害化管理的能力。

第十二条

污染场地

一、各缔约方均应努力制定适宜战略，用以识别和评估受到汞或汞化合物污染的场地。

二、任何旨在降低此类场地所造成的风险的行动，均应以环境无害化的方式进行，并酌情囊括一项针对其中所含汞或汞化合物对人体健康和环境所构成风险的评估。

三、缔约方大会应针对污染场地的管理问题通过指导意见，其中可附有针对以下问题的解决方法和办法：

(一) 场地识别与特征鉴别；

(二) 公众参与；

(三) 人体健康与环境风险评估；

(四) 污染场地风险管理的选择方案；

(五) 惠益与成本评估；以及

(六) 成果验证。

四、鼓励缔约方针对污染场地的识别、评估、确定优先次序、管理和视情修复问题合作制定战略并开展活动。

第十三条

财政资源和财务机制

一、每一缔约方均承诺在其能力范围内根据其国家政策、优先重点、计划和方案为旨在执行本公约而开展的国家活动提供资源。此种资源可包括通过相关政策、发展战略和国家预算、以及双边和多边供资和私营部门参与获得的国内供资。

二、发展中国家缔约方执行本公约的总体成效与本条的有效执行具有相关性。

三、迫切鼓励各方通过多边、区域和双边来源提供技术、财政和技术援助、以及能力建设和技术转让，用以增强和增加针对汞采取的行动，以期从财政资源、技术援助和技术转让诸方面为协助发展中国家缔约方执行本公约提供支持。

四、缔约方在其供资行动中，应当充分考虑到那些小岛屿发展中国家或最不发达国家缔约方的具体需要和特殊国情。

五、兹此确立一提供充足的、可预测的和及时的财政资源的机制。这一机制旨在支持发展中国家缔约方和经济转型缔约方履行其依照本公约承担的各项义务。

六、这一机制应当包括:

(一) 全球环境基金信托基金; 以及

(二) 一项旨在支持能力建设和技术援助的专门国际方案。

七、全球环境基金信托基金应当提供新的、可预测的、充足的和及时的财政资源，用于支付为执行缔约方大会所商定的、旨在支持本公约的执行工作而涉及的费用。为了本公约之目的，全球环境基金信托基金应当在缔约方大会的指导下运作并对缔约方大会负责。缔约方大会应当对此种财政资源的获得和使用所涉及的总体战略、政策、方案优先重点和资格提供指导。此外，缔约方大会还应当对能够从全球环境基金信托基金获得资助的活动类别的指示清单提供指导。全球环境基金信托基金应当提供资源，用于支付所商定的全球环境惠益所涉及的增量成本、以及所商定的某些基础活动的全部费用。

八、在为一项活动提供资源过程中，全球环境基金信托基金应当考虑到这一拟议活动在减少汞方面所具有的潜力及其所涉及的费用。

九、为了本公约之目的，第六条第二款中所提及的国际方案应当在缔约方大会的指导下运作并对缔约方大会负责。缔约方大会应当在其首次会议上就这一方案的东道机构作出决定——这一东道机构应是一个现有的实体单位，并负责向该机构提供指导，包括该方案的期限。邀请所有缔约方和其他利益攸关方在自愿基础上向这一方案提供财政资源。

十、缔约方大会以及构成这一财务机制的各实体应当在缔约方大会的首次会议上商定实行上述各款的相关安排。

十一、缔约方大会应当最迟在其第三次会议上、并于嗣后定期审查供资水平、缔约方大会向那些受托运行依照本条设立的财务机制的实体所提供的指导及它们的成效、它们满足发展中国家缔约方和经济转型缔约方不断变化的需要的能力。缔约方大会应当根据此种审查结果为改进财务机制的成效采取适当的行动。

十二、邀请所有缔约方在其能力范围内向这一财务机制提供捐助。财务机制应当鼓励由其他来源提供资源，包括私营部门，并应寻求为它所支持的各种活动撬动此种资源。

第十四条

能力建设、技术援助和技术转让

一、缔约方应协同合作，在其各自的能力范围内，向发展中国家缔约方、尤其是最不发达国家或小岛屿发展中国家缔约方，以及经济转型缔约方提供及时和适宜的能力建设和技术援助，以协助它们履行本公约所规定的各项义务。

二、依照本条第一款以及第十三条开展的能力建设和技术援助可通过区域、次区域以及国家一级的安排，包括现有的区域和次区域中心，通过其他多边和双边手段，以及通过伙伴关系，包括涉及私营部门的伙伴关系，予以提供。应寻求与化学品和废物领域内其他多边环境协定之间开展合作与协调，以提高技术援助及其结果的成效。

三、发达国家缔约方和其他缔约方在其能力范围内，酌情在私营部门及其他相关利益攸关方的支持下，应向发展中国家缔约方、尤其是最不发达国家和小岛屿发展中国家、以及经济转型缔约方推动和促进最新的环境无害化替代技术的开发、转让、普及和获取，以增强它们有效执行本公约的能力。

四、缔约方大会应虑及缔约方提交的呈文和报告，包括按照第二十一条的规定提交的呈文和报告，以及其他利益攸关方提供的信息，在其第二次会议前并于嗣后定期:

(一) 考虑关于替代技术现行举措及所取得进展的相关信息;

(二) 考虑缔约方、尤其是发展中国家缔约方对替代技术的需求; 以及

(三) 查明缔约方、尤其是发展中国家缔约方在技术转让方面遇到的各种挑战;

五、缔约方大会应就如何依照本条的规定进一步加强能力建设、技术援助和技术转让工作提出建议。

第十五条

履行与遵约委员会

一、兹此设立一项机制，其中包括一个作为缔约方大会附属机构的委员会，负责推动本公约各项条款的履行并审查本公约各项条款的遵约情况。这一机制，包括上述委员会，在本质上应具促进性，并应特别注重缔约方各自的国家能力和具体国情。

二、委员会应促进本公约所有条款的履行，并审议所有条款的遵守。委员会应审查履行和遵约方面的个体性问题和系统性问题，并酌情向缔约方大会提出建议。

三、委员会应当在充分考虑以联合国五大区域为基础的公平地域代表性原则的情况下，由缔约方提名并由缔约方大会选出的 15 名成员组成；其首批成员应在缔约方大会第一次会议上选举产生，并于嗣后依照缔约方大会根据第五款批准的议事规则选举产生；委员会各成员应当在与本公约相关的某一领域内具有专业能力，而且委员会的成员构成应能反映出专业知识间的适当平衡。

四、委员会可在如下基础上考虑问题：

(一) 任何缔约方提交的有关其自身遵约事项的书面呈文；

(二) 依照第二十一条提交的国家报告；以及

(三) 缔约方大会提出的要求；

五、委员会应当详细制订其议事规则，供缔约方大会在其第二次会议上批准；缔约方大会可通过委员会的进一步的工作大纲。

六、委员会应尽一切努力以协商一致的方式通过其建议。如已竭尽一切努力仍无法达成一致意见，则应作为最后手段，根据其成员的三分之二法定人数，以出席会议并参加表决的成员的四分之三多数票通过此类建议。

第十六条

健康方面

一、鼓励各缔约方：

(一) 推动制定并落实战略和方案，以查明和保护处于风险之中的群体、尤其是那些脆弱群体，其中可包括在公共卫生部门及其他相关部门的参与下：针对接触汞和汞化合物的问题，制定以科学为依据的健康导则；在适用情况下确立减少汞接触的目标；以及开展公共教育；

（二）针对职业接触汞和汞化合物的问题，推动制定并落实以科学为依据的教育和防范方案；

（三）推动因接触汞和汞化合物而受到影响的群体的预防、治疗和护理提供适当的医疗保健服务；以及

（四）酌情建立和加强机构和医务人员在因接触汞和汞化合物而导致的健康风险方面的预防、诊断、治疗和监测能力。

二、在考虑与健康有关的议题或活动时，缔约方大会应：

（一）酌情与世界卫生组织、国际劳工组织及其他相关政府间组织开展咨询与协作；

（二）酌情促进与世界卫生组织、国际劳工组织、以及其他相关国际组织的合作与信息交流。

第十七条

信息交流

一、各缔约方应促进以下信息的交流：

（一）有关汞和汞化合物的科学、技术、经济和法律信息，包括毒理学、生态毒理学和安全信息；

（二）有关减少或消除汞和汞化合物的生产、使用、贸易、排放和释放的信息；

（三）在技术和经济上可行的对下列产品和工艺的替代信息：

1. 添汞产品；

2. 使用汞或汞化合物的生产工艺；以及

3. 排放或释放汞或汞化合物的活动和工艺；

包括此类替代产品和工艺的健康与环境风险以及经济和社会成本与惠益方面的信息；以及

（四）接触汞和汞化合物的健康影响方面的流行病学信息，可酌情与世界卫生组织和其他相关组织密切合作。

二、缔约方可直接、或通过秘书处、或酌情与其他相关组织，包括化学品和废物公约的秘书处合作，交流第一款所述及的信息。

三、秘书处应促进本条所述信息交流方面的合作，同时促进与相关组织之间的合作，包括多边环境协定以及其他国际倡议的秘书处。除缔约方提供的信息外，上述信息还应包括在汞问题领域拥有专长的政府间组织和非政府组织以及拥有上述专长的国家机构和国际机构提供的信息。

四、各缔约方均应指定一个国家联络点，负责在本公约下交流信息，包括有关第三条所规定的进口缔约方同意问题的信息。

五、就本公约而言，人体健康与安全以及环境方面的相关信息不得视为机密信息。依照本公约交流其他信息的缔约方应按照双方约定保护任何机密信息。

第十八条

公共信息、认识和教育

一、各缔约方均应在其能力范围内推动和促进：

(一) 向公众提供以下方面的现有信息：

1. 汞和汞化合物对健康和环境的影响；
2. 汞和汞化合物的替代品；
3. 第十七条第一款所确定的各项主题；
4. 第十九条所要求的研究、开发和监测活动的结果；以及
5. 为履行本公约各项义务而开展的活动；

(二) 酌情与相关政府间组织和非政府组织以及脆弱群体协作，针对接触汞和汞化合物对人体健康和环境的影响问题所开展的教育、培训以及提高公众认识的活动。

二、每一缔约方均应利用现行机制或考虑建立相关机制，如在适用情况下建立污染物释放和转移登记簿等，以收集和传播其通过人为活动排放、释放或处置的汞和汞化合物的年度估计数量方面的相关信息。

第十九条

研究、开发和监测

一、缔约方应考虑到其各自的国情和能力，努力合作开发并改进：

(一) 汞和汞化合物的使用、消费以及向空气中的人为排放和向水和土地中的人为释放方面的清单；

(二) 针对脆弱群体以及包括诸如鱼类、海洋哺乳动物、海龟和鸟类等生物媒介在内的环境介质当中的汞和汞化合物含量建立的模型和进行的具有地域代表性的监测活动，以及在收集和交换适当的相关样本方面所开展的协作；

(三) 除汞和汞化合物对社会、经济和文化影响评估外，其对人体健康与环境的影响评估，尤其是对脆弱群体而言；

(四) 用于本款第一、二、三项下所开展活动的协调统一的方法学；

(五) 汞和汞化合物在一系列生态系统中的环境周期、迁移(包括远程迁移和沉降)、转化与归宿方面的信息，其中适当考虑到人为的与自然的汞排放和释放之间的区别，以及历史性沉降中的汞的再活化问题；

(六) 汞和汞化合物以及添汞产品的商业及贸易信息；以及

(七) 无汞产品和工艺技术经济可得性方面的信息与研究，以及减少和监测汞和汞化合物释放的最佳可得技术和最佳环境实践方面的信息与研究。

二、缔约方在开展本条第一款所确定的行动时，应酌情依托现有的监测网络和研究项目。

第二十条

实施计划

一、每一缔约方在进行初步评估后，考虑到其本国国情，可制定并执行一项实施计划，用以履行本公约下的义务。任何此类计划均应在制定完毕后尽快递交秘书处。

二、每一缔约方，虑及其国内情况并参考缔约方大会的指导意见及其他相关指导意见，可审查和更新其实施计划。

三、在开展本条第一款和第二款所述工作时，缔约方应咨询本国利益攸关方，以促进其实施计划的制定、实施、审查和更新工作。

四、缔约方亦可围绕区域计划协调配合，以促进本公约的实施。

第二十一条

报告

一、各缔约方均应通过秘书处向缔约方大会报告其为实施本公约各条款而采取的措施，并报告上述措施在实现本公约目标方面的成效以及可能遇到的挑战。

二、各缔约方均应在其报告中纳入本公约第三、五、七、八和九条所要求的信息。

三、缔约方大会应考虑与其他相关的化学品和废物公约协同报告是否可取，在其第一次会议上决定缔约方应遵守的报告时间与格式。

第二十二条

成效评估

一、缔约方大会应在本公约生效后 6 年内开始，并于嗣后按照它所确定的时间间隔定期对本公约的成效进行评估。

二、为便于开展评估工作，缔约方大会应在其第一次会议上着手做出安排，以为其提供以下方面的可比监测数据：环境中汞和汞化合物的存在和迁移情况，以及生物媒介和脆弱群体当中观察到的汞和汞化合物的含量趋势。

三、评估工作应在现有的科学、环境、技术、财政和经济信息基础上进行，包括：

(一) 依照本条第二款向缔约方大会提供的报告及其他监测信息；

(二) 依照第二十一条提交的报告；

(三) 依照第十五条提供的信息和建议；以及

(四) 依照本公约的规定编制的财政援助、技术转让和能力建设安排的运作情况诸方面的报告及其他相关信息。

第二十三条

缔约方大会

一、兹此设立缔约方大会。

二、缔约方大会第一次会议应当自本公约生效日期起 1 年内由联合国环境规划署执行主任召集举行。嗣后，缔约方大会的常会应当按照缔约方大会所确定的时间间隔定期举行。

三、缔约方大会的特别会议应当在缔约方大会认为必要的其他时间举行，或应任何缔约方的书面请求，在秘书处将该请求通报所有缔约方后的 6 个月内，并在该请求得到至少三分之一缔约方支持的情况下举行。

四、缔约方大会应当在其第一次会议上以协商一致的方式商定并通过缔约方大会及其任何附属机构的议事规则和财务细则，以及有关秘书处运作的财务条例。

五、缔约方大会应不断审查和评价本公约的实施情况和履行本公约为其规定的各项职责，并应为此目的：

(一) 为实施本公约设立它认为必要的附属机构；

(二) 酌情与相关的国际组织、政府间组织和非政府组织开展合作；

(三) 定期审查大会及秘书处依照第二十一条获得的所有信息；

(四) 考虑履行与遵约委员会提交的任何建议；

(五) 考虑并采取为实现本公约各项目标可能需要采取的任何额外行动；

(六) 依照第四条和第五条审查附件 A 和附件 B。

六、联合国及其专门机构、国际原子能机构以及任何非本公约缔约方的国家均可作为观察员出席缔约方大会的会议。任何组织或机构，无论是国家或国际性质、政府或非政府性质，只要在本公约所涉事项方面具有资格，并已通知秘书处愿意以观察员身份出席缔约方大会的会议，均可被接纳参加会议，除非有至少三分之一的出席缔约方对此表示反对。观察员的接纳和出席应遵守缔约方大会所通过的议事规则。

第二十四条

秘书处

一、兹此设立秘书处。

二、秘书处的职能应当包括：

(一) 为缔约方大会及其附属机构的会议做出安排，并为之提供所需的服务；

(二) 根据要求，为协助缔约方、特别是发展中国家缔约方和经济转型缔约方实施本公约提供便利；

(三) 酌情与相关国际组织的秘书处、特别是其他化学品和废物公约的秘书处进行协调；

(四) 协助缔约方相互交流与实施本公约有关的信息；

(五) 基于根据第十五条和第二十一条收到的信息以及其他现有信息，定期编制并向缔约方提交报告；

(六) 在缔约方大会的总体指导下，做出为切实履行其职能所需的行政和合同安排；以及

(七) 履行本公约明文规定的其他秘书处职能以及缔约方大会可能为之规定的其他职能。

三、本公约的秘书处职能应当由联合国环境规划署执行主任负责履行，除非缔约方大会以出席会议并参加表决的缔约方的四分之三多数票决定委托另一个或几个国际组织履行上述职能。

四、缔约方大会，经与适当国际机构磋商，可加强秘书处与其他化学品和废物公约秘书处之间的合作与协调。缔约方大会，经与适当国际机构磋商，可就此提供进一步的指导。

第二十五条

争端解决

一、缔约方应争取通过谈判或其自行选择的其他和平方式解决彼此之间因本公约的解释或适用问题而产生的任何争端。

二、非区域经济一体化组织的缔约方在批准、接受、核准或加入本公约时，或在其后任何时候，可在交给保存人的一份书面文书中声明，对于因本公约的解释或适用问题而产生的任何争端，该缔约方承认在涉及接受同样义务的任何其他缔约方时，下列一种或两种争端解决方式具有强制性：

(一) 按照载于附件 E 第一部分中的程序进行仲裁；

(二) 将争端提交国际法院审理。

三、区域经济一体化组织缔约方可针对第二款所述裁决方式，发表类似的声明。

四、依照第二款或第三款所发表的声明，在其中所规定的有效期内或自其撤销声明的书面通知交存于保存人后 3 个月内，应一直有效。

五、除非争端各方另有协议，否则声明的失效、撤销声明的通知或作出新的声明均不得在任何方面影响仲裁庭或国际法院正在进行的审理。

六、如果争端各方尚未依照第二款或第三款接受同样的争端解决方法，且它们未能在一方通知另一方它们之间存在争端后的 12 个月内根据第一款规定的方式解决争端，

则该争端应在争端任何一方的要求之下提交调解委员会。载于附件 E 第二部分的程序应适用于在本条文下进行的调解。

第二十六条

公约的修正

一、任何缔约方均可针对本公约提出修正案。

二、本公约的修正案应在缔约方大会的会议上通过。对本公约提出的任何修正案文均应由秘书处在建议通过该项修正案的会议举行之前至少提前 6 个月通报各缔约方。秘书处还应将该拟议修正案通报本公约所有签署方，并呈交保存人阅存。

三、缔约方应尽一切努力以协商一致的方式就针对本公约提出的任何修正案达成协议。如已竭尽一切努力仍无法达成一致意见，则应作为最后手段，以出席会议并参加表决的缔约方的四分之三多数票通过所涉修正案。

四、已获通过的修正案应由保存人通报所有缔约方，供其批准、接受或核准。

五、对修正案的批准、接受或核准应以书面形式通知保存人。按照第三款通过的修正案，应自该修正案通过之时缔约方的至少四分之三多数交存批准、接受或核准文书之日起第 90 天对同意接受该修正案约束的各缔约方生效。其后，任何其他缔约方自交存批准、接受或核准该修正案的文书之日起第 90 天，该修正案即开始对其生效。

第二十七条

附件的通过和修正

一、本公约各项附件构成本公约不可分割的组成部分。除非另有明文规定，凡提及本公约时，亦包括其所有附件在内。

二、在本公约生效之后通过的任何增补附件均应仅限于程序、科学、技术或行政事项。

三、下列程序应适用于本公约增补附件的提出、通过和生效：

(一) 增补附件应按照第二十六条第一至第三款规定的程序提出和通过；

(二) 何缔约方如无法接受某一增补附件，则应在保存人就通过该增补附件发出通知之日起一年内将此种情况书面通知保存人。保存人应在接获任何此类通知后立即通知所有缔约方。缔约方可随时书面通知保存人撤销先前对某一增补附件提出的不予接受通知，据此该附件即应根据第三项的规定对该缔约方生效；且

(三) 保存人就通过某一增补附件发出通知之日起 1 年后，该附件便应对尚未按照第二项的规定提交不予接受通知的本公约所有缔约方生效。

四、本公约各附件修正案的提出、通过和生效均应与本公约增补附件的提出、通过和生效遵循相同的程序，但如果任何缔约方已按照第三十条第五款的规定就附件修正案作出声明，则该附件修正案不得对该缔约方生效。此种情况下，任何此类修正案均将自该缔约方向保存人交存该修正案的批准、接受、核准或加入文书之日起的第 90 天起对该缔约方生效。

五、若某新增附件或某附件的修正案与本公约某个修正案有关，则在本公约上述修正案生效以前，该新增附件或附件修正案不得生效。

第二十八条
表决权

一、除第二款规定者外，本公约各缔约方均拥有一票表决权。

二、区域经济一体化组织在就其权限范围内的事项行使表决权时，其票数应与其作为本公约缔约方的成员国数目相同。如果此类组织的任何成员国行使表决权，则该组织便不得行使表决权，反之亦然。

第二十九条
签署

本公约应自 2013 年 10 月 10 日至 11 日在日本熊本、嗣后直至 2014 年 10 月 9 日在纽约联合国总部开放供所有国家和区域经济一体化组织签署。

第三十条
批准、接受、核准或加入

一、本公约须经各国和各区域经济一体化组织批准、接受或核准。本公约应自签署截止之日的次日起开放供各国和各区域经济一体化组织加入。批准、接受、核准或加入文书应当交存于保存人。

二、任何已成为本公约缔约方、但其成员国却均未成为缔约方的区域经济一体化组织，均应受本公约所规定的一切义务约束。若此类组织的一个或多个成员国是本公约缔约方，则该组织及其成员国应决定其各自为履行本公约规定的义务而承担的责任。在此种情形中，该组织及其成员国无权共同行使本公约所规定的权利。

三、区域经济一体化组织应当在其批准、接受、核准或加入文书中声明其在本公约所规定事项上的权限范围。任何此类组织亦应将其权限范围的任何相关变更通知保存人，再由保存人通知各缔约方。

四、鼓励每一国家或区域经济一体化组织在其批准、接受、核准或加入本公约时向秘书处转交其关于为执行本公约而采取的措施的信息。

五、任何缔约方均可在其批准、接受、核准或加入文书中声明，就该缔约方而言，对某一附件的任何修正只有在其交存了批准、接受、核准或加入文书之后方能对其生效。

第三十一条
生效

一、本公约应自第 50 份批准、接受、核准或加入文书交存之日起第 90 天开始生效。

二、对于在第 50 份批准、接受、核准或加入文书交存之后批准、接受、核准本公约或加入本公约的各国家或区域经济一体化组织，本公约应自该国或该区域经济一体化组织交存其批准、接受、核准或加入文书之日起第 90 天开始生效。

三、就第一款和第二款而言，区域经济一体化组织所交存的任何文书均不得视为该组织成员国所交存文书之外的额外文书。

第三十二条
保留

不得对本公约提出任何保留。

第三十三条
退出

一、自本公约对某一缔约方生效之日起 3 年后，该缔约方可随时向保存人发出书面通知，退出本公约。

二、任何此种退出均应在保存人收到退出通知之日起 1 年后开始生效，或在退出通知中可能指定的一个更晚日期开始生效。

第三十四条

保存人

应当由联合国秘书长担任本公约的保存人。

第三十五条

作准文本

本公约的正本应当交存于保存人，其阿拉伯文、中文、英文、法文、俄文和西班牙文文本均同为作准文本。

下列签署人，经正式授权，在本公约上签字，以昭信守。

公历两千零一十三年十月十日订于日本熊本。

附件 A
添汞产品

本附件不涵盖下列产品:

(一) 民事保护和军事用途所必需的产品;

(二) 用于研究、仪器校准或用于参照标准的产品;

(三) 在无法获得可行的无汞替代品的情况下,开关和继电器、用于电子显示的冷阴极荧光灯和外置电极荧光灯以及测量仪器;

(四) 传统或宗教所用产品;以及

(五) 以硫柳汞作为防腐剂的疫苗。

第一部分:受第四条第一款管制的产品

添汞产品	开始禁止产品生产、进口或出口的时间(淘汰日期)
电池,不包括含汞量低于 2%的扣式锌氧化银电池以及含汞量低于 2%的扣式锌空气电池	2020 年
开关和继电器,不包括每个电桥、开关或继电器的最高含汞量为 20 毫克的极高精确度电容和损耗测量电桥及用于监控仪器的高频射频开关和继电器	2020 年
用于普通照明用途、不超过 30 瓦、单支含汞量超过 5 毫克的紧凑型荧光灯	2020 年
下列用于普通照明用途的直管型荧光灯: (一) 低于 60 瓦、单支含汞量超过 5 毫克的直管型荧光灯(使用三基色荧光粉) (二) 低于 40 瓦(含 40 瓦)、单支含汞量超过 10 毫克的直管型荧光灯(使用卤磷酸盐荧光粉)	2020 年

添汞产品	开始禁止产品生产、进口或出口的时间（淘汰日期）
用于普通照明用途的高压汞灯	2020 年
用于电子显示的冷阴极荧光灯和外置电极荧光灯中使用的汞: （一） 长度较短(≤500 毫米)，单支含汞量超过 3.5 毫克 （二） 中等长度(>500 毫米且≤1500 毫米)，单支含汞量超过 5 毫克 （三） 长度较长(>1500 毫米)，单支含汞量超过 13 毫克	2020 年
化妆品(含汞量超过百万分之一)，包括亮肤肥皂和乳霜，不包括以汞为防腐剂且无有效安全替代防腐剂的眼部化妆品[1]	2020 年
农药、生物杀虫剂和局部抗菌剂	2020 年
下列非电子测量仪器，其中不包括在无法获得适当无汞替代品的情况下、安装在大型设备中或用于高精度测量的非电子测量设备: （一） 气压计; （二） 湿度计; （三） 压力表; （四） 温度计; （五） 血压计。	2020 年

[1] 意在不把含有痕量汞污染物的化妆品、肥皂和乳霜包含在内。

第二部分：受第四条第三款管制的产品

添汞产品	规定
牙科汞合金	缔约方在采取措施以逐步减少牙科汞合金的使用时，应考虑到该缔约方的国内情况和相关国际指南，并应至少纳入下列措施中的两项： (一) 制定旨在促进龋齿预防和改善健康状况的国家目标，尽最大限度降低牙科修复的需求； (二) 制定旨在尽最大限度减少牙科汞合金使用的国家目标； (三) 推动使用具有成本效益且有临床疗效的无汞替代品进行牙科修复； (四) 推动研究和开发高质量的无汞材料用于牙科修复； (五) 鼓励有代表性的专业机构和牙科学校就无汞牙科修复替代材料的使用及最佳管理实践的推广，对牙科专业人员和学生进行教育和培训； (六) 不鼓励在牙科修复中优先使用牙科汞合金而非无汞材料的保险政策和方案； (七) 鼓励在牙科修复中优先使用高质量的替代材料而非牙科汞合金的保险政策和方案； (八) 规定牙科汞合金只能以封装形式使用； (九) 推动在牙科设施中采用最佳环境实践，以减少汞和汞化合物向水和土地的释放。

附件 B
使用汞或汞化合物的生产工艺

第一部分：受第五条第二款管制的工艺

使用汞或汞化合物的生产工艺	淘汰日期
氯碱生产	2025年
使用汞或汞化合物作为催化剂的乙醛生产	2018年

第二部分：受第五条第三款管制的工艺

使用汞的生产工艺	规定
氯乙烯单体的生产	拟由缔约方采取的措施应当包括，但不限于如下各项： (一) 至2020年时在2010年用量的基础上每单位产品汞用量减少50%; (二) 促进采取各种措施，减轻对源自原生汞矿开采的汞的依赖; (三) 采取措施，减少汞向环境中的排放和释放: (四) 支持无汞催化剂和工艺的研究与开发; (五) 在缔约方大会确定基于现有工艺无汞催化剂技术和经济均可行5年后，不允许继续使用汞; (六) 向缔约方大会报告其为依照第二十一条开发和/或查明汞替代品以及淘汰汞使用所做出的努力。
甲醇钠、甲醇钾、乙醇钠或乙醇钾	拟由缔约方采取的措施应当包括，但不限于如下各项： (一) 采取措施减少汞的使用，争取尽快、且在本公约开始生效之后10年之内淘汰这一使用; (二) 至2020年时以2010年的用量为基础把每生产单位排放量和释放量减少50%; (三) 禁止使用源自原生汞矿开采的新的汞;

使用汞的生产工艺	规定
	(四) 支持无汞工艺的研究与开发; (五) 在缔约方大会确认无汞工艺已在技术和经济上均可行 5 年后不再允许使用汞; (六) 向缔约方大会报告其为依照第二十一条开发和/或查明汞替代品以及淘汰汞的使用所做出的努力。
使用含汞催化剂进行的聚氨酯生产	拟由缔约方采取的措施应当包括，但不限于如下各项: (一) 采取各种措施减少汞的使用，争取尽快、且在本公约开始生效之日起 10 年之内淘汰这一用途; (二) 采取各种措施减少对来自原生汞矿开采的汞的依赖; (三) 采取各种措施，减少汞向环境中的排放和释放; (四) 鼓励研究和开发无汞催化剂和工艺; (五) 向缔约方大会报告其为依照第二十一条开发和/或查明汞替代品以及淘汰汞的使用所做出的努力。 第五条第六款不得适用于这一生产工艺。

附件 C
手工和小规模采金业

国家行动计划

一、适用第七条第三款规定的每一缔约方均应在其国家行动计划中纳入：

(一) 国家目标和减排指标；

(二) 采取行动消除：

1. 整体矿石汞齐化；

2. 露天焚烧汞合金或经过加工的汞合金；

3. 在居民区焚烧汞合金；以及

4. 在没有首先去除汞的情况下，对添加了汞的沉积物、矿石或尾矿石进行氰化物沥滤；

(三) 为推动手工和小规模采金行业正规化或对其进行监管而采取的措施；

(四) 对其领土范围内手工和小规模黄金开采和加工活动中使用的汞的数量以及采用的实践所开展的基准估算；

(五) 促进减少手工和小规模黄金开采和加工活动中汞排放、汞释放和汞接触的战略，包括推广无汞方法的战略；

(六) 用于管理贸易并防止将源自国外和国内的汞和汞化合物挪用于手工和小规模黄金开采与加工活动的战略；

(七) 在实施和不断完善国家行动计划的过程中，吸引利益攸关方参与的战略；

(八) 手工和小规模采金工人及其社区汞接触问题的公共卫生战略。此类战略应包括，但不限于，健康数据的采集、医疗保健工作者的培训以及通过医疗单位开展的意识提高活动；

(九) 旨在防止脆弱群体、尤其是儿童和育龄妇女，特别是孕妇接触到手工和小规模采金活动中使用的汞的战略；

(十) 旨在向手工和小规模采金工人和受影响的社区提供信息的战略；以及

(十一) 实施国家行动计划的时间表。

二、每一缔约方均可在其国家行动计划中纳入为实现其目标而制定的额外战略，包括采用或引进无汞手工和小规模采金标准以及市场化的机制或营销手段。

附件 D
汞及其化合物的大气排放点源名目

点源类别：

燃煤电厂

燃煤工业锅炉

有色金属生产当中使用的冶炼和焙烧工艺[1]

废物焚烧设施

水泥熟料生产设施

[1] 就本附件而言，“有色金属”系指铅、锌、铜和工业黄金。

附件 E
仲裁和调解程序

第一部分：仲裁程序

为本公约第二十五条第二款第一项之目的，兹订立仲裁程序如下：

第一条

一、任何缔约方均可根据本公约第二十五条以书面形式通知争端的其他当事方，将争端交付仲裁。此种书面通知应附有关于追索要求的说明以及任何佐证文件，应阐明仲裁的主题事项并特别列明在解释或适用方面引发争端的本公约条款。
二、原告一方应向秘书处发出通知，说明其正在依照本公约第二十五条的规定将争端提交仲裁。通知中应附有原告一方的书面通知、追索声明以及以上第一款所述及的佐证文件。秘书处应将所收到的资料转送本公约所有缔约方。

第二条

一、如果按照以上第一条将争端交付仲裁，应为此设立仲裁庭。仲裁庭应由三名仲裁员组成。
二、争端所涉各方均应指派仲裁员一名，其以此种方式指派的这两名仲裁员应协议指定第三名仲裁员，并应由该名仲裁员担任仲裁庭庭长。在涉及两个以上当事方的争端中，所涉利害关系相同的当事方应协议共同指定一名仲裁员。仲裁庭庭长不应是争端的任何一方的国民，其惯常居所亦不应在争端的任何一方领土范围内或受雇于其中任何一方，且从未以任何其他身份涉及该案件。
三、仲裁员的任何空缺均应以最初的指派方式予以填补。

第三条

一、如果争端当事方之一在被告一方接获仲裁通知 2 个月之内仍未指派其仲裁员，则另一当事方可就此通知联合国秘书长，秘书长应于其后 2 个月内指定一名仲裁员。
二、如自指派第二名仲裁员的日期起 2 个月内仍未指定仲裁庭庭长，则应由联合国秘书长，经任何一方的请求，在其后的 2 个月内指定仲裁庭庭长。

第四条

仲裁庭应依照本公约的条款以及国际法的规定做出裁决。

第五条

除非争端各方另有协议，仲裁庭应自行确定其审理程序。

第六条

仲裁庭可应争端一当事方提出的请求，建议采取必要的临时保护措施。

第七条

争端所涉各方应便利仲裁庭的工作，尤应以一切可用手段：

(一) 向仲裁庭提供所有相关文件、资料和便利；和

(二) 于必要时使仲裁庭得以传唤证人或专家并接受其提供的证词。

第八条

争端各方和仲裁员均有义务保护其在仲裁庭审理案件期间秘密收到的任何资料或文件的机密性。

第九条

除非仲裁庭因案情特殊而另有决定，否则仲裁庭的费用应由争端所涉各方平均分担。仲裁庭应负责保存所涉全部费用的记录，并应向各当事方送交一份费用决算表。

第十条

任何因其与争端主题事项有法律性质的利害关系而可能由于该案件裁决结果而受到影响的缔约方，经仲裁庭同意可介入仲裁过程。

第十一条

仲裁庭可就争端的主题事项所直接引起的反诉听取陈诉并做出裁决。

第十二条

仲裁庭关于程序和实质问题的裁决均应以其仲裁员的多数票做出。

第十三条

一、如果争端的当事方之一不出庭或未能做出答辩，则另一当事方可要求仲裁庭继续进行仲裁程序并做出裁决。一方缺席或未能做出答辩，不得成为停止仲裁程序的理由。

二、仲裁庭在做出最后裁决之前，必须确切查明所提出的追索要求在事实和法律上均有确切的依据。

第十四条

除非仲裁庭认定有必要延长做出最后裁决的期限，否则它应在完全设立后 5 个月之内做出最后裁决；决定予以延长的期限不得超过其后 5 个月。

第十五条

仲裁庭的最后裁决应以争端所涉主题事项的范围为限，并应阐明其裁决所依据的理由。裁决书应载明参与做出裁决的仲裁员姓名和做出最后裁决的日期。仲裁庭的任何仲裁员均可在最后裁决书中附上单独的意见或异议。

第十六条

最后裁决应对争端各方具有约束力。对于上文第十条所述介入仲裁过程的当事方，在其介入所涉事项上，最后裁决书中对本公约的解释也应对该当事方具有约束力。最后裁决不得上诉，除非争端各方已事前议定了上诉程序。

第十七条

按照上文第十六条受最后裁决约束的当事方之间如对最后裁决的解释或其执行方式发生任何争执，其中任何一方均可就此提请做出裁决的仲裁庭对之做出裁定。

第二部分：调解程序

为本公约第二十五条第六款之目的，兹订立调解程序如下：

第一条

争端任何一方如按本公约第二十六条第六款提出设立调解委员会要求，应以书面形式向秘书处提出此种要求，同时抄送争端的其他当事方。秘书处应旋即将此事通知所有缔约方。

第二条

一、除非争端各方另有协议，否则调解委员会应由3名成员组成，由每一有关缔约方分别指定一名成员并由这些成员共同选定一名委员会主席。

二、对于涉及2个以上当事方的争端，所涉利害关系相同的当事方应通过协议共同指派其调解委员会成员。

第三条

如自秘书处收到上文第一条提到的书面要求之日起2个月内，尚有任何争端当事方未指定其委员会成员，则应由联合国秘书长根据任一当事方的请求，于其后2个月内指定委员会成员。

第四条

如自任命了调解委员会第2名成员之日起2个月内尚未选定调解委员会主席，则应由联合国秘书长根据争端任一当事方的请求，于其后2个月内指定委员会主席。

第五条

调解委员会应以独立且中立的方式协助争端各方努力友好解决争端。

第六条

一、调解委员会可按自认为合适的方式执行调解程序，同时充分考虑到案件的情况和争端当事各方希望表达的意见，包括其提出的任何关于迅速解决争端的要求。必要时，它可通过其本身的议事规则，除非当事方另有约定。

二、调解委员会在调解程序期间的任何时候均可以提出关于解决争端的提议或建议。

第七条

争端当事各方应配合调解委员会。尤其是，它们应务力按照委员会提出的要求提交书面材料、提供证据，并出席会议。当事各方及调解委员会成员有义务对委员会议事期间所收到的机密材料或文件保守机密。

第八条

调解委员会应按其成员的多数票作出决定。

第九条

除非争端已经解决，调解委员会应最迟在其完全设立后的 12 个月内提出一份报告，就解决争端的办法提出建议，各当事方应认真考虑那些建议。

第十条

对于调解委员会是否对所涉事项拥有审理权限的意见分歧，应由委员会予以裁定。

第十一条

调解委员会的费用应由争端各方平摊，除非它们另有约定。调解委员会应负责保存其所有费用的记录，并向各方提供一份最后的费用决算表。

[TEXT IN ENGLISH – TEXTE EN ANGLAIS]

MINAMATA CONVENTION ON MERCURY

The Parties to this Convention,

Recognizing that mercury is a chemical of global concern owing to its long-range atmospheric transport, its persistence in the environment once anthropogenically introduced, its ability to bioaccumulate in ecosystems and its significant negative effects on human health and the environment,

Recalling decision 25/5 of 20 February 2009 of the Governing Council of the United Nations Environment Programme to initiate international action to manage mercury in an efficient, effective and coherent manner,

Recalling paragraph 221 of the outcome document of the United Nations Conference on Sustainable Development "The future we want", which called for a successful outcome of the negotiations on a global legally binding instrument on mercury to address the risks to human health and the environment,

Recalling the United Nations Conference on Sustainable Development's reaffirmation of the principles of the Rio Declaration on Environment and Development, including, inter alia, common but differentiated responsibilities, and acknowledging States' respective circumstances and capabilities and the need for global action,

Aware of the health concerns, especially in developing countries, resulting from exposure to mercury of vulnerable populations, especially women, children, and, through them, future generations,

Noting the particular vulnerabilities of Arctic ecosystems and indigenous communities because of the biomagnification of mercury and contamination of traditional foods, and concerned about indigenous communities more generally with respect to the effects of mercury,

Recognizing the substantial lessons of Minamata Disease, in particular the serious health and environmental effects resulting from the mercury pollution, and the need to ensure proper management of mercury and the prevention of such events in the future,

Stressing the importance of financial, technical, technological, and capacity-building support, particularly for developing countries, and countries with economies in transition, in order to strengthen national capabilities for the management of mercury and to promote the effective implementation of the Convention,

Recognizing also the activities of the World Health Organization in the protection of human health related to mercury and the roles of relevant multilateral environmental agreements, especially the Basel Convention on the Control of Transboundary Movements of Hazardous Wastes and Their Disposal and the Rotterdam Convention on the Prior Informed Consent Procedure for Certain Hazardous Chemicals and Pesticides in International Trade,

Recognizing that this Convention and other international agreements in the field of the environment and trade are mutually supportive,

Emphasizing that nothing in this Convention is intended to affect the rights and obligations of any Party deriving from any existing international agreement,

Understanding that the above recital is not intended to create a hierarchy between this Convention and other international instruments,

Noting that nothing in this Convention prevents a Party from taking additional domestic measures consistent with the provisions of this Convention in an effort to protect human health and the environment from exposure to mercury in accordance with that Party's other obligations under applicable international law,

Have agreed as follows:

Article 1

Objective

The objective of this Convention is to protect the human health and the environment from anthropogenic emissions and releases of mercury and mercury compounds.

Article 2

Definitions

For the purposes of this Convention:

(a) "Artisanal and small-scale gold mining" means gold mining conducted by individual miners or small enterprises with limited capital investment and production;

(b) "Best available techniques" means those techniques that are the most effective to prevent and, where that is not practicable, to reduce emissions and releases of mercury to air, water and land and the impact of such emissions and releases on the environment as a whole, taking into account economic and technical considerations for a given Party or a given facility within the territory of that Party. In this context:

(i) "Best" means most effective in achieving a high general level of protection of the environment as a whole;

(ii) "Available" techniques means, in respect of a given Party and a given facility within the territory of that Party, those techniques developed on a scale that allows implementation in a relevant industrial sector under economically and technically viable conditions, taking into consideration the costs and benefits, whether or not those techniques are used or developed within the territory of that Party, provided that they are accessible to the operator of the facility as determined by that Party; and

(iii) "Techniques" means technologies used, operational practices and the ways in which installations are designed, built, maintained, operated and decommissioned;

(c) "Best environmental practices" means the application of the most appropriate combination of environmental control measures and strategies;

(d) "Mercury" means elemental mercury (Hg(0), CAS No. 7439-97-6);

(e) "Mercury compound" means any substance consisting of atoms of mercury and one or more atoms of other chemical elements that can be separated into different components only by chemical reactions;

(f) "Mercury-added product" means a product or product component that contains mercury or a mercury compound that was intentionally added;

(g) "Party" means a State or regional economic integration organization that has consented to be bound by this Convention and for which the Convention is in force;

(h) "Parties present and voting" means Parties present and casting an affirmative or negative vote at a meeting of the Parties;

(i) "Primary mercury mining" means mining in which the principal material sought is mercury;

(j) "Regional economic integration organization" means an organization constituted by sovereign States of a given region to which its member States have transferred competence in respect of matters governed by this Convention and which has been duly authorized, in accordance with its internal procedures, to sign, ratify, accept, approve or accede to this Convention; and

(k) "Use allowed" means any use by a Party of mercury or mercury compounds consistent with this Convention, including, but not limited to, uses consistent with Articles 3, 4, 5, 6 and 7.

Article 3

Mercury supply sources and trade

1. For the purposes of this Article:

(a) References to "mercury" include mixtures of mercury with other substances, including alloys of mercury, with a mercury concentration of at least 95 per cent by weight; and

(b) "Mercury compounds" means mercury (I) chloride (known also as calomel), mercury (II) oxide, mercury (II) sulphate, mercury (II) nitrate, cinnabar and mercury sulphide.

2. The provisions of this Article shall not apply to:

(a) Quantities of mercury or mercury compounds to be used for laboratory-scale research or as a reference standard; or

(b) Naturally occurring trace quantities of mercury or mercury compounds present in such products as non-mercury metals, ores, or mineral products, including coal, or products derived from these materials, and unintentional trace quantities in chemical products; or

(c) Mercury-added products.

3. Each Party shall not allow primary mercury mining that was not being conducted within its territory at the date of entry into force of the Convention for it.

4. Each Party shall only allow primary mercury mining that was being conducted within its territory at the date of entry into force of the Convention for it for a period of up to fifteen years after that date. During this period, mercury from such mining shall only be used in manufacturing of mercury-added products in accordance with Article 4, in manufacturing processes in accordance with Article 5, or be disposed in accordance with Article 11, using operations which do not lead to recovery, recycling, reclamation, direct re-use or alternative uses.

5. Each Party shall:

(a) Endeavour to identify individual stocks of mercury or mercury compounds exceeding 50 metric tons, as well as sources of mercury supply generating stocks exceeding 10 metric tons per year, that are located within its territory;

(b) Take measures to ensure that, where the Party determines that excess mercury from the decommissioning of chlor-alkali facilities is available, such mercury is disposed of in accordance with the guidelines for environmentally sound management referred to in paragraph 3 (a) of Article 11, using operations that do not lead to recovery, recycling, reclamation, direct re-use or alternative uses.

6. Each Party shall not allow the export of mercury except:

(a) To a Party that has provided the exporting Party with its written consent, and only for the purpose of:

(i) A use allowed to the importing Party under this Convention; or

(ii) Environmentally sound interim storage as set out in Article 10; or

(b) To a non-Party that has provided the exporting Party with its written consent, including certification demonstrating that:

(i) The non-Party has measures in place to ensure the protection of human health and the environment and to ensure its compliance with the provisions of Articles 10 and 11; and

(ii) Such mercury will be used only for a use allowed to a Party under this Convention or for environmentally sound interim storage as set out in Article 10.

7. An exporting Party may rely on a general notification to the Secretariat by the importing Party or non-Party as the written consent required by paragraph 6. Such general notification shall set out any terms and conditions under which the importing Party or non-Party provides its consent. The notification may be revoked at any time by that Party or non-Party. The Secretariat shall keep a public register of all such notifications.

8. Each Party shall not allow the import of mercury from a non-Party to whom it will provide its written consent unless the non-Party has provided certification that the mercury is not from sources identified as not allowed under paragraph 3 or paragraph 5 (b).

9. A Party that submits a general notification of consent under paragraph 7 may decide not to apply paragraph 8, provided that it maintains comprehensive restrictions on the export of mercury and has domestic measures in place to ensure that imported mercury is managed in an environmentally sound manner. The Party shall provide a notification of such decision to the Secretariat, including information describing its export restrictions and domestic regulatory measures, as well as information on the quantities and countries of origin of mercury imported from non-Parties. The Secretariat shall maintain a public register of all such notifications. The Implementation and Compliance Committee shall review and evaluate any such notifications and supporting information in accordance with Article 15 and may make recommendations, as appropriate, to the Conference of the Parties.

10. The procedure set out in paragraph 9 shall be available until the conclusion of the second meeting of the Conference of the Parties. After that time, it shall cease to be available, unless the Conference of the Parties decides otherwise by simple majority of the Parties present and voting, except with respect to a Party that has provided a notification under paragraph 9 before the end of the second meeting of the Conference of the Parties.

11. Each Party shall include in its reports submitted pursuant to Article 21 information showing that the requirements of this Article have been met.

12. The Conference of the Parties shall at its first meeting provide further guidance in regard to this Article, particularly in regard to paragraphs 5 (a), 6 and 8, and shall develop and adopt the required content of the certification referred to in paragraphs 6 (b) and 8.

13. The Conference of the Parties shall evaluate whether the trade in specific mercury compounds compromises the objective of this Convention and consider whether specific mercury compounds should, by their listing in an additional annex adopted in accordance with Article 27, be made subject to paragraphs 6 and 8.

ARTICLE 4

MERCURY-ADDED PRODUCTS

1. Each Party shall not allow, by taking appropriate measures, the manufacture, import or export of mercury-added products listed in Part I of Annex A after the phase-out date specified for those products, except where an exclusion is specified in Annex A or the Party has a registered exemption pursuant to Article 6.

2. A Party may, as an alternative to paragraph 1, indicate at the time of ratification or upon entry into force of an amendment to Annex A for it, that it will implement different measures or strategies to address products listed in Part I of Annex A. A Party may only choose this alternative if it can demonstrate that it has already reduced to a de minimis level the manufacture, import, and export of the large majority of the products listed in Part I of Annex A and that it has implemented measures or strategies to reduce the use of mercury in additional products not listed in Part I of Annex A at the time it notifies the Secretariat of its decision to use this alternative. In addition, a Party choosing this alternative shall:

(a) Report at the first opportunity to the Conference of the Parties a description of the measures or strategies implemented, including a quantification of the reductions achieved;

(b) Implement measures or strategies to reduce the use of mercury in any products listed in Part I of Annex A for which a de minimis value has not yet been obtained;

(c) Consider additional measures to achieve further reductions; and

(d) Not be eligible to claim exemptions pursuant to Article 6 for any product category for which this alternative is chosen.

No later than five years after the date of entry into force of the Convention, the Conference of the Parties shall, as part of the review process under paragraph 8, review the progress and the effectiveness of the measures taken under this paragraph.

3. Each Party shall take measures for the mercury-added products listed in Part II of Annex A in accordance with the provisions set out therein.

4. The Secretariat shall, on the basis of information provided by Parties, collect and maintain information on mercury-added products and their alternatives, and shall make such information publicly available. The Secretariat shall also make publicly available any other relevant information submitted by Parties.

5. Each Party shall take measures to prevent the incorporation into assembled products of mercury-added products the manufacture, import and export of which are not allowed for it under this Article.

6. Each Party shall discourage the manufacture and the distribution in commerce of mercury-added products not covered by any known use of mercury-added products prior to the date of entry into force of the Convention for it, unless an assessment of the risks and benefits of the product demonstrates environmental or human health benefits. A Party shall provide to the Secretariat, as appropriate, information on any such product, including any information on the environmental and human health risks and benefits of the product. The Secretariat shall make such information publicly available.

7. Any Party may submit a proposal to the Secretariat for listing a mercury-added product in Annex A, which shall include information related to the availability, technical and economic feasibility and environmental and health risks and benefits of the non-mercury alternatives to the product, taking into account information pursuant to paragraph 4.

8. No later than five years after the date of entry into force of the Convention, the Conference of the Parties shall review Annex A and may consider amendments to that Annex in accordance with Article 27.

9. In reviewing Annex A pursuant to paragraph 8, the Conference of the Parties shall take into account at least:

(a) Any proposal submitted under paragraph 7;

(b) The information made available pursuant to paragraph 4; and

(c) The availability to the Parties of mercury-free alternatives that are technically and economically feasible, taking into account the environmental and human health risks and benefits.

Article 5

Manufacturing processes in which mercury or mercury compounds are used

1. For the purposes of this Article and Annex B, manufacturing processes in which mercury or mercury compounds are used shall not include processes using mercury-added products, processes for manufacturing mercury-added products or processes that process mercury-containing waste.

2. Each Party shall not allow, by taking appropriate measures, the use of mercury or mercury compounds in the manufacturing processes listed in Part I of Annex B after the phase-out date specified in that Annex for the individual processes, except where the Party has a registered exemption pursuant to Article 6.

3. Each Party shall take measures to restrict the use of mercury or mercury compounds in the processes listed in Part II of Annex B in accordance with the provisions set out therein.

4. The Secretariat shall, on the basis of information provided by Parties, collect and maintain information on processes that use mercury or mercury compounds and their alternatives, and shall make such information publicly available. Other relevant information may also be submitted by Parties and shall be made publicly available by the Secretariat.

5. Each Party with one or more facilities that use mercury or mercury compounds in the manufacturing processes listed in Annex B shall:

(a) Take measures to address emissions and releases of mercury or mercury compounds from those facilities;

(b) Include in its reports submitted pursuant to Article 21 information on the measures taken pursuant to this paragraph; and

(c) Endeavour to identify facilities within its territory that use mercury or mercury compounds for processes listed in Annex B and submit to the Secretariat, no later than three years after the date of entry into force of the Convention for it, information on the number and types of such facilities and the estimated annual amount of mercury or mercury compounds used in those facilities. The Secretariat shall make such information publicly available.

6. Each Party shall not allow the use of mercury or mercury compounds in a facility that did not exist prior to the date of entry into force of the

Convention for it using the manufacturing processes listed in Annex B. No exemptions shall apply to such facilities.

7. Each Party shall discourage the development of any facility using any other manufacturing process in which mercury or mercury compounds are intentionally used that did not exist prior to the date of entry into force of the Convention, except where the Party can demonstrate to the satisfaction of the Conference of the Parties that the manufacturing process provides significant environmental and health benefits and that there are no technically and economically feasible mercury-free alternatives available providing such benefits.

8. Parties are encouraged to exchange information on relevant new technological developments, economically and technically feasible mercury-free alternatives, and possible measures and techniques to reduce and where feasible to eliminate the use of mercury and mercury compounds in, and emissions and releases of mercury and mercury compounds from, the manufacturing processes listed in Annex B.

9. Any Party may submit a proposal to amend Annex B in order to list a manufacturing process in which mercury or mercury compounds are used. It shall include information related to the availability, technical and economic feasibility and environmental and health risks and benefits of the non-mercury alternatives to the process.

10. No later than five years after the date of entry into force of the Convention, the Conference of the Parties shall review Annex B and may consider amendments to that Annex in accordance with Article 27.

11. In any review of Annex B pursuant to paragraph 10, the Conference of the Parties shall take into account at least:

(a) Any proposal submitted under paragraph 9;

(b) The information made available under paragraph 4; and

(c) The availability for the Parties of mercury-free alternatives which are technically and economically feasible taking into account the environmental and health risks and benefits.

Article 6

Exemptions available to a Party upon request

1. Any State or regional economic integration organization may register for one or more exemptions from the phase-out dates listed in Annex A and Annex B, hereafter referred to as an "exemption", by notifying the Secretariat in writing:

(a) On becoming a Party to this Convention; or

(b) In the case of any mercury-added product that is added by an amendment to Annex A or any manufacturing process in which mercury is used that is added by an amendment to Annex B, no later than the date upon which the applicable amendment enters into force for the Party.

Any such registration shall be accompanied by a statement explaining the Party's need for the exemption.

2. An exemption can be registered either for a category listed in Annex A or B or for a sub-category identified by any State or regional economic integration organization.

3. Each Party that has one or more exemptions shall be identified in a register. The Secretariat shall establish and maintain the register and make it available to the public.

4. The register shall include:

(a) A list of the Parties that have one or more exemptions;

(b) The exemption or exemptions registered for each Party; and

(c) The expiration date of each exemption.

5. Unless a shorter period is indicated in the register by a Party, all exemptions pursuant to paragraph 1 shall expire five years after the relevant phase-out date listed in Annex A or B.

6. The Conference of the Parties may, at the request of a Party, decide to extend an exemption for five years unless the Party requests a shorter period. In making its decision, the Conference of the Parties shall take due account of:

(a) A report from the Party justifying the need to extend the exemption and outlining activities undertaken and planned to eliminate the need for the exemption as soon as feasible;

(b) Available information, including in respect of the availability of alternative products and processes that are free of mercury or that involve the consumption of less mercury than the exempt use; and

(c) Activities planned or under way to provide environmentally sound storage of mercury and disposal of mercury wastes.

An exemption may only be extended once per product per phase-out date.

7. A Party may at any time withdraw an exemption upon written notification to the Secretariat. The withdrawal of an exemption shall take effect on the date specified in the notification.

8. Notwithstanding paragraph 1, no State or regional economic integration organization may register for an exemption after five years after the phase-out date for the relevant product or process listed in Annex A or B, unless one or more Parties remain registered for an exemption for that product or process, having received an extension pursuant to paragraph 6. In that case, a State or regional economic integration organization may, at the times set out in paragraphs 1 (a) and (b), register for an exemption for that product or process, which shall expire ten years after the relevant phase-out date.

9. No Party may have an exemption in effect at any time after 10 years after the phase-out date for a product or process listed in Annex A or B.

Article 7

Artisanal and small-scale gold mining

1. The measures in this Article and in Annex C shall apply to artisanal and small-scale gold mining and processing in which mercury amalgamation is used to extract gold from ore.

2. Each Party that has artisanal and small-scale gold mining and processing subject to this Article within its territory shall take steps to reduce, and where feasible eliminate, the use of mercury and mercury compounds in, and the emissions and releases to the environment of mercury from, such mining and processing.

3. Each Party shall notify the Secretariat if at any time the Party determines that artisanal and small-scale gold mining and processing in its territory is more than insignificant. If it so determines the Party shall:

(a) Develop and implement a national action plan in accordance with Annex C;

(b) Submit its national action plan to the Secretariat no later than three years after entry into force of the Convention for it or three years after the notification to the Secretariat, whichever is later; and

(c) Thereafter, provide a review every three years of the progress made in meeting its obligations under this Article and include such reviews in its reports submitted pursuant to Article 21.

4. Parties may cooperate with each other and with relevant intergovernmental organizations and other entities, as appropriate, to achieve the objectives of this Article. Such cooperation may include:

(a) Development of strategies to prevent the diversion of mercury or mercury compounds for use in artisanal and small-scale gold mining and processing;

(b) Education, outreach and capacity-building initiatives;

(c) Promotion of research into sustainable non-mercury alternative practices;

(d) Provision of technical and financial assistance;

(e) Partnerships to assist in the implementation of their commitments under this Article; and

(f) Use of existing information exchange mechanisms to promote knowledge, best environmental practices and alternative technologies that are environmentally, technically, socially and economically viable.

Article 8

Emissions

1. This Article concerns controlling and, where feasible, reducing emissions of mercury and mercury compounds, often expressed as "total

mercury", to the atmosphere through measures to control emissions from the point sources falling within the source categories listed in Annex D.

2. For the purposes of this Article:

(a) "Emissions" means emissions of mercury or mercury compounds to the atmosphere;

(b) "Relevant source" means a source falling within one of the source categories listed in Annex D. A Party may, if it chooses, establish criteria to identify the sources covered within a source category listed in Annex D so long as those criteria for any category include at least 75 per cent of the emissions from that category;

(c) "New source" means any relevant source within a category listed in Annex D, the construction or substantial modification of which is commenced at least one year after the date of:

(i) Entry into force of this Convention for the Party concerned; or

(ii) Entry into force for the Party concerned of an amendment to Annex D where the source becomes subject to the provisions of this Convention only by virtue of that amendment;

(d) "Substantial modification" means modification of a relevant source that results in a significant increase in emissions, excluding any change in emissions resulting from by-product recovery. It shall be a matter for the Party to decide whether a modification is substantial or not;

(e) "Existing source" means any relevant source that is not a new source;

(f) "Emission limit value" means a limit on the concentration, mass or emission rate of mercury or mercury compounds, often expressed as "total mercury", emitted from a point source.

3. A Party with relevant sources shall take measures to control emissions and may prepare a national plan setting out the measures to be taken to control emissions and its expected targets, goals and outcomes. Any plan shall be submitted to the Conference of the Parties within four years of the date of entry into force of the Convention for that Party. If a Party develops an implementation plan in accordance with Article 20, the Party may include in it the plan prepared pursuant to this paragraph.

4. For its new sources, each Party shall require the use of best available techniques and best environmental practices to control and, where feasible, reduce emissions, as soon as practicable but no later than five years after the date of entry into force of the Convention for that Party. A Party may use emission limit values that are consistent with the application of best available techniques.

5. For its existing sources, each Party shall include in any national plan, and shall implement, one or more of the following measures, taking into account its national circumstances, and the economic and technical feasibility and affordability of the measures, as soon as practicable but no more than ten years after the date of entry into force of the Convention for it:

(a) A quantified goal for controlling and, where feasible, reducing emissions from relevant sources;

(b) Emission limit values for controlling and, where feasible, reducing emissions from relevant sources;

(c) The use of best available techniques and best environmental practices to control emissions from relevant sources;

(d) A multi-pollutant control strategy that would deliver co-benefits for control of mercury emissions;

(e) Alternative measures to reduce emissions from relevant sources.

6. Parties may apply the same measures to all relevant existing sources or may adopt different measures in respect of different source categories. The objective shall be for those measures applied by a Party to achieve reasonable progress in reducing emissions over time.

7. Each Party shall establish, as soon as practicable and no later than five years after the date of entry into force of the Convention for it, and maintain thereafter, an inventory of emissions from relevant sources.

8. The Conference of the Parties shall, at its first meeting, adopt guidance on:

(a) Best available techniques and on best environmental practices, taking into account any difference between new and existing sources and the need to minimize cross-media effects; and

(b) Support for Parties in implementing the measures set out in paragraph 5, in particular in determining goals and in setting emission limit values.

9. The Conference of the Parties shall, as soon as practicable, adopt guidance on:

(a) Criteria that Parties may develop pursuant to paragraph 2 (b);

(b) The methodology for preparing inventories of emissions.

10. The Conference of the Parties shall keep under review, and update as appropriate, the guidance developed pursuant to paragraphs 8 and 9. Parties shall take the guidance into account in implementing the relevant provisions of this Article.

11. Each Party shall include information on its implementation of this Article in its reports submitted pursuant to Article 21, in particular information concerning the measures it has taken in accordance with paragraphs 4 to 7 and the effectiveness of the measures.

Article 9

Releases

1. This Article concerns controlling and, where feasible, reducing releases of mercury and mercury compounds, often expressed as "total mercury", to land and water from the relevant point sources not addressed in other provisions of this Convention.

2. For the purposes of this Article:

(a) "Releases" means releases of mercury or mercury compounds to land or water;

(b) "Relevant source" means any significant anthropogenic point source of release as identified by a Party that is not addressed in other provisions of this Convention;

(c) "New source" means any relevant source, the construction or substantial modification of which is commenced at least one year after the date of entry into force of this Convention for the Party concerned;

(d) "Substantial modification" means modification of a relevant source that results in a significant increase in releases, excluding any change in releases resulting from by-product recovery. It shall be a matter for the Party to decide whether a modification is substantial or not;

(e) "Existing source" means any relevant source that is not a new source;

(f) "Release limit value" means a limit on the concentration or mass of mercury or mercury compounds, often expressed as "total mercury", released from a point source.

3. Each Party shall, no later than three years after the date of entry into force of the Convention for it and on a regular basis thereafter, identify the relevant point source categories.

4. A Party with relevant sources shall take measures to control releases and may prepare a national plan setting out the measures to be taken to control releases and its expected targets, goals and outcomes. Any plan shall be submitted to the Conference of the Parties within four years of the date of entry into force of the Convention for that Party. If a Party develops an implementation plan in accordance with Article 20, the Party may include in it the plan prepared pursuant to this paragraph.

5. The measures shall include one or more of the following, as appropriate:

(a) Release limit values to control and, where feasible, reduce releases from relevant sources;

(b) The use of best available techniques and best environmental practices to control releases from relevant sources;

(c) A multi-pollutant control strategy that would deliver co-benefits for control of mercury releases;

(d) Alternative measures to reduce releases from relevant sources.

6. Each Party shall establish, as soon as practicable and no later than five years after the date of entry into force of the Convention for it, and maintain thereafter, an inventory of releases from relevant sources.

7. The Conference of the Parties shall, as soon as practicable, adopt guidance on:

(a) Best available techniques and on best environmental practices, taking into account any difference between new and existing sources and the need to minimize cross-media effects;

(b) The methodology for preparing inventories of releases.

8. Each Party shall include information on its implementation of this Article in its reports submitted pursuant to Article 21, in particular information concerning the measures it has taken in accordance with paragraphs 3 to 6 and the effectiveness of the measures.

Article 10

Environmentally sound interim storage of mercury, other than waste mercury

1. This Article shall apply to the interim storage of mercury and mercury compounds as defined in Article 3 that do not fall within the meaning of the definition of mercury wastes set out in Article 11.

2. Each Party shall take measures to ensure that the interim storage of such mercury and mercury compounds intended for a use allowed to a Party under this Convention is undertaken in an environmentally sound manner, taking into account any guidelines, and in accordance with any requirements, adopted pursuant to paragraph 3.

3. The Conference of the Parties shall adopt guidelines on the environmentally sound interim storage of such mercury and mercury compounds, taking into account any relevant guidelines developed under the Basel Convention on the Control of Transboundary Movements of Hazardous Wastes and Their Disposal and other relevant guidance. The Conference of the Parties may adopt requirements for interim storage in an additional annex to this Convention in accordance with Article 27.

4. Parties shall cooperate, as appropriate, with each other and with relevant intergovernmental organizations and other entities, to enhance capacity-building for the environmentally sound interim storage of such mercury and mercury compounds.

Article 11

Mercury wastes

1. The relevant definitions of the Basel Convention on the Control of Transboundary Movements of Hazardous Wastes and Their Disposal shall apply to wastes covered under this Convention for Parties to the Basel Convention. Parties to this Convention that are not Parties to the Basel Convention shall use those definitions as guidance as applied to wastes covered under this Convention.

2. For the purposes of this Convention, mercury wastes means substances or objects:

(a) Consisting of mercury or mercury compounds;

(b) Containing mercury or mercury compounds; or

(c) Contaminated with mercury or mercury compounds,

in a quantity above the relevant thresholds defined by the Conference of the Parties, in collaboration with the relevant bodies of the Basel Convention in a harmonized manner, that are disposed of or are intended to be disposed of or are required to be disposed of by the provisions of national law or this Convention. This definition excludes overburden, waste rock and tailings from mining, except from primary mercury mining, unless they contain mercury or mercury compounds above thresholds defined by the Conference of the Parties.

3. Each Party shall take appropriate measures so that mercury waste is:

(a) Managed in an environmentally sound manner, taking into account the guidelines developed under the Basel Convention and in accordance with requirements that the Conference of the Parties shall adopt in an additional annex in accordance with Article 27. In developing requirements, the Conference of the Parties shall take into account Parties' waste management regulations and programmes;

(b) Only recovered, recycled, reclaimed or directly re-used for a use allowed to a Party under this Convention or for environmentally sound disposal pursuant to paragraph 3 (a);

(c) For Parties to the Basel Convention, not transported across international boundaries except for the purpose of environmentally sound disposal in conformity with this Article and with that Convention. In circumstances where the Basel Convention does not apply to transport across international boundaries, a Party shall allow such transport only after taking into account relevant international rules, standards, and guidelines.

4. The Conference of the Parties shall seek to cooperate closely with the relevant bodies of the Basel Convention in the review and update, as appropriate, of the guidelines referred to in paragraph 3 (a).

5. Parties are encouraged to cooperate with each other and with relevant intergovernmental organizations and other entities, as appropriate, to develop and maintain global, regional and national capacity for the management of mercury wastes in an environmentally sound manner.

Article 12

Contaminated sites

1. Each Party shall endeavour to develop appropriate strategies for identifying and assessing sites contaminated by mercury or mercury compounds.

2. Any actions to reduce the risks posed by such sites shall be performed in an environmentally sound manner incorporating, where appropriate, an assessment of the risks to human health and the environment from the mercury or mercury compounds they contain.

3. The Conference of the Parties shall adopt guidance on managing contaminated sites that may include methods and approaches for:

(a) Site identification and characterization;

(b) Engaging the public;

(c) Human health and environmental risk assessments;

(d) Options for managing the risks posed by contaminated sites;

(e) Evaluation of benefits and costs; and

(f) Validation of outcomes.

4. Parties are encouraged to cooperate in developing strategies and implementing activities for identifying, assessing, prioritizing, managing and, as appropriate, remediating contaminated sites.

Article 13

Financial resources and mechanism

1. Each Party undertakes to provide, within its capabilities, resources in respect of those national activities that are intended to implement this Convention, in accordance with its national policies, priorities, plans and programmes. Such resources may include domestic funding through relevant policies, development strategies and national budgets, and bilateral and multilateral funding, as well as private sector involvement.

2. The overall effectiveness of implementation of this Convention by developing country Parties will be related to the effective implementation of this Article.

3. Multilateral, regional and bilateral sources of financial and technical assistance, as well as capacity-building and technology transfer, are encouraged, on an urgent basis, to enhance and increase their activities on mercury in support of developing country Parties in the implementation of this Convention relating to financial resources, technical assistance and technology transfer.

4. The Parties, in their actions with regard to funding, shall take full account of the specific needs and special circumstances of Parties that are small island developing States or least developed countries.

5. A Mechanism for the provision of adequate, predictable, and timely financial resources is hereby defined. The Mechanism is to support developing country Parties and Parties with economies in transition in implementing their obligations under this Convention.

6. The Mechanism shall include:

(a) The Global Environment Facility Trust Fund; and

(b) A specific international Programme to support capacity-building and technical assistance.

7. The Global Environment Facility Trust Fund shall provide new, predictable, adequate and timely financial resources to meet costs in support of

implementation of this Convention as agreed by the Conference of the Parties. For the purposes of this Convention, the Global Environment Facility Trust Fund shall be operated under the guidance of and be accountable to the Conference of the Parties. The Conference of the Parties shall provide guidance on overall strategies, policies, programme priorities and eligibility for access to and utilization of financial resources. In addition, the Conference of the Parties shall provide guidance on an indicative list of categories of activities that could receive support from the Global Environment Facility Trust Fund. The Global Environment Facility Trust Fund shall provide resources to meet the agreed incremental costs of global environmental benefits and the agreed full costs of some enabling activities.

8. In providing resources for an activity, the Global Environment Facility Trust Fund should take into account the potential mercury reductions of a proposed activity relative to its costs.

9. For the purposes of this Convention, the Programme referred to in paragraph 6 (b) will be operated under the guidance of and be accountable to the Conference of the Parties. The Conference of the Parties shall, at its first meeting, decide on the hosting institution for the Programme, which shall be an existing entity, and provide guidance to it, including on its duration. All Parties and other relevant stakeholders are invited to provide financial resources to the Programme, on a voluntary basis.

10. The Conference of the Parties and the entities comprising the Mechanism shall agree upon, at the first meeting of the Conference of the Parties, arrangements to give effect to the above paragraphs.

11. The Conference of the Parties shall review, no later than at its third meeting, and thereafter on a regular basis, the level of funding, the guidance provided by the Conference of the Parties to the entities entrusted to operationalize the Mechanism established under this Article and their effectiveness, and their ability to address the changing needs of developing country Parties and Parties with economies in transition. It shall, based on such review, take appropriate action to improve the effectiveness of the Mechanism.

12. All Parties, within their capabilities, are invited to contribute to the Mechanism. The Mechanism shall encourage the provision of resources from other sources, including the private sector, and shall seek to leverage such resources for the activities it supports.

Article 14

Capacity-building, technical assistance and technology transfer

1. Parties shall cooperate to provide, within their respective capabilities, timely and appropriate capacity-building and technical assistance to developing country Parties, in particular Parties that are least developed countries or small island developing States, and Parties with economies in transition, to assist them in implementing their obligations under this Convention.

2. Capacity-building and technical assistance pursuant to paragraph 1 and Article 13 may be delivered through regional, subregional and national arrangements, including existing regional and subregional centres, through other multilateral and bilateral means, and through partnerships, including partnerships involving the private sector. Cooperation and coordination with other multilateral environmental agreements in the field of chemicals and wastes should be sought to increase the effectiveness of technical assistance and its delivery.

3. Developed country Parties and other Parties within their capabilities shall promote and facilitate, supported by the private sector and other relevant stakeholders as appropriate, development, transfer and diffusion of, and access to, up-to-date environmentally sound alternative technologies to developing country Parties, in particular the least developed countries and small island developing States, and Parties with economies in transition, to strengthen their capacity to effectively implement this Convention.

4. The Conference of the Parties shall, by its second meeting and thereafter on a regular basis, and taking into account submissions and reports from Parties including those as provided for in Article 21 and information provided by other stakeholders:

(a) Consider information on existing initiatives and progress made in relation to alternative technologies;

(b) Consider the needs of Parties, particularly developing country Parties, for alternative technologies; and

(c) Identify challenges experienced by Parties, particularly developing country Parties, in technology transfer.

5. The Conference of the Parties shall make recommendations on how capacity-building, technical assistance and technology transfer could be further enhanced under this Article.

Article 15

Implementation and Compliance Committee

1. A mechanism, including a Committee as a subsidiary body of the Conference of the Parties, is hereby established to promote implementation of, and review compliance with, all provisions of this Convention. The mechanism, including the Committee, shall be facilitative in nature and shall pay particular attention to the respective national capabilities and circumstances of Parties.

2. The Committee shall promote implementation of, and review compliance with, all provisions of this Convention. The Committee shall examine both individual and systemic issues of implementation and compliance and make recommendations, as appropriate, to the Conference of the Parties.

3. The Committee shall consist of 15 members, nominated by Parties and elected by the Conference of the Parties, with due consideration to equitable geographical representation based on the five regions of the United Nations; the first members shall be elected at the first meeting of the Conference of the Parties and thereafter in accordance with the rules of procedure approved by the Conference of the Parties pursuant to paragraph 5; the members of the Committee shall have competence in a field relevant to this Convention and reflect an appropriate balance of expertise.

4. The Committee may consider issues on the basis of:

(a) Written submissions from any Party with respect to its own compliance;

(b) National reports in accordance with Article 21; and

(c) Requests from the Conference of the Parties.

5. The Committee shall elaborate its rules of procedure, which shall be subject to approval by the second meeting of the Conference of the Parties; the Conference of the Parties may adopt further terms of reference for the Committee.

6. The Committee shall make every effort to adopt its recommendations by consensus. If all efforts at consensus have been exhausted and no consensus is reached, such recommendations shall as a last resort be adopted by a three-

fourths majority vote of the members present and voting, based on a quorum of two-thirds of the members.

Article 16

Health aspects

1. Parties are encouraged to:

(a) Promote the development and implementation of strategies and programmes to identify and protect populations at risk, particularly vulnerable populations, and which may include adopting science-based health guidelines relating to the exposure to mercury and mercury compounds, setting targets for mercury exposure reduction, where appropriate, and public education, with the participation of public health and other involved sectors;

(b) Promote the development and implementation of science-based educational and preventive programmes on occupational exposure to mercury and mercury compounds;

(c) Promote appropriate health-care services for prevention, treatment and care for populations affected by the exposure to mercury or mercury compounds; and

(d) Establish and strengthen, as appropriate, the institutional and health professional capacities for the prevention, diagnosis, treatment and monitoring of health risks related to the exposure to mercury and mercury compounds.

2. The Conference of the Parties, in considering health-related issues or activities, should:

(a) Consult and collaborate with the World Health Organization, the International Labour Organization and other relevant intergovernmental organizations, as appropriate; and

(b) Promote cooperation and exchange of information with the World Health Organization, the International Labour Organization and other relevant intergovernmental organizations, as appropriate.

Article 17

Information exchange

1. Each Party shall facilitate the exchange of:

(a) Scientific, technical, economic and legal information concerning mercury and mercury compounds, including toxicological, ecotoxicological and safety information;

(b) Information on the reduction or elimination of the production, use, trade, emissions and releases of mercury and mercury compounds;

(c) Information on technically and economically viable alternatives to:

(i) Mercury-added products;

(ii) Manufacturing processes in which mercury or mercury compounds are used; and

(iii) Activities and processes that emit or release mercury or mercury compounds;

including information on the health and environmental risks and economic and social costs and benefits of such alternatives; and

(d) Epidemiological information concerning health impacts associated with exposure to mercury and mercury compounds, in close cooperation with the World Health Organization and other relevant organizations, as appropriate.

2. Parties may exchange the information referred to in paragraph 1 directly, through the Secretariat, or in cooperation with other relevant organizations, including the secretariats of chemicals and wastes conventions, as appropriate.

3. The Secretariat shall facilitate cooperation in the exchange of information referred to in this Article, as well as with relevant organizations, including the secretariats of multilateral environmental agreements and other international initiatives. In addition to information from Parties, this information shall include information from intergovernmental and non-governmental organizations with expertise in the area of mercury, and from national and international institutions with such expertise.

4. Each Party shall designate a national focal point for the exchange of information under this Convention, including with regard to the consent of importing Parties under Article 3.

5. For the purposes of this Convention, information on the health and safety of humans and the environment shall not be regarded as confidential. Parties that exchange other information pursuant to this Convention shall protect any confidential information as mutually agreed.

Article 18

Public information, awareness and education

1. Each Party shall, within its capabilities, promote and facilitate:

(a) Provision to the public of available information on:

(i) The health and environmental effects of mercury and mercury compounds;

(ii) Alternatives to mercury and mercury compounds;

(iii) The topics identified in paragraph 1 of Article 17;

(iv) The results of its research, development and monitoring activities under Article 19; and

(v) Activities to meet its obligations under this Convention;

(b) Education, training and public awareness related to the effects of exposure to mercury and mercury compounds on human health and the environment in collaboration with relevant intergovernmental and non-governmental organizations and vulnerable populations, as appropriate.

2. Each Party shall use existing mechanisms or give consideration to the development of mechanisms, such as pollutant release and transfer registers where applicable, for the collection and dissemination of information on estimates of its annual quantities of mercury and mercury compounds that are emitted, released or disposed of through human activities.

Article 19

Research, development and monitoring

1. Parties shall endeavour to cooperate to develop and improve, taking into account their respective circumstances and capabilities:

(a) Inventories of use, consumption, and anthropogenic emissions to air and releases to water and land of mercury and mercury compounds;

(b) Modelling and geographically representative monitoring of levels of mercury and mercury compounds in vulnerable populations and in environmental media, including biotic media such as fish, marine mammals, sea turtles and birds, as well as collaboration in the collection and exchange of relevant and appropriate samples;

(c) Assessments of the impact of mercury and mercury compounds on human health and the environment, in addition to social, economic and cultural impacts, particularly in respect of vulnerable populations;

(d) Harmonized methodologies for the activities undertaken under subparagraphs (a), (b) and (c);

(e) Information on the environmental cycle, transport (including long-range transport and deposition), transformation and fate of mercury and mercury compounds in a range of ecosystems, taking appropriate account of the distinction between anthropogenic and natural emissions and releases of mercury and of remobilization of mercury from historic deposition;

(f) Information on commerce and trade in mercury and mercury compounds and mercury-added products; and

(g) Information and research on the technical and economic availability of mercury-free products and processes and on best available techniques and best environmental practices to reduce and monitor emissions and releases of mercury and mercury compounds.

2. Parties should, where appropriate, build on existing monitoring networks and research programmes in undertaking the activities identified in paragraph 1.

Article 20

Implementation plans

1. Each Party may, following an initial assessment, develop and execute an implementation plan, taking into account its domestic circumstances, for meeting the obligations under this Convention. Any such plan should be transmitted to the Secretariat as soon as it has been developed.

2. Each Party may review and update its implementation plan, taking into account its domestic circumstances and referring to guidance from the Conference of the Parties and other relevant guidance.

3. Parties should, in undertaking work in paragraphs 1 and 2, consult national stakeholders to facilitate the development, implementation, review and updating of their implementation plans.

4. Parties may also coordinate on regional plans to facilitate implementation of this Convention.

Article 21

Reporting

1. Each Party shall report to the Conference of the Parties, through the Secretariat, on the measures it has taken to implement the provisions of this Convention and on the effectiveness of such measures and the possible challenges in meeting the objectives of the Convention.

2. Each Party shall include in its reporting the information as called for in Articles 3, 5, 7, 8 and 9 of this Convention.

3. The Conference of the Parties shall, at its first meeting, decide upon the timing and format of the reporting to be followed by the Parties, taking into account the desirability of coordinating reporting with other relevant chemicals and wastes conventions.

Article 22

Effectiveness evaluation

1. The Conference of the Parties shall evaluate the effectiveness of this Convention, beginning no later than six years after the date of entry into force of the Convention and periodically thereafter at intervals to be decided by it.

2. To facilitate the evaluation, the Conference of the Parties shall, at its first meeting, initiate the establishment of arrangements for providing itself with comparable monitoring data on the presence and movement of mercury and mercury compounds in the environment as well as trends in levels of mercury and mercury compounds observed in biotic media and vulnerable populations.

3. The evaluation shall be conducted on the basis of available scientific, environmental, technical, financial and economic information, including:

(a) Reports and other monitoring information provided to the Conference of the Parties pursuant to paragraph 2;

(b) Reports submitted pursuant to Article 21;

(c) Information and recommendations provided pursuant to Article 15; and

(d) Reports and other relevant information on the operation of the financial assistance, technology transfer and capacity-building arrangements put in place under this Convention.

Article 23

Conference of the Parties

1. A Conference of the Parties is hereby established.

2. The first meeting of the Conference of the Parties shall be convened by the Executive Director of the United Nations Environment Programme no later than one year after the date of entry into force of this Convention. Thereafter, ordinary meetings of the Conference of the Parties shall be held at regular intervals to be decided by the Conference.

3. Extraordinary meetings of the Conference of the Parties shall be held at such other times as may be deemed necessary by the Conference, or at the written request of any Party, provided that, within six months of the request being communicated to the Parties by the Secretariat, it is supported by at least one third of the Parties.

4. The Conference of the Parties shall by consensus agree upon and adopt at its first meeting rules of procedure and financial rules for itself and any of its subsidiary bodies, as well as financial provisions governing the functioning of the Secretariat.

5. The Conference of the Parties shall keep under continuous review and evaluation the implementation of this Convention. It shall perform the functions assigned to it by this Convention and, to that end, shall:

(a) Establish such subsidiary bodies as it considers necessary for the implementation of this Convention;

(b) Cooperate, where appropriate, with competent international organizations and intergovernmental and non-governmental bodies;

(c) Regularly review all information made available to it and to the Secretariat pursuant to Article 21;

(d) Consider any recommendations submitted to it by the Implementation and Compliance Committee;

(e) Consider and undertake any additional action that may be required for the achievement of the objectives of this Convention; and

(f) Review Annexes A and B pursuant to Article 4 and Article 5.

6. The United Nations, its specialized agencies and the International Atomic Energy Agency, as well as any State not a Party to this Convention, may be represented at meetings of the Conference of the Parties as observers. Any body or agency, whether national or international, governmental or non-governmental, that is qualified in matters covered by this Convention and has informed the Secretariat of its wish to be represented at a meeting of the Conference of the Parties as an observer may be admitted unless at least one third of the Parties present object. The admission and participation of observers shall be subject to the rules of procedure adopted by the Conference of the Parties.

Article 24

Secretariat

1. A Secretariat is hereby established.

2. The functions of the Secretariat shall be:

(a) To make arrangements for meetings of the Conference of the Parties and its subsidiary bodies and to provide them with services as required;

(b) To facilitate assistance to Parties, particularly developing country Parties and Parties with economies in transition, on request, in the implementation of this Convention;

(c) To coordinate, as appropriate, with the secretariats of relevant international bodies, particularly other chemicals and waste conventions;

(d) To assist Parties in the exchange of information related to the implementation of this Convention;

(e) To prepare and make available to the Parties periodic reports based on information received pursuant to Articles 15 and 21 and other available information;

(f) To enter, under the overall guidance of the Conference of the Parties, into such administrative and contractual arrangements as may be required for the effective discharge of its functions; and

(g) To perform the other secretariat functions specified in this Convention and such other functions as may be determined by the Conference of the Parties.

3. The secretariat functions for this Convention shall be performed by the Executive Director of the United Nations Environment Programme, unless the Conference of the Parties decides, by a three-fourths majority of the Parties present and voting, to entrust the secretariat functions to one or more other international organizations.

4. The Conference of the Parties, in consultation with appropriate international bodies, may provide for enhanced cooperation and coordination between the Secretariat and the secretariats of other chemicals and wastes conventions. The Conference of the Parties, in consultation with appropriate international bodies, may provide further guidance on this matter.

Article 25

Settlement of disputes

1. Parties shall seek to settle any dispute between them concerning the interpretation or application of this Convention through negotiation or other peaceful means of their own choice.

2. When ratifying, accepting, approving or acceding to this Convention, or at any time thereafter, a Party that is not a regional economic integration

organization may declare in a written instrument submitted to the Depositary that, with regard to any dispute concerning the interpretation or application of this Convention, it recognizes one or both of the following means of dispute settlement as compulsory in relation to any Party accepting the same obligation:

(a) Arbitration in accordance with the procedure set out in Part I of Annex E;

(b) Submission of the dispute to the International Court of Justice.

3. A Party that is a regional economic integration organization may make a declaration with like effect in relation to arbitration in accordance with paragraph 2.

4. A declaration made pursuant to paragraph 2 or 3 shall remain in force until it expires in accordance with its terms or until three months after written notice of its revocation has been deposited with the Depositary.

5. The expiry of a declaration, a notice of revocation or a new declaration shall in no way affect proceedings pending before an arbitral tribunal or the International Court of Justice, unless the parties to the dispute otherwise agree.

6. If the parties to a dispute have not accepted the same means of dispute settlement pursuant to paragraph 2 or 3, and if they have not been able to settle their dispute through the means mentioned in paragraph 1 within twelve months following notification by one Party to another that a dispute exists between them, the dispute shall be submitted to a conciliation commission at the request of any party to the dispute. The procedure set out in Part II of Annex E shall apply to conciliation under this Article.

Article 26

Amendments to the Convention

1. Amendments to this Convention may be proposed by any Party.

2. Amendments to this Convention shall be adopted at a meeting of the Conference of the Parties. The text of any proposed amendment shall be communicated to the Parties by the Secretariat at least six months before the meeting at which it is proposed for adoption. The Secretariat shall also communicate the proposed amendment to the signatories to this Convention and, for information, to the Depositary.

3. The Parties shall make every effort to reach agreement on any proposed amendment to this Convention by consensus. If all efforts at consensus have been exhausted, and no agreement reached, the amendment shall as a last resort be adopted by a three-fourths majority vote of the Parties present and voting at the meeting.

4. An adopted amendment shall be communicated by the Depositary to all Parties for ratification, acceptance or approval.

5. Ratification, acceptance or approval of an amendment shall be notified to the Depositary in writing. An amendment adopted in accordance with paragraph 3 shall enter into force for the Parties having consented to be bound by it on the ninetieth day after the date of deposit of instruments of ratification, acceptance or approval by at least three-fourths of the Parties that were Parties at the time at which the amendment was adopted. Thereafter, the amendment shall enter into force for any other Party on the ninetieth day after the date on which that Party deposits its instrument of ratification, acceptance or approval of the amendment.

Article 27

Adoption and amendment of annexes

1. Annexes to this Convention shall form an integral part thereof and, unless expressly provided otherwise, a reference to this Convention constitutes at the same time a reference to any annexes thereto.

2. Any additional annexes adopted after the entry into force of this Convention shall be restricted to procedural, scientific, technical or administrative matters.

3. The following procedure shall apply to the proposal, adoption and entry into force of additional annexes to this Convention:

(a) Additional annexes shall be proposed and adopted according to the procedure laid down in paragraphs 1-3 of Article 26;

(b) Any Party that is unable to accept an additional annex shall so notify the Depositary, in writing, within one year from the date of communication by the Depositary of the adoption of such annex. The Depositary shall without delay notify all Parties of any such notification received. A Party may at any time notify the Depositary, in writing, that it withdraws a previous notification of non-acceptance in respect of an additional annex, and the annex shall thereupon enter into force for that Party subject to subparagraph (c); and

(c) On the expiry of one year from the date of the communication by the Depositary of the adoption of an additional annex, the annex shall enter into force for all Parties that have not submitted a notification of non-acceptance in accordance with the provisions of subparagraph (b).

4. The proposal, adoption and entry into force of amendments to annexes to this Convention shall be subject to the same procedures as for the proposal, adoption and entry into force of additional annexes to the Convention, except that an amendment to an annex shall not enter into force with regard to any Party that has made a declaration with regard to amendment of annexes in accordance with paragraph 5 of Article 30, in which case any such amendment shall enter into force for such a Party on the ninetieth day after the date it has deposited with the Depositary its instrument of ratification, acceptance, approval or accession with respect to such amendment.

5. If an additional annex or an amendment to an annex is related to an amendment to this Convention, the additional annex or amendment shall not enter into force until such time as the amendment to the Convention enters into force.

Article 28

Right to vote

1. Each Party to this Convention shall have one vote, except as provided for in paragraph 2.

2. A regional economic integration organization, on matters within its competence, shall exercise its right to vote with a number of votes equal to the number of its member States that are Parties to this Convention. Such an organization shall not exercise its right to vote if any of its member States exercises its right to vote, and vice versa.

Article 29

Signature

This Convention shall be opened for signature at Kumamoto, Japan, by all States and regional economic integration organizations on 10 and 11 October 2013, and thereafter at the United Nations Headquarters in New York until 9 October 2014.

Article 30

Ratification, acceptance, approval or accession

1. This Convention shall be subject to ratification, acceptance or approval by States and by regional economic integration organizations. It shall be open for accession by States and by regional economic integration organizations from the day after the date on which the Convention is closed for signature. Instruments of ratification, acceptance, approval or accession shall be deposited with the Depositary.

2. Any regional economic integration organization that becomes a Party to this Convention without any of its member States being a Party shall be bound by all the obligations under the Convention. In the case of such organizations, one or more of whose member States is a Party to this Convention, the organization and its member States shall decide on their respective responsibilities for the performance of their obligations under the Convention. In such cases, the organization and the member States shall not be entitled to exercise rights under the Convention concurrently.

3. In its instrument of ratification, acceptance, approval or accession, a regional economic integration organization shall declare the extent of its competence in respect of the matters governed by this Convention. Any such organization shall also inform the Depositary, who shall in turn inform the Parties, of any relevant modification of the extent of its competence.

4. Each State or regional economic integration organization is encouraged to transmit to the Secretariat at the time of its ratification, acceptance, approval or accession of the Convention information on its measures to implement the Convention.

5. In its instrument of ratification, acceptance, approval or accession, any Party may declare that, with regard to it, any amendment to an annex shall enter into force only upon the deposit of its instrument of ratification, acceptance, approval or accession with respect thereto.

Article 31

Entry into force

1. This Convention shall enter into force on the ninetieth day after the date of deposit of the fiftieth instrument of ratification, acceptance, approval or accession.

2. For each State or regional economic integration organization that ratifies, accepts or approves this Convention or accedes thereto after the deposit of the fiftieth instrument of ratification, acceptance, approval or accession, the Convention shall enter into force on the ninetieth day after the date of deposit by such State or regional economic integration organization of its instrument of ratification, acceptance, approval or accession.

3. For the purposes of paragraphs 1 and 2, any instrument deposited by a regional economic integration organization shall not be counted as additional to those deposited by member States of that organization.

Article 32

Reservations

No reservations may be made to this Convention.

Article 33

Withdrawal

1. At any time after three years from the date on which this Convention has entered into force for a Party, that Party may withdraw from the Convention by giving written notification to the Depositary.

2. Any such withdrawal shall take effect upon expiry of one year from the date of receipt by the Depositary of the notification of withdrawal, or on such later date as may be specified in the notification of withdrawal.

Article 34

Depositary

The Secretary-General of the United Nations shall be the Depositary of this Convention.

Article 35

Authentic texts

The original of this Convention, of which the Arabic, Chinese, English, French, Russian and Spanish texts are equally authentic, shall be deposited with the Depositary.

IN WITNESS WHEREOF the undersigned, being duly authorized to that effect, have signed this Convention.

Done at Kumamoto, Japan, on this tenth day of October, two thousand and thirteen.

Annex A

Mercury-added products

The following products are excluded from this Annex:

(a) Products essential for civil protection and military uses;

(b) Products for research, calibration of instrumentation, for use as reference standard;

(c) Where no feasible mercury-free alternative for replacement is available, switches and relays, cold cathode fluorescent lamps and external electrode fluorescent lamps (CCFL and EEFL) for electronic displays, and measuring devices;

(d) Products used in traditional or religious practices; and

(e) Vaccines containing thiomersal as preservatives.

Part I: Products subject to Article 4, paragraph 1

Mercury-added products	**Date after which the manufacture, import or export of the product shall not be allowed (phase-out date)**
Batteries, except for button zinc silver oxide batteries with a mercury content < 2% and button zinc air batteries with a mercury content < 2%	2020
Switches and relays, except very high accuracy capacitance and loss measurement bridges and high frequency radio frequency switches and relays in monitoring and control instruments with a maximum mercury content of 20 mg per bridge, switch or relay	2020
Compact fluorescent lamps (CFLs) for general lighting purposes that are ≤ 30 watts with a mercury content exceeding 5 mg per lamp burner	2020
Linear fluorescent lamps (LFLs) for general lighting purposes: (a) Triband phosphor < 60 watts with a mercury content exceeding 5 mg per lamp; (b) Halophosphate phosphor ≤ 40 watts with a mercury content exceeding 10 mg per lamp	2020
High pressure mercury vapour lamps (HPMV) for general lighting purposes	2020
Mercury in cold cathode fluorescent lamps and external electrode fluorescent lamps (CCFL and EEFL) for electronic displays: (a) short length (≤ 500 mm) with mercury content exceeding 3.5 mg per lamp (b) medium length (> 500 mm and ≤ 1 500 mm) with mercury content exceeding 5 mg per lamp (c) long length (> 1 500 mm) with mercury content exceeding 13 mg per lamp	2020
Cosmetics (with mercury content above 1ppm), including skin lightening soaps and creams, and not including eye area cosmetics where mercury is used as a preservative and no effective and safe substitute preservatives are available[1/]	2020

Mercury-added products	Date after which the manufacture, import or export of the product shall not be allowed (phase-out date)
Pesticides, biocides and topical antiseptics	2020
The following non-electronic measuring devices except non-electronic measuring devices installed in large-scale equipment or those used for high precision measurement, where no suitable mercury-free alternative is available: (a) barometers; (b) hygrometers; (c) manometers; (d) thermometers; (e) sphygmomanometers.	2020

[1/] The intention is not to cover cosmetics, soaps or creams with trace contaminants of mercury.

Part II: Products subject to Article 4, paragraph 3

Mercury-added products	Provisions
Dental amalgam	Measures to be taken by a Party to phase down the use of dental amalgam shall take into account the Party's domestic circumstances and relevant international guidance and shall include two or more of the measures from the following list: (i) Setting national objectives aiming at dental caries prevention and health promotion, thereby minimizing the need for dental restoration; (ii) Setting national objectives aiming at minimizing its use; (iii) Promoting the use of cost-effective and clinically effective mercury-free alternatives for dental restoration; (iv) Promoting research and development of quality mercury-free materials for dental restoration; (v) Encouraging representative professional organizations and dental schools to educate and train dental professionals and students on the use of mercury-free dental restoration alternatives and on promoting best management practices; (vi) Discouraging insurance policies and programmes that favour dental amalgam use over mercury-free dental restoration; (vii) Encouraging insurance policies and programmes that favour the use of quality alternatives to dental amalgam for dental restoration; (viii) Restricting the use of dental amalgam to its encapsulated form; (ix) Promoting the use of best environmental practices in dental facilities to reduce releases of mercury and mercury compounds to water and land.

Annex B

Manufacturing processes in which mercury or mercury compounds are used

Part I: Processes subject to Article 5, paragraph 2

Manufacturing processes using mercury or mercury compounds	Phase-out date
Chlor-alkali production	2025
Acetaldehyde production in which mercury or mercury compounds are used as a catalyst	2018

Part II: Processes subject to Article 5, paragraph 3

Mercury using process	**Provisions**
Vinyl chloride monomer production	Measures to be taken by the Parties shall include but not be limited to: (i) Reduce the use of mercury in terms of per unit production by 50 per cent by the year 2020 against 2010 use; (ii) Promoting measures to reduce the reliance on mercury from primary mining; (iii) Taking measures to reduce emissions and releases of mercury to the environment; (iv) Supporting research and development in respect of mercury-free catalysts and processes; (v) Not allowing the use of mercury five years after the Conference of the Parties has established that mercury-free catalysts based on existing processes have become technically and economically feasible; (vi) Reporting to the Conference of the Parties on its efforts to develop and/or identify alternatives and phase out mercury use in accordance with Article 21.
Sodium or Potassium Methylate or Ethylate	Measures to be taken by the Parties shall include but not be limited to: (i) Measures to reduce the use of mercury aiming at the phase out of this use as fast as possible and within 10 years of the entry into force of the Convention; (ii) Reduce emissions and releases in terms of per unit production by 50 per cent by 2020 compared to 2010; (iii) Prohibiting the use of fresh mercury from primary mining; (iv) Supporting research and development in respect of mercury-free processes; (v) Not allowing the use of mercury five years after the Conference of the Parties has established that mercury-free processes have become technically and economically feasible; (vi) Reporting to the Conference of the Parties on its efforts to develop and/or identify alternatives and phase out mercury use in accordance with Article 21.
Production of polyurethane using mercury containing catalysts	Measures to be taken by the Parties shall include but not be limited to: (i) Taking measures to reduce the use of mercury, aiming at the phase out of this use as fast as possible, within 10 years of the entry into force of the Convention; (ii) Taking measures to reduce the reliance on mercury from primary mercury mining; (iii) Taking measures to reduce emissions and releases of mercury to the environment; (iv) Encouraging research and development in respect of mercury-free catalysts and processes; (v) Reporting to the Conference of the Parties on its efforts to develop and/or identify alternatives and phase out mercury use in accordance with Article 21. Paragraph 6 of Article 5 shall not apply to this manufacturing process.

Annex C

Artisanal and small-scale gold mining

National action plans

1. Each Party that is subject to the provisions of paragraph 3 of Article 7 shall include in its national action plan:

(a) National objectives and reduction targets;

(b) Actions to eliminate:

(i) Whole ore amalgamation;

(ii) Open burning of amalgam or processed amalgam;

(iii) Burning of amalgam in residential areas; and

(iv) Cyanide leaching in sediment, ore or tailings to which mercury has been added without first removing the mercury;

(c) Steps to facilitate the formalization or regulation of the artisanal and small-scale gold mining sector;

(d) Baseline estimates of the quantities of mercury used and the practices employed in artisanal and small-scale gold mining and processing within its territory;

(e) Strategies for promoting the reduction of emissions and releases of, and exposure to, mercury in artisanal and small-scale gold mining and processing, including mercury-free methods;

(f) Strategies for managing trade and preventing the diversion of mercury and mercury compounds from both foreign and domestic sources to use in artisanal and small scale gold mining and processing;

(g) Strategies for involving stakeholders in the implementation and continuing development of the national action plan;

(h) A public health strategy on the exposure of artisanal and small-scale gold miners and their communities to mercury. Such a strategy should include, inter alia, the gathering of health data, training for health-care workers and awareness-raising through health facilities;

(i) Strategies to prevent the exposure of vulnerable populations, particularly children and women of child-bearing age, especially pregnant women, to mercury used in artisanal and small-scale gold mining;

(j) Strategies for providing information to artisanal and small-scale gold miners and affected communities; and

(k) A schedule for the implementation of the national action plan.

2. Each Party may include in its national action plan additional strategies to achieve its objectives, including the use or introduction of standards for mercury-free artisanal and small-scale gold mining and market-based mechanisms or marketing tools.

Annex D

List of point sources of emissions of mercury and mercury compounds to the atmosphere

Point source category:

Coal-fired power plants;

Coal-fired industrial boilers;

Smelting and roasting processes used in the production of non-ferrous metals;[1]

Waste incineration facilities;

Cement clinker production facilities.

---

[1] For the purpose of this Annex, "non-ferrous metals" refers to lead, zinc, copper and industrial gold.

Annex E

Arbitration and conciliation procedures

Part I: Arbitration procedure

The arbitration procedure for purposes of paragraph 2 (a) of Article 25 of this Convention shall be as follows:

Article 1

1. A Party may initiate recourse to arbitration in accordance with Article 25 of this Convention by written notification addressed to the other party or parties to the dispute. The notification shall be accompanied by a statement of claim, together with any supporting documents. Such notification shall state the subject matter of arbitration and include, in particular, the Articles of this Convention the interpretation or application of which are at issue.

2. The claimant party shall notify the Secretariat that it is referring a dispute to arbitration pursuant to Article 25 of this Convention. The notification shall be accompanied by the written notification of the claimant party, the statement of claim, and the supporting documents referred to in paragraph 1 above. The Secretariat shall forward the information thus received to all Parties.

Article 2

1. If a dispute is referred to arbitration in accordance with Article 1 above, an arbitral tribunal shall be established. It shall consist of three members.

2. Each party to the dispute shall appoint an arbitrator, and the two arbitrators so appointed shall designate by agreement the third arbitrator, who shall be the President of the tribunal. In disputes between more than two parties, parties in the same interest shall appoint one arbitrator jointly by agreement. The President of the tribunal shall not be a national of any of the parties to the dispute, nor have his or her usual place of residence in the territory of any of these parties, nor be employed by any of them, nor have dealt with the case in any other capacity.

3. Any vacancy shall be filled in the manner prescribed for the initial appointment.

Article 3

1. If one of the parties to the dispute does not appoint an arbitrator within two months of the date on which the respondent party receives the notification of the arbitration, the other party may inform the Secretary-General of the United Nations, who shall make the designation within a further two-month period.

2. If the President of the arbitral tribunal has not been designated within two months of the date of the appointment of the second arbitrator, the Secretary-General of the United Nations shall, at the request of a party, designate the President within a further two-month period.

Article 4

The arbitral tribunal shall render its decisions in accordance with the provisions of this Convention and international law.

Article 5

Unless the parties to the dispute otherwise agree, the arbitral tribunal shall determine its own rules of procedure.

Article 6

The arbitral tribunal may, at the request of one of the parties to the dispute, recommend essential interim measures of protection.

Article 7

The parties to the dispute shall facilitate the work of the arbitral tribunal and, in particular, using all means at their disposal, shall:

(a) Provide it with all relevant documents, information and facilities; and

(b) Enable it, when necessary, to call witnesses or experts and receive their evidence.

Article 8

The parties to the dispute and the arbitrators are under an obligation to protect the confidentiality of any information or documents that they receive in confidence during the proceedings of the arbitral tribunal.

Article 9

Unless the arbitral tribunal determines otherwise because of the particular circumstances of the case, the costs of the tribunal shall be borne by the parties to the dispute in equal shares. The tribunal shall keep a record of all its costs and shall furnish a final statement thereof to the parties.

Article 10

A Party that has an interest of a legal nature in the subject matter of the dispute that may be affected by the decision may intervene in the proceedings with the consent of the arbitral tribunal.

Article 11

The arbitral tribunal may hear and determine counterclaims arising directly out of the subject matter of the dispute.

Article 12

Decisions of the arbitral tribunal on both procedure and substance shall be taken by a majority vote of its members.

Article 13

1. If one of the parties to the dispute does not appear before the arbitral tribunal or fails to defend its case, the other party may request the tribunal to continue the proceedings and to make its decision. Absence of a party or a failure of a party to defend its case shall not constitute a bar to the proceedings.

2. Before rendering its final decision, the arbitral tribunal must satisfy itself that the claim is well founded in fact and law.

Article 14

The arbitral tribunal shall render its final decision within five months of the date on which it is fully constituted, unless it finds it necessary to extend the time limit for a period that should not exceed five more months.

Article 15

The final decision of the arbitral tribunal shall be confined to the subject matter of the dispute and shall state the reasons on which it is based. It shall contain the names of the members who have participated and the date of the final decision. Any member of the tribunal may attach a separate or dissenting opinion to the final decision.

Article 16

The final decision shall be binding on the parties to the dispute. The interpretation of this Convention given by the final decision shall also be binding upon a Party intervening under Article 10 above insofar as it relates to matters in respect of which that Party intervened. The final decision shall be without appeal unless the parties to the dispute have agreed in advance to an appellate procedure.

Article 17

Any disagreement that may arise between those bound by the final decision in accordance with Article 16 above, as regards the interpretation or manner of implementation of that final decision, may be submitted by any of them for decision to the arbitral tribunal that rendered it.

Part II: Conciliation procedure

The conciliation procedure for purposes of paragraph 6 of Article 25 of this Convention shall be as follows:

Article 1

A request by a party to a dispute to establish a conciliation commission pursuant to paragraph 6 of Article 25 of this Convention shall be addressed in writing to the Secretariat, with a copy to the other party or parties to the dispute. The Secretariat shall forthwith inform all Parties accordingly.

Article 2

1. The conciliation commission shall, unless the parties to the dispute otherwise agree, comprise three members, one appointed by each party concerned and a President chosen jointly by those members.

2. In disputes between more than two parties, parties in the same interest shall appoint their member of the commission jointly by agreement.

Article 3

If any appointment by the parties to the dispute is not made within two months of the date of receipt by the Secretariat of the written request referred to in Article 1 above, the Secretary-General of the United Nations shall, upon request by any party, make such appointment within a further two-month period.

Article 4

If the President of the conciliation commission has not been chosen within two months of the appointment of the second member of the commission, the Secretary-General of the United Nations shall, upon request by any party to the dispute, designate the President within a further two-month period.

Article 5

The conciliation commission shall assist the parties to the dispute in an independent and impartial manner in their attempt to reach an amicable resolution.

Article 6

1. The conciliation commission may conduct the conciliation proceedings in such a manner as it considers appropriate, taking fully into account the circumstances of the case and the views the parties to the dispute may express, including any request for a swift resolution. It may adopt its own rules of procedure as necessary, unless the parties otherwise agree.

2. The conciliation commission may, at any time during the proceedings, make proposals or recommendations for a resolution of the dispute.

Article 7

The parties to the dispute shall cooperate with the conciliation commission. In particular, they shall endeavour to comply with requests by the commission to submit written materials, provide evidence and attend meetings. The parties and the members of the conciliation commission are under an obligation to protect the confidentiality of any information or documents they receive in confidence during the proceedings of the commission.

Article 8

The conciliation commission shall take its decisions by a majority vote of its members.

Article 9

Unless the dispute has already been resolved, the conciliation commission shall render a report with recommendations for resolution of the dispute no later than twelve months of being fully constituted, which the parties to the dispute shall consider in good faith.

Article 10

Any disagreement as to whether the conciliation commission has competence to consider a matter referred to it shall be decided by the commission.

Article 11

The costs of the conciliation commission shall be borne by the parties to the dispute in equal shares, unless they agree otherwise. The commission shall keep a record of all its costs and shall furnish a final statement thereof to the parties.

[TEXT IN FRENCH – TEXTE EN FRANÇAIS]

CONVENTION DE MINAMATA SUR LE MERCURE

Les Parties à la présente Convention,

Reconnaissant que le mercure est une substance chimique préoccupante à l'échelle mondiale vu sa propagation atmosphérique à longue distance, sa persistance dans l'environnement dès lors qu'il a été introduit par l'homme, son potentiel de bioaccumulation dans les écosystèmes et ses effets néfastes importants sur la santé humaine et l'environnement,

Rappelant la décision 25/5 adoptée le 20 février 2009 par le Conseil d'administration du Programme des Nations Unies pour l'environnement, demandant d'engager une action internationale pour gérer le mercure de manière efficiente, effective et cohérente,

Rappelant le paragraphe 221 du document final de la Conférence des Nations Unies sur le développement durable « L'avenir que nous voulons », qui espérait l'aboutissement des négociations pour l'élaboration d'un instrument international juridiquement contraignant sur le mercure, propre à éliminer les risques que ce dernier présente pour la santé humaine et l'environnement,

Rappelant la réaffirmation par la Conférence des Nations Unies sur le développement durable des principes de la Déclaration de Rio sur l'environnement et le développement incluant, entre autres, les responsabilités communes mais différenciées, et reconnaissant les situations et capacités respectives des États ainsi que la nécessité d'agir au niveau mondial,

Conscientes des préoccupations en matière de santé, en particulier dans les pays en développement, résultant d'une exposition au mercure des populations vulnérables, notamment les femmes, les enfants et, par leur intermédiaire, les générations futures,

Notant la vulnérabilité particulière des écosystèmes arctiques et des communautés autochtones du fait de la bioamplification du mercure et de la contamination des aliments traditionnels, et préoccupées plus généralement par la situation des communautés autochtones eu égard aux effets du mercure,

Reconnaissant les leçons importantes tirées de la maladie de Minamata, en particulier les effets graves sur la santé et l'environnement résultant de la pollution par le mercure, ainsi que la nécessité d'assurer une gestion appropriée du mercure et d'empêcher que de tels événements ne se reproduisent à l'avenir,

Soulignant l'importance d'une assistance financière, technique et technologique ainsi que d'un renforcement des capacités, en particulier pour les pays en développement et les pays à économie en transition, en vue de renforcer les capacités nationales aux fins de la gestion du mercure et de promouvoir la mise en œuvre effective de la Convention,

Reconnaissant également les activités relatives au mercure menées par l'Organisation mondiale de la Santé en matière de protection de la santé humaine et le rôle des accords multilatéraux sur l'environnement pertinents, en particulier la Convention de Bâle sur le contrôle des mouvements transfrontières de déchets dangereux et de leur élimination et la Convention de Rotterdam sur la procédure de consentement préalable en connaissance de cause applicable à certains produits chimiques et pesticides dangereux qui font l'objet d'un commerce international,

Reconnaissant que la présente Convention ainsi que d'autres accords internationaux relatifs à l'environnement et au commerce sont complémentaires,

Soulignant qu'aucune disposition de la présente Convention ne vise à modifier les droits et obligations de toute Partie découlant de tout accord international existant,

Étant entendu que le préambule qui précède n'a pas pour objet de créer une hiérarchie entre la présente Convention et d'autres instruments internationaux,

Notant que rien dans la présente Convention n'empêche une Partie de prendre d'autres mesures nationales conformes aux dispositions de la présente Convention dans le souci de protéger la santé humaine et l'environnement contre l'exposition au mercure conformément aux autres obligations incombant à cette Partie en vertu du droit international applicable,

Sont convenues de ce qui suit :

Article premier

Objectif

L'objectif de la présente Convention est de protéger la santé humaine et l'environnement contre les émissions et rejets anthropiques de mercure et de composés du mercure.

Article 2

Définitions

Aux fins de la présente Convention :

a) Par « extraction minière artisanale et à petite échelle d'or », on entend l'extraction minière d'or par des mineurs individuels ou de petites entreprises dont les investissements et la production sont limités;

b) Par « meilleures techniques disponibles », on entend les techniques les plus efficaces pour prévenir et, lorsque cela s'avère impossible, réduire les émissions atmosphériques et les rejets de mercure dans l'eau et le sol et leur incidence sur l'environnement dans son ensemble, en tenant compte des paramètres économiques et techniques entrant en considération pour une Partie donnée ou une installation donnée située sur le territoire de cette Partie. Dans ce contexte :

i) Par « meilleures », on entend les techniques les plus efficaces pour atteindre un niveau général élevé de protection de l'environnement dans son ensemble;

ii) Par techniques « disponibles », on entend, s'agissant d'une Partie donnée et d'une installation donnée située sur le territoire de cette Partie, les techniques développées à une échelle permettant de les mettre en œuvre dans un secteur industriel pertinent, dans des conditions économiquement et techniquement viables, compte tenu des coûts et des avantages, que ces techniques soient ou non utilisées ou développées sur le territoire de cette Partie, pour autant qu'elles soient accessibles à l'exploitant de l'installation, tel que déterminé par cette Partie; et

iii) Par « techniques », on entend les technologies utilisées, les modes d'exploitation et la façon dont les installations sont conçues, construites, entretenues, exploitées et mises hors service;

c) Par « meilleures pratiques environnementales », on entend l'application de la combinaison la plus appropriée de mesures de contrôle et de stratégies environnementales;

d) Par « mercure », on entend le mercure élémentaire (Hg(0), n° CAS : 7439 97 6);

e) Par « composé du mercure », on entend toute substance composée d'atomes de mercure et d'un ou de plusieurs atomes d'autres éléments chimiques qui ne peut être séparée en ses différents composants que par réaction chimique;

f) Par « produit contenant du mercure ajouté », on entend un produit ou composant d'un produit qui contient du mercure ou un composé du mercure ajouté intentionnellement;

g) Par « Partie », on entend un État ou une organisation régionale d'intégration économique qui a consenti à être lié par la présente Convention et à l'égard duquel la Convention est en vigueur;

h) Par « Parties présentes et votantes », on entend les Parties présentes qui expriment un vote affirmatif ou négatif à une réunion des Parties;

i) Par « extraction minière primaire de mercure », on entend une activité d'extraction minière dans laquelle la principale substance recherchée est le mercure;

j) Par « organisation régionale d'intégration économique », on entend une organisation constituée d'États souverains d'une région donnée, à laquelle ses États membres ont transféré des compétences en ce qui concerne les questions régies par la présente Convention et qui a été dûment autorisée, conformément à ses procédures internes, à signer, ratifier, accepter ou approuver la présente Convention, ou à y adhérer; et

k) Par « utilisation permise », on entend toute utilisation, par une Partie, de mercure ou de composés du mercure qui est conforme à la présente Convention, y compris, entre autres, les utilisations conformes aux articles 3, 4, 5, 6 et 7.

Article 3

Sources d'approvisionnement en mercure et commerce

1. Aux fins du présent article :

a) Le terme « mercure » désigne également les mélanges de mercure avec d'autres substances, y compris les alliages présentant une teneur en mercure d'au moins 95 % en poids; et

b) Le terme « composés du mercure » désigne le chlorure de mercure (I) ou calomel, l'oxyde de mercure (II), le sulfate de mercure (II), le nitrate de mercure (II), le cinabre et le sulfure de mercure.

2. Les dispositions du présent article ne s'appliquent pas :

a) Aux quantités de mercure ou de composés du mercure destinées à être utilisées pour la recherche en laboratoire ou comme étalon de référence;

b) Au mercure et aux composés du mercure naturellement présents à l'état de traces dans des produits tels que certains métaux, minerais ou produits minéraux sans mercure, dont le charbon, ou dans des produits dérivés de ces matériaux, ni aux quantités présentes non intentionnellement à l'état de traces dans des produits chimiques;

c) Aux produits contenant du mercure ajouté.

3. Chaque Partie fait en sorte qu'aucune activité d'extraction minière primaire de mercure en dehors de celles qui existaient à la date d'entrée en vigueur de la Convention à son égard ne soit menée sur son territoire.

4. Chaque Partie ne permet la poursuite des activités d'extraction minière primaire de mercure qui étaient menées sur son territoire à la date d'entrée en vigueur de la Convention à son égard que pendant une période maximale de 15 ans après cette date. Au cours de cette période, le mercure ainsi obtenu ne peut servir qu'à fabriquer des produits contenant du mercure ajouté, conformément à l'article 4, ou être utilisé dans des procédés visés à l'article 5. À défaut, il doit être éliminé conformément aux dispositions de l'article 11, par des opérations qui ne débouchent pas sur la récupération, le recyclage, la régénération, la réutilisation directe ou toute autre utilisation.

5. Chaque Partie :

a) S'efforce de recenser les stocks individuels de mercure ou composés du mercure de plus de 50 tonnes métriques ainsi que les sources d'approvisionnement en mercure produisant des stocks de plus de 10 tonnes métriques par an qui se trouvent sur son territoire;

b) Prend des mesures pour faire en sorte, si cette Partie établit l'existence de mercure excédentaire provenant de la mise hors service d'usines de chlore-alcali, que celui-ci soit éliminé conformément aux directives sur la gestion écologiquement rationnelle mentionnées à l'alinéa a) du paragraphe 3 de l'article 11, par des opérations qui ne débouchent pas sur la récupération, le recyclage, la régénération, la réutilisation directe ou toute autre utilisation.

6. Chaque Partie fait en sorte qu'il n'y ait aucune exportation de mercure sauf :

a) À destination d'une Partie qui a donné son consentement écrit à la Partie exportatrice, et uniquement en vue :

i) D'une utilisation permise à la Partie importatrice dans le cadre de la présente Convention; ou

ii) D'un stockage provisoire écologiquement rationnel comme indiqué à l'article 10; ou

b) À destination d'un État non Partie qui a donné son consentement écrit à la Partie exportatrice, y compris une attestation du fait que :

i) Cet État non Partie a pris des mesures pour garantir la protection de la santé humaine et de l'environnement et l'application des dispositions des articles 10 et 11; et

ii) Le mercure sera uniquement destiné à une utilisation permise à une Partie au titre de la présente Convention ou à un stockage provisoire écologiquement rationnel comme indiqué à l'article 10.

7. Une Partie exportatrice peut se baser sur une notification générale transmise au Secrétariat par l'État importateur Partie ou non Partie, en tant que consentement écrit tel que requis au paragraphe 6. Une telle notification générale établit les modalités et conditions du consentement de l'État importateur Partie ou non Partie. La notification peut être révoquée à tout moment par cet État Partie ou non Partie. Le Secrétariat tient un registre public de toutes ces notifications.

8. Chaque Partie fait en sorte qu'il n'y ait aucune importation de mercure en provenance d'un État non Partie auquel elle donnera son consentement écrit à moins que l'État non Partie lui ait certifié que le mercure ne provient pas de sources identifiées comme non autorisées au titre du paragraphe 3 ou de l'alinéa b) du paragraphe 5.

9. Une Partie qui soumet une notification générale de consentement au titre du paragraphe 7 peut décider de ne pas appliquer le paragraphe 8, à condition que des restrictions étendues portant sur les exportations de mercure et des mesures nationales soient en place pour faire en sorte que le mercure importé soit géré d'une manière écologiquement rationnelle. La Partie transmet au Secrétariat une notification concernant cette décision, qui contient des informations décrivant ses restrictions à l'exportation et ses mesures de

réglementation nationales ainsi que des informations sur les quantités de mercure et les pays d'origine du mercure importé d'États non Parties. Le Secrétariat tient un registre public de toutes ces notifications. Le Comité de mise en œuvre et du respect des obligations examine et évalue l'ensemble des notifications et des informations à l'appui de ces dernières conformément à l'article 15 et peut faire des recommandations à la Conférence des Parties, selon qu'il convient.

10. Il est possible de recourir à la procédure visée au paragraphe 9 jusqu'à la conclusion de la deuxième réunion de la Conférence des Parties. Après cette réunion, il ne sera plus possible de recourir à la procédure susmentionnée, à moins que la Conférence des Parties en décide autrement à la majorité simple des Parties présentes et votantes, sauf pour une Partie qui a fourni une notification au titre du paragraphe 9 avant la fin de la deuxième réunion de la Conférence des Parties.

11. Chaque Partie fait figurer dans ses rapports transmis conformément à l'article 21 des informations montrant que les exigences du présent article ont été respectées.

12. La Conférence des Parties énonce, à sa première réunion, des orientations supplémentaires concernant le présent article, en particulier l'alinéa a) du paragraphe 5, le paragraphe 6 et le paragraphe 8, et élabore et adopte les éléments requis de l'attestation visée à l'alinéa b) du paragraphe 6 et au paragraphe 8.

13. La Conférence des Parties évalue si le commerce de certains composés du mercure compromet l'objectif de la présente Convention et examine la question de savoir si ces composés du mercure devraient, par leur inscription à une annexe supplémentaire adoptée conformément à l'article 27, être soumis aux paragraphes 6 et 8.

Article 4

Produits contenant du mercure ajouté

1. Chaque Partie fait en sorte, en prenant des mesures appropriées, qu'aucun des produits contenant du mercure ajouté figurant dans la première partie de l'Annexe A ne soit fabriqué, importé ou exporté après la date d'abandon définitif fixée pour ces produits, sauf en cas d'exclusion spécifiée à l'Annexe A ou en vertu d'une dérogation enregistrée pour une Partie conformément à l'article 6.

2. Une Partie peut, en lieu et place du paragraphe 1, indiquer au moment de la ratification ou de l'entrée en vigueur d'un amendement à l'Annexe A à son égard qu'elle met en œuvre différentes mesures ou stratégies pour traiter les produits inscrits dans la première partie de l'Annexe A. Une Partie peut choisir la présente option uniquement si elle peut démontrer qu'elle a déjà réduit la fabrication, l'importation et l'exportation de la grande majorité des produits inscrits dans la première partie de l'Annexe A à un niveau de minimis et qu'elle a mis en œuvre des mesures ou des stratégies visant à réduire l'utilisation de mercure dans d'autres produits non inscrits dans la première partie de l'Annexe A au moment où elle notifie au Secrétariat sa décision de choisir la présente option. En outre, une Partie qui choisit la présente option :

a) Fournit à la Conférence des Parties, à la première occasion, une description des mesures ou stratégies mises en œuvre, y compris une quantification des réductions réalisées;

b) Met en œuvre des mesures ou stratégies visant à réduire l'utilisation de mercure dans les produits inscrits dans la première partie de l'Annexe A pour lesquels une valeur de minimis n'a pas encore été obtenue;

c) Envisage des mesures supplémentaires afin de réaliser de nouvelles réductions; et

d) Ne peut prétendre à des dérogations au titre de l'article 6 pour aucune des catégories de produits pour lesquelles la présente option est choisie.

Au plus tard cinq ans après la date d'entrée en vigueur de la Convention, la Conférence des Parties examine, dans le cadre de la procédure d'examen prévue au paragraphe 8, les progrès et l'efficacité des mesures prises en application du présent paragraphe.

3. Chaque Partie prend des mesures à l'égard des produits contenant du mercure ajouté inscrits dans la deuxième partie de l'Annexe A, conformément aux dispositions de cette Annexe.

4. À partir d'informations fournies par les Parties, le Secrétariat recueille et tient à jour des informations sur les produits contenant du mercure ajouté et sur leurs solutions de remplacement, et met ces informations à la disposition du public. Le Secrétariat met également à la disposition du public toute autre information pertinente communiquée par les Parties.

5. Chaque Partie prend des mesures pour empêcher que des produits contenant du mercure ajouté dont la fabrication, l'importation et l'exportation

ne lui sont pas permises en vertu du présent article soient incorporés dans des produits assemblés.

6. Chaque Partie décourage la fabrication et la distribution dans le commerce de produits contenant du mercure ajouté à des fins qui ne cadrent avec aucune des utilisations connues de tels produits avant la date d'entrée en vigueur de la présente Convention à son égard, à moins qu'une évaluation des risques et avantages du produit prouve que celui-ci procure des bienfaits aux plans de l'environnement ou de la santé humaine. Les Parties fournissent au Secrétariat, le cas échéant, des informations sur chaque produit de ce genre, y compris toute information concernant les risques et les avantages qu'il présente pour l'environnement et la santé humaine. Le Secrétariat met ces informations à la disposition du public.

7. Toute Partie peut soumettre au Secrétariat une proposition d'inscription à l'Annexe A d'un produit contenant du mercure ajouté, dans laquelle doivent figurer des informations sur la disponibilité de solutions de remplacement sans mercure, la faisabilité technique et économique de ces dernières ainsi que les risques et avantages qu'elles présentent pour l'environnement et la santé, en tenant compte des informations visées au paragraphe 4.

8. Au plus tard cinq ans après la date d'entrée en vigueur de la Convention, la Conférence des Parties examine l'Annexe A et peut envisager de l'amender conformément à l'article 27.

9. Lors de l'examen de l'Annexe A conformément au paragraphe 8, la Conférence des Parties tient compte, au minimum :

a) De toute proposition présentée conformément au paragraphe 7;

b) Des informations mises à disposition en application du paragraphe 4; et

c) De la disponibilité pour les Parties de solutions de remplacement sans mercure qui sont techniquement et économiquement viables, eu égard aux risques et avantages pour l'environnement et la santé humaine.

Article 5

Procédés de fabrication utilisant du mercure ou des composés du mercure

1. Aux fins du présent article et de l'Annexe B, les procédés de fabrication utilisant du mercure ou des composés du mercure n'incluent pas les procédés

qui utilisent ou servent à fabriquer des produits contenant du mercure ajouté ni les procédés de traitement de déchets contenant du mercure.

2. Chaque Partie fait en sorte, en prenant des mesures appropriées, qu'aucun mercure ou composé du mercure ne soit utilisé dans les procédés de fabrication inscrits dans la première partie de l'Annexe B après la date d'abandon définitif spécifiée dans cette Annexe pour chaque procédé, sauf en vertu d'une dérogation enregistrée conformément à l'article 6.

3. Chaque Partie prend des mesures pour limiter l'utilisation de mercure ou de composés du mercure dans les procédés énumérés dans la deuxième partie de l'Annexe B conformément aux dispositions de cette Annexe.

4. À partir d'informations fournies par les Parties, le Secrétariat recueille et tient à jour des informations sur les procédés utilisant du mercure ou des composés du mercure et leurs solutions de remplacement, et met ces informations à la disposition du public. Le Secrétariat met également à la disposition du public toute autre information pertinente communiquée par les Parties.

5. Chaque Partie disposant d'une ou de plusieurs installations qui utilisent du mercure ou des composés du mercure dans des procédés de fabrication inscrits à l'Annexe B :

a) Prend des mesures pour lutter contre les émissions et rejets de mercure ou de composés du mercure provenant de ces installations;

b) Fait figurer dans les rapports qu'elle soumet conformément à l'article 21 des informations sur les mesures prises en application du présent paragraphe; et

c) S'efforce de recenser les installations situées sur son territoire qui utilisent du mercure ou des composés du mercure dans des procédés inscrits à l'Annexe B et soumet au Secrétariat, au plus tard trois ans après la date d'entrée en vigueur de la Convention à son égard, des informations sur le nombre et le type de ces installations ainsi que sur leur consommation estimative annuelle de mercure ou de composés du mercure. Le Secrétariat met ces informations à la disposition du public.

6. Chaque Partie fait en sorte qu'aucune installation qui n'existait pas avant la date d'entrée en vigueur de la Convention à son égard n'utilise du mercure ou des composés du mercure dans des procédés de fabrication inscrits à l'Annexe B. Aucune dérogation n'est applicable à ces installations.

7. Chaque Partie décourage le développement de toute installation ayant recours à un quelconque autre procédé de fabrication dans lequel du mercure ou des composés du mercure sont utilisés intentionnellement, qui n'existait pas avant la date d'entrée en vigueur de la Convention, sauf si cette Partie peut démontrer à la satisfaction de la Conférence des Parties que le procédé concerné procure d'importants avantages pour l'environnement et la santé et qu'il n'existe pas de solutions de remplacement sans mercure techniquement et économiquement faisables qui apportent de tels bienfaits.

8. Les Parties sont encouragées à échanger des informations sur les nouveaux développements techniques pertinents, les solutions de remplacement sans mercure qui sont économiquement et techniquement faisables, les mesures et techniques envisageables pour réduire et, si possible, éliminer l'utilisation de mercure et de composés du mercure dans les procédés de fabrication inscrits à l'Annexe B, et les émissions et rejets de mercure et de composés du mercure provenant de ces procédés.

9. Toute Partie peut soumettre une proposition d'amendement de l'Annexe B aux fins d'inscription d'un procédé de fabrication utilisant du mercure ou des composés du mercure, dans laquelle doivent figurer des informations sur la disponibilité de solutions de remplacement sans mercure pour le procédé concerné, la faisabilité technique et économique de ces solutions, et les risques et avantages qu'elles comportent pour l'environnement et la santé.

10. Au plus tard cinq ans après la date d'entrée en vigueur de la Convention, la Conférence des Parties examine l'Annexe B et peut envisager de l'amender conformément à l'article 27.

11. Lors de tout examen de l'Annexe B conformément au paragraphe 10, la Conférence des Parties tient compte, au minimum :

a) De toute proposition présentée conformément au paragraphe 9;

b) Des informations mises à disposition en application du paragraphe 4; et

c) De la disponibilité pour les Parties de solutions de remplacement sans mercure qui sont techniquement et économiquement faisables, eu égard aux risques et avantages pour l'environnement et la santé.

Article 6

Dérogations accessibles aux Parties sur demande

1. Tout État ou organisation régionale d'intégration économique peut faire enregistrer une ou plusieurs dérogations aux dates d'abandon définitif figurant dans l'Annexe A et l'Annexe B, ci-après dénommée « dérogation », moyennant notification écrite adressée au Secrétariat :

a) Lorsqu'il ou elle devient Partie à la présente Convention; ou

b) Dans le cas d'un produit contenant du mercure ajouté qui est inscrit par amendement à l'annexe A ou d'un procédé de fabrication utilisant du mercure qui est inscrit par amendement à l'annexe B, au plus tard à la date d'entrée en vigueur de l'amendement concerné pour cette Partie.

Un tel enregistrement est accompagné d'une déclaration expliquant les raisons pour lesquelles la Partie a besoin de la dérogation.

2. Une dérogation peut être enregistrée soit pour une catégorie figurant à l'Annexe A ou B soit pour une sous-catégorie identifiée par tout État ou organisation régionale d'intégration économique.

3. Chaque Partie qui a une ou plusieurs dérogations est inscrite dans un registre établi et tenu à jour par le Secrétariat, qui le rend accessible au public.

4. Le registre comprend :

a) Une liste des Parties qui ont une ou plusieurs dérogations;

b) La ou les dérogations enregistrées pour chaque Partie; et

c) La date d'expiration de chaque dérogation.

5. À moins qu'une période plus courte ne soit indiquée dans le registre par une Partie, toutes les dérogations en vertu du paragraphe 1 expirent cinq ans après la date d'abandon définitif pertinente figurant à l'Annexe A ou B.

6. La Conférence des Parties peut, à la demande d'une Partie, décider de proroger une dérogation pour une durée de cinq ans, à moins que la Partie ne demande une durée plus courte. Dans sa décision, la Conférence des Parties tient dûment compte des éléments ci-après :

a) Le rapport de la Partie justifiant la nécessité de proroger la dérogation et donnant un aperçu des activités entreprises et prévues pour éliminer cette nécessité dès que possible;

b) Les informations disponibles, y compris sur la disponibilité de produits et procédés de remplacement qui ne font pas appel au mercure ou en consomment moins que l'utilisation faisant l'objet de la dérogation; et

c) Les activités prévues ou en cours pour stocker le mercure et éliminer les déchets de mercure d'une manière écologiquement rationnelle.

Une dérogation ne peut être prorogée qu'une fois par produit par date d'abandon définitif.

7. Une Partie peut à tout moment, sur notification écrite adressée au Secrétariat, faire annuler une dérogation. L'annulation de la dérogation prend effet à la date indiquée dans la notification.

8. Nonobstant le paragraphe 1, aucun État ni aucune organisation régionale d'intégration économique ne peut faire enregistrer une dérogation après cinq ans à compter de la date d'abandon définitif du produit ou procédé concerné inscrit à l'Annexe A ou B, à moins qu'une ou plusieurs Parties soient encore enregistrées au titre d'une dérogation afférente à ce produit ou procédé, ayant bénéficié d'une prorogation conformément au paragraphe 6. Dans ce cas, un État ou une organisation régionale d'intégration économique peut, aux moments spécifiés aux alinéas a) et b) du paragraphe 1, faire enregistrer une dérogation pour ce produit ou procédé, qui expire dix ans après la date d'abandon définitif pertinente.

9. Aucune Partie ne peut disposer d'une dérogation en vigueur à l'égard d'un produit ou procédé inscrit à l'Annexe A ou B à un quelconque moment après dix ans à compter de la date d'abandon définitif spécifiée dudit produit ou procédé.

Article 7

Extraction minière artisanale et à petite échelle d'or

1. Les mesures énoncées dans le présent article et dans l'Annexe C s'appliquent à l'extraction minière et à la transformation artisanales et à petite échelle d'or utilisant l'amalgamation au mercure pour extraire l'or du minerai.

2. Chaque Partie sur le territoire de laquelle sont menées des activités d'extraction minière et de transformation artisanales et à petite échelle d'or

visées au présent article prend des mesures pour réduire et, si possible, éliminer l'utilisation de mercure et de composés du mercure dans le cadre de ces activités ainsi que les émissions et rejets consécutifs de mercure dans l'environnement.

3. Toute Partie qui, à n'importe quel moment, constate que les activités d'extraction minière et de transformation artisanales et à petite échelle d'or menées sur son territoire sont non négligeables notifie ce fait au Secrétariat. Dans ce cas, la Partie :

a) Élabore et met en œuvre un plan d'action national conformément à l'Annexe C;

b) Soumet son plan d'action national au Secrétariat au plus tard trois ans après l'entrée en vigueur de la Convention à son égard ou dans un délai de trois ans à compter de la date de la notification adressée au Secrétariat, la date la plus tardive étant retenue; et

c) Par la suite, fournit tous les trois ans un compte rendu des progrès qu'elle a accomplis dans le respect de ses obligations au titre du présent article et fait figurer ces comptes rendus dans ses rapports soumis en application de l'article 21.

4. Les Parties peuvent coopérer entre elles ainsi qu'avec des organisations intergouvernementales compétentes et d'autres entités, selon qu'il convient, pour atteindre les objectifs du présent article. Cette coopération peut porter, entre autres, sur :

a) L'élaboration de stratégies visant à prévenir le détournement de mercure ou de composés du mercure en vue d'une utilisation dans l'extraction minière et la transformation artisanales et à petite échelle d'or;

b) Des initiatives en matière d'éducation, de sensibilisation et de renforcement des capacités;

c) La promotion de la recherche de solutions de remplacement durables sans mercure;

d) La fourniture d'une assistance technique et financière;

e) Des partenariats pour les aider à mettre en œuvre leurs engagements au titre du présent article; et

f) L'utilisation des mécanismes d'échange d'informations existants pour promouvoir les connaissances, les meilleures pratiques environnementales et les technologies de remplacement viables aux plans environnemental, technique, social et économique.

Article 8

Émissions

1. Le présent article porte sur le contrôle et, dans la mesure du possible, sur la réduction des émissions atmosphériques de mercure et composés du mercure, souvent exprimées en « quantité totale de mercure », à l'aide de mesures de contrôle visant les sources ponctuelles appartenant aux catégories énumérées à l'Annexe D.

2. Aux fins du présent article :

a) Par « émissions », on entend les émissions atmosphériques de mercure ou composés du mercure;

b) Par « source pertinente », on entend une source appartenant à une des catégories de sources mentionnées dans l'Annexe D. Une Partie peut, si elle le souhaite, établir des critères pour identifier les sources relevant d'une catégorie de sources inscrite à l'Annexe D, tant que les critères retenus pour chaque catégorie couvrent au moins 75 % des émissions de cette dernière;

c) Par « nouvelle source », on entend toute source pertinente appartenant à une catégorie inscrite à l'Annexe D, dont la construction ou une modification importante a débuté au moins un an après :

i) La date d'entrée en vigueur de la présente Convention à l'égard de la Partie concernée; ou

ii) La date d'entrée en vigueur à l'égard de la Partie concernée d'un amendement à l'Annexe D si les dispositions de la présente Convention deviennent applicables à cette source uniquement en vertu dudit amendement;

d) Par « modification importante », on entend une modification d'une source pertinente entraînant une augmentation notable des émissions, à l'exclusion de tout changement au niveau des émissions résultant de la récupération de sous-produits. Il revient à la Partie de déterminer si une modification est importante ou non;

e) Par « source existante », on entend toute source pertinente qui n'est pas une nouvelle source;

f) Par « valeur limite d'émission », on entend un plafond, souvent exprimé en « quantité totale de mercure », fixé pour la concentration, la masse ou le taux des émissions de mercure ou de composés du mercure d'une source ponctuelle.

3. Une Partie disposant de sources pertinentes prend des mesures pour contrôler les émissions et peut élaborer un plan national énonçant les mesures à prendre à cette fin ainsi que les objectifs, les buts et les résultats escomptés. Ce plan est soumis à la Conférence des Parties dans un délai de quatre ans à compter de la date d'entrée en vigueur de la Convention à l'égard de cette Partie. Si une Partie élabore un plan de mise en œuvre conformément à l'article 20, elle peut y faire figurer le plan établi en application du présent paragraphe.

4. S'agissant de ses nouvelles sources, chaque Partie exige l'utilisation des meilleures techniques disponibles et des meilleures pratiques environnementales pour contrôler, et dans la mesure du possible, réduire les émissions, dès que possible mais au plus tard cinq ans après la date d'entrée en vigueur de la Convention à son égard. Une Partie peut utiliser des valeurs limites d'émission compatibles avec l'application des meilleures techniques disponibles.

5. S'agissant de ses sources existantes, chaque Partie inclut dans tout plan national et met en œuvre une ou plusieurs des mesures ci-après, en tenant compte de sa situation nationale ainsi que de la faisabilité technique et économique et du caractère abordable des mesures, dès que possible mais au plus tard dix ans après la date d'entrée en vigueur de la Convention à son égard :

a) Un objectif quantifié pour contrôler et, dans la mesure du possible, réduire les émissions des sources pertinentes;

b) Des valeurs limites d'émission pour contrôler et, dans la mesure du possible, réduire les émissions des sources pertinentes;

c) L'utilisation des meilleures techniques disponibles et des meilleures pratiques environnementales pour contrôler les émissions des sources pertinentes;

d) Une stratégie de contrôle multipolluants qui présenterait des avantages connexes en matière de contrôle des émissions de mercure;

e) D'autres mesures pour réduire les émissions des sources pertinentes.

6. Les Parties peuvent appliquer les mêmes mesures à toutes les sources existantes pertinentes ou adopter des mesures différentes pour chaque catégorie de sources. L'objectif de ces mesures appliquées par une Partie est de réaliser, au fil du temps, des progrès raisonnables en matière de réduction des émissions.

7. Chaque Partie établit, dès que possible mais au plus tard cinq ans après la date d'entrée en vigueur de la Convention à son égard, un inventaire des émissions des sources pertinentes qu'elle tient à jour par la suite.

8. La Conférence des Parties adopte, à sa première réunion, des orientations concernant :

a) Les meilleures techniques disponibles et les meilleures pratiques environnementales, en tenant compte des différences entre les nouvelles sources et les sources existantes ainsi que de la nécessité de réduire au minimum les effets entre différents milieux; et

b) L'aide nécessaire aux Parties pour mettre en œuvre les mesures énoncées au paragraphe 5, en particulier en ce qui concerne la détermination des objectifs et la fixation des valeurs limites d'émission.

9. La Conférence des Parties adopte, dès que possible, des orientations concernant :

a) Les critères que les Parties peuvent définir conformément à l'alinéa b) du paragraphe 2;

b) La méthode à suivre pour établir les inventaires des émissions.

10. La Conférence des Parties examine régulièrement et met à jour, au besoin, les orientations élaborées conformément aux paragraphes 8 et 9. Les Parties tiennent compte de ces orientations dans la mise en œuvre des dispositions pertinentes du présent article.

11. Chaque Partie fait figurer des informations concernant la mise en œuvre du présent article dans les rapports qu'elle soumet conformément à l'article 21, notamment des informations sur les mesures qu'elle a prises conformément aux paragraphes 4 à 7 et sur l'efficacité de ces mesures.

Article 9

Rejets

1. Le présent article porte sur le contrôle et, dans la mesure du possible, sur la réduction des rejets de mercure et composés du mercure, souvent exprimés en « quantité totale de mercure », dans le sol et l'eau par des sources ponctuelles pertinentes qui ne sont pas traitées dans d'autres dispositions de la présente Convention.

2. Aux fins du présent article :

a) Par « rejets », on entend les rejets de mercure ou de composés du mercure dans le sol ou l'eau;

b) Par « source pertinente », on entend toute source anthropique ponctuelle notable de rejets identifiée par une Partie, qui n'est pas traitée dans d'autres dispositions de la présente Convention;

c) Par « nouvelle source », on entend toute source pertinente dont la construction ou une modification importante a débuté au moins un an après la date d'entrée en vigueur de la présente Convention pour la Partie concernée;

d) Par « modification importante », on entend une modification d'une source pertinente entraînant une augmentation notable des rejets, à l'exclusion de tout changement au niveau des rejets résultant de la récupération de sous-produits. Il revient à la Partie de déterminer si une modification est importante ou non;

e) Par « source existante », on entend toute source pertinente qui n'est pas une nouvelle source;

f) Par « valeur limite de rejet », on entend un plafond, souvent exprimé en « quantité totale de mercure », fixé pour la concentration ou la masse de mercure ou de composés du mercure rejetés par une source ponctuelle.

3. Chaque Partie identifie, au plus tard trois ans après la date d'entrée en vigueur de la Convention à son égard et, par la suite, à intervalles réguliers, les catégories de sources ponctuelles pertinentes.

4. Une Partie disposant de sources pertinentes prend des mesures pour contrôler les rejets et peut élaborer un plan national énonçant les mesures à prendre à cette fin ainsi que les objectifs, les buts et les résultats escomptés. Le plan est soumis à la Conférence des Parties dans un délai de quatre ans à

compter de la date d'entrée en vigueur de la Convention à l'égard de cette Partie. Si une Partie élabore un plan de mise en œuvre conformément à l'article 20, elle peut y faire figurer le plan établi en application du présent paragraphe.

5. Les mesures comprennent, selon qu'il convient, une ou plusieurs des mesures suivantes :

a) Des valeurs limites de rejet pour contrôler et, dans la mesure du possible, réduire les rejets des sources pertinentes;

b) L'utilisation des meilleures techniques disponibles et des meilleures pratiques environnementales pour contrôler les rejets des sources pertinentes;

c) Une stratégie de contrôle multipolluants qui présenterait des avantages connexes en matière de contrôle des rejets de mercure;

d) D'autres mesures pour réduire les rejets des sources pertinentes.

6. Chaque Partie établit, dès que possible et au plus tard cinq ans après la date d'entrée en vigueur de la Convention à son égard, un inventaire des rejets des sources pertinentes qu'elle tient à jour par la suite.

7. La Conférence des Parties adopte, dès que possible, des orientations concernant :

a) Les meilleures techniques disponibles et les meilleures pratiques environnementales, en tenant compte des différences entre les nouvelles sources et les sources existantes ainsi que de la nécessité de réduire au minimum les effets entre différents milieux;

b) La méthode à suivre pour établir les inventaires des rejets.

8. Chaque Partie fait figurer des informations concernant la mise en œuvre du présent article dans les rapports qu'elle soumet conformément à l'article 21, notamment des informations sur les mesures qu'elle a prises conformément aux paragraphes 3 à 6 et sur l'efficacité de ces mesures.

Article 10

Stockage provisoire écologiquement rationnel du mercure, à l'exclusion des déchets de mercure

1. Le présent article s'applique au stockage provisoire du mercure et des composés du mercure définis à l'article 3 qui ne répondent pas à la définition des déchets de mercure figurant à l'article 11.

2. Chaque Partie prend des mesures pour faire en sorte que le stockage provisoire du mercure et des composés du mercure destinés à une utilisation permise à une Partie en vertu de la présente Convention soit assuré d'une manière écologiquement rationnelle, en tenant compte de toutes les directives et conformément à toutes les exigences adoptées en vertu du paragraphe 3.

3. La Conférence des Parties adopte des directives concernant le stockage provisoire écologiquement rationnel du mercure et des composés du mercure, en tenant compte de toute directive pertinente élaborée au titre de la Convention de Bâle sur le contrôle des mouvements transfrontières de déchets dangereux et de leur élimination et d'autres orientations pertinentes. La Conférence des Parties peut adopter des exigences concernant le stockage provisoire sous la forme d'une annexe supplémentaire à la présente Convention conformément à l'article 27.

4. Les Parties coopèrent, s'il y a lieu, entre elles et avec des organisations intergouvernementales compétentes et d'autres entités afin de renforcer le développement des capacités en vue du stockage provisoire écologiquement rationnel du mercure et des composés du mercure.

Article 11

Déchets de mercure

1. Pour les Parties à la Convention de Bâle sur le contrôle des mouvements transfrontières de déchets dangereux et de leur élimination, les définitions pertinentes de la Convention de Bâle s'appliquent aux déchets visés par la présente Convention. Les Parties à la présente Convention qui ne sont pas Parties à la Convention de Bâle utilisent ces définitions comme des orientations applicables aux déchets visés par la présente Convention.

2. Aux fins de la présente Convention, par « déchets de mercure », on entend les substances ou objets :

a) Constitués de mercure ou de composés du mercure;

b) Contenant du mercure ou des composés du mercure; ou

c) Contaminés par du mercure ou des composés du mercure,

en quantité supérieure aux seuils pertinents définis par la Conférence des Parties, en collaboration avec les organes compétents de la Convention de Bâle, de manière harmonisée, qu'on élimine, qu'on a l'intention d'éliminer ou qu'on est tenu d'éliminer en vertu des dispositions du droit national ou de la présente Convention. La présente définition exclut les morts-terrains, les déchets de rocs et les résidus provenant de l'extraction minière, à l'exception de l'extraction minière primaire de mercure, à moins qu'ils ne contiennent du mercure ou des composés du mercure en quantité supérieure aux seuils définis par la Conférence des Parties.

3. Chaque Partie prend des mesures appropriées pour que les déchets de mercure :

a) Fassent l'objet d'une gestion écologiquement rationnelle, en tenant compte des directives élaborées au titre de la Convention de Bâle et conformément aux exigences que la Conférence des Parties adopte dans une annexe supplémentaire, conformément à l'article 27. En élaborant ces exigences, la Conférence des Parties prend en compte les réglementations et programmes des Parties en matière de gestion des déchets;

b) Ne soient récupérés, recyclés, régénérés ou réutilisés directement qu'en vue d'une utilisation permise à une Partie en vertu de la présente Convention ou d'une élimination écologiquement rationnelle conformément à l'alinéa a) du paragraphe 3;

c) Pour les Parties à la Convention de Bâle, ne soient pas transportés par-delà les frontières internationales, sauf à des fins d'élimination écologiquement rationnelle conformément aux dispositions du présent article et de la Convention de Bâle. Dans le cas des transports par-delà les frontières internationales auxquels la Convention de Bâle ne s'applique pas, une Partie n'autorise un tel transport qu'après avoir tenu compte des règles, normes et directives internationales pertinentes.

4. La Conférence des Parties s'attache à coopérer étroitement avec les organes compétents de la Convention de Bâle pour examiner et actualiser, selon qu'il convient, les directives visées à l'alinéa a) du paragraphe 3.

5. Les Parties sont encouragées à coopérer entre elles et avec des organisations intergouvernementales compétentes et d'autres entités, s'il y a lieu, pour développer et maintenir les capacités mondiales, régionales et

nationales en vue de la gestion écologiquement rationnelle des déchets de mercure.

Article 12

Sites contaminés

1. Chaque Partie s'efforce d'élaborer des stratégies appropriées pour identifier et évaluer les sites contaminés par du mercure ou des composés du mercure.

2. Les actions visant à réduire les risques présentés par ces sites sont menées d'une manière écologiquement rationnelle comprenant, au besoin, une évaluation des risques pour la santé humaine et l'environnement posés par le mercure ou les composés du mercure qu'ils recèlent.

3. La Conférence des Parties adopte des orientations sur la gestion des sites contaminés qui peuvent inclure des méthodes et des approches pour :

a) L'identification et la caractérisation des sites contaminés;

b) La mobilisation du public;

c) Les évaluations des risques pour la santé humaine et l'environnement;

d) Les options de gestion des risques présentés par les sites contaminés;

e) L'évaluation des avantages et des coûts; et

f) La validation des résultats.

4. Les Parties sont encouragées à coopérer à l'élaboration de stratégies et à l'exécution d'activités visant à identifier, évaluer, classer par ordre de priorité, gérer et, s'il y a lieu, remettre en état les sites contaminés.

Article 13

Ressources financières et mécanisme de financement

1. Chaque Partie s'engage à fournir, dans la mesure de ses moyens et conformément à ses politiques, priorités, plans et programmes nationaux, des ressources pour les activités nationales prévues aux fins de la mise en œuvre de la présente Convention. Ces ressources peuvent inclure des financements nationaux dans le cadre de politiques, stratégies de développement et budgets

nationaux pertinents, des financements bilatéraux et multilatéraux, ainsi que la participation du secteur privé.

2. L'efficacité globale de la mise en œuvre de la présente Convention par les Parties qui sont des pays en développement sera liée à la mise en œuvre effective du présent article.

3. Les sources multilatérales, régionales et bilatérales d'assistance dans les domaines financier et technique et dans ceux du renforcement des capacités et du transfert de technologies sont encouragées de façon urgente à renforcer et intensifier leurs activités se rapportant au mercure visant à appuyer les Parties qui sont des pays en développement dans la mise en œuvre de la présente Convention pour ce qui est des ressources financières, de l'assistance technique et du transfert de technologies.

4. Lorsqu'elles prennent des mesures concernant le financement, les Parties tiennent pleinement compte des besoins spécifiques et de la situation particulière des Parties comptant parmi les petits États insulaires en développement ou les pays les moins avancés.

5. Il est institué par les présentes un mécanisme destiné à fournir en temps voulu des ressources financières adéquates et prévisibles pour aider les Parties qui sont des pays en développement ou des pays à économie en transition dans la mise en œuvre de leurs obligations au titre de la présente Convention.

6. Le mécanisme inclut :

a) La Caisse du Fonds pour l'environnement mondial; et

b) Un programme international spécifique visant à soutenir le renforcement des capacités et l'assistance technique.

7. La Caisse du Fonds pour l'environnement mondial fournit en temps voulu des ressources financières nouvelles, prévisibles et adéquates pour couvrir les coûts de l'aide à la mise en œuvre de la présente Convention, comme convenu par la Conférence des Parties. Aux fins de la présente Convention, la Caisse du Fonds pour l'environnement mondial est placée sous la direction de la Conférence des Parties à laquelle elle rend compte. La Conférence des Parties énonce des orientations sur les stratégies, politiques et priorités programmatiques globales ainsi que sur les conditions requises pour avoir accès aux ressources financières et utiliser ces dernières. En outre, la Conférence des Parties énonce des orientations sur une liste indicative des catégories d'activités qui pourraient bénéficier du soutien de la Caisse du Fonds pour l'environnement mondial. La Caisse du Fonds pour

l'environnement mondial fournit des ressources pour couvrir les surcoûts convenus liés aux avantages environnementaux mondiaux et l'ensemble des coûts convenus de certaines activités habilitantes.

8. Lorsqu'elle fournit des ressources pour une activité, la Caisse du Fonds pour l'environnement mondial devrait tenir compte du potentiel de réduction du mercure de l'activité proposée par rapport à ses coûts.

9. Aux fins de la présente Convention, le programme visé à l'alinéa b) du paragraphe 6 sera placé sous la direction de la Conférence des Parties à laquelle il rendra compte. La Conférence des Parties décide, à sa première réunion, de l'institution d'accueil du programme, qui doit être une institution existante, et fournit à cette dernière des orientations, y compris sur la durée dudit programme. Toutes les Parties et autres parties prenantes concernées sont invitées à fournir, sur une base volontaire, des ressources financières au programme.

10. La Conférence des Parties et les entités constituant le mécanisme conviennent, à la première réunion de la Conférence des Parties, d'arrangements pour donner effet aux paragraphes ci-dessus.

11. La Conférence des Parties examine, au plus tard à sa troisième réunion et, par la suite, à intervalles réguliers, le niveau de financement, les orientations fournies par la Conférence des Parties aux entités chargées d'assurer le fonctionnement du mécanisme institué en vertu du présent article et leur efficacité, et leur capacité à répondre aux besoins en évolution des Parties qui sont des pays en développement et des pays à économie en transition. Sur la base de cet examen, la Conférence des Parties prend des mesures appropriées pour améliorer l'efficacité du mécanisme.

12. Toutes les Parties sont invitées à apporter des contributions au mécanisme, dans la mesure de leurs moyens. Le mécanisme encourage la fourniture de ressources provenant d'autres sources, y compris du secteur privé, et cherche à mobiliser ces ressources pour les activités qu'il soutient.

Article 14

Renforcement des capacités, assistance technique et transfert de technologies

1. Les Parties coopèrent en vue de fournir, dans les limites de leurs capacités respectives, un renforcement des capacités et une assistance technique appropriés, en temps utile, aux Parties qui sont des pays en développement, en particulier aux pays les moins avancés et aux petits États insulaires en

développement, et aux Parties qui sont des pays à économie en transition, pour les aider à mettre en œuvre leurs obligations au titre de la présente Convention.

2. Le renforcement des capacités et l'assistance technique visés au paragraphe 1 et à l'article 13 peuvent être fournis par le biais d'arrangements aux niveaux régional, sous-régional et national, y compris par les centres régionaux et sous-régionaux existants, par le biais d'autres moyens multilatéraux et bilatéraux, et par le biais de partenariats, y compris avec le secteur privé. La coopération et la coordination avec d'autres accords multilatéraux sur l'environnement concernant les produits chimiques et les déchets devraient être recherchées en vue d'améliorer l'efficacité de l'assistance technique et de la fourniture de celle-ci.

3. Les Parties qui sont des pays développés et les autres Parties, dans les limites de leurs capacités, encouragent et facilitent, avec le soutien du secteur privé et d'autres parties prenantes concernées, selon qu'il convient, la mise au point, le transfert et la diffusion de technologies de remplacement écologiquement rationnelles de pointe, ainsi que l'accès à ces technologies, au bénéfice des Parties qui sont des pays en développement, en particulier les pays les moins avancés et les petits États insulaires en développement, et des Parties qui sont des pays à économie en transition, en vue de renforcer leur capacité de mise en œuvre effective de la présente Convention.

4. La Conférence des Parties, au plus tard à sa deuxième réunion et, par la suite, à intervalles réguliers, en tenant compte des communications et des rapports soumis par les Parties, y compris ceux requis à l'article 21, ainsi que des informations fournies par d'autres parties prenantes :

a) Examine les informations sur les initiatives en cours et les progrès accomplis dans le domaine des technologies de remplacement;

b) Évalue les besoins des Parties en matière de technologies de remplacement, en particulier ceux des Parties qui sont des pays en développement; et

c) Identifie les défis rencontrés par les Parties, en particulier celles qui sont des pays en développement, en matière de transfert de technologies.

5. La Conférence des Parties émet des recommandations sur la manière dont le renforcement des capacités, l'assistance technique et le transfert de technologies pourraient être encore améliorés au titre du présent article.

Article 15

Comité de mise en œuvre et du respect des obligations

1. Il est institué par les présentes un mécanisme, comprenant un Comité ayant qualité d'organe subsidiaire de la Conférence des Parties, en vue de promouvoir la mise en œuvre et d'examiner le respect de toutes les dispositions de la présente Convention. Le mécanisme, y compris le Comité, est de nature facilitatrice et accorde une attention particulière à la situation et aux capacités nationales respectives des Parties.

2. Le Comité encourage la mise en œuvre et examine le respect de toutes les dispositions de la présente Convention. Il examine tant les questions individuelles que systémiques ayant trait à la mise en œuvre et au respect des dispositions et fait des recommandations à la Conférence des Parties, selon qu'il convient.

3. Le Comité est composé de 15 membres désignés par les Parties et élus par la Conférence des Parties, en tenant dûment compte d'une représentation géographique équitable fondée sur les cinq régions de l'Organisation des Nations Unies; les premiers membres sont élus à la première réunion de la Conférence des Parties et ensuite conformément au règlement intérieur approuvé par la Conférence des Parties en vertu du paragraphe 5; les membres du Comité possèdent des compétences dans un domaine en rapport avec la présente Convention et reflètent un équilibre approprié des expertises.

4. Le Comité peut examiner des questions sur la base :

a) De communications écrites transmises par toute Partie concernant son respect des dispositions;

b) De rapports nationaux soumis conformément à l'article 21; et

c) De demandes formulées par la Conférence des Parties.

5. Le Comité élabore son règlement intérieur, qui est soumis à l'approbation de la Conférence des Parties, à sa deuxième réunion; la Conférence des Parties peut ajouter des clauses supplémentaires au mandat du Comité.

6. Le Comité met tout en œuvre pour adopter ses recommandations par consensus. Si tous les efforts en ce sens sont demeurés vains et qu'aucun consensus n'est atteint, les recommandations sont adoptées en dernier recours par vote à la majorité des trois quarts des membres présents et votants, sur la base d'un quorum de deux tiers des membres.

Article 16

Aspects sanitaires

1. Les Parties sont encouragées à :

a) Promouvoir l'élaboration et la mise en œuvre de stratégies et de programmes visant à identifier et protéger les populations à risques, en particulier les populations vulnérables, qui pourraient comprendre l'adoption de directives sanitaires à caractère scientifique sur l'exposition au mercure et aux composés du mercure fixant des objectifs pour la réduction de l'exposition au mercure, le cas échéant, et l'éducation du public, avec la participation du secteur de la santé publique et d'autres secteurs concernés;

b) Promouvoir l'élaboration et la mise en œuvre de programmes d'éducation et de prévention à fondement scientifique portant sur l'exposition professionnelle au mercure et aux composés du mercure;

c) Promouvoir les services de soins de santé appropriés pour la prévention, le traitement et les soins des populations affectées par l'exposition au mercure ou aux composés de mercure; et

d) Mettre en place et renforcer, selon qu'il convient, les capacités institutionnelles et les moyens dont disposent les professionnels de la santé pour la prévention, le diagnostic, le traitement et la surveillance des risques pour la santé de l'exposition au mercure et aux composés du mercure.

2. La Conférence des Parties, dans le cadre de l'examen de questions ou activités liées à la santé, devrait :

a) Consulter l'Organisation mondiale de la Santé, l'Organisation internationale du Travail et d'autres organisations intergouvernementales compétentes et collaborer avec celles-ci, selon qu'il convient; et

b) Promouvoir la coopération et l'échange d'informations avec l'Organisation mondiale de la Santé, l'Organisation internationale du Travail et d'autres organisations intergouvernementales compétentes, selon qu'il convient.

Article 17

Échange d'informations

1. Chaque Partie facilite l'échange :

a) D'informations scientifiques, techniques, économiques et juridiques concernant le mercure et les composés du mercure, y compris des informations toxicologiques, écotoxicologiques et relatives à la sécurité;

b) D'informations sur la réduction ou l'élimination de la production, de l'utilisation, du commerce, des émissions et des rejets de mercure et de composés du mercure;

c) D'informations concernant les solutions de remplacement techniquement et économiquement viables pour :

i) Les produits contenant du mercure ajouté;

ii) Les procédés de fabrication dans lesquels du mercure ou des composés du mercure sont utilisés; et

iii) Les activités et procédés qui émettent ou rejettent du mercure ou des composés du mercure;

y compris des informations relatives aux risques pour la santé et l'environnement et aux coûts et avantages socioéconomiques de ces solutions de remplacement; et

d) D'informations épidémiologiques concernant les effets sur la santé de l'exposition au mercure et aux composés du mercure, en étroite coopération avec l'Organisation mondiale de la Santé et d'autres organisations compétentes, au besoin.

2. Les Parties peuvent échanger les informations visées au paragraphe 1 directement, par l'intermédiaire du Secrétariat ou en coopération avec d'autres organisations compétentes, notamment les Secrétariats des conventions relatives aux produits chimiques et aux déchets, selon qu'il convient.

3. Le Secrétariat facilite la coopération en matière d'échange d'informations mentionnée dans le présent article et la coopération avec des organisations compétentes, notamment les Secrétariats des accords multilatéraux sur l'environnement et d'autres initiatives internationales. Les informations en question comprennent non seulement celles fournies par les Parties, mais aussi

celles obtenues des organisations intergouvernementales et non gouvernementales et des institutions nationales et internationales qui possèdent une expertise dans le domaine du mercure.

4. Chaque Partie désigne un correspondant national pour l'échange d'informations au titre de la présente Convention, notamment en ce qui concerne le consentement des Parties importatrices mentionné à l'article 3.

5. Aux fins de la présente Convention, les informations concernant la santé et la sécurité des personnes ainsi que l'environnement ne sont pas considérées comme confidentielles. Les Parties qui échangent d'autres informations en application de la présente Convention respectent le caractère confidentiel des informations de façon mutuellement convenue.

Article 18

Information, sensibilisation et éducation du public

1. Chaque Partie, dans les limites de ses moyens, encourage et facilite :

a) La mise à la disposition du public des informations disponibles concernant :

i) Les effets du mercure et des composés du mercure sur la santé et l'environnement;

ii) Les solutions de remplacement du mercure et des composés du mercure;

iii) Les sujets identifiés au paragraphe 1 de l'article 17;

iv) Les résultats de ses activités de recherche développement et de surveillance au titre de l'article 19; et

v) Les activités qu'elle mène pour s'acquitter de ses obligations au titre de la présente Convention;

b) L'éducation, la formation et la sensibilisation du public en ce qui concerne les effets de l'exposition au mercure et aux composés du mercure sur la santé humaine et l'environnement, en collaboration avec les organisations intergouvernementales et non gouvernementales compétentes et les populations vulnérables, le cas échéant.

2. Chaque Partie utilise des mécanismes existants ou envisage d'élaborer des mécanismes, tels que des registres des rejets et transferts de polluants, s'il y a lieu, aux fins de la collecte et de la diffusion d'informations sur les estimations des quantités annuelles de mercure et de composés du mercure qui sont émises, rejetées ou éliminées par des activités humaines sur son territoire.

Article 19

Recherche-développement et surveillance

1. Les Parties s'efforcent de coopérer pour développer et améliorer, compte tenu de leur situation et de leurs moyens respectifs :

a) Des inventaires recensant les utilisations, la consommation, les émissions atmosphériques et les rejets dans l'eau et le sol, d'origine anthropique, de mercure et de composés du mercure;

b) La modélisation et la surveillance géographiquement représentative des concentrations de mercure et de composés du mercure chez les populations vulnérables et dans les milieux naturels, notamment chez les biotes tels que les poissons, les mammifères marins, les tortues de mer et les oiseaux, ainsi que la collaboration en matière de collecte et d'échange d'échantillons appropriés et pertinents;

c) Des évaluations de l'impact du mercure et des composés du mercure sur la santé humaine et l'environnement, ainsi que dans les domaines social, économique et culturel, en particulier chez les populations vulnérables;

d) Des méthodes harmonisées pour les activités menées au titre des alinéas a), b) et c);

e) L'information concernant le cycle environnemental, la propagation (notamment la propagation à longue distance et le dépôt), la transformation et le devenir du mercure et des composés du mercure dans différents écosystèmes, en tenant dûment compte de la distinction entre, d'une part, les émissions et rejets anthropiques et, d'autre part, les émissions et rejets naturels de mercure ainsi que de la remobilisation de mercure provenant de dépôts anciens;

f) L'information sur le commerce et les échanges de mercure et de composés du mercure, et de produits contenant du mercure ajouté; et

g) L'information et la recherche concernant la disponibilité technique et économique de produits et procédés sans mercure, ainsi que les meilleures techniques disponibles et les meilleures pratiques environnementales pour réduire et surveiller les émissions et les rejets de mercure et de composés du mercure.

2. Les Parties devraient, au besoin, s'appuyer sur les réseaux de surveillance et programmes de recherche existants lors de l'exécution des activités mentionnées au paragraphe 1.

Article 20

Plans de mise en œuvre

1. Chaque Partie peut, à l'issue d'une première évaluation, élaborer et appliquer un plan de mise en œuvre tenant compte de sa situation nationale pour s'acquitter de ses obligations au titre de la présente Convention. Ce plan devrait être transmis au Secrétariat dès qu'il aura été élaboré.

2. Chaque Partie peut réviser et mettre à jour son plan de mise en œuvre, en tenant compte de sa situation nationale, des orientations données par la Conférence des Parties et des autres orientations pertinentes.

3. Les Parties devraient, lorsqu'elles entreprennent les activités mentionnées aux paragraphes 1 et 2, consulter les parties prenantes nationales pour faciliter l'élaboration, la mise en œuvre, la révision et la mise à jour de leurs plans de mise en œuvre.

4. Les Parties peuvent également se concerter sur des plans régionaux afin de faciliter la mise en œuvre de la présente Convention.

Article 21

Établissement de rapports

1. Chaque Partie fait rapport à la Conférence des Parties, par l'intermédiaire du Secrétariat, sur les mesures qu'elle a prises pour mettre en œuvre les dispositions de la présente Convention et l'efficacité de ces mesures ainsi que sur les éventuelles difficultés qu'elle a rencontrées dans la réalisation des objectifs de la Convention.

2. Chaque Partie inclut, dans ses rapports, les informations requises par les articles 3, 5, 7, 8 et 9 de la présente Convention.

3. La Conférence des Parties décide, à sa première réunion, de la périodicité et de la présentation des rapports, à respecter par les Parties, en tenant compte

du caractère souhaitable d'une coordination avec les autres conventions pertinentes relatives aux produits chimiques et aux déchets pour la communication des informations.

Article 22

Évaluation de l'efficacité

1. La Conférence des Parties évalue l'efficacité de la présente Convention au plus tard six ans après sa date d'entrée en vigueur et, par la suite, périodiquement, à des intervalles dont elle décidera.

2. Afin de faciliter cette évaluation, la Conférence des Parties lance, à sa première réunion, la mise en place d'arrangements pour obtenir des données de surveillance comparables sur la présence et les mouvements de mercure et de composés du mercure dans l'environnement ainsi que sur les tendances des concentrations de mercure et de composés du mercure observées dans les milieux biotiques et chez les populations vulnérables.

3. L'évaluation est effectuée sur la base des informations scientifiques, environnementales, techniques, financières et économiques disponibles, incluant :

a) Des rapports et d'autres données de surveillance fournis à la Conférence des Parties conformément au paragraphe 2;

b) Des rapports soumis conformément à l'article 21;

c) Des informations et des recommandations fournies conformément à l'article 15; et

d) Des rapports et d'autres informations pertinentes sur le fonctionnement des arrangements en matière d'assistance financière, de transfert de technologies et de renforcement des capacités mis en place au titre de la présente Convention.

Article 23

Conférence des Parties

1. Il est institué par les présentes une Conférence des Parties.

2. La première réunion de la Conférence des Parties est convoquée par le Directeur exécutif du Programme des Nations Unies pour l'environnement au

plus tard un an après la date d'entrée en vigueur de la présente Convention. Par la suite, les réunions ordinaires de la Conférence des Parties se tiennent à des intervalles réguliers à décider par la Conférence.

3. Des réunions extraordinaires de la Conférence des Parties ont lieu à tout autre moment si la Conférence le juge nécessaire, ou à la demande écrite d'une Partie, sous réserve que, dans un délai de six mois suivant sa communication aux Parties par le Secrétariat, cette demande soit appuyée par un tiers au moins des Parties.

4. La Conférence des Parties arrête et adopte par consensus, à sa première réunion, son règlement intérieur et ses règles de gestion financière et ceux de tout organe subsidiaire, ainsi que les dispositions financières régissant le fonctionnement du Secrétariat.

5. La Conférence des Parties suit et évalue en permanence la mise en œuvre de la présente Convention. Elle s'acquitte des fonctions qui lui sont assignées par la présente Convention et, à cette fin :

a) Crée les organes subsidiaires qu'elle juge nécessaires à la mise en œuvre de la présente Convention;

b) Coopère, au besoin, avec les organisations internationales et les organismes intergouvernementaux et non gouvernementaux compétents;

c) Examine périodiquement toutes les informations qui lui sont communiquées ainsi que toutes celles communiquées au Secrétariat en application de l'article 21;

d) Examine toutes les recommandations qui lui sont transmises par le Comité de mise en œuvre et du respect des obligations;

e) Examine et prend toute autre mesure nécessaire à la réalisation des objectifs de la présente Convention; et

f) Examine les Annexes A et B conformément aux articles 4 et 5.

6. L'Organisation des Nations Unies, ses institutions spécialisées et l'Agence internationale de l'énergie atomique, de même que tout État qui n'est pas Partie à la présente Convention, peuvent se faire représenter aux réunions de la Conférence des Parties en qualité d'observateurs. Tout organe ou organisme, national ou international, gouvernemental ou non gouvernemental, compétent dans les domaines visés par la présente Convention et qui a informé le Secrétariat de son souhait de se faire représenter à une réunion de la

Conférence des Parties en qualité d'observateur peut être admis à y prendre part à moins qu'un tiers au moins des Parties présentes n'y fassent objection. L'admission et la participation des observateurs sont subordonnées au respect du règlement intérieur adopté par la Conférence des Parties.

Article 24

Secrétariat

1. Il est institué par les présentes un Secrétariat.

2. Les fonctions du Secrétariat sont les suivantes :

a) Organiser les réunions de la Conférence des Parties et de ses organes subsidiaires et leur fournir les services requis;

b) Faciliter l'octroi, sur demande, d'une assistance aux Parties, en particulier aux Parties qui sont des pays en développement ou à économie en transition, aux fins de la mise en œuvre de la présente Convention;

c) Assurer la coordination, si besoin est, avec les secrétariats d'organismes internationaux compétents, en particulier avec ceux d'autres conventions sur les produits chimiques et les déchets;

d) Soutenir les Parties dans le cadre de l'échange d'informations concernant la mise en œuvre de la présente Convention;

e) Établir et mettre à la disposition des Parties des rapports périodiques fondés sur les informations reçues en vertu des articles 15 et 21 ainsi que d'autres informations disponibles;

f) Conclure, sous la supervision générale de la Conférence des Parties, les arrangements administratifs et contractuels qui pourraient lui être nécessaires pour s'acquitter efficacement de ses fonctions; et

g) S'acquitter des autres fonctions de secrétariat spécifiées dans la présente Convention et de toute fonction supplémentaire qui pourrait lui être confiée par la Conférence des Parties.

3. Les fonctions de secrétariat de la présente Convention sont assurées par le Directeur exécutif du Programme des Nations Unies pour l'environnement, sauf si la Conférence des Parties décide, à une majorité des trois quarts des Parties présentes et votantes, de confier les fonctions de secrétariat à une ou plusieurs autres organisations internationales.

4. La Conférence des Parties peut, en consultation avec des organismes internationaux compétents, prévoir une coopération et une coordination renforcées entre le Secrétariat et les secrétariats d'autres conventions sur les produits chimiques et les déchets. La Conférence des Parties peut, en consultation avec des organismes internationaux compétents, énoncer d'autres orientations sur ce sujet.

Article 25

Règlement des différends

1. Les Parties s'efforcent de régler tout différend surgissant entre elles concernant l'interprétation ou l'application de la présente Convention par voie de négociation ou par tout autre moyen pacifique de leur choix.

2. Lorsqu'elle ratifie, accepte ou approuve la présente Convention ou y adhère, ou à tout autre moment par la suite, toute Partie qui n'est pas une organisation régionale d'intégration économique peut déclarer dans un instrument écrit soumis au Dépositaire que, pour tout différend concernant l'interprétation ou l'application de la présente Convention, elle reconnaît comme obligatoires, à l'égard de toute Partie acceptant la même obligation, l'un des deux ou les deux moyens de règlement des différends suivants :

a) L'arbitrage, conformément à la procédure énoncée dans la première partie de l'Annexe E;

b) La saisine de la Cour internationale de Justice.

3. Toute organisation régionale d'intégration économique Partie à la Convention peut faire une déclaration ayant le même effet concernant l'arbitrage, conformément au paragraphe 2.

4. Toute déclaration faite en application du paragraphe 2 ou du paragraphe 3 reste en vigueur jusqu'à l'expiration du délai stipulé dans cette déclaration ou jusqu'à l'expiration d'un délai de trois mois à compter du dépôt, auprès du Dépositaire, de la notification écrite de sa révocation.

5. L'expiration d'une déclaration, la notification de la révocation d'une déclaration ou le dépôt d'une nouvelle déclaration n'affecte en rien la procédure engagée devant un tribunal arbitral ou devant la Cour internationale de Justice, à moins que les parties au différend n'en conviennent autrement.

6. Si les parties à un différend n'ont pas accepté le même moyen de règlement des différends conformément au paragraphe 2 ou au paragraphe 3, et

si elles ne sont pas parvenues à régler leur différend par les moyens indiqués au paragraphe 1 dans les douze mois suivant la notification par une Partie à une autre Partie de l'existence d'un différend entre elles, le différend est porté devant une commission de conciliation, à la demande de l'une des parties au différend. La procédure énoncée dans la deuxième partie de l'Annexe E s'applique à la conciliation au titre du présent article.

Article 26

Amendements à la Convention

1. Toute Partie peut proposer des amendements à la présente Convention.

2. Les amendements à la présente Convention sont adoptés à une réunion de la Conférence des Parties. Le texte de tout projet d'amendement est communiqué aux Parties par le Secrétariat six mois au moins avant la réunion à laquelle il est présenté pour adoption. Le Secrétariat communique également les projets d'amendement aux signataires de la présente Convention et, à titre d'information, au Dépositaire.

3. Les Parties mettent tout en œuvre pour parvenir à un accord par consensus sur tout amendement proposé à la présente Convention. Si tous les efforts en ce sens sont demeurés vains et qu'aucun accord n'est intervenu, l'amendement est adopté en dernier recours par vote à la majorité des trois quarts des Parties présentes et votantes participant à la réunion.

4. Le Dépositaire communique tout amendement adopté à toutes les Parties aux fins de ratification, d'acceptation ou d'approbation.

5. La ratification, l'acceptation ou l'approbation d'un amendement est notifiée par écrit au Dépositaire. Un amendement adopté conformément au paragraphe 3 entre en vigueur à l'égard des Parties ayant accepté d'être liées par ses dispositions le quatre vingt dixième jour à compter de la date du dépôt des instruments de ratification, d'acceptation ou d'approbation par les trois quarts au moins des Parties qui étaient Parties au moment où l'amendement a été adopté. Par la suite, l'amendement entre en vigueur à l'égard de toute autre Partie le quatre vingt dixième jour à compter de la date du dépôt par cette Partie de son instrument de ratification, d'acceptation ou d'approbation de l'amendement.

Article 27

Adoption et amendements des annexes

1. Les annexes à la présente Convention en font partie intégrante et, sauf disposition contraire expresse, toute référence à la Convention constitue également une référence à ses annexes.

2. Les annexes supplémentaires adoptées après l'entrée en vigueur de la présente Convention ont exclusivement trait à des questions de procédure ou à des questions d'ordre scientifique, technique ou administratif.

3. La proposition, l'adoption et l'entrée en vigueur d'annexes supplémentaires à la présente Convention sont régies par la procédure suivante :

a) Les annexes supplémentaires sont proposées et adoptées selon la procédure énoncée aux paragraphes 1 à 3 de l'article 26;

b) Toute Partie qui ne peut accepter une annexe supplémentaire en informe le Dépositaire par notification écrite dans l'année qui suit la date de communication par le Dépositaire de l'adoption de cette annexe. Ce dernier informe sans délai toutes les Parties de toute notification reçue en ce sens. Une Partie peut à tout moment informer le Dépositaire par notification écrite qu'elle retire une notification antérieure de non acceptation d'une annexe supplémentaire; l'annexe considérée entre alors en vigueur à l'égard de cette Partie sous réserve des dispositions de l'alinéa c) ci après; et

c) À l'expiration d'un délai d'un an à compter de la date de la communication par le Dépositaire de l'adoption d'une annexe supplémentaire, celle ci entre en vigueur à l'égard de toutes les Parties qui n'ont pas communiqué de notification de non acceptation en application des dispositions de l'alinéa b).

4. La proposition, l'adoption et l'entrée en vigueur d'amendements aux annexes à la présente Convention sont soumises à la même procédure que la proposition, l'adoption et l'entrée en vigueur d'annexes supplémentaires à la Convention, sous réserve qu'un amendement à une annexe n'entre pas en vigueur à l'égard d'une Partie qui a fait une déclaration concernant un amendement à des annexes conformément au paragraphe 5 de l'article 30, auquel cas cet amendement entre en vigueur à l'égard de la Partie en question le quatre vingt dixième jour à compter de la date à laquelle celle-ci dépose, auprès du Dépositaire, son instrument de ratification, d'acceptation, d'approbation ou d'adhésion concernant un tel amendement.

5. Si une annexe supplémentaire ou un amendement à une annexe se rapporte à un amendement à la présente Convention, cette annexe supplémentaire ou cet amendement n'entre en vigueur que lorsque l'amendement à la Convention entre lui-même en vigueur.

Article 28

Droit de vote

1. Sous réserve des dispositions du paragraphe 2, chaque Partie à la présente Convention dispose d'une voix.

2. Les organisations régionales d'intégration économique disposent, pour exercer leur droit de vote dans les domaines qui relèvent de leur compétence, d'un nombre de voix égal au nombre de leurs États membres qui sont Parties à la présente Convention. Elles n'exercent pas leur droit de vote si l'un de leurs États membres exerce le sien, et inversement.

Article 29

Signature

La présente Convention est ouverte à la signature de tous les États et organisations régionales d'intégration économique à Kumamoto (Japon) les 10 et 11 octobre 2013, et ensuite au siège de l'Organisation des Nations Unies, à New York, jusqu'au 9 octobre 2014.

Article 30

Ratification, acceptation, approbation ou adhésion

1. La présente Convention est soumise à la ratification, à l'acceptation ou à l'approbation des États et des organisations régionales d'intégration économique. Elle est ouverte à l'adhésion des États et des organisations régionales d'intégration économique à compter du jour qui suit la date où elle cesse d'être ouverte à la signature. Les instruments de ratification, d'acceptation, d'approbation ou d'adhésion sont déposés auprès du Dépositaire.

2. Toute organisation régionale d'intégration économique qui devient Partie à la présente Convention sans qu'aucun de ses États membres n'y soit Partie est liée par toutes les obligations énoncées dans la Convention. Lorsqu'un ou plusieurs États membres d'une de ces organisations sont Parties à la Convention, l'organisation et ses États membres décident de leurs

responsabilités respectives en ce qui concerne l'exécution des obligations qui leur incombent en vertu de la Convention. En pareil cas, l'organisation et ses États membres ne sont pas habilités à exercer concurremment leurs droits au titre de la Convention.

3. Dans leurs instruments de ratification, d'acceptation, d'approbation ou d'adhésion, les organisations régionales d'intégration économique indiquent l'étendue de leur compétence à l'égard des questions régies par la présente Convention. En outre, ces organisations informent le Dépositaire, qui en informe à son tour les Parties, de toute modification pertinente de l'étendue de leur compétence.

4. Chaque État ou organisation régionale d'intégration économique est encouragé à transmettre au Secrétariat, au moment de sa ratification, de son acceptation ou de son approbation de la Convention ou de son adhésion à celle-ci, des informations sur les mesures qu'il ou elle a prises pour mettre en œuvre la Convention.

5. Dans son instrument de ratification, d'acceptation, d'approbation ou d'adhésion, toute Partie peut déclarer que tout amendement à une annexe n'entre en vigueur à son égard qu'après le dépôt de son instrument de ratification, d'acceptation ou d'approbation dudit amendement ou d'adhésion à celui-ci.

Article 31

Entrée en vigueur

1. La présente Convention entre en vigueur le quatre-vingt-dixième jour suivant la date du dépôt du cinquantième instrument de ratification, d'acceptation, d'approbation ou d'adhésion.

2. Pour chaque État ou organisation régionale d'intégration économique qui ratifie, accepte ou approuve la Convention, ou y adhère, après le dépôt du cinquantième instrument de ratification, d'acceptation, d'approbation ou d'adhésion, la Convention entre en vigueur le quatre vingt dixième jour suivant la date du dépôt, par cet État ou cette organisation, de son instrument de ratification, d'acceptation, d'approbation ou d'adhésion.

3. Aux fins des paragraphes 1 et 2, tout instrument déposé par une organisation régionale d'intégration économique n'est pas considéré comme venant s'ajouter aux instruments déjà déposés par les États membres de cette organisation.

Article 32

Réserves

Aucune réserve ne peut être faite à la présente Convention.

Article 33

Retrait

1. À l'expiration d'un délai de trois ans à compter de la date d'entrée en vigueur de la présente Convention à l'égard d'une Partie, cette dernière peut à tout moment se retirer de la Convention par notification écrite adressée au Dépositaire.

2. Tout retrait prend effet à l'expiration d'un délai d'un an à compter de la date de réception de la notification de retrait par le Dépositaire, ou à toute autre date ultérieure spécifiée dans la notification de retrait.

Article 34

Dépositaire

Le Secrétaire général de l'Organisation des Nations Unies est le Dépositaire de la présente Convention.

Article 35

Textes faisant foi

L'original de la présente Convention, dont les textes anglais, arabe, chinois, espagnol, français et russe font également foi, est déposé auprès du Dépositaire.

EN FOI DE QUOI les soussignés, dûment autorisés à cet effet, ont signé la présente Convention.

Fait à Kumamoto (Japon), le dix octobre deux mil treize.

Annexe A

Produits contenant du mercure ajouté

Les produits ci-après sont exclus de la présente Annexe :

a) Produits essentiels à des fins militaires et de protection civile;

b) Produits utilisés pour la recherche, pour l'étalonnage d'instruments, comme étalon de référence;

c) Lorsqu'aucune solution de remplacement faisable sans mercure n'est disponible, commutateurs et relais, lampes fluorescentes à cathode froide et lampes fluorescentes à électrodes externes pour affichages électroniques et appareils de mesure;

d) Produits utilisés dans des pratiques traditionnelles ou religieuses; et

e) Vaccins contenant du thimérosal comme conservateur.

Première partie : Produits soumis au paragraphe 1 de l'article 4

Produits contenant du mercure ajouté	**Date à compter de laquelle la production, l'importation ou l'exportation du produit n'est plus autorisée (date d'abandon définitif)**
Piles, à l'exception des piles boutons zinc-oxyde d'argent et zinc-air à teneur en mercure < 2 %	2020
Commutateurs et relais, à l'exception des ponts de mesure de capacité et de perte à très haute précision et des commutateurs et relais radio haute fréquence pour instruments de surveillance et de contrôle possédant une teneur maximale en mercure de 20 mg par pont, commutateur ou relais	2020
Lampes fluorescentes compactes d'éclairage ordinaire de puissance ≤ 30 W à teneur en mercure supérieure à 5 mg par bec de lampe	2020
Tubes fluorescents linéaires d'éclairage ordinaire : a) au phosphore à trois bandes de puissance < 60 W à teneur en mercure supérieure à 5 mg par lampe; b) au phosphore d'halophosphate de puissance ≤ 40 W à teneur en mercure supérieure à 10 mg par lampe	2020
Lampes d'éclairage ordinaire à vapeur de mercure sous haute pression	2020

Produits contenant du mercure ajouté	**Date à compter de laquelle la production, l'importation ou l'exportation du produit n'est plus autorisée (date d'abandon définitif)**
Mercure contenu dans les lampes fluorescentes à cathode froide et à électrodes externes pour affichages électroniques : a) de faible longueur (≤ 500 mm) à teneur en mercure supérieure à 3,5 mg par lampe b) de longueur moyenne (> 500 mm et ≤ 1 500 mm) à teneur en mercure supérieure à 5 mg par lampe c) de grande longueur (> 1 500 mm) à teneur en mercure supérieure à 13 mg par lampe	2020
Cosmétiques (à teneur en mercure supérieure à 1 ppm), y compris les savons et crèmes de blanchissement de la peau, mais à l'exclusion des cosmétiques pour la zone oculaire dans lesquels le mercure est utilisé comme agent de conservation pour lequel aucun substitut efficace et sans danger n'est disponible[1/]	2020
Pesticides, biocides et antiseptiques locaux	2020
Les instruments de mesure non électroniques ci-après, à l'exception de ceux incorporés dans des équipements de grande taille ou utilisés pour des mesures à haute précision, lorsqu'aucune solution de remplacement convenable sans mercure n'est disponible : a) baromètres; b) hygromètres; c) manomètres; d) thermomètres; e) sphygmomanomètres.	2020

1 Les cosmétiques, savons et crèmes qui contiennent du mercure sous forme de contaminant à l'état de traces ne sont pas visés.

Deuxième partie : Produits soumis au paragraphe 3 de l'article 4

Produits contenant du mercure ajouté	**Dispositions**
Amalgames dentaires	Les mesures qu'une Partie doit prendre pour éliminer progressivement l'utilisation d'amalgames dentaires doivent tenir compte de sa situation nationale et des orientations internationales pertinentes et comprendre deux ou plusieurs des mesures suivantes : i) Définir des objectifs nationaux de prévention des caries et de promotion de l'hygiène dentaire pour réduire autant que possible le besoin de restauration dentaire; ii) Définir des objectifs nationaux visant à réduire autant que possible leur utilisation; iii) Promouvoir l'utilisation de matériaux de restauration dentaire économiques et cliniquement efficaces qui ne contiennent pas de mercure; iv) Promouvoir les activités de recherche-développement axées sur des matériaux de restauration dentaire de qualité qui ne contiennent pas de mercure; v) Encourager les organisations professionnelles représentatives et les écoles de médecine dentaire à éduquer et former les professionnels du secteur dentaire et les étudiants à l'utilisation de matériaux de restauration dentaire sans mercure et à la promotion des meilleures pratiques de gestion; vi) Décourager les polices d'assurance et programmes qui privilégient les amalgames plutôt que les matériaux de restauration dentaire sans mercure; vii) Encourager les polices d'assurance et programmes qui favorisent l'utilisation de matériaux de restauration dentaire de qualité sans mercure; viii) Restreindre l'utilisation d'amalgames dentaires à leur forme encapsulée; ix) Promouvoir l'utilisation des meilleures pratiques environnementales dans les établissements de soins dentaires afin de réduire les rejets de mercure et de composés du mercure dans l'eau et le sol.

Annexe B

Procédés de fabrication dans lesquels du mercure ou des composés du mercure sont utilisés

Première partie : Procédés soumis au paragraphe 2 de l'article 5

Procédés de fabrication utilisant du mercure ou des composés du mercure	**Date d'abandon définitif**
Production de chlore alcali	2025
Production d'acétaldéhyde dans laquelle du mercure ou des composés du mercure sont utilisés comme catalyseurs	2018

Deuxième partie : Procédés soumis au paragraphe 3 de l'article 5

Procédé utilisant du mercure	Dispositions
Production de chlorure de vinyle monomère	Les mesures devant être prises par les Parties consistent, entre autres, à : i) Réduire, d'ici à 2020, l'utilisation de mercure de 50 % par unité de production par rapport à l'année 2010; ii) Promouvoir des mesures visant à réduire la dépendance à l'égard du mercure provenant de l'extraction primaire; iii) Prendre des mesures pour réduire les émissions et les rejets de mercure dans l'environnement; iv) Appuyer la recherche-développement dans le domaine des catalyseurs et procédés sans mercure; v) Ne pas permettre l'utilisation de mercure cinq ans après que la Conférence des Parties a établi l'existence de catalyseurs sans mercure techniquement et économiquement faisables basés sur des procédés existants; vi) Faire rapport à la Conférence des Parties sur les efforts déployés pour développer et/ou identifier des solutions de remplacement et éliminer l'utilisation du mercure conformément à l'article 21.
Production de méthylate ou d'éthylate de sodium ou de potassium	Les mesures devant être prises par les Parties consistent, entre autres, à : i) Réduire l'utilisation de mercure dans le but de la faire cesser le plus rapidement possible et au plus tard 10 ans après l'entrée en vigueur de la Convention; ii) Réduire, d'ici à 2020, les émissions et les rejets de 50 % par unité de production par rapport à l'année 2010; iii) Interdire l'utilisation de nouveau mercure provenant de l'extraction primaire; iv) Appuyer la recherche-développement dans le domaine des procédés sans mercure; v) Ne pas permettre l'utilisation de mercure cinq ans après que la Conférence des Parties a établi l'existence de procédés sans mercure techniquement et économiquement faisables; vi) Faire rapport à la Conférence des Parties sur les efforts déployés pour développer et/ou identifier des solutions de remplacement et éliminer l'utilisation de mercure conformément à l'article 21.

Procédé utilisant du mercure	**Dispositions**
Production de polyuréthane utilisant des catalyseurs contenant du mercure	Les mesures devant être prises par les Parties consistent, entre autres, à : i) Réduire l'utilisation de mercure dans le but de la faire cesser le plus rapidement possible et au plus tard 10 ans après l'entrée en vigueur de la Convention; ii) Réduire la dépendance à l'égard du mercure provenant de l'extraction primaire; iii) Réduire les émissions et les rejets de mercure dans l'environnement; iv) Appuyer la recherche-développement dans le domaine des catalyseurs et procédés sans mercure; v) Faire rapport à la Conférence des Parties sur les efforts déployés pour développer et/ou identifier des solutions de remplacement et éliminer l'utilisation de mercure conformément à l'article 21. Le paragraphe 6 de l'article 5 ne s'applique pas à ce procédé de fabrication.

Annexe C

Extraction minière artisanale et à petite échelle d'or

Plans d'action nationaux

1. Chaque Partie soumise aux dispositions du paragraphe 3 de l'article 7 fait figurer dans son plan d'action national :

a) Des objectifs nationaux et des objectifs de réduction;

b) Des mesures visant à éliminer :

i) L'amalgamation de minerai brut;

ii) Le brûlage à l'air libre d'amalgames ou d'amalgames transformés;

iii) Le brûlage d'amalgames dans des zones résidentielles; et

iv) La lixiviation au cyanure de sédiments, minerais et résidus auxquels du mercure a été ajouté, sans en avoir au préalable retiré ce dernier;

c) Des mesures pour faciliter la formalisation ou la réglementation du secteur de l'extraction minière artisanale et à petite échelle d'or;

d) Des estimations initiales des quantités de mercure et des pratiques utilisées sur son territoire dans le secteur de l'extraction minière et de la transformation artisanales et à petite échelle d'or;

e) Des stratégies pour promouvoir la réduction des émissions et rejets de mercure et de l'exposition à cette substance dans le secteur de l'extraction minière et de la transformation artisanales et à petite échelle d'or et, en particulier, des méthodes ne faisant pas appel au mercure;

f) Des stratégies visant à gérer les échanges commerciaux et à empêcher le détournement de mercure et composés du mercure provenant de sources étrangères et nationales destinés à être utilisés pour l'extraction minière et la transformation artisanales et à petite échelle d'or;

g) Des stratégies visant à impliquer les parties prenantes dans la mise en œuvre et l'amélioration continue du plan d'action national;

h) Une stratégie de santé publique relative à l'exposition des mineurs travaillant dans l'extraction aurifère artisanale et à petite échelle et de leurs communautés au mercure. Une telle stratégie devrait prévoir, entre autres, la collecte de données sanitaires, la formation du personnel des services de santé et la sensibilisation par l'intermédiaire des établissements de santé;

i) Des stratégies visant à prévenir l'exposition des populations vulnérables, notamment les enfants et les femmes en âge de procréer, en particulier les femmes enceintes, au mercure utilisé dans l'extraction minière artisanale et à petite échelle d'or;

j) Des stratégies pour informer les mineurs travaillant dans l'extraction aurifère artisanale et à petite échelle et les communautés touchées; et

k) Un calendrier pour la mise en œuvre du plan d'action national.

2. Chaque Partie peut faire figurer dans son plan d'action national des stratégies supplémentaires pour atteindre ses objectifs comme, par exemple, l'utilisation ou l'introduction de normes relatives à l'extraction minière artisanale et à petite échelle d'or par des procédés ne faisant pas appel au mercure et de mécanismes reposant sur le marché ou d'outils de marketing.

Annexe D

Liste des sources ponctuelles d'émissions atmosphériques de mercure et de composés du mercure

Catégorie de sources ponctuelles :

Centrales électriques alimentées au charbon;

Chaudières industrielles alimentées au charbon;

Procédés de fusion et de grillage utilisés dans la production de métaux non ferreux[1/];

Installations d'incinération de déchets;

Installations de production de clinker de ciment.

[1/] Aux fins de la présente Annexe, on entend par « métaux non ferreux » le plomb, le zinc, le cuivre et l'or industriel.

Annexe E

Procédures d'arbitrage et de conciliation

Première partie : Procédure d'arbitrage

Aux fins de l'alinéa a) du paragraphe 2 de l'article 25 de la présente Convention, la procédure d'arbitrage est la suivante :

Article premier

1. Toute Partie peut prendre l'initiative de recourir à l'arbitrage, conformément à l'article 25 de la présente Convention, par notification écrite adressée à l'autre partie ou aux autres parties au différend. Une telle notification est accompagnée de l'exposé des conclusions, ainsi que de toutes pièces justificatives, et indique l'objet de l'arbitrage, notamment les articles de la présente Convention dont l'interprétation ou l'application font l'objet du litige.

2. La partie requérante notifie au Secrétariat qu'elle renvoie un différend à l'arbitrage conformément à l'article 25 de la présente Convention. La notification est accompagnée de la notification écrite de la partie requérante, de l'exposé des conclusions et des pièces justificatives visés au paragraphe 1 ci-dessus. Le Secrétariat communique les informations ainsi reçues à toutes les Parties.

Article 2

1. Si un différend est renvoyé à l'arbitrage conformément à l'article premier ci dessus, un tribunal arbitral composé de trois membres est institué.

2. Chaque partie au différend nomme un arbitre et les deux arbitres ainsi nommés désignent d'un commun accord le troisième arbitre, qui exerce la présidence du tribunal. En cas de différends entre plus de deux parties, les parties qui font cause commune nomment un arbitre d'un commun accord. Le Président du tribunal ne doit pas être ressortissant de l'une des parties au différend, ni avoir sa résidence habituelle sur le territoire de l'une de ces parties, ni se trouver au service de l'une d'elles, ni s'être déjà occupé de l'affaire à un autre titre.

3. Il est pourvu à tout siège vacant de la manière prévue pour la nomination initiale.

Article 3

1. Si, dans un délai de deux mois après la date de réception de la notification d'arbitrage par la partie défenderesse, l'une des parties au différend ne procède pas à la nomination d'un arbitre, l'autre partie peut saisir le Secrétaire général de l'Organisation des Nations Unies, qui procède à cette désignation dans un nouveau délai de deux mois.

2. Si, dans un délai de deux mois après la nomination du deuxième arbitre, le Président du tribunal arbitral n'est pas désigné, le Secrétaire général de l'Organisation des Nations Unies procède, à la requête d'une partie, à sa désignation dans un nouveau délai de deux mois.

Article 4

Le tribunal arbitral rend ses décisions conformément aux dispositions de la présente Convention et au droit international.

Article 5

Sauf si les parties au différend en conviennent autrement, le tribunal arbitral établit ses propres règles de procédure.

Article 6

À la demande de l'une des parties au différend, le tribunal arbitral peut recommander les mesures conservatoires indispensables.

Article 7

Les parties au différend facilitent le déroulement des travaux du tribunal arbitral et, en particulier, utilisent tous les moyens à leur disposition pour :

a) Fournir au tribunal tous les documents, renseignements et facilités nécessaires; et

b) Permettre au tribunal, en cas de besoin, de citer des témoins ou des experts et d'enregistrer leur déposition.

Article 8

Les parties au différend et les arbitres sont tenus de protéger la confidentialité de tout renseignement ou document qu'ils obtiennent à titre confidentiel au cours de la procédure du tribunal arbitral.

Article 9

À moins que le tribunal arbitral n'en décide autrement en raison des circonstances particulières de l'affaire, les frais du tribunal sont supportés à parts égales par les parties au différend. Le tribunal tient un relevé de tous ses frais et en fournit un état final aux parties.

Article 10

Toute Partie ayant, en ce qui concerne l'objet du différend, un intérêt d'ordre juridique susceptible d'être affecté par la décision peut intervenir dans la procédure avec le consentement du tribunal arbitral.

Article 11

Le tribunal arbitral peut instruire et trancher les demandes reconventionnelles directement liées à l'objet du différend.

Article 12

Les décisions du tribunal arbitral, tant sur la procédure que sur le fond, sont prises à la majorité des voix de ses membres.

Article 13

1. Si l'une des parties au différend ne se présente pas devant le tribunal arbitral ou ne fait pas valoir ses moyens, l'autre partie peut demander au tribunal de poursuivre la procédure et de rendre sa sentence. L'absence d'une partie ou le fait pour une partie de ne pas faire valoir ses moyens ne fait pas obstacle au déroulement de la procédure.

2. Avant de prononcer sa sentence définitive, le tribunal arbitral doit s'assurer que la demande est fondée en fait et en droit.

Article 14

Le tribunal arbitral prononce sa sentence définitive au plus tard cinq mois après la date à laquelle il a été créé, à moins qu'il estime nécessaire de prolonger ce délai d'une durée qui ne devrait pas excéder cinq mois.

Article 15

La sentence définitive du tribunal arbitral est limitée à l'objet du différend et est motivée. Elle contient le nom des membres qui y ont pris part et la date à laquelle elle a été prononcée. Tout membre du tribunal peut joindre à la sentence l'exposé de son opinion individuelle ou dissidente.

Article 16

La sentence définitive lie les parties au différend. L'interprétation qui est faite de la présente Convention dans la sentence définitive lie également toute Partie intervenant conformément à l'article 10 dans la mesure où elle a trait à des questions au sujet desquelles cette Partie est intervenue. La sentence définitive est sans appel, à moins que les parties au différend ne soient convenues à l'avance d'une procédure d'appel.

Article 17

Tout désaccord pouvant surgir entre les parties liées par la sentence définitive en application de l'article 16 concernant l'interprétation ou la mise en œuvre de cette sentence peut être soumis par l'une ou l'autre de ces parties à la décision du tribunal arbitral qui a prononcé la sentence.

Deuxième partie : Procédure de conciliation

Aux fins du paragraphe 6 de l'article 25 de la présente Convention, la procédure de conciliation est la suivante :

Article premier

Toute demande d'une partie à un différend visant à créer une commission de conciliation en application du paragraphe 6 de l'article 25 de la présente Convention est adressée par écrit au Secrétariat avec copie à l'autre partie ou aux autres parties au différend. Le Secrétariat en informe immédiatement toutes les Parties.

Article 2

1. La commission de conciliation se compose, à moins que les parties au différend n'en conviennent autrement, de trois membres, chaque partie concernée en nommant un et le Président étant choisi conjointement par les membres ainsi nommés.

2. En cas de différend entre plus de deux parties, les parties faisant cause commune nomment leur membre de la commission d'un commun accord.

Article 3

Si, dans un délai de deux mois après la date de réception par le Secrétariat de la demande écrite visée à l'article premier ci dessus, tous les membres n'ont pas été nommés par les parties au différend, le Secrétaire général de l'Organisation des Nations Unies procède, à la requête d'une partie quelconque, aux nominations nécessaires dans un nouveau délai de deux mois.

Article 4

Si, dans un délai de deux mois après la nomination du deuxième membre de la commission, le Président de celle-ci n'a pas été choisi, le Secrétaire général de l'Organisation des Nations Unies procède, à la requête d'une partie au différend, à sa désignation dans un nouveau délai de deux mois.

Article 5

La commission de conciliation aide les parties au différend, de façon indépendante et impartiale, à parvenir à un règlement à l'amiable.

Article 6

1. La commission de conciliation peut mener la procédure de la manière qu'elle juge appropriée, compte pleinement tenu des circonstances de l'affaire et des vues éventuellement exprimées par les parties au différend, notamment de toute demande visant à obtenir un règlement rapide du différend. Elle peut adopter son propre règlement intérieur, si nécessaire, à moins que les parties n'en conviennent autrement.

2. La commission de conciliation peut, à tout moment de la procédure, faire des propositions ou des recommandations en vue d'un règlement du différend.

Article 7

Les parties au différend coopèrent avec la commission de conciliation. Elles s'efforcent, en particulier, de satisfaire à ses demandes concernant la présentation de documents écrits et d'éléments de preuve et la participation aux réunions. Les parties au différend et les membres de la commission de conciliation sont tenus de protéger la confidentialité de tout renseignement ou document qu'ils obtiennent à titre confidentiel au cours de la procédure de conciliation.

Article 8

La commission de conciliation prend ses décisions à la majorité des voix de ses membres.

Article 9

À moins que le différend n'ait déjà été résolu, la commission de conciliation présente, au plus tard douze mois après sa création, un rapport contenant ses recommandations pour le règlement du différend, que les parties au différend examinent de bonne foi.

Article 10

En cas de désaccord au sujet de la compétence de la commission de conciliation pour examiner une question dont elle est saisie, celle-ci décide si elle est ou non compétente.

Article 11

Les frais de la commission de conciliation sont supportés par les parties au différend à parts égales, à moins qu'elles n'en conviennent autrement. La commission tient un relevé de tous ses frais et en fournit un état final aux parties.

[TEXT IN RUSSIAN – TEXTE EN RUSSE]

МИНАМАТСКАЯ КОНВЕНЦИЯ О РТУТИ

Стороны настоящей Конвенции,

признавая, что ртуть является химическим веществом, вызывающим обеспокоенность в глобальном масштабе вследствие ее переноса в атмосфере на большие расстояния, ее стойкости в окружающей среде после попадания в нее в результате антропогенной деятельности, ее способности к биоаккумуляции в экосистемах, а также вследствие обусловленных ее воздействием значительных негативных последствий для здоровья человека и окружающей среды,

ссылаясь на решение 25/5 Совета управляющих Программы Организации Объединенных Наций по окружающей среде от 20 февраля 2009 года о том, чтобы инициировать международные меры по регулированию ртути эффективным, действенным и последовательным образом,

ссылаясь на пункт 221 итогового документа Конференции Организации Объединенных Наций по устойчивому развитию «Будущее, которого мы хотим», в котором содержится призыв к успешному завершению переговоров по имеющему обязательную юридическую силу глобальному документу по ртути в целях устранения рисков для здоровья человека и окружающей среды,

ссылаясь на то, что Конференция Организации Объединенных Наций по устойчивому развитию подтвердила принципы Рио-де-Жанейрской декларации по окружающей среде и развитию, включая в том числе принцип общей, но дифференцированной ответственности, и признавая соответствующие условия и возможности государств и необходимость действий в глобальном масштабе,

осознавая риски для здоровья, особенно в развивающихся странах, являющиеся результатом воздействия ртути на уязвимые группы населения, особенно на женщин, детей и, через них, на будущие поколения,

отмечая, что экосистемы и коренные общины Арктики являются особенно уязвимыми вследствие биомагнификации ртути и заражения традиционных продуктов питания, и будучи озабочены последствиями воздействия ртути на коренные общины в целом,

принимая во внимание существенные уроки болезни Минамата, в частности, серьезные последствия загрязнения ртутью для здоровья человека и окружающей среды, и необходимость обеспечить надлежащее регулирование ртути и предотвратить повторение подобного в будущем, *подчеркивая* важное значение финансовой, технической, технологической поддержки и поддержки в создании потенциала, в частности, в случае развивающихся стран и стран с переходной экономикой, в целях расширения их национальных возможностей в области регулирования ртути и содействия эффективному осуществлению Конвенции,

признавая также связанную с ртутью деятельность Всемирной организации здравоохранения по охране здоровья человека и роль соответствующих многосторонних природоохранных соглашений, особенно Базельской конвенции о контроле за трансграничной перевозкой опасных отходов и их удалением и Роттердамской конвенции о процедуре предварительного обоснованного согласия в отношении отдельных опасных химических веществ и пестицидов в международной торговле,

признавая, что настоящая Конвенция и другие международные соглашения в области окружающей среды и торговли носят взаимодополняющий характер,

подчеркивая, что ничто в настоящей Конвенции не преследует цель повлиять на права и обязательства любой Стороны, вытекающие из любого действующего международного соглашения,

осознавая, что вышеизложенное констатирующее положение не имеет целью установление иерархии между настоящей Конвенцией и другими международными документами,

отмечая, что ничто в настоящей Конвенции не препятствует принятию любой Стороной дополнительных внутренних мер, согласующихся с положениями настоящей Конвенции, в рамках усилий по охране здоровья человека и окружающей среды от воздействия ртути в соответствии с другими обязательствами Сторон согласно применимому международному праву,

договорились о нижеследующем:

Статья 1
Цель

Цель настоящей Конвенции заключается в охране здоровья человека и окружающей среды от антропогенных выбросов и высвобождений ртути и ее соединений.

Статья 2
Определения

Для целей настоящей Конвенции:

a) «кустарная и мелкомасштабная золотодобыча» означает добычу золота, которая осуществляется отдельными старателями или небольшими предприятиями при ограниченных капитальных инвестициях и в ограниченных объемах;

b) «наилучшие имеющиеся методы» означает наиболее эффективные методы предотвращения и, если это не представляется практически возможным, сокращения выбросов и высвобождений ртути в атмосферу, в воды и на землю и их воздействия на окружающую среду в целом с учетом экономических и технических обстоятельств в данной Стороне или на данном объекте на ее территории. В этом контексте:

i) «наилучшие» означает наиболее эффективные для достижения высокого общего уровня охраны окружающей среды в целом;

ii) «имеющиеся» означает в отношении данной Стороны и данного объекта на ее территории методы, разработанные в таких масштабах, которые позволяют применять их в соответствующем секторе промышленности на экономически и технически осуществимых условиях с учетом затрат и выгод, независимо от того, используются ли и разрабатываются ли такие методы в пределах территории рассматриваемой Стороны, при условии, что они доступны для оператора объекта, как это определено данной Стороной; и

iii) «методы» означает применяемые технологии, оперативные методы работы и способы проектирования, сооружения, обслуживания и функционирования установок и вывода их из эксплуатации;

c) «наилучшие виды природоохранной деятельности» означает применение наиболее целесообразного сочетания мер и стратегий экологического контроля;

d) «ртуть» означает элементарную ртуть (Hg(0), КАС № 7439-97-6);

e) «ртутные соединения» означает любое вещество, состоящее из атомов ртути и еще одного или более чем одного атома других химических элементов, которые могут быть разделены на различные компоненты только с помощью химических реакций;

f) «продукт с добавлением ртути» означает продукт или компонент продукта, которые содержат ртуть или ртутное соединение, намеренно добавленные в них;

g) «Сторона» означает государство или региональную организацию экономической интеграции, которые дали свое согласие быть связанными обязательствами по настоящей Конвенции и для которых эта Конвенция вступила в силу;

h) «Стороны, присутствующие и участвующие в голосовании» означает Стороны, присутствующие и голосующие «за» или «против» на совещании Сторон;

i) «первичная добыча ртути» означает добычу, при которой основным добываемым материалом является ртуть;

j) «региональная организация экономической интеграции» означает организацию, созданную суверенными государствами какого-либо региона, которой ее государствами-членами поручено заниматься вопросами, регулируемыми настоящей Конвенцией, и которая должным образом уполномочена в соответствии со своими внутренними процедурами подписать, ратифицировать, принять или одобрить настоящую Конвенцию или присоединиться к ней; и

k) «разрешенный вид использования» означает любой вид использования какой-либо Стороной ртути или ртутных соединений, соответствующий настоящей Конвенции, включая виды использования, соответствующие статьям 3, 4, 5, 6 и 7, но не ограничиваясь ими.

Статья 3
Источники поставок ртути и торговля ею

1. Для целей настоящей статьи:

a) ссылки на «ртуть» включают смеси ртути с другими веществами, в том числе сплавы ртути с концентрацией ртути как минимум в 95 весовых процентов;

b) «ртутные соединения» означает хлорид ртути (I) (также известный как каломель), оксид ртути (II), сульфат ртути (II), нитрат ртути (II), киноварь и сульфид ртути.

2. Положения настоящей статьи не применяются к:

a) объемам ртути и ртутных соединений, подлежащих использованию в исследованиях лабораторного масштаба или в качестве эталонного стандарта;

b) естественным следовым количествам ртути или ртутных соединений, присутствующим в таких продуктах, как нертутные металлы, руды или минеральные продукты, включая уголь, или продукты, получаемые из этих материалов, и непреднамеренные следовые количества в химических продуктах; или

c) продуктам с добавлением ртути.

3. Ни одна Сторона не разрешает первичную добычу ртути, если она не велась на ее территории на дату вступления в силу настоящей Конвенции для этой Стороны.

4. Каждая Сторона разрешает первичную добычу ртути, только если она велась на ее территории на дату вступления в силу настоящей Конвенции для этой Стороны, на период до пятнадцати лет после этой даты. В течение этого периода ртуть, полученная в ходе такой добычи, используется исключительно в производстве продуктов с добавлением ртути в соответствии со статьей 4, в производственных процессах в соответствии со статьей 5 или удаляется в соответствии со статьей 11 с применением операций, которые не ведут к рекуперации, рециркуляции, утилизации, прямому повторному или альтернативному использованию.

5. Каждая Сторона:

a) предпринимает шаги для выявления отдельных запасов ртути или ртутных соединений в объеме свыше 50 метрических тонн, а также источников поставок ртути, обеспечивающих создание запасов ртути в объеме свыше 10 метрических тонн в год, которые находятся на ее территории;

b) принимает меры для обеспечения того, чтобы в тех случаях, когда данная Сторона устанавливает наличие избыточного количества ртути в результате вывода из эксплуатации установок для хлорно-щелочного производства, эта ртуть удалялась в соответствии с руководящими принципами экологически обоснованного регулирования, указанными в пункте 3(a) статьи 11, с применением операций, которые не ведут к рекуперации, рециркуляции, утилизации, прямому повторному или альтернативному использованию.

6. Ни одна Сторона не разрешает экспорт ртути, кроме как:

a) в Сторону, предоставившую экспортирующей Стороне свое письменное согласие, и только для целей;

i) вида использования, разрешенного импортирующей Стороне в соответствии с настоящей Конвенцией; или

ii) экологически безопасного временного хранения, как это предусмотрено в статье 10; или

b) в государство, не являющееся Стороной, предоставившее экспортирующей Стороне свое письменное согласие, включая подтверждение того, что:

i) данное государство, не являющееся Стороной, приняло меры для обеспечения охраны здоровья человека и окружающей среды и для обеспечения соблюдения ею положений статей 10 и 11; и

ii) эта ртуть будет применяться только для вида использования, разрешенного Стороне в соответствии с настоящей Конвенцией, или для экологически безопасного временного хранения, как это предусмотрено в статье 10.

7. Экспортирующая Сторона может рассматривать общее уведомление, направленное импортирующей Стороной или государством, не являющимся Стороной, секретариату, в качестве письменного согласия, требуемого в соответствии с пунктом 6. В этом общем уведомлении указываются любые условия, на которых импортирующая Сторона или государство, не являющееся Стороной, дает свое согласие. Данное уведомление может быть в любой момент отозвано импортирующей Стороной или государством, не являющимся Стороной. Секретариат ведет открытый реестр всех таких уведомлений.

8. Ни одна Сторона не разрешает импорт ртути из государства, не являющегося Стороной, которому она предоставит свое письменное согласие, за исключением тех случаев, когда данное государство, не являющееся Стороной, предоставило подтверждение того, что эта ртуть получена не из источников, указанных в пункте 3 или пункте 5(b) как неразрешенные.

9. Сторона, представляющая общее уведомление о согласии в соответствии с пунктом 7, может принять решение о неприменении пункта 8, если она применяет всеобъемлющие ограничения экспорта ртути и ввела внутренние меры, обеспечивающие экологически безопасное регулирование импортируемой ртути. Такая Сторона направляет уведомление о та-

ком решении секретариату, включив в него информацию с описанием ее экспортных ограничений и внутренних мер регулирования, а также информацию о количествах и странах происхождения ртути, импортируемой из государств, не являющихся Сторонами. Секретариат ведет открытый реестр всех таких уведомлений. Комитет по осуществлению и соблюдению рассматривает и оценивает любые такие уведомления и вспомогательную информацию в соответствии со статьей 15 и может, если это целесообразно, выносить рекомендации Конференции Сторон.

10. Процедура, изложенная в пункте 9, может применяться вплоть до завершения второго совещания Конференции Сторон. После этого она применяться не может, если только Конференция Сторон не примет иного решения простым большинством присутствующих и участвующих в голосовании Сторон, исключая любую Сторону, предоставившую уведомление в соответствии с пунктом 9 до завершения второго совещания Конференции Сторон.

11. Каждая Сторона включает в свою отчетность, представляемую в соответствии со статьей 21, информацию о выполнении требований настоящей статьи.

12. Конференция Сторон на своем первом совещании предоставляет дополнительные указания в отношении настоящей статьи, особенно в отношении пунктов 5(a), 6 и 8, и разрабатывает и принимает требования в отношении содержания уведомления, о котором говорится в пунктах 6(b) и 8.

13. Конференция Сторон проводит оценку того, не противоречит ли цели настоящей Конвенции торговля конкретными ртутными соединениями, и рассматривает вопрос о том, не следует ли распространить действие пунктов 6 и 8 на конкретные ртутные соединения путем их включения в перечень дополнительного приложения, принятого в соответствии со статьей 27.

Статья 4
Продукты с добавлением ртути

1. Ни одна Сторона не разрешает посредством принятия соответствующих мер производство, импорт или экспорт продуктов с добавлением ртути, перечисленных в части I приложения A, после наступления предусмотренного для этих продуктов срока поэтапного вывода из обращения, кроме случаев, когда в приложении A предусмотрено исключение, или случаев наличия у Стороны зарегистрированного исключения в соответствии со статьей 6.

2. Сторона может в качестве альтернативы пункту 1 во время ратификации или при вступлении для нее в силу поправки к приложению А указать, что она будет реализовывать различные мероприятия или стратегии в отношении продуктов, перечисленных в части I приложения А. Сторона может воспользоваться такой альтернативой только в том случае, если она в состоянии подтвердить, что она уже сократила до минимального уровня объемы производства, импорта и экспорта подавляющего большинства продуктов, перечисленных в части I приложения А, и что она реализовывает мероприятия и стратегии, направленные на сокращение использования ртути в дополнительных продуктах, не перечисленных в части I приложения А, на момент ее уведомления секретариата о своем решении воспользоваться данной альтернативой. Кроме того, Сторона, решившая воспользоваться данной альтернативой:

a) сообщает при первой возможности Конференции Сторон описание реализуемых мероприятий или стратегий, в том числе данные о количественных показателях достигнутых сокращений;

b) реализует мероприятия или стратегии, направленные на сокращение использования ртути в любых продуктах, перечисленных в части I приложения А, в отношении которых минимальный уровень еще не достигнут;

c) рассматривает дополнительные меры по достижению дальнейших сокращений; и

d) не обладает правом обращаться с просьбой о предоставлении исключений в соответствии со статьей 6 для любой категории продуктов, в отношении которой избрана данная альтернатива.

Не позднее чем через пять лет после даты вступления Конвенции в силу, Конференция Сторон в рамках процесса обзора согласно пункту 8 рассматривает прогресс и эффективность мер, принятых в соответствии с настоящим пунктом.

3. Каждая Сторона принимает меры в отношении продуктов с добавлением ртути, перечисленных в части II приложения А, в соответствии с изложенными в ней положениями.

4. На основании представленной Сторонами информации секретариат собирает и хранит информацию о продуктах с добавлением ртути и альтернативах им и обеспечивает общедоступность такой информации. Секретариат также делает общедоступной любую иную соответствующую информацию, представленную Сторонами.

5. Каждая Сторона принимает меры для предотвращения включения в составные продукты продуктов с добавлением ртути, производство, импорт или экспорт которых не разрешены для нее в соответствии с настоящей статьей.

6. Каждая Сторона противодействует производству и распределению через систему торговли продуктов с добавлением ртути, не охватываемых ни одним известным видом использования продуктов с добавлением ртути, до даты вступления для нее в силу Конвенции, если только оценка рисков и преимуществ данного продукта не свидетельствует о пользе для окружающей среды или здоровья человека. Сторона представляет в секретариат, если это целесообразно, информацию о любом таком продукте, включая любую информацию о рисках и пользе воздействия этого продукта на окружающую среду и здоровье человека. Эта информация делается секретариатом общедоступной.

7. Любая Сторона может представить в секретариат предложение о включении продукта с добавлением ртути в приложение А с указанием информации о наличии, технической и экономической обоснованности безртутных альтернатив продукту и обусловленных этими альтернативами рисках и выгодах для окружающей среды и здоровья человека, с учетом информации в соответствии с пунктом 4.

8. Не позднее чем через пять лет с даты вступления Конвенции в силу Конференция Сторон проводит обзор приложения А и может рассмотреть поправки к нему в соответствии со статьей 27.

9. При проведении обзора приложения А в соответствии с пунктом 8 Конференция Сторон учитывает как минимум:

a) любое предложение, представляемое в соответствии с пунктом 7;

b) информацию, представленную в соответствии с пунктом 4; и

c) наличие для Сторон безртутных альтернатив, которые являются технически и экономически осуществимыми, с учетом рисков и пользы воздействия на окружающую среду и здоровье человека.

Статья 5
Производственные процессы, в которых применяются ртуть или ртутные соединения

1. Для целей настоящей статьи и приложения В производственные процессы, в которых применяются ртуть или ртутные соединения, не включают процессы, в которых используются продукты с добавлением ртути, процессы производства продуктов с добавлением ртути или процессы по переработке содержащих ртуть отходов.

2. Ни одна Сторона не разрешает путем принятия надлежащих мер применение ртути или ртутных соединений в производственных процессах, перечисленных в части I приложения В, после наступления срока поэтапного вывода из обращения, указанного в этом приложении для отдельного процесса, кроме случаев, когда у Стороны имеется зарегистрированное исключение, как это предусмотрено в статье 6.

3. Каждая Сторона принимает меры для ограничения применения ртути или ртутных соединений в процессах, перечисленных в части II приложения В, в соответствии с изложенными в нем положениями.

4. На основании представленной Сторонами информации секретариат собирает и хранит информацию о процессах, в которых используются ртуть или ртутные соединения, и альтернативах им, и обеспечивает общедоступность такой информации. Иная соответствующая информация может также направляться Сторонами и предоставляться секретариатом для общего пользования.

5. Каждая Сторона, располагающая одним или более объектом, где ртуть или ртутные соединения применяются в производственных процессах, перечисленных в приложении В:

a) принимает меры для решения вопроса выбросов и высвобождений ртути или ртутных соединений с этих объектов;

b) включает в свою отчетность, представляемую в соответствии со статьей 21, информацию о мерах, принятых в рамках настоящего пункта; и

c) принимает меры для определения на своей территории объектов, где ртуть или ртутные соединения применяются в производственных процессах, перечисленных в приложении В, и не позднее чем через три года после даты вступления для нее в силу настоящей Конвенции представляет в секретариат информацию о количестве и видах таких объектов, в том числе расчетный ежегодный объем потребляемой ими ртути или ртутных соединений. Эта информация делается секретариатом общедоступной.

6. Ни одна Сторона не разрешает использование ртути или ртутных соединений на объектах, которые не существовали до даты вступления в силу настоящей Конвенции для этой Стороны, использующих производственные процессы, перечисленные в приложении В. В отношении таких объектов исключения не применяются.

7. Каждая Сторона противодействует созданию любого объекта, использующего любой иной производственный процесс, при котором намеренно используются ртуть или ртутные соединения, если он не существовал до даты вступления в силу Конвенции, кроме случаев, когда Сторона может убедительно доказать Конференции Сторон, что этот производственный процесс обеспечивает существенную пользу для окружающей среды и здоровья человека и что технически и экономически возможные безртутные альтернативы, обеспечивающие такую пользу, отсутствуют.

8. Сторонам рекомендуется обмениваться информацией, касающейся соответствующих технологических новшеств, экономически и технически осуществимых безртутных альтернатив и возможных мер и методов для сокращения и, где это возможно, исключения применения ртути и ртутных соединений в производственных процессах, перечисленных в приложении В, а также выбросов и высвобождений ртути и ртутных соединений в результате этих производственных процессов.

9. Любая Сторона может представить предложение о внесении поправок в приложение В с целью включения в него производственных процессов, в которых используется ртуть или ртутные соединения. В нем указывается информация о наличии, технической и экономической обоснованности безртутных альтернатив этим процессам, и обусловленных этими альтернативами рисках и выгодах для окружающей среды и здоровья человека.

10. Не позднее чем через пять лет после даты вступления в силу Конвенции Конференция Сторон проводит обзор приложения В и может рассмотреть поправки к нему в соответствии со статьей 27.

11. При любом рассмотрении приложения В в соответствии с пунктом 10 Конференция Сторон учитывает как минимум:

a) любое предложение, представляемое в соответствии с пунктом 9;

b) информацию, являющуюся доступной в соответствии с пунктом 4; и

c) наличие для Сторон безртутных альтернатив, которые являются технически и экономически осуществимыми, с учетом рисков и пользы для окружающей среды и здоровья человека.

Статья 6
Исключения, предоставляемые Стороне по запросу

1. Любое государство или региональная организация экономической интеграции могут зарегистрировать одно или несколько исключений в отношении сроков поэтапного вывода из обращения, указанных в приложении А и приложении В, далее именуемых «исключение», путем письменного уведомления секретариата:

a) став Стороной настоящей Конвенции; или

b) если какой-либо продукт с добавлением ртути дополнительно включается на основании поправки в приложение А или какой-либо производственный процесс, в котором используется ртуть, дополнительно включается на основании поправки в приложение В не позднее даты вступления в силу для этой Стороны применимой поправки.

Регистрация любого исключения должна сопровождаться заявлением, в котором будет обоснована необходимость исключения для этой Стороны.

2. Исключение может регистрироваться либо по категориям, перечисленным в приложении А или В, либо по подкатегориям, определяемым любым государством или региональной организацией экономической интеграции.

3. Каждая Сторона, которая обладает исключением или исключениями, указывается в реестре. Секретариат формирует и ведет реестр и предоставляет его для использования в общедоступном режиме.

4. Реестр включает в себя:

a) перечень Сторон, обладающих исключением или исключениями;

b) исключение или исключения, зарегистрированные в отношении каждой Стороны; и

c) дату истечения срока действия каждого исключения.

5. В случае если в реестре Стороной не указан более короткий срок, срок действия всех исключений в соответствии с пунктом 1 истекает че-

рез пять лет после наступления соответствующего срока поэтапного вывода из обращения, указанного в приложении А или приложении В.

6. По просьбе Стороны Конференция Сторон может принять решение о продлении срока действия исключения на пять лет, если только эта Сторона не просит о более коротком сроке. Принимая свое решение, Конференция Сторон должным образом учитывает:

a) доклад Стороны с обоснованием необходимости продления срока действия исключения и изложением осуществленных и запланированных мероприятий по максимально быстрому устранению потребности в исключении;

b) имеющуюся информацию, в том числе в отношении наличия альтернативных продуктов и процессов, которые позволяют обходиться без ртути или связаны с применением меньших количеств ртути, чем вид использования, охватываемый исключением; и

c) планируемые или осуществляемые мероприятия по обеспечению экологически безопасного хранения ртути и удаления ртутных отходов.

Срок действия исключения может продлеваться не более одного раза в отношении одного продукта и срока его поэтапного вывода из обращения.

7. Сторона может в любой момент отозвать исключение путем письменного уведомления секретариата. Отзыв исключения вступает в силу в дату, указанную в уведомлении.

8. Несмотря на положения пункта 1, никакое государство или региональная организация экономической интеграции не могут зарегистрировать исключение в отношении соответствующего продукта или процесса, включенного в приложение А или В, по истечении пяти лет после наступления срока его поэтапного вывода из обращения, если только одна или несколько Сторон не сохраняют зарегистрированное исключение в отношении данного продукта или процесса, получив продление в соответствии с пунктом 6. В этом случае государство или региональная организация экономической интеграции могут в сроки, указанные в пунктах 1(a) и (b), зарегистрировать исключение в отношении данного продукта или процесса, срок действия которого истекает через десять лет после наступления соответствующего срока поэтапного вывода из обращения.

9. Никакая Сторона ни в какое время не может иметь действующее исключение в отношении продукта или процесса, указанного в приложении А или В, через десять лет после истечения срока поэтапного вывода из обращения этого продукта или процесса.

Статья 7
Кустарная и мелкомасштабная золотодобыча

1. Меры, указанные в настоящей статье и в приложении С, применяются в отношении кустарной и мелкомасштабной добычи и обработки золота, где для извлечения золота из руды используется ртутное амальгамирование.

2. Каждая Сторона, на территории которой осуществляются кустарная и мелкомасштабная добыча и обработка золота, на которую распространяются положения настоящей статьи, принимает меры с целью сокращения и, где это возможно, прекращения применения ртути и ртутных соединений и образования выбросов и высвобождений ртути в окружающую среду при такой добыче и обработке.

3. Если в любой момент времени Сторона определяет, что кустарная и мелкомасштабная добыча и обработка золота на ее территории выходит за рамки незначительной, она сообщает об этом секретариату. Если Стороной будет это определено, она:

a) разрабатывает и осуществляет национальный план действий в соответствии с приложением С;

b) представляет свой национальный план действий секретариату не позднее чем через три года после вступления для нее в силу Конвенции или через три года после направления уведомления секретариату, в зависимости от того, что происходит позднее; и

c) впоследствии каждые три года проводит обзор хода выполнения своих обязательств в соответствии с настоящей статьей и включает такие обзоры в свою отчетность, представляемую в соответствии со статьей 21.

4. Стороны могут сотрудничать друг с другом и, если это целесообразно, с соответствующими межправительственными организациями и другими учреждениями для достижения целей настоящей статьи. Такое сотрудничество может включать:

a) разработку стратегий предотвращения перенаправления ртути или ртутных соединений для использования в кустарной и мелкомасштабной добыче и обработке золота;

b) инициативы по учебной подготовке, информационно-просветительской деятельности и созданию потенциала;

c) содействие научным исследованиям в области устойчивых альтернативных видов деятельности, не предполагающих применения ртути;

d) оказание технической и финансовой помощи;

e) партнерства для оказания содействия в выполнении их обязательств в соответствии с настоящей статьей; и

f) использование существующих механизмов обмена информацией с целью распространения знаний, наилучших видов природоохранной деятельности и альтернативных технологий, приемлемых с экологической, технической, социальной и экономической точек зрения.

Статья 8
Выбросы

1. Настоящая статья касается контроля и, где это осуществимо, сокращения выбросов ртути и ртутных соединений, обычно обозначаемых как «суммарный объем ртути», в атмосферу с помощью мер контроля выбросов из точечных источников, относящихся к категориям источников, перечисленным в приложении D.

2. Для целей настоящей статьи:

a) «выбросы» означает выбросы ртути или ртутных соединений в атмосферу;

b) «соответствующий источник» означает источник, относящийся к одной из категорий источников, перечисленных в приложении D. Стороной, по ее выбору, могут быть установлены критерии для определения источников, относящихся к категории источников, перечисленных в приложении D, если эти критерии по любой категории распространяются по крайней мере на 75 процентов выбросов для этой категории;

c) «новый источник» означает любой соответствующий источник в одной из категорий, перечисленных в приложении D, строительство или существенная модификация которого начинается не ранее чем через один год после даты:

i) вступления в силу настоящей Конвенции для соответствующей Стороны; или

ii) вступления в силу для соответствующей Стороны поправки к приложению D, если действие положений настоящей Конвенции начинает распространяться на источник лишь в силу этой поправки;

d) «существенная модификация» означает изменение соответствующего источника, приводящее к значительному увеличению выбросов, за исключением любого изменения объема выбросов в результате извлечения побочного продукта. Вопрос о том, является ли модификация существенной, решает сама Сторона;

e) «существующий источник» означает любой соответствующий источник, который не является новым источником;

f) «предельное значение выбросов» означает предел в отношении концентрации, массы или интенсивности выбросов ртути или ртутных соединений из точечного источника выбросов, обычно обозначаемых как «суммарный объем ртути»;

3. Сторона, располагающая соответствующими источниками, принимает меры по контролю выбросов и может подготовить национальный план с изложением мер, которые будут приниматься для контроля выбросов, и ожидаемых ею целевых показателей, целей и результатов. Любой план представляется Конференции Сторон в течение четырех лет после даты вступления в силу Конвенции для этой Стороны. Если Сторона разрабатывает план осуществления в соответствии со статьей 20, то она может включить в него план, подготовленный в соответствии с настоящим пунктом.

4. Применительно к своим новым источникам каждая Сторона требует использования наилучших имеющихся методов и наилучших видов природоохранной деятельности для контроля и, где это выполнимо, сокращения выбросов как только это становится осуществимым, но не позднее чем через пять лет после даты вступления в силу Конвенции для этой Стороны. Стороной могут использоваться показатели предельных значений выбросов, которые согласуются с применением наилучших имеющихся методов.

5. В отношении своих существующих источников каждая Сторона включает в любой национальный план и осуществляет одну или более из следующих мер с учетом ее национальной ситуации, экономической и технической обоснованности, а также финансовой доступности этих мер, как только это становится осуществимым, но не позднее чем через десять лет после даты вступления для нее в силу Конвенции:

a) установление количественных целевых показателей для контроля и, там, где это практически возможно, сокращения выбросов из соответствующих источников;

b) установление предельных значений выбросов для контроля и, там, где это практически возможно, сокращения выбросов из соответствующих источников;

c) использование наилучших имеющихся методов и наилучших видов природоохранной деятельности для контроля выбросов из соответствующих источников;

d) осуществление стратегии контроля одновременного воздействия нескольких загрязнителей, которая обеспечит сопутствующие выгоды для контроля выбросов ртути;

e) принятие альтернативных мер по сокращению выбросов из соответствующих источников.

6. Стороны могут применять либо одинаковые меры ко всем соответствующим существующим источникам, либо разные меры в отношении разных категорий источников. Целью этих мер, принимаемых Стороной, должно быть достижение разумного прогресса в сокращении со временем выбросов ртути.

7. Каждая Сторона формирует, как только это становится осуществимым, но не позднее чем через пять лет после даты вступления в силу для нее Конвенции, и в дальнейшем ведет кадастр выбросов из соответствующих источников.

8. Конференция Сторон принимает на своем первом совещании руководящие принципы в отношении:

a) наилучших имеющихся методов и наилучших видов природоохранной деятельности с учетом любых различий между новыми и существующими источниками, а также необходимости сведения к минимуму последствий межсредовых загрязнений; и

b) поддержки Сторон при осуществлении мер, предусмотренных в пункте 5, в частности, при определении целевых показателей и установлении предельных значений выбросов.

9. Конференция Сторон, как только это становится осуществимым, принимает руководящие принципы в отношении:

a) критериев, которые Стороны могут разработать в соответствии с пунктом 2(b);

b) методологии формирования кадастров выбросов.

10. Конференция Сторон на постоянной основе проводит обзор и при необходимости обновляет руководящие принципы, разработанные в соответствии с пунктами 8 и 9. Стороны принимают данные руководящие принципы во внимание при осуществлении соответствующих положений настоящей статьи.

11. Каждая Сторона включает в свои доклады, представляемые согласно статье 21, информацию об осуществлении ею настоящей статьи, в частности, информацию о мерах, принимаемых ею в соответствии с пунктами 4–7, и об эффективности этих мер.

Статья 9
Высвобождения

1. Настоящая статья касается контроля и, где это осуществимо, сокращения высвобождений ртути и ртутных соединений, обычно обозначаемых как «суммарный объем ртути», на землю и в воды из соответствующих точечных источников, не охватываемых другими положениями настоящей Конвенции.

2. Для целей настоящей статьи:

a) «высвобождения» означает поступление ртути или ртутных соединений на землю или в воду;

b) «соответствующий источник» означает любой значительный антропогенный точечный источник выбросов, выявленный Стороной, не охватываемый другими положениями настоящей Конвенции;

c) «новый источник» означает любой соответствующий источник, строительство или существенная модификация которого начинается не ранее чем через один год после даты вступления в силу настоящей Конвенции для соответствующей Стороны;

d) «существенная модификация» означает изменение соответствующего источника, приводящее к значительному увеличению высвобождений, за исключением любого изменения объема высвобождений в результате извлечения побочного продукта. Вопрос о том, является ли модификация существенной, решается самой Стороной;

e) «существующий источник» означает любой соответствующий источник, который не является новым источником;

f) «предельное значение высвобождений» означает предел концентрации или массы ртути или ртутных соединений, высвобождаемых из точечного источника, обычно обозначаемых как «суммарный объем ртути».

3. Каждая Сторона, не позднее чем через три года после даты вступления для нее в силу Конвенции и далее на регулярной основе, выявляет соответствующие категории точечных источников.

4. Сторона, располагающая соответствующими источниками, принимает меры по контролю высвобождений и может подготовить национальный план с изложением мер, которые будут приниматься для контроля высвобождений ртути, и ожидаемых ею целевых показателей, целей и результатов. Любой план представляется Конференции Сторон в течение четырех лет после даты вступления в силу Конвенции для этой Стороны. Если Сторона разрабатывает план осуществления согласно статье 20, то она может включить в него план, подготовленный в соответствии с настоящим пунктом.

5. В число мер входит, в зависимости от целесообразности, осуществление одного или нескольких из следующих мероприятий:

a) установление предельных значений высвобождений для контроля и, там, где это практически возможно, сокращения высвобождений из соответствующих источников;

b) использование наилучших имеющихся методов и наилучших видов природоохранной деятельности для контроля высвобождений из соответствующих источников;

c) осуществление стратегии контроля одновременного воздействия нескольких загрязнителей, которая обеспечит сопутствующие выгоды для контроля высвобождений ртути;

d) принятие альтернативных мер по сокращению высвобождений из соответствующих источников.

6. Каждая Сторона формирует, как только это становится практически возможным, но не позднее чем через пять лет после даты вступления для нее в силу Конвенции, и в дальнейшем ведет кадастр высвобождений из соответствующих источников.

7. Конференция Сторон, как только это становится практически возможным, принимает руководящие принципы в отношении:

a) наилучших имеющихся методов и наилучших видов природоохранной деятельности с учетом любых различий между новыми и существующими источниками, а также необходимости сведения к минимуму последствий межсредовых загрязнений;

b) методологии формирования кадастров высвобождений.

8. Каждая Сторона включает в свои доклады, представляемые согласно статье 21, информацию об осуществлении ею настоящей статьи, в частности, информацию о мерах, принимаемых ею в соответствии с пунктами 3–6, и об эффективности этих мер.

Статья 10
Экологически безопасное временное хранение ртути, кроме ртутных отходов

1. Настоящая статья применяется к временному хранению ртути и ртутных соединений, как они определены в статье 3, на которые не распространяется приведенное в статье 11 определение ртутных отходов.

2. Каждая Сторона принимает меры для обеспечения того, чтобы временное хранение такой ртути и ртутных соединений, предназначенных для вида использования, разрешенного Стороне в соответствии с настоящей Конвенцией, осуществлялось экологически безопасным образом с учетом любых руководящих принципов и в соответствии с любыми требованиями, принятыми в соответствии с пунктом 3.

3. Конференция Сторон принимает руководящие принципы по экологически безопасному временному хранению такой ртути и ртутных соединений с учетом любых соответствующих руководящих принципов, разработанных в соответствии с Базельской конвенцией о контроле за трансграничной перевозкой опасных отходов и их удалением, и других соответствующих руководств. Конференцией Сторон в дополнительном приложении к настоящей Конвенции могут приниматься требования в отношении временного хранения, как это предусмотрено в статье 27.

4. Стороны по мере необходимости сотрудничают друг с другом, с соответствующими межправительственными организациями и другими учреждениями в целях наращивания потенциала экологически безопасного временного хранения такой ртути и ртутных соединений.

Статья 11
Ртутные отходы

1. В отношении Сторон Базельской конвенции к отходам, охватываемым настоящей Конвенцией, применяются соответствующие определения Базельской конвенции о контроле за трансграничной перевозкой опасных

отходов и их удалением. Стороны настоящей Конвенции, не являющиеся Сторонами Базельской конвенции, используют эти определения в качестве руководства применительно к отходам, охватываемым настоящей Конвенцией.

2. Для целей настоящей Конвенции «ртутные отходы» означает вещества или предметы:

a) состоящие из ртути или ртутных соединений;

b) содержащие ртуть или ртутные соединения; или

c) загрязненные ртутью или ртутными соединениями,

в количестве, превышающем соответствующие пороговые значения, установленные Конференцией Сторон в гармоничном взаимодействии с соответствующими органами Базельской конвенции, которые удаляются, предназначены для удаления или должны быть удалены в соответствии с положениями национального законодательства или настоящей Конвенции. Данное определение не включает вскрышные и пустые породы и отвалы, образующиеся в процессе горной добычи за исключением первичной добычи ртути, если только они не содержат ртуть или ртутные соединения в количестве, превышающем пороговые значения, установленные Конференцией Сторон.

3. Каждая Сторона принимает соответствующие меры для того, чтобы ртутные отходы:

a) регулировались экологически безопасным образом с учетом руководящих принципов, разработанных в соответствии с Базельской конвенцией и в соответствии с требованиями, которые будут приняты Конференцией Сторон в дополнительном приложении, как это предусмотрено в статье 27. При разработке требований Конференция Сторон принимает во внимание положения и программы Сторон, касающиеся регулирования отходов;

b) подвергались регенерации, рециркуляции, восстановлению или непосредственному повторному использованию исключительно в рамках вида использования, разрешенного Стороне в соответствии с настоящей Конвенцией, или в целях экологически безопасного удаления в соответствии с пунктом 3(a);

c) для Сторон Базельской конвенции не перемещались через международные границы, кроме как для цели экологически безопасного удаления в соответствии с настоящей статьей и в соответствии с Базельской конвенцией. В обстоятельствах, когда положения Базельской конвенции не применяются к перемещению через национальные границы, Стороны разрешают такое перемещение только после принятия во внимание соответствующих международных норм, стандартов и руководящих принципов.

4. Конференция Сторон стремится тесно сотрудничать с соответствующими органами Базельской конвенции в области проведения обзора и при необходимости обновления руководящих принципов, указанных в пункте 3(a).

5. Сторонам рекомендуется при необходимости сотрудничать друг с другом, с соответствующими межправительственными организациями и другими учреждениями в целях развития и поддержания глобального, регионального и национального потенциала регулирования ртутных отходов экологически безопасным способом.

Статья 12
Загрязненные участки

1. Каждая Сторона прилагает усилия для разработки надлежащих стратегий по выявлению и оценке участков, загрязненных ртутью или ртутными соединениями.

2. Любые действия по снижению рисков, которые представляют собой такие участки, осуществляются экологически безопасным способом и включают, в случае целесообразности, оценку рисков для здоровья человека и окружающей среды, обусловленных содержащимися в них ртутью или ртутными соединениями.

3. Конференция Сторон принимает руководство по принципам регулирования загрязненных участков, которое может включать методы и подходы в отношении:

a) выявления участков и снятия их характеристик;

b) привлечения общественности;

c) оценки рисков для здоровья человека и окружающей среды;

d) вариантов регулирования рисков, обусловленных загрязненными участками;

e) оценки выгод и затрат; и

f) аттестации результатов.

4. Сторонам рекомендуется сотрудничать в разработке стратегий и осуществлении мероприятий по выявлению, оценке, определению приоритетности, регулированию и, при необходимости, восстановлению загрязненных участков.

Статья 13
Финансовые ресурсы и механизм финансирования

1. Каждая Сторона обязуется обеспечивать в рамках своих возможностей ресурсы в связи с теми национальными мероприятиями, которые направлены на осуществление настоящей Конвенции, в соответствии со своей национальной политикой, приоритетами, планами и программами. Такие ресурсы могут включать внутреннее финансирование в рамках соответствующей политики, стратегий развития и национальных бюджетов, а также двустороннее и многостороннее финансирование наряду с привлечением частного сектора.

2. Совокупная эффективность осуществления настоящей Конвенции Сторонами, являющимися развивающимися странами, будет связана с эффективным осуществлением настоящей статьи.

3. Многосторонним, региональным и двусторонним источникам финансовой и технической помощи, а также создания потенциала и передачи технологии рекомендуется на безотлагательной основе расширять и активизировать свою деятельность в вопросах ртути в поддержку Сторон, являющихся развивающимися странами, в осуществлении положений настоящей Конвенции, касающихся финансовых ресурсов, технической помощи и передачи технологии.

4. Стороны в своей деятельности, касающейся финансирования, в полной мере учитывают конкретные потребности и особое положение Сторон, являющихся малыми островными развивающимися государствами или наименее развитыми странами.

5. Настоящим определяется механизм для своевременного обеспечения достаточных финансовых ресурсов на предсказуемой основе. Этот механизм призван оказывать поддержку Сторонам, являющимся развивающимися странами и странами с переходной экономикой, в соблюдении ими своих обязательств в соответствии с настоящей Конвенцией.

6. В состав механизма входят:

a) Целевой фонд Фонда глобальной окружающей среды и

b) Целевая международная программа для поддержки процессов создания потенциала и оказания технической помощи.

7. Целевой фонд Фонда глобальной окружающей среды своевременно обеспечивает новые и достаточные финансовые ресурсы на предсказуемой основе для покрытия расходов по поддержке осуществления настоящей Конвенции в соответствии с решениями Конференции Сторон. Для целей настоящей Конвенции Целевой фонд Фонда глобальной окружающей среды функционирует под руководством Конференции Сторон и подотчетен ей. Конференция Сторон обеспечивает указания относительно общих стратегий, политики, программных приоритетов и правомочности доступа к финансовым ресурсам и их использования. Кроме того, Конференция Сторон обеспечивает указания относительно ориентировочного перечня категорий видов деятельности для получения поддержки от Целевого фонда Фонда глобальной окружающей среды. Целевой фонд Фонда глобальной окружающей среды предоставляет ресурсы для покрытия согласованных дополнительных издержек, связанных с получением глобальных экологических преимуществ, и согласованных полных расходов на некоторые стимулирующие мероприятия.

8. Предоставляя ресурсы на мероприятия, Целевой фонд Фонда глобальной окружающей среды должен принимать во внимание соотношение потенциального сокращения ртути в результате осуществления предлагаемого мероприятия с расходами на него.

9. Для целей настоящей Конвенции Программа, о которой говорится в пункте 6(b), функционирует под руководством Конференции Сторон и подотчетна ей. На своем первом совещании Конференция Сторон принимает решение относительно уже существующего зонтичного учреждения для Программы и обеспечивает указания для нее, в том числе относительно сроков ее деятельности. Всем Сторонам и другим соответствующим заинтересованным субъектам рекомендуется предоставлять финансовые ресурсы Программе на добровольной основе.

10. Конференция Сторон и органы, входящие в состав механизма, на первом совещании Конференции Сторон согласовывают процедуры для выполнения вышеуказанных пунктов.

11. Конференция Сторон, не позднее чем на своем третьем совещании, а далее — через регулярные промежутки времени, рассматривает уровень финансирования, руководящие указания Конференции Сторон в адрес органов, которым поручено обеспечить работоспособность механизма, учрежденного в соответствии с настоящей статьей, и их эффективность, а также их способность удовлетворять изменяющиеся потребности Сторон, являющихся развивающимися странами и странами с переходной экономикой. На основе такого рассмотрения она принимает соответствующие меры для повышения эффективности механизма.

12. Всем Сторонам в рамках имеющихся у них возможностей рекомендуется способствовать деятельности механизма. Механизм содействует привлечению ресурсов из других источников, включая частный сектор, и стремится использовать такие ресурсы на мероприятия, поддержку которым он оказывает.

Статья 14
Создание потенциала, техническое содействие и передача технологии

1. Стороны осуществляют сотрудничество с целью оказания, в пределах их соответствующих возможностей, своевременной и надлежащей помощи в создании потенциала и технического содействия Сторонам, являющимся развивающимися странами, в частности Сторонам, являющимся наименее развитыми странами или малыми островными развивающимися государствами, и Сторонам, являющимся странами с переходной экономикой, в порядке способствования им в осуществлении их обязательств в соответствии с настоящей Конвенцией.

2. Создание потенциала и техническое содействие в соответствии с пунктом 1 и статьей 13 могут осуществляться в рамках региональных, субрегиональных и национальных механизмов, включая существующие региональные и субрегиональные центры, посредством других многосторонних и двусторонних средств, а также посредством партнерств, в том числе партнерств с участием частного сектора. Следует стремиться к сотрудничеству и координации с другими многосторонними природоохранными соглашениями в области химических веществ и отходов для повышения эффективности оказания технического содействия.

3. Стороны, являющиеся развитыми странами, и другие Стороны в пределах своих возможностей развивают и облегчают при поддержке частного сектора и других соответствующих заинтересованных субъектов, когда это уместно, разработку, передачу и распространение современных экологически обоснованных альтернативных видов технологии, а также доступ к ним Сторон, являющихся развивающимися странами, в частности наименее развитыми странами и малыми островными развивающимися государствами, и Сторон, являющихся странами с переходной экономикой, в целях укрепления их потенциала эффективного осуществления настоящей Конвенции.

4. К своему второму совещанию и впоследствии на регулярной основе и с учетом представлений и докладов Сторон, в том числе предусмотренных в статье 21, и информации, представленной другими заинтересованными субъектами, Конференция Сторон:

a) рассматривает информацию о существующих инициативах и о достигнутом прогрессе в области альтернативных технологий;

b) рассматривает потребности Сторон, особенно Сторон, являющихся развивающимися странами, в альтернативных технологиях; и

c) выявляет проблемы, с которыми сталкиваются Стороны, особенно Стороны, являющиеся развивающимися странами, в области передачи технологии.

5. Конференция Сторон выносит рекомендации о путях дальнейшего укрепления работы по созданию потенциала, техническому содействию и передаче технологии в соответствии с настоящей статьей.

Статья 15
Комитет по осуществлению и соблюдению

1. Настоящим учреждается механизм, включающий Комитет в качестве вспомогательного органа Конференции Сторон, для поощрения осуществления и проведения обзора соблюдения всех положений настоящей Конвенции. Механизм, включающий Комитет, по своему характеру предполагает оказание содействия и уделяет особое внимание соответствующему национальному потенциалу и ситуации Сторон.

2. Комитет поощряет осуществление и проводит обзор соблюдения всех положений настоящей Конвенции. Комитет рассматривает как индивидуальные, так и системные вопросы осуществления и соблюдения и по мере необходимости выносит рекомендации Конференции Сторон.

3. Комитет состоит из 15 членов, назначаемых Сторонами и избираемых Конференцией Сторон с должным учетом справедливого географического представительства на основе 5 регионов Организации Объединенных Наций; первые члены Комитета избираются на первом совещании Конференции Сторон, после чего — в соответствии с правилами процедуры, утвержденными Конференцией Сторон согласно пункту 5; члены Комитета обладают компетенцией в области, связанной с настоящей Конвенцией, и отражают надлежащий баланс экспертного потенциала.

4. Комитет может рассматривать вопросы на основании:

a) письменных представлений любой Стороны в связи с ее соблюдением;

b) национальных докладов, представляемых согласно статье 21; и

c) просьб Конференции Сторон.

5. Комитет разрабатывает свои правила процедуры, которые подлежат утверждению Конференцией Сторон на ее втором совещании; Конференция Сторон может утверждать дополнительные положения круга ведения Комитета.

6. Комитет прилагает все усилия к утверждению своих рекомендаций на основе консенсуса. Если исчерпаны все средства для достижения консенсуса, а консенсус не достигнут, то в качестве последней меры такая рекомендация утверждается большинством в три четверти голосов членов, присутствующих и участвующих в голосовании, при наличии кворума в две трети членов.

Статья 16
Медико-санитарные аспекты

1. Сторонам рекомендуется:

a) содействовать разработке и осуществлению стратегий и программ для выявления и защиты населения, относящегося к группе риска, особенно уязвимых групп, включая разработку научно обоснованных руководящих принципов по охране здоровья, касающихся воздействия ртути и ртутных соединений, определение целевых заданий для сокращения воздействия ртути там, где это применимо, и просвещение общественности при участии государственной системы здравоохранения и других соответствующих секторов;

b) содействовать разработке и осуществлению научно обоснованных учебных и профилактических программ, касающихся воздействия ртути и ртутных соединений на рабочем месте;

c) содействовать оказанию надлежащих медицинских услуг для предупреждения, лечения и ухода за населением, пострадавшим от воздействия ртути и ртутных соединений; и

d) создавать и укреплять, по мере необходимости, институциональный и профессиональный медицинский потенциал для предупреждения, диагностики, лечения и мониторинга рисков для здоровья, связанных с воздействием ртути и ртутных соединений.

2. При рассмотрении связанных со здоровьем вопросов или мероприятий Конференции Сторон следует:

a) по мере необходимости консультироваться и сотрудничать с Всемирной организацией здравоохранения, Международной организацией труда и другими соответствующими межправительственными организациями; и

b) по мере необходимости содействовать сотрудничеству и обмену информацией с Всемирной организацией здравоохранения, Международной организацией труда и другими соответствующими межправительственными организациями.

Статья 17
Обмен информацией

1. Каждая Сторона содействует обмену:

a) научной, технической, экономической и правовой информацией, касающейся ртути и ртутных соединений, включая информацию токсикологического и экотоксикологического характера, а также информацию по вопросам безопасности;

b) информацией о сокращении или ликвидации производства, применения, торговли, выбросов и высвобождений ртути и ртутных соединений;

c) информацией о технически и экономически осуществимых альтернативах:

i) продуктам с добавлением ртути;

ii) производственным процессам, в которых применяются ртуть или ртутные соединения; и

iii) видам деятельности и процессам, при которых происходят выбросы или высвобождения ртути или ртутных соединений,

включая информацию о рисках для здоровья и окружающей среды и социально-экономических затратах и выгодах, связанных с такими альтернативами; и

d) эпидемиологической информацией, касающейся последствий для здоровья, связанных с воздействием ртути и ртутных соединений, в тесном сотрудничестве с Всемирной организацией здравоохранения и другими соответствующими организациями, по мере целесообразности.

2. Стороны могут обмениваться указанной в пункте 1 информацией напрямую, через секретариат или в сотрудничестве с другими соответствующими организациями, включая секретариаты существующих конвенций о химических веществах и отходах, по мере целесообразности.

3. Секретариат содействует сотрудничеству в области обмена информацией, указанной в настоящей статье, а также сотрудничеству с соответ-

ствующими организациями, включая секретариаты многосторонних природоохранных соглашений и других международных инициатив. Помимо информации от Сторон такая информация включает информацию от межправительственных и неправительственных организаций, обладающих экспертным потенциалом в области ртути, и существующих национальных и международных учреждений, обладающих таким потенциалом.

4. Каждая Сторона назначает национальный координационный центр для обмена информацией в соответствии с настоящей Конвенцией, в том числе в отношении согласия импортирующих Сторон согласно статье 3.

5. Для целей настоящей Конвенции информация, касающаяся вопросов здоровья и безопасности человека и окружающей среды, не считается конфиденциальной. Стороны, осуществляющие обмен иной информацией в соответствии с настоящей Конвенцией, обеспечивают защиту любой конфиденциальной информации на основе взаимных договоренностей.

Статья 18
Информирование, повышение осведомленности и просвещение общественности

1. Каждая Сторона в рамках своих возможностей содействует и способствует:

a) предоставлению общественности имеющейся информации о:

i) воздействии ртути и ртутных соединений на здоровье человека и окружающую среду;

ii) альтернативах ртути и ртутным соединениям;

iii) темах, определенных в пункте 1 статьи 17;

iv) результатах своей деятельности в области научных исследований, разработок и мониторинга в соответствии со статьей 19; и

v) деятельности по выполнению своих обязательств по настоящей Конвенции;

b) просвещению, обучению и обеспечению осведомленности населения о последствиях воздействия ртути и ртутных соединений для здоровья человека и окружающей среды в сотрудничестве с соответствующими межправительственными и неправительственными организациями и уязвимыми группами населения, по мере целесообразности.

2. Каждая Сторона использует существующие механизмы или рассматривает возможность разработки таких механизмов, как реестры высвобождения и переноса загрязнителей, где это применимо, для сбора и распространения информации относительно оценочных показателей своих ежегодных объемов ртути и ртутных соединений, которые выбрасываются, высвобождаются или удаляются вследствие деятельности человека.

Статья 19
Научные исследования, разработки и мониторинг

1. Стороны с учетом своих условий и возможностей осуществляют сотрудничество в деле разработки и улучшения:

a) кадастров применения, потребления и антропогенных атмосферных выбросов и высвобождений в воды и на землю ртути и ртутных соединений;

b) моделирования и географически репрезентативного мониторинга уровней ртути и ртутных соединений в уязвимых группах населения и компонентах окружающей среды, включая биоту, например, в рыбе, морских млекопитающих, морских черепахах и птицах, а также сотрудничества в области отбора соответствующих и надлежащих проб и обмена ими;

c) оценок воздействия ртути и ртутных соединений на здоровье человека и окружающую среду, наряду с социальным, экономическим и культурным воздействием, особенно в отношении уязвимых групп населения;

d) согласованных методологий в отношении мероприятий, проводимых в соответствии с подпунктами (a), (b) и (c);

e) информации об экологическом цикле, переносе (включая перенос на большие расстояния и осаждение), преобразовании и круговороте ртути и ртутных соединений в различных экосистемах, с должным учетом различия между антропогенными и природными выбросами и высвобождениями ртути и ремобилизацией ртути из ранее образовавшихся осаждений;

f) информации о торговле ртутью, ртутными соединениями и продуктами с добавлением ртути; и

g) информации и научных исследований в отношении технической и экономической доступности безртутных продуктов и процессов, а также наилучших имеющихся методов и наилучших видов природоохранной деятельности для сокращения и мониторинга выбросов и высвобождений ртути и ртутных соединений.

2. В процессе осуществления мероприятий, указанных в пункте 1, Сторонам следует, где это целесообразно, опираться на существующие сети мониторинга и научно-исследовательские программы.

Статья 20
Планы осуществления

1. Каждая Сторона может, после первоначальной оценки, разрабатывать и выполнять с учетом своих внутренних обстоятельств план осуществления, направленный на выполнение обязательств по настоящей Конвенции. Любые такие планы следует представлять в секретариат сразу после их разработки.

2. Каждая Сторона может пересматривать и обновлять свой план осуществления с учетом ее внутренних обстоятельств и в соответствии с руководящими принципами Конференции Сторон и другими соответствующими руководящими принципами.

3. При проведении работы в соответствии с пунктами 1 и 2 Сторонам следует консультироваться с национальными заинтересованными субъектами по вопросам содействия разработке, осуществлению, обзору и обновлению своих планов осуществления.

4. Стороны могут также координировать планы на региональном уровне с целью содействия осуществлению настоящей Конвенции.

Статья 21
Представление информации

1. Каждая Сторона представляет Конференции Сторон через секретариат информацию о принимаемых ею мерах по осуществлению положений настоящей Конвенции и об эффективности таких мер и возможных проблемах с точки зрения достижения целей настоящей Конвенции.

2. Каждая Сторона включает в свою отчетность информацию, предусмотренную статьями 3, 5, 7, 8 и 9 настоящей Конвенции.

3. Конференция Сторон на своем первом совещании определяет периодичность и форму представления Сторонами отчетности с учетом желательности координации представления отчетности с другими соответствующими конвенциями о химических веществах и отходах.

Статья 22
Оценка эффективности

1. Конференция Сторон проводит оценку эффективности настоящей Конвенции, начиная не позднее чем через шесть лет после даты вступления Конвенции в силу, а затем с периодичностью, определяемой ею.

2. В целях содействия проведению оценки Конференция Сторон на своем первом совещании инициирует формирование механизмов для обеспечения себя сравнимыми данными мониторинга о наличии и перемещении ртути и ртутных соединений в окружающей среде, а также об изменении уровней ртути и ртутных соединений, наблюдаемых в биоте и в уязвимых группах населения.

3. Оценка проводится на основании имеющейся научной, экологической, технической, финансовой и экономической информации, включающей:

a) отчетность и другую информацию о мониторинге, представляемую Конференции Сторон в соответствии с пунктом 2;

b) отчетность, представленную в соответствии со статьей 21;

c) информацию и рекомендации, представленные в соответствии со статьей 15; и

d) отчетность и другую соответствующую информацию о работе механизмов финансовой помощи, передачи технологий и создания потенциала, созданных в соответствии с настоящей Конвенцией.

Статья 23
Конференция Сторон

1. Настоящим учреждается Конференция Сторон.

2. Первое совещание Конференции Сторон созывается Директором-исполнителем Программы Организации Объединенных Наций по окружающей среде не позднее чем через один год после даты вступления в силу настоящей Конвенции. После этого очередные совещания Конференции Сторон созываются с периодичностью, которую установит Конференция.

3. Внеочередные совещания Конференции Сторон созываются в случаях, когда Конференция может счесть это необходимым, или по письменной просьбе любой Стороны, при условии, что в течение шести меся-

цев с момента информирования Сторон секретариатом эта просьба будет поддержана не менее чем одной третью Сторон.

4. Конференция Сторон на своем первом совещании консенсусом согласовывает и принимает правила процедуры и финансовые правила для себя и любых своих вспомогательных органов, а также финансовые положения, регулирующие функционирование секретариата.

5. Конференция Сторон на постоянной основе контролирует и оценивает осуществление настоящей Конвенции. Она выполняет функции, возложенные на нее в соответствии с настоящей Конвенцией, и с этой целью:

a) учреждает такие вспомогательные органы, которые она считает необходимыми для осуществления настоящей Конвенции;

b) сотрудничает в соответствующих случаях с компетентными международными организациями, а также межправительственными и неправительственными органами;

c) проводит регулярный обзор всей информации, представляемой ей и секретариату в соответствии со статьей 21;

d) рассматривает любые рекомендации, представленные ей Комитетом по осуществлению и соблюдению;

e) рассматривает и принимает любые дополнительные меры, которые могут потребоваться для достижения целей настоящей Конвенции; и

f) проводит обзор приложений A и B в соответствии со статьями 4 и 5.

6. Организация Объединенных Наций, ее специализированные учреждения и Международное агентство по атомной энергии, а также любое государство, не являющееся Стороной настоящей Конвенции, могут быть представлены на совещаниях Конференции Сторон в качестве наблюдателей. Любые национальные или международные правительственные или неправительственные органы или учреждения, которые обладают компетенцией в вопросах, охватываемых настоящей Конвенцией, и известили секретариат о своем желании быть представленными на совещании Конференции Сторон в качестве наблюдателей, могут быть допущены к участию в нем, если против этого не возражает по меньшей мере одна треть Сторон, присутствующих на совещании. Допуск и участие наблюдателей регулируются правилами процедуры, принятыми Конференцией Сторон.

Статья 24
Секретариат

1. Настоящим учреждается секретариат.

2. На секретариат возлагаются следующие функции:

a) организация совещаний Конференции Сторон и ее вспомогательных органов и их обслуживание в случае необходимости;

b) содействие оказанию Сторонам, особенно Сторонам, являющимся развивающимися странами, и Сторонам, являющимся странами с переходной экономикой, содействия, по их просьбе, в осуществлении настоящей Конвенции;

c) обеспечение необходимой координации деятельности с секретариатами других соответствующих международных органов, особенно других конвенций о химических веществах и отходах;

d) оказание Сторонам помощи в обмене информацией, связанной с осуществлением настоящей Конвенции;

e) подготовка и представление Сторонам периодических докладов, основанных на информации, полученной в соответствии со статьями 15 и 21, и другой имеющейся информации;

f) заключение под общим руководством Конференции Сторон таких административных и договорных соглашений, которые могут потребоваться для эффективного выполнения его функций; и

g) выполнение других функций секретариата, определенных в настоящей Конвенции, и таких других функций, которые могут быть определены Конференцией Сторон.

3. Функции секретариата настоящей Конвенции обеспечиваются Директором-исполнителем Программы Организации Объединенных Наций по окружающей среде, если Конференция Сторон не примет большинством в три четверти присутствующих и участвующих в голосовании Сторон решение поручить выполнение функций секретариата какой-либо другой международной организации или нескольким другим таким организациям.

4. Конференция Сторон в консультации с соответствующими международными органами может обеспечивать укрепление сотрудничества и координации между секретариатом и секретариатами других конвенций о химических веществах и отходах. Конференция Сторон в консультации с

соответствующими международными органами может давать дополнительные руководящие указания по этому вопросу.

Статья 25
Урегулирование споров

1. Стороны стремятся урегулировать любой возникающий между ними спор относительно толкования или применения настоящей Конвенции путем переговоров или другими мирными средствами по своему выбору.

2. При ратификации, принятии, одобрении настоящей Конвенции или присоединении к ней или в любое время после этого любая Сторона, не являющаяся региональной организацией экономической интеграции, может направить Депозитарию письменное заявление о том, что в отношении любого спора, касающегося толкования или применения настоящей Конвенции, она признает одно или оба из следующих средств урегулирования спора как обязательные в отношении любой Стороны, принимающей на себя такие же обязательства:

a) арбитражное разбирательство в соответствии с процедурой, предусмотренной в части I приложения E;

b) передачу спора в Международный Суд.

3. Сторона, являющаяся региональной организацией экономической интеграции, может сделать подобное заявление в отношении арбитражного разбирательства в соответствии с пунктом 2.

4. Заявление, сделанное в соответствии с пунктом 2 или 3, остается в силе до истечения срока действия в соответствии с его условиями или в течение трех месяцев после сдачи на хранение Депозитарию письменного уведомления о его аннулировании.

5. Истечение срока действия заявления, уведомление об аннулировании или новое заявление никоим образом не влияют на разбирательство, ведущееся в арбитражном суде или в Международном Суде, если стороны спора не договорились об ином.

6. Если стороны спора не приняли в соответствии с пунктом 2 или 3 одно и то же средство урегулирования спора и если они не смогли урегулировать свой спор с помощью средств, упомянутых в пункте 1, в течение двенадцати месяцев после направления одной из Сторон другой Стороне уведомления о наличии спора между ними, этот спор, по просьбе любой из сторон спора, передается на рассмотрение согласительной комиссии. Процедура, изложенная в части II приложения E, применяется к согласительному процессу в рамках настоящей статьи.

Статья 26
Поправки к Конвенции

1. Любая Сторона может предлагать поправки к настоящей Конвенции.

2. Поправки к настоящей Конвенции принимаются на совещании Конференции Сторон. Текст любой предложенной поправки направляется секретариатом Сторонам не позднее чем за шесть месяцев до проведения совещания, на котором ее предлагается принять. Секретариат также направляет текст предложенной поправки сигнатариям настоящей Конвенции и для информации — Депозитарию.

3. Стороны прилагают все усилия к достижению согласия в отношении любой предлагаемой поправки к настоящей Конвенции путем консенсуса. Если все усилия, направленные на достижение консенсуса, исчерпаны, а согласие не достигнуто, то поправка в качестве последней меры принимается большинством в три четверти голосов Сторон, присутствующих и участвующих в голосовании на данном совещании.

4. Принятая поправка направляется Депозитарием всем Сторонам для ратификации, принятия или одобрения.

5. Депозитарию направляются письменные уведомления о ратификации, принятии или одобрении поправки. Поправка, принятая в соответствии с пунктом 3, вступает в силу для тех Сторон, которые дали свое согласие быть связанными обязательствами в рамках Конвенции, на девяностый день после сдачи на хранение документов о ратификации, принятии или одобрении по меньшей мере тремя четвертями числа Сторон, являвшихся Сторонами в момент принятия поправки. После этого поправка вступает в силу для любой другой Стороны на девяностый день после сдачи данной Стороной на хранение документа о ратификации, принятии или одобрении этой поправки.

Статья 27
Принятие и изменение приложений

1. Приложения к настоящей Конвенции составляют ее неотъемлемую часть, и, если прямо не предусматривается иное, ссылка на настоящую Конвенцию одновременно представляет собой ссылку на любые приложения к ней.

2. Любые дополнительные приложения, принятые после вступления в силу настоящей Конвенции, ограничиваются процедурными, научными, техническими или административными вопросами.

3. В отношении предложения, принятия или вступления в силу дополнительных приложений к настоящей Конвенции применяется следующая процедура:

a) дополнительные приложения предлагаются и принимаются в соответствии с процедурой, оговоренной в пунктах 1–3 статьи 26;

b) любая Сторона, которая не может принять дополнительное приложение, письменно уведомляет об этом Депозитария в течение одного года со дня сообщения Депозитарием о принятии дополнительного приложения. Депозитарий незамедлительно уведомляет все Стороны о любом таком полученном им уведомлении. Любая Сторона может в любое время отозвать ранее направленное уведомление о непринятии любого дополнительного приложения, после чего это приложение вступает в силу для данной Стороны при соблюдении положений подпункта (c); и

c) по истечении одного года со дня сообщения Депозитарием о принятии дополнительного приложения это приложение вступает в силу для всех Сторон, которые не представили уведомление в соответствии с положениями подпункта (b).

4. Предложение, принятие и вступление в силу поправок к приложениям к настоящей Конвенции регулируются такими же процедурами, какие установлены для предложения, принятия и вступления в силу дополнительных приложений к Конвенции, кроме случаев, когда поправка к приложению не вступает в силу в отношении любой Стороны, сделавшей заявление по поправке к приложениям в соответствии с пунктом 5 статьи 30; в этом случае любая такая поправка вступает в силу для такой Стороны на девяностый день после даты сдачи ею Депозитарию своего документа о ратификации, принятии, одобрении или присоединении к такой поправке.

5. Если дополнительное приложение или поправка к приложению связаны с поправкой к настоящей Конвенции, то дополнительное приложение или поправка к приложению не вступают в силу до тех пор, пока не вступила в силу поправка к Конвенции.

Статья 28
Право голоса

1. За исключением случаев, предусмотренных в пункте 2, каждая Сторона настоящей Конвенции имеет один голос.

2. Региональная организация экономической интеграции участвует в голосовании по вопросам, входящим в ее компетенцию, с числом голосов, равным числу ее государств-членов, являющихся Сторонами настоящей

Конвенции. Такая организация не пользуется правом голоса, если им пользуется какое-либо ее государство-член, и наоборот.

Статья 29
Подписание

Настоящая Конвенция открыта для подписания всеми государствами и региональными организациями экономической интеграции в Кумамото, Япония, 10 и 11 октября 2013 года и позднее, до 9 октября 2014 года, в Центральных учреждениях Организации Объединенных Наций в Нью-Йорке.

Статья 30
Ратификация, принятие, одобрение или присоединение

1. Настоящая Конвенция подлежит ратификации, принятию или одобрению государствами и региональными организациями экономической интеграции. Она открыта для присоединения государств и региональных организаций экономической интеграции со следующего дня после того, когда Конвенция закрывается для подписания. Документы о ратификации, принятии, одобрении или присоединении сдаются на хранение Депозитарию.

2. Любая организация экономической интеграции, которая становится Стороной настоящей Конвенции в то время, как ни одно из ее государств-членов не является ее Стороной, связана всеми обязательствами, вытекающими из Конвенции. В случае, когда одно или несколько государств-членов такой организации являются Сторонами настоящей Конвенции, эта организация и ее государства-члены принимают решение в отношении соответствующих обязанностей по выполнению своих обязательств, вытекающих из Конвенции. В таких случаях организация и государства-члены не могут одновременно пользоваться правами, предусмотренными Конвенцией.

3. В своих документах о ратификации, принятии, одобрении или присоединении региональные организации экономической интеграции заявляют о сфере своей компетенции в отношении вопросов, регулируемых настоящей Конвенцией. Любая такая организация уведомляет также о любом соответствующем изменении сферы своей компетенции Депозитария, который, в свою очередь, информирует об этом Стороны.

4. Каждому государству или региональной организации экономической интеграции рекомендуется представить в секретариат во время ратификации, принятия и одобрения Конвенции или присоединения к ней информацию о своих мерах по осуществлению Конвенции.

5. В своем документе о ратификации, принятии, одобрении или присоединении любая Сторона может заявить, что в отношении нее любая поправка к приложению вступает в силу лишь после сдачи на хранение ее документа о ратификации, принятии, утверждении или присоединении к ней.

Статья 31
Вступление в силу

1. Настоящая Конвенция вступает в силу на девяностый день после сдачи на хранение пятидесятого документа о ратификации, принятии, одобрении или присоединении.

2. Для каждого государства или региональной организации экономической интеграции, которые ратифицируют, принимают или одобряют настоящую Конвенцию, либо присоединяются к ней после сдачи на хранение пятидесятого документа о ратификации, принятии, одобрении или присоединении, Конвенция вступает в силу на девяностый день после сдачи на хранение таким государством или региональной организацией экономической интеграции своего документа о ратификации, принятии, одобрении или присоединении.

3. Для целей пунктов 1 и 2 любой документ, сданный на хранение региональной организацией экономической интеграции, не считается дополнительным по отношению к документам, сданным на хранение государствами-членами такой организации.

Статья 32
Оговорки

Оговорки к настоящей Конвенции не допускаются.

Статья 33
Выход

1. В любое время по истечении трех лет с даты вступления настоящей Конвенции в силу для Стороны эта Сторона может выйти из Конвенции, направив письменное уведомление Депозитарию.

2. Любой такой выход вступает в силу по истечении одного года после получения Депозитарием уведомления о выходе или в такой более поздний срок, который может быть указан в уведомлении о выходе.

Статья 34
Депозитарий

Функции Депозитария настоящей Конвенции выполняет Генеральный секретарь Организации Объединенных Наций.

Статья 35
Аутентичные тексты

Подлинник настоящей Конвенции, тексты которого на английском, арабском, испанском, китайском, русском и французском языках являются равно аутентичными, сдается на хранение Депозитарию.

В УДОСТОВЕРЕНИЕ ЧЕГО нижеподписавшиеся, должным образом на то уполномоченные, подписали настоящую Конвенцию.

Совершено в Кумамото, Япония, сего десятого дня октября две тысячи тринадцатого года.

Приложение A
Продукты с добавлением ртути

Из настоящего приложения исключаются следующие продукты:

a) продукты, необходимые для защиты гражданского населения и для военного применения;

b) продукты для исследований, калибровки приборов, для применения в качестве эталона;

c) при отсутствии приемлемых безртутных альтернатив для замены — переключатели и реле, люминесцентные лампы с холодным катодом и люминесцентные лампы с внешним электродом (ЛЛХК и ЛЛВЭ) для электронных дисплеев, измерительные устройства;

d) продукты, применяемые в традиционной или религиозной практике; и

e) вакцины, содержащие тиомерсал в качестве консервантов.

Часть I: Продукты, на которые распространяется пункт 1 статьи 4

Продукты с добавлением ртути	*Срок, после которого производство, импорт или экспорт продукта не разрешается (срок поэтапного вывода из обращения)*
Аккумуляторы, кроме серебряно-цинковых таблеточных аккумуляторов с содержанием ртути менее 2% и воздушно-цинковых таблеточных аккумуляторов с содержанием ртути менее 2%	2020 год
Переключатели и реле, за исключением высокоточных конденсаторных мостов и мостов для измерения потерь и высокочастотных радиочастотных переключателей и реле контрольных приборов и регуляторов с максимальным содержанием ртути 20 мг на каждый мост, переключатель или реле	2020 год
Лампы люминесцентные малогабаритные (ЛЛМ) общего освещения мощностью 30 ватт или менее и содержанием ртути свыше 5 мг в колбе лампы	2020 год
Лампы люминесцентные трубчатые (ЛМТ) общего освещения: a) с трехцветным люминофором мощностью менее 60 ватт с содержанием ртути свыше 5 мг в лампе; b) с галофосфатным люминофором мощностью 40 ватт или менее и содержанием ртути свыше 10 мг в лампе	2020 год
Лампы общего освещения ртутные высокого давления паросветные (РВДП)	2020 год

Продукты с добавлением ртути	*Срок, после которого производство, импорт или экспорт продукта не разрешается (срок поэтапного вывода из обращения)*
Ртуть в лампах люминесцентных с холодным катодом и лампах люминесцентных с внешним электродом (ЛЛХК и ЛЛВЭ) для электронных дисплеев: a) коротких (≤ 500 мм), с содержанием ртути свыше 3,5 мг в лампе; b) средних (> 500 мм и ≤ 1500 мм), с содержанием ртути свыше 5 мг в лампе; c) длинных (> 1500 мм), с содержанием ртути свыше 13 мг в лампе	2020 год
Косметика (с содержанием ртути свыше 1 части на миллион), включая мыло и кремы для осветления кожи, за исключением косметики для зоны глаз, в которой ртуть применяется в качестве консерванта и для которой эффективные и безопасные консерванты-заменители не существуют[1]	2020 год
Пестициды, биоциды и локальные антисептики	2020 год
Перечисленные ниже неэлектронные измерительные устройства, кроме неэлектронных измерительных устройств, установленных на крупногабаритном оборудовании или используемых для высокоточного измерения, если отсутствуют приемлемые безртутные альтернативы: a) барометры; b) гигрометры; c) манометры; d) термометры; e) сфигмоманометры.	2020 год

[1] Предполагается не учитывать косметику, мыло или кремы, имеющие следовые загрязнения ртутью.

Часть II: Продукты, на которые распространяется пункт 3 статьи 4

Продукты с добавлением ртути	*Положения*
Амальгама для зубных пломб	Мероприятия, проводимые Стороной для сокращения использования амальгамы для зубных пломб, учитывают внутренние обстоятельства Стороны и соответствующие международные руководящие принципы, а также предусматривают два или более мероприятий из следующего перечня: i) установление национальных целей, направленных на профилактику кариеса зубов и поощрение здорового образа жизни, которые, таким образом, сводят к минимуму потребность в восстановлении зубов; ii) установление национальных целей, направленных на минимизацию ее использования; iii) содействие использованию рентабельных и клинически эффективных безртутных альтернатив для восстановления зубов; iv) содействие проведению исследований и разработке качественных безртутных материалов для восстановления зубов;

Продукты с добавлением ртути	*Положения*
	v) стимулирование профильных профессиональных организаций и стоматологических учебных заведений к обучению и подготовке специалистов и студентов-стоматологов в области использования безртутных альтернатив при восстановлении зубов, а также содействие применению передовых практических методов управления;
	vi) препятствование использованию договоров и программ страхования, которыми поощряется применение амальгамы для зубных пломб вместо восстановления зубов без использования ртути;
	vii) стимулирование договоров и программ страхования, которыми поощряется применение качественных альтернатив амальгаме для зубных пломб при восстановлении зубов;
	viii) ограничение использования амальгамы для зубных пломб ее герметизированной формой;
	ix) поощрение использования наилучших видов природоохранной деятельности в стоматологических учреждениях в целях сокращения высвобождений ртути и ртутных соединений в воды и на землю.

Приложение В
Производственные процессы, в которых применяются ртуть или ртутные соединения

Часть I: Процессы, на которые распространяется пункт 2 статьи 5

Производственные процессы, в которых применяются ртуть или ртутные соединения	*Срок поэтапного вывода из обращения*
Хлорно-щелочное производство	2025 год
Производство ацетальдегида, в котором ртуть или ртутные соединения применяются в качестве катализатора	2018 год

Часть II: Процессы, на которые распространяется пункт 3 статьи 5

Процессы с использованием ртути	*Положения*
Производство мономера винилхлорида	Принимаемые Сторонами меры включают, не ограничиваясь перечисленными, следующие мероприятия: i) сокращение использования ртути в расчете на единицу продукции на 50% к 2020 году по сравнению с объемом использования в 2010 году; ii) содействие мероприятиям по сокращению использования ртути, полученной в результате первичной добычи ртути; iii) принятие мер для сокращения выбросов и высвобождений ртути в окружающую среду; iv) оказание поддержки исследованиям и разработкам в области безртутных катализаторов и процессов; v) недопущение использования ртути по истечении пяти лет после того как Конференцией Сторон установлено, что безртутные катализаторы, основанные на существующих процессах, стали практически реализуемыми в техническом и экономическом отношении; vi) представление Конференции Сторон информации о своих усилиях по разработке и/или определению альтернатив и поэтапному отказу от применения ртути в соответствии со статьей 21.
Метилат или этилат натрия или калия	Принимаемые Сторонами меры включают, не ограничиваясь перечисленными, следующие мероприятия: i) проведение мероприятий по сокращению применения ртути с целью поэтапного отказа от ее применения в максимально сжатые сроки и в течение 10 лет с момента вступления Конвенции в силу; ii) сокращение выбросов и высвобождений ртути в расчете на единицу продукции на 50% к 2020 году по сравнению с 2010 годом; iii) запрещение использования новой ртути, полученной в результате первичной добычи; iv) оказание поддержки исследованиям и разработкам в области безртутных процессов; v) недопущение использования ртути по истечении пяти лет после того как Конференцией Сторон установлено, что безртутные процессы стали практически реализуемыми в техническом и экономическом отношении;

Процессы с использованием ртути	*Положения*
	vi) представление Конференции Сторон информации об усилиях Стороны по разработке/выявлению альтернатив и поэтапному отказу от применения ртути в соответствии со статьей 21.
Производство полиуретана с применением содержащих ртуть катализаторов	Принимаемые Сторонами меры включают, не ограничиваясь перечисленными, следующие мероприятия: i) проведение мероприятий по сокращению применения ртути с целью поэтапного отказа от ее применения в максимально сжатые сроки и в течение 10 лет с момента вступления Конвенции в силу; ii) проведение мероприятий по сокращению использования ртути, полученной в результате первичной добычи ртути; iii) проведение мероприятий по сокращению выбросов и высвобождений ртути в окружающую среду; iv) поощрение исследований и разработок в области безртутных катализаторов и процессов; v) представление Конференции Сторон информации об усилиях Стороны по разработке и/или выявлению альтернатив и поэтапному отказу от применения ртути в соответствии со статьей 21. В отношении данного производственного процесса положения пункта 6 статьи 5 не применяются.

Приложение C
Кустарная и мелкомасштабная золотодобыча

Национальные планы действий

1. Каждая Сторона, на которую распространяется действие пункта 3 статьи 7, включает в свой национальный план действий:

a) национальные цели и целевые показатели сокращения;

b) меры по отказу от:

i) амальгамирования цельной руды;

ii) открытого сжигания амальгамы или переработанной амальгамы;

iii) сжигания амальгамы в жилых районах; и

iv) выщелачивания цианированием осадочных пород, руды или шлама, куда была добавлена ртуть, без первоначального удаления ртути;

c) меры по содействию упорядочению или регулированию сектора кустарной и мелкомасштабной золотодобычи;

d) базовые оценки использованных количеств ртути и методов, применяемых при кустарной и мелкомасштабной добыче и обработке золота на ее территории;

e) стратегии поощрения сокращения выбросов и высвобождений, а также уменьшения воздействия ртути при кустарной и мелкомасштабной добыче и обработке золота, включая безртутные методы;

f) стратегии регулирования торговли и предупреждения утечки ртути и ртутных соединений как из иностранных, так и из отечественных источников для использования при кустарной и мелкомасштабной добыче и обработке золота;

g) стратегии привлечения заинтересованных субъектов к осуществлению и продолжению разработки национального плана действий;

h) стратегию в области здравоохранения по борьбе с воздействием ртути на старателей, занимающихся кустарной и мелкомасштабной золотодобычей, и на их общины. Такая стратегия должна предусматривать, в частности, сбор данных о состоянии здоровья, обучение работников здравоохранения и повышение осведомленности через учреждения здравоохранения;

i) стратегии предотвращения воздействия ртути, используемой при кустарной и мелкомасштабной золотодобыче, на уязвимые группы населения, в частности, на детей и женщин детородного возраста, особенно беременных женщин;

j) стратегии предоставления информации старателям, занимающимся кустарной и мелкомасштабной золотодобычей, и затрагиваемым общинам; и

k) график выполнения национального плана действий.

2. Каждая Сторона может включать в свой национальный план действий дополнительные стратегии для достижения своих целей, включая применение и внедрение стандартов безртутной кустарной и мелкомасштабной золотодобычи, а также рыночных механизмов или маркетинговых инструментов.

Приложение D
Перечень точечных источников выбросов в атмосферу ртути и ртутных соединений

Категория точечного источника:

угольные электростанции;

угольные промышленные котлоагрегаты;

плавильные и прокаливающие процессы, применяемые при производстве цветных металлов[1];

установки для сжигания отходов;

установки для производства цементного клинкера.

[1] Для целей настоящего приложения «цветные металлы» означает свинец, цинк, медь и производимое промышленным способом золото.

Приложение Е
Процедура арбитражного разбирательства и согласительная процедура

Часть I: Процедура арбитражного разбирательства

Для целей пункта 2(а) статьи 25 настоящей Конвенции устанавливается следующая процедура арбитражного разбирательства:

Статья 1

1. Любая Сторона может возбудить арбитражное разбирательство в соответствии со статьей 25 настоящей Конвенции путем письменного уведомления на имя другой стороны или сторон спора. Уведомление сопровождается исковым заявлением вместе с любыми подкрепляющими документами. В таком уведомлении излагается предмет арбитражного разбирательства и приводятся, в частности, статьи настоящей Конвенции, относительно толкования или применения которых возник спор.

2. Сторона-истец уведомляет секретариат о том, что она передает спор на арбитражное разбирательство в соответствии со статьей 25 настоящей Конвенции. Уведомление сопровождается письменным уведомлением стороны-истца, исковым заявлением и подкрепляющими документами, упомянутыми в пункте 1 выше. Секретариат препровождает полученную таким образом информацию всем Сторонам.

Статья 2

1. Если спор передается на арбитражное разбирательство в соответствии со статьей 1 выше, создается арбитражный суд. Он состоит из трех членов.

2. Каждая сторона спора назначает одного арбитра, и два назначенных таким образом арбитра по взаимному согласию назначают третьего арбитра, выполняющего функции Председателя суда. При возникновении споров, в которых участвуют более двух сторон, те стороны, которые имеют общий интерес, по взаимному согласию вместе назначают одного арбитра. Председатель суда не может быть гражданином любой из сторон спора, не может иметь своим обычным местом жительства территорию любой из этих сторон, не может находиться у них на службе или в каком-либо ином качестве иметь отношение к этому делу.

3. Любая вакансия заполняется согласно процедуре, предусмотренной для первоначального назначения.

Статья 3

1. Если одна из сторон спора не назначает арбитра в течение двух месяцев после даты получения стороной-ответчиком уведомления об арбитражном разбирательстве, другая сторона вправе информировать об этом Генерального секретаря Организации Объединенных Наций, который производит назначение в течение следующих двух месяцев.

2. Если по истечении двух месяцев после назначения второго арбитра Председатель арбитражного суда не назначается, то по просьбе одной из сторон Генеральный секретарь Организации Объединенных Наций назначает его в течение следующих двух месяцев.

Статья 4

Арбитражный суд выносит свои решения в соответствии с положениями настоящей Конвенции и международным правом.

Статья 5

Если стороны спора не договорились об ином, арбитражный суд устанавливает свои собственные правила процедуры.

Статья 6

Арбитражный суд может, по просьбе одной из сторон спора, рекомендовать необходимые временные меры защиты.

Статья 7

Стороны спора содействуют работе арбитражного суда и, в частности, с использованием всех имеющихся в их распоряжении возможностей:

a) представляют ему все соответствующие документы, информацию и средства;

b) в случае необходимости дают ему возможность вызвать свидетелей или экспертов и ознакомиться с их показаниями.

Статья 8

Стороны спора и арбитры обязаны обеспечивать конфиденциальность любой информации или документов, которые они получают в конфиденциальном порядке в ходе разбирательства в арбитражном суде.

Статья 9

Если арбитражный суд не примет иного решения исходя из конкретных обстоятельств дела, судебные издержки распределяются между сторонами спора поровну. Суд регистрирует все свои издержки и представляет сторонам окончательный отчет об этих издержках.

Статья 10

Любая Сторона, имеющая в предмете спора интерес правового характера, который может быть затронут решением, имеет право с согласия арбитражного суда участвовать в разбирательстве.

Статья 11

Арбитражный суд может заслушивать встречные иски, вытекающие непосредственно из предмета спора, и принимать по ним решения.

Статья 12

Решения арбитражного суда по вопросам как процедуры, так и существа принимаются большинством голосов его членов.

Статья 13

1. При неявке одной из сторон спора в арбитражный суд или непредставлении ею своей аргументации по делу другая сторона может просить суд продолжить разбирательство и вынести свое решение. Отсутствие стороны или непредставление ею аргументации по делу не является препятствием для разбирательства.

2. До вынесения своего окончательного решения арбитражный суд должен убедиться в том, что иск является фактически и юридически обоснованным.

Статья 14

Арбитражный суд выносит окончательное решение в течение пяти месяцев после даты своего окончательного учреждения, если только он не сочтет необходимым продлить этот срок еще на один период, не превышающий пяти месяцев.

Статья 15

Окончательное решение арбитражного суда ограничивается предметом спора и сопровождается изложением мотивов, на которых оно основывается. Оно содержит имена членов, которые участвовали в его принятии, и дату принятия окончательного решения. Любой член суда может приложить отдельное или особое мнение к окончательному решению.

Статья 16

Окончательное решение является обязательным для сторон спора. Толкование настоящей Конвенции, приведенное в окончательном решении, также является обязательным для Стороны, участвующей в разбирательстве в соответствии со статьей 10 выше, постольку, поскольку оно касается вопросов, по поводу которых такая Сторона участвовала в разбирательстве. Окончательное решение не подлежит обжалованию, если только стороны спора не договорились заранее о процедуре обжалования.

Статья 17

Любые разногласия, которые могут возникнуть между участниками, для которых окончательное решение относительно толкования или порядка выполнения этого окончательного решения является обязательным в соответствии со статьей 16 выше, могут быть переданы любым из этих участников на рассмотрение арбитражного суда, который вынес это решение.

Часть II: Согласительная процедура

Для целей пункта 6 статьи 25 настоящей Конвенции устанавливается следующая согласительная процедура:

Статья 1

Просьба одной из сторон спора о создании согласительной комиссии в соответствии с пунктом 6 статьи 25 настоящей Конвенции направляется в письменном виде секретариату, а копия просьбы направляется другой стороне или другим сторонам спора. Секретариат незамедлительно информирует об этом все Стороны.

Статья 2

1. Если стороны спора не договорились об ином, согласительная комиссия состоит из трех членов, по одному из которых назначаются каждой заинтересованной стороной, а Председатель выбирается совместно этими членами.

2. При споре, в котором участвуют более двух сторон, стороны, имеющие общий интерес, по взаимному согласию вместе назначают своего члена комиссии.

Статья 3

Если стороны спора не производят какого-либо назначения в течение двух месяцев с даты получения секретариатом письменной просьбы, о которой говорится в статье 1 выше, то Генеральный секретарь Организации Объединенных Наций, по просьбе любой стороны, производит такое назначение в течение следующих двух месяцев.

Статья 4

Если Председатель согласительной комиссии не был выбран в течение двух месяцев после назначения второго члена комиссии, то Генеральный секретарь Организации Объединенных Наций, по просьбе любой из сторон спора, назначает Председателя в течение следующих двух месяцев.

Статья 5

Согласительная комиссия оказывает содействие сторонам спора независимо и беспристрастно в их стремлении достичь урегулирования по взаимному согласию.

Статья 6

1. Согласительная комиссия вправе проводить согласительные процедуры, как она сочтет это целесообразным, с полным учетом обстоятельств дела и мнений, которые могут выразить стороны спора, включая любые просьбы об ускоренном урегулировании. Она может, по мере необходимости, принимать собственные правила процедуры, если стороны не договорились об ином.

2. Согласительная комиссия вправе в любой момент в ходе разбирательства вынести предложения или рекомендации по урегулированию спора.

Статья 7

Стороны спора сотрудничают с согласительной комиссией. В частности, они стремятся выполнять просьбы комиссии о представлении письменных материалов, предъявлении доказательств и посещении заседаний. Стороны и члены согласительной комиссии обязаны обеспечивать конфиденциальность любой информации или документов, которые они получают в конфиденциальном порядке в ходе работы комиссии.

Статья 8

Согласительная комиссия принимает свои решения большинством голосов своих членов.

Статья 9

Если только спор еще не урегулирован, согласительная комиссия не позднее чем через двенадцать месяцев после сформирования в полном составе представляет доклад с рекомендациями относительно разрешения спора, который стороны спора добросовестно рассматривают.

Статья 10

Любые разногласия относительно компетенции согласительной комиссии рассматривать переданный ей вопрос разрешаются самой комиссией.

Статья 11

Издержки согласительной комиссии распределяются между сторонами спора в равной пропорции, если они не договорились об ином. Комиссия регистрирует все свои издержки и представляет сторонам окончательный отчет о них.

[TEXT IN SPANISH – TEXTE EN ESPAGNOL]

CONVENIO DE MINAMATA SOBRE EL MERCURIO

Las Partes en el presente Convenio,

Reconociendo que el mercurio es un producto químico de preocupación mundial debido a su transporte a larga distancia en la atmósfera, su persistencia en el medio ambiente tras su introducción antropógena, su capacidad de bioacumulación en los ecosistemas y sus importantes efectos adversos para la salud humana y el medio ambiente,

Recordando la decisión 25/5 del Consejo de Administración del Programa de las Naciones Unidas para el Medio Ambiente, de 20 de febrero de 2009, en la que se pedía emprender medidas internacionales para gestionar el mercurio de manera eficaz, efectiva y coherente,

Recordando el párrafo 221 del documento final de la Conferencia de las Naciones Unidas sobre el Desarrollo Sostenible, "El futuro que queremos", donde se pidió que se procurara que concluyeran con éxito las negociaciones de un instrumento mundial jurídicamente vinculante sobre el mercurio a fin de hacer frente a los riesgos que representaba para la salud humana y el medio ambiente,

Recordando que la Conferencia de las Naciones Unidas sobre el Desarrollo Sostenible reafirmó los principios de la Declaración de Río sobre el Medio Ambiente y el Desarrollo incluido, entre otros, el de las responsabilidades comunes pero diferenciadas, y reconociendo las circunstancias y las capacidades de cada Estado, así como la necesidad de adoptar medidas de alcance mundial,

Conscientes de los problemas de salud, especialmente en los países en desarrollo, derivados de la exposición al mercurio de las poblaciones vulnerables, en particular las mujeres, los niños y, a través de ellos, las generaciones venideras,

Señalando la vulnerabilidad especial de los ecosistemas árticos y las comunidades indígenas debido a la biomagnificación del mercurio y a la contaminación de sus alimentos tradicionales, y preocupadas en general por las comunidades indígenas debido a los efectos del mercurio,

Reconociendo las lecciones importantes aprendidas de la enfermedad de Minamata, en particular los graves efectos adversos para la salud y el medio ambiente derivados de la contaminación por mercurio, y la necesidad de garantizar una gestión adecuada del mercurio y de prevenir incidentes de esa índole en el futuro,

Destacando la importancia del apoyo financiero, técnico, tecnológico y de creación de capacidad, en especial para los países en desarrollo y los países con economías en transición, a fin de fortalecer las capacidades nacionales destinadas a la gestión del mercurio y de promover la aplicación eficaz del Convenio,

Reconociendo también las actividades desplegadas por la Organización Mundial de la Salud en la protección de la salud humana de los efectos del mercurio y la función de los acuerdos ambientales multilaterales pertinentes, en especial el Convenio de Basilea sobre el control de los movimientos transfronterizos de los desechos peligrosos y su eliminación y el Convenio de Rotterdam sobre el procedimiento de consentimiento fundamentado previo aplicable a ciertos plaguicidas y productos químicos peligrosos objeto de comercio internacional,

Reconociendo también que el presente Convenio y otros acuerdos internacionales en el ámbito del medio ambiente y el comercio se apoyan mutuamente,

Poniendo de relieve que nada de lo dispuesto en el presente Convenio tiene por objeto afectar los derechos ni las obligaciones de que gocen o que hayan contraído las Partes en virtud de cualquier otro acuerdo internacional existente,

Entendiendo que lo expuesto más arriba no tiene por objeto crear una jerarquía entre el presente Convenio y otros instrumentos internacionales,

Haciendo notar que nada de lo dispuesto en el presente Convenio impide a las Partes adoptar otras medidas nacionales que estén en consonancia con las disposiciones del presente Convenio, como parte de los esfuerzos por proteger la salud humana y el medio ambiente de la exposición al mercurio, de conformidad con otras obligaciones de las Partes dimanantes del derecho internacional aplicable,

Han acordado lo siguiente:

Artículo 1

Objetivo

El objetivo del presente Convenio es proteger la salud humana y el medio ambiente de las emisiones y liberaciones antropógenas de mercurio y compuestos de mercurio.

Artículo 2

Definiciones

A los efectos del presente Convenio:

a) Por "extracción de oro artesanal y en pequeña escala" se entiende la extracción de oro llevada a cabo por mineros particulares o pequeñas empresas con una inversión de capital y una producción limitadas;

b) Por “mejores técnicas disponibles” se entienden las técnicas que son más eficaces para evitar y, cuando eso no es factible, reducir las emisiones y liberaciones de mercurio a la atmósfera, al agua y al suelo, y los efectos de esas emisiones y liberaciones para el medio ambiente en su conjunto, teniendo en cuenta consideraciones económicas y técnicas para una Parte dada o una instalación dada en el territorio de esa Parte. En ese contexto:

i) Por “mejores” se entiende más eficaces para lograr un alto grado general de protección del medio ambiente en su conjunto;

ii) Por “disponibles” se entienden, en relación con una Parte dada y una instalación dada en el territorio de esa Parte, las técnicas que se han desarrollado a una escala que permite su aplicación en un sector industrial pertinente en condiciones de viabilidad económica y técnica, tomando en consideración los costos y los beneficios, ya sean técnicas que se utilicen o produzcan en el territorio de esa Parte o no, siempre y cuando sean accesibles al operador de la instalación como determine esa Parte; y

iii) Por “técnicas” se entienden tanto las tecnologías utilizadas como las prácticas operacionales y la manera en que se diseñan, construyen, mantienen, operan y desmantelan las instalaciones;

c) Por “mejores prácticas ambientales” se entiende la aplicación de la combinación más adecuada de medidas y estrategias de control ambiental;

d) Por “mercurio” se entiende el mercurio elemental (Hg(0), núm. de CAS 7439-97-6);

e) Por “compuesto de mercurio” se entiende toda sustancia que consiste en átomos de mercurio y uno o más átomos de elementos químicos distintos que puedan separarse en componentes diferentes solo por medio de reacciones químicas;

f) Por “producto con mercurio añadido” se entiende un producto o componente de un producto al que se haya añadido mercurio o un compuesto de mercurio de manera intencional;

g) Por “Parte” se entiende un Estado o una organización de integración económica regional que haya consentido en someterse a las obligaciones establecidas en el presente Convenio y en el que el presente Convenio esté en vigor;

h) Por “Partes presentes y votantes” se entiende las Partes que estén presentes y emitan un voto afirmativo o negativo en una reunión de las Partes;

i) Por “extracción primaria de mercurio” se entiende la extracción en la que el principal material que se busca es mercurio;

j) Por “organización de integración económica regional” se entiende una organización constituida por Estados soberanos de una región determinada a la cual los Estados miembros hayan cedido su competencia respecto de los asuntos regidos por el presente Convenio y que haya sido debidamente facultada, de conformidad con sus procedimientos internos, para firmar, ratificar, aceptar o aprobar el presente Convenio o adherirse a él; y

k) Por “uso permitido” se entiende cualquier uso por una Parte de mercurio o de compuestos de mercurio que esté en consonancia con el presente Convenio, incluidos, aunque no únicamente, los usos que estén en consonancia con los artículos 3, 4, 5, 6 y 7.

Artículo 3

Fuentes de suministro y comercio de mercurio

1. A los efectos del presente artículo:

a) Toda referencia al “mercurio” incluye las mezclas de mercurio con otras sustancias, incluidas las aleaciones de mercurio, que tengan una concentración de mercurio de al menos 95% por peso; y

b) Por “compuestos de mercurio” se entiende cloruro de mercurio (I) o calomelanos, óxido de mercurio (II), sulfato de mercurio (II), nitrato de mercurio (II), mineral de cinabrio y sulfuro de mercurio.

2. Las disposiciones del presente artículo no se aplicarán a:

a) Las cantidades de mercurio o compuestos de mercurio que se utilicen para investigaciones a nivel de laboratorio o como patrón de referencia; o

b) Las cantidades traza naturalmente presentes de mercurio o compuestos de mercurio en productos distintos del mercurio tales como metales, mineral en bruto o productos minerales, incluido el carbón, o bien en productos derivados de esos materiales, y las cantidades traza no intencionales presentes en productos químicos; o

c) Los productos con mercurio añadido.

3. Ninguna Parte permitirá la extracción primaria de mercurio que no se estuviera realizando en su territorio en la fecha de entrada en vigor del Convenio para ella.

4. Cada Parte en cuyo territorio se estuvieran realizando actividades de extracción primaria de mercurio en la fecha de entrada en vigor del presente Convenio para ella permitirá esa extracción únicamente por un período de hasta 15 años después de esa fecha. Durante ese período, el mercurio producido por esa extracción solamente se utilizará en la fabricación de productos con mercurio añadido de conformidad con el artículo 4 o en los procesos de fabricación de conformidad con el artículo 5, o bien se eliminará de conformidad con el artículo 11, mediante operaciones que no conduzcan a la recuperación, el reciclado, la regeneración, la reutilización directa u otros usos.

5. Cada Parte:

a) Se esforzará por identificar cada una de las existencias de mercurio o compuestos de mercurio superiores a 50 toneladas métricas, así como las fuentes de suministro de mercurio que generen existencias superiores a 10 toneladas métricas por año, que estén situadas en su territorio;

b) Adoptará medidas para asegurar que, cuando la Parte determine la existencia de exceso de mercurio procedente del desmantelamiento de plantas de producción de cloro-álcali, ese mercurio se deseche de conformidad con las directrices para la gestión ambientalmente racional a que se hace referencia en el párrafo 3 a) del artículo 11, mediante operaciones que no conduzcan a la recuperación, el reciclado, la regeneración, la utilización directa u otros usos.

6. Ninguna Parte permitirá la exportación de mercurio, salvo:

a) A una Parte que haya proporcionado a la Parte exportadora su consentimiento por escrito y únicamente para:

i) Un uso permitido a esa Parte importadora en virtud del presente Convenio; o

ii) Su almacenamiento provisional ambientalmente racional de acuerdo con lo dispuesto en el artículo 10; o

b) A un Estado u organización que no sea Parte que haya proporcionado a la Parte exportadora su consentimiento por escrito en el que se incluya una certificación que demuestre que:

i) El Estado o la organización que no es Parte ha adoptado medidas para garantizar la protección de la salud humana y el medio ambiente, así como el cumplimiento de las disposiciones de los artículos 10 y 11; y

ii) Ese mercurio se destinará únicamente a un uso permitido a una Parte en virtud del presente Convenio o a su almacenamiento provisional ambientalmente racional de acuerdo con lo dispuesto en el artículo 10.

7. Una Parte exportadora podrá considerar que una notificación general a la Secretaría por la Parte importadora, o por un Estado u organización importador que no sea Parte, constituye el consentimiento por escrito exigido en el párrafo 6. En esa notificación general se enunciarán las cláusulas y las condiciones en virtud de las cuales la Parte importadora, o el Estado u organización importador que no sea Parte, proporciona el consentimiento. La notificación podrá ser revocada en cualquier momento por dicha Parte o dicho Estado u organización que no sea Parte. La Secretaría mantendrá un registro público de esas notificaciones.

8. Ninguna Parte permitirá la importación de mercurio de un Estado u organización que no sea Parte a quien comunique su consentimiento por escrito a menos que dicho Estado u organización que no sea Parte haya aportado una certificación de que el mercurio no procede de fuentes no permitidas en virtud del párrafo 3 o del párrafo 5 b).

9. Una Parte que presente una notificación general de consentimiento en virtud del párrafo 7 podrá decidir no aplicar el párrafo 8, siempre y cuando mantenga amplias restricciones a la exportación de mercurio y aplique medidas internas encaminadas a asegurar que el mercurio importado se gestiona de manera ambientalmente racional. La Parte notificará esa decisión a la Secretaría, aportando información que describa las restricciones a la exportación y las medidas normativas internas, así como información sobre las cantidades y los países de origen del mercurio importado de Estados u organizaciones que no sean Parte. La Secretaría mantendrá un registro público de todas las notificaciones de esa índole. El Comité de Aplicación y Cumplimiento examinará y evaluará todas las notificaciones y la información justificativa de conformidad con el artículo 15 y podrá formular recomendaciones, según corresponda, a la Conferencia de las Partes.

10. El procedimiento establecido en el párrafo 9 estará disponible hasta la clausura de la segunda reunión de la Conferencia de las Partes. A partir de ese momento, dejará de estar disponible, a menos que la Conferencia de las Partes decida lo contrario por mayoría simple de las Partes presentes y votantes, excepto en lo que respecta a una Parte que haya presentado una notificación con arreglo al párrafo 9 antes de la clausura de la segunda reunión de la Conferencia de las Partes.

11. Cada Parte incluirá en sus informes presentados con arreglo al artículo 21 información que demuestre que se han cumplido los requisitos fijados en el presente artículo.

12. La Conferencia de las Partes proporcionará, en su primera reunión, orientación ulterior con respecto al presente artículo, especialmente con respecto a los párrafos 5 a), 6 y 8, y elaborará y aprobará el contenido requerido de la certificación a que se hace referencia en los párrafos 6 b) y 8.

13. La Conferencia de las Partes evaluará si el comercio de compuestos de mercurio específicos compromete el objetivo del presente Convenio y examinará si tales compuestos de mercurio específicos deben someterse a los párrafos 6 y 8 mediante su inclusión en un anexo adicional aprobado de conformidad con el artículo 27.

Artículo 4

Productos con mercurio añadido

1. Cada Parte prohibirá, adoptando las medidas pertinentes, la fabricación, la importación y la exportación de los productos con mercurio añadido incluidos en la parte I del anexo A después de la fecha de eliminación especificada para esos productos, salvo cuando se haya especificado una exclusión en el anexo A o cuando la Parte se haya inscrito para una exención conforme al artículo 6.

2. Como alternativa a lo dispuesto en el párrafo 1, una Parte podría indicar, en el momento de la ratificación o en la fecha de entrada en vigor de una enmienda del anexo A para ella, que aplicará medidas o estrategias diferentes en relación con los productos incluidos en la parte I del anexo A. La Parte solamente podrá optar por esta alternativa si puede demostrar que ya ha reducido a un nivel mínimo la fabricación, la importación y la exportación de la gran mayoría de los productos incluidos en la parte I del anexo A y que ha aplicado medidas o estrategias para reducir el uso de mercurio en otros productos no incluidos en la parte I del anexo A en el momento en que notifique a la Secretaría su decisión de usar esa alternativa. Además, una Parte que opte por esta alternativa:

a) Presentará un informe a la Conferencia de las Partes, a la primera oportunidad, con una descripción de las medidas o estrategias adoptadas, incluida la cuantificación de las reducciones alcanzadas;

b) Aplicará medidas o estrategias destinadas a reducir el uso de mercurio en los productos incluidos en la parte I del anexo A para los que todavía no haya obtenido un nivel mínimo;

c) Considerará la posibilidad de aplicar medidas adicionales para lograr mayores reducciones; y

d) No tendrá derecho a hacer uso de exenciones de conformidad con el artículo 6 para ninguna categoría de productos a la cual aplique esta alternativa.

A más tardar cinco años después de la entrada en vigor del Convenio, la Conferencia de las Partes, dentro del proceso de examen establecido en el párrafo 8, examinará los progresos y la eficacia de las medidas adoptadas de conformidad con el presente párrafo.

3. Las Partes adoptarán medidas en relación con los productos con mercurio añadido incluidos en la parte II del anexo A de conformidad con las disposiciones establecidas en dicho anexo.

4. Sobre la base de la información proporcionada por las Partes, la Secretaría reunirá y mantendrá información sobre los productos con mercurio añadido y sus alternativas, y pondrá esa información a disposición del público. La Secretaría hará también pública cualquier otra información pertinente presentada por las Partes.

5. Cada Parte adoptará medidas para impedir la utilización en productos ensamblados de los productos con mercurio añadido cuya fabricación, importación y exportación no estén permitidas en virtud del presente artículo.

6. Cada Parte desincentivará la fabricación y la distribución con fines comerciales de productos con mercurio añadido para usos que no estén comprendidos en ninguno de los usos conocidos de esos productos antes de la fecha de entrada en vigor del presente Convenio para ella, a menos que una evaluación de los riesgos y beneficios de ese producto demuestre beneficios para la salud humana o el medio ambiente. La Parte proporcionará a la Secretaría, según proceda, información sobre cualquier producto de ese tipo, incluida cualquier información sobre los riesgos y beneficios para la salud humana y el medio ambiente. La Secretaría pondrá esa información a disposición del público.

7. Cualquiera de las Partes podrá presentar a la Secretaría una propuesta de inclusión de un producto con mercurio añadido en el anexo A, en la que figurará información relacionada con la disponibilidad, la viabilidad técnica y económica, y los riesgos y beneficios para la salud y el medio ambiente de las alternativas a este producto sin mercurio, teniendo en cuenta la información conforme al párrafo 4.

8. A más tardar cinco años después de la fecha de entrada en vigor del Convenio, la Conferencia de las Partes examinará el anexo A y podrá considerar la posibilidad de introducir enmiendas a ese anexo de acuerdo con lo dispuesto en el artículo 27.

9. En el examen del anexo A conforme a lo dispuesto en el párrafo 8, la Conferencia de las Partes tendrá en cuenta, como mínimo:

a) Cualquier propuesta presentada con arreglo al párrafo 7;

b) La información hecha pública con arreglo al párrafo 4; y

c) El acceso de las Partes a alternativas sin mercurio que sean viables desde el punto de vista técnico y económico y que tengan en cuenta los riesgos y beneficios para el medio ambiente y la salud humana.

Artículo 5

Procesos de fabricación en los que se utiliza mercurio o compuestos de mercurio

1. A los efectos del presente artículo y del anexo B, los procesos de fabricación en los que se utiliza mercurio o compuestos de mercurio no comprenderán los procesos en los que se utilizan productos con mercurio añadido ni los procesos de fabricación de productos con mercurio añadido ni los procesos en que se traten desechos que contengan mercurio.

2. Ninguna Parte permitirá, tomando para ello las medidas apropiadas, el uso de mercurio ni de compuestos de mercurio en los procesos de fabricación incluidos en la parte I del anexo B tras la fecha de eliminación especificada en dicho anexo para cada proceso, salvo cuando la Parte se haya inscrito para una exención conforme al artículo 6.

3. Cada Parte adoptará medidas para restringir el uso de mercurio o compuestos de mercurio en los procesos incluidos en la parte II del anexo B de conformidad con las disposiciones que allí se establecen.

4. Sobre la base de la información proporcionada por las Partes, la Secretaría reunirá y mantendrá información sobre los procesos en los que se utiliza mercurio o compuestos de mercurio y sus alternativas, y pondrá esa información a disposición del público. Las Partes podrán presentar otra información pertinente, que la Secretaría pondrá a disposición del público.

5. Cada Parte que cuente con una o más instalaciones que utilicen mercurio o compuestos de mercurio en los procesos de fabricación incluidos en el anexo B:

a) Adoptará medidas para ocuparse de las emisiones y liberaciones de mercurio o compuestos de mercurio de esas instalaciones;

b) Incluirá en los informes que presente de conformidad con el artículo 21 información sobre las medidas adoptadas en cumplimiento del presente párrafo; y

c) Se esforzará por identificar las instalaciones ubicadas dentro de su territorio que utilizan mercurio o compuestos de mercurio en los procesos incluidos en el anexo B y, a más tardar tres años después de la fecha de entrada en vigor del presente Convenio para la Parte, presentará a la Secretaría información sobre el número y los tipos de instalaciones y una estimación de la cantidad de mercurio o compuestos de mercurio que utiliza anualmente. La Secretaría pondrá esa información a disposición del público.

6. Ninguna Parte permitirá el uso de mercurio ni de compuestos de mercurio en instalaciones que no existieran antes de la fecha de entrada en vigor del presente Convenio para la Parte y que utilicen procesos de fabricación incluidos en el anexo B. A esas instalaciones no se les otorgará exención alguna.

7. Las Partes desincentivarán el establecimiento de instalaciones, no existentes antes de la fecha de entrada en vigor del presente Convenio, que usen cualquier otro proceso de fabricación en el que se utilice mercurio o compuestos de mercurio de manera intencional, salvo que la Parte pueda demostrar, a satisfacción de la Conferencia de las Partes, que el proceso de fabricación reporta un beneficio importante para el medio ambiente y la salud, y que no existen alternativas sin mercurio viables desde el punto de vista económico y técnico que ofrezcan ese beneficio.

8. Se alienta a las Partes a intercambiar información sobre nuevos avances tecnológicos pertinentes, alternativas sin mercurio viables desde el punto de vista económico y técnico, y posibles medidas y técnicas para reducir y, cuando sea factible, eliminar el uso de mercurio y compuestos de mercurio de los procesos de fabricación incluidos en el anexo B, así como las emisiones y las liberaciones de mercurio y compuestos de mercurio procedentes de esos procesos.

9. Cualquiera de las Partes podrá presentar una propuesta de modificación del anexo B con objeto de incluir un proceso de fabricación en el que se utilice mercurio o compuestos de mercurio. La propuesta incluirá información relacionada con la disponibilidad, la viabilidad técnica y económica, y los riesgos y beneficios para la salud humana y el medio ambiente de las alternativas sin mercurio.

10. A más tardar cinco años después de la fecha de entrada en vigor del Convenio, la Conferencia de las Partes examinará el anexo B y podrá considerar la posibilidad de introducir enmiendas en ese anexo de acuerdo con lo dispuesto en el artículo 27.

11. Al examinar el anexo B conforme a lo dispuesto en el párrafo 10, en su caso, la Conferencia de las Partes tendrá en cuenta, como mínimo:

a) Cualquier propuesta presentada con arreglo al párrafo 9;

b) La información puesta a disposición conforme al párrafo 4; y

c) El acceso de las Partes a alternativas sin mercurio que sean viables desde el punto de vista técnico y económico, teniendo en cuenta los riesgos y beneficios para el medio ambiente y la salud.

Artículo 6

Exenciones de las que puede hacer uso una Parte previa solicitud

1. Cualquier Estado u organización de integración económica regional podrá inscribirse para una o más exenciones a partir de las fechas de eliminación que figuran en el anexo A y en el anexo B, en adelante denominadas "exenciones", notificándolo por escrito a la Secretaría:

a) Al pasar a ser Parte en el presente Convenio; o

b) En el caso de los productos con mercurio añadido que se añadan por una enmienda del anexo A o de los procesos de fabricación en los que se utilice mercurio y que se añadan por una enmienda del anexo B, a más tardar en la fecha en que entre en vigor para la Parte la enmienda aplicable.

Toda inscripción de ese tipo irá acompañada de una declaración en la que se explique la necesidad de la Parte de hacer uso de la exención.

2. Será posible inscribirse para una exención respecto de una de las categorías incluidas en el anexo A o B, o respecto de una subcategoría determinada por cualquier Estado u organización de integración económica regional.

3. Cada Parte que tenga una o varias exenciones se identificará en un registro. La Secretaría establecerá y mantendrá ese registro y lo pondrá a disposición del público.

4. El registro constará de:

a) Una lista de las Partes que tienen una o varias exenciones;

b) La exención o exenciones inscritas para cada Parte; y

c) La fecha de expiración de cada exención.

5. A menos que una Parte indique en el registro una fecha anterior, todas las exenciones inscritas con arreglo al párrafo 1 expirarán transcurridos cinco años de la fecha de eliminación correspondiente indicada en los anexos A o B.

6. La Conferencia de las Partes podrá, a petición de una Parte, decidir prorrogar una exención por cinco años, a menos que la Parte pida un período más breve. Al adoptar su decisión, la Conferencia de las Partes tendrá debidamente en cuenta:

a) Un informe de la Parte en el que justifique la necesidad de prorrogar la exención e indique las actividades emprendidas y planificadas para eliminar la necesidad de esa exención lo antes posible;

b) La información disponible, incluida la disponibilidad de productos y procesos alternativos que no utilicen mercurio o para los cuales se consuma menos mercurio que para el uso exento; y

c) Las actividades planificadas o en curso para almacenar mercurio y eliminar desechos de mercurio de manera ambientalmente racional.

Las exenciones solo se podrán prorrogar una única vez por producto por fecha de eliminación.

7. Una Parte podrá, en cualquier momento, retirar una exención mediante notificación por escrito a la Secretaría. El retiro de la exención será efectivo en la fecha que se especifique en la notificación.

8. No obstante lo dispuesto en el párrafo 1, ningún Estado ni organización de integración económica regional podrá inscribirse para una exención transcurridos cinco años desde la fecha de eliminación del producto o proceso correspondiente incluido en los anexos A o B, a menos que una o varias Partes continúen inscritas para una exención respecto de ese producto o proceso por haber recibido una prórroga de conformidad con el párrafo 6. En ese caso, un Estado o una organización de integración económica regional podrá, en las fechas establecidas en el párrafo 1 a) y b), inscribirse para una exención respecto de ese producto o proceso, exención que expirará transcurridos diez años desde la fecha de eliminación correspondiente.

9. Ninguna Parte tendrá exenciones en vigor en ningún momento transcurridos diez años desde la fecha de eliminación de un producto o proceso incluido en los anexos A o B.

Artículo 7

Extracción de oro artesanal y en pequeña escala

1. Las medidas que figuran en el presente artículo y en el anexo C se aplicarán a las actividades de extracción y tratamiento de oro artesanales y en pequeña escala en las que se utilice amalgama de mercurio para extraer oro de la mina.

2. Cada Parte en cuyo territorio se realicen actividades de extracción y tratamiento de oro artesanales y en pequeña escala sujetas al presente artículo adoptará medidas para reducir y, cuando sea viable, eliminar el uso de mercurio y de compuestos de mercurio de esas actividades y las emisiones y liberaciones de mercurio en el medio ambiente provenientes de ellas.

3. Cada Parte notificará a la Secretaría si en cualquier momento determina que las actividades de extracción y tratamiento de oro artesanales y en pequeña escala realizadas en su territorio son más que insignificantes. Si así lo determina, la Parte:

a) Elaborará y aplicará un plan de acción nacional de conformidad con el anexo C;

b) Presentará su plan de acción nacional a la Secretaría a más tardar tres años después de la entrada en vigor del Convenio para esa Parte o tres años después de la notificación a la Secretaría, si esa fecha fuese posterior; y

c) En lo sucesivo, presentará un examen, cada tres años, de los progresos realizados en el cumplimiento de las obligaciones contraídas en virtud del presente artículo e incluirá esos exámenes en los informes que presente de conformidad con el artículo 21.

4. Las Partes podrán cooperar entre sí y con las organizaciones intergubernamentales y otras entidades pertinentes, según proceda, para lograr los objetivos del presente artículo. Esa cooperación podría incluir:

a) La formulación de estrategias para prevenir el desvío de mercurio o compuestos de mercurio para su uso en la extracción y el tratamiento de oro artesanales y en pequeña escala;

b) Las iniciativas de educación, divulgación y creación de capacidad;

c) La promoción de investigaciones sobre prácticas alternativas sostenibles en las que no se utilice mercurio;

d) La prestación de asistencia técnica y financiera;

e) El establecimiento de modalidades de asociación para facilitar el cumplimiento de los compromisos contraídos en virtud del presente artículo; y

f) El uso de los mecanismos de intercambio de información existentes para promover conocimientos, mejores prácticas ambientales y tecnologías alternativas que sean viables desde el punto de vista ambiental, técnico, social y económico.

Artículo 8

Emisiones

1. El presente artículo trata del control y, cuando sea viable, la reducción de las emisiones de mercurio y compuestos de mercurio, a menudo expresadas como "mercurio total", a la atmósfera mediante medidas encaminadas a controlar las emisiones procedentes de las fuentes puntuales que entran dentro de las categorías enumeradas en el anexo D.

2. A los efectos del presente artículo:

a) Por “emisiones” se entienden las emisiones de mercurio o compuestos de mercurio a la atmósfera;

b) Por “fuente pertinente” se entiende una fuente que entra dentro de una de las categorías enumeradas en el anexo D. Una Parte podrá, si así lo desea, establecer criterios para identificar las fuentes incluidas en una de las categorías enumeradas en el anexo D, siempre que esos criterios incluyan al menos el 75% de las emisiones procedentes de esa categoría;

c) Por “nueva fuente” se entiende cualquier fuente pertinente de una categoría enumerada en el anexo D, cuya construcción o modificación sustancial comience como mínimo un año después de la fecha de:

i) La entrada en vigor del presente Convenio para la Parte de que se trate; o

ii) La entrada en vigor para la Parte de que se trate de una enmienda del anexo D en virtud de la cual la fuente de emisiones quede sujeta a las disposiciones del presente Convenio únicamente en virtud de esa enmienda;

d) Por “modificación sustancial” se entiende la modificación de una fuente pertinente cuyo resultado sea un aumento significativo de las emisiones, con exclusión de cualquier variación en las emisiones resultante de la recuperación de subproductos. Corresponderá a la Parte decidir si una modificación es o no sustancial;

e) Por “fuente existente” se entiende cualquier fuente pertinente que no sea una nueva fuente;

f) Por “valor límite de emisión” se entiende un límite a la concentración, la masa o la tasa de emisión de mercurio o compuestos de mercurio, a menudo expresadas como “mercurio total”, emitida por una fuente puntual.

3. Una Parte en la que haya fuentes pertinentes adoptará medidas para controlar las emisiones y podrá preparar un plan nacional en el que se expongan las medidas que deben adoptarse para controlar las emisiones, así como las metas, los objetivos y los resultados que prevé obtener. Esos planes se presentarán a la Conferencia de las Partes en un plazo de cuatro años desde la fecha de entrada en vigor del Convenio para esa Parte. Si una Parte decidiera elaborar un plan de aplicación con arreglo a lo establecido en el artículo 20, podrá incluir en su texto el plan que se contempla en el presente párrafo.

4. En lo relativo a las nuevas fuentes, cada Parte exigirá el uso de las mejores técnicas disponibles y las mejores prácticas ambientales para controlar y, cuando sea viable, reducir las emisiones lo antes posible, pero en cualquier caso antes de que

transcurran cinco años desde la entrada en vigor del Convenio para esa Parte. Una Parte podrá utilizar valores límite de emisión que sean compatibles con la aplicación de las mejores técnicas disponibles.

5. En lo relativo a las fuentes existentes, cada Parte incluirá una o más de las siguientes medidas en cualquier plan nacional y las aplicará lo antes posible, pero en cualquier caso antes de que transcurran diez años desde la fecha de entrada en vigor del Convenio para ella, teniendo en cuenta las circunstancias nacionales y la viabilidad económica y técnica, así como la asequibilidad, de las medidas:

a) Un objetivo cuantificado para controlar y, cuando sea viable, reducir las emisiones procedentes de las fuentes pertinentes;

b) Valores límite de emisión para controlar y, cuando sea viable, reducir las emisiones procedentes de las fuentes pertinentes;

c) El uso de las mejores técnicas disponibles y las mejores prácticas ambientales para controlar las emisiones procedentes de las fuentes pertinentes;

d) Una estrategia de control de múltiples contaminantes que aporte beneficios paralelos para el control de las emisiones de mercurio;

e) Otras medidas encaminadas a reducir las emisiones procedentes de las fuentes pertinentes.

6. Las Partes podrán aplicar las mismas medidas a todas las fuentes existentes pertinentes o podrán adoptar medidas diferentes con respecto a diferentes categorías de fuentes. El objetivo será que las medidas aplicadas por una Parte permitan lograr, con el tiempo, progresos razonables en la reducción de las emisiones.

7. Cada Parte establecerá, tan pronto como sea factible y a más tardar cinco años después de la fecha de entrada en vigor del Convenio para ella, un inventario de las emisiones de las fuentes pertinentes, que mantendrá a partir de entonces.

8. La Conferencia de las Partes, en su primera reunión, aprobará directrices sobre:

a) Las mejores técnicas disponibles y las mejores prácticas ambientales, teniendo en cuenta las posibles diferencias entre las fuentes nuevas y las existentes, así como la necesidad de reducir al mínimo los efectos cruzados entre los distintos medios; y

b) La prestación de apoyo a las Partes en la aplicación de las medidas que figuran en el párrafo 5, especialmente en la determinación de los objetivos y el establecimiento de los valores límite de emisión.

9. La Conferencia de las Partes, tan pronto como sea factible, aprobará directrices sobre:

a) Los criterios que las Partes pueden establecer con arreglo al párrafo 2 b);

b) La metodología para la preparación de inventarios de emisiones.

10. La Conferencia de las Partes mantendrá en examen, y actualizará según proceda, las directrices elaboradas con arreglo a lo establecido en los párrafos 8 y 9. Las Partes tendrán en cuenta esas directrices al aplicar las disposiciones pertinentes del presente artículo.

11. Cada Parte incluirá información sobre la aplicación del presente artículo en los informes que presente en virtud de lo establecido en el artículo 21, en particular información relativa a las medidas que haya adoptado con arreglo a los párrafos 4 a 7, y a la eficacia de esas medidas.

Artículo 9

Liberaciones

1. El presente artículo trata del control y, cuando sea viable, la reducción de las liberaciones de mercurio y compuestos de mercurio, a menudo expresadas como "mercurio total", al suelo y al agua procedentes de fuentes puntuales pertinentes no consideradas en otras disposiciones del presente Convenio.

2. A los efectos del presente artículo:

a) Por "liberaciones" se entienden las liberaciones de mercurio o compuestos de mercurio al suelo o al agua;

b) Por "fuente pertinente" se entiende toda fuente puntual antropógena significativa de liberaciones detectada por una Parte y no considerada en otras disposiciones del presente Convenio;

c) Por "nueva fuente" se entiende cualquier fuente pertinente cuya construcción o modificación sustancial comience como mínimo un año después de la fecha de entrada en vigor del presente Convenio para la Parte de que se trate;

d) Por "modificación sustancial" se entiende la modificación de una fuente pertinente cuyo resultado sea un aumento significativo de las liberaciones, con exclusión de cualquier variación en las liberaciones resultante de la recuperación de subproductos. Corresponderá a la Parte decidir si una modificación es o no sustancial;

e) Por "fuente existente" se entiende cualquier fuente pertinente que no sea una nueva fuente;

f) Por "valor límite de liberación" se entiende un límite a la concentración o la masa de mercurio o compuestos de mercurio, a menudo expresadas como "mercurio total", liberada por una fuente puntual.

3. Cada Parte determinará las categorías pertinentes de fuentes puntuales a más tardar tres años después de la entrada en vigor para ella del Convenio y periódicamente a partir de entonces.

4. Una Parte en la que haya fuentes pertinentes adoptará medidas para controlar las liberaciones y podrá preparar un plan nacional en el que se expongan las medidas que deben adoptarse para controlar las liberaciones, así como las metas, los objetivos y los resultados que prevé obtener. Esos planes se presentarán a la Conferencia de las Partes en un plazo de cuatro años desde la fecha de entrada en vigor del Convenio para esa Parte. Si una Parte decidiera elaborar un plan de aplicación con arreglo a lo establecido en el artículo 20, podrá incluir en su texto el plan que se contempla en el presente párrafo.

5. Las medidas incluirán una o varias de las siguientes, según corresponda:

a) Valores límite de liberación para controlar y, cuando sea viable, reducir las liberaciones procedentes de las fuentes pertinentes;

b) El uso de las mejores técnicas disponibles y las mejores prácticas ambientales para controlar las liberaciones procedentes de las fuentes pertinentes;

c) Una estrategia de control de múltiples contaminantes que aporte beneficios paralelos para el control de las liberaciones de mercurio;

d) Otras medidas encaminadas a reducir las liberaciones procedentes de las fuentes pertinentes.

6. Cada Parte establecerá, tan pronto como sea factible y a más tardar cinco años después de la fecha de entrada en vigor del Convenio para ella, un inventario de las liberaciones de las fuentes pertinentes, que mantendrá a partir de entonces.

7. La Conferencia de las Partes, tan pronto como sea factible, aprobará directrices sobre:

a) Las mejores técnicas disponibles y las mejores prácticas ambientales, teniendo en cuenta las posibles diferencias entre las fuentes nuevas y las existentes, así como la necesidad de reducir al mínimo los efectos cruzados entre los distintos medios;

b) La metodología para la preparación de inventarios de liberaciones.

8. Cada Parte incluirá información sobre la aplicación del presente artículo en los informes que presente en virtud de lo establecido en el artículo 21, en particular información relativa a las medidas que haya adoptado con arreglo a los párrafos 3 a 6, y a la eficacia de esas medidas.

Artículo 10

Almacenamiento provisional ambientalmente racional de mercurio, distinto del mercurio de desecho

1. El presente artículo se aplicará al almacenamiento provisional de mercurio y compuestos de mercurio definidos en el artículo 3 que no estén comprendidos en el significado de la definición de desechos de mercurio que figura en el artículo 11.

2. Cada Parte adoptará medidas para velar por que el almacenamiento provisional de mercurio y de compuestos de mercurio destinados a un uso permitido a una Parte en virtud del presente Convenio se lleve a cabo de manera ambientalmente racional, teniendo en cuenta toda directriz y de acuerdo con todo requisito que se apruebe con arreglo al párrafo 3.

3. La Conferencia de las Partes adoptará directrices sobre el almacenamiento provisional ambientalmente racional de dicho mercurio y compuestos de mercurio, teniendo en cuenta las directrices pertinentes elaboradas en el marco del Convenio de Basilea sobre el control de los movimientos transfronterizos de los desechos peligrosos y su eliminación y toda otra orientación pertinente. La Conferencia de las Partes podrá aprobar requisitos para el almacenamiento provisional en un anexo adicional del presente Convenio, con arreglo al artículo 27.

4. Las Partes cooperarán, según proceda, entre sí y con las organizaciones intergubernamentales y otras entidades pertinentes a fin de aumentar la creación de capacidad para el almacenamiento provisional ambientalmente racional de ese mercurio y compuestos de mercurio.

Artículo 11

Desechos de mercurio

1. Las definiciones pertinentes del Convenio de Basilea sobre el control de los movimientos transfronterizos de los desechos peligrosos y su eliminación se aplicarán a los desechos incluidos en el presente Convenio para las Partes en el Convenio de Basilea. Las Partes en el presente Convenio que no sean Partes en el Convenio de Basilea harán uso de esas definiciones como orientación aplicada a los desechos a que se refiere el presente Convenio.

2. A los efectos del presente Convenio, por desechos de mercurio se entienden sustancias u objetos:

a) que constan de mercurio o compuestos de mercurio;

b) que contienen mercurio o compuestos de mercurio; o

c) contaminados con mercurio o compuestos de mercurio,

en una cantidad que exceda los umbrales pertinentes definidos por la Conferencia de las Partes, en colaboración con los órganos pertinentes del Convenio de Basilea de manera armonizada, a cuya eliminación se procede, se propone proceder o se está obligado a proceder en virtud de lo dispuesto en la legislación nacional o en el presente Convenio. Se excluyen de esta definición la roca de recubrimiento, de desecho y los desechos de la minería, salvo los derivados de la extracción primaria de mercurio, a menos que contengan cantidades de mercurio o compuestos de mercurio que excedan los umbrales definidos por la Conferencia de las Partes.

3. Cada Parte adoptará las medidas apropiadas para que los desechos de mercurio:

a) Sean gestionados, de manera ambientalmente racional, teniendo en cuenta las directrices elaboradas en el marco del Convenio de Basilea y de conformidad con los requisitos que la Conferencia de las Partes aprobará en un anexo adicional, de acuerdo con lo dispuesto en el artículo 27. En la elaboración de los requisitos, la Conferencia de las Partes tendrá en cuenta los reglamentos y programas de las Partes en materia de gestión de desechos;

b) Sean recuperados, reciclados, regenerados o reutilizados directamente solo para un uso permitido a la Parte en virtud del presente Convenio o para la eliminación ambientalmente racional con arreglo al párrafo 3 a);

c) En el caso de las Partes en el Convenio de Basilea, no sean transportados a través de fronteras internacionales salvo con fines de su eliminación ambientalmente racional, de conformidad con las disposiciones del presente artículo y con dicho Convenio. En circunstancias en las que las disposiciones del Convenio de Basilea no se apliquen al transporte a través de fronteras internacionales, las Partes permitirán ese transporte únicamente después de haber tomado en cuenta los reglamentos, normas y directrices internacionales pertinentes.

4. La Conferencia de las Partes procurará cooperar estrechamente con los órganos pertinentes del Convenio de Basilea en el examen y la actualización, según proceda, de las directrices a que se hace referencia en el párrafo 3 a).

5. Se alienta a las Partes a cooperar entre sí y con las organizaciones intergubernamentales y otras entidades pertinentes, según proceda, a fin de crear y

mantener la capacidad de gestionar los desechos de mercurio de manera ambientalmente racional a nivel mundial, regional y nacional.

Artículo 12

Sitios contaminados

1. Cada Parte procurará elaborar estrategias adecuadas para identificar y evaluar los sitios contaminados con mercurio o compuestos de mercurio.

2. Toda medida adoptada para reducir los riesgos que generan esos sitios se llevará a cabo de manera ambientalmente racional incorporando, cuando proceda, una evaluación de los riesgos para la salud humana y el medio ambiente derivados del mercurio o de los compuestos de mercurio que contengan.

3. La Conferencia de las Partes aprobará orientaciones sobre la gestión de sitios contaminados, que podrán incluir métodos y criterios en relación con:

a) La identificación y caracterización de sitios;

b) La participación del público;

c) La evaluación de los riesgos para la salud humana y el medio ambiente;

d) Las opciones para gestionar los riesgos que plantean los sitios contaminados;

e) La evaluación de los costos y beneficios; y

f) La validación de los resultados.

4. Se alienta a las Partes a cooperar en la formulación de estrategias y la ejecución de actividades para detectar, evaluar, priorizar, gestionar y, según proceda, rehabilitar sitios contaminados.

Artículo 13

Recursos financieros y mecanismo financiero

1. Cada Parte, con arreglo a sus posibilidades y de conformidad con sus políticas, prioridades, planes y programas nacionales, se compromete a facilitar recursos respecto de las actividades nacionales cuya finalidad sea aplicar el presente Convenio. Esos recursos podrán comprender la financiación nacional mediante políticas al respecto, estrategias de desarrollo y presupuestos nacionales, así como la financiación multilateral y bilateral, además de la participación del sector privado.

2. La eficacia general en la aplicación del presente Convenio por las Partes que son países en desarrollo estará relacionada con la aplicación efectiva del presente artículo.

3. Se alienta a las fuentes multilaterales, regionales y bilaterales de asistencia técnica y financiera, así como de creación de capacidad y transferencia de tecnología, a que mejoren y aumenten con carácter urgente sus actividades relacionadas con el mercurio en apoyo de las Partes que son países en desarrollo con miras a la aplicación del presente Convenio en lo que respecta a los recursos financieros, la asistencia técnica y la transferencia de tecnología.

4. En las medidas relacionadas con la financiación, las Partes tendrán plenamente en cuenta las necesidades específicas y las circunstancias especiales de las Partes que son pequeños Estados insulares en desarrollo o países menos adelantados.

5. Por el presente se define un Mecanismo para facilitar recursos financieros adecuados, previsibles y oportunos. El Mecanismo está dirigido a apoyar a las Partes que son países en desarrollo y a las Partes con economías en transición en el cumplimiento de las obligaciones contraídas en virtud del presente Convenio.

6. El Mecanismo incluirá lo siguiente:

a) El Fondo Fiduciario del Fondo para el Medio Ambiente Mundial; y

b) Un Programa internacional específico para apoyar la creación de capacidad y la asistencia técnica.

7. El Fondo Fiduciario del Fondo para el Medio Ambiente Mundial aportará nuevos recursos financieros previsibles, adecuados y oportunos para sufragar los costos de apoyo a la aplicación del presente Convenio conforme a lo acordado por la Conferencia de las Partes. A los efectos del presente Convenio, el Fondo Fiduciario del Fondo para el Medio Ambiente Mundial funcionará bajo la orientación de la Conferencia de las Partes, a la que rendirá cuentas. La Conferencia de las Partes facilitará orientaciones sobre las estrategias generales, las políticas, las prioridades programáticas y las condiciones que otorguen el derecho a acceder a los recursos financieros y utilizarlos. Además, la Conferencia de las Partes brindará orientación sobre una lista indicativa de categorías de actividades que podrán recibir apoyo del Fondo Fiduciario del Fondo para el Medio Ambiente Mundial. El Fondo Fiduciario aportará recursos para sufragar los costos adicionales convenidos que permitan obtener beneficios ambientales mundiales y la totalidad de los costos convenidos de algunas actividades de apoyo.

8. Al aportar recursos para una actividad, el Fondo Fiduciario del Fondo para el Medio Ambiente Mundial debería tener en cuenta el potencial de reducción de mercurio de una actividad propuesta en relación con su costo.

9. A los efectos del presente Convenio, el Programa mencionado en el párrafo 6 b) funcionará bajo la orientación de la Conferencia de las Partes, a la que rendirá cuentas. La Conferencia de las Partes, en su primera reunión, tomará una decisión sobre la institución anfitriona del Programa, que será una entidad existente, y facilitará orientaciones a esta, incluso en lo relativo a la duración del mismo. Se invita a todas las Partes y otros grupos de interés a que aporten recursos financieros para el Programa, con carácter voluntario.

10. En su primera reunión, la Conferencia de las Partes acordará con las entidades integrantes del Mecanismo las disposiciones necesarias para dar efecto a los párrafos anteriores.

11. La Conferencia de las Partes examinará, a más tardar en su tercera reunión, y de ahí en adelante de manera periódica, el nivel de financiación, la orientación facilitada por la Conferencia de las Partes a las entidades encargadas del funcionamiento del Mecanismo establecido conforme al presente artículo y la eficacia de tales entidades, así como su capacidad para atender a las cambiantes necesidades de las Partes que son países en desarrollo y las Partes con economías en transición. Sobre la base de ese examen, la Conferencia adoptará las medidas apropiadas a fin de incrementar la eficacia del Mecanismo.

12. Se invita a todas las Partes a que hagan contribuciones al Mecanismo, en la medida de sus posibilidades. El Mecanismo promoverá el suministro de recursos provenientes de otras fuentes, incluido el sector privado, y tratará de atraer ese tipo de recursos para las actividades a las que presta apoyo.

Artículo 14

Creación de capacidad, asistencia técnica y transferencia de tecnología

1. Las Partes cooperarán, en la medida de sus respectivas posibilidades y de manera oportuna y adecuada, en la creación de capacidad y la prestación de asistencia técnica en beneficio de las Partes que son países en desarrollo, en particular las Partes que son países menos adelantados o pequeños Estados insulares en desarrollo, y las Partes con economías en transición, a fin de ayudarlas a cumplir las obligaciones contraídas en virtud del presente Convenio.

2. La creación de capacidad y la asistencia técnica previstas en el párrafo 1 y el artículo 13 se podrán proporcionar a través de arreglos regionales, subregionales y nacionales, incluidos los centros regionales y subregionales existentes, a través de otros medios multilaterales y bilaterales, y a través de asociaciones, incluidas aquellas en las que participe el sector privado. Con el fin de aumentar la eficacia de la asistencia técnica y su prestación, debería procurarse la cooperación y la

coordinación con otros acuerdos ambientales multilaterales en la esfera de los productos químicos y los desechos.

3. Las Partes que son países desarrollados y otras Partes promoverán y facilitarán, en la medida de sus posibilidades, con el apoyo del sector privado y otros grupos de interés, según corresponda, el desarrollo, la transferencia y la difusión de tecnologías alternativas ambientalmente racionales actualizadas, así como el acceso a estas, a las Partes que son países en desarrollo, en particular las Partes que son países menos adelantados y pequeños Estados insulares en desarrollo, y las Partes con economías en transición, para reforzar su capacidad de aplicar con eficacia el presente Convenio.

4. La Conferencia de las Partes, a más tardar en su segunda reunión y en lo sucesivo en forma periódica, teniendo en cuenta los documentos presentados y los informes de las Partes, incluidos los previstos en el artículo 21, así como la información proporcionada por otros grupos de interés:

a) Examinará la información sobre iniciativas existentes y progresos realizados en relación con las tecnologías alternativas;

b) Examinará las necesidades de las Partes, en particular las Partes que son países en desarrollo, en cuanto a tecnologías alternativas; y

c) Determinará los retos a que se enfrentan las Partes, especialmente las Partes que son países en desarrollo, en lo que respecta a la transferencia de tecnología.

5. La Conferencia de las Partes formulará recomendaciones sobre la manera de seguir mejorando la creación de capacidad, la asistencia técnica y la transferencia de tecnología según lo dispuesto en el presente artículo.

Artículo 15

Comité de Aplicación y Cumplimiento

1. Por el presente artículo queda establecido un mecanismo, que incluye un Comité como órgano subsidiario de la Conferencia de las Partes, para promover la aplicación y examinar el cumplimiento de todas las disposiciones del presente Convenio. El mecanismo, incluido el Comité, tendrá un carácter facilitador y prestará especial atención a las capacidades y circunstancias nacionales de cada una de las Partes.

2. El Comité promoverá la aplicación y examinará el cumplimiento de todas las disposiciones del presente Convenio. El Comité examinará las cuestiones específicas y sistémicas relacionadas con la aplicación y el cumplimiento, y formulará recomendaciones, según proceda, a la Conferencia de las Partes.

3. El Comité estará integrado por 15 miembros propuestos por las Partes y elegidos por la Conferencia de las Partes teniendo debidamente en cuenta la representación geográfica equitativa de las cinco regiones de las Naciones Unidas; los primeros miembros serán elegidos en la primera reunión de la Conferencia de las Partes y, en adelante, se seguirá el reglamento aprobado por la Conferencia de las Partes en virtud del párrafo 5; los miembros del Comité tendrán competencia en una esfera pertinente para el presente Convenio y reflejarán un equilibro de conocimientos especializados apropiado.

4. El Comité podrá examinar cuestiones sobre la base de:

a) Los documentos presentados remitidos por escrito por cualquier Parte en relación con su propio cumplimiento;

b) Los informes nacionales presentado de conformidad con el artículo 21; y

c) Las solicitudes de la Conferencia de las Partes.

5. El Comité elaborará su propio reglamento, que estará sujeto a la aprobación de la Conferencia de las Partes en su segunda reunión; la Conferencia de las Partes podrá aprobar mandatos adicionales para el Comité.

6. El Comité hará todo lo que esté a su alcance para aprobar sus recomendaciones por consenso. Una vez agotados todos los esfuerzos por llegar a un consenso sin lograrlo, las recomendaciones se aprobarán, como último recurso, por el voto de tres cuartas partes de los miembros presentes y votantes, con un quórum de dos terceras partes de los miembros.

Artículo 16

Aspectos relacionados con la salud

1. Se alienta a las Partes a:

a) Promover la elaboración y la ejecución de estrategias y programas que sirvan para identificar y proteger a las poblaciones en situación de riesgo, especialmente las vulnerables, que podrán incluir la aprobación de directrices sanitarias de base científica relacionadas con la exposición al mercurio y los compuestos de mercurio, el establecimiento de metas para la reducción de la exposición al mercurio, según corresponda, y la educación del público, con la participación del sector de la salud pública y otros sectores interesados;

b) Promover la elaboración y la ejecución de programas educativos y preventivos de base científica sobre la exposición ocupacional al mercurio y los compuestos de mercurio;

c) Promover servicios adecuados de atención sanitaria para la prevención, el tratamiento y la atención de las poblaciones afectadas por la exposición al mercurio o los compuestos de mercurio; y

d) Establecer y fortalecer, según corresponda, la capacidad institucional y de los profesionales de la salud para prevenir, diagnosticar, tratar y vigilar los riesgos para la salud relacionados con la exposición al mercurio y los compuestos de mercurio.

2. Al examinar cuestiones o actividades relacionadas con la salud, la Conferencia de las Partes debería:

a) Consultar y colaborar con la Organización Mundial de la Salud, la Organización Internacional del Trabajo y otras organizaciones intergubernamentales pertinentes, según proceda; y

b) Promover la cooperación y el intercambio de información con la Organización Mundial de la Salud, la Organización Internacional del Trabajo y otras organizaciones intergubernamentales pertinentes, según proceda.

Artículo 17

Intercambio de información

1. Cada Parte facilitará el intercambio de:

a) Información científica, técnica, económica y jurídica relativa al mercurio y los compuestos de mercurio, incluida información toxicológica, ecotoxicológica y sobre seguridad;

b) Información sobre la reducción o eliminación de la producción, el uso, el comercio, las emisiones y las liberaciones de mercurio y compuestos de mercurio;

c) Información sobre alternativas viables desde el punto de vista técnico y económico a:

i) los productos con mercurio añadido;

ii) los procesos de fabricación en los que se utiliza mercurio o compuestos de mercurio; y

iii) las actividades y los procesos que emiten o liberan mercurio o compuestos de mercurio;

incluida información relativa a los riesgos para la salud y el medio ambiente y a los costos y beneficios económicos y sociales de esas alternativas; e

d) Información epidemiológica relativa a los efectos para la salud asociados con la exposición al mercurio y los compuestos de mercurio, en estrecha cooperación con la Organización Mundial de la Salud y otras organizaciones pertinentes, según proceda.

2. Las Partes podrán intercambiar la información a que se hace referencia en el párrafo 1 directamente, a través de la Secretaría o en cooperación con otras organizaciones pertinentes, incluidas las secretarías de los convenios sobre productos químicos y desechos, según proceda.

3. La Secretaría facilitará la cooperación en el intercambio de información al que se hace referencia en el presente artículo, así como con las organizaciones pertinentes, incluidas las secretarías de los acuerdos ambientales multilaterales y otras iniciativas internacionales. Además de la información proporcionada por las Partes, esta información incluirá la proporcionada por organizaciones intergubernamentales y no gubernamentales que tengan conocimientos especializados en la esfera del mercurio, y por instituciones nacionales e internacionales que tengan esos conocimientos.

4. Cada Parte designará un coordinador nacional para el intercambio de información en el marco del presente Convenio, incluso en relación con el consentimiento de las Partes importadoras en virtud del artículo 3.

5. A los efectos del presente Convenio, la información sobre la salud y la seguridad humanas y del medio ambiente no se considerará confidencial. Las Partes que intercambien otro tipo de información de conformidad con el presente Convenio protegerán toda información confidencial en la forma que convengan mutuamente.

Artículo 18

Información, sensibilización y formación del público

1. Cada Parte, con arreglo a sus capacidades, promoverá y facilitará:

a) El acceso del público a información disponible sobre:

i) Los efectos del mercurio y los compuestos de mercurio para la salud y el medio ambiente;

ii) Alternativas al mercurio y los compuestos de mercurio;

iii) Los temas que figuran en el párrafo 1 del artículo 17;

iv) Los resultados de las actividades de investigación, desarrollo y vigilancia que realice de conformidad con el artículo 19; y

v) Las actividades destinadas a cumplir las obligaciones contraídas en virtud del presente Convenio;

b) La formación, la capacitación y la sensibilización del público en relación con los efectos de la exposición al mercurio y los compuestos de mercurio para la salud humana y el medio ambiente, en colaboración con organizaciones intergubernamentales y no gubernamentales pertinentes y con poblaciones vulnerables, según proceda.

2. Cada Parte utilizará los mecanismos existentes o considerará la posibilidad de establecer mecanismos, tales como registros de liberaciones y transferencias de contaminantes, si procede, para la recopilación y difusión de información sobre estimaciones de las cantidades anuales de mercurio y compuestos de mercurio que se emiten, liberan o eliminan a través de actividades humanas.

Artículo 19

Investigación, desarrollo y vigilancia

1. Las Partes se esforzarán por cooperar, teniendo en consideración sus respectivas circunstancias y capacidades, en la elaboración y el mejoramiento de:

a) Los inventarios del uso, el consumo y las emisiones antropógenas al aire, y de las liberaciones al agua y al suelo, de mercurio y compuestos de mercurio;

b) La elaboración de modelos y la vigilancia geográficamente representativa de los niveles de mercurio y compuestos de mercurio en poblaciones vulnerables y el entorno, incluidos medios bióticos como los peces, los mamíferos marinos, las tortugas marinas y los pájaros, así como la colaboración en la recopilación y el intercambio de muestras pertinentes y apropiadas;

c) Las evaluaciones de los efectos del mercurio y los compuestos de mercurio para la salud humana y el medio ambiente, además de los efectos sociales, económicos y culturales, especialmente en lo que respecta a las poblaciones vulnerables;

d) Las metodologías armonizadas para las actividades realizadas en el ámbito de los apartados a), b) y c) precedentes;

e) La información sobre el ciclo ambiental, el transporte (incluidos el transporte y la deposición a larga distancia), la transformación y el destino del mercurio y los compuestos de mercurio en un conjunto de ecosistemas, teniendo debidamente en cuenta la distinción entre las emisiones y liberaciones antropógenas y naturales de mercurio y la nueva movilización de mercurio procedente de su deposición histórica;

f) La información sobre el comercio y el intercambio de mercurio y compuestos de mercurio y productos con mercurio añadido; y

g) La información e investigación sobre la disponibilidad técnica y económica de productos y procesos que no utilicen mercurio, y sobre las mejores técnicas disponibles y las mejores prácticas ambientales para reducir y monitorizar las emisiones y liberaciones de mercurio y compuestos de mercurio.

2. Cuando corresponda, las Partes deberán aprovechar las redes de vigilancia y los programas de investigación existentes al realizar las actividades definidas en el párrafo 1.

Artículo 20

Planes de aplicación

1. Cada Parte, después de efectuar una evaluación inicial, podrá elaborar y ejecutar un plan de aplicación, teniendo en cuenta sus circunstancias nacionales, para cumplir las obligaciones contraídas con arreglo al presente Convenio. Ese plan se debe transmitir a la Secretaría en cuanto se elabore.

2. Cada Parte podrá examinar y actualizar su plan de aplicación teniendo en cuenta sus circunstancias nacionales y ajustándose a la orientación brindada por la Conferencia de las Partes y otras orientaciones pertinentes.

3. Al efectuar la labor indicada en los párrafos 1 y 2, las Partes deberían consultar a los grupos de interés nacionales con miras a facilitar la elaboración, la aplicación, el examen y la actualización de sus planes de aplicación.

4. Las Partes también podrán coordinar los planes regionales para facilitar la aplicación del presente Convenio.

Artículo 21

Presentación de informes

1. Cada Parte informará, a través de la Secretaría, a la Conferencia de las Partes sobre las medidas que haya adoptado para aplicar las disposiciones del presente Convenio y sobre la eficacia de esas medidas y los posibles desafíos para el logro de los objetivos del Convenio.

2. Cada Parte incluirá en sus informes la información solicitada con arreglo a los artículos 3, 5, 7, 8 y 9 del presente Convenio.

3. En su primera reunión, la Conferencia de las Partes decidirá las fechas y el formato para la presentación de informes que habrán de cumplir las Partes, teniendo

en cuenta la conveniencia de coordinar la presentación de informes con otros convenios pertinentes sobre productos químicos y desechos.

Artículo 22

Evaluación de la eficacia

1. La Conferencia de las Partes evaluará la eficacia del presente Convenio antes de que hayan transcurrido como máximo seis años a partir de la fecha de su entrada en vigor, y en lo sucesivo de manera periódica a intervalos que esta ha de fijar.

2. Con el fin de facilitar la evaluación, en su primera reunión, la Conferencia de las Partes dará comienzo al establecimiento de arreglos para proveerse de datos monitorizados comparables sobre la presencia y los movimientos de mercurio y compuestos de mercurio en el medio ambiente, así como sobre las tendencias de los niveles de mercurio y compuestos de mercurio observados en los medios bióticos y las poblaciones vulnerables.

3. La evaluación deberá fundamentarse en la información científica, ambiental, técnica, financiera y económica disponible, que incluirá:

a) Informes y otros datos monitorizados suministrados a la Conferencia de las Partes de conformidad con el párrafo 2;

b) Informes presentados con arreglo al artículo 21;

c) Información y recomendaciones que se formulen de conformidad con el artículo 15; e

d) Informes y otra información pertinente sobre el funcionamiento de los arreglos de asistencia financiera, transferencia de tecnología y creación de capacidad establecidos en el marco del presente Convenio.

Artículo 23

Conferencia de las Partes

1. Queda establecida una Conferencia de las Partes.

2. El Director Ejecutivo del Programa de las Naciones Unidas para el Medio Ambiente convocará la primera reunión de la Conferencia de las Partes a más tardar un año después de la fecha de entrada en vigor del presente Convenio. En lo sucesivo, se celebrarán reuniones ordinarias de la Conferencia de las Partes a los intervalos regulares que decida la Conferencia.

3. Se celebrarán reuniones extraordinarias de la Conferencia de las Partes cuando esta lo estime necesario o cuando cualquiera de las Partes lo solicite por escrito,

siempre que, en un plazo de seis meses desde que la Secretaría haya comunicado esa solicitud a las Partes, un tercio de las Partes, como mínimo, apoye esa solicitud.

4. En su primera reunión, la Conferencia de las Partes acordará y aprobará por consenso su reglamento interno y su reglamentación financiera y los de cualquiera de sus órganos subsidiarios, además de las disposiciones financieras que han de regir el funcionamiento de la Secretaría.

5. La Conferencia de las Partes mantendrá en examen y evaluación permanentes la aplicación del presente Convenio. Se encargará de las funciones que le asigne el presente Convenio y, a ese efecto:

a) Establecerá los órganos subsidiarios que considere necesarios para la aplicación del presente Convenio;

b) Cooperará, cuando proceda, con las organizaciones internacionales y los órganos intergubernamentales y no gubernamentales competentes;

c) Examinará periódicamente toda la información que se ponga a su disposición y a disposición de la Secretaría de conformidad con el artículo 21;

d) Considerará toda recomendación que le presente el Comité de Aplicación y Cumplimiento;

e) Examinará y adoptará las medidas adicionales que sean necesarias para alcanzar los objetivos del presente Convenio; y

f) Revisará los anexos A y B de conformidad con lo dispuesto en el artículo 4 y el artículo 5.

6. Las Naciones Unidas, sus organismos especializados y el Organismo Internacional de Energía Atómica, así como los Estados que no sean Partes en el presente Convenio, podrán estar representados en calidad de observadores en las reuniones de la Conferencia de las Partes. Todo órgano u organismo con competencia en las esferas que abarca el presente Convenio, ya sea nacional o internacional, gubernamental o no gubernamental, que haya comunicado a la Secretaría su deseo de estar representado en una reunión de la Conferencia de las Partes en calidad de observador podrá ser admitido, salvo que se oponga a ello al menos un tercio de las Partes presentes. La admisión y la participación de observadores estarán sujetas al reglamento aprobado por la Conferencia de las Partes.

Artículo 24

Secretaría

1. Queda establecida una secretaría.

2. Las funciones de la Secretaría serán las siguientes:

a) Organizar las reuniones de la Conferencia de las Partes y sus órganos subsidiarios y prestarles los servicios necesarios;

b) Facilitar la prestación de asistencia a las Partes, en especial las Partes que son países en desarrollo y países con economías en transición, cuando lo soliciten, para la aplicación del presente Convenio;

c) Coordinar su labor, si procede, con las secretarías de los órganos internacionales pertinentes, en particular otros convenios sobre productos químicos y desechos;

d) Prestar asistencia a las Partes en el intercambio de información relacionada con la aplicación del presente Convenio;

e) Preparar y poner a disposición de las Partes informes periódicos basados en la información recibida con arreglo a los artículos 15 y 21 y otra información disponible;

f) Concertar, con la orientación general de la Conferencia de las Partes, los arreglos administrativos y contractuales que puedan ser necesarios para el desempeño eficaz de sus funciones; y

g) Realizar las demás funciones de secretaría especificadas en el presente Convenio y otras funciones que determine la Conferencia de las Partes.

3. Las funciones de secretaría para el presente Convenio serán desempeñadas por el Director Ejecutivo del Programa de las Naciones Unidas para el Medio Ambiente, salvo que la Conferencia de las Partes, por una mayoría de tres cuartos de las Partes presentes y votantes, decida encomendarlas a otra u otras organizaciones internacionales.

4. La Conferencia de las Partes, en consulta con los órganos internacionales pertinentes, podrá adoptar disposiciones para fomentar el aumento de la cooperación y la coordinación entre la Secretaría y las secretarías de otros convenios sobre productos químicos y desechos. La Conferencia de las Partes, en consulta con los órganos internacionales pertinentes, podrá impartir orientación adicional sobre esta cuestión.

Artículo 25

Solución de controversias

1. Las Partes procurarán resolver cualquier controversia suscitada entre ellas en relación con la interpretación o la aplicación del presente Convenio mediante negociación u otros medios pacíficos de su propia elección.

2. Al ratificar, aceptar o aprobar el presente Convenio, o adherirse a él, o en cualquier momento posterior, toda Parte que no sea una organización de integración económica regional podrá declarar en un instrumento escrito presentado al Depositario que, respecto de cualquier controversia sobre la interpretación o la aplicación del presente Convenio, reconoce como obligatorios, en relación con cualquier Parte que acepte la misma obligación, uno o los dos medios para la solución de controversias siguientes:

a) Arbitraje de conformidad con el procedimiento establecido en la parte I del anexo E;

b) Sometimiento de la controversia a la Corte Internacional de Justicia.

3. Una Parte que sea una organización de integración económica regional podrá hacer una declaración de efecto similar en relación con el arbitraje, de conformidad con el párrafo 2.

4. Toda declaración formulada con arreglo al párrafo 2 o al párrafo 3 permanecerá en vigor hasta que expire de conformidad con sus propios términos o hasta que hayan transcurrido tres meses después de haberse depositado en poder del Depositario una notificación escrita de su revocación.

5. Ni la expiración de una declaración, ni una notificación de revocación ni una nueva declaración afectarán en modo alguno los procedimientos pendientes ante un tribunal arbitral o ante la Corte Internacional de Justicia, a menos que las Partes en la controversia acuerden otra cosa.

6. Si las Partes en una controversia no han aceptado el mismo medio para la solución de controversias de conformidad con el párrafo 2 o el párrafo 3, y si no han podido dirimir la controversia por los medios mencionados en el párrafo 1 en un plazo de 12 meses a partir de la notificación de una Parte a otra de que existe entre ellas una controversia, la controversia se someterá a una comisión de conciliación a solicitud de cualquiera de las Partes en ella. El procedimiento que figura en la parte II del anexo E se aplicará a la conciliación con arreglo al presente artículo.

Artículo 26

Enmiendas del Convenio

1. Cualquier Parte podrá proponer enmiendas del presente Convenio.

2. Las enmiendas del presente Convenio se aprobarán en una reunión de la Conferencia de las Partes. La Secretaría comunicará el texto de toda propuesta de enmienda a las Partes al menos seis meses antes de la reunión en que se proponga su aprobación. La Secretaría comunicará también las propuestas de enmienda a los signatarios del presente Convenio y al Depositario, para su información.

3. Las Partes harán todo lo posible por llegar a un acuerdo por consenso sobre cualquier propuesta de enmienda del presente Convenio. Una vez agotados todos los esfuerzos por llegar a un consenso, sin lograrlo, la enmienda se aprobará, como último recurso, por una mayoría de tres cuartos de las Partes presentes y votantes en la reunión.

4. El Depositario comunicará la enmienda aprobada a todas las Partes para su ratificación, aceptación o aprobación.

5. La ratificación, aceptación o aprobación de una enmienda se notificará por escrito al Depositario. La enmienda que se apruebe con arreglo al párrafo 3 entrará en vigor para las Partes que hayan consentido en someterse a las obligaciones establecidas en ella el nonagésimo día contado a partir de la fecha de depósito de los instrumentos de ratificación, aceptación o aprobación de al menos tres cuartos de las Partes que lo eran en el momento en que se aprobó la enmienda. De ahí en adelante, la enmienda entrará en vigor para cualquier otra Parte el nonagésimo día contado a partir de la fecha en que haya depositado su instrumento de ratificación, aceptación o aprobación de la enmienda.

Artículo 27

Aprobación y enmienda de los anexos

1. Los anexos del presente Convenio formarán parte integrante del mismo y, a menos que se disponga expresamente otra cosa, toda referencia al presente Convenio constituirá a la vez una referencia a ellos.

2. Todo anexo adicional aprobado tras la entrada en vigor del presente Convenio estará limitado a cuestiones de procedimiento, científicas, técnicas o administrativas.

3. Para la propuesta, aprobación y entrada en vigor de nuevos anexos del presente Convenio se aplicará el siguiente procedimiento:

a) Los anexos adicionales se propondrán y aprobarán de conformidad con el procedimiento que se establece en los párrafos 1 a 3 del artículo 26;

b) Las Partes que no puedan aceptar un anexo adicional lo notificarán por escrito al Depositario dentro del plazo de un año contado a partir de la fecha en que el Depositario haya comunicado la aprobación de dicho anexo. El Depositario comunicará sin demora a todas las Partes cualquier notificación recibida. Una Parte podrá, en cualquier momento, notificar por escrito al Depositario la retirada de una notificación de no aceptación que haya hecho anteriormente respecto de un anexo adicional y, en tal caso, el anexo entrará en vigor respecto de esa Parte con arreglo al apartado c); y

c) Al cumplirse el plazo de un año contado a partir de la fecha en que el Depositario haya comunicado la aprobación de un anexo adicional, el anexo entrará en vigor para todas las Partes que no hayan presentado una notificación de no aceptación de conformidad con las disposiciones del apartado b).

4. La propuesta, aprobación y entrada en vigor de enmiendas de los anexos del presente Convenio estarán sujetas a los mismos procedimientos previstos para la propuesta, aprobación y entrada en vigor de los anexos adicionales del Convenio, con la salvedad de que una enmienda de un anexo no entrará en vigor para una Parte que haya formulado una declaración con respecto a la enmienda de anexos de conformidad con el párrafo 5 del artículo 30, en cuyo caso cualquier enmienda de ese tipo entrará en vigor con respecto a dicha Parte el nonagésimo día contado a partir de la fecha del depósito en poder del Depositario de su instrumento de ratificación, aceptación, aprobación o adhesión con respecto a tal enmienda.

5. Si un anexo adicional o una enmienda de un anexo guarda relación con una enmienda del presente Convenio, el anexo adicional o la enmienda no entrará en vigor hasta que entre en vigor la enmienda del Convenio.

Artículo 28

Derecho de voto

1. Cada Parte en el presente Convenio tendrá un voto, salvo lo dispuesto en el párrafo 2.

2. En los asuntos de su competencia, las organizaciones de integración económica regional ejercerán su derecho de voto con un número de votos igual al número de sus Estados miembros que sean Partes en el presente Convenio. Dichas organizaciones no ejercerán su derecho de voto si cualquiera de sus Estados miembros ejerce el suyo, y viceversa.

Artículo 29

Firma

El presente Convenio estará abierto a la firma en Kumamoto (Japón) para todos los Estados y organizaciones de integración económica regional los días 10 y 11 de octubre de 2013, y posteriormente en la Sede de las Naciones Unidas en Nueva York hasta el 9 de octubre de 2014.

Artículo 30

Ratificación, aceptación aprobación o adhesión

1. El presente Convenio estará sujeto a la ratificación, la aceptación o la aprobación de los Estados y las organizaciones de integración económica regional. El Convenio estará abierto a la adhesión de los Estados y de las organizaciones de integración económica regional a partir del día siguiente a la fecha en que expire el plazo para la firma del Convenio. Los instrumentos de ratificación, aceptación, aprobación o adhesión se depositarán en poder del Depositario.

2. Toda organización de integración económica regional que pase a ser Parte en el presente Convenio sin que ninguno de sus Estados miembros sea Parte quedará vinculada por todas las obligaciones contraídas en virtud del Convenio. En el caso de dichas organizaciones, cuando uno o varios de sus Estados miembros sean Partes en el presente Convenio, la organización y sus Estados miembros decidirán acerca de sus responsabilidades respectivas en cuanto al cumplimiento de las obligaciones contraídas en virtud del Convenio. En tales casos, la organización y los Estados miembros no estarán facultados para ejercer simultáneamente los derechos que establezca el Convenio.

3. En sus instrumentos de ratificación, aceptación, aprobación o adhesión, las organizaciones de integración económica regional declararán el ámbito de su competencia en relación con los asuntos regidos por el presente Convenio. Esas organizaciones también informarán al Depositario sobre cualquier modificación importante de su ámbito de competencia y este, a su vez, informará de ello a las Partes.

4. Se alienta a los Estados y a las organizaciones de integración económica regional a que, en el momento de su ratificación, aceptación o aprobación del Convenio o de su adhesión al mismo, transmitan a la Secretaría información sobre las medidas que vayan a aplicar para cumplir las disposiciones del Convenio.

5. En su instrumento de ratificación, aceptación, aprobación o adhesión, una Parte podrá declarar que, con respecto a ella, una enmienda de un anexo solo entrará

en vigor una vez que haya depositado su instrumento de ratificación, aceptación, aprobación o adhesión con respecto a dicha enmienda.

Artículo 31

Entrada en vigor

1. El presente Convenio entrará en vigor el nonagésimo día contado a partir de la fecha en que haya sido depositado el quincuagésimo instrumento de ratificación, aceptación, aprobación o adhesión.

2. Respecto de cada Estado u organización de integración económica regional que ratifique, acepte o apruebe el presente Convenio o que se adhiera a él después de haber sido depositado el quincuagésimo instrumento de ratificación, aceptación, aprobación o adhesión, el Convenio entrará en vigor el nonagésimo día contado a partir de la fecha en que dicho Estado u organización de integración económica regional haya depositado su instrumento de ratificación, aceptación, aprobación o adhesión.

3. A los efectos de los párrafos 1 y 2, los instrumentos depositados por una organización de integración económica regional no se considerarán adicionales con respecto a los depositados por los Estados miembros de esa organización.

Artículo 32

Reservas

No podrán formularse reservas al presente Convenio.

Artículo 33

Denuncia

1. En cualquier momento después de la expiración de un plazo de tres años contados a partir de la fecha de entrada en vigor del presente Convenio respecto de una Parte, esa Parte podrá denunciar el Convenio mediante notificación hecha por escrito al Depositario.

2. La denuncia cobrará efecto al cabo de un año contado desde la fecha en que el Depositario haya recibido la notificación correspondiente o, posteriormente, en la fecha que se indique en la notificación.

Artículo 34

Depositario

El Secretario General de las Naciones Unidas será el Depositario del presente Convenio.

Artículo 35

Autenticidad de los textos

El original del presente Convenio, cuyos textos en los idiomas árabe, chino, español, francés, inglés y ruso son igualmente auténticos, se depositará en poder del Depositario.

EN TESTIMONIO DE LO CUAL, los infrascritos, debidamente autorizados a esos efectos, han firmado el presente Convenio.

Hecho en Kumamoto (Japón) el décimo día de octubre de dos mil trece.

Anexo A

Productos con mercurio añadido

Se excluyen del presente anexo los productos siguientes:

a) Productos esenciales para usos militares y protección civil;

b) Productos para investigación, calibración de instrumentos, para su uso como patrón de referencia;

c) Cuando no haya disponible ninguna alternativa sin mercurio viable para piezas de repuesto, interruptores y relés, lámparas fluorescentes de cátodo frío y lámparas fluorescentes de electrodo externo (CCFL y EEFL) para pantallas electrónicas, y aparatos de medición;

d) Productos utilizados en prácticas tradicionales o religiosas; y

e) Vacunas que contengan timerosal como conservante.

Parte I: Productos sujetos al artículo 4, párrafo 1

Productos con mercurio añadido	**Fecha después de la cual no estará permitida la producción, importación ni exportación del producto (fecha de eliminación)**
Baterías, salvo pilas de botón de óxido de plata con un contenido de mercurio < 2% y pilas de botón zinc-aire con un contenido de mercurio < 2%	2020
Interruptores y relés, con excepción de puentes medidores de capacitancia y pérdida de alta precisión e interruptores y relés radio frecuencia de alta frecuencia utilizados en instrumentos de monitorización y control con un contenido máximo de mercurio de 20 mg por puente, interruptor o relé	2020
Lámparas fluorescentes compactas (CFL) para usos generales de iluminación de ≤ 30 vatios con un contenido de mercurio superior a 5 mg por quemador de lámpara	2020
Lámparas fluorescentes lineales (LFL) para usos generales de iluminación: a) fósforo tribanda de < 60 vatios con un contenido de mercurio superior a 5 mg por lámpara; b) fósforo en halofosfato de ≤ 40 vatios con un contenido de mercurio superior a 10 mg por lámpara.	2020

Productos con mercurio añadido	Fecha después de la cual no estará permitida la producción, importación ni exportación del producto (fecha de eliminación)
Lámparas de vapor de mercurio a alta presión (HPMV) para usos generales de iluminación	2020
Mercurio en lámparas fluorescentes de cátodo frío y lámparas fluorescentes de electrodo externo (CCFL y EEFL) para pantallas electrónicas: a) de longitud corta (≤ 500 mm) con un contenido de mercurio superior a 3,5 mg por lámpara; b) de longitud media (> 500 mm y ≤ 1 500 mm) con un contenido de mercurio superior a 5 mg por lámpara; c) de longitud larga (> 1 500 mm) con un contenido de mercurio superior a 13 mg por lámpara.	2020
Cosméticos (con un contenido de mercurio superior a 1 ppm), incluidos los jabones y las cremas para aclarar la piel, pero sin incluir los cosméticos para la zona de alrededor de los ojos que utilicen mercurio como conservante y para los que no existan conservantes alternativos eficaces y seguros[1/]	2020
Plaguicidas, biocidas y antisépticos de uso tópico	2020
Los siguientes aparatos de medición no electrónicos, a excepción de los aparatos de medición no electrónicos instalados en equipo de gran escala o los utilizados para mediciones de alta precisión, cuando no haya disponible ninguna alternativa adecuada sin mercurio: a) barómetros; b) higrómetros; c) manómetros; d) termómetros; e) esfigmomanómetros.	2020

[1/] La intención es no abarcar los cosméticos, los jabones o las cremas que contienen trazas contaminantes de mercurio.

Parte II: Productos sujetos al artículo 4, párrafo 3

Productos con mercurio añadido	**Disposiciones**
Amalgama dental	Las medidas que ha de adoptar la Parte para reducir el uso de la amalgama dental tendrán en cuenta las circunstancias nacionales de la Parte y las orientaciones internacionales pertinentes e incluirán dos o más de las medidas que figuran en la lista siguiente: i) Establecer objetivos nacionales destinados a la prevención de la caries dental y a la promoción de la salud, a fin de reducir al mínimo la necesidad de restauración dental; ii) Establecer objetivos nacionales encaminados a reducir al mínimo su uso; iii) Promover el uso de alternativas sin mercurio eficaces en función de los costos y clínicamente efectivas para la restauración dental; iv) Promover la investigación y el desarrollo de materiales de calidad sin mercurio para la restauración dental; v) Alentar a las organizaciones profesionales representativas y a las escuelas odontológicas para que eduquen e impartan capacitación a dentistas profesionales y estudiantes sobre el uso de alternativas sin mercurio en la restauración dental y la promoción de las mejores prácticas de gestión; vi) Desincentivar las políticas y los programas de seguros que favorezcan el uso de amalgama dental en lugar de la restauración dental sin mercurio; vii) Alentar las políticas y los programas de seguros que favorezcan el uso de alternativas de calidad a la amalgama dental para la restauración dental; viii) Limitar el uso de amalgama dental en su forma encapsulada; ix) Promover el uso de las mejores prácticas ambientales en los gabinetes dentales para reducir las liberaciones de mercurio y compuestos de mercurio al agua y al suelo.

Anexo B

Procesos de fabricación en los que se utiliza mercurio o compuestos de mercurio

Parte I: Procesos sujetos al artículo 5, párrafo 2

Procesos de fabricación en los que utiliza mercurio o compuestos de mercurio	**Fecha de eliminación**
Producción de cloro-álcali	2025
Producción de acetaldehído en la que se utiliza mercurio o compuestos de mercurio como catalizador	2018

Parte II: Procesos sujetos al artículo 5, párrafo 3

Proceso que utiliza mercurio	**Disposiciones**
Producción de monómeros de cloruro de vinilo	Las Partes habrán de adoptar, entre otras, las medidas siguientes: i) Reducir el uso de mercurio en términos de producción por unidad en un 50% antes del año 2020 en relación con el uso en 2010; ii) Promover medidas para reducir la dependencia del mercurio procedente de la extracción primaria; iii) Tomar medidas para reducir las emisiones y liberaciones de mercurio al medio ambiente; iv) Apoyar la investigación y el desarrollo de catalizadores y procesos sin mercurio; v) No permitir el uso de mercurio cinco años después de que la Conferencia de las Partes haya determinado que catalizadores sin mercurio basados en procesos existentes se han vuelto viables desde el punto de vista económico y técnico; vi) Presentar informes a la Conferencia de las Partes sobre sus esfuerzos por producir y/o encontrar alternativas y para eliminar el uso del mercurio de conformidad con el artículo 21.
Metilato o etilato sódico o potásico	Las Partes habrán de adoptar, entre otras, las medidas siguientes: i) Adoptar medidas para reducir el uso de mercurio encaminadas a eliminar este uso lo antes posible y en un plazo de diez años a partir de la entrada en vigor del Convenio; ii) Reducir las emisiones y liberaciones en términos de producción por unidad en un 50% antes del año 2020 en relación con 2010; iii) Prohibir el uso de mercurio nuevo procedente de la extracción primaria; iv) Apoyar la investigación y el desarrollo relativos a procesos sin mercurio; v) No permitir el uso de mercurio cinco años después de que la Conferencia de las Partes haya determinado que procesos sin mercurio se han vuelto viables desde el punto de vista económico y técnico; vi) Presentar informes a la Conferencia de las Partes sobre sus esfuerzos por producir y/o encontrar alternativas y para eliminar el uso del mercurio de conformidad con el artículo 21.
Producción de poliuretano en la que se utilizan catalizadores que contienen mercurio	Las Partes habrán de adoptar, entre otras, las medidas siguientes: i) Adoptar medidas para reducir el uso de mercurio encaminadas a eliminar este uso lo antes posible y en un plazo de diez años a partir de la entrada en vigor del Convenio; ii) Adoptar medidas para reducir la dependencia del mercurio procedente de la extracción primaria;

Proceso que utiliza mercurio	Disposiciones
	iii) Tomar medidas para reducir las emisiones y liberaciones de mercurio al medio ambiente; iv) Alentar la investigación y el desarrollo de catalizadores y procesos sin mercurio; v) Presentar informes a la Conferencia de las Partes sobre sus esfuerzos por producir y/o encontrar alternativas y para eliminar el uso del mercurio de conformidad con el artículo 21. El párrafo 6 del artículo 5 no será de aplicación para este proceso de fabricación.

Anexo C

Extracción de oro artesanal y en pequeña escala

Planes nacionales de acción

1. Cada Parte que esté sujeta a las disposiciones del párrafo 3 del artículo 7 incluirá en su plan nacional de acción:

a) Las metas de reducción y los objetivos nacionales;

b) Medidas para eliminar:

i) La amalgamación del mineral en bruto;

ii) La quema expuesta de la amalgama o amalgama procesada;

iii) La quema de la amalgama en zonas residenciales; y

iv) La lixiviación de cianuro en sedimentos, mineral en bruto o rocas a los que se ha agregado mercurio, sin eliminar primero el mercurio;

c) Medidas para facilitar la formalización o reglamentación del sector de la extracción de oro artesanal y en pequeña escala;

d) Estimaciones de referencia de las cantidades de mercurio utilizadas y las prácticas empleadas en la extracción y el tratamiento de oro artesanales y en pequeña escala en su territorio;

e) Estrategias para promover la reducción de emisiones y liberaciones de mercurio, y la exposición a esa sustancia, en la extracción y el tratamiento de oro artesanales y en pequeña escala, incluidos métodos sin mercurio;

f) Estrategias para gestionar el comercio y prevenir el desvío de mercurio y compuestos de mercurio procedentes de fuentes extranjeras y nacionales para su uso en la extracción y el tratamiento de oro artesanales y en pequeña escala;

g) Estrategias para atraer la participación de los grupos de interés en la aplicación y el perfeccionamiento permanente del plan de acción nacional;

h) Una estrategia de salud pública sobre la exposición al mercurio de los mineros artesanales y que extraen oro en pequeña escala y sus comunidades. Dicha estrategia debería incluir, entre otras cosas, la reunión de datos de salud, la capacitación de trabajadores de la salud y campañas de sensibilización a través de los centros de salud;

i) Estrategias para prevenir la exposición de las poblaciones vulnerables al mercurio utilizado en la extracción de oro artesanal y en pequeña escala, en particular los niños y las mujeres en edad fértil, especialmente las embarazadas;

j) Estrategias para proporcionar información a los mineros artesanales y que extraen oro en pequeña escala y las comunidades afectadas; y

k) Un calendario de aplicación del plan de acción nacional

2. Cada Parte podrá incluir en su plan de acción nacional estrategias adicionales para alcanzar sus objetivos, por ejemplo la utilización o introducción de normas para la extracción de oro artesanal y en pequeña escala sin mercurio y mecanismos de mercado o herramientas de comercialización.

Anexo D

Lista de fuentes puntuales de emisiones de mercurio y compuestos de mercurio a la atmósfera

Categoría de fuente puntual:

Centrales eléctricas de carbón;

Calderas industriales de carbón;

Procesos de fundición y calcinación utilizados en la producción de metales no ferrosos[1/];

Plantas de incineración de desechos;

Fábricas de cemento clínker.

[1/] A los efectos del presente anexo, por "metales no ferrosos" se entiende plomo, zinc, cobre y oro industrial.

Anexo E

Procedimientos de arbitraje y conciliación

Parte I: Procedimiento arbitral

El procedimiento arbitral, a los efectos de lo dispuesto en el párrafo 2 a) del artículo 25 del presente Convenio, será el siguiente:

Artículo 1

1. Cualquier Parte podrá recurrir al arbitraje de conformidad con lo dispuesto en el artículo 25 del presente Convenio mediante notificación escrita a la otra Parte o las otras Partes en la controversia. La notificación irá acompañada de un escrito de demanda, junto con cualesquiera documentos justificativos. En esa notificación se definirá la cuestión que ha de ser objeto de arbitraje y se hará referencia específica a los artículos del presente Convenio de cuya interpretación o aplicación se trate.

2. La Parte demandante notificará a la Secretaría que somete la controversia a arbitraje de conformidad con lo dispuesto en el artículo 25 del presente Convenio. La notificación deberá incluir una notificación escrita de la Parte demandante, el escrito de demanda y los documentos justificativos a que se hace referencia en el párrafo 1 del presente artículo. La Secretaría transmitirá la información así recibida a todas las Partes.

Artículo 2

1. Si la controversia se somete a arbitraje de conformidad con el artículo 1, se establecerá un tribunal arbitral. El tribunal arbitral estará integrado por tres miembros.

2. Cada una de las Partes en la controversia nombrará un árbitro, y los dos árbitros así nombrados designarán mediante acuerdo al tercer árbitro, quien asumirá la Presidencia del tribunal. En controversias entre más de dos Partes, las Partes que compartan un mismo interés nombrarán un solo árbitro mediante acuerdo. El Presidente del tribunal no deberá tener la nacionalidad de ninguna de las Partes en la controversia, ni tener residencia habitual en el territorio de ninguna de esas Partes, ni estar al servicio de ninguna de ellas, ni haberse ocupado del asunto en ningún otro concepto.

3. Toda vacante que se produzca se cubrirá en la forma prescrita para el nombramiento inicial.

Artículo 3

1. Si una de las Partes en la controversia no nombra un árbitro en un plazo de dos meses contados a partir de la fecha de la recepción de la notificación de arbitraje por la Parte demandada, la otra Parte podrá informar de ello al Secretario General de las Naciones Unidas, quien procederá a la designación en un nuevo plazo de dos meses.

2. Si el Presidente del tribunal arbitral no ha sido designado en un plazo de dos meses a partir de la fecha de nombramiento del segundo árbitro, el Secretario General de las Naciones Unidas, a instancia de una Parte, designará al Presidente en un nuevo plazo de dos meses.

Artículo 4

El tribunal arbitral emitirá sus decisiones de conformidad con las disposiciones del presente Convenio y del derecho internacional.

Artículo 5

A menos que las Partes en la controversia dispongan otra cosa, el tribunal arbitral establecerá su propio reglamento.

Artículo 6

El tribunal arbitral podrá, a solicitud de una de las Partes en la controversia, recomendar medidas de protección básicas provisionales.

Artículo 7

Las Partes en la controversia facilitarán la labor del tribunal arbitral y, en especial, utilizando todos los medios a su disposición:

a) Le proporcionarán todos los documentos, información y facilidades pertinentes; y

b) Le permitirán, cuando sea necesario, convocar a testigos o peritos para oír sus declaraciones.

Artículo 8

Las Partes en la controversia y los árbitros quedan obligados a proteger el carácter confidencial de cualquier información o documento que se les comunique con ese carácter durante el proceso del tribunal arbitral.

Artículo 9

A menos que el tribunal arbitral decida otra cosa debido a las circunstancias particulares del caso, los gastos del tribunal serán sufragados en porcentajes iguales por las Partes en la controversia. El tribunal llevará una relación de todos sus gastos y presentará a las Partes un estado final de los mismos.

Artículo 10

Una Parte que tenga un interés de carácter jurídico en la materia objeto de la controversia y que pueda verse afectada por el fallo podrá intervenir en las actuaciones, con el consentimiento del tribunal arbitral.

Artículo 11

El tribunal arbitral podrá conocer de las demandas de reconvención directamente relacionadas con el objeto de la controversia, y resolverlas.

Artículo 12

Los fallos del tribunal arbitral, tanto en materia de procedimiento como sobre el fondo, se adoptarán por mayoría de votos de sus miembros.

Artículo 13

1. Si una de las Partes en la controversia no comparece ante el tribunal arbitral o no defiende su caso, la otra Parte podrá solicitar al tribunal que continúe el procedimiento y proceda a dictar su fallo. El hecho de que una Parte no comparezca o no defienda su posición no constituirá un obstáculo para el procedimiento.

2. Antes de emitir su fallo definitivo, el tribunal arbitral deberá cerciorarse de que la demanda está bien fundada de hecho y de derecho.

Artículo 14

El tribunal arbitral dictará su fallo definitivo en un plazo de cinco meses contados a partir de la fecha en que esté ya plenamente constituido, a menos que considere necesario prorrogar el plazo por un período que no excederá de otros cinco meses.

Artículo 15

El fallo definitivo del tribunal arbitral se limitará al objeto de la controversia y será motivado. Incluirá los nombres de los miembros que han participado y la fecha del fallo definitivo. Cualquier miembro del tribunal podrá adjuntar al fallo definitivo una opinión separada o discrepante.

Artículo 16

El fallo definitivo será vinculante respecto de las Partes en la controversia. La interpretación del presente Convenio formulada mediante el fallo definitivo también será vinculante para toda Parte que intervenga con arreglo al artículo 10 del presente procedimiento, en la medida en que guarde relación con cuestiones respecto de las cuales esa Parte haya intervenido. El fallo definitivo no podrá ser impugnado, a menos que las Partes en la controversia hayan convenido de antemano un procedimiento de apelación.

Artículo 17

Todo desacuerdo que surja entre las Partes sujetas al fallo definitivo de conformidad con el artículo 16 del presente procedimiento respecto de la interpretación o forma de aplicación de dicho fallo definitivo podrá ser presentado por cualquiera de las Partes al tribunal arbitral que emitió el fallo definitivo para que éste se pronuncie al respecto.

Parte II: Procedimiento de conciliación

El procedimiento de conciliación a los efectos del párrafo 6 del artículo 25 del presente Convenio será el siguiente:

Artículo 1

Una solicitud de una Parte en una controversia para establecer una comisión de conciliación con arreglo al párrafo 6 del artículo 25 del presente Convenio será dirigida, por escrito, a la Secretaría, con una copia a la otra Parte u otras Partes en la controversia. La Secretaría informará inmediatamente a todas las Partes según proceda.

Artículo 2

1. A menos que las Partes en la controversia decidan otra cosa, la comisión de conciliación estará integrada por tres miembros, uno nombrado por cada Parte interesada y un Presidente elegido conjuntamente por esos miembros.

2. En las controversias entre más de dos Partes, las que compartan un mismo interés nombrarán de común acuerdo a un miembro en la comisión.

Artículo 3

Si en un plazo de dos meses a partir de la fecha de recepción por la Secretaría de la solicitud por escrito a que se hace referencia en el artículo 1 del presente procedimiento, las Partes en la controversia no han nombrado a un miembro de la comisión, el Secretario General de las Naciones Unidas, a instancia de cualquiera de las Partes, procederá a su nombramiento en un nuevo plazo de dos meses.

Artículo 4

Si el Presidente de la comisión de conciliación no hubiera sido designado dentro de los dos meses siguientes al nombramiento del segundo miembro de la comisión, el Secretario General de las Naciones Unidas, a instancia de cualquiera de las Partes en la controversia, procederá a su designación en un nuevo plazo de dos meses.

Artículo 5

La comisión de conciliación prestará asistencia a las Partes en la controversia de manera independiente e imparcial en los esfuerzos que realicen para tratar de llegar a una solución amistosa.

Artículo 6

1. La comisión de conciliación podrá realizar sus actuaciones de conciliación de la manera que considere adecuada, teniendo cabalmente en cuenta las circunstancias del caso y las opiniones que las Partes en la controversia puedan expresar, incluida toda solicitud de resolución rápida. La comisión podrá aprobar su propio reglamento según sea necesario, a menos que las Partes acuerden otra cosa.

2. La comisión de conciliación podrá, en cualquier momento durante sus actuaciones, formular propuestas o recomendaciones para la solución de la controversia.

Artículo 7

Las Partes en la controversia cooperarán con la comisión de conciliación. En especial, procurarán atender a las solicitudes de la comisión relativas a la presentación de material escrito y pruebas y a la asistencia a reuniones. Las Partes y los miembros de la comisión de conciliación quedan obligados a proteger el carácter confidencial de cualquier información o documento que se les comunique con ese carácter durante las actuaciones de la comisión

Artículo 8

La comisión de conciliación tomará sus decisiones por mayoría de votos de sus miembros.

Artículo 9

A menos que la controversia se haya resuelto, la comisión de conciliación redactará un informe con recomendaciones para la resolución de la controversia en un plazo no mayor de 12 meses contados a partir de la fecha de su constitución plena, que las Partes en la controversia examinarán de buena fe.

Artículo 10

Cualquier desacuerdo en cuanto a la competencia de la comisión de conciliación para examinar la cuestión que se le haya remitido será decidido por la comisión.

Artículo 11

A menos que acuerden otra cosa, las Partes en la controversia sufragarán en porcentajes iguales los gastos de la comisión de conciliación. La comisión llevará una relación de todos sus gastos y presentará a las Partes un estado final de los mismos.

No. 54670

Turkey
and
Guinea

Agreement between the Government of the Republic of Turkey and the Government of the Republic of Guinea on cooperation in the field of tourism. Conakry, 3 March 2016

Entry into force: *16 November 2016 by notification, in accordance with article 8*

Authentic texts: *French and Turkish*

Registration with the Secretariat of the United Nations: *Turkey, 29 August 2017*

Turquie
et
Guinée

Accord de coopération dans le domaine du tourisme entre le Gouvernement de la République turque et le Gouvernement de la République de Guinée. Conakry, 3 mars 2016

Entrée en vigueur : *16 novembre 2016 par notification, conformément à l'article 8*

Textes authentiques : *français et turc*

Enregistrement auprès du Secrétariat de l'Organisation des Nations Unies : *Turquie, 29 août 2017*

[TEXT IN FRENCH – TEXTE EN FRANÇAIS]

ACCORD DE COOPERATION DANS LE DOMAINE DU TOURISME ENTRE LE GOUVERNEMENT DE LA REPUBLIQUE DE TURQUIE ET LE GOUVERNEMENT DE LA REPUBLIQUE DE GUINEE.

Le Gouvernement de la République de Turquie d'une part;

Et

Le Gouvernement de la République de Guinée, d'autre part;

Ci-après désignés « les parties contractantes » ;

- ✓ Considérant les liens historiques d'amitié et de fraternité qui unissent nos deux Peuples;
- ✓ Désireuses de renforcer les liens de coopération notamment dans le domaine de Tourisme;
- ✓ Convaincus que le Tourisme constitue un facteur de Développement Economique et Social et un facteur de resserrement des liens d'amitié ;
- ✓ Soucieuses d'établir une base de coopération mutuellement avantageuse,

SONT CONVENUS DE CE QUI SUIT:

ARTICLE 1 :

Les parties contractantes prendront les mesures nécessaires pour favoriser et renforcer les échanges touristiques entre la République de Turquie et la République de Guinée.

A cet effet, elles s'attacheront; promouvoir la coopération entre leurs organismes centraux de tourisme, entre leurs établissements nationaux du Tourisme et du Transport ainsi qu'entre leurs Agences et Associations Professionnelles de Tourisme.

ARTICLE 2 :

Les parties contractantes décident d'instaurer et de développer la coopération technique et l'échange d'informations entre les deux pays :

- ✓ Sur l'organisation administrative et les stratégies de développement et de promotion du Tourisme ;
- ✓ Sur les avantages et mesures d'encouragement à l'investissement touristique dans les deux pays ;
- ✓ Sur les systèmes de formation à tous les niveaux ;
- ✓ Sur les échanges de documentations (statistiques, études, brochures, films etc.).
- ✓ Sur la législation du tourisme,
- ✓ Sur la certification des installations touristiques certifiées (classification, projet d'étoile verte etc.)

ARTICLE 3 :

Les parties contractantes décident de renforcer leur coopération dans le domaine des manifestations touristiques notamment par la participation aux salons et foires du tourisme dans chacun des deux pays.

ARTICLE 4 :

Dans le but de développer les flux touristiques internationaux à destination des deux pays, les parties contractantes décident de tout mettre en œuvre pour inciter leurs Offices Nationaux de Tourisme, leurs Compagnies Nationales de Transport et leurs Professionnels du Tourisme, à collaborer et à se prêter assistance pour la promotion de leurs produits touristiques respectifs.

ARTICLE 5 :

Les parties contractantes conviennent de procéder à l'échange d'informations technique en faisant échange d'experts en matière de formation de tourisme entre les deux pays et elles s'attacheront à promouvoir la coopération en matière de programme de formation professionnelle aux personnels travaillant dans les entreprises d'hébergement et de restauration opérant dans le secteur du tourisme.

ARTICLE 6 :

Les parties contractantes conviennent d'harmoniser les positions des deux pays sur le plan international, notamment au niveau de l'Organisation Mondiale du Tourisme.

ARTICLE 7 :

Les parties contractantes décident de constituer un Comité Technique, chargé d'étudier et de faire appliquer les mesures susceptibles de contribuer à la réalisation des objectifs fixés dans le cadre du présent Accord.

Ce Comité se réunira une fois tous les deux ans, alternativement dans l'un et l'autre pays. Elle pourra tenir, au besoin, des réunions extraordinaires, sur décision prise d'un commun accord par les parties contractantes.

ARTICLE 8 :

Chacune des Parties Contractantes notifiera à l'autre par voie diplomatique l'accomplissement des procédures juridiques internes requises pour l'entré en vigueur du présent accord. Celui-ci entera en vigueur à la date de réception de la dernière notification.

Le présent Accord est conclu pour une durée de cinq ans, à moins que l'une des parties contractantes ne le dénonce par voie diplomatique avec un préavis de six mois avant l'expiration de la période de validité en cours, le présent Accord sera prorogé par tacite reconduction pour des périodes successives d'un an.

Le Présent Accord pourra être modifié à tout moment par le consentement mutuel écrit des Parties Contractantes. Les modifications seront mises en vigueur selon la procédure prévue à l'alinéa 1 du présent article.

Fait le 3 mars 2016 à Conakry en deux exemplaires originaux, en langues Turque et en Français les deux textes faisant également foi.

Pour Le Gouvernement de la République de Turquie

Mevlüt ÇAVUŞOĞLU

Ministre des Affaires Etrangères de la République de Turquie

Pour Le Gouvernement de la République de Guinée

Thierno Ousmane DIALLO

Ministre d'Etat, Ministre de l'Hôtellerie, du Tourisme et de l'Artisanat de la République de Guinée

[TEXT IN TURKISH – TEXTE EN TURC]

TÜRKİYE CUMHURİYETİ HÜKÜMETİ İLE GİNE CUMHURİYETİ HÜKÜMETİ ARASINDA TURİZM ALANINDA İŞBİRLİĞİ ANLAŞMASI

Türkiye Cumhuriyeti Hükümeti ile Gine Cumhuriyeti Hükümeti bundan böyle "Akit Taraflar" olarak adlandırılacaktır.

✓ İki halkı birleştiren dostluk ve kardeşliğin tarihi bağlarını göz önünde tutarak,

✓ Özellikle Turizm alanında işbirliği bağların güçlendirilmesi isteğiyle,

✓ Turizmin, Ekonomik ve Sosyal Gelişimde ve dostluk bağlarının güçlendirilmesinde bir etken olduğu hususunda kani olarak,

✓ Karşılıklı olarak avantajlı bir işbirliği temelinin yerleştirilmesi temennisiyle,

AŞAĞIDAKİ HUSUSLARDA ANLAŞMAYA VARMIŞLARDIR:

MADDE 1:

Akit Taraflar, Türkiye Cumhuriyeti ile Gine Cumhuriyeti arasında karşılıklı turistik değişimleri desteklemek ve güçlendirmek için gerekli olan bütün önlemleri alacaklardır.

Taraflar, bu amaçla kendilerine ait merkezi turizm kuruluşları, ulusal turizm ve taşıma kuruluşları arasında ve profesyonel turizm acenteleri ve birlikleri arasında işbirliğini geliştirmeye imkân vereceklerdir.

MADDE 2:

Akit Taraflar, aşağıda belirtilen konularda her iki ülke arasında teknik işbirliğini ve bilgi alışverişini tesis etmek ve geliştirmek hususunda mutabakata varmışlardır:

✓ Turizm idari organizasyonu, gelişme stratejileri ve tanıtım alanlarında,

✓ Her iki ülkede turizm yatırımlarına yönelik kolaylıklar ve teşvikler,

✓ Her düzeyde eğitim sistemleri,

✓ Belge alışverişi (istatistikler, incelemeler, broşürler, filmler vs.)

✓ Turizm mevzuatı,

✓ Turizm belgeli tesislere ilişkin sertifikasyon (sınıflandırma, yeşil yıldız projesi, vb.)

MADDE 3:

Akit Taraflar, turistik etkinlikler alanında özellikle her iki ülkede turizm fuar ve salonlarına katılmak suretiyle işbirliğini güçlendireceklerdir.

MADDE 4:

Her iki ülkeye yönelik uluslararası turistik akımlarını geliştirmek amacıyla, Akit Taraflar kendilerine ait ulusal turizm bürolarını, ulusal taşımacılık şirketlerini ve turizm alanında çalışan profesyonelleri karşılıklı turistik ürünlerin tanıtımı için birbirleriyle yardımlaşmaları ve işbirliği yapmalarına teşvik etmek amacıyla gerekli bütün çabayı göstereceklerdir.

MADDE 5:

Akit Taraflar, turizm eğitimi konusunda birbirleriyle karşılıklı uzman değişimi gerçekleştirerek teknik bilgi alışverişinde bulunacak ve turizm sektöründe konaklama ve yeme-içme işletmelerinde çalışan personele yönelik mesleki turizm eğitim programları konularında işbirliğini geliştirmeye yönelik gerekli önlemleri alacaklardır.

MADDE 6:

Akit Taraflar, uluslararası planda, özellikle Dünya Turizm Örgütü düzeyinde her iki ülke konumunu birbiri ile uyumlu kılma konusunda mutabakata varmışlardır.

MADDE 7:

Akit Taraflar, işbu Anlaşmanın gerçekleştirilmesine katkıda bulunacak gerekli önlemlerin araştırılması ve uygulanmasından sorumlu bir teknik komite oluşturulması hususunda mutabakata varmışlardır.

Bu komite, dönüşümlü olarak, her iki ülkede iki yılda bir toplanacaktır. Bu komite gerekli durumlarda Akit Taraflarca alınan ortak karar doğrultusunda olağanüstü toplantı düzenleyebilecektir.

MADDE 8:

Akit Taraflardan her biri, işbu anlaşmanın yürürlüğe girmesi için gerekli iç hukuk işlemlerinin tamamlandığını diplomatik yollarla diğerlerine bildirecektir. Anlaşma son bildirimin alındığı tarihte yürürlüğe girecektir.

İşbu Anlaşma beş yıl süre için akdedilmiştir. Akit Taraflardan biri, bu anlaşmanın geçerlilik sürecinin bitiminden 6 ay öncesinde feshini diplomatik kanal yoluyla bildirmedikçe, işbu Anlaşma 1 yıllık sürelerle, zımni olarak uzatılacaktır.

İşbu Anlaşma Akit Tarafların karşılıklı yazılı rızasıyla herhangi bir zamanda değiştirilebilir. Değişiklikler bu maddenin birinci fıkrasında belirtilen usule göre yürürlüğe girecektir.

İşbu Anlaşma 3 Mart 2016 tarihinde Konakri'de 2 orijinal nüsha halinde her biri eşit derecede geçerli olmak üzere Türkçe ve Fransızca imzalanmıştır.

Türkiye Cumhuriyeti Hükümeti Adına	Gine Cumhuriyeti Hükümeti Adına
Mevlüt ÇAVUŞOĞLU	Thierno Ousmane DIALLO
Türkiye Cumhuriyeti Dışişleri Bakanı	Gine Cumhuriyeti Otelcilik, Turizm ve El Sanatlarından Sorumlu Devlet Bakanı

[TRANSLATION – TRADUCTION]

AGREEMENT BETWEEN THE GOVERNMENT OF THE REPUBLIC OF TURKEY AND THE GOVERNMENT OF THE REPUBLIC OF GUINEA ON COOPERATION IN THE FIELD OF TOURISM

The Government of the Republic of Turkey, of the one part, and the Government of the Republic of Guinea, of the other part, hereinafter referred to as "the Contracting Parties",

Considering the historical bonds of friendship and fraternity that unite our two peoples,

Desirous to strengthen cooperation, particularly in the field of tourism,

Convinced that tourism is a factor in economic and social development and contributes to reinforcing the bonds of friendship,

Striving to establish a mutually beneficial basis for cooperation,

Have agreed as follows:

Article 1

The Contracting Parties shall take the necessary measures to foster and strengthen tourist exchanges between the Republic of Turkey and the Republic of Guinea.

To that end, they shall work to promote cooperation between their central tourism bodies, their national tourism and transport institutions, and their professional tourism agencies and associations.

Article 2

The Contracting Parties decide to establish and develop technical cooperation and information-sharing between the two countries in the following areas:

- Administrative organization and strategies for the development and promotion of tourism;
- Benefits and incentives for investment in tourism in the two countries;
- Training systems at all levels;
- Information exchange (statistics, studies, pamphlets, films, etc.);
- Tourism legislation;
- Certification of accredited tourist facilities (classification, the Green Star project, etc.).

Article 3

The Contracting Parties decide to strengthen their cooperation in the area of tourism-related events, in particular by participating in tourism fairs and exhibitions in each of the two countries.

Article 4

In order to boost international tourist flows to both countries, the Contracting Parties decide to make every effort to encourage their national tourism offices, their national transport companies and their tourism professionals to collaborate and assist each other in promoting their respective tourism products.

Article 5

The Contracting Parties agree to share technical information by exchanging experts in tourism training between the two countries, and shall work to promote cooperation in the area of vocational training programmes for personnel working in accommodation and food service enterprises operating in the tourism sector.

Article 6

The Contracting Parties agree to harmonize the positions of the two countries at the international level, in particular in the context of the World Tourism Organization.

Article 7

The Contracting Parties decide to establish a Technical Committee, to examine and enforce measures that may contribute to the achievement of the objectives set out in this Agreement.

The Committee shall meet once every two years, alternately in each country. It may, if necessary, hold extraordinary meetings, based on mutual agreement between the Contracting Parties.

Article 8

Each Contracting Party shall notify the other, through the diplomatic channel, of the completion of the internal legal procedures required for the entry into force of this Agreement. It shall enter into force on the date of receipt of the last notification.

This Agreement is concluded for a period of five years; unless one of the Contracting Parties terminates it through the diplomatic channel by virtue of a six-month notification prior to the expiry of the current period of validity, this Agreement shall be tacitly extended for successive one-year periods.

This Agreement may be amended at any time by the mutual written consent of the Contracting Parties. The amendments shall enter into force in accordance with the procedure set out in paragraph 1 of this article.

DONE on 3 March 2016 at Conakry in two original copies, in Turkish and French, both texts being equally authentic.

For the Government of the Republic of Turkey:

MEVLÜT ÇAVUŞOĞLU

Minister for Foreign Affairs of the Republic of Turkey

For the Government of the Republic of Guinea:

THIERNO OUSMANE DIALLO

Minister of State, Minister of Hotels, Tourism and Crafts of the Republic of Guinea

No. 54671

Turkey and Guinea

Agreement between the Government of the Republic of Turkey and the Government of the Republic of Guinea on cooperation in the fields of health and medical sciences. Conakry, 3 March 2016

Entry into force: *16 November 2016 by notification, in accordance with article 7*

Authentic texts: *English, French and Turkish*

Registration with the Secretariat of the United Nations: *Turkey, 29 August 2017*

Turquie et Guinée

Accord de coopération dans les domaines de la santé et des sciences médicales entre le Gouvernement de la République turque et le Gouvernement de la République de Guinée. Conakry, 3 mars 2016

Entrée en vigueur : *16 novembre 2016 par notification, conformément à l'article 7*

Textes authentiques : *anglais, français et turc*

Enregistrement auprès du Secrétariat de l'Organisation des Nations Unies : *Turquie, 29 août 2017*

[TEXT IN ENGLISH – TEXTE EN ANGLAIS]

AGREEMENT BETWEEN THE GOVERNMENT OF THE REPUBLIC OF TURKEY AND THE GOVERNMENT OF THE REPUBLIC OF GUINEA ON COOPERATION IN THE FIELDS OF HEALTH AND MEDICAL SCIENCES

The Government of the Republic of Turkey and the Government of the Republic of Guinea (hereinafter referred to as the "Parties"),

Considering that the two countries have declared their intention to cooperate in the fields of health and medical sciences,

Recognizing that this cooperation will contribute to the improvement of the health of their people,

Have agreed as follows:

ARTICLE 1
Objective

The Parties, based on the principles of equality and reciprocity and in conformity with their mutual benefits, shall promote cooperation in the fields of health and medical sciences.

ARTICLE 2
Areas of Cooperation

The Parties shall encourage cooperation in the fields of health and medical sciences in the following areas:

a) Strengthening their healthcare systems, infrastructures and organizations,
b) Primary health care services and public health,
c) Secondary and tertiary level of healthcare services,
d) Drugs, pharmaceutical products and medical devices,
e) Short term training of health personnel,
f) Health tourism.

ARTICLE 3
Cooperation Methods

The Parties shall carry out the cooperation specified in Article 2 of this Agreement, through mutual exchange of experts and promotion of the participation in meetings at national and international level in the fields of health and medical sciences.

The Parties shall establish a Joint Working Committee to determine and assess the cooperation activities between themselves The Committee shall meet once a year on alternating basis as required.

ARTICLE 4
Financial Arrangements

For visits of experts and other personnel of both countries within the framework of this Agreement:

a) The Sending Party shall cover round trip travel expenses;
b) The Hosting Country shall cover board, lodging and (if necessary) domestic travel expenses of the Sending Party. This period shall not be longer than two (2) weeks;
c) The Hosting Party shall provide medical treatment in case of emergency for the visiting experts and other personnel (excluding dental prosthesis).

ARTICLE 5
Implementing Authorities

The Ministry of Health of the Republic of Turkey and the Ministry of Health of the Republic of Guinea shall implement the provisions of this Agreement.

ARTICLE 6
Settlement of Disputes

Any dispute arising from the interpretation or implementation of this Agreement shall be settled amicably by negotiations or consultations by the Parties through diplomatic channels.

ARTICLE 7
Entry into Force and Duration

This Agreement shall enter into force on the date of the receipt of the last written notification by which The Parties notify each other, through diplomatic channels, of the completion of their internal legal procedures required for its entry into force.

This Agreement shall be concluded for a period of three (3) years. The Agreement shall be renewed implicitly for one-year periods unless one of the Contracting Parties notifies the other in writing through diplomatic channels of its intention to terminate the Agreement six (6) months prior to the date of expiration. The termination of this Agreement shall not affect the implementation of initiated or on-going activities and projects.

This Agreement may be amended by mutual written consent of the Contracting Parties at any time. The amendments shall enter into force in accordance with the same legal procedure prescribed under paragraph 1of this Article.

Done in Conakry, on 3 March 2016, in three original copies in Turkish, French and English, all texts being equally authentic. In case of any divergence of interpretation, the English text shall prevail.

On Behalf of The Government of The Republic of Turkey

Fatma Güldemet SARI
Minister of Environment and Urbanization of The Republic of Turkey

On Behalf of The Government of The Republic of Guinea

Dr. Abdourahmane DIALLO
Minister of Health of The Republic of Guinea

[TEXT IN FRENCH – TEXTE EN FRANÇAIS]

ACCORD DE COOPERATION DANS LES DOMAINES DE LA SANTÉ ET DES SCIENCES MÉDICALES ENTRE LE GOUVERNEMENT DE LA RÉPUBLIQUE DE TURQUIE ET LE GOUVERNEMENT DE LA RÉPUBLIQUE DE GUÌNEE

Le Gouvernement de la République de Turquie et le Gouvernement de la République de Guinée, désignés ci-après "les Parties",

Considérant que les deux pays expriment leur volonté de coopérer dans les domaines de la Santé et les sciences médicales,

Tenant compte que cette coopération contribuera à l'amélioration de la santé de leur peuples,

Sont convenus de ce qui suit:

ARTICLE 1
Objectif

Les Parties encouragent la coopération dans les domaines des sciences médicales et de la santé sur la base des principes de la réciprocité et de l'égalité et conformément au bénéfice mutuel.

ARTICLE 2
Domaines de Coopération

Les Parties encouragent la coopération dans les domaines de la santé et des sciences médicales par les sujets suivants:

a) Le renforcement de leurs organisations, des infrastructures et des systèmes de santé,
b) Services de santé primaire et la santé publique,
c) Services de santé secondaire et tertiaire,
d) Le médicament, produits pharmaceutiques et appareils médicaux,
e) Formation à court terme du personnel de santé,
f) Tourisme de santé.

ARTICLE 3
Méthodes de Coopération

Les Parties réalisent la coopération conformément à l'article 2 du présent Accord, en échangeant mutuellement les experts et en promouvant la participation à des réunions au niveau national et international dans les domaines de la santé et des sciences médicales.

Les Parties établissent un comité de travail commun afin de désigner et d'évaluer les activités de coopération. Si nécessaire ce comité se réunira alternativement une fois par an.

ARTICLE 4
Dispositions Financières

En ce qui concerne les visites des experts et autres personnels des deux pays dans le cadre du présent Accord;

a) La Partie qui envoie prend en charge les frais du voyage aller-retour.
b) La Partie d'accueil prend en charge les frais d'hébergement, d'alimentation et de transport à l'intérieur du pays (si nécessaire) de la Partie d'envoi. Cette période ne doit pas dépasser deux (02) semaines.
c) L'Etat Hôte fournit la prise en charge médical, en cas d'urgence, aux experts en visite et autres personnels (les prothèses dentaires ne sont pas comprises.)

ARTICLE 5
Organismes d'Exécution

La mise en œuvre des dispositions du présent Accord est faite par le Ministère de la Santé de la République de Turquie et le Ministère de la Santé de la République de Guinée.

ARTICLE 6
Règlement des Litiges

Tout différend résultant de l'interprétation ou de la mise en œuvre du présent Accord est réglé entre les Parties à l'amiable par des consultations ou des négociations par voie diplomatique.

ARTICLE 7
Entrée en Vigueur et Durée

Le présent Accord entre en vigueur à la date de réception de la dernière notification par laquelle chacune des Parties notifie à l'autre par voie diplomatique l'accomplissement des procédures juridiques internes requises pour l'entrée en vigueur du présent Accord.

Le présent Accord est conclu pour une durée de trois (3) ans. A moins que l'une des Parties ne le dénonce par voie diplomatique avec un préavis de six (6) mois avant l'expiration de la période de validité en cours, le présent Accord est prorogé par tacite reconduction pour des périodes successives d'un (1) ans. En cas de la résiliation du présent Accord, les projets et les activités ayant été entrepris ou qui sont en cours de mise en œuvre ne sont pas affectés.

Le présent Accord peut être modifié à tout moment par les Parties par consentement mutuel écrit. Toute modification entrera en vigueur conformément à la procédure énoncée dans le premier paragraphe de cet article.

Fait à Conakry le 3 mars 2016 en trois exemplaires, en langues Turc, Français et Anglais, chacun des textes faisant également foi. En cas de divergence d'interprétation, le texte anglais fera foi.

Pour Le Gouvernement de la République de Turquie

Fatma Güldemet SARI
Ministre de l'Environnement et de l'Urbanisme de la République de Turquie

Pour Le Gouvernement de la République de Guinée

Dr. Abdourahmane DIALLO
Ministre de la Santé de la République de Guinée

[TEXT IN TURKISH – TEXTE EN TURC]

TÜRKİYE CUMHURİYETİ HÜKÜMETİ İLE GİNE CUMHURİYETİ HÜKÜMETİ ARASINDA SAĞLIK VE TIP BİLİMLERİ ALANLARINDA İŞBİRLİĞİNE DAİR ANLAŞMA

Türkiye Cumhuriyeti Hükümeti ile Gine Cumhuriyeti Hükümeti (bundan sonra "Taraflar" şeklinde anılacaklardır),

İki ülkenin sağlık ve tıp bilimleri alanlarında işbirliğinde bulunma iradelerini beyan ettiklerini göz önünde bulundurarak,

Bu işbirliğinin halklarının sağlığının gelişmesine katkıda bulunacağını dikkate alarak,

Aşağıdaki hususlarda anlaşmaya varmışlardır:

MADDE 1
Amaç

Taraflar, eşitlik ve karşılıklılık ilkelerine dayalı ve karşılıklı faydalarına uygun olarak, sağlık ve tıp bilimleri alanlarında işbirliğini teşvik ederler.

MADDE 2
İşbirliği Alanları

Taraflar, sağlık ve tıp bilimleri alanlarında aşağıdaki konularda işbirliğini teşvik ederler:

a. Sağlık sistemleri, altyapıları ve organizasyonlarının güçlendirilmesi,
b. Birinci basamak sağlık hizmetleri ve halk sağlığı,
c. İkinci ve üçüncü basamak sağlık hizmetleri,
d. İlaç, eczacılık ve tıbbı cihaz,
e. Sağlık personelinin kısa süreli eğitimi,
f. Sağlık turizmi,

MADDE 3
İşbirliği Yöntemleri

Taraflar İşbu Anlaşma'nın 2. maddesinde belirtilen işbirliğini, karşılıklı uzman değişimi, sağlık ve tıp bilimleri alanlarında ulusal ve uluslararası düzeyde toplantılara katılımın teşvik edilmesi yolları ile yaparlar.

Taraflar aralarındaki işbirliği faaliyetlerini belirlemek ve değerlendirmek üzere bir Ortak Çalışma Komitesi kurarlar. Bu Komite gerektiğinde yılda bir kez dönüşümlü olarak toplanır.

MADDE 4
Mali Düzenlemeler

İşbu Anlaşma çerçevesinde her iki ülkenin uzman ve diğer personellerinin ziyaretlerinde:

a) Gönderen Taraf gidiş-dönüş seyahat masraflarını karşılar.
b) Ev sahibi ülke ziyaretçi ülkenin iaşe ve ibate giderleri ile ülke içi yolculuk giderlerini (gerekli olduğu takdirde) karşılar. Bu süre iki (2) haftayı geçmez.
c) Ev Sahibi Taraf, ziyaretçi uzman ve diğer personele acil durumlarda tıbbi tedavi (diş protezi hariç) sağlar.

MADDE 5
Uygulayıcı Kurumlar

İşbu Anlaşma'nın hükümlerinin uygulanmasını Türkiye Cumhuriyeti Sağlık Bakanlığı ile Gine Cumhuriyeti Sağlık Bakanlığı yürütür.

MADDE 6
İhtilafların Halli

İşbu Anlaşma'nın yorumundan veya uygulanmasından doğabilecek tüm uyuşmazlıklar Taraflarca dostane bir şekilde görüşülerek veya müzakereler yoluyla diplomatik kanaldan çözümlenir.

MADDE 7
Yürürlüğe Giriş ve Süre

İşbu Anlaşma, yürürlüğe girmesi için gerekli iç yasal usullerin tamamlandığını Tarafların birbirlerine diplomatik yollarla bildirdikleri son yazılı bildirimin alındığı tarihte yürürlüğe girer.

İşbu Anlaşma, üç (3) yıl süre için akdedilmiştir. Akit Taraflardan biri, bu Anlaşma'nın geçerlilik süresinin bitiminden altı (6) ay önce feshini diplomatik kanaldan ihbar etmedikçe, iş bu anlaşma süresi bir (1) yıllık sürelerle, zımni olarak uzatılır. İşbu Anlaşma'nın sona ermesi, başlatılmış veya devam eden faaliyetleri ve projeleri etkilemez.

İşbu Anlaşma, Akit Tarafların karşılıklı yazılı rızalarıyla herhangi bir zamanda değiştirilebilir. Değişiklikler, bu maddenin 1. paragrafında belirtilen usule uygun şekilde yürürlüğe girer.

İşbu Anlaşma, Konakri'de, 3 Mart 2016 tarihinde, Türkçe, Fransızca ve İngilizce dillerinde üç asıl nüsha halinde ve tüm metinler eşit geçerlikte olmak üzere imzalanmıştır. Yorum farklılıkları olması halinde İngilizce metin esas alınır.

Türkiye Cumhuriyeti
Hükümeti Adına

Fatma Güldemet SARI
Türkiye Cumhuriyeti Çevre ve
Şehircilik Bakanı

Gine Cumhuriyeti
Hükümeti Adına

Dr. Abdourahmane DIALLO
Gine Cumhuriyeti Sağlık Bakanı

ANNEX A

Ratifications, accessions, subsequent agreements, etc., concerning treaties and international agreements registered in August 2017 with the Secretariat of the United Nations

ANNEXE A

Ratifications, adhésions, accords ultérieurs, etc., concernant des traités et accords internationaux enregistrés en août 2017 au Secrétariat de l'Organisation des Nations Unies

No. 5742. Multilateral

CONVENTION ON THE CONTRACT FOR THE INTERNATIONAL CARRIAGE OF GOODS BY ROAD (CMR). GENEVA, 19 MAY 1956 [*United Nations, Treaty Series, vol. 399, I-5742.*]

ADDITIONAL PROTOCOL TO THE CONVENTION ON THE CONTRACT FOR THE INTERNATIONAL CARRIAGE OF GOODS BY ROAD (CMR) CONCERNING THE ELECTRONIC CONSIGNMENT NOTE. GENEVA, 20 FEBRUARY 2008 [*United Nations, Treaty Series, vol. 2762, A-5742.*]

ACCESSION

Slovenia

Deposit of instrument with the Secretary-General of the United Nations: 15 August 2017

Date of effect: 13 November 2017

Registration with the Secretariat of the United Nations: ex officio, 15 August 2017

N° 5742. Multilatéral

CONVENTION RELATIVE AU CONTRAT DE TRANSPORT INTERNATIONAL DE MARCHANDISES PAR ROUTE (CMR). GENÈVE, 19 MAI 1956 [*Nations Unies, Recueil des Traités, vol. 399, I-5742.*]

PROTOCOLE ADDITIONNEL À LA CONVENTION RELATIVE AU CONTRAT DE TRANSPORT INTERNATIONAL DE MARCHANDISES PAR ROUTE (CMR) CONCERNANT LA LETTRE DE VOITURE ÉLECTRONIQUE. GENÈVE, 20 FÉVRIER 2008 [*Nations Unies, Recueil des Traités, vol. 2762, A-5742.*]

ADHÉSION

Slovénie

Dépôt de l'instrument auprès du Secrétaire général de l'Organisation des Nations Unies : 15 août 2017

Date de prise d'effet : 13 novembre 2017

Enregistrement auprès du Secrétariat de l'Organisation des Nations Unies : d'office, 15 août 2017

No. 14458. Multilateral

CONVENTION ON THE REDUCTION OF STATELESSNESS. NEW YORK, 30 AUGUST 1961 [*United Nations, Treaty Series, vol. 989, I-14458.*]

ACCESSION

Burkina Faso

Deposit of instrument with the Secretary-General of the United Nations: 3 August 2017

Date of effect: 1 November 2017

Registration with the Secretariat of the United Nations: ex officio, 3 August 2017

Nº 14458. Multilatéral

CONVENTION SUR LA RÉDUCTION DES CAS D'APATRIDIE. NEW YORK, 30 AOÛT 1961 [*Nations Unies, Recueil des Traités, vol. 989, I-14458.*]

ADHÉSION

Burkina Faso

Dépôt de l'instrument auprès du Secrétaire général de l'Organisation des Nations Unies : 3 août 2017

Date de prise d'effet : 1er novembre 2017

Enregistrement auprès du Secrétariat de l'Organisation des Nations Unies : d'office, 3 août 2017

No. 16396. United Kingdom of Great Britain and Northern Ireland and Indonesia

AGREEMENT BETWEEN THE GOVERNMENT OF THE UNITED KINGDOM OF GREAT BRITAIN AND NORTHERN IRELAND AND THE GOVERNMENT OF THE REPUBLIC OF INDONESIA FOR THE PROMOTION AND PROTECTION OF INVESTMENTS. LONDON, 27 APRIL 1976 [*United Nations, Treaty Series, vol. 1074, I-16396.*]

TERMINATION

Date of effect: 23 March 2017

Information provided by the Secretariat of the United Nations: 21 August 2017

N° 16396. Royaume-Uni de Grande-Bretagne et d'Irlande du Nord et Indonésie

ACCORD ENTRE LE GOUVERNEMENT DU ROYAUME-UNI DE GRANDE-BRETAGNE ET D'IRLANDE DU NORD ET LE GOUVERNEMENT DE LA RÉPUBLIQUE D'INDONÉSIE RELATIF À LA PROMOTION ET À LA PROTECTION DES INVESTISSEMENTS. LONDRES, 27 AVRIL 1976 [*Nations Unies, Recueil des Traités, vol. 1074, I-16396.*]

ABROGATION

Date de prise d'effet : 23 mars 2017

Information fournie par le Secrétariat de l'Organisation des Nations Unies : 21 août 2017

No. 20378. Multilateral

CONVENTION ON THE ELIMINATION OF ALL FORMS OF DISCRIMINATION AGAINST WOMEN. NEW YORK, 18 DECEMBER 1979 [*United Nations, Treaty Series, vol. 1249, I-20378.*]

OBJECTION TO THE RESERVATIONS MADE BY BAHRAIN

Germany

Notification deposited with the Secretary-General of the United Nations: 1 August 2017

Registration with the Secretariat of the United Nations: ex officio, 1 August 2017

N° 20378. Multilatéral

CONVENTION SUR L'ÉLIMINATION DE TOUTES LES FORMES DE DISCRIMINATION À L'ÉGARD DES FEMMES. NEW YORK, 18 DÉCEMBRE 1979 [*Nations Unies, Recueil des Traités, vol. 1249, I-20378.*]

OBJECTION AUX RÉSERVES FORMULÉES PAR LE BAHREÏN

Allemagne

Dépôt de la notification auprès du Secrétaire général de l'Organisation des Nations Unies : 1er août 2017

Enregistrement auprès du Secrétariat de l'Organisation des Nations Unies : d'office, 1er août 2017

[TEXT IN GERMAN – TEXTE EN ALLEMAND]

Die Regierung der Bundesrepublik Deutschland hat die von Bahrain am 5. August 2016 hinsichtlich des Übereinkommens zur Beseitigung jeder Form von Diskriminierung der Frau vom 18. Dezember 1979 abgegebenen Vorbehalte geprüft.

Die Regierung der Bundesrepublik Deutschland ist der Auffassung, dass die Vorbehalte mit Ziel und Zweck des Übereinkommens unvereinbar sind. Die Regierung der Bundesrepublik Deutschland erhebt daher Einspruch gegen diese Vorbehalte.

Dieser Einspruch schließt das Inkrafttreten des Übereinkommens zwischen der Bundesrepublik Deutschland und Bahrain nicht aus.

[TRANSLATION – TRADUCTION][1]

The Government of the Federal Republic of Germany has examined the reservations submitted on August 5, 2016 by Bahrain regarding the Convention on the Elimination of All Forms of Discrimination against Women of December 18, 1979.

The Government of the Federal Republic of Germany considers that the reservations are incompatible with the object and purpose of the Convention. The Government of the Federal Republic of Germany therefore objects to these reservations.

This objection shall not preclude the entry into force of the Convention between the Federal Republic of Germany and Bahrain.

[TRANSLATION – TRADUCTION]

Le Gouvernement de la République fédérale d'Allemagne a examiné les réserves formulées le 5 août 2016 par le Bahreïn à la Convention sur l'élimination de toutes les formes de discrimination à l'égard des femmes du 18 décembre 1979.

Le Gouvernement de la République fédérale d'Allemagne considère que les réserves sont incompatibles avec l'objet et le but de la Convention. En conséquence, le Gouvernement de la République fédérale d'Allemagne fait objection à ces réserves.

Cette objection ne fait pas obstacle à l'entrée en vigueur de la Convention entre la République fédérale d'Allemagne et le Bahreïn.

OBJECTION TO THE RESERVATIONS MADE BY BAHRAIN

Netherlands

Notification deposited with the Secretary-General of the United Nations: 3 August 2017

Registration with the Secretariat of the United Nations: ex officio, 3 August 2017

OBJECTION AUX RÉSERVES FORMULÉES PAR BAHREÏN

Pays-Bas

Dépôt de la notification auprès du Secrétaire général de l'Organisation des Nations Unies : 3 août 2017

Enregistrement auprès du Secrétariat de l'Organisation des Nations Unies : d'office, 3 août 2017

[1] Translation provided by the Government of Germany – Traduction fournie par le Gouvernement de l'Allemagne.

OBJECTION TO THE MODIFICATION OF RESERVATIONS MADE BY BAHRAIN

United Kingdom of Great Britain and Northern Ireland

Notification deposited with the Secretary-General of the United Nations: 1 August 2017

Registration with the Secretariat of the United Nations: ex officio, 1 August 2017

OBJECTION À LA MODIFICATION DES RÉSERVES FORMULÉES PAR BAHREÏN

Royaume-Uni de Grande-Bretagne et d'Irlande du Nord

Dépôt de la notification auprès du Secrétaire général de l'Organisation des Nations Unies : 1er août 2017

Enregistrement auprès du Secrétariat de l'Organisation des Nations Unies : d'office, 1er août 2017

[TEXT IN ENGLISH – TEXTE EN ANGLAIS]

The Government of the United Kingdom notes that a modification of the Kingdom of Bahrain's reservations to the Convention on the Elimination of All Forms of Discrimination Against Women ("the Convention") was received on 5 August 2016.

The Government of the United Kingdom notes that the Kingdom of Bahrain has substantively modified its reservations in respect of Article 2; Article 15, paragraph 4; and Article 16, stating that the implementation of these Articles will be "*without breaching the provisions of the Islamic Shariah*".

Notwithstanding that the Government of Bahrain has indicated that the modifications do not imply an extension of the original reservations, and that they instead constitute editorial amendments that do not place any limitations on Bahrain's commitments upon accession, the Government of the United Kingdom notes that a condition of compatibility with another system of law has been added to the reservation to Article 15, paragraph 4; and has been reformulated in respect of the reservations to Articles 2 and 16. The Government of the United Kingdom further notes that a reservation which consists of a general reference to a system of law without specifying its contents does not clearly define for the other States Parties to the Convention the extent to which the reserving State has accepted the obligations of the Convention. The Government of the United Kingdom of Great Britain and Northern Ireland therefore objects to the aforesaid reservations in respect of Article 2; Article 15, paragraph 4; and Article 16.

[TRANSLATION – TRADUCTION]

Le Gouvernement du Royaume-Uni relève qu'une modification des réserves faites par le Royaume de Bahreïn à la Convention sur l'élimination de toutes les formes de discrimination à l'égard des femmes (« la Convention ») a été reçue le 5 août 2016.

Le Gouvernement du Royaume-Uni note que le Royaume de Bahreïn a apporté des modifications de fond à ses réserves à l'égard de l'article 2, du paragraphe 4 de l'article 15 et de l'article 16 de la Convention, la nouvelle formulation indiquant que la mise en œuvre de ces dispositions « ne doit pas enfreindre les dispositions de la loi islamique ».

Bien que le Gouvernement bahreïnite ait indiqué que les modifications en question ne donnent pas lieu à une extension des réserves initiales, et qu'elles constituent au contraire des modifications d'ordre rédactionnel qui n'imposent aucune restriction aux engagements du Bahreïn lors de l'adhésion, le Gouvernement du Royaume-Uni fait observer qu'une condition de compatibilité avec un autre système de droit a été ajoutée à la réserve à l'égard du paragraphe 4 de l'article 15, et qu'une telle condition a été reformulée en ce qui concerne les réserves à l'égard des articles 2 et 16. Le Gouvernement du Royaume-Uni fait en outre observer qu'une réserve consistant en un renvoi général à un système de droit dont elle ne précise pas la teneur n'indique pas clairement aux autres États parties à la Convention dans quelle mesure l'État réservataire a accepté les obligations au titre de celle-ci. Le Gouvernement du Royaume-Uni de Grande-Bretagne et d'Irlande du Nord fait donc objection aux réserves susmentionnées à l'égard de l'article 2, du paragraphe 4 de l'article 15 et de l'article 16 de la Convention.

No. 21584. Czechoslovakia and Turkey

INTERNATIONAL ROAD TRANSPORT AGREEMENT BETWEEN THE GOVERNMENT OF THE CZECHOSLOVAK SOCIALIST REPUBLIC AND THE GOVERNMENT OF THE REPUBLIC OF TURKEY. PRAGUE, 30 JUNE 1981 [*United Nations, Treaty Series, vol. 1299, I-21584.*]

TERMINATION IN THE RELATIONS BETWEEN THE REPUBLIC OF TURKEY AND THE SLOVAK REPUBLIC

Date: 12 April 2017

Date of effect: 12 April 2017

Information provided by the Secretariat of the United Nations: 21 August 2017

Nº 21584. Tchécoslovaquie et Turquie

ACCORD RELATIF AUX TRANSPORTS ROUTIERS INTERNATIONAUX CONCLU ENTRE LE GOUVERNEMENT DE LA RÉPUBLIQUE SOCIALISTE TCHÉCOSLOVAQUE ET LE GOUVERNEMENT DE LA RÉPUBLIQUE TURQUE. PRAGUE, 30 JUIN 1981 [*Nations Unies, Recueil des Traités, vol. 1299, I-21584.*]

ABROGATION DANS LES RAPPORTS ENTRE LA RÉPUBLIQUE TURQUE ET LA RÉPUBLIQUE SLOVAQUE

Date : 12 avril 2017

Date de prise d'effet : 12 avril 2017

Information fournie par le Secrétariat de l'Organisation des Nations Unies : 21 août 2017

No. 22495. Multilateral

CONVENTION ON PROHIBITIONS OR RESTRICTIONS ON THE USE OF CERTAIN CONVENTIONAL WEAPONS WHICH MAY BE DEEMED TO BE EXCESSIVELY INJURIOUS OR TO HAVE INDISCRIMINATE EFFECTS (WITH PROTOCOLS I, II AND III). GENEVA, 10 OCTOBER 1980 [*United Nations, Treaty Series, vol. 1342, I-22495.*]

RATIFICATION

Afghanistan

Deposit of instrument with the Secretary-General of the United Nations: 9 August 2017

Date of effect: 9 February 2018

Registration with the Secretariat of the United Nations: ex officio, 9 August 2017

Nº 22495. Multilatéral

CONVENTION SUR L'INTERDICTION OU LA LIMITATION DE L'EMPLOI DE CERTAINES ARMES CLASSIQUES QUI PEUVENT ÊTRE CONSIDÉRÉES COMME PRODUISANT DES EFFETS TRAUMATIQUES EXCESSIFS OU COMME FRAPPANT SANS DISCRIMINATION (AVEC PROTOCOLES I, II ET III). GENÈVE, 10 OCTOBRE 1980 [*Nations Unies, Recueil des Traités, vol. 1342, I-22495.*]

RATIFICATION

Afghanistan

Dépôt de l'instrument auprès du Secrétaire général de l'Organisation des Nations Unies : 9 août 2017

Date de prise d'effet : 9 février 2018

Enregistrement auprès du Secrétariat de l'Organisation des Nations Unies : d'office, 9 août 2017

ADDITIONAL PROTOCOL TO THE CONVENTION ON PROHIBITIONS OR RESTRICTIONS ON THE USE OF CERTAIN CONVENTIONAL WEAPONS WHICH MAY BE DEEMED TO BE EXCESSIVELY INJURIOUS OR TO HAVE INDISCRIMINATE EFFECTS (PROTOCOL IV, ENTITLED PROTOCOL ON BLINDING LASER WEAPONS). VIENNA, 13 OCTOBER 1995 [*United Nations, Treaty Series, vol. 2024, A-22495.*]

CONSENT TO BE BOUND

Afghanistan

Deposit of instrument with the Secretary-General of the United Nations: 9 August 2017

Date of effect: 9 February 2018

Registration with the Secretariat of the United Nations: ex officio, 9 August 2017

PROTOCOLE ADDITIONNEL À LA CONVENTION SUR L'INTERDICTION OU LA LIMITATION DE L'EMPLOI DE CERTAINES ARMES CLASSIQUES QUI PEUVENT ÊTRE CONSIDÉRÉES COMME PRODUISANT DES EFFETS TRAUMATIQUES EXCESSIFS OU COMME FRAPPANT SANS DISCRIMINATION (PROTOCOLE IV, INTITULÉ PROTOCOLE RELATIF AUX ARMES À LASER AVEUGLANTES). VIENNE, 13 OCTOBRE 1995 [*Nations Unies, Recueil des Traités, vol. 2024, A-22495.*]

CONSENTEMENT À ÊTRE LIÉ

Afghanistan

Dépôt de l'instrument auprès du Secrétaire général de l'Organisation des Nations Unies : 9 août 2017

Date de prise d'effet : 9 février 2018

Enregistrement auprès du Secrétariat de l'Organisation des Nations Unies : d'office, 9 août 2017

PROTOCOL ON PROHIBITIONS OR RESTRICTIONS ON THE USE OF MINES, BOOBY-TRAPS AND OTHER DEVICES AS AMENDED ON 3 MAY 1996 (PROTOCOL II, AS AMENDED ON 3 MAY 1996) ANNEXED TO THE CONVENTION ON PROHIBITIONS OR RESTRICTIONS ON THE USE OF CERTAIN CONVENTIONAL WEAPONS WHICH MAY BE DEEMED TO BE EXCESSIVELY INJURIOUS OR TO HAVE INDISCRIMINATE EFFECTS. GENEVA, 3 MAY 1996 [*United Nations, Treaty Series, vol. 2048, A-22495.*]

CONSENT TO BE BOUND

Afghanistan

Deposit of instrument with the Secretary-General of the United Nations: 9 August 2017

Date of effect: 9 February 2018

Registration with the Secretariat of the United Nations: ex officio, 9 August 2017

PROTOCOLE SUR L'INTERDICTION OU LA LIMITATION DE L'EMPLOI DES MINES, PIÈGES ET AUTRES DISPOSITIFS, TEL QU'IL A ÉTÉ MODIFIÉ LE 3 MAI 1996 (PROTOCOLE II, TEL QU'IL A ÉTÉ MODIFIÉ LE 3 MAI 1996) ANNEXÉ À LA CONVENTION SUR L'INTERDICTION OU LA LIMITATION DE L'EMPLOI DE CERTAINES ARMES CLASSIQUES QUI PEUVENT ÊTRE CONSIDÉRÉES COMME PRODUISANT DES EFFETS TRAUMATIQUES EXCESSIFS OU COMME FRAPPANT SANS DISCRIMINATION. GENÈVE, 3 MAI 1996 [*Nations Unies, Recueil des Traités, vol. 2048, A-22495.*]

CONSENTEMENT À ÊTRE LIÉ

Afghanistan

Dépôt de l'instrument auprès du Secrétaire général de l'Organisation des Nations Unies : 9 août 2017

Date de prise d'effet : 9 février 2018

Enregistrement auprès du Secrétariat de l'Organisation des Nations Unies : d'office, 9 août 2017

AMENDMENT TO ARTICLE I OF THE CONVENTION ON PROHIBITIONS OR RESTRICTIONS ON THE USE OF CERTAIN CONVENTIONAL WEAPONS WHICH MAY BE DEEMED TO BE EXCESSIVELY INJURIOUS OR TO HAVE INDISCRIMINATE EFFECTS. GENEVA, 21 DECEMBER 2001 [*United Nations, Treaty Series, vol. 2260, A-22495.*]

ACCESSION

Afghanistan

Deposit of instrument with the Secretary-General of the United Nations: 9 August 2017

Date of effect: 9 February 2018

Registration with the Secretariat of the United Nations: ex officio, 9 August 2017

AMENDEMENT À L'ARTICLE PREMIER DE LA CONVENTION SUR L'INTERDICTION OU LA LIMITATION DE L'EMPLOI DE CERTAINES ARMES CLASSIQUES QUI PEUVENT ÊTRE CONSIDÉRÉES COMME PRODUISANT DES EFFETS TRAUMATIQUES EXCESSIFS OU COMME FRAPPANT SANS DISCRIMINATION. GENÈVE, 21 DÉCEMBRE 2001 [*Nations Unies, Recueil des Traités, vol. 2260, A-22495.*]

ADHÉSION

Afghanistan

Dépôt de l'instrument auprès du Secrétaire général de l'Organisation des Nations Unies : 9 août 2017

Date de prise d'effet : 9 février 2018

Enregistrement auprès du Secrétariat de l'Organisation des Nations Unies : d'office, 9 août 2017

PROTOCOL ON EXPLOSIVE REMNANTS OF WAR TO THE CONVENTION ON PROHIBITIONS OR RESTRICTIONS ON THE USE OF CERTAIN CONVENTIONAL WEAPONS WHICH MAY BE DEEMED TO BE EXCESSIVELY INJURIOUS OR TO HAVE INDISCRIMINATE EFFECTS (PROTOCOL V). GENEVA, 28 NOVEMBER 2003 [*United Nations, Treaty Series, vol. 2399, A-22495.*]

CONSENT TO BE BOUND

Afghanistan

Deposit of instrument with the Secretary-General of the United Nations: 9 August 2017

Date of effect: 9 February 2018

Registration with the Secretariat of the United Nations: ex officio, 9 August 2017

PROTOCOLE RELATIF AUX RESTES EXPLOSIFS DE GUERRE À LA CONVENTION SUR L'INTERDICTION OU LA LIMITATION DE L'EMPLOI DE CERTAINES ARMES CLASSIQUES QUI PEUVENT ÊTRE CONSIDÉRÉES COMME PRODUISANT DES EFFETS TRAUMATIQUES EXCESSIFS OU COMME FRAPPANT SANS DISCRIMINATION (PROTOCOLE V). GENÈVE, 28 NOVEMBRE 2003 [*Nations Unies, Recueil des Traités, vol. 2399, A-22495.*]

CONSENTEMENT À ÊTRE LIÉ

Afghanistan

Dépôt de l'instrument auprès du Secrétaire général de l'Organisation des Nations Unies : 9 août 2017

Date de prise d'effet : 9 février 2018

Enregistrement auprès du Secrétariat de l'Organisation des Nations Unies : d'office, 9 août 2017

No. 24631. Multilateral

CONVENTION ON THE PHYSICAL PROTECTION OF NUCLEAR MATERIAL. VIENNA, 3 MARCH 1980, AND NEW YORK, 3 MARCH 1980 [*United Nations, Treaty Series, vol. 1456, I-24631.*]

AMENDMENT TO THE CONVENTION ON THE PHYSICAL PROTECTION OF NUCLEAR MATERIAL. VIENNA, 8 JULY 2005 [*United Nations, Treaty Series, vol. 3132, A-24631.*]

RATIFICATION

Namibia

Deposit of instrument with the Director-General of the International Atomic Energy Agency: 16 August 2017

Date of effect: 16 August 2017

Registration with the Secretariat of the United Nations: International Atomic Energy Agency, 23 August 2017

Nº 24631. Multilatéral

CONVENTION SUR LA PROTECTION PHYSIQUE DES MATIÈRES NUCLÉAIRES. VIENNE, 3 MARS 1980, ET NEW YORK, 3 MARS 1980 [*Nations Unies, Recueil des Traités, vol. 1456, I-24631.*]

AMENDEMENT À LA CONVENTION SUR LA PROTECTION PHYSIQUE DES MATIÈRES NUCLÉAIRES. VIENNE, 8 JUILLET 2005 [*Nations Unies, Recueil des Traités, vol. 3132, A-24631.*]

RATIFICATION

Namibie

Dépôt de l'instrument auprès du Directeur général de l'Agence internationale de l'énergie atomique : 16 août 2017

Date de prise d'effet : 16 août 2017

Enregistrement auprès du Secrétariat de l'Organisation des Nations Unies : Agence internationale de l'énergie atomique, 23 août 2017

No. 27531. Multilateral

CONVENTION ON THE RIGHTS OF THE CHILD. NEW YORK, 20 NOVEMBER 1989 [*United Nations, Treaty Series, vol. 1577, I-27531.*]

PARTIAL WITHDRAWAL OF RESERVATION

Republic of Korea

Notification effected with the Secretary-General of the United Nations: 11 August 2017

Registration with the Secretariat of the United Nations: ex officio, 11 August 2017

Nº 27531. Multilatéral

CONVENTION RELATIVE AUX DROITS DE L'ENFANT. NEW YORK, 20 NOVEMBRE 1989 [*Nations Unies, Recueil des Traités, vol. 1577, I-27531.*]

RETRAIT PARTIEL DE RÉSERVE

République de Corée

Notification effectuée auprès du Secrétaire général de l'Organisation des Nations Unies : 11 août 2017

Enregistrement auprès du Secrétariat de l'Organisation des Nations Unies : d'office, 11 août 2017

[TEXT IN ENGLISH – TEXTE EN ANGLAIS]

On 11 August 2017, the Government of the Republic of Korea informed the Secretary-General that it had decided to withdraw the reservation in respect of article 21, paragraph (a), made upon ratification.

[TRANSLATION – TRADUCTION]

Le 11 août 2017, le Gouvernement de la République de Corée a informé le Secrétaire général qu'il a décidé de retirer la réserve au paragraphe (a) de l'article 21, formulée lors de la ratification.

No. 33545. Multilateral

CONVENTION ON NUCLEAR SAFETY. VIENNA, 20 SEPTEMBER 1994 [*United Nations, Treaty Series, vol. 1963, I-33545.*]

ACCEPTANCE

Cuba

Deposit of instrument with the Director-General of the International Atomic Energy Agency: 3 July 2017

Date of effect: 1 October 2017

Registration with the Secretariat of the United Nations: International Atomic Energy Agency, 22 August 2017

Nº 33545. Multilatéral

CONVENTION SUR LA SÛRETÉ NUCLÉAIRE. VIENNE, 20 SEPTEMBRE 1994 [*Nations Unies, Recueil des Traités, vol. 1963, I-33545.*]

ACCEPTATION

Cuba

Dépôt de l'instrument auprès du Directeur général de l'Agence internationale de l'énergie atomique : 3 juillet 2017

Date de prise d'effet : 1er octobre 2017

Enregistrement auprès du Secrétariat de l'Organisation des Nations Unies : Agence internationale de l'énergie atomique, 22 août 2017

No. 37605. Multilateral

JOINT CONVENTION ON THE SAFETY OF SPENT FUEL MANAGEMENT AND ON THE SAFETY OF RADIOACTIVE WASTE MANAGEMENT. VIENNA, 5 SEPTEMBER 1997 [*United Nations, Treaty Series, vol. 2153, I-37605.*]

ACCESSION

Cuba

Deposit of instrument with the Director-General of the International Atomic Energy Agency: 3 July 2017

Date of effect: 1 October 2017

Registration with the Secretariat of the United Nations: International Atomic Energy Agency, 22 August 2017

Nº 37605. Multilatéral

CONVENTION COMMUNE SUR LA SÛRETÉ DE LA GESTION DU COMBUSTIBLE USÉ ET SUR LA SÛRETÉ DE LA GESTION DES DÉCHETS RADIOACTIFS. VIENNE, 5 SEPTEMBRE 1997 [*Nations Unies, Recueil des Traités, vol. 2153, I-37605.*]

ADHÉSION

Cuba

Dépôt de l'instrument auprès du Directeur général de l'Agence internationale de l'énergie atomique : 3 juillet 2017

Date de prise d'effet : 1er octobre 2017

Enregistrement auprès du Secrétariat de l'Organisation des Nations Unies : Agence internationale de l'énergie atomique, 22 août 2017

No. 39574. Multilateral

N° 39574. Multilatéral

UNITED NATIONS CONVENTION AGAINST TRANSNATIONAL ORGANIZED CRIME. NEW YORK, 15 NOVEMBER 2000 [*United Nations, Treaty Series, vol. 2225, I-39574.*]

CONVENTION DES NATIONS UNIES CONTRE LA CRIMINALITÉ TRANSNATIONALE ORGANISÉE. NEW YORK, 15 NOVEMBRE 2000 [*Nations Unies, Recueil des Traités, vol. 2225, I-39574.*]

PROTOCOL AGAINST THE SMUGGLING OF MIGRANTS BY LAND, SEA AND AIR, SUPPLEMENTING THE UNITED NATIONS CONVENTION AGAINST TRANSNATIONAL ORGANIZED CRIME. NEW YORK, 15 NOVEMBER 2000 [*United Nations, Treaty Series, vol. 2241, A-39574.*]

PROTOCOLE CONTRE LE TRAFIC ILLICITE DE MIGRANTS PAR TERRE, AIR ET MER, ADDITIONNEL À LA CONVENTION DES NATIONS UNIES CONTRE LA CRIMINALITÉ TRANSNATIONALE ORGANISÉE. NEW YORK, 15 NOVEMBRE 2000 [*Nations Unies, Recueil des Traités, vol. 2241, A-39574.*]

OBJECTION TO THE RESERVATION MADE BY AFGHANISTAN UPON ACCESSION

Austria

Notification deposited with the Secretary-General of the United Nations: 18 August 2017

Registration with the Secretariat of the United Nations: ex officio, 18 August 2017

OBJECTION À LA RÉSERVE FORMULÉE PAR L'AFGHANISTAN LORS DE L'ADHÉSION

Autriche

Dépôt de la notification auprès du Secrétaire général de l'Organisation des Nations Unies : 18 août 2017

Enregistrement auprès du Secrétariat de l'Organisation des Nations Unies : d'office, 18 août 2017

[TEXT IN ENGLISH – TEXTE EN ANGLAIS]

The Government of Austria has carefully examined the reservation made by the Islamic Republic of Afghanistan upon accession to the Protocol against the Smuggling of Migrants by Land, Sea and Air, supplementing the United Nations Convention against Transnational Organized Crime.

By seeking to exclude the application of Article 18 of the Protocol in its entirety, the reservation contravenes the purpose of the Protocol, namely to protect the rights of migrants and to promote cooperation among States Parties. It generally excludes a central issue the Protocol intends to govern.

Austria therefore considers the reservation to be incompatible with the object and purpose of the Protocol and objects to it. This objection shall not preclude the entry into force of the Protocol between Austria and the Islamic Republic of Afghanistan. The Protocol will thus become operative between the two States without the Islamic Republic of Afghanistan benefitting from the aforementioned reservation.

[TRANSLATION – TRADUCTION]

Le Gouvernement autrichien a examiné avec attention la réserve formulée par la République islamique d'Afghanistan lors de l'adhésion au Protocole contre le trafic illicite de migrants par terre, mer et air, additionnel à la Convention des Nations Unies contre la criminalité transnationale organisée.

En cherchant à exclure l'application de l'article 18 du Protocole dans son intégralité, la réserve est contraire au but du Protocole, à savoir la protection des droits des migrants et la promotion de la coopération entre les États parties. La réserve exclut, de façon générale, une question centrale que le Protocole vise à régir.

Par conséquent, l'Autriche considère que la réserve est incompatible avec l'objet et le but du Protocole et s'y oppose. Cette objection ne fait pas obstacle à l'entrée en vigueur du Protocole entre l'Autriche et la République islamique d'Afghanistan. Le Protocole entrera donc en vigueur entre les deux États sans que la République islamique d'Afghanistan ne puisse se prévaloir de la réserve susmentionnée.

No. 40757. Indonesia and Netherlands

AGREEMENT BETWEEN THE GOVERNMENT OF THE REPUBLIC OF INDONESIA AND THE GOVERNMENT OF THE KINGDOM OF THE NETHERLANDS FOR THE AVOIDANCE OF DOUBLE TAXATION AND THE PREVENTION OF FISCAL EVASION WITH RESPECT TO TAXES ON INCOME. JAKARTA, 29 JANUARY 2002 [*United Nations, Treaty Series, vol. 2287, I-40757.*]

PROTOCOL AMENDING THE AGREEMENT BETWEEN THE GOVERNMENT OF THE KINGDOM OF THE NETHERLANDS AND THE GOVERNMENT OF THE REPUBLIC OF INDONESIA FOR THE AVOIDANCE OF DOUBLE TAXATION AND THE PREVENTION OF FISCAL EVASION WITH RESPECT TO TAXES ON INCOME, AND ITS PROTOCOL, SIGNED AT JAKARTA ON JANUARY 29, 2002. JAKARTA, 30 JULY 2015

Entry into force: 1 August 2017, in accordance with article 10

Authentic texts: Dutch, English and Indonesian

Registration with the Secretariat of the United Nations: Netherlands, 9 August 2017

N° 40757. Indonésie et Pays-Bas

ACCORD ENTRE LE GOUVERNEMENT DE LA RÉPUBLIQUE D'INDONÉSIE ET LE GOUVERNEMENT DU ROYAUME DES PAYS-BAS TENDANT À ÉVITER LA DOUBLE IMPOSITION ET À PRÉVENIR L'ÉVASION FISCALE EN MATIÈRE D'IMPÔTS SUR LE REVENU. JAKARTA, 29 JANVIER 2002 [*Nations Unies, Recueil des Traités, vol. 2287, I-40757.*]

PROTOCOLE AMENDANT L'ACCORD ENTRE LE GOUVERNEMENT DU ROYAUME DES PAYS-BAS ET LE GOUVERNEMENT DE LA RÉPUBLIQUE D'INDONÉSIE TENDANT À ÉVITER LA DOUBLE IMPOSITION ET À PRÉVENIR L'ÉVASION FISCALE EN MATIÈRE D'IMPÔTS SUR LE REVENU, ET SON PROTOCOLE, SIGNÉ À JAKARTA LE 29 JANVIER 2002. JAKARTA, 30 JUILLET 2015

Entrée en vigueur : 1er août 2017, conformément à l'article 10

Textes authentiques : néerlandais, anglais et indonésien

Enregistrement auprès du Secrétariat de l'Organisation des Nations Unies : Pays-Bas, 9 août 2017

[TEXT IN DUTCH – TEXTE EN NÉERLANDAIS]

Protocol tot wijziging van het Verdrag tussen de Regering van het Koninkrijk der Nederlanden en de Regering van de Republiek Indonesië tot het vermijden van dubbele belasting en het voorkomen van het ontgaan van belasting met betrekking tot belastingen naar het inkomen, en het Protocol daarbij, ondertekend te Jakarta op 29 januari 2002

De Regering van het Koninkrijk der Nederlanden

en

de Regering van de Republiek Indonesië,

Geleid door de wens een Protocol te sluiten tot wijziging van het Verdrag tussen de Regering van het Koninkrijk der Nederlanden en de Regering van de Republiek Indonesië tot het vermijden van dubbele belasting en het voorkomen van het ontgaan van belasting met betrekking tot belastingen naar het inkomen, en het Protocol daarbij, ondertekend te Jakarta op 29 februari 2002 (hierna te noemen „het Verdrag"),

Zijn het volgende overeengekomen:

Artikel 1

Artikel 10, tweede lid, van het Verdrag wordt vervangen door het volgende artikellid:

„2. Deze dividenden mogen echter ook in de Staat waarvan het lichaam dat de dividenden betaalt inwoner is overeenkomstig de wetgeving van die Staat worden belast, maar indien de uiteindelijk gerechtigde tot de dividenden een inwoner van de andere Staat is, mag de aldus geheven belasting:
a. 5 percent van het brutobedrag van de dividenden niet overschrijden, indien de uiteindelijk gerechtigde een lichaam is (niet zijnde een samenwerkingsverband) dat onmiddellijk ten minste 25 percent bezit van het kapitaal van het lichaam dat de dividenden betaalt;
b. 10 percent van het brutobedrag van de dividenden niet overschrijden, indien de uiteindelijk gerechtigde een pensioenfonds is dat ingevolge de wettelijke bepalingen van een van beide Staten erkend is en onder toezicht staat en waarvan het inkomen in het algemeen is vrijgesteld van belasting in de Staat waarin het ingevolge de wettelijke bepalingen is erkend en onder toezicht staat;
c. in alle overige gevallen 15 percent van het brutobedrag van de dividenden niet overschrijden.".

Artikel 2

Artikel 11, vierde lid, van het Verdrag wordt vervangen door het volgende artikellid:

„4. Niettegenstaande de bepalingen van het tweede lid, mag interest afkomstig uit een van beide Staten ook in de Staat waaruit hij afkomstig is overeenkomstig de wetgeving van die Staat worden belast, maar indien de uiteindelijk gerechtigde tot de interest een inwoner van de andere Staat is en de interest wordt betaald ter zake van een lening met een looptijd van meer dan twee jaar of wordt betaald in verband met de verkoop op afbetaling van nijverheids- of handelsuitrusting of wetenschappelijke uitrusting, mag de aldus geheven belasting 5 percent van het brutobedrag van de interest niet overschrijden.".

Artikel 3

a. In artikel 24, derde lid, van het Verdrag worden de woorden „artikel 16, eerste lid," vervangen door de woorden: „artikel 16, eerste en derde lid,";

b. In artikel 24, vierde lid, van het Verdrag worden de woorden „artikel 11, tweede lid," vervangen door de woorden: „artikel 11, tweede en vierde lid,".

Artikel 4

Artikel 28 wordt in zijn geheel vervangen door het volgende artikel:

„Artikel 28

Uitwisseling van informatie

1. De bevoegde autoriteiten van de beide Staten wisselen informatie uit die naar verwachting van belang is voor de uitvoering van de bepalingen van dit Verdrag of voor de administratie of de tenuitvoerlegging van de nationale wetgeving met betrekking tot belastingen van elke soort en benaming die worden geheven ten behoeve van beide Staten, of van de staatkundige onderdelen of plaatselijke publiekrechtelijke lichamen daarvan, voor zover de heffing van die belastingen niet in strijd is met het Verdrag. De uitwisseling van informatie wordt niet beperkt door de artikelen 1 en 2.

2. Alle uit hoofde van het eerste lid door een van beide Staten ontvangen informatie wordt op dezelfde wijze geheim gehouden als informatie die volgens de nationale wetgeving van die Staat is verkregen en wordt alleen ter kennis gebracht van personen of autoriteiten (daaronder begrepen rechterlijke instanties en administratiefrechtelijke lichamen) die betrokken zijn bij de vaststelling of invordering van, de tenuitvoerlegging of vervolging ter zake van, of de beslissing in beroepszaken betrekking hebbende op de in het eerste lid bedoelde belastingen, of het toezicht daarop. Deze personen of autoriteiten mogen van de informatie alleen voor deze doeleinden gebruikmaken. Zij mogen de informatie bekendmaken in openbare rechtszittingen of in gerechtelijke beslissingen.

3. In geen geval worden de bepalingen van de voorgaande leden zo uitgelegd dat zij een Staat de verplichting opleggen:
a. administratieve maatregelen te nemen die in strijd zijn met de wetgeving of de administratieve praktijk van die of van de andere Staat;
b. informatie te verstrekken die niet verkrijgbaar is volgens de wetgeving of in de normale administratieve gang van zaken van die of van de andere Staat;

c. informatie te verstrekken die een handels-, bedrijfs-, nijverheids- of beroepsgeheim of een fabrieks- of handelswerkwijze zou onthullen, dan wel informatie waarvan het verstrekken in strijd zou zijn met de openbare orde (ordre public).

4. Indien informatie wordt verzocht door een van beide Staten in overeenstemming met dit artikel, wendt de andere Staat zijn maatregelen inzake het verzamelen van informatie aan om de verlangde informatie te verkrijgen, ongeacht het feit dat die andere Staat ten behoeve van zijn eigen belastingheffing niet over dergelijke informatie behoeft te beschikken. Op de in de vorige zin vervatte verplichting zijn de beperkingen van het derde lid van toepassing, maar deze beperkingen mogen in geen geval zodanig worden uitgelegd dat het een Staat is toegestaan uitsluitend op grond van het feit dat hij geen nationaal belang heeft bij dergelijke informatie te weigeren informatie te verstrekken.

5. De bepalingen van het derde lid mogen in geen geval zodanig worden uitgelegd dat het een Staat is toegestaan het verschaffen van informatie te weigeren uitsluitend op grond van het feit dat de betreffende gegevens berusten bij een bank, een andere financiële instelling, een gevolmachtigde, of een persoon die bij wijze van vertegenwoordiging of als vertrouwenspersoon optreedt, dan wel omdat deze betrekking hebben op eigendomsbelangen in een persoon.".

Artikel 5

Het volgende artikel wordt na artikel 28 van het Verdrag ingevoegd:

„Artikel 28A

Bijstand bij de invordering van belastingen

1. De Staten verlenen elkaar bijstand bij de invordering van belastingvorderingen. Deze bijstand wordt niet beperkt door de artikelen 1 en 2. De bevoegde autoriteiten van de Staten kunnen in onderlinge overeenstemming de wijze van toepassing van dit artikel regelen. Er mag geen verzoek om bijstand worden ingediend indien het totale bedrag van de betreffende vordering minder is dan EUR 1.500.

2. Onder de uitdrukking „belastingvordering" als gebezigd in dit artikel wordt verstaan een bedrag verschuldigd in verband met belastingen van elke soort en benaming die worden geheven ten behoeve van de Staten, voor zover de belastingheffing uit hoofde daarvan niet in strijd is met dit Verdrag of met een ander instrument waarbij de Staten partij zijn, alsmede interest, administratieve boetes en de kosten van invordering of van conservatoire maatregelen die verband houden met dat bedrag.

3. De bepalingen van dit artikel zijn slechts van toepassing op een belastingvordering die onderwerp is van een executoriale titel in de verzoekende Staat en die, tenzij anders overeengekomen tussen de bevoegde autoriteiten, niet wordt bestreden. Indien de vordering echter een belastingverplichting betreft van een persoon die geen inwoner van de verzoekende Staat is, is dit artikel slechts van toepassing indien de vordering niet langer kan worden bestreden, tenzij anders overeengekomen tussen de bevoegde autoriteiten. De belastingvordering wordt door die andere Staat ingevorderd in overeenstemming met de bepalingen van zijn wetgeving die van toepassing zijn op de tenuitvoerlegging en invordering van zijn eigen belastingen als ware de belastingvordering een belastingvordering van die andere Staat.

4. Indien een belastingvordering van een Staat een vordering is ter zake waarvan die Staat uit hoofde van zijn wetgeving conservatoire maatregelen kan nemen teneinde de invordering te waarborgen, kan die belastingvordering op verzoek van de bevoegde autoriteit van die Staat worden aanvaard ten behoeve van het nemen van conservatoire maatregelen door de bevoegde autoriteit van die andere Staat. Die andere Staat neemt ter zake van die belastingvordering conservatoire maatregelen in overeenstemming met de bepalingen van zijn wetgeving, als ware de belastingvordering een belastingvordering van die andere Staat, ook wanneer de belastingvordering op het tijdstip waarop deze maatregelen worden genomen niet invorderbaar is in de eerstbedoelde Staat of verschuldigd is door een persoon die gerechtigd is de invordering ervan te beletten.

5. Onverminderd de bepalingen van het derde en vierde lid, zijn op een door een Staat voor de toepassing van het derde of vierde lid aanvaarde belastingvordering niet de termijnen van toepassing noch wordt aan een belastingvordering voorrang verleend uit hoofde van de wetgeving van die Staat op grond van haar aard als zodanig en, tenzij anders overeengekomen tussen de bevoegde autoriteiten, kunnen belastingvorderingen niet worden ingevorderd door middel van inhechtenisneming wegens schuld van de schuldenaar. Voorts wordt aan een door een Staat voor de toepassing van het derde of vierde lid aanvaarde belastingvordering in die Staat geen voorrang verleend, die uit hoofde van de wetgeving van de andere Staat op die belastingvordering van toepassing is.

6. Procedures inzake het bestaan, de geldigheid of het bedrag van een belastingvordering van een Staat worden niet aanhangig gemaakt bij de rechterlijke instanties of administratiefrechtelijke lichamen van de andere Staat.

7. Indien te eniger tijd nadat uit hoofde van het derde of vierde lid een verzoek is gedaan door een Staat en voordat de andere Staat de desbetreffende belastingvordering heeft ingevorderd en overgemaakt aan de eerstbedoelde Staat, de desbetreffende belastingvordering:
a. in het geval van een verzoek ingevolge het derde lid, ophoudt een belastingvordering van de eerstbedoelde Staat te zijn die invorderbaar is uit hoofde van de wetgeving van die Staat en die verschuldigd is door een persoon die, op dat tijdstip, uit hoofde van de wetgeving van die Staat de invordering ervan niet kan beletten; of
b. in het geval van een verzoek uit hoofde van het vierde lid, ophoudt een belastingvordering van de eerstbedoelde Staat te zijn ter zake waarvan die Staat uit hoofde van zijn wetgeving conservatoire maatregelen kan treffen teneinde de invordering ervan te waarborgen,

stelt de bevoegde autoriteit van de eerstbedoelde Staat de bevoegde autoriteit van de andere Staat onverwijld daarvan in kennis, en, naar keuze van de andere Staat, wordt het verzoek door de eerstbedoelde Staat uitgesteld of ingetrokken.

8. In geen geval worden de bepalingen van dit artikel zo uitgelegd dat zij een Staat de verplichting opleggen:
a. administratieve maatregelen te nemen die in strijd zijn met de wetgeving of de administratieve praktijk van die of van de andere Staat;
b. maatregelen te nemen die in strijd zouden zijn met de openbare orde (ordre public);
c. bijstand te verlenen indien de andere Staat niet alle redelijke invorderings- of conservatoire maatregelen heeft aangewend die hem naargelang van het geval uit hoofde van zijn wetgeving of bestuurlijke praktijk, ter beschikking staan;
d. bijstand te verlenen in gevallen waarin de administratieve last voor die Staat kennelijk niet in verhouding staat tot het voordeel te behalen door de andere Staat.".

Artikel 6

Het volgende artikel wordt voor artikel I van het Protocol bij het Verdrag ingevoegd:

„Algemeen

Met inachtneming van mogelijke voorbehouden, opmerkingen of standpunten, naargelang van het geval, bij of ten aanzien van het OESO model belastingverdrag of het commentaar daarbij van een van de twee Staten, leggen de beide Staten de bepalingen van het Verdrag die gelijk zijn of in hoofdzaak gelijk zijn aan de bepalingen van het OESO-model belastingverdrag inzake dubbele belasting naar het inkomen en naar het vermogen uit overeenkomstig het commentaar van de OESO op deze bepalingen op het tijdstip van ondertekening van het Verdrag en overeenkomstig latere wijzigingen ter verduidelijking van dit commentaar van de OESO. De beide Staten leggen met name het in het Verdrag gebezigde begrip „uiteindelijk gerechtigde" uit overeenkomstig de uitlegging daarvan die door de OESO is gepubliceerd op het tijdstip van ondertekening van het Verdrag en overeenkomstig latere wijzigingen ter verduidelijking van een dergelijke uitlegging door de OESO.".

Artikel 7

Het volgende artikel wordt na artikel X van het Protocol bij het Verdrag ingevoegd:

„XI

Ad artikel 28:

De bepalingen van artikel 28 zijn dienovereenkomstig van toepassing op inlichtingen die naar verwachting van belang zijn voor de tenuitvoerlegging van inkomensafhankelijke regelingen indien de Nederlandse belastingadministratie verantwoordelijk is voor de uitvoering en naleving van dergelijke inkomensafhankelijke regelingen. Inlichtingen die uit hoofde van dit Protocol worden verkregen worden uitsluitend gebruikt ten behoeve van het innen van bijdragen, toekennen van voordelen of vaststellen van de omvang van deze bijdragen en voordelen die voortvloeien uit inkomensafhankelijk regelingen.".

Artikel 8

Artikel VIII van het Protocol bij het Verdrag wordt vervangen door:

„1. Indien aan de bron belasting is geheven die het belastingbedrag dat ingevolge de bepalingen van de artikelen 10, 11 en 12 mag worden geheven te boven gaat, moeten verzoeken om teruggaaf van het daarboven uitgaande belastingbedrag worden ingediend bij de bevoegde autoriteit van de Staat die de belasting heeft geheven, binnen een tijdvak van drie jaar na afloop van het kalenderjaar waarin de belasting is geheven.

2. Het is wel te verstaan dat er geen onderlinge overeenstemming over de wijze van toepassing van de artikelen 10, 11 en 12 vereist is voor de toepassing van deze artikelen.".

Artikel 9

Dit Protocol vormt een integrerend onderdeel van het Verdrag en het Protocol daarbij.

Artikel 10

Elke Staat stelt de andere in kennis van de voltooiing van de op grond van zijn wetgeving vereiste procedures voor het in werking doen treden van dit Protocol. Het Protocol treedt in werking op de eerste dag van de tweede maand volgend op de laatste datum waarop de onderscheiden Regeringen elkaar schriftelijk langs diplomatieke weg in kennis hebben gesteld. De bepalingen van dit Protocol zijn voor het eerst van toepassing op bedragen betaald of betaalbaar gesteld op de eerste dag van de tweede maand volgend op de datum waarop het Protocol in werking treedt.

TEN BLIJKE WAARVAN de ondergetekenden, daartoe naar behoren gemachtigd door hun onderscheiden Regeringen, dit Protocol hebben ondertekend.

GEDAAN te Jakarta op 30 juli 2015, in tweevoud, in de Engelse, de Nederlandse en de Indonesische taal, zijnde de drie teksten gelijkelijk authentiek. In geval van verschil in interpretatie en toepassing van dit Protocol is de Engelse tekst doorslaggevend.

Voor het Koninkrijk der Nederlanden,

ROB SWARTBOL

Voor de Republiek Indonesië

SUAHASIL NAZARA

[TEXT IN ENGLISH – TEXTE EN ANGLAIS]

Protocol amending the Agreement between the Government of the Kingdom of the Netherlands and the Government of the Republic of Indonesia for the avoidance of double taxation and the prevention of fiscal evasion with respect to taxes on income, and its Protocol, signed at Jakarta on January 29, 2002

The Government of the Kingdom of the Netherlands

and

the Government of the Republic of Indonesia,

Desiring to conclude a Protocol to amend the Agreement between the Government of the Kingdom of the Netherlands and the Government of the Republic of Indonesia for the avoidance of double taxation and the prevention of fiscal evasion with respect to taxes on income, and its Protocol, signed at Jakarta on January 29, 2002 (hereinafter referred to as "the Agreement"),

Have agreed as follows:

Article 1

Paragraph 2 of Article 10 shall be replaced by the following paragraph:

"2. However, such dividends may also be taxed in the State of which the company paying the dividends is a resident and according to the laws of that State, but if the beneficial owner of the dividends is a resident of the other State, the tax so charged shall not exceed:

a) 5 per cent of the gross amount of the dividends if the beneficial owner is a company (other than a partnership) which holds directly at least 25 per cent of the capital of the company paying the dividends;
b) 10 per cent of the gross amount of the dividends if the beneficial owner is a pension fund that is recognized and controlled according to the statutory provisions of one of the two States and the income of which is generally exempt from tax in the State according to whose statutory provisions it is recognized and controlled;
c) 15 per cent of the gross amount of the dividends in all other cases.".

Article 2

Paragraph 4 of Article 11 shall be replaced by the following paragraph:

"4. Notwithstanding the provisions of paragraph 2, interest arising in one of the two States may also be taxed in the State in which it arises and according to the laws of that State, but if the beneficial owner of the interest is a resident of the other State and if the interest is paid on a loan made for a period of more than 2 years or is paid in connection with the sale on credit of any industrial, commercial or scientific equipment, the tax so charged shall not exceed 5 per cent of the gross amount of the interest.".

---

1) De Indonesische tekst is niet opgenomen.

2) Het voor eensluidend gewaarmerkt afschrift is nog niet ontvangen. In de tekst kunnen derhalve onjuistheden voorkomen die in een volgend Tractatenblad zullen worden gecorrigeerd.

Article 3

a) In paragraph 3 of Article 24 of the Agreement, the words "paragraph 1 of Article 16" shall be replaced by the words: "paragraphs 1 and 3 of Article 16";

b) In paragraph 4 of Article 24 of the Agreement, the words "paragraph 2 of Article 11" shall be replaced by the words: "paragraphs 2 and 4 of Article 11".

Article 4

Article 28 shall be replaced in its entirety by the following Article:

"Article 28

Exchange of information

1. The competent authorities of the two States shall exchange such information as is foreseeably relevant for carrying out the provisions of this Agreement or to the administration or enforcement of the domestic laws concerning taxes of every kind and description imposed on behalf of the two States, or of their political subdivisions or local authorities, insofar as the taxation thereunder is not contrary to the Agreement. The exchange of information is not restricted by Articles 1 and 2.

2. Any information received under paragraph 1 by one of the two States shall be treated as secret in the same manner as information obtained under the domestic laws of that State and shall be disclosed only to persons or authorities (including courts and administrative bodies) concerned with the assessment or collection of, the enforcement or prosecution in respect of, the determination of appeals in relation to the taxes referred to in paragraph 1, or the oversight of the above. Such persons or authorities shall use the information only for such purposes. They may disclose the information in public court proceedings or in judicial decisions.

3. In no case shall the provisions of the previous paragraphs be construed so as to impose on either State the obligation:
a) to carry out administrative measures at variance with the laws and administrative practice of that or of the other State;
b) to supply information which is not obtainable under the laws or in the normal course of the administration of that or of the other State;
c) to supply information which would disclose any trade, business, industrial, commercial or professional secret or trade process, or information the disclosure of which would be contrary to public policy (ordre public).

4. If information is requested by one of the two States in accordance with this Article, the other State shall use its information gathering measures to obtain the requested information, even though that other State may not need such information for its own tax purposes. The obligation contained in the preceding sentence is subject to the limitations of paragraph 3 but in no case shall such limitations be construed to permit either State to decline to supply information solely because it has no domestic interest in such information.

5. In no case shall the provisions of paragraph 3 be construed to permit either State to decline to supply information solely because the information is held by a bank, other financial institution, nominee or person acting in an agency or a fiduciary capacity or because it relates to ownership interests in a person.".

Article 5

The following Article shall be inserted after Article 28 of the Agreement:

"Article 28A

Assistance in the collection of taxes

1. The two States shall lend assistance to each other in the collection of revenue claims. This assistance is not restricted by Articles 1 and 2. The competent authorities of the two States may by mutual agreement settle the mode of application of this Article. No request for assistance may be made if the total amount of the relevant claim is less than EUR 1,500.

2. The term "revenue claim" as used in this Article means an amount owed in respect of taxes of every kind and description imposed on behalf of the States, insofar as the taxation thereunder is not contrary to this Agreement or any other instrument to which the States are parties, as well as interest, administrative penalties and costs of collection or conservancy related to such amount.

3. The provisions of this Article shall apply only to a revenue claim that forms the subject of an instrument permitting enforcement in the applicant State and, unless otherwise agreed between the competent authorities, that is not contested. However, where the claim relates to a liability to tax of a person as a non-resident of the applicant State, this Article shall only apply, unless otherwise agreed between the competent authorities, where the claim may no longer be contested. The revenue claim shall be collected by that other State in accordance with the provisions of its laws applicable to the enforcement and collection of its own taxes as if the revenue claim were a revenue claim of that other State.

4. When a revenue claim of a State is a claim in respect of which that State may, under its law, take measures of conservancy with a view to ensure its collection, that revenue claim shall, at the request of the competent authority of that State, be accepted for purposes of taking measures of conservancy by the competent authority of the other State. That other State shall take measures of conservancy in respect of that revenue claim in accordance with the provisions of its laws as if the revenue claim were a revenue claim of that other State even if, at the time when such measures are applied, the revenue claim is not enforceable in the first-mentioned State or is owed by a person who has a right to prevent its collection.

5. Notwithstanding the provisions of paragraphs 3 and 4, a revenue claim accepted by a State for purposes of paragraph 3 or 4 shall not, in that State, be subject to the time limits or accorded any priority applicable to a revenue claim under the laws of that State by reason of its nature as such and, unless otherwise agreed between the competent authorities, cannot be collected by imprisonment for debt of the debtor. In addition, a revenue claim accepted by a State for the purposes of paragraph 3 or 4 shall not, in that State, have any priority applicable to that revenue claim under the laws of the other State.

6. Proceedings with respect to the existence, validity or the amount of a revenue claim of a State shall not be brought before the courts or administrative bodies of the other State.

7. Where, at any time after a request has been made by a State under paragraph 3 or 4 and before the other State has collected and remitted the relevant revenue claim to the first-mentioned State, the relevant revenue claim ceases to be

a) in the case of a request under paragraph 3, a revenue claim of the first-mentioned State that is enforceable under the laws of that State and is owed by a person who, at that time, cannot, under the laws of that State, prevent its collection, or
b) in the case of a request under paragraph 4, a revenue claim of the first-mentioned State in respect of which that State may, under its laws, take measures of conservancy with a view to ensure its collection,

the competent authority of the first-mentioned State shall promptly notify the competent authority of the other State of that fact and, at the option of the other State, the first-mentioned State shall either suspend or withdraw its request.

8. In no case shall the provisions of this Article be construed so as to impose on a State the obligation:

a) to carry out administrative measures at variance with the laws and administrative practice of that or of the other State;
b) to carry out measures which would be contrary to public policy (ordre public);
c) to provide assistance if the other State has not pursued all reasonable measures of collection or conservancy, as the case may be, available under its laws or administrative practice;
d) to provide assistance in those cases where the administrative burden for that State is clearly disproportionate to the benefit to be derived by the other State.".

Article 6

The following Article shall be inserted before Article I of the Protocol to the Agreement:

"General

Subject to any reservations, observations or positions as the case may be to the OECD Model Tax Convention or its Commentary made by either State, the two States shall interpret the provisions of the Agreement which are identical or in substance similar to the provisions of the OECD Model Tax Convention on Income and on Capital, in accordance with the OECD Commentary thereon at the moment of signing the Agreement and any subsequent clarifying modifications of such Commentary. Especially, the two States shall interpret the term 'beneficial owner' used in the Agreement in accordance with the interpretation thereof as published by the OECD at the moment of signing the Agreement and any subsequent clarifying modifications of such OECD interpretation.".

Article 7

The following Article shall be inserted after Article X of the Protocol to the Agreement:

"XI

With reference to Article 28

The provisions of Article 28 shall also apply accordingly to information that is foreseeable relevant for carrying out income-related regulations if the Netherlands tax administration is in charge of implementing and enforcing such income-related regulations. Information received under this Protocol shall be used only for the purpose of levying the contributions, granting the benefits or determining the extent of these contributions and benefits derived from income-related regulations.".

Article 8

Article VIII of the Protocol to the Agreement shall be replaced by:

"1. Where tax has been levied at source in excess of the amount of tax chargeable under the provisions of Articles 10, 11 and 12, applications for the refund of the excess amount of tax have to be lodged with the competent authority of the State having levied the tax, within a period of three years after the expiration of the calendar year in which the tax has been levied.

2. It is understood that no mutual agreement on the mode of application of Articles 10, 11 and 12, is required for the application of these Articles.".

Article 9

This Protocol shall form an integral part of the Agreement, and its Protocol.

Article 10

Each State shall notify to the other the completion of the procedures required by its law for the bringing into force of this Protocol. It shall enter into force on the first day of the second month following the later of the dates on which the respective Governments have notified each other in writing through diplomatic channels. The provisions of this Protocol shall for the first time have effect for amounts paid or credited on or after the first day of the second month next following the date on which the Protocol enters into force.

IN WITNESS WHEREOF the undersigned, being duly authorised thereto by their respective Governments, have signed this Protocol.

DONE at Jakarta this 30th day of July 2015, in duplicate, in the English, Netherlands and Indonesian languages, the three texts being equally authentic. In the event of there being a divergence in the interpretation and the application of this Protocol, the English text shall prevail.

For the Kingdom of the Netherlands,

ROB SWARTBOL

For the Republic of Indonesia,

SUAHASIL NAZARA

[TEXT IN INDONESIAN – TEXTE EN INDONÉSIEN]

PROTOKOL PERUBAHAN PERSETUJUAN

ANTARA

PEMERINTAH KERAJAAN BELANDA

DAN

PEMERINTAH REPUBLIK INDONESIA

UNTUK PENGHINDARAN PAJAK BERGANDA DAN PENCEGAHAN PENGELAKAN PAJAK YANG BERKENAAN DENGAN PAJAK ATAS PENGHASILAN DAN PROTOKOLNYA YANG DITANDATANGANI DI JAKARTA PADA TANGGAL 29 JANUARI 2002

Pemerintah Kerajaan Belanda

dan

Pemerintah Republik Indonesia,

Berkeinginan untuk menyepakati Protokol untuk mengubah Persetujuan antara Pemerintah Republik Indonesia dan Pemerintah Kerajaan Belanda untuk Penghindaran Pajak Berganda dan Pencegahan Pengelakan Pajak yang Berkenaan dengan Pajak atas Penghasilan dan Protokolnya yang ditandatangani di Jakarta pada tanggal 29 Januari 2002 (untuk selanjutnya disebut sebagai "Persetujuan"),

Telah menyetujui sebagai berikut:

Pasal 1

Pasal 10 ayat 2 diganti menjadi sebagai berikut:

"2. Namun demikian, dividen tersebut dapat juga dikenai pajak di Negara di mana perusahaan pembayar dividen menjadi penduduknya dengan tarif pajak sesuai dengan perundang-undangan Negara tersebut, tetapi jika pemilik manfaat sebenarnya dari dividen tersebut adalah penduduk Negara lainnya, maka pajak yang dikenakan tidak boleh melebihi:

a) 5 persen dari jumlah bruto dividen jika pemilik manfaat sebenarnya dari dividen adalah suatu perusahaan (selain persekutuan) yang memiliki secara langsung sedikitnya 25 persen dari modal perusahaan pembayar dividen;
b) 10 persen dari jumlah bruto dividen jika pemilik manfaat sebenarnya dari dividen adalah dana pensiun yang diakui dan diatur menurut ketentuan hukum yang berlaku di salah satu Negara dan yang penghasilannya secara umum dikecualikan dari pajak di Negara yang menurut ketentuan hukumnya dana pensiun tersebut diakui dan diatur;
c) 15 persen dari jumlah bruto dividen untuk jenis dividen lainnya."

Pasal 2

Pasal 11 ayat 4 diganti menjadi sebagai berikut:

"4. Menyimpang dari ketentuan dalam ayat 2, bunga yang timbul di salah satu Negara dapat juga dikenai pajak di Negara di mana bunga tersebut timbul dan menurut perundang-undangan Negara tersebut, tetapi jika pemilik manfaat sebenarnya dari bunga tersebut adalah penduduk dari Negara lainnya dan jika bunga dibayar atas pinjaman yang diberikan untuk jangka waktu lebih dari 2 tahun atau dibayar sehubungan dengan penjualan peralatan industri, komersial atau ilmiah secara kredit, pajak yang dikenakan tidak boleh melebihi 5 persen dari jumlah bruto bunga."

Pasal 3

a) Dalam Pasal 24 ayat 3 dari Persetujuan, kata-kata "Pasal 16 ayat 1" diganti menjadi "Pasal 16 ayat 1 dan 3".
b) Dalam Pasal 24 ayat 4 dari Persetujuan, kata-kata "Pasal 11 ayat 2" diganti menjadi "Pasal 11 ayat 2 dan 4".

Pasal 4

Pasal 28 diganti seluruhnya dengan Pasal berikut:

"Pasal 28
Pertukaran Informasi

1. Pejabat berwenang dari kedua Negara akan melakukan pertukaran informasi yang dipandang relevan untuk melaksanakan ketentuan-ketentuan

dalam Persetujuan ini atau untuk pengadministrasian atau penerapan hukum domestik yang berkaitan dengan perpajakan dalam bentuk dan nama apapun yang dikenakan atas nama kedua Negara tersebut, atau bagian ketatanegaraannya atau pemerintah daerahnya, sepanjang pengaturan perpajakan tersebut tidak bertentangan dengan Persetujuan ini. Pertukaran informasi ini tidak dibatasi oleh Pasal 1 dan Pasal 2.

2. Setiap informasi yang diterima berdasarkan ayat 1 oleh salah satu dari kedua Negara akan dijaga kerahasiaannya dengan cara yang sama seperti informasi yang diperoleh berdasarkan perundang-undangan domestik Negara tersebut dan hanya boleh diungkapkan kepada orang-orang atau pihak-pihak berwenang (termasuk pengadilan dan badan-badan administratif) yang berkepentingan dalam penetapan atau penagihan, penegakan hukum atau penuntutan, pengambilan keputusan banding sehubungan pajak-pajak yang merujuk ayat 1, atau lembaga yang mengawasi orang-orang atau pihak-pihak berwenang di atas. Orang-orang atau pihak-pihak berwenang tersebut hanya boleh menggunakan informasi dimaksud untuk tujuan-tujuan di atas. Mereka boleh mengungkapkan informasi dimaksud dalam proses pengadilan atau pembuatan keputusan pengadilan.

3. Ketentuan-ketentuan pada ayat sebelumnya tidak boleh ditafsirkan sebagai mewajibkan suatu Negara:
   a) untuk melakukan tindakan-tindakan administrasi yang menyimpang dari ketentuan perundang-undangan atau praktik administrasi yang berlaku di Negara tersebut atau Negara lainnya;
   b) untuk memberikan informasi yang tidak dapat diperoleh berdasarkan perundang-undangan atau dalam pelaksanaan administrasi yang lazim di Negara tersebut atau di Negara lainnya;
   c) untuk memberikan informasi yang akan mengungkapkan rahasia perniagaan, usaha, industri, komersial atau profesi, atau proses dagang, atau informasi yang pengungkapannya akan bertentangan dengan kebijakan publik (*ordre public*).

4. Apabila informasi yang diminta oleh salah satu dari kedua Negara berkesesuaian dengan Pasal ini, Negara lainnya akan menggunakan tindakan-tindakan pengumpulan informasi untuk memperoleh informasi yang diminta tersebut, meskipun Negara lainnya tersebut tidak memerlukan informasi dimaksud untuk kepentingan perpajakannya. Kewajiban yang terkandung dalam kalimat sebelum ini harus memperhatikan pembatasan-pembatasan dalam ayat 3 namun sama sekali tidak boleh ditafsirkan sebagai mengizinkan suatu Negara untuk menolak memberikan informasi semata-mata karena tidak memiliki kepentingan domestik atas informasi yang diminta tersebut.

5. Ketentuan-ketentuan pada ayat 3 tidak boleh ditafsirkan sebagai mengizinkan suatu Negara untuk menolak memberikan informasi semata-mata karena informasi dimaksud dimiliki oleh bank, lembaga keuangan lainnya, wakil atau pihak yang bertindak sebagai agen atau dalam kapasitas

sebagai perantara atau karena berkaitan dengan kepemilikan suatu pihak terhadap informasi tersebut."

Pasal 5

Setelah Pasal 28, disisipkan Pasal berikut ini:

"Pasal 28A
Bantuan dalam Penagihan Pajak

1. Kedua Negara akan saling memberi bantuan satu sama lain dalam penagihan klaim penerimaan pajak. Bantuan ini tidak dibatasi oleh Pasal 1 dan Pasal 2. Pejabat berwenang kedua Negara melalui persetujuan bersama dapat menentukan metode penerapan Pasal ini. Permintaan bantuan tidak dapat dilakukan jika total nilai klaim penerimaan pajak yang ditagih kurang dari 1.500 Euro.

2. Istilah "klaim penerimaan pajak" yang digunakan dalam Pasal ini adalah jumlah utang pajak dalam bentuk dan nama apapun yang dikenakan atas nama Negara, sepanjang pengenaan pajak tersebut tidak bertentangan dengan Persetujuan ini atau instrumen lain di mana kedua Negara merupakan Negara pihak, termasuk juga bunga, sanksi administrasi dan biaya penagihan atau biaya pengamanan terkait jumlah tersebut.

3. Ketentuan-ketentuan dalam Pasal ini berlaku hanya terhadap klaim penerimaan pajak yang berbentuk instrumen yang dapat dieksekusi di Negara pemohon dan, kecuali bila disepakati berbeda oleh para pejabat berwenang, yang tidak dipersengketakan. Namun demikian, apabila klaim tersebut berkaitan dengan kewajiban pajak seseorang/badan yang bukan penduduk Negara pemohon, Pasal ini hanya berlaku, kecuali disepakati berbeda oleh para pejabat berwenang, apabila klaim tersebut tidak lagi dipersengketakan. Klaim penerimaan pajak harus ditagih oleh Negara lainnya sesuai dengan ketentuan perundang-undangan Negara lainnya tersebut yang berlaku terhadap penerapan dan penagihan pajak-pajaknya seakan-akan klaim penerimaan pajak dimaksud adalah klaim penerimaan pajak Negara lainnya tersebut.

4. Apabila klaim penerimaan pajak suatu Negara merupakan klaim yang berkenaan dengan kondisi dimana Negara tersebut dapat, berdasarkan undang-undangnya, melakukan tindakan-tindakan pengamanan dengan maksud untuk memastikan penagihannya, klaim penerimaan pajak dimaksud harus, atas permintaan pejabat berwenang Negara tersebut, dipenuhi untuk tujuan pengambilan langkah-langkah pengamanan oleh pejabat berwenang Negara lainnya. Negara lainnya tersebut harus melakukan tindakan-tindakan pengamanan atas klaim penerimaan pajak tersebut sesuai dengan ketentuan perundang-undangan Negara lainnya seakan-akan klaim penerimaan pajak tersebut adalah klaim penerimaan pajak Negara lainnya tersebut meskipun, pada saat tindakan-tindakan pengamanan tersebut dilakukan, klaim penerimaan pajak tersebut tidak

dapat ditagih di Negara yang disebutkan pertama atau terhutang oleh orang/badan yang berhak untuk mencegah upaya penagihannya.

5. Menyimpang dari ketentuan-ketentuan pada ayat 3 dan ayat 4, klaim penerimaan pajak yang dipenuhi oleh suatu Negara untuk tujuan sebagaimana dimaksud pada ayat 3 dan ayat 4 tidak boleh, di Negara tersebut, terikat oleh batasan waktu atau pemberian prioritas yang berlaku atas suatu klaim penerimaan pajak berdasarkan perundang-undangan Negara tersebut karena sifatnya yang sedemikian dan, kecuali disepakati berbeda oleh para pejabat berwenang, tidak dapat ditagih dengan memenjarakan debitur. Selain itu, klaim penerimaan pajak yang dipenuhi oleh suatu Negara untuk tujuan sebagaimana dimaksud pada ayat 3 dan ayat 4 tidak boleh, di Negara tersebut, mempunyai prioritas yang berlaku atas klaim penerimaan pajak berdasarkan perundang-undangan Negara lainnya tersebut.

6. Catatan-catatan yang berkenaan dengan keberadaan, validitas atau jumlah suatu klaim penerimaan pajak di suatu Negara tidak dapat diajukan ke pengadilan atau badan-badan administrasi Negara lainnya.

7. Dalam hal, kapan pun setelah suatu permintaan telah diajukan oleh suatu Negara berdasarkan ayat 3 atau ayat 4 dan sebelum Negara lainnya telah mengumpulkan dan mengirimkan hasil penagihan klaim penerimaan pajak dimaksud kepada Negara yang disebutkan pertama, klaim penerimaan pajak dimaksud tidak lagi merupakan klaim:
   a) dalam hal permintaan sebagaimana dimaksud pada ayat 3, suatu klaim penerimaan pajak dari Negara yang disebutkan pertama yang dapat ditagih berdasarkan perundang-undangan Negara tersebut dan terutang oleh seseorang atau badan yang, pada saat itu, tidak dapat, berdasarkan perundang-undangan Negara tersebut, mencegah tindakan penagihannya, atau
   b) dalam hal permintaan sebagaimana dimaksud pada ayat 4, suatu klaim penerimaan pajak dari Negara yang disebutkan pertama yang berkenaan dengan kondisi dimana Negara tersebut dapat, berdasarkan perundang-undangannya, melakukan tindakan-tindakan pengamanan dengan maksud untuk memastikan penagihannya,

   pejabat berwenang Negara yang disebutkan pertama harus segera memberitahukan pejabat berwenang Negara lainnya tentang fakta tersebut dan, berdasarkan pilihan Negara lainnya, Negara yang disebutkan pertama harus menunda atau membatalkan permintaannya.

8. Ketentuan-ketentuan dalam Pasal ini tidak boleh ditafsirkan sebagai mewajibkan suatu Negara:
   a) untuk melakukan tindakan-tindakan administrasi yang menyimpang dari ketentuan perundang-undangan dan praktik administrasi yang berlaku di Negara tersebut atau Negara lainnya;
   b) melakukan tindakan-tindakan yang bertentangan dengan kebijakan publik (*ordre public*);
   c) memberikan bantuan jika Negara lainnya belum mengupayakan semua tindakan penagihan atau pengamanan yang memadai, tergantung

kasusnya, yang tersedia berdasarkan perundang-undangannya atau praktik administrasinya;

d) menyediakan bantuan dalam kasus-kasus tersebut dimana beban administrasi bagi Negara tersebut secara jelas tidak sebanding dengan manfaat yang akan diterima oleh Negara lainnya."

Pasal 6

Pasal berikut disisipkan sebelum Pasal I Protokol pada Persetujuan:

"Ketentuan Umum
Kecuali disebutkan lain dalam reservasi, observasi atau posisi yang mungkin ada dalam *OECD Model Tax Convention* atau Penjelasannya yang dibuat oleh salah satu Negara, kedua Negara tersebut harus menafsirkan ketentuan-ketentuan dalam Persetujuan ini yang identik atau serupa secara substansi dengan ketentuan-ketentuan dalam *OECD Model Tax Convention on Income and on Capital*, sesuai dengan Penjelasan model tersebut yang ada pada saat penandatanganan Persetujuan ini dan modifikasi Penjelasan terkait yang terbit setelah itu. Khususnya, kedua Negara harus menafsirkan istilah 'pemilik manfaat sebenarnya' yang digunakan dalam Persetujuan ini sesuai dengan penafsiran sebagaimana dipublikasikan oleh OECD pada saat penandatanganan Persetujuan ini dan modifikasi Penjelasan terkait yang terbit setelah itu."

Pasal 7

Pasal berikut disisipkan setelah Pasal X Protokol pada Persetujuan:

"XI Dengan mengacu pada Pasal 28
Ketentuan-ketentuan dalam Pasal 28 maka berlaku juga untuk informasi yang dipandang relevan untuk melaksanakan peraturan-peraturan terkait penghasilan jika otoritas pajak Belanda bertanggung jawab dalam penerapan dan pemberlakuan peraturan-peraturan terkait penghasilan tersebut. Informasi yang diterima berdasarkan Protokol ini hanya akan digunakan untuk tujuan pengenaan kontribusi, pemberian manfaat atau penentuan sejauh mana kontribusi dan manfaat tersebut didapatkan dari peraturan-peraturan terkait penghasilan."

Pasal 8

Pasal VIII Protokol pada Persetujuan diubah menjadi:

1. Apabila pajak yang telah dikenakan di Negara sumber melebihi jumlah pajak yang seharusnya dikenakan berdasarkan ketentuan-ketentuan dalam Pasal 10, 11 dan 12, permohonan pengembalian jumlah kelebihan pembayaran pajak tersebut harus diajukan kepada pejabat berwenang Negara yang memajaki tersebut, dalam jangka waktu tiga tahun setelah berakhirnya tahun kalender dimana pajak tersebut dikenakan.

2. Dipahami bahwa persetujuan bersama tentang tata cara penerapan Pasal 10, 11 dan 12 tidak diperlukan dalam rangka pelaksanaan Pasal-Pasal tersebut."

Pasal 9

Protokol ini merupakan bagian yang tidak terpisahkan dari Persetujuan, dan Protokolnya.

Pasal 10

Masing-masing Negara memberitahukan Negara lainnya tentang penyelesaian prosedur-prosedur yang diperlukan oleh perundang-undangannya untuk memberlakukan Protokol ini. Protokol ini mulai berlaku pada hari pertama dari bulan kedua setelah tanggal saat masing-masing Pemerintah telah memberitahu satu sama lain secara tertulis melalui saluran diplomatik. Ketentuan-ketentuan dalam Protokol ini akan berlaku untuk pertama kalinya terhadap jumlah yang dibayarkan atau dikreditkan pada saat atau setelah hari pertama dari bulan kedua berikutnya setelah tanggal saat Protokol ini berlaku efektif.

SEBAGAI BUKTI yang bertandatangan di bawah ini, yang telah diberikan kuasa oleh Pemerintahnya masing-masing, telah menandatangani Protokol ini.

Dibuat di Jakarta pada 30 Juli tanggal dalam rangkap dua, masing-masing dalam Bahasa Inggris, Bahasa Belanda, dan Bahasa Indonesia, ketiga naskah tersebut mempunyai kekuatan hukum yang sama. Dalam hal terjadi perbedaan penafsiran dan pelaksanaan atas Protokol ini, maka naskah dalam bahasa Inggris yang berlaku.

UNTUK PEMERINTAH KERAJAAN BELANDA	UNTUK PEMERINTAH REPUBLIK INDONESIA

[TRANSLATION – TRADUCTION]

PROTOCOLE AMENDANT L'ACCORD ENTRE LE GOUVERNEMENT DU ROYAUME DES PAYS-BAS ET LE GOUVERNEMENT DE LA RÉPUBLIQUE D'INDONÉSIE TENDANT À ÉVITER LA DOUBLE IMPOSITION ET À PRÉVENIR L'ÉVASION FISCALE EN MATIÈRE D'IMPÔTS SUR LE REVENU, ET SON PROTOCOLE, SIGNÉ À JAKARTA LE 29 JANVIER 2002

Le Gouvernement du Royaume des Pays-Bas et le Gouvernement de la République d'Indonésie,

Désireux de conclure un Protocole amendant l'Accord entre le Gouvernement du Royaume des Pays-Bas et le Gouvernement de la République d'Indonésie tendant à éviter la double imposition et à prévenir l'évasion fiscale en matière d'impôts sur le revenu, et son Protocole, signé à Jakarta le 29 janvier 2002 (ci-après dénommé l'« Accord »),

Sont convenus de ce qui suit :

Article premier

Le paragraphe 2 de l'Article 10 est remplacé par le paragraphe suivant :

« 2. Toutefois, ces dividendes sont également imposables dans l'État dont la société qui paie les dividendes est un résident et selon la législation en vigueur dans cet État, mais si le bénéficiaire effectif des dividendes est un résident de l'autre État contractant, l'impôt ainsi établi ne peut excéder :

a) 5 % du montant brut des dividendes si le bénéficiaire effectif est une société (autre qu'une société de personnes) qui détient directement au moins 25 % du capital de la société qui paie les dividendes ;

b) 10 % du montant brut des dividendes si le bénéficiaire effectif est un fonds de pension reconnu et contrôlé selon les dispositions législatives de l'un des deux États et dont les revenus sont généralement exonérés d'impôts dans l'État selon les dispositions législatives duquel il est reconnu et contrôlé ;

c) 15 % du montant brut des dividendes dans tous les autres cas. »

Article 2

Le paragraphe 4 de l'Article 11 est remplacé par le paragraphe suivant :

« 4. Nonobstant les dispositions du paragraphe 2, les intérêts provenant de l'un des deux États sont aussi imposables dans l'État d'où ils proviennent et selon la législation de cet État, mais si le bénéficiaire effectif des intérêts est un résident de l'autre État et si les intérêts sont payés sur un prêt consenti pour une période de plus de deux ans ou sont payés au titre de la vente à crédit d'un équipement industriel, commercial ou scientifique, l'impôt ainsi établi ne peut excéder 5 % du montant brut des intérêts. »

Article 3

a) Au paragraphe 3 de l'Article 24 de l'Accord, les mots « paragraphe 1 de l'Article 16 » sont remplacés par les mots « paragraphes 1 et 3 de l'Article 16 » ;

b) Au paragraphe 4 de l'Article 24 de l'Accord, les mots « paragraphe 2 de l'Article 11 » sont remplacés par les mots « paragraphes 2 et 4 de l'Article 11 ».

Article 4

L'Article 28 est remplacé dans son intégralité par l'Article suivant :

« Article 28. Échange de renseignements

1. Les autorités compétentes des deux États échangent les renseignements vraisemblablement pertinents pour appliquer les dispositions du présent Accord ou celles de la législation interne relative aux impôts de toute nature ou dénomination perçus pour le compte des deux États, de leurs subdivisions politiques ou de leurs collectivités locales, dans la mesure où l'imposition qu'elle prévoit n'est pas contraire à l'Accord. L'échange de renseignements n'est pas restreint par les Articles premier et 2.

2. Les renseignements reçus en vertu du paragraphe 1 par l'un des deux États contractants sont tenus secrets de la même manière que les renseignements obtenus en application de la législation interne de cet État, et ils ne sont communiqués qu'aux personnes ou autorités (y compris les tribunaux et organes administratifs) concernées par l'établissement ou le recouvrement des impôts visés au paragraphe 1, par les procédures ou poursuites concernant ces impôts, par les décisions sur les recours relatifs à ces impôts, ou par le contrôle de ce qui précède. Ces personnes ou autorités n'utilisent ces renseignements qu'à ces fins, mais peuvent en faire état au cours d'audiences publiques de tribunaux ou dans des jugements.

3. Les dispositions des paragraphes précédents ne peuvent en aucun cas être interprétées comme imposant à l'un ou l'autre État l'obligation :

a) de prendre des mesures administratives dérogeant à sa législation et à sa pratique administrative ou à celles de l'autre État ;

b) de fournir des renseignements qui ne pourraient être obtenus sur la base de sa législation ou dans le cadre de sa pratique administrative normale ou de celles de l'autre État ;

c) de fournir des renseignements qui révéleraient un secret commercial, industriel ou professionnel, ou un procédé commercial, ou des renseignements dont la communication serait contraire à l'ordre public.

4. Si des renseignements sont demandés par l'un des deux États conformément au présent Article, l'autre État utilise ses mesures de collecte de renseignements pour obtenir les renseignements demandés quand bien même cet autre État n'aurait pas besoin de ces renseignements à ses propres fins fiscales. L'obligation contenue dans la phrase précédente est subordonnée aux limitations prévues au paragraphe 3, mais en aucun cas ces limitations ne doivent être interprétées comme autorisant un État contractant à refuser de fournir des renseignements pour la seule raison qu'il ne détient aucun intérêt national dans de tels renseignements.

5. Les dispositions du paragraphe 3 ne doivent en aucun cas être interprétées comme autorisant un État à refuser de fournir des renseignements pour la seule raison que les

renseignements sont tenus par une banque, une autre institution financière, un mandataire ou une personne agissant en qualité d'agent ou à titre fiduciaire ou parce que cela concerne les intérêts fonciers d'une personne. »

Article 5

L'Article suivant est inséré après l'Article 28 de l'Accord :

« Article 28A. Assistance en matière de recouvrement des impôts

1. Les deux États se prêtent mutuellement assistance pour le recouvrement de leurs créances fiscales. Cette assistance n'est pas limitée par les Articles premier et 2. Les autorités compétentes des deux États peuvent régler d'un commun accord les modalités d'application du présent Article. Aucune demande d'assistance ne peut être formulée si le montant total de la créance concernée est inférieur à 1 500 euros.

2. L'expression "créance fiscale" utilisée dans le présent Article désigne une somme due au titre des impôts de toute nature ou dénomination perçus pour le compte des États, dans la mesure où l'imposition prévue n'est pas contraire au présent Accord ou à tout autre instrument auquel les États sont parties, ainsi que les intérêts, pénalités administratives et coûts de recouvrement ou de conservation afférents à ce montant.

3. Les dispositions du présent Article ne s'appliquent qu'aux créances fiscales qui font l'objet d'un instrument permettant l'exécution dans l'État requérant et qui, sauf convention contraire entre les autorités compétentes, ne sont pas contestées. Toutefois, lorsque la créance porte sur l'assujettissement à l'impôt d'une personne en tant que non-résident de l'État requérant, le présent Article ne s'applique, sauf convention contraire entre les autorités compétentes, que lorsque la créance ne peut plus être contestée. Cette créance fiscale est recouvrée par cet autre État conformément aux dispositions de sa législation applicable en matière de recouvrement de ses propres impôts comme si la créance en question était une créance fiscale de cet autre État.

4. Lorsqu'une créance fiscale d'un État est une créance à l'égard de laquelle cet État peut, en vertu de sa législation, prendre des mesures conservatoires pour assurer son recouvrement, cette créance doit, à la demande des autorités compétentes de cet État, être acceptée aux fins d'adoption de mesures conservatoires par les autorités compétentes de l'autre État. Cet autre État doit prendre des mesures conservatoires à l'égard de cette créance fiscale conformément aux dispositions de sa législation comme s'il s'agissait d'une créance fiscale de cet autre État même si, au moment où ces mesures sont appliquées, la créance fiscale n'est pas recouvrable dans le premier État ou est due par une personne qui a le droit d'empêcher son recouvrement.

5. Nonobstant les dispositions des paragraphes 3 et 4, les délais de prescription et la priorité applicables, en vertu de la législation d'un État, à une créance fiscale en raison de sa nature en tant que telle ne s'appliquent pas à une créance fiscale acceptée par cet État aux fins du paragraphe 3 ou 4 et, à moins que les autorités compétentes n'en conviennent autrement, ne peut être recouvrée en ayant recours à l'incarcération du débiteur pour dettes. En outre, une créance fiscale acceptée par un État aux fins du paragraphe 3 ou du paragraphe 4 ne peut se voir appliquer aucune priorité dans cet État en vertu de la législation de l'autre État.

6. Les procédures concernant l'existence, la validité ou le montant d'une créance fiscale d'un État ne sont pas soumises aux tribunaux ou organismes administratifs de l'autre État.

7. Lorsque, à tout moment après qu'une demande a été formulée par un État en vertu du paragraphe 3 ou 4 et avant que l'autre État ait recouvré et transmis le montant de la créance fiscale en question au premier État, cette créance fiscale cesse d'être :

a) dans le cas d'une demande présentée en vertu du paragraphe 3, une créance fiscale du premier État qui est recouvrable en vertu de la législation de cet État et est due par une personne qui, à ce moment, ne peut, en vertu des lois de cet État, empêcher son recouvrement ; ou

b) dans le cas d'une demande présentée en vertu du paragraphe 4, une créance fiscale du premier État à l'égard de laquelle cet État peut, en vertu de sa législation, prendre des mesures conservatoires pour assurer son recouvrement ;

les autorités compétentes du premier État notifient promptement ce fait aux autorités compétentes de l'autre État et le premier État, au choix de l'autre État, suspend ou retire sa demande.

8. Les dispositions du présent Article ne peuvent en aucun cas être interprétées comme imposant à un État l'obligation :

a) de prendre des mesures administratives dérogeant à sa propre législation et à sa pratique administrative ou à celles de l'autre État ;

b) de prendre des mesures qui seraient contraires à l'ordre public ;

c) de prêter assistance si l'autre État n'a pas pris toutes les mesures raisonnables de recouvrement ou de conservation, selon le cas, qui sont disponibles en vertu de sa législation ou de sa pratique administrative ;

d) de prêter assistance dans les cas où la charge administrative qui en résulte pour cet État est nettement disproportionnée par rapport aux avantages que peut en tirer l'autre État. »

Article 6

L'Article suivant est inséré avant l'Article premier du Protocole à l'Accord :

« Généralités

Sous réserve des réserves, observations ou positions éventuelles de l'un ou l'autre État à l'égard du Modèle de convention fiscale de l'OCDE ou de ses commentaires, les deux États interprètent les dispositions de l'Accord qui sont identiques ou similaires en substance aux dispositions du Modèle de convention fiscale de l'OCDE concernant le revenu et la fortune, conformément aux commentaires de l'OCDE s'y rapportant au moment de la signature de l'Accord et à toute modification ultérieure apportée à ces commentaires afin de les clarifier. En particulier, les deux États interprètent l'expression "bénéficiaire effectif" utilisée dans l'Accord conformément à l'interprétation qui en est donnée par l'OCDE au moment de la signature de l'Accord et à toute modification ultérieure clarifiant cette interprétation de l'OCDE. »

Article 7

L'Article suivant est inséré après l'Article X du Protocole à l'Accord :

« XI. En ce qui concerne l'Article 28 :

Les dispositions de l'Article 28 s'appliquent également, en conséquence, aux renseignements qui sont vraisemblablement pertinents pour l'application des réglementations liées aux revenus si l'administration fiscale des Pays-Bas est chargée de mettre en œuvre et d'appliquer lesdites réglementations. Les renseignements reçus en vertu du présent Protocole ne sont utilisés qu'aux fins de la perception des cotisations, de l'octroi des avantages ou de la détermination de l'étendue de ces cotisations et avantages découlant des réglementations liées aux revenus. »

Article 8

L'Article VIII du Protocole à l'Accord est remplacé par ce qui suit :

« 1. Lorsque l'impôt prélevé à la source est supérieur au montant exigible en vertu des dispositions des Articles 10, 11 et 12, une demande de restitution du montant excédentaire d'impôt sera présentée à l'autorité compétente de l'État ayant prélevé l'impôt, dans les trois ans à partir de l'expiration de l'année civile pendant laquelle l'impôt a été perçu.

2. Il est entendu qu'aucun accord mutuel sur le mode d'application des Articles 10, 11 et 12 n'est requis pour l'application de ces Articles. »

Article 9

Le présent Protocole fait partie intégrante de l'Accord, et de son Protocole.

Article 10

Chaque État notifie à l'autre l'accomplissement des procédures requises par sa législation pour l'entrée en vigueur du présent Protocole, lequel entre en vigueur le premier jour du deuxième mois suivant la dernière des dates auxquelles les Gouvernements respectifs se sont notifiés par écrit et par la voie diplomatique. Les dispositions du présent Protocole s'appliquent pour la première fois aux montants payés ou crédités le premier jour du deuxième mois suivant la date d'entrée en vigueur du Protocole ou après cette date.

EN FOI DE QUOI, les soussignés, à ce dûment autorisés par leurs Gouvernements respectifs, ont signé le présent Protocole.

FAIT à Jakarta, le 30 juillet 2015, en double exemplaire, en langues anglaise, néerlandaise et indonésienne, les trois textes faisant également foi. En cas de divergence concernant l'interprétation et l'application du présent Protocole, le texte anglais prévaut.

Pour le Royaume des Pays-Bas :
ROB SWARTBOL

Pour la République d'Indonésie :
SUAHASIL NAZARA

No. 44004. Multilateral

INTERNATIONAL CONVENTION FOR THE SUPPRESSION OF ACTS OF NUCLEAR TERRORISM. NEW YORK, 13 APRIL 2005 [*United Nations, Treaty Series, vol. 2445, I-44004.*]

RATIFICATION (WITH RESERVATION AND DECLARATIONS)

Singapore

Deposit of instrument with the Secretary-General of the United Nations: 2 August 2017

Date of effect: 1 September 2017

Registration with the Secretariat of the United Nations: ex officio, 2 August 2017

N° 44004. Multilatéral

CONVENTION INTERNATIONALE POUR LA RÉPRESSION DES ACTES DE TERRORISME NUCLÉAIRE. NEW YORK, 13 AVRIL 2005 [*Nations Unies, Recueil des Traités, vol. 2445, I-44004.*]

RATIFICATION (AVEC RÉSERVE ET DÉCLARATIONS)

Singapour

Dépôt de l'instrument auprès du Secrétaire général de l'Organisation des Nations Unies : 2 août 2017

Date de prise d'effet : 1er septembre 2017

Enregistrement auprès du Secrétariat de l'Organisation des Nations Unies : d'office, 2 août 2017

Reservation and declarations:

Réserve et déclarations :

[TEXT IN ENGLISH – TEXTE EN ANGLAIS]

Reservation

Pursuant to Article 23, paragraph 2, of the Convention, the Republic of Singapore declares that it does not consider itself bound by the provisions of Article 23, paragraph 1 of the Convention.

Declarations

1. The Republic of Singapore understands that the term 'armed conflict' in Article 4, paragraph 2, of the Convention does not include internal disturbances and tensions, such as riots, isolated and sporadic acts of violence, and other acts of a similar nature.

2. The Republic of Singapore understands that, under Article 4 and Article 1, paragraph 6, the Convention does not apply to:

a. the military forces of a state in the exercise of their official duties;

b. civilians who direct or organise the official activities of military forces of a state; or

c. civilians acting in support of the official activities of the military forces of a state, if the civilians are under the formal command, control, and responsibility of those forces.

3. The Republic of Singapore understands Article 11, paragraph 1, of the Convention to include the right of competent authorities to decide not to submit any particular case for prosecution before the judicial authorities if the alleged offender is dealt with under national security and preventive detention laws.

[TRANSLATION – TRADUCTION]

Réserve

Conformément au paragraphe 2 de l'article 23 de la Convention, la République de Singapour déclare qu'elle ne se considère pas liée par le paragraphe 1 de l'article 23 de la Convention.

Déclarations

1. La République de Singapour considère qu'au paragraphe 2 de l'article 4 de la Convention, le terme « conflit armé » n'inclut pas les situations de tensions internes ni de troubles intérieurs, comme les émeutes, actes isolés et sporadiques de violence et autres actes de nature analogue.

2. La République de Singapour considère qu'en vertu de l'article 4 et du paragraphe 6 de l'article premier, la Convention ne s'applique pas:

a. Aux forces militaires d'un État dans l'exercice de leurs fonctions officielles ;

b. à des civils qui dirigent ou organisent les activités officielles de forces militaires d'un État ; ou

c. à des civils agissant à l'appui des activités officielles des forces militaires d'un État, si ces civils sont placés officiellement sous le commandement, le contrôle et la responsabilité de ces forces.

3. La République de Singapour considère que le paragraphe 1 de l'article 11 de la Convention inclut le droit des autorités compétentes à décider de ne pas engager de poursuites auprès des autorités judiciaires si l'auteur allégué de l'infraction relève des lois en matière de détention préventive et de sécurité nationale.

No. 48656. Austria, Liechtenstein and Switzerland

AGREEMENT BETWEEN THE REPUBLIC OF AUSTRIA, THE SWISS CONFEDERATION AND THE PRINCIPALITY OF LIECHTENSTEIN ON TRANSBOUNDARY COOPERATION OF SECURITY AND CUSTOMS AUTHORITIES. BERN, 27 APRIL 1999 [*United Nations, Treaty Series, vol. 2759, I-48656.*]

Termination in accordance with:

54652. Agreement between the Republic of Austria, the Swiss Confederation and the Principality of Liechtenstein on cross-border police cooperation. Vaduz, 4 June 2012 [*United Nations, Treaty Series, vol. 3200, I-54652.*]

Entry into force: 1 July 2017

Registration with the Secretariat of the United Nations: Austria, 10 August 2017

Information provided by the Secretariat of the United Nations: 10 August 2017

N° 48656. Autriche, Liechtenstein et Suisse

ACCORD ENTRE LA CONFÉDÉRATION SUISSE, LA RÉPUBLIQUE D'AUTRICHE ET LA PRINCIPAUTÉ DU LIECHTENSTEIN CONCERNANT LA COOPÉRATION TRANSFRONTALIÈRE DES AUTORITÉS COMPÉTENTES EN MATIÈRE DE SÉCURITÉ ET DE DOUANE. BERNE, 27 AVRIL 1999 [*Nations Unies, Recueil des Traités, vol. 2759, I-48656.*]

Abrogation conformément à :

54652. Accord entre la République d'Autriche, la Confédération suisse et la Principauté du Liechtenstein relatif à la coopération policière transfrontalière. Vaduz, 4 juin 2012 [*Nations Unies, Recueil des Traités, vol. 3200, I-54652.*]

Entrée en vigueur : 1er juillet 2017

Enregistrement auprès du Secrétariat de l'Organisation des Nations Unies : Autriche, 10 août 2017

Information fournie par le Secrétariat de l'Organisation des Nations Unies : 10 août 2017

No. 49361. Argentina and Brazil

AGREEMENT BETWEEN THE ARGENTINE REPUBLIC AND THE FEDERATIVE REPUBLIC OF BRAZIL ON INTEGRATED BORDER COMMUNITIES. PUERTO IGUAZÚ, 30 NOVEMBER 2005 [*United Nations, Treaty Series, vol. 2814, I-49361.*]

EXCHANGE OF NOTES CONSTITUTING AN AGREEMENT BETWEEN THE ARGENTINE REPUBLIC AND THE FEDERATIVE REPUBLIC OF BRAZIL ADDING SAN ANTONIO AND SANTO ANTÔNIO DO SUDOESTE TO THE LIST OF INTEGRATED BORDER COMMUNITIES ANNEXED TO THE AGREEMENT BETWEEN THE ARGENTINE REPUBLIC AND THE FEDERATIVE REPUBLIC OF BRAZIL ON INTEGRATED BORDER COMMUNITIES. BUENOS AIRES, 3 OCTOBER 2016 AND 20 OCTOBER 2016

Entry into force: 18 January 2017, in accordance with the provisions of the said letters

Authentic texts: Portuguese and Spanish

Registration with the Secretariat of the United Nations: Argentina, 14 August 2017

N° 49361. Argentine et Brésil

ACCORD ENTRE LA RÉPUBLIQUE ARGENTINE ET LA RÉPUBLIQUE FÉDÉRATIVE DU BRÉSIL RELATIF AUX COMMUNAUTÉS FRONTALIÈRES INTÉGRÉES. PUERTO IGUAZÚ, 30 NOVEMBRE 2005 [*Nations Unies, Recueil des Traités, vol. 2814, I-49361.*]

ÉCHANGE DE LETTRES CONSTITUANT UN ACCORD ENTRE LA RÉPUBLIQUE ARGENTINE ET LA RÉPUBLIQUE FÉDÉRATIVE DU BRÉSIL AJOUTANT SAN ANTONIO ET SANTO ANTÔNIO DO SUDOESTE À LA LISTE DES COMMUNAUTÉS FRONTALIÈRES INTÉGRÉES ANNEXÉE À L'ACCORD ENTRE LA RÉPUBLIQUE ARGENTINE ET LA RÉPUBLIQUE FÉDÉRATIVE DU BRÉSIL RELATIF AUX COMMUNAUTÉS FRONTALIÈRES INTÉGRÉES. BUENOS AIRES, 3 OCTOBRE 2016 ET 20 OCTOBRE 2016

Entrée en vigueur : 18 janvier 2017, conformément aux dispositions desdites lettres

Textes authentiques : portugais et espagnol

Enregistrement auprès du Secrétariat de l'Organisation des Nations Unies : Argentine, 14 août 2017

[TEXT IN PORTUGUESE – TEXTE EN PORTUGAIS]

I

Ministra de Relaciones Exteriores y Culto

Buenos Aires, 3 OCT 2013

Senhor Embaixador,

Tenho a honra de dirigir-me a Vossa Excelência com o propósito de referir-me ao "Acordo entre a República Argentina e a República Federativa do Brasil sobre Localidades Fronteiriças Vinculadas", assinado em Puerto Iguazú, em 30 de novembro de 2005.

Em virtude de o Artigo X, Inciso 1, do Acordo prever a ampliação ou redução da lista de Localidades Fronteiriças Vinculadas por troca de notas diplomáticas, tenho a honra de propor, em nome do Governo Argentino, a incorporação de San Antonio (Departamento Geral Manuel Belgrano, Província de Misiones, República Argentina) e de Santo Antônio do Sudoeste (Estado do Paraná, República Federativa do Brasil) à mencionada nômina.

Se o antes exposto for aceitável para o Governo da República Federativa do Brasil, a presente Nota e a de resposta de Vossa Excelência na qual conste a referida conformidade constituirão um Acordo entre os dois Governos, que entrará em vigor a partir de noventa (90) dias de sua Nota de resposta.

Aproveito a oportunidade para reiterar a Vossa Excelência os protestos da minha mais alta e distinta consideração.

SUSANA MALCORRA
Ministra de Relaciones Exteriores
y Culto

A SUA EXCELÊNCIA O EMBAIXADOR
DA REPÚBLICA FEDERATIVA DO BRASIL
SENHOR SÉRGIO FRANÇA DANESE
BUENOS AIRES

II

Buenos Aires, 20 de outubro de 2016

Nº169/PFRO-BRAS-ARGT

Senhora Chanceler,

Tenho a honra de referir-me à Nota de Vossa Excelência, do dia 3 de outubro de 2016, cujo teor em português é o seguinte:

[See letter I - Voir lettre I]

Em resposta, tenho a honra de transmitir, em nome do Governo da República Federativa do Brasil, a aceitação dos termos propostos por Vossa Excelência. Nesse sentido, esta Nota e a de Vossa Excelência constituem Acordo entre a República Argentina e a República Federativa do Brasil para a incorporação de San Antonio (Departamento Geral Manuel Belgrano, Província de Misiones, República Argentina) e de Santo Antônio do Sudoeste (Estado do Paraná, República Federativa do Brasil) ao Acordo sobre Localidades Fronteriças Vinculadas, com vigência a partir de 90 dias a contar da presente data.

Aproveito a oportunidade para reiterar a Vossa Excelência os protestos da minha mais alta e distinta consideração.

EMBAIXADA DA REPÚBLICA FEDERATIVA DO BRASIL ORDEM E PROGRESSO BUENOS AIRES

Sérgio França Danese
(Embaixador do Brasil)

A Sua Excelência a Senhora Susana Malcorra,
Ministra de Relações Exteriores e Culto.

[TEXT IN SPANISH – TEXTE EN ESPAGNOL]

I

Ministra de Relaciones Exteriores y Culto

Buenos Aires, 3 OCT 2016

Señor Embajador,

Tengo el honor de dirigirme a Vuestra Excelencia, con el propósito de referirme al "Acuerdo entre la República Argentina y la República Federativa del Brasil sobre Localidades Fronterizas Vinculadas", suscrito en Puerto Iguazú el 30 de noviembre de 2005.

En virtud de que el Artículo X, Inciso 1, del Acuerdo prevé la ampliación o reducción de la lista de Localidades Fronterizas Vinculadas por intercambio de notas diplomáticas, tengo el honor de proponer, en nombre del Gobierno Argentino, la incorporación de San Antonio (Departamento General Manuel Belgrano, Provincia de Misiones, República Argentina) y de Santo Antonio do Sudoeste (Estado de Paraná, República Federativa del Brasil), a la mencionada nómina.

Si lo antes expuesto fuese aceptable para el Gobierno de la República Federativa del Brasil, la presente Nota y la de respuesta de Vuestra Excelencia donde conste dicha conformidad constituirán un Acuerdo entre los dos Gobiernos, que entrará en vigor a partir de los noventa (90) días de vuestra Nota de respuesta.

Hago propicia la oportunidad para reiterar a Vuestra Excelencia las seguridades de mi más alta y distinguida consideración.

SUSANA MALCORRA
Ministra de Relaciones Exteriores
y Culto

A SU EXCELENCIA EL SEÑOR EMBAJADOR
DE LA REPÚBLICA FEDERATIVA DEL BRASIL
D. SÉRGIO FRANÇA DANESE
BUENOS AIRES

II

Buenos Aires, 20 de octubre del 2016

N°169 / PFRO-BRAS-ARGT

Señora Canciller,

Tengo el honor de referirme a la Nota de Vuestra Excelencia, del día 3 de octubre de 2016, cuyo contenido en español es el siguiente:

[See letter I - Voir lettre I]

En respuesta, tengo el honor de transmitir, en nombre de la República Federativa del Brasil, la aceptación de los términos propuestos por Vuestra Excelencia. En ese sentido, esta Nota y la de Vuestra Excelencia constituyen Acuerdo entre la República Argentina y la República Federativa del Brasil para la incorporación de San Antonio (Departamento General Manuel Belgrano, Provincia de Misiones, República Argentina) y de Santo Antonio do Sudoeste (Estado de Paraná, República Federativa del Brasil), al Acuerdo sobre Localidades Fronterizas Vinculadas, con vigencia a partir de 90 días a contar de esta fecha.

Hago propicia la oportunidad para reiterar a Vuestra Excelencia las seguridades de mi más alta y distinguida consideración.

EMBAIXADA DA REPÚBLICA FEDERATIVA DO BRASIL · BUENOS AIRES · ORDEM E PROGRESSO

Sérgio França Danese
(Embajador del Brasil)

A Su Excelencia la Señora Susana Malcorra,
Ministra de Relaciones Exteriores y Culto.

[TRANSLATION – TRADUCTION]

I

MINISTER FOR FOREIGN AFFAIRS AND WORSHIP

Buenos Aires, 3 October 2016

Excellency,

I have the honour of writing to you with reference to the "Agreement between the Argentine Republic and the Federative Republic of Brazil on integrated border communities", signed at Puerto Iguazú on 30 November 2005.

By virtue of the fact that article X, paragraph 1, of the Agreement provides for additions to or deletions from the list of integrated border communities through an exchange of diplomatic notes, I have the honour to propose, on behalf of the Government of Argentina, that San Antonio (General Manuel Belgrano Department, Misiones Province, Argentine Republic) and Santo Antônio do Sudoeste (State of Paraná, Federative Republic of Brazil) be added to that list.

If the foregoing provisions are acceptable to the Government of the Federative Republic of Brazil, this Note and your reply expressing your approval thereto shall constitute an Agreement between the two Governments, which shall enter into force 90 days from the date of your reply Note.

I avail myself of this opportunity to convey to you, Excellency, the renewed assurances of my highest consideration.

SUSANA MALCORRA
Minister for Foreign Affairs and Worship

His Excellency
Mr. Sérgio França Danese
Ambassador of the Federative Republic of Brazil
Buenos Aires

II

Buenos Aires, 20 October 2016

No.169/PFRO-BRAS-ARGT

Madam,

I have the honour of referring to your Note, in Spanish, of 3 October 2016, which reads as follows:

[See note I]

In reply, I have the honour of transmitting, on behalf of the Federative Republic of Brazil, acceptance of the terms you have proposed. In that regard, this Note and your Note shall constitute an Agreement between the Argentine Republic and the Federative Republic of Brazil for the addition of San Antonio (General Manuel Belgrano Department, Misiones Province, Argentine Republic) and Santo Antônio do Sudoeste (State of Paraná, Federative Republic of Brazil) to the Agreement on integrated border communities, effective 90 days from today's date.

I avail myself of this opportunity to convey to you, Madam, the renewed assurances of my highest consideration.

SÉRGIO FRANÇA DANESE
Ambassador of Brazil

Her Excellency
Ms. Susana Malcorra
Minister for Foreign Affairs and Worship

[TRANSLATION – TRADUCTION]

I

MINISTÈRE DES AFFAIRES ÉTRANGÈRES ET DU CULTE

Buenos Aires, le 3 octobre 2016

Monsieur l'Ambassadeur,

J'ai l'honneur de me référer à l'Accord entre la République argentine et la République fédérative du Brésil relatif aux communautés frontalières intégrées, signé à Puerto Iguazú le 30 novembre 2005.

Le paragraphe 1 de l'article X de l'Accord prévoyant l'allongement ou la réduction de la liste des communautés frontalières intégrées par échange de notes diplomatiques, j'ai le plaisir de proposer, au nom du Gouvernement argentin, l'ajout de San Antonio (département General Manuel Belgrano, province de Misiones, République argentine) et de Santo Antônio do Sudoeste (État du Paraná, République fédérative du Brésil) à ladite liste.

Si les dispositions qui précèdent rencontrent l'agrément de la République fédérative du Brésil, la présente note et votre réponse de confirmation constitueront un Accord entre les deux Gouvernements qui entrera en vigueur 90 jours à compter de la date de votre réponse.

Veuillez agréer, Monsieur l'Ambassadeur, les assurances de ma très haute considération.

SUSANA MALCORRA
Ministre des affaires étrangères et du culte

Son Excellence
Monsieur Sérgio França Danese
Ambassadeur
République fédérative du Brésil
Buenos Aires

II

Buenos Aires, le 20 octobre 2016

N° 169/PFRO-BRAS-ARGT

Madame la Ministre,

J'ai l'honneur de me référer à votre note du 3 octobre 2016, libellée comme suit en langue espagnole :

[Voir note I]

En réponse, j'ai le plaisir de vous informer, au nom de la République fédérative du Brésil, de l'acceptation des conditions que vous avez proposées. À cet égard, la présente note ainsi que votre note constituent un Accord entre la République argentine et la République fédérative du Brésil concernant l'ajout de San Antonio (département General Manuel Belgrano, province de Misiones, République argentine) et de Santo Antônio do Sudoeste (État du Paraná, République fédérative du Brésil) à l'Accord relatif aux communautés frontalières intégrées, qui prend effet 90 jours à compter de la date d'aujourd'hui.

Veuillez agréer, Madame la Ministre, les assurances de ma très haute considération.

SÉRGIO FRANÇA DANESE
Ambassadeur

Son Excellence
Madame Susana Malcorra
Ministre des affaires étrangères et du culte

No. 51620. Peru and United States of America

ASSISTANCE AGREEMENT BETWEEN THE UNITED STATES OF AMERICA AND THE REPUBLIC OF PERU. LIMA, 20 SEPTEMBER 2012 [*United Nations, Treaty Series, vol. 2970, I-51620.*]

AMENDMENT NO. 9 TO THE ASSISTANCE AGREEMENT BETWEEN THE UNITED STATES OF AMERICA AND THE REPUBLIC OF PERU (WITH TABLE). LIMA, 16 MARCH 2017

Entry into force: 16 March 2017 by signature

Authentic texts: English and Spanish

Registration with the Secretariat of the United Nations: Peru, 21 August 2017

Not published in print, in accordance with article 12(2) of the General Assembly regulations to give effect to Article 102 of the Charter of the United Nations, as amended, and the publication practice of the Secretariat.

Nº 51620. Pérou et États-Unis d'Amérique

ACCORD D'ASSISTANCE ENTRE LES ÉTATS-UNIS D'AMÉRIQUE ET LA RÉPUBLIQUE DU PÉROU. LIMA, 20 SEPTEMBRE 2012 [*Nations Unies, Recueil des Traités, vol. 2970, I-51620.*]

AMENDEMENT Nº 9 À L'ACCORD D'ASSISTANCE ENTRE LES ÉTATS-UNIS D'AMÉRIQUE ET LA RÉPUBLIQUE DU PÉROU (AVEC TABLEAU). LIMA, 16 MARS 2017

Entrée en vigueur : 16 mars 2017 par signature

Textes authentiques : anglais et espagnol

Enregistrement auprès du Secrétariat de l'Organisation des Nations Unies : Pérou, 21 août 2017

Non disponible en version imprimée, conformément au paragraphe 2 de l'article 12 du règlement de l'Assemblée générale destiné à mettre en application l'Article 102 de la Charte des Nations Unies, tel qu'amendé, et à la pratique du Secrétariat en matière de publication.

No. 54113. Multilateral

PARIS AGREEMENT. PARIS, 12 DECEMBER 2015 [*United Nations, Treaty Series, vol. 3156, I-54113.*]

RATIFICATION

Sudan

Deposit of instrument with the Secretary-General of the United Nations: 2 August 2017

Date of effect: 1 September 2017

Registration with the Secretariat of the United Nations: ex officio, 2 August 2017

RATIFICATION

Timor-Leste

Deposit of instrument with the Secretary-General of the United Nations: 16 August 2017

Date of effect: 15 September 2017

Registration with the Secretariat of the United Nations: ex officio, 16 August 2017

RATIFICATION

Zimbabwe

Deposit of instrument with the Secretary-General of the United Nations: 7 August 2017

Date of effect: 6 September 2017

Registration with the Secretariat of the United Nations: ex officio, 7 August 2017

N° 54113. Multilatéral

ACCORD DE PARIS. PARIS, 12 DÉCEMBRE 2015 [*Nations Unies, Recueil des Traités, vol. 3156, I-54113.*]

RATIFICATION

Soudan

Dépôt de l'instrument auprès du Secrétaire général de l'Organisation des Nations Unies : 2 août 2017

Date de prise d'effet : 1er septembre 2017

Enregistrement auprès du Secrétariat de l'Organisation des Nations Unies : d'office, 2 août 2017

RATIFICATION

Timor-Leste

Dépôt de l'instrument auprès du Secrétaire général de l'Organisation des Nations Unies : 16 août 2017

Date de prise d'effet : 15 septembre 2017

Enregistrement auprès du Secrétariat de l'Organisation des Nations Unies : d'office, 16 août 2017

RATIFICATION

Zimbabwe

Dépôt de l'instrument auprès du Secrétaire général de l'Organisation des Nations Unies : 7 août 2017

Date de prise d'effet : 6 septembre 2017

Enregistrement auprès du Secrétariat de l'Organisation des Nations Unies : d'office, 7 août 2017

No. 54225. Argentina and China

FRAMEWORK AGREEMENT FOR ECONOMIC AND INVESTMENT COOPERATION BETWEEN THE GOVERNMENT OF THE ARGENTINE REPUBLIC AND THE GOVERNMENT OF THE PEOPLE'S REPUBLIC OF CHINA. BUENOS AIRES, 18 JULY 2014 [*United Nations, Treaty Series, vol. 3171, I-54225.*]

COMPLEMENTARY AGREEMENT FOR INDUSTRIAL INVESTMENT COOPERATION BETWEEN THE GOVERNMENT OF THE ARGENTINE REPUBLIC AND THE GOVERNMENT OF THE PEOPLE'S REPUBLIC OF CHINA. BUENOS AIRES, 18 JULY 2014

Entry into force: 7 November 2016, in accordance with article 5

Authentic texts: Chinese, English and Spanish

Registration with the Secretariat of the United Nations: Argentina, 14 August 2017

Nº 54225. Argentine et Chine

ACCORD-CADRE DE COOPÉRATION EN MATIÈRE ÉCONOMIQUE ET D'INVESTISSEMENT ENTRE LE GOUVERNEMENT DE LA RÉPUBLIQUE ARGENTINE ET LE GOUVERNEMENT DE LA RÉPUBLIQUE POPULAIRE DE CHINE. BUENOS AIRES, 18 JUILLET 2014 [*Nations Unies, Recueil des Traités, vol. 3171, I-54225.*]

ACCORD COMPLÉMENTAIRE DE COOPÉRATION EN MATIÈRE D'INVESTISSEMENT INDUSTRIEL ENTRE LE GOUVERNEMENT DE LA RÉPUBLIQUE ARGENTINE ET LE GOUVERNEMENT DE LA RÉPUBLIQUE POPULAIRE DE CHINE. BUENOS AIRES, 18 JUILLET 2014

Entrée en vigueur : 7 novembre 2016, conformément à l'article 5

Textes authentiques : chinois, anglais et espagnol

Enregistrement auprès du Secrétariat de l'Organisation des Nations Unies : Argentine, 14 août 2017

[TEXT IN CHINESE – TEXTE EN CHINOIS]

阿根廷共和国政府与中华人民共和国政府
关于产业投资合作的补充协议

阿根廷共和国政府与中华人民共和国政府（下称“双方”），

意欲在对等互利的基础上发展并加强双边经济关系；

鉴于双方达成的《阿根廷共和国政府与中华人民共和国政府与经济和投资合作框架协议》（下称“框架协议”,本协议在其下达成）表明两国政府愿为加强两国及两国人民联系做出努力；

考虑到双方之间已签署并生效的双边经济合作协议，特别是于 2013 年 9 月 5 日签署的《阿根廷共和国政府与中华人民共和国政府关于建立经济合作与协调战略对话机制的谅解备忘录》；

鉴于根据阿根廷共和国政府与中华人民共和国政府之间经济合作与协调战略对话机制（下称“阿中经济对话机制”）的指导原则，两国有关部门保持了密切交流和协调，联合组织推介重大基础设施项目的活动，并就扩展和加强经济技术合作、联合制定一份阿根廷与中国之间的产业投资合作框架达成一致；

知悉加强两国间双边经济关系需要考虑团结一致、对等互补、互相尊重和领土主权的原则；

认识到双方有加强合作关系的共同愿望；

鉴此，双方就《框架协议》下《阿根廷共和国政府与中华人民共和国政府关于产业投资合作的补充协议》达成一致：

第一条　总体目标

本补充协议的目标如下：

一、进一步落实两国元首达成的重要共识，规划、设计和着力推进未来中期（5 年）两国产业投资合作，增加出口部门的附加值，促进双边经济关系的动态平衡。

二、结合两国各自经济发展重点和产业结构调整规划，加强产业投资合作；创造更多就业机会，推动技术进步，并为中国实施创新驱动发展、构建开放型经济新体制等战略和阿根廷在工业化基础上将社会包容性与经济增长进程融合创造有利条件。

三、为两国企业在各领域开展优势互补、互利共赢的合作创造良好环境和条件；在落实好现有重大项目的基础上，循序渐进、突出重点，积极有序地扩大产业投资项目合作。

四、根据《阿根廷共和国政府与中华人民共和国政府共同行动计划》跟踪有关合作事项。

五、通过加强产业投资合作，丰富双边经济技术务实合作和战略伙伴关系的内涵，实现两国经济社会共同发展并造福两国人民。

第二条　重点领域

双方认识到，阿中同为发展中国家和新兴市场国家，在经济转型、产业现代化、改善民生、实现经济社会可持续发展面临重要的挑战，在资源禀赋、产业结构、资金技术等方面形成互补，形成了产业投资合作的良好基础。在此基础上，双方确定的产业投资合作重点领域包括但不限于：

一、能源领域

双方将促进两国企业在油气勘探、开发、提升采收率、炼化、运输和销售，以及核能、水电、风电、太阳能、电网、清洁煤等方面开展投资合作，共同努力加快清洁能源的发展和能源效率的提高，推动能源装备制造方面的合作。

二、矿业领域

双方将推动两国企业在具有发展潜力地区的矿业勘探开发合作，开展铁、锂、铜等矿产品的产业化合作投资项目；此外，双方将鼓励在生产、冶炼、提纯以及制造的各个阶段增加产品附加值。

三、制造业领域

双方将推动两国企业在生产过程能够吸纳本地内容的行业和产业现代化改造项目中的投资合作。合作重点包括：钢铁；铝材；水泥和平板玻璃等；汽车整车和零部件；铁路装备；制药；塑料；电子信息产业，包括电信设备、计算机、医疗设备和其他电子设备的生产制造等；纺织、服装、制鞋、家电等轻工业等。

四、农业及粮食流通等相关领域

双方将促进两国企业在农业及粮食流通等相关领域的投资合作，促进农业现代化和农产品产业链的发展，以保障粮食安全和促进高附加值农产品的出口。合作重点包括：农业种植；农业生物技术；良种培育；农产品加工和生产；渔业和畜牧业产品；林业产品、粮油食品；粮食仓储、运输和物流等相关基础设施建设和运营；质量检测技术等。

五、配套和支持体系

双方将鼓励两国企业在设立研发实验室、设计中心、销售中心、技术支持中心和建立服务体系方面加强合作，以支持和促进两国产业投资合作。

双方将探索以共同建设工业园的方式推动两国产业合作，分享园区规划、建设和管理的经验，支持两国企业通过形成产业价值链上的更紧密联系和融合，实现共同发展。

六、其他领域

双方同意就共同感兴趣的其他领域的产业投资合作进行沟通交流，推动具体项目合作。

七、重点项目

双方同意，在本补充协议签署后，根据第四条由双方实施部门就重点项目进行交流，并拟形成一份未来 5 年重点领域的产业投资合作重点项目清单。

第三条　组织实施

一、双方将通过阿中经济对话机制，协调、推动和实施《阿根廷共和国政府与中华人民共和国政府经济和投资合作协议》和《阿根廷共和国政府与中华人民共和国政府关于建立经济合作与协调战略对话机制的谅解备忘录》框架下各相关领域的合作。

二、双方将通过以下活动推动产业投资合作：

（一）交流两国产业政策和投资政策，探讨为两国企业开展产业投资合作创造良好的政策环境和有利条件，最大程度地提供投资便利化；

（二）开展产业投资合作研究，提出促进合作的政策建议，规范和引导两国企业开展合作；根据双边关系发展、合作需求变化等因素，调整重点合作项目清单；

（三）制定产业投资合作指南，为企业开展合作提供信息服务，指导企业依法经营并履行必要的社会责任；

（四）组织项目推介会等投资促进活动，为企业合作搭建平台，推动信息交流、项目对接和最佳实践分享；

（五）鼓励两国金融机构、研究机构、中介组织和培训机构等为企业开展投资合作提供融资、研究和人力资源等方面的服务和支持。

（六）在政府层面引导促进合作，指导和推动企业在对方国家潜在的投资合作项目。根据政府引导、商业运作原则，企业将作为投资合作的主体。

第四条　实施部门

双方同意，将由阿方的经济和公共财政部与中方的国家发展和改革委员会，在阿中经济对话机制的框架下，批准可能有助于本补充协议执行的安排、计划、协议和特别合作项目。

第五条 生效和终止

一、框架协议生效时，本补充协议将同时生效。

二、在框架协议的有效期内，本补充协议一直有效，除非有一方通过书面方式通知另一方终止本补充协议。协议终止将于书面通知发出的六个月后生效。

三、本补充协议的终止不影响正在执行的项目，这些项目将根据相关时间表完成。

本补充协议于二 O 一四年七月十八日在布宜诺斯艾利斯签订，一式两份，每份都用中文、英文和西班牙文写成，三种文本同等作准。如对文本解释发生分歧，以英文文本为准。

阿根廷共和国政府 代表	中华人民共和国政府 代表

[TEXT IN ENGLISH – TEXTE EN ANGLAIS]

COMPLEMENTARY AGREEMENT
FOR INDUSTRIAL INVESTMENT COOPERATION
BETWEEN
THE GOVERNMENT OF THE ARGENTINE REPUBLIC
AND
THE GOVERNMENT OF THE PEOPLE'S REPUBLIC OF CHINA

The Government of the Argentine Republic and the Government of the People's Republic of China (hereinafter referred to as the "Parties");

WHEREAS the Parties intend to develop and intensify the bilateral economic relations between them, on the basis of reciprocity and mutual benefit;

WHEREAS the *Framework Agreement for Economic and Investment Cooperation* entered into by the Government of the Argentine Republic and the Government of the People's Republic of China (hereinafter "the Framework Agreement"), under which framework the present Agreement is concluded, expresses the willing efforts of both governments to intensify and strengthen the links between both countries and their people;

WHEREAS the Parties take into consideration the bilateral agreements on economic cooperation between them which are currently in force, in particular, the *Memorandum of Understanding on Establishing a Mechanism for Strategic Dialogue for Economic Cooperation and Coordination between the Government of the Argentine Republic and the Government of the People's Republic of China* signed on 5 September 2013;

WHEREAS the ministerial authorities of both countries have maintained close coordination exchanges, taking into account the guidelines of the mechanism for the Strategic Dialogue for Economic Cooperation and Coordination between the governments of the Argentine Republic and the People's Republic of China (hereinafter referred to as the "SDECC"), have organized joint road shows to present important infrastructure projects and have entered into agreements related to the expansion and strengthening of economic and technical bilateral cooperation and the joint development of a framework for industrial investment cooperation between both countries;

WHEREAS the Parties are aware of the need to consider the principles of solidarity, reciprocity and complementation, mutual respect and territorial sovereignty with the purpose of strengthening the bilateral economic relation between them;

WHEREAS the Parties acknowledge the mutual wish to strengthen their cooperation relations.

THEREFORE, the Parties have agreed to enter into this *Complementary Agreement for Industrial Investment Cooperation between the Government of the Argentine Republic and the Government of the People's Republic of China* under the framework of the *Framework Agreement* under the following terms:

ARTICLE 1
General objectives

The purposes of this Complementary Agreement shall be the following:

1. Plan, design and vigorously promote the industrial investment cooperation between both countries to achieve industrial integration in the medium term (five years) with the purpose of increasing the added value in export sectors to promote the dynamic balance in the bilateral economic relation, so as to implement the important agreements entered into by the Presidents of both countries.

2. Strengthen industrial investment cooperation in line with the economic development priorities and the industrial restructuring plans of both countries; create more job opportunities and boost technological advances, and create favorable conditions for China to carry out its strategies, including, for example, Driving Development with Innovation and Fostering a New Open-Economy System, and for Argentina to advance in consolidating its economic growth process with social inclusion based on industrialization.

3. Create favorable environment and conditions so that the enterprises of both countries can carry out mutual, complementary and beneficial cooperation in different areas; expand industrial investment project cooperation in an orderly and gradual fashion and with appropriate priorities, on the basis of the correct implementation of the important existing projects.

4. Monitor cooperation in accordance with the *Joint Action Plan between the Government of the Argentine Republic and the Government of the People's Republic of China.*

5. Enrich the content of the economic and technical bilateral cooperation and strategic partnership, and achieve the social and economic development of both countries; benefit both countries though strengthening industrial investment cooperation.

ARTICLE 2
Priority areas

The Parties recognize that both Argentina and China are developing countries and emerging market economies; that both countries face important challenges in connection with economic transformation, industry modernization, improvement of the population's well-being, and achievement of sustained economic and social development; that both countries complement each other in terms of natural resources, industrial structure, finances and technology, which constitutes a solid foundation for industrial investment cooperation. Based on the foregoing, the Parties have identified priority areas for industrial investment cooperation, including, but not limited to:

1. Energy
The Parties shall facilitate enterprise of both countries to carry out investment cooperation in areas including oil and gas exploration and development, enhanced recovery, refinery, transportation and sales, and nuclear power, hydropower, wind power, solar energy, power grid, and clean coal. The Parties shall make joint efforts to accelerate clean energy development and improve energy efficiency, and promote cooperation in energy equipment manufacturing.

2. Minerals
The Parties shall promote cooperation among enterprises of both countries in mining exploration and development in areas with development potential, as well as carry out industrialization and investment cooperation projects related to mineral resources, including iron, lithium and copper; furthermore, the Parties shall encourage increasing the added value of the products in all stages, including production, smelting, purification and manufacture.

3. Manufactures
The Parties shall promote investment cooperation among enterprises of both countries in those industries and industrial modernization projects that promote the incorporation of local content into manufacturing. Such cooperation shall focus on the following areas, among others: iron and steel; aluminum

products; cement and plate glasses; automobiles and auto parts; railway equipment; medicines; plastic industry; electronic, information technology and communications industries, including the manufacture of telecommunication equipment, computers, medical equipment and other electronic equipment; light industries, including textiles, apparels, footwear and household appliances.

4. Agriculture, logistics and distribution of farming products and related areas

The Parties shall facilitate investment cooperation among enterprises of both countries in agriculture, logistics and distribution of farming products and related areas in order to promote agriculture modernization and the development of agricultural product's industrial chains with a view to guaranteeing food safety and the export of high value-added farming products. Such cooperation shall focus on the following areas, among others: farming; agricultural biotechnology; cultivation of good seed varieties; processing and production of agricultural products; fishery and livestock products; forestry products, cereals and oils; infrastructure construction and operation, including grain storage, transportation and logistics; and quality inspection and testing.

5. Support systems

The Parties shall encourage enterprises of both countries to strengthen cooperation in areas related to the establishment of Research and Development (R&D) laboratories, design, sales, and technical support centers and the establishment of service systems with a view to supporting and promoting industrial investment cooperation between both countries.

The Parties shall consider and analyze establishing industrial parks to promote industrial cooperation between both countries, share experiences in industrial park planning, building and management, and support enterprises of both countries to achieve common development by building closer links and greater integration throughout the industrial value chain.

6. Other areas

The Parties agree to communicate and exchange ideas on industrial investment cooperation in other areas of common interest and to promote cooperation in concrete projects.

7. Priority projects

The Parties agree to exchange priority projects to the applicable authority in accordance with the Article 4, once the Complementary Agreement is signed, with a view to forming a list of priority projects of industrial investment cooperation to be implemented in the next five years in the priority areas.

ARTICLE 3
Organization and implementation

1. The Parties shall coordinate, promote and implement cooperation through the SDECC in all relevant areas under the frame work of the *Agreement for Economic and Investment Cooperation between the Government of the Argentine Republic and the Government of the People's Republic of China* and the *Memorandum of Understanding on Establishing a Mechanism for Strategic Dialogue for Economic Cooperation and Coordination between the Government of the Argentine Republic and the Government of the People's Republic of China.*

2. The Parties shall promote industrial investment cooperation through the following activities:

(1) Exchanging industrial and investment policies between both countries, exploring ways to create a favorable policy environment and conditions for the enterprises of both countries to conduct industrial investment cooperation, and providing investment facilitation to the maximum extent possible;

(2) Conducting industrial investment research and making recommendations on cooperation promotion policies in order to regulate and guide cooperation among enterprises of both countries; adjusting the list of priority industrial investment cooperation projects to the development of bilateral relations, changes in cooperation needs and other factors;

(3) Creating guidelines for industrial investment cooperation, which guidelines shall provide information services for enterprises engaged in cooperation, and instruct enterprises on how to do business in accordance with the law and to adhere to the respective corporate social responsibility as required;

(4) Organizing investment promotion activities such as project road shows in order to build platforms for industrial cooperation and facilitate information exchange, seeking project match and best practice sharing;

(5) Encouraging financial institutions, research institutes, intermediary agencies, and training and other organizations of both countries to provide financing, research and human resources, and other services, as well as support to investment cooperation among enterprises of both countries;

(6) Introducing collaboration at a governmental level and guiding and facilitating enterprises in the identification of potential partners in the country of the other Party; in accordance with the principle of government guidance and business operation, enterprises shall be the major players in investment cooperation.

ARTICLE 4
Applicable authorities

The Parties agree that the following authorities shall approve the programs, plans, agreements and special cooperation projects as may be convenient to execute this Complementary Agreement, under the framework of the SDECC: in the case of Argentina, the Ministry of Economy and Public Finances, and in the case of China, the National Development and Reform Commission.

ARTICLE 5
Entry into force and termination

1. This Complementary Agreement shall enter into force when the Framework Agreement enters into force.

2. This Complementary Agreement shall remain in force for as long as the Framework Agreement is in force, unless either party denounces this Complementary Agreement at any time through written notice to the other Party. The denunciation shall be effective six (06) months after notice thereof is given to the other Party.

3. The termination of this Complementary Agreement shall not affect the execution of any ongoing project, which shall be completed as per the relevant schedule.

This Complementary Agreement is signed in Buenos Aires, on 18 July 2014 in two counterparts in the Spanish, Chinese and English languages, all texts being equally authentic. In the event of any divergence of interpretation, the English text shall prevail.

FOR THE GOVERNMENT OF THE ARGENTINE REPUBLIC	**FOR THE GOVERNMENT OF THE PEOPLE'S REPUBLIC OF CHINA**

[TEXT IN SPANISH – TEXTE EN ESPAGNOL]

CONVENIO COMPLEMENTARIO DE COOPERACIÓN EN MATERIA DE INVERSIÓN INDUSTRIAL ENTRE EL GOBIERNO DE LA REPÚBLICA ARGENTINA Y EL GOBIERNO DE LA REPÚBLICA POPULAR CHINA

El Gobierno de la República Argentina y el Gobierno de la República Popular China (en adelante denominados "las Partes");

CONSIDERANDO

Que las Partes tienen la intención de desarrollar e intensificar la relación económica bilateral entre ellas sobre la base de la reciprocidad y el beneficio mutuo;

Que el *Convenio Marco de Cooperación en Materia Económica y de Inversiones* celebrado entre el Gobierno de la República Argentina y el Gobierno de la República Popular China (en adelante, el "Convenio Marco"), dentro de cuyo marco se ha concluido el presente Acuerdo, expresa los esmerados esfuerzos de ambos gobiernos para intensificar y fortalecer los lazos entre los dos países y sus pueblos;

Que las Partes tienen en cuenta los acuerdos bilaterales sobre cooperación económica entre ellas que se encuentran actualmente vigentes, en particular el *Memorándum de Entendimiento sobre el Establecimiento de un Mecanismo de Diálogo Estratégico para la Cooperación y la Coordinación Económica entre el Gobierno de la República Argentina y el Gobierno de la República Popular China*, suscripto el 5 de septiembre de 2013

Que las autoridades ministeriales de ambos países han mantenido estrechos intercambios de coordinación, teniendo en cuenta las pautas del mecanismo de Diálogo Estratégico para la Cooperación y Coordinación Económica entre los gobiernos de la República Argentina y la República Popular China (en adelante, el "DECCE"), han organizado *road shows* conjuntos para presentar proyectos de infraestructura de relevancia, y han celebrado acuerdos relacionados con la expansión y el fortalecimiento de la cooperación bilateral económica y técnica y el desarrollo conjunto de un marco para la cooperación en materia de inversión industrial entre ambos países;

Que las Partes son conscientes de la necesidad de tener en cuenta los principios de solidaridad, reciprocidad y complementariedad, respeto mutuo y soberanía territorial, con el fin de fortalecer la relación económica bilateral entre las partes; y

Que las Partes reconocen el deseo mutuo de fortalecer su relación de cooperación;

POR LO TANTO, las Partes han acordado celebrar el siguiente Convenio Complementario de Cooperación en materia de Inversión Industrial entre el Gobierno de la República Argentina y el Gobierno de la República Popular China, en línea con el Convenio Marco:

Artículo 1
Objetivos generales

Los objetivos del presente Convenio Complementario son:

1. Planear, diseñar y promover vigorosamente la cooperación en materia de inversión industrial entre los dos países para lograr la integración industrial en el mediano plazo (cinco años), con el objeto de incrementar el valor agregado en los sectores exportadores, a fin de promover el equilibrio dinámico en la relación económica bilateral, de manera tal de implementar los importantes convenios concluidos por los Presidentes de ambos países.

2. Fortalecer la cooperación en materia de inversión industrial en línea con las prioridades de desarrollo económico y los planes de reestructuración industrial de ambos países, crear más oportunidades de trabajo e impulsar los avances tecnológicos, así como crear condiciones favorables para que China lleve a cabo sus estrategias, entre ellas, Impulsar el Desarrollo con Innovación y Promover un Nuevo Sistema de Economía Abierta, y para que la Argentina avance en la consolidación de su proceso de crecimiento económico con inclusión social basado en la industrialización.

3. Crear un ambiente y condiciones favorables para que las empresas de ambos países puedan llevar a cabo una cooperación mutua, complementaria y beneficiosa para ambas partes en diversas áreas; ampliar la cooperación en materia de proyectos de inversión industrial de forma ordenada y gradual y con

prioridades adecuadas, sobre la base de la correcta implementación de los importantes proyectos ya existentes.

4. Realizar un seguimiento de la cooperación de conformidad con el *Plan de Acción Conjunta entre el Gobierno de la República Popular China y el Gobierno de la República Argentina.*

5. Enriquecer el contenido de la cooperación bilateral en materia económica y técnica, y de la asociación estratégica, y lograr el desarrollo económico y social de los dos países; beneficiar a ambos pueblos mediante el fortalecimiento de la cooperación en materia de inversión industrial.

Artículo 2
Áreas prioritarias

Las Partes reconocen que tanto Argentina como China son países en desarrollo y economías de mercados emergentes; que ambos países enfrentan importantes desafíos en cuanto a transformación económica, modernización de la industria, mejora del bienestar de la población y logro de un desarrollo económico y social sostenible; y que ambos países se complementan en materia de dotación de recursos naturales, estructura industrial, finanzas y tecnología, lo cual constituye una base sólida para la cooperación en materia de inversión industrial. Sobre estas premisas, las Partes han identificado áreas prioritarias para la cooperación en materia de inversión industrial, incluidas, entre otras, las siguientes:

1. Energía
Las Partes facilitarán la actividad de las empresas de ambos países para el desarrollo de la cooperación en materia de inversiones en áreas como exploración y desarrollo de petróleo y gas, recuperación mejorada, refinería, transporte y ventas, así como energía nuclear, hidroeléctrica, eólica y solar, las redes eléctricas, biocombustibles y carbón limpio. Las Partes emprenderán esfuerzos conjuntos para acelerar el desarrollo de energías limpias y mejorar la eficiencia energética, así como para promover la cooperación en la fabricación de equipamiento energético.

2. Minerales
Las Partes promoverán la cooperación entre empresas de ambos países en materia de exploración y desarrollo minero en áreas con potencial de desarrollo, llevarán a cabo proyectos de cooperación en materia de industrialización e inversión en recursos mineros, incluidos hierro, litio y cobre. Asimismo, las Partes promoverán el aumento del valor agregado de los productos en todas las etapas, incluidas la producción, fundición, purificación y fabricación.

3. Manufacturas

Las Partes promoverán la cooperación entre las empresas de ambos países en materia de inversiones en industrias y proyectos de modernización industrial que promuevan la incorporación de contenido local a la producción. Dicha cooperación se centrará, entre otras, en las siguientes áreas: hierro y acero, productos de aluminio, placas de cemento y de vidrio; automóviles y autopartes; equipamiento ferroviario; medicamentos; industria plástica; industria electrónica y de tecnologías de la información y la comunicación, incluida la fabricación de equipos de telecomunicaciones, computadoras, equipos médicos y otros equipos electrónicos; industrias livianas, incluida la textil, de vestimenta, calzado y electrodomésticos.

4. Agricultura, logística y distribución de productos agropecuarios y áreas relacionadas

Las Partes facilitarán la cooperación entre las empresas de ambos países en materia de inversión en agricultura, logística y distribución de productos agropecuarios y áreas relacionadas con el objetivo de promover la modernización de la agricultura y el desarrollo de la cadena industrial de los productos agrícolas, a fin de garantizar la seguridad alimentaria y la exportación de productos agropecuarios de alto valor agregado. La cooperación se focalizará, entre otras, en las siguientes áreas: actividades agropecuarias; biotecnología agrícola; cultivo de variedades de semillas de buena calidad; procesamiento y producción de productos agrícolas; productos pesqueros y ganaderos; productos silvícolas, cereales y aceites; construcción y operación de infraestructuras, incluido el almacenamiento de granos, transporte y logística; e inspección y pruebas de calidad.

5. Sistemas de apoyo

Las Partes impulsarán a las empresas de ambos países a fortalecer la cooperación en áreas de instalación de laboratorios de Investigación y Desarrollo (I+D), centros de diseño, de ventas, de soporte técnico y de establecimiento de sistemas de servicios, con el objetivo de apoyar y promover la cooperación en materia de inversión industrial entre los dos países.

Las Partes considerarán y analizarán la instalación de parques industriales para promover la cooperación industrial entre los dos países, compartir experiencias en el planeamiento, la construcción y la administración de parques industriales, y apoyar a empresas de los dos países, con el objetivo de alcanzar un desarrollo común a través del establecimiento de lazos más estrechos y de una mayor integración en toda la cadena de valor industrial.

6. Otras áreas

Las partes acuerdan comunicarse e intercambiar ideas sobre cooperación en materia de inversión industrial en otras áreas de interés común, así como promover la cooperación en proyectos concretos.

7. Proyectos prioritarios

Las Partes se comprometen a intercambiar proyectos prioritarios entre las autoridades correspondientes de conformidad con el Artículo 4, una vez suscrito el Convenio Complementario, con el objetivo de elaborar una lista de proyectos prioritarios de cooperación en materia de inversión industrial que serán implementados dentro de los próximos cinco años en las áreas prioritarias.

Artículo 3
Organización e implementación

1 Las Partes coordinarán, promocionarán e implementarán la cooperación a través del DECCE en todas las áreas relevantes, dentro del marco del *Convenio de Cooperación Económica e Inversiones entre el Gobierno de la República Argentina y el Gobierno de la República Popular China* y el *Memorándum de Entendimiento sobre el Establecimiento de un Mecanismo de Diálogo Estratégico para la Cooperación y la Coordinación Económica entre el Gobierno de la República Argentina y el Gobierno de la República Popular China.*

2. Las Partes promocionarán la cooperación en materia de inversión industrial mediante las siguientes actividades:

1) Intercambio de políticas industriales y de inversión entre los dos países, estudio de modalidades para crear un entorno de políticas favorables y condiciones para que las empresas de ambos países lleven a cabo la cooperación en materia de inversión industrial, y facilitación de la inversión en la mayor medida posible;

2) Investigación sobre inversión industrial y formulación de recomendaciones sobre políticas de promoción de cooperación, con el objetivo de regular y guiar la cooperación entre empresas de ambos países; adaptación de la lista de proyectos prioritarios de cooperación en materia de inversión industrial en función del desarrollo de las relaciones bilaterales, los cambios de las necesidades de cooperación y otros factores;

3) Creación de pautas para la cooperación en materia de inversión industrial, que proveerán servicios de información para empresas involucradas en la cooperación y guiarán a las empresas respecto de la forma de llevar a cabo

actividades comerciales en cumplimiento de la ley y de conformidad con la respectiva responsabilidad social empresaria, según corresponda;

4) Organización de actividades de promoción de inversiones como *road shows* para crear plataformas para la cooperación industrial y facilitar el intercambio de información, buscando la coincidencia de proyectos y el intercambio de buenas prácticas;

5) Instar a entidades financieras, institutos de investigación, organismos intermediarios y organizaciones de capacitación y de otra índole de ambos países para proveer financiamiento, recursos humanos y de investigación, y otros servicios, así como apoyo para la cooperación en materia de inversión entre empresas de los dos países;

6) Implementar la colaboración a nivel gubernamental y brindar asistencia a la esfera empresarial a fin de facilitar la identificación de potenciales socios en los respectivos Estados Parte. Sobre la base del principio de la operación empresarial y la orientación gubernamental, las empresas serán los principales actores de cooperación en materia de inversión.

ARTICULO 4
Autoridades competentes

Las partes facultan a las siguientes autoridades a aprobar, en el marco del DECCE, los programas, planes, convenios y proyectos especiales de cooperación que resulten necesarios para la ejecución del presente Convenio Complementario: en el caso de la Argentina, al Ministerio de Economía y Finanzas Públicas y, en el caso de China, a la Comisión Nacional de Desarrollo y Reforma.

Artículo 5
Entrada en vigor y terminación

1. El presente Convenio Complementario entrará en vigor en la fecha en que entre en vigor el Convenio Marco.

2. El presente Convenio Complementario permanecerá en vigencia mientras el Convenio Marco se encuentre en vigencia, salvo que alguna de las Partes notifique a la otra por escrito de su voluntad de finalizar el presente Convenio en

cualquier momento. La denuncia del Convenio será efectiva 6 (seis) meses luego de cursada la notificación a la Parte correspondiente.

3. La terminación de este Convenio no afectará la ejecución de ninguno de los proyectos en curso, que serán completados según el cronograma estipulado.

Se firma el presente Convenio Complementario en Buenos Aires, el 18 de julio de 2014, en dos ejemplares originales, cada uno de ellos en los idiomas español, chino e inglés, siendo todos los textos igualmente auténticos. En caso de divergencia de interpretación, prevalecerá la versión en inglés.

POR
EL GOBIERNO DE
LA REPÚBLICA ARGENTINA

POR
EL GOBIERNO DE
LA REPÚBLICA POPULAR CHINA

[TRANSLATION – TRADUCTION]

ACCORD COMPLÉMENTAIRE DE COOPÉRATION EN MATIÈRE D'INVESTISSEMENT INDUSTRIEL ENTRE LE GOUVERNEMENT DE LA RÉPUBLIQUE ARGENTINE ET LE GOUVERNEMENT DE LA RÉPUBLIQUE POPULAIRE DE CHINE

Le Gouvernement de la République argentine et le Gouvernement de la République Populaire de Chine (ci-après dénommés les « Parties »),

Considérant que les Parties ont l'intention de développer et d'intensifier les relations économiques bilatérales entre elles, en se fondant sur les principes de réciprocité et d'avantage mutuel,

Considérant l'Accord-cadre de coopération en matière économique et d'investissement conclu entre le Gouvernement de la République argentine et le Gouvernement de la République populaire de Chine (ci-après dénommé l'« Accord-cadre »), dans le cadre duquel le présent Accord est conclu, qui exprime les efforts volontaires des deux Gouvernements visant à intensifier et à renforcer les liens entre les deux pays et leurs peuples,

Considérant que les Parties prennent en considération les accords bilatéraux de coopération économique conclus entre elles qui sont actuellement en vigueur, en particulier le Mémorandum d'accord sur la création d'un mécanisme de dialogue stratégique pour la coopération et la coordination économiques entre le Gouvernement de la République argentine et le Gouvernement de la République populaire de Chine signé le 5 septembre 2013,

Considérant que les autorités ministérielles des deux pays ont maintenu d'étroits échanges de coordination, en tenant compte des lignes directrices du mécanisme de dialogue stratégique pour la coopération et la coordination économiques entre les Gouvernements de la République argentine et de la République populaire de Chine (ci-après dénommé « mécanisme de dialogue stratégique »), organisé des tournées de promotion conjointes pour présenter d'importants projets d'infrastructure et conclu des accords relatifs à l'expansion et au renforcement de la coopération économique et technique bilatérale et à l'élaboration conjointe d'un cadre de coopération en matière d'investissement industriel entre les deux pays,

Considérant que les Parties sont conscientes de la nécessité de prendre en compte les principes de solidarité, de réciprocité et de complémentarité, de respect mutuel et de souveraineté territoriale aux fins du renforcement de la relation économique bilatérale entre elles,

Considérant que les Parties reconnaissent leur volonté mutuelle de renforcer leurs relations de coopération,

Par conséquent, les Parties sont convenues de conclure le présent Accord complémentaire de coopération en matière d'investissement industriel entre le Gouvernement de la République argentine et le Gouvernement de la République populaire de Chine au titre de l'Accord-cadre, selon les termes suivants :

Article premier. Objectifs généraux

Les objectifs du présent Accord complémentaire sont les suivants :

1. Planifier, concevoir et encourager vivement la coopération en matière d'investissement industriel entre les deux pays afin de parvenir à une intégration industrielle à moyen terme (au bout de cinq ans) dans le but d'accroître la valeur ajoutée dans les secteurs de l'exportation en vue de promouvoir l'équilibre dynamique de la relation économique bilatérale aux fins de la mise en œuvre des accords importants conclus par les Présidents des deux pays ;

2. Renforcer la coopération en matière d'investissement industriel conformément aux priorités de développement économique et aux programmes de restructuration industrielle des deux pays ; créer davantage d'opportunités d'emploi et stimuler les avancées technologiques, et créer des conditions favorables afin de donner à la Chine les moyens de mener à bien ses stratégies, y compris, par exemple, le pilotage du développement par l'innovation et la promotion d'un nouveau système d'économie ouverte, et à l'Argentine les moyens de progresser dans la consolidation de son processus de croissance économique avec une inclusion sociale basée sur l'industrialisation ;

3. Créer un environnement et des conditions favorables afin que les entreprises des deux pays puissent instaurer une coopération mutuelle, complémentaire et bénéfique dans différents domaines ; étendre la coopération en matière de projets d'investissement industriel de manière ordonnée et progressive en définissant des priorités appropriées, sur la base de la mise en œuvre convenable des projets majeurs existants ;

4. Effectuer un suivi de la coopération conformément au Plan d'action commun entre le Gouvernement de la République argentine et le Gouvernement de la République populaire de Chine ;

5. Enrichir le contenu de la coopération économique et technique bilatérale et du partenariat stratégique et réussir le développement social et économique des deux pays ; renforcer la coopération en matière d'investissement industriel au profit des deux pays.

Article 2. Domaines prioritaires

Les Parties reconnaissent que l'Argentine et la Chine sont des pays en développement et des économies de marché émergentes ; que les deux pays sont confrontés à des défis majeurs en matière de transformation économique, de modernisation de l'industrie, d'amélioration du bien-être de la population et de réalisation d'un développement économique et social durable ; que les deux pays se complètent en termes de ressources naturelles, de structure industrielle, de finances et de technologie, ce qui constitue une base solide pour la coopération en matière d'investissement industriel. Sur la base de ce qui précède, les Parties ont recensé des domaines prioritaires pour la coopération en matière d'investissement industriel, qui comprennent notamment, mais sans s'y limiter :

1. L'énergie

Les Parties favorisent la coopération en matière d'investissement entre les entreprises des deux pays dans des domaines tels que l'exploration et l'exploitation du pétrole et du gaz, la récupération assistée, le raffinage, le transport et la vente, ainsi que l'énergie nucléaire, l'hydroélectricité, l'énergie éolienne, l'énergie solaire, les réseaux électriques et le charbon propre. Les Parties déploient des efforts conjoints visant à accélérer le développement des énergies propres et à améliorer le rendement énergétique, ainsi qu'à promouvoir la coopération dans le domaine de la fabrication d'équipements d'énergie.

2. Les minéraux

Les Parties encouragent la coopération entre les entreprises des deux pays en matière d'exploration et d'exploitation minières dans les zones présentant un potentiel de développement, ainsi que la réalisation de projets d'industrialisation et de coopération en matière d'investissement liés aux ressources minérales, notamment le fer, le lithium et le cuivre ; en outre, les Parties encouragent l'augmentation de la valeur ajoutée des produits à tous les stades, notamment la production, la fusion, la purification et la fabrication.

3. Les produits finis

Les Parties encouragent la coopération en matière d'investissement entre les entreprises des deux pays autour des industries et des projets de modernisation industrielle qui favorisent l'intégration de contenu local dans la fabrication. Cette coopération devra s'intéresser, entre autres, aux domaines suivants : fer et acier, produits en aluminium, ciment et verres à plaque, automobiles et pièces détachées, matériel ferroviaire, médicaments, industrie plastique, électronique, technologie de l'information et secteurs des communications, notamment la fabrication d'équipements de télécommunication, d'ordinateurs, d'équipements médicaux et d'autres équipements électroniques, industries légères, notamment les textiles, les vêtements, les chaussures et les appareils ménagers.

4. L'agriculture, la logistique et la distribution de produits agricoles et les domaines connexes

Les Parties favorisent la coopération en matière d'investissement entre les entreprises des deux pays dans le domaine de l'agriculture, de la logistique et de la distribution des produits agricoles et dans des domaines connexes en vue de promouvoir la modernisation de l'agriculture et le développement des chaînes industrielles de produits agricoles afin de garantir la sécurité sanitaire des aliments et l'exportation de produits agricoles à forte valeur ajoutée. Cette coopération s'intéresse, entre autres, aux domaines suivants : agriculture, biotechnologie agricole, culture de bonnes variétés de semences, transformation et production de produits agricoles, produits de la pêche et de l'élevage, produits de la sylviculture, céréales et huiles, construction et exploitation d'infrastructures, notamment le stockage des céréales, le transport et la logistique, l'inspection et les tests qualité.

5. Les systèmes d'accompagnement

Les Parties encouragent les entreprises des deux pays à renforcer la coopération dans les domaines liés à la création de laboratoires de recherche-développement, de centres de conception, de vente et d'assistance technique et à la mise en place de dispositifs de services destinés à soutenir et à promouvoir la coopération en matière d'investissement industriel entre les deux pays.

Les Parties envisagent la création de parcs industriels et en débattent en vue de promouvoir la coopération industrielle entre les deux pays, de partager leurs expériences en matière de planification, de construction et de gestion de parcs industriels et d'aider les entreprises des deux pays à parvenir à un développement commun en tissant des liens plus étroits et en intensifiant l'intégration tout au long de la chaîne de valeur industrielle.

6. D'autres domaines

Les Parties conviennent de communiquer et d'échanger des idées sur la coopération en matière d'investissement industriel dans d'autres domaines d'intérêt commun et de promouvoir la coopération dans le cadre de projets concrets.

7. Les domaines prioritaires

Les Parties conviennent d'échanger les projets prioritaires avec l'autorité compétente conformément à l'article 4, une fois l'Accord complémentaire signé, en vue de dresser une liste des projets prioritaires de coopération en matière d'investissement industriel à mettre en œuvre au cours des cinq prochaines années dans les domaines prioritaires.

Article 3. Organisation et mise en œuvre

1. Les Parties coordonnent, encouragent et mettent en œuvre la coopération par l'intermédiaire du mécanisme de dialogue stratégique dans tous les domaines pertinents de l'Accord-cadre de coopération en matière économique et d'investissement entre le Gouvernement de la République argentine et le Gouvernement de la République populaire de Chine et du Mémorandum d'accord sur la création d'un mécanisme de dialogue stratégique pour la coopération et la coordination économiques entre le Gouvernement de la République argentine et le Gouvernement de la République populaire de Chine.

2. Les Parties encouragent la coopération en matière d'investissement industriel par l'entremise des activités suivantes :

1) L'échange de politiques industrielles et d'investissement entre les deux pays, le recensement des moyens de créer un environnement politique et des conditions favorables pour que les entreprises des deux pays puissent mener une coopération en matière d'investissement industriel, et la facilitation des investissements dans toute la mesure du possible ;

2) La conduite de recherches sur les investissements industriels et la formulation de recommandations sur les politiques de promotion de la coopération en vue de réglementer et d'orienter la coopération entre les entreprises des deux pays ; l'adaptation de la liste des projets de coopération prioritaires en matière d'investissement industriel au développement des relations bilatérales, à l'évolution des besoins de coopération et à d'autres facteurs ;

3) La création de lignes directrices pour la coopération en matière d'investissement industriel sur la base desquelles des services d'information aux entreprises engagées dans la coopération seront mis en place, et l'instruction des entreprises sur la manière de faire des affaires conformément à la législation et à assurer la responsabilité sociale des entreprises le cas échéant ;

4) L'organisation d'activités de promotion de l'investissement, telles que des tournées de présentation de projets en vue de créer des plateformes de coopération industrielle et de faciliter l'échange de renseignements, la recherche de correspondances entre projets et le partage des meilleures pratiques ;

5) L'incitation des organismes de financement, des instituts de recherche, des organismes intermédiaires et des instituts de formation et autres organisations des deux pays à fournir le financement, l'effort de recherche et les ressources humaines,

ainsi que d'autres services, et à soutenir la coopération en matière d'investissement entre les entreprises des deux pays ;

6) L'introduction de la collaboration au niveau gouvernemental et l'orientation et l'accompagnement des entreprises dans le recensement de partenaires potentiels dans le pays de l'autre Partie ; conformément au principe de directives gouvernementales et d'exploitation commerciale, les entreprises sont les principaux acteurs de la coopération en matière d'investissement.

Article 4. Autorités compétentes

Les Parties conviennent que les autorités suivantes approuvent les programmes, les plans, les accords et les projets spéciaux de coopération pouvant être utiles à l'exécution du présent Accord complémentaire, au titre du mécanisme de dialogue stratégique : pour l'Argentine, le Ministère de l'économie et des finances publiques, et pour la Chine, la Commission nationale du développement et de la réforme.

Article 5. Entrée en vigueur et dénonciation

1. Le présent Accord complémentaire entre en vigueur à la date de l'entrée en vigueur de l'Accord-cadre.

2. Le présent Accord complémentaire reste en vigueur aussi longtemps que l'Accord-cadre est en vigueur, sauf si l'une des Parties dénonce le présent Accord complémentaire à tout moment par notification écrite adressée à l'autre Partie. La dénonciation prend effet six mois après la notification de l'autre Partie.

3. La dénonciation du présent Accord complémentaire n'affecte pas l'exécution de tout projet en cours qui doit être achevé conformément au calendrier établi.

SIGNÉ à Buenos Aires, le 18 juillet 2014, en deux exemplaires, en langues espagnole, chinoise et anglaise, tous les textes faisant également foi. En cas de divergence d'interprétation, le texte anglais prévaut.

Pour le Gouvernement de la République argentine :

[SIGNÉ]

Pour le Gouvernement de la République populaire de Chine :

[SIGNÉ]

COMPLEMENTARY AGREEMENT FOR INFRASTRUCTURE COOPERATION BETWEEN THE GOVERNMENT OF THE ARGENTINE REPUBLIC AND THE GOVERNMENT OF THE PEOPLE'S REPUBLIC OF CHINA. BUENOS AIRES, 18 JULY 2014

Entry into force: 7 November 2016, in accordance with article 8

Authentic texts: Chinese, English and Spanish

Registration with the Secretariat of the United Nations: Argentina, 14 August 2017

ACCORD COMPLÉMENTAIRE DE COOPÉRATION EN MATIÈRE D'INFRASTRUCTURES ENTRE LE GOUVERNEMENT DE LA RÉPUBLIQUE ARGENTINE ET LE GOUVERNEMENT DE LA RÉPUBLIQUE POPULAIRE DE CHINE. BUENOS AIRES, 18 JUILLET 2014

Entrée en vigueur : 7 novembre 2016, conformément à l'article 8

Textes authentiques : chinois, anglais et espagnol

Enregistrement auprès du Secrétariat de l'Organisation des Nations Unies : Argentine, 14 août 2017

[TEXT IN CHINESE – TEXTE EN CHINOIS]

阿根廷共和国政府与中华人民共和国政府
关于基础设施领域合作的补充协议

阿根廷共和国政府与中华人民共和国政府（下称“双方”），

希望通过联合实施经济项目，在新的合作愿景框架下加强双边关系；

鉴于双方达成的《阿根廷共和国政府与中华人民共和国政府与经济和投资合作框架协议》（下称“框架协议”，本协议在其下达成）表明两国政府愿为加强两国及两国人民联系做出努力；

鉴于开展基础设施工程建设有助于提高系统性竞争力，完善国家的整体生产体系，提升出口能力，为平衡双边贸易关系创造更好条件；

鉴于根据阿根廷共和国政府与中华人民共和国政府之间经济合作与协调战略对话机制（下称“阿中经济对话机制”）的指导原则，两国有关部门保持了密切交流和协调，联合组织推介重大基础设施项目的活动，并就扩展和加强经济技术合作、联合制定一份阿根廷与中国之间的公共基础设施合作框架达成一致；

鉴此，基于上述前提，双方就《框架协议》下《阿根廷共和国政府与中华人民共和国政府关于基础设施领域合作的补充协议》达成一致：

第一条 总体目标

双方将促进合作，在阿根廷国内立法和本补充协议条款基础上，共同制定一份关于与阿根廷产业发展关键领域直接相关的公共基础设施整体投资合作计划，包括但不限于：能源生产、电信、陆地运输以及港口基础设施建设等。

双方同意为两国企业在各领域开展互补互利的合作创造有利环境和合适条件，在落实好现有重大项目的基础上，突出重点、积极有序地扩大基础设施投资与合作。

第二条 合作原则

双方同意，根据优势互补、平等互利、共同发展的总体原则，考虑到双方各自具体情况，推动双边经济关系实现更大的均衡，并在符合各自国内法律法规、发展规划和经济政策的前提下，促进两国基础设施合作。

双方将发挥政府、企业、金融机构、研究机构等各方面积极性推动合作。根据政府引导、商业运作的原则，企业将作为以市场为导向的合作的主体。

双方将鼓励两国金融机构基于市场运作及对项目的谨慎评估，对项目合作提供优惠融资和多样化的金融服务。另外，双方将鼓励研究机构、培训机构等发挥自身优势参与合作。

基础设施建设工程的实施和执行应尽量有利于吸纳阿根廷本土员工、资本货物和零部件。

第三条 重点领域

双方同意合作的重点领域为能源生产、电信、陆地运输以及港口基础设施建设等方面的项目。

双方同意，在本补充协议签署后，根据第五条由双方实施部门就重点项目进行交流，并拟形成一份未来 5 年重点领域的基础设施合作重点项目清单。

第四条 组织实施

本补充协议下的合作应通过阿中经济对话机制，以下列方式进行：

中华人民共和国政府将通过以下机构推动中国的公有和民营企业参与阿根廷的基础设施建设项目：

（一）中国国家发展和改革委员会将会同有关部门为中方有关企业提供官方支持。

（二）中国有关银行和其他中国金融机构将为本补充协议所包括的项目的开展提供融资选项。

（三）中国出口信用保险公司将根据其可用保险额度和国家境外投资保险相关法律规定，在与阿根廷方面共同努力尽可能优化阿根廷主权信用风险评级的基础上，积极为中国居民或法人对阿根廷的投融资提供适用的保险支持。

阿根廷共和国政府可做到：

（一）对包含在本补充协议框架内的阿根廷公共部门项目，依据《框架协议》第五条进行授标。

（二）促进中国和阿根廷本地企业之间的合作伙伴关系，开展技术转让，雇佣本地员工。

与本补充协议相关的活动，可通过两国有关公共或民营团体、机构和组织之间的合同、安排或项目实施。在任何情况下，两国有关机构达成的这些文件一旦被两国相关机关批准，应包括详细的工作计划、资金接收和使用流程和其他条款。

第五条 实施机构

双方同意由阿方的经济和公共财政部与中方的国家发展和改革委员会，在阿中经济对话机制的框架下，商议并达成执行本补充协议所需的安排、计划、协议和特别合作项目。

第六条 便利条件

双方应根据各自国内立法相互为赴各自国家开展协议中活动的对方人员提供出入境和逗留的便利。

第七条 修订

经双方同意，可对本补充协议进行修改，所做修订应根据第八条规定生效。

第八条 生效和终止

一、框架协议生效时，本补充协议将同时生效。

二、在框架协议的有效期内，本补充协议一直有效，除非有一方通过书面方式通知另一方终止本补充协议。协议终止将于书面通知发出的六个月后生效。

三、除非双方另有约定，否则终止本补充协议不对正在执行的项目、安排和活动造成影响。

本补充协议于二 O 一四年七月十八日在布宜诺斯艾利斯签订，一式两份，每份都用中文、英文和西班牙文写成，三种文本同等作准。如对文本解释发生分歧，以英文文本为准。

阿根廷共和国政府

代表

中华人民共和国政府

代表

[TEXT IN ENGLISH – TEXTE EN ANGLAIS]

COMPLEMENTARY AGREEMENT FOR INFRAESTRUCTURE COOPERATION BETWEEN THE GOVERNMENT OF THE ARGENTINE REPUBLIC AND THE GOVERNMENT OF THE PEOPLE'S REPUBLIC OF CHINA

The Government of the Argentine Republic and the Government of the People's Republic of China (hereinafter referred to as the "Parties")

WHEREAS the Parties wish to consolidate their bilateral relations by boosting them within the framework of a new vision of cooperation through joint economic projects;

WHEREAS the *Framework Agreement for Economic and Investment Cooperation* entered into by the Government of the Argentine Republic and the Government of the People's Republic of China (hereinafter "the Framework Agreement"), under which framework the present Agreement is concluded, expresses the willing efforts of both governments to intensify and strengthen the links between both countries and their people;

WHEREAS the development of infrastructure works contributes to increasing systemic competitiveness, hence leading to a more integrated productive machine, with greater export capacity and better conditions for balancing bilateral trade relations;

WHEREAS the ministerial authorities of both countries have maintained close coordination exchanges, taking into account the guidelines of the mechanism for the Strategic Dialogue for Economic Cooperation and Coordination between governments of the People's Republic of China and the Argentine Republic (hereinafter referred to as "SDECC"), have organized joint road shows to present important infrastructure projects and have entered into agreements related to the expansion and strengthening of economic and technical bilateral cooperation and the joint development of a framework for public infrastructure cooperation between Argentina and China.

THEREFORE, based on the abovementioned premises, the Parties have AGREED to enter into this *Complementary Agreement for Infrastructure Cooperation between the Government of the Argentine Republic and the Government of the People's Republic of China* within *the Framework Agreement* under the following terms:

ARTICLE 1
General objectives

The Parties shall promote the cooperation for the joint development of an Integrated Investment Cooperation Plan in Public Infrastructure directed to key areas for Argentina's industrial development, including, but not limited to, energy generation, telecommunications, land transport, and port infrastructure, in accordance with Argentina's domestic law and the provisions of this Agreement.

The Parties agree to create favorable environment and suitable conditions so that enterprises of both countries may carry out mutual, complementary and beneficial cooperation in different areas; expand infrastructure project investment and cooperation in an orderly fashion and with appropriate priorities, on the basis of the correct implementation of the important existing projects.

ARTICLE 2
Principles of cooperation

The Parties agree to follow the general principles of complementing each Party's advantages, mutual benefits and common development, considering each Party's specifities so as to achieve greater equilibrium in the bilateral economic relation; and to promote infrastructure cooperation between both countries, in accordance with their domestic laws and regulations and the development plans and economic policies of both countries.

The Parties shall take advantage of the initiatives of the different players, such as government instrumentalities, companies, financial institutions and research institutes in order to boost cooperation. In accordance with the principle of government guidance and business operation, enterprises shall be the major players in market-oriented cooperation.

The Parties shall encourage financial institutions to provide concessional financing and diversified financial services for project cooperation on the basis of market operation and cautious project assessment. Furthermore, the Parties shall encourage research institutes, training and other organizations to participate in cooperation by bringing their advantages into full play.

The particular conditions of application and execution of the infrastructure works shall attempt to favor the incorporation of employees, capital goods and components of local origin.

ARTICLE 3
Priority areas

The Parties agree that the cooperation priority shall be oriented to projects related to energy generation, telecommunications, land transport and port infrastructure, among others.

The Parties agree to exchange priority projects to the applicable authority in accordance with the Article 5, once the Complementary Agreement is signed, with a view to forming a list of priority projects of infrastructure cooperation to be implemented in the next five years in the priority areas.

ARTICLE 4
Organization and implementation

Cooperation under this Complementary Agreement shall be carried out through the SDECC in the following forms:

The Government of the People's Republic of China shall promote the participation of public and private Chinese enterprises in Argentina's infrastructure projects through:

- The National Development and Reform Commission and other relevant government agencies, which shall provide formal support to the interested Chinese enterprises.
- Chinese banks and other Chinese financial institutions, which shall provide financing options for the development of the projects included in this Complementary Agreement.
- SINOSURE, according to its availability and state regulations regarding overseas investment insurance, shall actively provide the applicable credit insurance facilities to Argentina concerning investment financing by individuals or legal entities residing in China, pursuant to the joint efforts with Argentina to achieve the most advantageous rating possible in terms of Sovereign risk.

The Government of the Argentine Republic may:

- Award procurement contracts related to Argentina's public sector projects, within the framework of this Complementary Agreement in accordance with Article 5 of the Framework Agreement.

- Promote the partnership between Chinese and local enterprises, favoring technology transfer and employment for local people.

The different activities related to this Agreement may be carried out through contracts, programs or projects to be developed by bodies, groups, institutions, or organizations of both countries, whether public or private. In any case, these documents shall contain a detail of the work plan, the procedure for use of the funds and other terms, once they have been agreed to by all appropriate authorities.

ARTICLE 5
Applicable authorities

The Parties agree that the following authorities shall approve the programs, plans, agreements and special cooperation projects as may be convenient to execute this Complementary Agreement, under the framework of the SDECC: in the case of Argentina, the Ministry of Economy and Public Finances, and in the case of China, the National Development and Reform Commission.

ARTICLE 6
Facilities

The Parties shall provide each other with mutual assistance to facilitate the entry, stay and exit from the country of the people authorized to carry out activities under this Agreement, pursuant to the respective domestic law of the each country.

ARTICLE 7
Amendments

This Complementary Agreement may be amended by mutual consent of the Parties.

ARTICLE 8
Entry into force and termination

This Complementary Agreement shall enter into force simultaneously with the Framework Agreement.

This Complementary Agreement shall remain in force as long as the Framework Agreement is in force unless either party denounces this Complementary Agreement at any time through written notice to the other Party. The denunciation shall be effective six (6) months after notice thereof is given to the other Party.

The termination of this Complementary Agreement shall not affect the application of ongoing programs, projects and activities, unless otherwise agreed by the Parties.

This Complementary Agreement is signed in Buenos Aires, on 18 July 2014 in two counterparts in the Spanish, Chinese and English languages, all texts being equally authentic. In the event of any divergence of interpretation, the English text shall prevail.

FOR THE GOVERNMENT OF THE ARGENTINE REPUBLIC	**FOR THE GOVERNMENT OF THE PEOPLE'S REPUBLIC OF CHINA**

[TEXT IN SPANISH – TEXTE EN ESPAGNOL]

CONVENIO COMPLEMENTARIO DE COOPERACIÓN EN MATERIA DE INFRAESTRUCTURA ENTRE EL GOBIERNO DE LA REPÚBLICA ARGENTINA Y EL GOBIERNO DE LA REPÚBLICA POPULAR CHINA

El Gobierno de la República Argentina y el Gobierno de la República Popular China (en adelante, "las Partes")

CONSIDERANDO:

Que las Partes desean consolidar sus relaciones bilaterales impulsándolas en el marco de una nueva visión de cooperación mediante proyectos económicos conjuntos;

Que el *Convenio Marco de Cooperación en materia Económica y de Inversiones*, suscripto por el Gobierno de la República Argentina y el Gobierno de la República Popular China (en adelante, "el Convenio Marco"), en cuyo marco se perfecciona el presente Convenio, expresa la voluntad de ambos gobiernos de intensificar y fortalecer los vínculos entre los dos países y sus pueblos;

Que el desarrollo de obras de infraestructura contribuye a incrementar la competitividad sistémica y, por lo tanto, conduce a un aparato productivo más integrado, con mayor capacidad exportadora y mejores condiciones para equilibrar las relaciones comerciales bilaterales;

Que las autoridades ministeriales de ambos países han mantenido estrechos intercambios de coordinación, teniendo en cuenta los lineamientos del Mecanismo de Diálogo Estratégico para la Cooperación y la Coordinación Económica entre los gobiernos de la República Popular China y la República Argentina (en adelante, "DECCE"), han organizado conjuntamente presentaciones de importantes proyectos de infraestructura y han celebrado acuerdos relativos a la expansión y profundización de la cooperación bilateral técnica y económica y al desarrollo conjunto de un marco para la cooperación en materia de infraestructura pública entre la República Argentina y la República Popular China.

POR LO TANTO, sobre la base de lo establecido precedentemente, las Partes CONVIENEN en celebrar el presente *Convenio Complementario de Cooperación en materia de Infraestructura entre el Gobierno de la República Argentina y el Gobierno de la República Popular China* dentro del *Convenio Marco* de conformidad con las siguientes cláusulas:

ARTÍCULO 1
Objetivos generales

Las Partes promoverán la cooperación para el desarrollo conjunto de un Plan de Cooperación Integrado en materia de Inversiones en Infraestructura Pública, destinado a áreas clave para el desarrollo industrial de la República Argentina, entre las que se incluyen la generación de energía, las telecomunicaciones, el transporte terrestre, y la infraestructura portuaria, conforme a la legislación interna argentina y las disposiciones del presente Convenio.

Las Partes acuerdan crear un entorno favorable y condiciones propicias a fin de que las empresas de ambos países puedan realizar acciones de cooperación mutua, complementaria y beneficiosa en diversas áreas; expandir de manera ordenada la inversión y la cooperación en proyectos de infraestructura, estableciendo prioridades adecuadas, sobre la base de la correcta implementación de los importantes proyectos ya existentes.

ARTÍCULO 2
Principios de cooperación

Las Partes se comprometen a seguir los principios generales relativos a la complementariedad de las ventajas de cada una, el beneficio mutuo y el desarrollo común, considerando las especificidades de cada una de las Partes de modo de lograr un mayor equilibrio en las relaciones económicas bilaterales; y a promover la cooperación en materia de infraestructura entre ambos países, de conformidad con sus leyes y reglamentaciones internas, así como con los planes de desarrollo y las políticas económicas de ambos países.

Las Partes aprovecharán las iniciativas de los diferentes actores, tales como organismos gubernamentales, empresas, entidades financieras e institutos de investigación, con el objeto de fomentar la cooperación. De acuerdo con el principio de orientación gubernamental y funcionamiento empresarial, las empresas serán los actores principales en la cooperación orientada al mercado.

Las Partes alentarán a las entidades financieras a brindar financiamiento concesional y servicios financieros diversificados para la cooperación en materia de proyectos sobre la base de las operaciones del mercado y una cautelosa evaluación de los proyectos. Asimismo, las Partes alentarán a los institutos de investigación, entidades de capacitación y a otras organizaciones a participar en la cooperación aprovechando sus ventajas al máximo.

Las condiciones particulares de aplicación y ejecución de las obras de infraestructura procurarán favorecer la incorporación de empleados, bienes de capital y componentes de origen local.

ARTÍCULO 3
Áreas prioritarias

Las Partes acuerdan que la prioridad en la cooperación se oriente a los proyectos relacionados con la generación de energía, las telecomunicaciones, el transporte terrestre y la infraestructura portuaria, entre otros.

Las Partes aceptan intercambiar proyectos prioritarios con las autoridades pertinentes de conformidad con el Artículo 5, una vez firmado el Convenio Complementario, con miras a confeccionar una lista de proyectos prioritarios sobre cooperación en materia de infraestructura, los que se implementarán durante los próximos cinco años en las áreas prioritarias.

ARTÍCULO 4
Organización e implementación

La cooperación en el marco del presente Convenio Complementario se llevará a cabo mediante el DECCE de las formas que se detallan a continuación.

El Gobierno de la República Popular China fomentará la participación de las empresas chinas públicas y privadas en los proyectos de infraestructura de la República Argentina mediante:

- La Comisión Nacional de Desarrollo y Reforma y otras dependencias gubernamentales pertinentes, que brindarán apoyo formal a las empresas chinas interesadas.
- Los bancos y otras entidades financieras de China, que brindarán opciones de financiamiento para el desarrollo de los proyectos incluidos en el presente Convenio Complementario.
- SINOSURE, de acuerdo con su disponibilidad y las reglamentaciones estatales sobre pólizas de seguro de inversión en el exterior, brindará activamente a la República Argentina los servicios de seguro de crédito relativos al financiamiento por parte de individuos o entidades financieras residentes en la República Popular China, de conformidad con los esfuerzos conjuntos con la República Argentina tendientes a lograr la calificación más ventajosa en materia de riesgo soberano.

El Gobierno de la República Argentina podrá:

- Adjudicar las contrataciones relacionadas con proyectos del sector público de la República Argentina en el marco del presente Convenio Complementario conforme al Artículo 5 del Convenio Marco.

- Promover la asociación de empresas chinas y argentinas, favoreciendo la transferencia de tecnología y el empleo a nivel local.

Las diversas actividades relacionadas con el presente Convenio podrán llevarse a cabo mediante contratos, programas o proyectos desarrollados por organismos, grupos, instituciones u organizaciones públicas o privadas de ambos países. En cualquier caso, los documentos en cuestión deberán especificar el plan de trabajo, el procedimiento para el uso de los fondos y otras disposiciones, una vez que hayan sido acordados por todas las autoridades competentes.

ARTÍCULO 5
Autoridades pertinentes

Las Partes acuerdan que los programas, planes, convenios y proyectos de cooperación especial deberán ser aprobados, según resulte conveniente a los fines de la ejecución del presente Convenio Complementario, en el marco del DECCE, por el Ministerio de Economía y Finanzas Públicas, en el caso de la República Argentina, y por la Comisión Nacional de Desarrollo y Reforma, en el caso de la República Popular China.

ARTÍCULO 6
Facilidades

Las Partes deberán brindarse asistencia mutua para facilitar el ingreso, la estadía y la salida del país de las personas autorizadas a llevar a cabo actividades en virtud del presente Convenio, en concordancia con la legislación interna de dicho país.

ARTÍCULO 7
Modificaciones

El presente Convenio podrá ser modificado de común acuerdo por las Partes.

ARTÍCULO 8
Entrada en vigencia y terminación

El presente Convenio Complementario entrará en vigencia simultáneamente con el Convenio Marco.

El presente Convenio permanecerá vigente durante el plazo de vigencia del Convenio Marco, a menos que una de las Partes denuncie el presente

Convenio Complementario mediante notificación escrita a la otra Parte. La denuncia surtirá efectos a los seis (6) meses de comunicada la otra Parte.

La terminación de este Convenio no afectará la implementación de programas, proyectos y actividades que se encuentren en curso, a menos que las Partes estipulen lo contrario.

Se suscribe el presente Convenio Complementario en Buenos Aires, el 18 de julio de 2014, por duplicado, en los idiomas español, chino e inglés, siendo todos los textos igualmente auténticos. En caso de divergencia en la interpretación, prevalecerá la versión en inglés.

POR **EL GOBIERNO DE** **LA REPÚBLICA ARGENTINA**	**POR** **EL GOBIERNO DE** **LA REPÚBLICA POPULAR CHINA**

[TRANSLATION – TRADUCTION]

ACCORD COMPLÉMENTAIRE DE COOPÉRATION EN MATIÈRE D'INFRASTRUCTURES ENTRE LE GOUVERNEMENT DE LA RÉPUBLIQUE ARGENTINE ET LE GOUVERNEMENT DE LA RÉPUBLIQUE POPULAIRE DE CHINE

Le Gouvernement de la République argentine et le Gouvernement de la République populaire de Chine (ci-après dénommés les « Parties »),

Attendu que les Parties souhaitent consolider leurs relations bilatérales en les dynamisant dans le cadre d'une nouvelle vision de la coopération à travers des projets économiques communs,

Attendu que l'Accord-cadre de coopération en matière économique et d'investissement entre le Gouvernement de la République argentine et le Gouvernement de la République populaire de Chine (ci-après dénommé l'« Accord-cadre »), dans le cadre duquel le présent Accord est conclu, exprime les efforts volontaires des deux Gouvernements visant à intensifier et à renforcer les liens entre les deux pays et leurs peuples,

Attendu que le développement des travaux d'infrastructure contribue à accroître la compétitivité systémique, ce qui conduit à une machine de production plus intégrée, avec une plus grande capacité d'exportation et de meilleures conditions pour équilibrer les relations commerciales bilatérales,

Attendu que les autorités ministérielles des deux pays ont maintenu d'étroits échanges de coordination, en tenant compte des lignes directrices du mécanisme de dialogue stratégique pour la coopération et la coordination économiques entre les Gouvernements de la République populaire de Chine et de la République argentine (ci-après dénommé « mécanisme de dialogue stratégique »), organisé des tournées de promotion conjointes pour présenter d'importants projets d'infrastructure et conclu des accords relatifs à l'expansion et au renforcement de la coopération économique et technique bilatérale et à l'élaboration conjointe d'un cadre de coopération en matière d'infrastructures publiques entre l'Argentine et la Chine,

Par conséquent, sur la base des prémisses susmentionnées, les Parties sont convenues de conclure le présent Accord complémentaire de coopération en matière d'infrastructures entre le Gouvernement de la République argentine et le Gouvernement de la République populaire de Chine au titre de l'Accord-cadre, selon les termes suivants :

Article premier. Objectifs généraux

Les Parties encouragent la coopération en vue de l'élaboration conjointe d'un plan de coopération intégré en matière d'investissements dans les infrastructures publiques axé sur des domaines clés pour le développement industriel de l'Argentine, y compris, mais sans s'y limiter, la production d'énergie, les télécommunications, les transports terrestres et les infrastructures portuaires, conformément au droit interne de l'Argentine et aux dispositions du présent Accord.

Les Parties conviennent de créer un environnement favorable et des conditions appropriées pour que les entreprises des deux pays puissent mener une coopération mutuelle, complémentaire et bénéfique dans différents domaines ; et d'accroître les investissements et la coopération en matière de projets d'infrastructure de manière ordonnée et avec des priorités appropriées, sur la base de la mise en œuvre correcte des projets existants importants.

Article 2. Principes de coopération

Les Parties conviennent de suivre les principes généraux de complémentarité des avantages de chaque Partie, de bénéfices mutuels et de développement commun, en tenant compte des spécificités de chaque Partie, afin de parvenir à un meilleur équilibre dans la relation économique bilatérale, et de promouvoir la coopération en matière d'infrastructures entre les deux pays, conformément à leurs lois et règlements internes ainsi qu'aux plans de développement et aux politiques économiques des deux pays.

Les Parties tirent parti des initiatives des différents acteurs, tels que les organes publics, les entreprises, les institutions financières et les instituts de recherche, afin de stimuler la coopération. Conformément au principe de l'orientation gouvernementale et de l'exploitation commerciale, les entreprises doivent être les principaux acteurs de la coopération axée sur le marché.

Les Parties encouragent les institutions financières à fournir des financements concessionnels et des services financiers diversifiés pour la coopération en matière de projets sur la base du fonctionnement du marché et d'une évaluation prudente des projets. En outre, les Parties encouragent les instituts de recherche, les organismes de formation et les autres organisations à participer à la coopération en mettant pleinement à profit leurs avantages.

Les conditions particulières d'application et d'exécution des travaux d'infrastructure ont pour but de favoriser l'incorporation de salariés, de biens d'équipement et de composants d'origine locale.

Article 3. Domaines prioritaires

Les Parties conviennent que la priorité de la coopération est orientée vers les projets liés à la production d'énergie, aux télécommunications, aux transports terrestres et aux infrastructures portuaires, entre autres.

Les Parties conviennent d'échanger les projets prioritaires avec l'autorité compétente conformément à l'article 5, une fois l'Accord complémentaire signé, en vue de dresser une liste des projets prioritaires de coopération en matière d'infrastructures à mettre en œuvre au cours des cinq prochaines années dans les domaines prioritaires.

Article 4. Organisation et mise en œuvre

La coopération au titre du présent Accord complémentaire s'effectue par l'intermédiaire du mécanisme de dialogue stratégique sous les formes suivantes :

Le Gouvernement de la République populaire de Chine encourage la participation des entreprises chinoises publiques et privées aux projets d'infrastructure de l'Argentine par l'intermédiaire :

- De la Commission nationale du développement et de la réforme et autres organismes publics concernés, qui apportent un soutien formel aux entreprises chinoises intéressées ;

- Des banques chinoises et autres institutions financières chinoises, qui fournissent des options de financement pour le développement des projets inclus dans le présent Accord complémentaire ;
- De SINOSURE, qui, en fonction de ses disponibilités et de la réglementation nationale concernant l'assurance des investissements à l'étranger, fournit activement les facilités d'assurance-crédit applicables à l'Argentine concernant le financement des investissements par des personnes physiques ou morales résidant en Chine, conformément aux efforts conjoints avec l'Argentine pour obtenir la notation la plus avantageuse possible eu égard au risque souverain.

Le Gouvernement de la République argentine peut :

- Attribuer les marchés relatifs aux projets du secteur public de l'Argentine, dans le cadre du présent Accord complémentaire, conformément à l'article 5 de l'Accord-cadre ;
- Promouvoir le partenariat entre les entreprises chinoises et locales, en favorisant le transfert de technologie et l'emploi pour la population locale.

Les différentes activités liées au présent Accord peuvent être réalisées grâce à des contrats, des programmes ou des projets qui seront développés par des organismes, des groupes, des institutions ou des organisations des deux pays, qu'ils soient publics ou privés. Dans tous les cas, ces documents contiennent des détails concernant le plan de travail, la procédure d'utilisation des fonds et d'autres conditions, une fois qu'ils ont été acceptés par toutes les autorités compétentes.

Article 5. Autorités compétentes

Les Parties conviennent que les autorités suivantes approuvent les programmes, les plans, les accords et les projets spéciaux de coopération qui peuvent être utiles à l'exécution du présent Accord complémentaire, dans le cadre du mécanisme de dialogue stratégique : dans le cas de l'Argentine, le Ministère de l'économie et des finances publiques, et dans le cas de la Chine, la Commission nationale du développement et de la réforme.

Article 6. Installations

Les Parties se prêtent mutuellement assistance pour faciliter l'entrée, le séjour et la sortie du pays des personnes autorisées à exercer des activités dans le cadre du présent Accord, en application du droit interne respectif de chaque pays.

Article 7. Amendements

Le présent Accord complémentaire peut être amendé par consentement mutuel des Parties.

Article 8. Entrée en vigueur et dénonciation

Le présent Accord complémentaire entre en vigueur en même temps que l'Accord-cadre.

Le présent Accord complémentaire reste en vigueur aussi longtemps que l'Accord-cadre est en vigueur, sauf si l'une des Parties dénonce le présent Accord complémentaire à tout moment par une notification écrite adressée à l'autre Partie. La dénonciation prend effet six mois après la notification de l'autre Partie.

La dénonciation du présent Accord complémentaire ne porte pas atteinte à la mise en œuvre des programmes, projets et activités en cours, sauf accord contraire des Parties.

SIGNÉ à Buenos Aires, le 18 juillet 2014, en deux exemplaires, en langues espagnole, chinoise et anglaise, tous les textes faisant également foi. En cas de divergence d'interprétation, le texte anglais prévaut.

Pour le Gouvernement de la République argentine :

[SIGNÉ]

Pour le Gouvernement de la République populaire de Chine :

[SIGNÉ]

No. 54629. Multilateral

ASEAN CONVENTION ON COUNTER TERRORISM. CEBU CITY, 13 JANUARY 2007 [*United Nations, Treaty Series, vol. 3199, I-54629.*]

RATIFICATION

Indonesia

Deposit of instrument with Secretary-General of the Association of Southeast Asian Nations: 14 May 2012

Date of effect: 14 May 2012

Registration with the Secretariat of the United Nations: Association of South-East Asian Nations, 17 August 2017

RATIFICATION

Lao People's Democratic Republic

Deposit of instrument with Secretary-General of the Association of Southeast Asian Nations: 28 November 2012

Date of effect: 28 November 2012

Registration with the Secretariat of the United Nations: Association of South-East Asian Nations, 17 August 2017

RATIFICATION

Malaysia

Deposit of instrument with Secretary-General of the Association of Southeast Asian Nations: 11 January 2013

Date of effect: 11 January 2013

Registration with the Secretariat of the United Nations: Association of South-East Asian Nations, 17 August 2017

N° 54629. Multilatéral

CONVENTION DE L'ASEAN SUR LA LUTTE CONTRE LE TERRORISME. CEBU, 13 JANVIER 2007 [*Nations Unies, Recueil des Traités, vol. 3199, I-54629.*]

RATIFICATION

Indonésie

Dépôt de l'instrument auprès de Secrétaire général de l'Association des nations de l'Asie du Sud-Est : 14 mai 2012

Date de prise d'effet : 14 mai 2012

Enregistrement auprès du Secrétariat de l'Organisation des Nations Unies : Association des nations de l'Asie du Sud-Est, 17 août 2017

RATIFICATION

République démocratique populaire lao

Dépôt de l'instrument auprès de Secrétaire général de l'Association des nations de l'Asie du Sud-Est : 28 novembre 2012

Date de prise d'effet : 28 novembre 2012

Enregistrement auprès du Secrétariat de l'Organisation des Nations Unies : Association des nations de l'Asie du Sud-Est, 17 août 2017

RATIFICATION

Malaisie

Dépôt de l'instrument auprès de Secrétaire général de l'Association des nations de l'Asie du Sud-Est : 11 janvier 2013

Date de prise d'effet : 11 janvier 2013

Enregistrement auprès du Secrétariat de l'Organisation des Nations Unies : Association des nations de l'Asie du Sud-Est, 17 août 2017

RATIFICATION

Myanmar

Deposit of instrument with Secretary-General of the Association of Southeast Asian Nations: 21 February 2012

Date of effect: 21 February 2012

Registration with the Secretariat of the United Nations: Association of South-East Asian Nations, 17 August 2017

RATIFICATION

Myanmar

Dépôt de l'instrument auprès de Secrétaire général de l'Association des nations de l'Asie du Sud-Est : 21 février 2012

Date de prise d'effet : 21 février 2012

Enregistrement auprès du Secrétariat de l'Organisation des Nations Unies : Association des nations de l'Asie du Sud-Est, 17 août 2017

No. 54635. Peru and Ecuador

AGREEMENT ON THE TRANSFER OF SENTENCED PERSONS BETWEEN THE REPUBLIC OF PERU AND THE REPUBLIC OF ECUADOR. LIMA, 11 AUGUST 1999 [*United Nations, Treaty Series, vol. 3199, I-54635.*]

PROTOCOL AMENDING THE AGREEMENT ON THE TRANSFER OF SENTENCED PERSONS BETWEEN THE REPUBLIC OF PERU AND THE REPUBLIC OF ECUADOR. ARENILLAS, 30 OCTOBER 2014

Entry into force: 30 October 2014 by notification, in accordance with article 2

Authentic text: Spanish

Registration with the Secretariat of the United Nations: Peru, 21 August 2017

Nº 54635. Pérou et Équateur

ACCORD RELATIF AU TRANSFÈREMENT DES PERSONNES CONDAMNÉES ENTRE LA RÉPUBLIQUE DU PÉROU ET LA RÉPUBLIQUE DE L'ÉQUATEUR. LIMA, 11 AOÛT 1999 [*Nations Unies, Recueil des Traités, vol. 3199, I-54635.*]

PROTOCOLE AMENDANT L'ACCORD RELATIF AU TRANSFÈREMENT DES PERSONNES CONDAMNÉES ENTRE LA RÉPUBLIQUE DU PÉROU ET LA RÉPUBLIQUE DE L'ÉQUATEUR. ARENILLAS, 30 OCTOBRE 2014

Entrée en vigueur : 30 octobre 2014 par notification, conformément à l'article 2

Texte authentique : espagnol

Enregistrement auprès du Secrétariat de l'Organisation des Nations Unies : Pérou, 21 août 2017

[TEXT IN SPANISH – TEXTE EN ESPAGNOL]

PROTOCOLO MODIFICATORIO AL CONVENIO SOBRE TRANSFERENCIA DE PERSONAS CONDENADAS ENTRE LA REPÚBLICA DEL PERÚ Y LA REPÚBLICA DEL ECUADOR

Visto el Convenio sobre la Transferencia de Personas Condenadas entre la República del Perú y la República del Ecuador, suscrito el 11 de agosto de 1999, en adelante "el Convenio";

Teniendo presente la importancia de reforzar y agilizar la cooperación judicial internacional en materia penal entre ambos países, especialmente si se tiene en cuenta el fin humanitario que impregna al instituto de traslado de condenados;

Considerando la necesidad de incorporar la institución de la Autoridad Central de modo que se torne más expedita la tramitación de los pedidos de transferencia con el fin de que, en el plazo más breve posible, quien ha sido condenado por uno de los Estados pueda cumplir su condena en su país de origen;

Por ello, la República del Perú y la República del Ecuador,

Acuerdan lo siguiente:

Artículo 1.- Incorpórese el artículo III-A con el siguiente texto:

"ARTÍCULO III-A

AUTORIDADES CENTRALES

1. Para los efectos de este Convenio, los Estados Parte designan como Autoridades Centrales:

a) Por la República del Perú, al Ministerio Público - Fiscalía de la Nación; y,

b) Por la República del Ecuador, al Ministerio de Justicia, Derechos Humanos y Cultos.

2. Las Autoridades Centrales de los Estados Parte mantendrán estrecha comunicación para asegurar el seguimiento de las solicitudes de transferencia de personas condenadas.

3. Cualquier modificación que afecte la designación de una Autoridad Central, se pondrá en conocimiento del otro Estado Parte por la vía diplomática.

Artículo 2.- El presente Protocolo Modificatorio entrará en vigor a partir de la fecha de su suscripción.

Hecho en Arenillas, el día 30 del mes de octubre del año 2014, en dos originales, siendo ambos igualmente auténticos.

Por la República del Perú

Gonzalo Gutiérrez Reinel
MINISTRO DE RELACIONES EXTERIORES

Por la República del Ecuador

Ricardo Patiño Aroca
MINISTRO DE RELACIONES EXTERIORES Y MOVILIDAD HUMANA

[TRANSLATION – TRADUCTION]

PROTOCOL AMENDING THE AGREEMENT ON THE TRANSFER OF SENTENCED PERSONS BETWEEN THE REPUBLIC OF PERU AND THE REPUBLIC OF ECUADOR

Having regard to the Agreement on the Transfer of Sentenced Persons between the Republic of Peru and the Republic of Ecuador, signed on 11 August 1999, hereinafter referred to as "the Agreement",

Bearing in mind the importance of strengthening and streamlining international legal cooperation in criminal matters between the two countries, especially considering the humanitarian purpose of the institution responsible for the transfer of sentenced persons,

Considering the need to include the Central Authority as a body in order to expedite the processing of requests for transfer so that, in the shortest possible time, persons sentenced by one of the States might serve their sentence in their country of origin,

The Republic of Peru and the Republic of Ecuador,

Have therefore agreed as follows:

Article 1. Add the following text to article III-A:

"Article III-A. Central Authorities

1. For the purposes of this Agreement, the States Parties designate as Central Authorities:
   (a) For the Republic of Peru, the Office of the Attorney General of the Nation in the Public Prosecution Service; and
   (b) For the Republic of Ecuador, the Ministry of Justice, Human Rights and Worship.
2. The Central Authorities of the States Parties shall remain in close communication to ensure requests for the transfer of sentenced persons are followed up.
3. Any change affecting the designation of a Central Authority shall be brought to the attention of the other State Party through the diplomatic channel.

Article 2. This Protocol shall enter into force on the date of its signature.

DONE at Arenillas on 30 October 2014, in two originals, both texts being equally authentic.

For the Republic of Peru:

GONZALO GUTIÉRREZ REINEL
Minister for Foreign Affairs

For the Republic of Ecuador:

RICARDO PATIÑO AROCA
Minister for Foreign Affairs and Human Mobility

[TRANSLATION – TRADUCTION]

PROTOCOLE AMENDANT L'ACCORD RELATIF AU TRANSFÈREMENT DES PERSONNES CONDAMNÉES ENTRE LA RÉPUBLIQUE DU PÉROU ET LA RÉPUBLIQUE DE L'ÉQUATEUR

La République du Pérou et la République de l'Équateur,

Vu l'Accord relatif au transfèrement des personnes condamnées entre la République du Pérou et la République de l'Équateur, signé le 11 août 1999, ci-après dénommé l'« Accord »,

Gardant à l'esprit la nécessité de renforcer et de simplifier la coopération juridique internationale en matière pénale entre les deux pays, compte tenu notamment de la finalité humanitaire du transfèrement des personnes condamnées,

Considérant qu'il est nécessaire d'inclure l'institution de l'autorité centrale en vue d'accélérer le traitement des demandes de transfèrement pour que, dans les meilleurs délais, une personne condamnée par l'un des États puisse purger sa peine dans son pays d'origine,

Sont convenues de ce qui suit :

Article premier. Le texte suivant est intégré à l'article III-A :

« Article III-A. Autorités centrales

1. Aux fins du présent Accord, les États parties désignent comme autorités centrales :
   a) Pour la République du Pérou, le Bureau du Procureur général de la Nation au sein du Ministère public ; et
   b) Pour la République de l'Équateur, le Ministère de la justice, des droits de l'homme et du culte.
2. Les autorités centrales des États parties maintiennent une communication étroite afin d'assurer le suivi des demandes de transfèrement des personnes condamnées.
3. Toute modification concernant la désignation d'une autorité centrale est portée à la connaissance de l'autre État Partie par la voie diplomatique. »

Article 2. Le présent Protocole d'amendement entre en vigueur à compter de la date de sa signature.

FAIT à Arenillas, le 30 octobre 2014, en deux exemplaires originaux, les deux textes faisant également foi.

Pour la République du Pérou :

GONZALO GUTIÉRREZ REINEL
Ministre des affaires étrangères

Pour la République de l'Équateur :

RICARDO PATIÑO AROCA
Ministre des affaires étrangères et de la mobilité humaine

No. 54637. Peru and Bolivia

AGREEMENT BETWEEN THE GOVERNMENT OF THE REPUBLIC OF PERU AND THE GOVERNMENT OF THE REPUBLIC OF BOLIVIA ON THE MUTUAL PROMOTION AND PROTECTION OF INVESTMENTS. ILO, 30 JULY 1993 [*United Nations, Treaty Series, vol. 3199, I-54637.*]

EXCHANGE OF NOTES CONSTITUTING AN AGREEMENT BETWEEN THE REPUBLIC OF PERU AND THE PLURINATIONAL STATE OF BOLIVIA AMENDING THE AGREEMENT BETWEEN THE GOVERNMENT OF THE REPUBLIC OF PERU AND THE GOVERNMENT OF THE REPUBLIC OF BOLIVIA ON THE MUTUAL PROMOTION AND PROTECTION OF INVESTMENTS. LIMA, 19 FEBRUARY 2015, AND LA PAZ, 19 FEBRUARY 2015

Entry into force: 19 February 2015 by the exchange of the said notes, in accordance with their provisions

Authentic text: Spanish

Registration with the Secretariat of the United Nations: Peru, 1 August 2017

N° 54637. Pérou et Bolivie

CONVENTION ENTRE LE GOUVERNEMENT DE LA RÉPUBLIQUE DU PÉROU ET LE GOUVERNEMENT DE LA RÉPUBLIQUE DE BOLIVIE RELATIF À LA PROMOTION ET À LA PROTECTION RÉCIPROQUES DES INVESTISSEMENTS. ILO, 30 JUILLET 1993 [*Nations Unies, Recueil des Traités, vol. 3199, I-54637.*]

ÉCHANGE DE NOTES CONSTITUANT UN ACCORD ENTRE LA RÉPUBLIQUE DU PÉROU ET L'ÉTAT PLURINATIONAL DE BOLIVIE AMENDANT LA CONVENTION ENTRE LE GOUVERNEMENT DE LA RÉPUBLIQUE DU PÉROU ET LE GOUVERNEMENT DE LA RÉPUBLIQUE DE BOLIVIE RELATIF À LA PROMOTION ET À LA PROTECTION RÉCIPROQUES DES INVESTISSEMENTS. LIMA, 19 FÉVRIER 2015, ET LA PAZ, 19 FÉVRIER 2015

Entrée en vigueur : 19 février 2015 par l'échange desdites notes, conformément à leurs dispositions

Texte authentique : espagnol

Enregistrement auprès du Secrétariat de l'Organisation des Nations Unies : Pérou, 1er août 2017

[TEXT IN SPANISH – TEXTE EN ESPAGNOL]

I

Nota RE (GAB) Nº 6/19

El Ministerio de Relaciones Exteriores del Perú saluda muy atentamente al Honorable Ministerio de Relaciones Exteriores del Estado Plurinacional de Bolivia y tiene a bien referirse al "Convenio entre el Gobierno de la República del Perú y el Gobierno de la República de Bolivia sobre Promoción y Protección Recíproca de Inversiones", suscrito el 30 de julio de 1993 y vigente desde el 20 de febrero de 1995.

Sobre el particular, el Ministerio de Relaciones Exteriores del Perú en el ánimo de superar por la vía diplomática la diferencia surgida a propósito de la vigencia del Convenio y que fue motivo de negociación desde mayo del año 2013 tiene a bien proponer a ese Honorable Ministerio, en virtud del numeral (1) del artículo 12 del Convenio, mantener la vigencia de dicho tratado por un (1) año adicional, computable a partir del 20 de febrero de 2015 hasta el 19 de febrero de 2016, a fin que, durante tal tiempo pueda negociarse un nuevo acuerdo de promoción y protección recíproca de inversiones que sustituya el actualmente vigente. Queda entendido que de no alcanzarse un nuevo Acuerdo, la vigencia del actual Convenio no será renovada y solo será extendible el periodo de ultraactividad por quince (15) años adicionales a favor de las inversiones realizadas antes del 19 de febrero de 2016, conforme a lo previsto en el segundo párrafo del artículo 14 del Convenio actualmente vigente.

Asimismo el Ministerio de Relaciones Exteriores del Perú propone al Honorable Ministerio de Relaciones Exteriores del Estado Plurinacional de Bolivia que en el transcurso de dicho período toda diferencia que pudiera surgir a propósito de la interpretación o aplicación del Convenio, será resuelta esencialmente a través de negociaciones directas entre las Partes Contratantes.

La presente Nota y la Nota que con el mismo tenor tuviera a bien remitir ese Honorable Ministerio constituirán un entendimiento entre los dos países

El Ministerio de Relaciones Exteriores del Perú hace propicia la oportunidad para renovar al Honorable Ministerio de Relaciones Exteriores del Estado Plurinacional de Bolivia las seguridades de su más alta y distinguida consideración.

Lima, 19 de febrero de 2015

Al Honorable
Ministerio de Relaciones Exteriores
Del Estado Plurinacional de Bolivia
La Paz.-

II

GM-DGAJ-UAJ-Cs-472/2015

EL MINISTERIO DE RELACIONES EXTERIORES – saluda muy atentamente al Ministerio de Relaciones Exteriores de la República del Perú y tiene a bien invocar el "Convenio entre el Gobierno de la República del Perú y el Gobierno de la República de Bolivia sobre Promoción y Protección Recíproca de Inversiones", suscrito el 30 de julio de 1993, que fuera ratificado en este Estado mediante Ley N° 1573 de 12 de julio de 1994 y, en la República del Perú, según Decreto Supremo N° 03-94-RE, de fecha 09 de marzo de 1994; y cobró vigor el 20 de febrero de 1995, en ocasión del intercambio de Notas Diplomáticas, según su Artículo 14.

Asimismo, tiene a bien referirse a su Nota de 19 de febrero de 2015, mediante la cual, se propone mantener la vigencia al Convenio referido, por el lapso de un año adicional, bajo el siguiente tenor:

[See note I - Voir note I]

EL MINISTERIO DE RELACIONES EXTERIORES – hace propicia la oportunidad para reiterar al Honorable Ministerio de Relaciones Exteriores de la República del Perú, las seguridades de su más alta y distinguida consideración.

La Paz, 19 de febrero de 2015.

Al Honorable
MINISTERIO DE RELACIONES EXTERIORES
DE LA REPÚBLICA DEL PERÚ
Lima.-

[TRANSLATION – TRADUCTION]

I

Lima, 19 February 2015

Note RE (GAB) No. 6/19

The Ministry of Foreign Affairs of Peru presents its compliments to the Ministry of Foreign Affairs of the Plurinational State of Bolivia and has the honour of referring to the Agreement between the Government of the Republic of Peru and the Government of the Republic of Bolivia on the mutual promotion and protection of investments, which was signed on 30 July 1993 and entered into force on 20 February 1995.

In this connection, the Ministry of Foreign Affairs of Peru, seeking a diplomatic resolution to the dispute concerning the period during which the Agreement is in force, which has been the subject of negotiations since May 2013, wishes to propose to the Ministry, by virtue of paragraph 1 of article 12 of the Agreement, that this treaty remain in force for one additional year, for the period from 20 February 2015 through 19 February 2016, in order to make it possible, during this period, to negotiate a new agreement on the mutual promotion and protection of investments to replace the one currently in force. It is understood that, should a new agreement not be reached, the current Agreement will not be renewed and will only be extended for a period of 15 additional years for investments made prior to 19 February 2016, in accordance with the second paragraph of article 14 of the Agreement currently in force.

Moreover, the Ministry of Foreign Affairs of Peru proposes to the Ministry of Foreign Affairs of the Plurinational State of Bolivia that, during the above-mentioned period, any disputes that might arise concerning the interpretation or application of the Agreement is to be resolved primarily through direct negotiations between the Contracting Parties.

This Note and a Note with the same contents submitted by the Ministry of Foreign Affairs of the Plurinational State of Bolivia shall constitute an understanding between the two countries.

The Ministry of Foreign Affairs of Peru takes this opportunity to convey to the Ministry of Foreign Affairs of the Plurinational State of Bolivia the renewed assurances of its highest consideration.

[SIGNED]

Ministry of Foreign Affairs
of the Plurinational State of Bolivia
La Paz

II

MINISTRY OF FOREIGN AFFAIRS

BOLIVIA

La Paz, 19 February 2015

GM-DGAJ-UAJ-Cs-472/2015

The Ministry of Foreign Affairs of the Plurinational State of Bolivia presents its compliments to the Ministry of Foreign Affairs of the Republic of Peru and wishes to refer to the Agreement between the Government of the Republic of Peru and the Government of the Republic of Bolivia on the mutual promotion and protection of investments, signed on 30 July 1993, which was ratified in this State by Act No. 1573 of 12 July 1994 and, in the Republic of Peru, by Supreme Decree No. 03-94-RE of 9 March 1994; and entered into force on 20 February 1995, on the occasion of the Exchange of Diplomatic Notes, in accordance with article 14 of the Agreement.

The Ministry has the honour of referring to your Note of 19 February 2015, in which you propose that the above-mentioned Agreement remain in force for a period of one additional year, as set out below:

[See note I]

The Ministry of Foreign Affairs of the Plurinational State of Bolivia takes this opportunity to convey to the Ministry of Foreign Affairs of the Republic of Peru the renewed assurances of its highest consideration.

[SIGNED]

Ministry of Foreign Affairs
of the Republic of Peru
Lima

[TRANSLATION – TRADUCTION]

I

MINISTÈRE DES AFFAIRES ÉTRANGÈRES DE LA RÉPUBLIQUE DU PÉROU

Lima, le 19 février 2015

Note RE (GAB) nº 6/19

Le Ministère des relations extérieures du Pérou présente ses compliments au Ministère des affaires étrangères de l'État plurinational de Bolivie et a l'honneur de se référer à la Convention entre le Gouvernement de la République du Pérou et le Gouvernement de la République de Bolivie relative à la promotion et à la protection réciproques des investissements, signée le 30 juillet 1993 et en vigueur depuis le 20 février 1995.

À cet égard, le Ministère des relations extérieures du Pérou, en vue de la résolution par la voie diplomatique du différend se rapportant à la période d'application de la Convention et qui fait l'objet de négociations depuis mai 2013, souhaite proposer au Ministère des affaires étrangères de l'État plurinational de Bolivie, en vertu du paragraphe 1 de l'article 12 de la Convention, que ledit traité reste en vigueur pour une année supplémentaire, qui va du 20 février 2015 au 19 février 2016, afin qu'il soit possible, au cours de ladite période, de négocier un nouvel accord relatif à la promotion et à la protection réciproques des investissements se substituant à celui actuellement en vigueur. Il est entendu que si aucun nouvel Accord n'est conclu, la Convention actuelle ne sera pas renouvelée et seule la période d'application différée sera prolongée pour 15 années supplémentaires au bénéfice des investissements réalisés avant le 19 février 2016, conformément aux dispositions du deuxième paragraphe de l'article 14 de la Convention actuellement en vigueur.

Le Ministère des relations extérieures du Pérou propose par ailleurs au Ministère des affaires étrangères de l'État plurinational de Bolivie que, pendant la période susmentionnée, les différends susceptibles de survenir au sujet de l'interprétation ou de l'application de la Convention soient principalement résolus par voie de négociations directes entre les Parties contractantes.

La présente note et une note de la même teneur présentée en réponse par le Ministère des affaires étrangères de l'État plurinational de Bolivie constituent un accord entre les deux pays.

Le Ministère péruvien des relations extérieures saisit cette occasion pour renouveler au Ministère des affaires étrangères de l'État plurinational de Bolivie les assurances de sa très haute considération.

[SIGNÉ]

Ministère des affaires étrangères
État plurinational de Bolivie
La Paz

II

MINISTÈRE DES AFFAIRES ÉTRANGÈRES

BOLIVIE

La Paz, le 19 février 2015

GM-DGAJ-UAJ-Cs-472/2015

Le Ministère des affaires étrangères présente ses compliments au Ministère des relations extérieures de la République du Pérou et souhaite se référer à la Convention entre le Gouvernement de la République du Pérou et le Gouvernement de la République de Bolivie relative à la promotion et à la protection réciproques des investissements, signée le 30 juillet 1993, ratifiée dans cet État par la loi nº 1573 du 12 juillet 1994, et en République du Pérou par le Décret suprême nº 03-94-RE du 9 mars 1994, et entrée en vigueur le 20 février 1995, par échange de notes diplomatiques, conformément à son article 14.

Le Ministère a par ailleurs l'honneur de se référer à votre note du 19 février 2015, par laquelle vous proposez que la Convention susmentionnée reste en vigueur pour une période d'une année supplémentaire, et dont la teneur est la suivante :

[Voir note I]

Le Ministère des affaires étrangères de l'État plurinational de Bolivie saisit cette occasion pour renouveler au Ministère des relations extérieures du Pérou les assurances de sa très haute considération.

[SIGNÉ]

Ministère des relations extérieures du Pérou
Lima

EXCHANGE OF NOTES CONSTITUTING AN AGREEMENT BETWEEN THE REPUBLIC OF PERU AND THE PLURINATIONAL STATE OF BOLIVIA AMENDING THE AGREEMENT BETWEEN THE GOVERNMENT OF THE REPUBLIC OF PERU AND THE GOVERNMENT OF THE REPUBLIC OF BOLIVIA ON THE MUTUAL PROMOTION AND PROTECTION OF INVESTMENTS (WITH CORRECTIONS). LA PAZ, 4 NOVEMBER 2016, AND LIMA, 4 NOVEMBER 2016

Entry into force: 4 November 2016 by the exchange of the said notes, in accordance with their provisions

Authentic text: Spanish

Registration with the Secretariat of the United Nations: Peru, 21 August 2017

ÉCHANGE DE NOTES CONSTITUANT UN ACCORD ENTRE LA RÉPUBLIQUE DU PÉROU ET L'ÉTAT PLURINATIONAL DE BOLIVIE AMENDANT L'ACCORD ENTRE LE GOUVERNEMENT DE LA RÉPUBLIQUE DU PÉROU ET LE GOUVERNEMENT DE LA RÉPUBLIQUE DE BOLIVIE RELATIF À LA PROMOTION ET À LA PROTECTION RÉCIPROQUES DES INVESTISSEMENTS (AVEC CORRECTIONS). LA PAZ, 4 NOVEMBRE 2016, ET LIMA, 4 NOVEMBRE 2016

Entrée en vigueur : 4 novembre 2016 par l'échange desdites notes, conformément à leurs dispositions

Texte authentique : espagnol

Enregistrement auprès du Secrétariat de l'Organisation des Nations Unies : Pérou, 21 août 2017

[TEXT IN SPANISH – TEXTE EN ESPAGNOL]

I

ESTADO PLURINACIONAL DE BOLIVIA
MINISTERIO DE RELACIONES EXTERIORES

GM-DGAJ-UAJ-Cs-2847/2016

EL MINISTERIO DE RELACIONES EXTERIORES – saluda muy atentamente al Ministerio de Relaciones Exteriores de la República del Perú y tiene a bien invocar al *"Convenio entre el Gobierno de la República del Perú y el Gobierno de la República de Bolivia sobre Promoción y Protección Recíproca de Inversiones"*, suscrito el 30 de julio de 1993, que fuera ratificado en este Estado, mediante Ley N° 1573 de 12 de julio de 1994 y, en la República del Perú, según Decreto Supremo N° 03-94-RE, de fecha 09 de marzo de 1994; y cobró vigor el 20 de febrero de 1995, en ocasión del intercambio de Notas Diplomáticas, según su Artículo 14.

Al respecto, propone el restablecimiento y modificación de lo acordado, mediante su Nota Re (GAB) N° 6/19, de propuesta de mantener la vigencia del referido Compromiso Internacional, por un año adicional y, la Nota GM-DGAJ-UAJ-Cs-472/2015 de respuesta y aceptación de este Estado, ambas de 19 de febrero de 2015, con el siguiente tenor:

"El Ministerio de Relaciones Exteriores del Perú saluda muy atentamente al Honorable Ministerio de Relaciones Exteriores del Estado Plurinacional de Bolivia y tiene a bien referirse al 'Convenio entre el Gobierno de la República del Perú y el Gobierno de la República de Bolivia sobre Promoción y Protección Recíproca de Inversiones', suscrito el 30 de julio de 1993 y vigente desde el 20 de febrero de 1995.

*Sobre el particular, el Ministerio de Relaciones Exteriores del Perú en el ánimo de superar por la vía diplomática la diferencia surgida a propósito de la vigencia del Convenio y que fue motivo de negociación desde mayo del año 2013, tiene a bien proponer a ese Honorable Ministerio, en virtud del numeral (1) del Artículo 12 del Convenio, mantener la vigencia del Convenio **hasta el 19 de febrero de 2018**, a fin que, durante tal tiempo pueda negociarse un nuevo acuerdo de promoción y protección recíproca de inversiones. Queda entendido que de no alcanzarse un nuevo Acuerdo, la vigencia del actual Convenio no será renovada y sólo será extensible el período de ultractividad por quince (15) años adicionales a favor de las inversiones realizadas antes del 31 de diciembre de 2017, conforme a lo previsto en el segundo párrafo del Artículo 14 del Convenio actualmente vigente"*

Al Honorable
MINISTERIO DE RELACIONES EXTERIORES DE LA REPÚBLICA DEL PERÚ
Lima.-

Asimismo, el Ministerio de Relaciones Exteriores del Estado Plurinacional de Bolivia sugiere al Honorable Ministerio de Relaciones Exteriores de la República del Perú que en el transcurso de dicho periodo toda diferencia que pueda surgir a propósito de la interpretación o aplicación del Convenio, será resuelta esencialmente a través de negociaciones directas entre las Partes Contratantes.

La presente Nota y la Nota que con el mismo tenor tuviera a bien remitir ese Honorable Ministerio constituirán un entendimiento formal entre los dos países.

EL MINISTERIO DE RELACIONES EXTERIORES – hace propicia la oportunidad para reiterar al Honorable Ministerio de Relaciones Exteriores de la República del Perú, las seguridades de su más alta y distinguida consideración.

La Paz, 04 de noviembre de 2016

II

Nota RE (GAB) N° 6/178

El Ministerio de Relaciones Exteriores del Perú saluda muy atentamente al Honorable Ministerio de Relaciones Exteriores del Estado Plurinacional de Bolivia y tiene a bien manifestar su conformidad con la propuesta realizada a través de su Nota GM-DGAJ-UAJ-Cs-2847/2016 de fecha 04 de noviembre de 2016, en relación al "Convenio entre el Gobierno de la República del Perú y el Gobierno de la República de Bolivia sobre Promoción y Protección Recíproca de Inversiones", según el siguiente tenor:

[See note I - Voir note I]

El Ministerio de Relaciones Exteriores del Perú tiene el honor de confirmar que la Nota del Honorable Ministerio de Relaciones Exteriores del Estado Plurinacional de Bolivia antes transcrita y la presente Nota de aceptación, constituirán un acuerdo entre los dos países.

El Ministerio de Relaciones Exteriores del Perú hace propicia la oportunidad para renovar al Honorable Ministerio de Relaciones Exteriores del Estado Plurinacional de Bolivia las seguridades de su más alta y distinguida consideración.

Lima, 04 de noviembre de 2016

Al **Honorable Ministerio de Relaciones Exteriores**
del Estado Plurinacional de Bolivia
Ciudad.-

III

Nota RE (GAB) N° 6/193.

El Ministerio de Relaciones Exteriores del Perú saluda muy atentamente al Honorable Ministerio de Relaciones Exteriores del Estado Plurinacional de Bolivia y tiene a bien referirse al restablecimiento y modificación del "Convenio entre el Gobierno de la República del Perú y el Gobierno de la República de Bolivia sobre Promoción y Protección Recíproca de Inversiones", suscrito el 30 de julio de 1993.

Sobre el particular, habiéndose percatado este Ministerio de errores materiales en el acuerdo por intercambio de notas celebrado mediante Nota boliviana GM-DGAJ-UAJ-Cs-2847/2016 y Nota peruana RE (GAB) N° 6/178, ambas de 4 de noviembre de 2016, e invocando lo dispuesto por el derecho internacional consuetudinario en la materia, precisa que la redacción correcta del acuerdo contenido en ellas es la siguiente:

" **EL MINISTERIO DE RELACIONES EXTERIORES** saluda muy atentamente al Ministerio de Relaciones Exteriores de la República del Perú y tiene a bien invocar el "Convenio entre el Gobierno de la República del Perú y el Gobierno de la República de Bolivia sobre Promoción y Protección Recíproca de Inversiones", suscrito el 30 de julio de 1993.

Al respecto, este Ministerio plantea el restablecimiento y modificación de lo acordado mediante su Nota (GAB) Nº 6/19 en la cual se propuso mantener la vigencia del referido compromiso internacional, por un año adicional, y la Nota GM-DGAJ-UAJ-Cs-472/2015 de respuesta y aceptación de este Estado, ambas de 19 de febrero de 2015, con el siguiente tenor:

'El Ministerio de Relaciones Exteriores del Perú saluda muy atentamente al Honorable Ministerio de Relaciones Exteriores del Estado Plurinacional de Bolivia y tiene a bien referirse al 'Convenio entre el Gobierno de la República del Perú y el Gobierno de la República de Bolivia sobre Promoción y Protección Recíproca de Inversiones", suscrito el 30 de julio de 1993 y vigente desde el 20 de febrero de 1995.

*Sobre el particular, el Ministerio de Relaciones Exteriores del Perú tiene a bien proponer a ese Honorable Ministerio mantener la vigencia del Convenio **hasta el 19 de febrero de 2018**, a fin que durante tal tiempo pueda negociarse un nuevo acuerdo de promoción y protección recíproca de inversiones. Queda entendido que de no alcanzarse un nuevo acuerdo, la vigencia del actual Convenio no será renovada y solo será extensible el periodo de ultraactividad por quince (15) años adicionales a favor de las inversiones realizadas hasta el 19 de febrero de 2018, conforme a lo previsto en el segundo párrafo del Artículo 14 del Convenio.' "*

Al Honorable
Ministerio de Relaciones Exteriores del
Estado Plurinacional de Bolivia
La Paz.-

La presente Nota y la Nota que con el mismo tenor tuviera a bien remitir ese Honorable Ministerio constituirán un entendimiento entre los dos países.

El Ministerio de Relaciones Exteriores del Perú hace propicia la oportunidad para renovar al Honorable Ministerio de Relaciones Exteriores del Estado Plurinacional de Bolivia las seguridades de su más alta y distinguida consideración.

Lima, 26 DIC. 2016

IV

GM-DGAJ-UAJ-Cs-94/2017

EL MINISTERIO DE RELACIONES EXTERIORES DEL ESTADO PLURINACIONAL DE BOLIVIA, saluda muy atentamente al Ministerio de Relaciones Exteriores de la República del Perú y, tiene a bien manifestar su Aceptación a la propuesta de Enmienda realizada en su Nota RE (GAB) Nº 6/193 de 26 de diciembre de 2016, del Acuerdo de restablecimiento y modificación del *"Convenio entre el Gobierno de la República del Perú y el Gobierno de la República de Bolivia sobre Promoción y Protección Reciproca de Inversiones"* de 30 de julio de 1993, efectuado el 04 de noviembre de 2016, mediante las Notas GM-DGAJ-UAJ-Cs-2847/2016 de la Parte boliviana y RE (GAB) Nº 6/178 de la Parte peruana, según el siguiente tenor:

[See note III - Voir note III]

El Ministerio de Relaciones Exteriores del Estado Plurinacional de Bolivia, confirma así, la Enmienda propuesta en la Nota RE (GAB) Nº 6/193 del Ministerio de Relaciones Exteriores del Perú, con una vigencia *ab initio*; constituyendo la precitada Nota y la presente Nota de aceptación, un Acuerdo Internacional entre los dos Estados.

El Ministerio de Relaciones Exteriores del Estado Plurinacional de Bolivia, hace propicia la oportunidad para renovar al Ministerio de Relaciones Exteriores de la República del Perú, las seguridades de más alta y distinguida consideración.

La Paz, 17 ENE. 2017

David Choquehuanca Céspedes
MINISTRO DE RELACIONES EXTERIORES

Al Honorable
Ricardo V. Luna Mendoza
Ministro de Relaciones Exteriores de la República del Perú
Lima.-

[TRANSLATION – TRADUCTION]

I

PLURINATIONAL STATE OF BOLIVIA

MINISTRY OF FOREIGN AFFAIRS

La Paz, 4 November 2016

GM-DGAJ-UAJ-Cs-2847/2016

The Ministry of Foreign Affairs presents its compliments to the Ministry of Foreign Affairs of the Republic of Peru and wishes to refer to the "Agreement between the Government of the Republic of Peru and the Government of the Republic of Bolivia on the mutual promotion and protection of investments" signed on 30 July 1993, which was ratified in this State by Act No. 1573 of 12 July 1994, and, in the Republic of Peru, by Supreme Decree No. 03-94-RE of 9 March 1994, and entered into force on 20 February 1995, by virtue of the Exchange of Diplomatic Notes, in accordance with article 14 of the Agreement.

In this regard, it hereby proposes to reestablish and modify that which has been agreed upon, by means of its Note Re (GAB) No. 6/19, namely, to extend the aforementioned International Commitment for one additional year, and Note No. GM-DGAJ-UAJ-Cs 472/2015, comprising this State's response and acceptance, both Notes dated 19 February 2015, which reads as follows:

"The Ministry of Foreign Affairs of Peru presents its compliments to the Ministry of Foreign Affairs of the Plurinational State of Bolivia and has the honour of referring to the "Agreement between the Government of the Republic of Peru and the Government of the Republic of Bolivia on the mutual promotion and protection of investments", which was signed on 30 July 1993 and entered into force on 20 February 1995.

In this connection, the Ministry of Foreign Affairs of Peru, seeking a diplomatic resolution to the dispute concerning the period during which the Agreement is in force, which has been the subject of negotiations since May 2013, wishes to propose to the Ministry, by virtue of paragraph 1 of article 12 of the Agreement, that the validity of Agreement be extended up until 19 February 2018, in order to make it possible, during this period, to negotiate a new agreement on the mutual promotion and protection of investments. It is understood that, should a new agreement not be reached, the current Agreement will not be renewed and will only be extended for a period of 15 additional years for investments made prior to 31 December 2017, in accordance with the second paragraph of article 14 of the Agreement currently in force."

Moreover, the Ministry of Foreign Affairs of the Plurinational State of Bolivia suggests to the Ministry of Foreign Affairs of Peru that, during the above-mentioned period, any disputes that might arise concerning the interpretation or application of the Agreement is to be resolved primarily through direct negotiations between the Contracting Parties.

This Note and a Note with the same content submitted by the Ministry of Foreign Affairs of the Plurinational State of Bolivia shall constitute a formal understanding between the two countries.

The Ministry of Foreign Affairs takes this opportunity to convey to the Ministry of Foreign Affairs of the Republic of Peru the renewed assurances of its highest consideration.

[SIGNED]

Ministry of Foreign Affairs
of the Republic of Peru
Lima

II

Lima, 4 November 2016

Note RE (GAB) No. 6/178

The Ministry of Foreign Affairs of Peru presents its compliments to the Ministry of Foreign Affairs of the Plurinational State of Bolivia and hereby agrees to the proposal made by means of your Note No. GM-DGAJ-UAJ-Cs-2847/2016, dated 4 November 2016, regarding the "Agreement between the Government of the Republic of Peru and the Government of the Republic of Bolivia on the mutual promotion and protection of investments", which reads as follows:

[See note I]

The Ministry of Foreign Affairs of Peru has the honour of confirming that the above-mentioned Note from the Ministry of Foreign Affairs of the Plurinational State of Bolivia and this Note of acceptance shall constitute an Agreement between the two countries.

The Ministry of Foreign Affairs of the Plurinational State of Bolivia takes this opportunity to convey to the Ministry of Foreign Affairs of the Republic of Peru the renewed assurances of its highest consideration.

[SIGNED]

Ministry of Foreign Affairs
of the Plurinational State of Bolivia

III

Lima, 26 December 2016

Note RE (GAB) No. 6/193

The Ministry of Foreign Affairs of Peru presents its compliments to the Ministry of Foreign Affairs of the Plurinational State of Bolivia and has the honour of referring to the reinstatement and modification of the “Agreement between the Government of the Republic of Peru and the Government of the Republic of Bolivia on the mutual promotion and protection of investments”, which was signed on 30 July 1993.

In this connection, this Ministry, having detected material errors in the Agreement constituted by the Exchange of Notes by means of Note No. GM-DGAJ-Cs-UAJ-2847/2016 from the Plurinational State of Bolivia and Note RE (GAB) No. 6/178 from Peru, both dated 4 November 2015, and invoking the provisions of customary international law, hereby specifies that the correct wording of the Agreement contained therein is as follows:

“The Ministry of Foreign Affairs presents its compliments to the Ministry of Foreign Affairs of the Republic of Peru and has the honour of referring to the Agreement between the Government of the Republic of Peru and the Government of the Republic of Bolivia on the mutual promotion and protection of investments, which was signed on 30 July 1993.

In this regard, this Ministry proposes to reestablish and modify the Agreement by means of its Note Re (GAB) No. 6/19, in which it was put forward that the validity of the aforementioned International Commitment be extended for one additional year, and Note No. GM-DGAJ-UAJ-Cs 472/2015, comprising this State’s response and acceptance, both Notes dated 19 February 2015, which reads as follows:

‘The Ministry of Foreign Affairs of Peru presents its compliments to the Ministry of Foreign Affairs of the Plurinational State of Bolivia and has the honour of referring to the “Agreement between the Government of the Republic of Peru and the Government of the Republic of Bolivia on the mutual promotion and protection of investments”, which was signed on 30 July 1993 and entered into force on 20 February 1995.

In this connection, the Ministry of Foreign Affairs of Peru wishes to propose to this Ministry that the validity of the Agreement be extended up until 19 February 2018, in order to make it possible, during this period, to negotiate a new agreement on the mutual promotion and protection of investments. It is understood that, should a new agreement not be reached, the current Agreement will not be renewed and may only be extended for a period of 15 years for investments made up until 19 February 2018, in accordance with the second paragraph of article 14 of the Agreement.’”

This Note and a Note with the same content submitted by this Ministry shall constitute an understanding between the two countries.

The Ministry of Foreign Affairs of the Republic of Peru takes this opportunity to convey to the Ministry of Foreign Affairs of the Plurinational State of Bolivia the renewed assurances of its highest consideration.

[SIGNED]

Ministry of Foreign Affairs
of the Plurinational State of Bolivia
La Paz

IV

PLURINATIONAL STATE OF BOLIVIA

MINISTRY OF FOREIGN AFFAIRS

La Paz, 17 January 2017

GM-DGAJ-UAJ-Cs-94/2017

The Ministry of Foreign Affairs of the Plurinational State of Bolivia presents its compliments to the Ministry of Foreign Affairs of the Republic of Peru and hereby confirms its acceptance of the proposed Amendment made in its Note RE (GAB) No. 6/193 of 26 December 2016 to reestablish and modify the "Agreement between the Government of the Republic of Peru and the Government of the Republic of Bolivia on the mutual promotion and protection of investments", which was signed on 30 July 1993, made on 4 November 2016, by means of Note No. GM-DGAJ-UAJ-Cs-2847/2016 from the Plurinational State of Bolivia and Note No. RE (GAB) No. 6/178 from Peru, which reads as follows:

[See note I]

The Ministry of Foreign Affairs of the Plurinational State of Bolivia hereby confirms the Amendment proposed in Note RE (GAB) No. 6/193 from the Ministry of Foreign Affairs of Peru, with effect ab initio; the above-mentioned Note and this Note of acceptance constitute an International Agreement between the two States.

The Ministry of Foreign Affairs of the Plurinational State of Bolivia takes this opportunity to convey to the Ministry of Foreign Affairs of the Republic of Peru the renewed assurances of its highest consideration.

DAVID CHOQUEHUANCA CÉSPEDES
Minister for Foreign Affairs

Ricardo V. Luna Mendoza
Minister for Foreign Affairs of the Republic of Peru
Lima

[TRANSLATION – TRADUCTION]

I

ÉTAT PLURINATIONAL DE BOLIVIE

MINISTÈRE DES RELATIONS EXTÉRIEURES

La Paz, le 4 novembre 2016

GM-DGAJ-UAJ-Cs-2847/2016

Le Ministère des relations extérieures présente ses compliments au Ministère des relations extérieures de la République du Pérou et se réfère à la Convention entre le Gouvernement de la République du Pérou et le Gouvernement de la République de Bolivie relative à la promotion et à la protection réciproques des investissements, signée le 30 juillet 1993, ratifiée dans cet État par la loi nº 1573 du 12 juillet 1994, et en République du Pérou par le Décret suprême nº 03-94-RE du 9 mars 1994, et entrée en vigueur le 20 février 1995, par échange de notes diplomatiques, conformément à son article 14.

À cet égard, le Ministère propose le rétablissement et la modification de l'accord, par sa note RE (GAB) nº 6/19, qui propose de maintenir la validité de l'engagement international susmentionné, pour une année supplémentaire, et par la note GM-DGAJ-UAJ-Cs-472/2015 de réponse et d'acceptation de cet État, toutes deux datées du 19 février 2015, dont la teneur est la suivante :

« Le Ministère des relations extérieures du Pérou présente ses compliments au Ministère des affaires étrangères de l'État plurinational de Bolivie et a l'honneur de se référer à la Convention entre le Gouvernement de la République du Pérou et le Gouvernement de la République de Bolivie relative à la promotion et à la protection réciproques des investissements, signée le 30 juillet 1993 et en vigueur depuis le 20 février 1995.

À cet égard, le Ministère des relations extérieures du Pérou, en vue de la résolution par la voie diplomatique du différend se rapportant à la période d'application de la Convention et qui fait l'objet de négociations depuis mai 2013, souhaite proposer au Ministère des affaires étrangères de l'État plurinational de Bolivie, en vertu du paragraphe 1 de l'article 12 de la Convention, de maintenir la Convention en vigueur jusqu'au 19 février 2018, afin qu'il soit possible, au cours de ladite période, de négocier un nouvel accord relatif à la promotion et à la protection réciproques des investissements. Il est entendu que si aucun nouvel Accord n'est conclu, la Convention actuelle ne sera pas renouvelée et seule la période d'application différée sera prolongée pour 15 années supplémentaires au bénéfice des investissements réalisés avant le 31 décembre 2017, conformément aux dispositions du deuxième paragraphe de l'article 14 de la Convention actuellement en vigueur. »

Le Ministère des relations extérieures de l'État plurinational de Bolivie propose par ailleurs au Ministère des relations extérieures du Pérou que, pendant la période susmentionnée, les différends susceptibles de survenir au sujet de l'interprétation ou de l'application de la Convention soient principalement résolus par voie de négociations directes entre les Parties contractantes.

La présente note et une note de même teneur qui sera envoyée par le Ministère de la République du Pérou constitueront un accord formel entre les deux pays.

Le Ministère des relations extérieures saisit cette occasion pour renouveler au Ministère des relations extérieures de la République du Pérou les assurances de sa très haute considération.

II

Lima, le 4 novembre 2016

Note RE (GAB) nº 6/178

Le Ministère des relations extérieures du Pérou présente ses compliments au Ministère des relations extérieures de l'État plurinational de Bolivie et indique par la présente qu'il accepte la proposition énoncée dans la note GM-DGAJ-UAJ-Cs-2847/2016 du 4 novembre 2016 concernant la Convention entre le Gouvernement de la République du Pérou et le Gouvernement de la République de Bolivie relative à la promotion et à la protection réciproques des investissements, libellée comme suit :

[Voir note I]

Le Ministère des relations extérieures du Pérou a l'honneur de confirmer que la note du Ministère des relations extérieures de l'État plurinational de Bolivie transcrite ci-dessus et la présente note de confirmation constituent un accord entre les deux pays.

Le Ministère des relations extérieures de la République du Pérou saisit cette occasion pour renouveler au Ministère des relations extérieures de l'État plurinational de Bolivie les assurances de sa très haute considération.

[SIGNÉ]

Ministère des relations extérieures
État plurinational de Bolivie
La Paz

III

Lima, le 26 décembre 2016

Note RE (GAB) n° 6/193

Le Ministère des relations extérieures du Pérou présente ses compliments au Ministère des relations extérieures de l'État plurinational de Bolivie et a l'honneur de se référer au rétablissement et à la modification de la Convention entre le Gouvernement de la République du Pérou et le Gouvernement de la République de Bolivie relative à la promotion et à la protection réciproques des investissements, signée le 30 juillet 1993.

À cet égard, le Ministère, ayant détecté des erreurs substantielles dans l'accord par échange de notes conclu par la note GM-DGAJ-Cs-UAJ-2847/2016 de l'État plurinational de Bolivie et la note RE (GAB) n° 6/178 du Pérou, toutes deux datées du 4 novembre 2015, et invoquant les dispositions du droit international coutumier en la matière, précise que le libellé correct de l'accord qui y figure est le suivant :

« Le Ministère des relations extérieures présente ses compliments au Ministère des relations extérieures de la République du Pérou et a l'honneur de se référer à la Convention entre le Gouvernement de la République du Pérou et le Gouvernement de la République de Bolivie relative à la promotion et à la protection réciproques des investissements, signée le 30 juillet 1993.

À cet égard, le Ministère propose le rétablissement et la modification de ce qui a été convenu par le biais de la note (GAB) n° 6/19, dans laquelle il était proposé de maintenir la validité de l'engagement international visé pour une année supplémentaire, et de la note GM-DGAl-UAI-Cs-472/2015 de réponse et d'acceptation de cet État, toutes deux datées du 19 février 2015, dont la teneur est la suivante :

"Le Ministère des relations extérieures du Pérou présente ses compliments au Ministère des affaires étrangères de l'État plurinational de Bolivie et a l'honneur de se référer à la Convention entre le Gouvernement de la République du Pérou et le Gouvernement de la République de Bolivie relative à la promotion et à la protection réciproques des investissements, signée le 30 juillet 1993 et en vigueur depuis le 20 février 1995.

À cet égard, le Ministère des relations extérieures du Pérou souhaite proposer au Ministère des relations extérieures de l'État plurinational de Bolivie de maintenir la Convention en vigueur jusqu'au 19 février 2018 afin qu'il soit possible, au cours de ladite période, de négocier un nouvel accord relatif à la promotion et à la protection réciproques des investissements. Il est entendu que si aucun nouvel accord n'est conclu, la Convention actuelle ne sera pas renouvelée et seule la période d'application différée sera prolongée pour 15 années supplémentaires au bénéfice des investissements réalisés jusqu'au le 19 février 2018, conformément aux dispositions du deuxième paragraphe de l'article 14 de la Convention." »

La présente note et une note de la même teneur qui sera envoyée par le Ministère des relations extérieures de l'État plurinational de Bolivie constitueront un accord entre les deux pays.

Le Ministère des relations extérieures de la République du Pérou saisit cette occasion pour renouveler au Ministère des relations extérieures de la République de l'État plurinational de Bolivie les assurances de sa très haute considération.

[SIGNÉ]

Ministère des relations extérieures
État plurinational de Bolivie
La Paz

IV

ÉTAT PLURINATIONAL DE BOLIVIE

MINISTÈRE DES RELATIONS EXTÉRIEURES

La Paz, le 17 janvier 2017

GM-DGAJ-UAJ-Cs-94/2017

Le Ministère des relations extérieures de l'État plurinational de Bolivie présente ses compliments au Ministère des relations extérieures de la République du Pérou et déclare qu'il accepte la proposition de modification formulée dans sa note RE (GAB) nº 6/193 du 26 décembre 2016 portant sur le rétablissement et la modification de la Convention entre le Gouvernement de la République du Pérou et le Gouvernement de la République de Bolivie relative à la promotion et à la protection réciproques des investissements du 30 juillet 1993, conclue le 4 novembre 2016 par les notes GM-DGAJ-UAJ-Cs-2847/2016 de l'État plurinational de Bolivie et RE (GAB) nº 6/178 du Pérou, dont la teneur est la suivante :

[Voir note III]

Le Ministère des relations extérieures de l'État plurinational de Bolivie confirme par la présente la modification proposée dans la note RE (GAB) nº 6/193 du Ministère des relations extérieures du Pérou, avec effet ab initio, la note susmentionnée et la présente note de confirmation constituant un accord international entre les deux États.

Le Ministère des relations extérieures de l'État plurinational de Bolivie saisit cette occasion pour renouveler au Ministère des relations extérieures de la République du Pérou les assurances de sa très haute considération.

DAVID CHOQUEHUANCA CÉSPEDES
Ministère des relations extérieures

Son Excellence
Monsieur Ricardo V. Luna Mendoza
Ministre des relations extérieures
République du Pérou
Lima

No. 54652. Austria, Liechtenstein and Switzerland

AGREEMENT BETWEEN THE REPUBLIC OF AUSTRIA, THE SWISS CONFEDERATION AND THE PRINCIPALITY OF LIECHTENSTEIN ON CROSS-BORDER POLICE COOPERATION. VADUZ, 4 JUNE 2012 [*United Nations, Treaty Series, vol. 3200, I-54652.*]

ARRANGEMENT BETWEEN THE GOVERNMENT OF THE REPUBLIC OF AUSTRIA, THE GOVERNMENT OF THE SWISS CONFEDERATION AND THE GOVERNMENT OF THE PRINCIPALITY OF LIECHTENSTEIN ON THE IMPLEMENTATION OF ARTICLE 13, PARAGRAPH 1, LITERA (C) AND OF CHAPTER VI OF THE AGREEMENT BETWEEN THE REPUBLIC OF AUSTRIA, THE SWISS CONFEDERATION AND PRINCIPALITY OF LIECHTENSTEIN ON CROSS-BORDER POLICE COOPERATION (WITH ANNEX AND DECLARATIONS, 04 APRIL 2016 AND 14 APRIL 2016). LUXEMBOURG, 10 SEPTEMBER 2015

Entry into force: 1 August 2017, in accordance with article 10

Authentic text: German

Registration with the Secretariat of the United Nations: Austria, 10 August 2017

Nº 54652. Autriche, Liechtenstein et Suisse

ACCORD ENTRE LA RÉPUBLIQUE D'AUTRICHE, LA CONFÉDÉRATION SUISSE ET LA PRINCIPAUTÉ DU LIECHTENSTEIN RELATIF À LA COOPÉRATION POLICIÈRE TRANSFRONTALIÈRE. VADUZ, 4 JUIN 2012 [*Nations Unies, Recueil des Traités, vol. 3200, I-54652.*]

ARRANGEMENT ENTRE LE GOUVERNEMENT DE LA RÉPUBLIQUE D'AUTRICHE, LE GOUVERNEMENT DE LA CONFÉDÉRATION SUISSE ET LE GOUVERNEMENT DE LA PRINCIPAUTÉ DU LIECHTENSTEIN RELATIF À LA MISE EN ŒUVRE DE L'ALINÉA C) DU PARAGRAPHE 1 DE L'ARTICLE 13 ET DU CHAPITRE VI DE L'ACCORD ENTRE LA RÉPUBLIQUE D'AUTRICHE, LA CONFÉDÉRATION SUISSE ET LA PRINCIPAUTÉ DU LIECHTENSTEIN RELATIF À LA COOPÉRATION POLICIÈRE TRANSFRONTALIÈRE (AVEC ANNEXE ET DÉCLARATIONS, 4 AVRIL 2016 ET 14 AVRIL 2016). LUXEMBOURG, 10 SEPTEMBRE 2015

Entrée en vigueur : 1er août 2017, conformément à l'article 10

Texte authentique : allemand

Enregistrement auprès du Secrétariat de l'Organisation des Nations Unies : Autriche, 10 août 2017

[TEXT IN GERMAN – TEXTE EN ALLEMAND]

Vereinbarung zwischen der Regierung der Republik Österreich, der Regierung der Schweizerischen Eidgenossenschaft sowie der Regierung des Fürstentums Liechtenstein über die Durchführung von

Artikel 13 Abs. 1 lit. c und Kapitel VI des Vertrages zwischen der Republik Österreich, der Schweizerischen Eidgenossenschaft und dem Fürstentum Liechtenstein über die grenzüberschreitende polizeiliche Zusammenarbeit

„Durchführungsvereinbarung"

KAPITEL I
Allgemeines

Artikel 1
Anwendungsbereich

Zweck dieser Durchführungsvereinbarung ist es, die notwendigen rechtlichen, administrativen und technischen Details für die Zusammenarbeit im Rahmen der Verfolgung von Zuwiderhandlungen gegen Vorschriften des Straßenverkehrs gemäß Kapitel VI des Vertrages zwischen der Republik Österreich, der Schweizerischen Eidgenossenschaft und dem Fürstentum Liechtenstein über die grenzüberschreitende polizeiliche Zusammenarbeit (im Weiteren: "Vertrag"), geschehen zu Vaduz am 4. Juni 2012, in Übereinstimmung mit Art. 13 Abs. 1 lit. c iVm Abs. 4 sowie Art. 47 des Vertrages festzulegen.

Artikel 2
Anwendbare Rechtsvorschriften

Die Zusammenarbeit gemäß Art. 39 des Vertrages umfasst auch Zuwiderhandlungen im Bereich gebührenpflichtiger Parkzonen bzw. Kurzparkzonen.

KAPITEL II
Datenaustausch

Artikel 3
Elektronischer Fahrzeug- und Halterdatenaustausch

(1) Der Halterdatenaustausch gemäß Art. 13 Abs. 1 lit. c iVm Art. 40 Abs. 1 des Vertrages erfolgt automatisiert durch ein Batch-Anfrageverfahren im elektronischen Wege über die jeweiligen zuständigen nationalen Stellen im Rahmen des vereinbarten Systems über gesicherte Datenleitungen. Die Befugnisse der zuständigen nationalen Stellen richten sich nach dem geltenden Recht des betreffenden Vertragsstaates. Diese Stellen werden gemäß Art. 46 des Vertrages bei Hinterlegung der Ratifikationsurkunden oder im diplomatischen Wege wechselseitig kundgetan.

(2) Für Ermittlungen gemäß Art. 13 Abs. 1 lit. c iVm Art. 40 Abs. 1 des Vertrages gestatten die Vertragsstaaten den zuständigen nationalen Stellen der anderen Vertragsstaaten den automatisierten Abruf der nationalen Fahrzeug- und Halterdaten.

Artikel 4
Abruf der Daten

(1) Der Abruf erfolgt unter Angabe des vollständigen Kennzeichens sowie der Art der Zuwiderhandlung.

(2) Im Übrigen erfolgt ein Abruf nach Maßgabe der Bestimmungen des Vertrages sowie dem nationalen Recht des abrufenden Staates.

Artikel 5

Datenspiegel

Die für den elektronischen Austausch der Fahrzeug- und Halterdaten vorgesehenen Elemente sind in dem in der Anlage beigefügten Datenspiegel festgehalten.

Artikel 6

Datenschutz beim elektronischen Fahrzeug- und Halterdatenaustausch

(1) Die Vertragsstaaten ergreifen die erforderlichen Maßnahmen um sicherzustellen, dass der elektronische Informationsaustausch ohne den Austausch von Daten, die andere, nicht für die Zwecke dieser Zusammenarbeit verwendete Datenbanken betreffen, erfolgt.

(2) Der übermittelte Datensatz ist nach Maßgabe der Bestimmungen des nationalen Rechts, spätestens jedoch fünf Jahre nach rechtskräftigem Abschluss der Verfahren, für deren Zweck die Daten abgerufen wurden bzw. für die sie verwendet wurden, zu löschen.

(3) Die Suchanfragen müssen gemäß Art. 52 des Vertrages automationsunterstützt protokolliert werden. Die Protokolldaten haben zumindest den Anlass, Inhalt, die Empfangsstelle sowie den Zeitpunkt der Datenübermittlung zu umfassen.

KAPITEL III

Nachermittlungen und Vollstreckung

Artikel 7

Lenkerermittlung und Lenkerbefragung

(1) Die Zusammenarbeit gemäß Art. 40 Abs. 2 des Vertrages erfolgt im direkten Behördenverkehr.

(2) Die Lenkerermittlung bzw. Lenkerbefragung durch die zuständige Behörde des Zulassungsstaates erfolgt nach Maßgabe der nationalen Rechtsvorschriften.

(3) Die Lenkerermittlung bzw. Lenkerbefragung gemäß Art. 40 Abs. 2 des Vertrages erfolgt nur, wenn seitens der zuständigen Behörde des Deliktsstaates eine Lenkerermittlung bzw. Lenkerbefragung ergebnislos verlaufen ist.

Artikel 8

Vollstreckungshilfe

Der ersuchende Staat übermittelt das Vollstreckungsersuchen an die zuständige Stelle des Vollstreckungsstaates im direkten Behördenverkehr.

KAPITEL IV

Schlussbestimmungen

Artikel 9

Elektronischer Datenaustausch mit dem Fürstentum Liechtenstein

Der elektronische Austausch der Fahrzeug- und Halterdaten zwischen dem Fürstentum Liechtenstein und der Republik Österreich erfolgt über die zuständige schweizerische Stelle analog zum Informationsaustausch zwischen der Schweizerischen Eidgenossenschaft und der Republik Österreich.

Artikel 10

Inkrafttreten

(1) Diese Durchführungsvereinbarung tritt am ersten Tag des zweiten Monats nach dem Tag in Kraft, an dem alle Vertragsstaaten dem Depositär gemäß Art. 61 des Vertrages den Abschluss der für das Inkrafttreten der Durchführungsvereinbarung erforderlichen innerstaatlichen Verfahren schriftlich mitgeteilt haben.

(2) Diese Durchführungsvereinbarung tritt gleichzeitig mit dem Vertrag außer Kraft. Dasselbe gilt bei einer Kündigung des Vertrages für den kündigenden Vertragsstaat.

Geschehen zu Luxemburg am 10. September 2015 in drei Urschriften in deutscher Sprache.

Für die Regierung der Republik Österreich

Mikl-Leitner m.p.

Für die Regierung der Schweizerischen Eidgenossenschaft

Sommaruga m.p.

Für die Regierung des Fürstentums Liechtenstein

Zwiefelhofer m.p.

ANLAGE:

Datenspiegel
gemäß Artikel 5 der Durchführungsvereinbarung

Für die Anfrage/Suche gemäß Artikel 4 erforderliche Einzeldaten:

Posten	O/F (1)	Bemerkungen
Angaben zum Fahrzeug		
Zulassungsstaat / Anfrageland	O	FL, A oder CH
Amtliches Kennzeichen	O	Amtliches Kennzeichen (Kontrollschild) des jeweiligen Landes, welches für die Halterermittlung angefragt wird. Die Spezifikationen der Kennzeichen/Kontrollschilder werden in der technischen Vereinbarung definiert.
Angaben zum Delikt		
Deliktsstaat	O	
Bezugsdatum des Delikts	O	
Zweck der Suche	O	Zuwiderhandlung im Straßenverkehr (ev. auch als Fall-Code, z. B. EUCARIS-Fall-Code 13)

Infolge der Suche gemäß Artikel 4 bereitgestellte Einzeldaten:

Abschnitt I: Angaben zum Fahrzeug

Posten	O/F (1)	Bemerkungen
Amtliches Kennzeichen	O	
Fahrgestellnummer/FIN	F	
Zulassungsstaat / Anfrageland	O	
Marke	O O	
Handelsbezeichnung des Fahrzeugs	O	
EU-Fahrzeugklasse	O	
Fahrzeugfarbe	F	ev. auch als Farb-Code

Abschnitt II: Angaben zum Halter des Fahrzeugs

Posten	O/F (1)	Bemerkungen
Name des Zulassungsinhabers (Firma)	O	Für Nachnamen, Infixe, Titel usw. sind getrennte Felder zu verwenden und der Name ist in druckbarem Format anzugeben. Bei juristischen Personen sind die entsprechenden Angaben zu liefern.
Vorname	O	Für den/die Vornamen und Initialen sind getrennte Felder zu verwenden und der Name ist in druckbarem Format anzugeben.
Anschrift	O	Für Straße, Hausnummer und Zusatz, Postleitzahl, Wohnort, Wohnsitzstaat usw. sind getrennte Felder zu verwenden und die Anschrift ist in druckbarem Format anzugeben.
Geburtsdatum	O	
Rechtsperson	O	

(1) O = obligatorisch, wenn (im nationalen Register) vorhanden; F = fakultativ.

[TRANSLATION – TRADUCTION]

ARRANGEMENT BETWEEN THE GOVERNMENT OF THE REPUBLIC OF AUSTRIA, THE GOVERNMENT OF THE SWISS CONFEDERATION AND THE GOVERNMENT OF THE PRINCIPALITY OF LIECHTENSTEIN ON THE IMPLEMENTATION OF ARTICLE 13, PARAGRAPH 1, LITERA (C), AND OF CHAPTER VI OF THE AGREEMENT BETWEEN THE REPUBLIC OF AUSTRIA, THE SWISS CONFEDERATION AND PRINCIPALITY OF LIECHTENSTEIN ON CROSS-BORDER POLICE COOPERATION

"IMPLEMENTATION ARRANGEMENT"

CHAPTER I. GENERAL PROVISIONS

Article 1. Scope

The purpose of this Implementation Arrangement shall be to lay down the necessary legal, administrative and technical details for cooperation in handling traffic offences in accordance with Chapter VI of the Agreement between the Republic of Austria, the Swiss Confederation and the Principality of Liechtenstein on cross-border police cooperation done at Vaduz on 4 June 2021 (hereinafter referred to as "the Agreement"), in accordance with article 13, paragraph 1, litera (c), in conjunction with paragraph 4 and article 47 of that Agreement.

Article 2. Applicable law

Cooperation under article 39 of the Agreement shall extend to offences related to paid parking zones and short-term parking zones.

CHAPTER II. EXCHANGE OF DATA

Article 3. Electronic exchange of vehicle and owner data

(1) The exchange of owner data referred to in article 13, paragraph 1, litera (c), in conjunction with article 40, paragraph 1, of the Agreement shall be implemented by means of an automated electronic batch query procedure over secure data connections through the respective competent national offices under the agreed-upon system. The powers vested in each competent national office shall be governed by the laws of the Contracting Party in question. The Contracting Parties shall inform each other of those offices, which shall have been designated in accordance with article 46 of the Agreement, through the diplomatic channel.

(2) The Contracting Parties shall grant the competent national offices of the other Contracting Parties automated access to their national vehicle and owner data for identification

purposes, in accordance with article 13, paragraph 1, litera (c), in conjunction with article 40, paragraph 1, of the Agreement.

Article 4. Data access

(1) When accessing data, the complete licence plate and the nature of the offence shall be provided.

(2) In all other respects, data access shall be governed by the provisions of the Agreement and the domestic laws of the State accessing the data.

Article 5. Data templates

The elements required in the electronic exchange of vehicle and owner data are indicated in the data templates provided in the Annex.

Article 6. Data protection in the electronic exchange of vehicle and owner data

(1) The Contracting Parties shall take the measures required to ensure that, in the electronic exchange of information, no data from databases other than those used for the purposes of this cooperation are exchanged.

(2) The data transmitted shall be erased as required under domestic law, but in any case no later than five years after the closure of the case for which the data were accessed or used has taken legal effect.

(3) As required in article 52 of the Agreement, an automated record shall be kept of each transmittal request. Records shall provide, at a minimum, the reason for each data transmittal, and details pertaining to its content, the receiving office and the date and time.

CHAPTER III. FOLLOW-UP INVESTIGATIONS AND ENFORCEMENT

Article 7. Driver identification and interviews

(1) The authorities cooperating under article 40, paragraph 2, of the Agreement shall communicate with each other directly.

(2) The identification and/or interviewing of a driver by the competent authority of the State of registration shall be subject to domestic legal requirements.

(3) A driver may be identified and/or interviewed in accordance with article 40, paragraph 2, of the Agreement only if the competent authority of the State in which the offence was committed has been unsuccessful in identifying and/or interviewing the driver.

Article 8. Enforcement assistance

The requesting State shall submit its request for enforcement to the competent authority of the enforcing State through direct communication between the authorities.

CHAPTER IV. FINAL PROVISIONS

Article 9. Electronic exchange of data with the Principality of Liechtenstein

The electronic exchange of vehicle and owner data between the Principality of Liechtenstein and the Republic of Austria shall be implemented through the competent Swiss office in the same manner in which information is exchanged between Swiss Confederation and the Republic of Austria.

Article 10. Entry into force

(1) This Implementation Arrangement shall enter into force on the first day of the second month following the date on which all Contracting Parties have provided written notification to the depositary, in accordance with article 61 of the Agreement, confirming that the domestic procedures required for the entry into force of this Implementation Arrangement have been fulfilled.

(2) This Implementation Arrangement shall cease to have effect at the same time as the Treaty. In the event of termination by one of the Contracting Parties, the same shall apply in respect of the terminating Contracting Party.

DONE at Luxembourg on 10 September 2015 in three originals in German.

For the Government of the Republic of Austria:

MIKL-LEITNER, M.P.

For the Government of the Swiss Confederation:

SOMMARUGA, M.P.

For the Government of the Principality of Liechtenstein:

ZWIEFELHOFER, M.P.

ANNEX

Data templates as referred to in article 5 of the Implementation Arrangement

For requests and searches in accordance with article 4, the following data shall be provided:

Item	C/O (1)	Remarks.
Vehicle details		
State of registration/requesting country	C	FL, A or CH.
Licence plate	C	Licence plate issued by the respective country being requested to provide owner data. The specifications for licence plates are defined in the technical arrangement.
Details of the offence		
State in which the offence was committed	C	
Reference date for the offence	C	
Purpose of the search	C	Traffic offence (may be indicated with a code, e.g. EUCARIS code 13.

Data made available for searches in accordance with article 4:

Section I: Vehicle details

Item	C/O (1)	Remarks.
Licence plate	C	
Vehicle identification number (VIN)	O	
State of registration / requesting country	C	
Make	C	
Commercial name of the vehicle	C	
EU vehicle class	C	
Vehicle colour	O	May be given as a colour code.

Section II: Vehicle owner details

Item	C/O ([1])	Remarks.
Name of the registration holder (company)	C	For the family name, infixes, titles, etc., separate fields shall be used, and the name shall be given in printable format. For legal persons, the relevant details shall be provided.
Given name	C	Separate fields shall be used for the given name(s) and initials, and the name shall be given in printable format.
Address	C	Separate fields shall be used for street, house number and suffix, postal code, place of residence, country of residence, etc., and the address shall be given in printable format.
Date of birth	C	
Legal person	C	

([1]) C: Compulsory where available (in the national register); O: Optional.

[TRANSLATION – TRADUCTION]

ARRANGEMENT ENTRE LE GOUVERNEMENT DE LA RÉPUBLIQUE D'AUTRICHE, LE GOUVERNEMENT DE LA CONFÉDÉRATION SUISSE ET LE GOUVERNEMENT DE LA PRINCIPAUTÉ DU LIECHTENSTEIN RELATIF À L'APPLICATION DE L'ALINÉA C) DU PARAGRAPHE 1 DE L'ARTICLE 13 ET DU CHAPITRE VI DE L'ACCORD ENTRE LA RÉPUBLIQUE D'AUTRICHE, LA CONFÉDÉRATION SUISSE ET LA PRINCIPAUTÉ DU LIECHTENSTEIN RELATIF À LA COOPÉRATION POLICIÈRE TRANSFRONTALIÈRE

« ARRANGEMENT DE MISE EN ŒUVRE »

CHAPITRE I. DISPOSITIONS GÉNÉRALES

Article premier. Champ d'application

Le présent Arrangement de mise en œuvre a pour objet de fixer les détails juridiques, administratifs et techniques nécessaires à la coopération en matière de traitement des infractions routières conformément au chapitre VI de l'Accord entre la République d'Autriche, la Confédération suisse et la Principauté du Liechtenstein relatif à la coopération policière transfrontalière conclu à Vaduz le 4 juin 2021 (ci-après dénommé « l'Accord »), conformément à l'alinéa c) du paragraphe 1 de l'article 13 dudit Accord, conjointement au paragraphe 4 de son article 47.

Article 2. Droit applicable

La coopération au titre de l'article 39 de l'Accord couvre les infractions relatives aux zones de stationnement payant et aux zones de stationnement de courte durée.

CHAPITRE II. ÉCHANGE DE DONNÉES

Article 3. Échange électronique de données sur les véhicules et leurs propriétaires

1) L'échange de données sur les propriétaires de véhicules visé à l'alinéa c) du paragraphe 1 de l'article 13 de l'Accord, conjointement au paragraphe 1 de son article 40, est mis en œuvre au moyen d'une procédure électronique automatisée d'interrogation par lots sur des connexions de données sécurisées par l'intermédiaire des bureaux nationaux compétents respectifs dans le cadre du système convenu. Les pouvoirs dévolus à chaque bureau national compétent sont régis par la législation de la Partie contractante en question. Les Parties contractantes s'informent

mutuellement, par la voie diplomatique, des bureaux qui ont été désignés conformément à l'article 46 de l'Accord.

2) Les Parties contractantes accordent aux bureaux nationaux compétents des autres Parties contractantes un accès automatisé à leurs données nationales sur les véhicules et les propriétaires à des fins d'identification, conformément à l'alinéa c) du paragraphe 1 de l'article 13 de l'Accord, conjointement au paragraphe 1 de son article 40.

Article 4. Accès aux données

1) Lors de l'accès aux données, la plaque d'immatriculation complète et la nature de l'infraction doivent être fournies.

2) À tous autres égards, l'accès aux données est régi par les dispositions de l'Accord et par le droit interne de l'État qui accède aux données.

Article 5. Modèles de données

Les éléments requis pour l'échange électronique des données relatives aux véhicules et à leurs propriétaires sont indiqués dans les modèles de données figurant en annexe.

Article 6. Protection des données dans l'échange électronique des données relatives aux véhicules et à leurs propriétaires

1) Les Parties contractantes prennent les mesures nécessaires pour que, dans l'échange électronique de renseignements, aucune donnée provenant de bases de données autres que celles utilisées aux fins de la présente coopération ne soit échangée.

2) Les données transmises sont effacées dans les conditions prévues par le droit interne, mais en tout état de cause au plus tard cinq ans après que la clôture de l'affaire pour laquelle les données ont été consultées ou utilisées a pris effet juridiquement.

3) Comme le prévoit l'article 52 de l'Accord, chaque demande de transmission fait l'objet d'un enregistrement automatisé. Les enregistrements comprennent, au minimum, la raison de chaque transmission de données, son contenu, le bureau destinataire, la date et l'heure.

CHAPITRE III. SUIVI DES ENQUÊTES ET APPLICATION DE LA LOI

Article 7. Identification des conducteurs et interrogatoires

1) Les autorités qui coopèrent en vertu du paragraphe 2 de l'article 40 de l'Accord communiquent directement entre elles.

2) L'identification et/ou les interrogatoires des conducteurs par l'autorité compétente de l'État d'enregistrement sont soumis aux exigences du droit interne de cet État.

3) Un conducteur ne peut être identifié et/ou interrogé conformément au paragraphe 2 de l'article 40 de l'Accord que si l'autorité compétente de l'État dans lequel l'infraction a été commise n'a pas réussi à identifier et/ou à interroger le conducteur.

Article 8. Assistance en matière d'application de la loi

L'État requérant soumet sa demande d'exécution à l'autorité compétente de l'État d'exécution par communication directe entre autorités.

CHAPITRE IV. DISPOSITIONS FINALES

Article 9. Échange électronique de données avec la Principauté du Liechtenstein

L'échange électronique des données sur les véhicules et leurs propriétaires entre la Principauté du Liechtenstein et la République d'Autriche se fait par l'intermédiaire du bureau suisse compétent, tout comme l'échange de renseignements entre la Confédération suisse et la République d'Autriche.

Article 10. Entrée en vigueur

1) Le présent Arrangement de mise en œuvre entre en vigueur le premier jour du deuxième mois suivant la date à laquelle toutes les Parties contractantes ont notifié par écrit au dépositaire, conformément à l'article 61 de l'Accord, que les procédures internes requises pour l'entrée en vigueur du présent Arrangement de mise en œuvre ont été accomplies.

2) Le présent Arrangement de mise en œuvre cesse de produire ses effets en même temps que le Traité. En cas de dénonciation par l'une des Parties contractantes, les mêmes modalités s'appliquent à l'égard de la Partie contractante qui dénonce.

FAIT à Luxembourg, le 10 septembre 2015, en deux exemplaires originaux en langue allemande.

Pour le Gouvernement de la République d'Autriche :

MIKL-LEITNER

Pour le Gouvernement de la Confédération suisse :

SOMMARUGA

Pour le Gouvernement de la Principauté du Liechtenstein :

ZWIEFELHOFER

ANNEXE

Modèles de données visés à l'article 5 de l'Arrangement de mise en œuvre

Pour les demandes et les recherches conformément à l'article 4, les données suivantes doivent être fournies :

Objet	O/F (1)	Remarques
Renseignements sur le véhicule		
État d'enregistrement/pays demandeur	O	FL, A ou CH
Plaque d'immatriculation	O	Plaque d'immatriculation délivrée par le pays auquel on demande de fournir les données sur le propriétaire. Les spécifications des plaques d'immatriculation sont définies dans les modalités techniques.
Renseignements sur l'infraction		
État dans lequel l'infraction a été commise	O	
Date de référence de l'infraction	O	
Objectif de la recherche	O	Infraction au code de la route (peut être indiquée par un code, comme EUCARIS 13)

Données mises à disposition pour des recherches conformément à l'article 4 :

Section I. Renseignements sur le véhicule

Objet	O/F (1)	Remarques
Plaque d'immatriculation	O	
Numéro d'immatriculation du véhicule	F	
État d'enregistrement/pays demandeur	O	
Fabrication	O	
Nom commercial du véhicule	O	
Classe de véhicule UE	O	
Couleur du véhicule	F	Peut être indiquée sous la forme d'un code de couleur

Section II. Renseignements sur le propriétaire du véhicule

Objet	O/F [1]	Remarques
Nom du titulaire de l'enregistrement (société)	O	Pour le nom de famille, les infixes, les titres, etc., des champs séparés doivent être utilisés et le nom doit être indiqué en format imprimable. Pour les personnes morales, des données pertinentes doivent être fournies.
Nom de famille	O	Des champs séparés doivent être utilisés pour le ou les prénom(s) et les initiales, et le nom doit être donné en format imprimable.
Adresse	O	Des champs séparés sont utilisés pour la rue, le numéro et le suffixe de la maison, le code postal, le lieu de résidence, le pays de résidence, etc., et l'adresse est indiquée en format imprimable.
Date de naissance	O	
Personne morale	O	

[1] O : obligatoire si disponible (dans le registre national) ; F : facultatif.

No. 54669. Multilateral

MINAMATA CONVENTION ON MERCURY. KUMAMOTO, 10 OCTOBER 2013

RATIFICATION (WITH DECLARATION)

Austria

Date: 12 June 2017

Date of effect: 10 September 2017

Registration with the Secretariat of the United Nations: ex officio, 16 August 2017

Nº 54669. Multilatéral

CONVENTION DE MINAMATA SUR LE MERCURE. KUMAMOTO, 10 OCTOBRE 2013

RATIFICATION (AVEC DÉCLARATION)

Autriche

Date : 12 juin 2017

Date de prise d'effet : 10 septembre 2017

Enregistrement auprès du Secrétariat de l'Organisation des Nations Unies : d'office, 16 août 2017

Declaration:

Déclaration :

[TEXT IN ENGLISH – TEXTE EN ANGLAIS]

"The Republic of Austria declares in accordance with Article 25 paragraph 2 of the Convention that, with regard to any dispute concerning the interpretation or application of this Convention, it recognizes both of means of dispute settlement mentioned in paragraph 2 as compulsory in relation to any party accepting the same obligation."

[TRANSLATION – TRADUCTION]

La République d'Autriche déclare, conformément au paragraphe 2 de l'article 25 de la Convention, que, à l'égard de tout différend concernant l'interprétation ou l'application de la présente Convention, elle reconnaît les deux moyens de règlement des différends mentionnés au paragraphe 2 comme obligatoires à l'égard de toute Partie acceptant la même obligation.

RATIFICATION

Brazil

Deposit of instrument with the Secretary-General of the United Nations: 8 August 2017

Date of effect: 6 November 2017

Registration with the Secretariat of the United Nations: ex officio, 16 August 2017

RATIFICATION

Brésil

Dépôt de l'instrument auprès du Secrétaire général de l'Organisation des Nations Unies : 8 août 2017

Date de prise d'effet : 6 novembre 2017

Enregistrement auprès du Secrétariat de l'Organisation des Nations Unies : d'office, 16 août 2017

RATIFICATION (WITH DECLARATION)

Czech Republic

Deposit of instrument with the Secretary-General of the United Nations: 19 June 2017

Date of effect: 17 September 2017

Registration with the Secretariat of the United Nations: ex officio, 16 August 2017

RATIFICATION (AVEC DÉCLARATION)

République tchèque

Dépôt de l'instrument auprès du Secrétaire général de l'Organisation des Nations Unies : 19 juin 2017

Date de prise d'effet : 17 septembre 2017

Enregistrement auprès du Secrétariat de l'Organisation des Nations Unies : d'office, 16 août 2017

Declaration:

Déclaration :

[TEXT IN CZECH – TEXTE EN TCHÈQUE]

Prozkoumavše tuto úmluvu a vědouce, že Parlament České republiky s ní souhlasí, schvalujeme a potvrzujeme ji a v souladu s článkem 30 odst. 5 Minamatské úmluvy o rtuti Česká republika prohlašuje, že pro ni vstupuje kterákoli změna přílohy Úmluvy v platnost pouze po uložení její ratifikační listiny, listiny o přijetí, schválení nebo přístupu vztahující se k této změně.

[TRANSLATION – TRADUCTION][1]

… in accordance with paragraph 5 of Article 30 of the Minamata Convention on Mercury, the Czech Republic declares that any amendment to an annex to the Convention shall enter into force for the Czech Republic only upon the deposit of its instrument of ratification, acceptance, approval or accession in respect thereto.

[1] Translation provided by the Government of the Czech Republic – Traduction fournie par le Gouvernement de la République tchèque.

[TRANSLATION – TRADUCTION]

... conformément au paragraphe 5 de l'article 30 de la Convention de Minamata sur le mercure, la République tchèque déclare que tout amendement à une annexe à la Convention n'entre en vigueur pour la République tchèque qu'après le dépôt de son instrument de ratification, d'acceptation, d'approbation ou d'adhésion à celui-ci.

TERRITORIAL EXCLUSION IN RESPECT OF GREENLAND AND THE FAROE ISLANDS

Denmark

Notification deposited with the Secretary-General of the United Nations: 18 May 2017

Registration with the Secretariat of the United Nations: ex officio, 16 August 2017

EXCLUSION TERRITORIALE À L'ÉGARD DU GROENLAND ET DES ÎLES FÉROÉ

Danemark

Dépôt de la notification auprès du Secrétaire général de l'Organisation des Nations Unies : 18 mai 2017

Enregistrement auprès du Secrétariat de l'Organisation des Nations Unies : d'office, 16 août 2017

ACCESSION

El Salvador

Deposit of instrument with the Secretary-General of the United Nations: 20 June 2017

Date of effect: 18 September 2017

Registration with the Secretariat of the United Nations: ex officio, 16 August 2017

ADHÉSION

El Salvador

Dépôt de l'instrument auprès du Secrétaire général de l'Organisation des Nations Unies : 20 juin 2017

Date de prise d'effet : 18 septembre 2017

Enregistrement auprès du Secrétariat de l'Organisation des Nations Unies : d'office, 16 août 2017

ACCESSION

Estonia

Deposit of instrument with the Secretary-General of the United Nations: 21 June 2017

Date of effect: 19 September 2017

Registration with the Secretariat of the United Nations: ex officio, 16 August 2017

ADHÉSION

Estonie

Dépôt de l'instrument auprès du Secrétaire général de l'Organisation des Nations Unies : 21 juin 2017

Date de prise d'effet : 19 septembre 2017

Enregistrement auprès du Secrétariat de l'Organisation des Nations Unies : d'office, 16 août 2017

ACCEPTANCE

Finland

Deposit of instrument with the Secretary-General of the United Nations: 1 June 2017

Date of effect: 30 August 2017

Registration with the Secretariat of the United Nations: ex officio, 16 August 2017

RATIFICATION

France

Deposit of instrument with the Secretary-General of the United Nations: 15 June 2017

Date of effect: 13 September 2017

Registration with the Secretariat of the United Nations: ex officio, 16 August 2017

RATIFICATION (WITH DECLARATIONS)

Iran (Islamic Republic of)

Deposit of instrument with the Secretary-General of the United Nations: 16 June 2017

Date of effect: 14 September 2017

Registration with the Secretariat of the United Nations: ex officio, 16 August 2017

ACCEPTATION

Finlande

Dépôt de l'instrument auprès du Secrétaire général de l'Organisation des Nations Unies : 1er juin 2017

Date de prise d'effet : 30 août 2017

Enregistrement auprès du Secrétariat de l'Organisation des Nations Unies : d'office, 16 août 2017

RATIFICATION

France

Dépôt de l'instrument auprès du Secrétaire général de l'Organisation des Nations Unies : 15 juin 2017

Date de prise d'effet : 13 septembre 2017

Enregistrement auprès du Secrétariat de l'Organisation des Nations Unies : d'office, 16 août 2017

RATIFICATION (AVEC DÉCLARATIONS)

Iran (République islamique d')

Dépôt de l'instrument auprès du Secrétaire général de l'Organisation des Nations Unies : 16 juin 2017

Date de prise d'effet : 14 septembre 2017

Enregistrement auprès du Secrétariat de l'Organisation des Nations Unies : d'office, 16 août 2017

[TEXT IN ENGLISH – TEXTE EN ANGLAIS]

"… pursuant to Article 30, paragraph 5 of the Convention, the Islamic Republic of Iran hereby declares that any amendment to an annex to the Convention shall enter into force for the Islamic Republic of Iran only upon the deposit of its instrument of ratification, acceptance, approval or accession with respect thereto…"

"Consistent with its principal policy of protecting and promoting the environment and human health, the Islamic Republic of Iran has ratified the Minamata Convention on Mercury.

Fulfilling the obligations enshrined in the Convention is a clear duty of all relevant stakeholders including governmental or non-governmental; the Ministry of Foreign Affairs as the National Focal Point and the Organization of Protection of Environment as the National Authority of the Convention are assigned with the task of handling and monitoring the national implementation of the Convention.

It is the understanding of the Islamic Republic of Iran that implementation of the Convention is subject to providing the developing countries with sustainable, adequate and accessible financial support, technical assistance, technology transfer as well as capacity building and proper training which are recognized in the Articles 13 and 14 of the Convention as part of responsibilities of all parties, specifically the developed country parties.

The Islamic Republic of Iran is of the view that full and accurate implementation of the said articles is as necessary as other articles of the Convention and non-implementation of the said Articles may raise the issue of compliance.

Should the above assistance and support fail to be adequate, timely and sustainable; the extension of the exemptions will be a necessity.

The Islamic Republic of Iran would like to encourage all countries that have not yet done so, in particular developed countries to join the Convention and emphasizes that the whole international community should work together to realize the accepted principle of 'Common But Differentiated Responsibilities'."

[TRANSLATION – TRADUCTION]

… en application du paragraphe 5 de l'article 30 de la Convention, la République islamique d'Iran déclare que tout amendement à une annexe n'entrera en vigueur à son égard qu'après le dépôt de son instrument de ratification, d'acceptation ou d'approbation dudit amendement ou d'adhésion à celui-ci.

Conformément à sa politique de protection et de promotion de l'environnement et de la santé humaine, la République islamique d'Iran a ratifié la Convention de Minamata sur le mercure.

Toutes les parties prenantes, y compris les organisations gouvernementales et non gouvernementales, doivent s'acquitter des obligations énoncées dans la Convention; le Ministère des affaires étrangères, en tant que correspondant national, et l'Organisation de protection de l'environnement, en tant qu'autorité nationale compétente en ce qui concerne la Convention, sont tenus de gérer et de contrôler l'application de la Convention au niveau national.

La République islamique d'Iran comprend qu'aux fins de l'application de la Convention, il doit être fourni aux pays en développement une assistance et un appui dans les domaines financier et technique et dans ceux du transfert de technologies, du renforcement des capacités et de la formation qui soit durable, suffisant et accessible, conformément aux articles 13 et 14 de la Convention, dans le cadre des responsabilités qui incombent à toutes les parties, en particulier aux pays développés qui sont parties à la Convention.

La République islamique d'Iran est d'avis que l'application intégrale et exacte de ces articles est aussi nécessaire que celle d'autres articles de la Convention et que la non-application de ces articles peut soulever la question du non-respect des dispositions.

Si l'assistance et l'appui susmentionnés ne sont pas suffisants, rapides et durables, il faudra proroger les exemptions.

La République islamique d'Iran tient à encourager tous les pays qui ne l'ont pas encore fait, en particulier les pays développés, à adhérer à la Convention et souligne que l'ensemble de la communauté internationale doit œuvrer de concert pour concrétiser le principe accepté de « responsabilités communes mais différenciées ».

RATIFICATION (WITH DECLARATION)

Jamaica

Deposit of instrument with the Secretary-General of the United Nations: 19 July 2017

Date of effect: 17 October 2017

Registration with the Secretariat of the United Nations: ex officio, 16 August 2017

RATIFICATION (AVEC DÉCLARATION)

Jamaïque

Dépôt de l'instrument auprès du Secrétaire général de l'Organisation des Nations Unies : 19 juillet 2017

Date de prise d'effet : 17 octobre 2017

Enregistrement auprès du Secrétariat de l'Organisation des Nations Unies : d'office, 16 août 2017

Declaration:

[TEXT IN ENGLISH – TEXTE EN ANGLAIS]

"... any amendment to an Annex to the Convention shall enter into force for Jamaica only upon the deposit of its instrument of ratification, acceptance, approval or accession with respect thereto."

Déclaration :

[TRANSLATION – TRADUCTION]

... tout amendement à une annexe à la Convention n'entrera en vigueur pour la Jamaïque qu'après le dépôt de son instrument de ratification, d'acceptation, d'approbation ou d'adhésion à celui-ci.

ACCESSION

Kiribati

Deposit of instrument with the Secretary-General of the United Nations: 28 July 2017

Date of effect: 26 October 2017

Registration with the Secretariat of the United Nations: ex officio, 16 August 2017

ADHÉSION

Kiribati

Dépôt de l'instrument auprès du Secrétaire général de l'Organisation des Nations Unies : 28 juillet 2017

Date de prise d'effet : 26 octobre 2017

Enregistrement auprès du Secrétariat de l'Organisation des Nations Unies : d'office, 16 août 2017

RATIFICATION

Latvia

Deposit of instrument with the Secretary-General of the United Nations: 20 June 2017

Date of effect: 18 September 2017

Registration with the Secretariat of the United Nations: ex officio, 16 August 2017

RATIFICATION

Lettonie

Dépôt de l'instrument auprès du Secrétaire général de l'Organisation des Nations Unies : 20 juin 2017

Date de prise d'effet : 18 septembre 2017

Enregistrement auprès du Secrétariat de l'Organisation des Nations Unies : d'office, 16 août 2017

RATIFICATION

Niger

Deposit of instrument with the Secretary-General of the United Nations: 9 June 2017

Date of effect: 7 September 2017

Registration with the Secretariat of the United Nations: ex officio, 16 August 2017

RATIFICATION

Niger

Dépôt de l'instrument auprès du Secrétaire général de l'Organisation des Nations Unies : 9 juin 2017

Date de prise d'effet : 7 septembre 2017

Enregistrement auprès du Secrétariat de l'Organisation des Nations Unies : d'office, 16 août 2017

RATIFICATION

Palau

Deposit of instrument with the Secretary-General of the United Nations: 21 June 2017

Date of effect: 19 September 2017

Registration with the Secretariat of the United Nations: ex officio, 16 August 2017

RATIFICATION

Palaos

Dépôt de l'instrument auprès du Secrétaire général de l'Organisation des Nations Unies : 21 juin 2017

Date de prise d'effet : 19 septembre 2017

Enregistrement auprès du Secrétariat de l'Organisation des Nations Unies : d'office, 16 août 2017

RATIFICATION (WITH DECLARATIONS)

Republic of Moldova

Deposit of instrument with the Secretary-General of the United Nations: 20 June 2017

Date of effect: 18 September 2017

Registration with the Secretariat of the United Nations: ex officio, 16 August 2017

RATIFICATION (AVEC DÉCLARATIONS)

République de Moldova

Dépôt de l'instrument auprès du Secrétaire général de l'Organisation des Nations Unies : 20 juin 2017

Date de prise d'effet : 18 septembre 2017

Enregistrement auprès du Secrétariat de l'Organisation des Nations Unies : d'office, 16 août 2017

Declarations:

Déclarations :

[TEXT IN MOLDOVAN – TEXTE EN MOLDAVE]

„În conformitate cu articolul 25 punctul 2 din Convenție, Republica Moldova acceptă ambele mijloace de soluționare a litigiilor menționate în acest punct ca fiind obligatorii în relațiile cu orice parte care acceptă aceeași obligație."

„În conformitate cu articolul 30 punctul 5 din Convenție, orice amendament la o anexă va intra în vigoare pentru Republica Moldova numai după depunerea instrumentului său de ratificare, acceptare, aprobare sau aderare cu privire la acest amendament."

[TRANSLATION – TRADUCTION][1]

In accordance with Article 25, paragraph 2 of the Convention, the Republic of Moldova accepts both means of dispute settlement referred to in this paragraph as compulsory in relation to any party accepting the same obligation.

In accordance with Article 30, paragraph 5 of the Convention, any amendment of an annex shall enter into force for the Republic of Moldova only after the deposit of its instrument of ratification, acceptance, approval or accession with respect thereto.

[TRANSLATION – TRADUCTION]

Conformément au paragraphe 2 de l'article 25 de la Convention, la République de Moldova accepte comme obligatoires les deux moyens de règlement des différends mentionnés audit paragraphe à l'égard de toute Partie acceptant la même obligation.

Conformément au paragraphe 5 de l'article 30 de la Convention, tout amendement à une annexe n'entrera en vigueur pour la République de Moldova qu'après le dépôt de son instrument de ratification, d'acceptation ou d'approbation dudit amendement ou d'adhésion à celui-ci.

ACCESSION

Rwanda

Deposit of instrument with the Secretary-General of the United Nations: 29 June 2017

Date of effect: 27 September 2017

Registration with the Secretariat of the United Nations: ex officio, 16 August 2017

ADHÉSION

Rwanda

Dépôt de l'instrument auprès du Secrétaire général de l'Organisation des Nations Unies : 29 juin 2017

Date de prise d'effet : 27 septembre 2017

Enregistrement auprès du Secrétariat de l'Organisation des Nations Unies : d'office, 16 août 2017

RATIFICATION

Slovakia

Deposit of instrument with the Secretary-General of the United Nations: 31 May 2017

Date of effect: 29 August 2017

Registration with the Secretariat of the United Nations: ex officio, 16 August 2017

RATIFICATION

Slovaquie

Dépôt de l'instrument auprès du Secrétaire général de l'Organisation des Nations Unies : 31 mai 2017

Date de prise d'effet : 29 août 2017

Enregistrement auprès du Secrétariat de l'Organisation des Nations Unies : d'office, 16 août 2017

[1] Translation provided by the Government of the Republic of Moldova – Traduction fournie par le Gouvernement de la République de Moldova.

RATIFICATION

Slovenia

Deposit of instrument with the Secretary-General of the United Nations: 23 June 2017

Date of effect: 21 September 2017

Registration with the Secretariat of the United Nations: ex officio, 16 August 2017

RATIFICATION

Sri Lanka

Deposit of instrument with the Secretary-General of the United Nations: 19 June 2017

Date of effect: 17 September 2017

Registration with the Secretariat of the United Nations: ex officio, 16 August 2017

ACCESSION

St. Kitts and Nevis

Deposit of instrument with the Secretary-General of the United Nations: 24 May 2017

Date of effect: 22 August 2017

Registration with the Secretariat of the United Nations: ex officio, 16 August 2017

RATIFICATION

Syrian Arab Republic

Deposit of instrument with the Secretary-General of the United Nations: 26 July 2017

Date of effect: 24 October 2017

Registration with the Secretariat of the United Nations: ex officio, 16 August 2017

RATIFICATION

Slovénie

Dépôt de l'instrument auprès du Secrétaire général de l'Organisation des Nations Unies : 23 juin 2017

Date de prise d'effet : 21 septembre 2017

Enregistrement auprès du Secrétariat de l'Organisation des Nations Unies : d'office, 16 août 2017

RATIFICATION

Sri Lanka

Dépôt de l'instrument auprès du Secrétaire général de l'Organisation des Nations Unies : 19 juin 2017

Date de prise d'effet : 17 septembre 2017

Enregistrement auprès du Secrétariat de l'Organisation des Nations Unies : d'office, 16 août 2017

ADHÉSION

Saint-Kitts-et-Nevis

Dépôt de l'instrument auprès du Secrétaire général de l'Organisation des Nations Unies : 24 mai 2017

Date de prise d'effet : 22 août 2017

Enregistrement auprès du Secrétariat de l'Organisation des Nations Unies : d'office, 16 août 2017

RATIFICATION

République arabe syrienne

Dépôt de l'instrument auprès du Secrétaire général de l'Organisation des Nations Unies : 26 juillet 2017

Date de prise d'effet : 24 octobre 2017

Enregistrement auprès du Secrétariat de l'Organisation des Nations Unies : d'office, 16 août 2017

ACCESSION (WITH DECLARATION)

Thailand

Deposit of instrument with the Secretary-General of the United Nations: 22 June 2017

Date of effect: 20 September 2017

Registration with the Secretariat of the United Nations: ex officio, 16 August 2017

ADHÉSION (AVEC DÉCLARATION)

Thaïlande

Dépôt de l'instrument auprès du Secrétaire général de l'Organisation des Nations Unies : 22 juin 2017

Date de prise d'effet : 20 septembre 2017

Enregistrement auprès du Secrétariat de l'Organisation des Nations Unies : d'office, 16 août 2017

Declaration:

Déclaration :

[TEXT IN ENGLISH – TEXTE EN ANGLAIS]

"... any amendment to an annex to the Convention shall enter into force only upon the deposit of [the Government of the Kingdom of Thailand's] instrument of ratification, acceptance, approval or accession in accordance with Article 30 paragraph 5."

[TRANSLATION – TRADUCTION]

... tout amendement à une annexe à la Convention n'entrera en vigueur qu'après le dépôt de l'instrument de ratification, d'acceptation, d'approbation ou d'adhésion du Gouvernement du Royaume de Thaïlande conformément au paragraphe 5 de l'article 30.

APPROVAL

Viet Nam

Deposit of instrument with the Secretary-General of the United Nations: 23 June 2017

Date of effect: 21 September 2017

Registration with the Secretariat of the United Nations: ex officio, 16 August 2017

APPROBATION

Viet Nam

Dépôt de l'instrument auprès du Secrétaire général de l'Organisation des Nations Unies : 23 juin 2017

Date de prise d'effet : 21 septembre 2017

Enregistrement auprès du Secrétariat de l'Organisation des Nations Unies : d'office, 16 août 2017

PROCÈS-VERBAL OF RECTIFICATION OF THE MINAMATA CONVENTION ON MERCURY. NEW YORK, 26 DECEMBER 2014

Entry into force: 26 December 2014

Authentic texts: Arabic, Chinese and Spanish

Registration with the Secretariat of the United Nations: ex officio, 16 August 2017

PROCÈS-VERBAL DE RECTIFICATION DE LA CONVENTION DE MINAMATA SUR LE MERCURE. NEW YORK, 26 DÉCEMBRE 2014

Entrée en vigueur : 26 décembre 2014

Textes authentiques : arabe, chinois et espagnol

Enregistrement auprès du Secrétariat de l'Organisation des Nations Unies : d'office, 16 août 2017

مكان التغيير	النص العربي الأصلي	التصويبات المقترح إدخالها على النص العربي
المادة 13-3	"تشجِّع المصادر المتعددة الأطراف والإقليمية والثنائية للمساعدة المالية والتقنية ولبناء القدرات ونقل التكنولوجيا، بصفة عاجلة، على تعزيز ..."	"تشجِّع المصادر المتعددة الأطراف والإقليمية والثنائية للمساعدة المالية والتقنية ولبناء القدرات ونقل التكنولوجيا، بصفة عاجلة، على تعزيز ..."
المادة 19-1 (ب)	"نماذج رصد تمثيلي للمناطق الجغرافية لمستويات الزئبق ومركبات الزئبق لدى الفئات السكانية الضعيفة وفي الأوساط البيئية، بما في ذلك ..."	"نماذج ورصد تمثيلي للمناطق الجغرافية لمستويات الزئبق ومركبات الزئبق لدى الفئات السكانية الضعيفة وفي الأوساط البيئية، بما في ذلك ..."
الصف الثاني من الجدول الوارد في الجزء الأول	"القواطع والمرحلات، ما عدا قناطر قياس السعة أو الفقد العالية الدقة والقواطع والمرحلات اللاسلكية ذات الذبذبة العالية، وأجهزة المراقبة والتحكُّم، على ألا يزيد ما تحتوي عليه من الزئبق عن 20 ملغ لكل قنطرة أو مفتاح أو مرحِّل"	"القواطع والمرحلات، ما عدا قناطر قياس السعة أو الفقد العالية الدقة والقواطع والمرحلات اللاسلكية ذات الذبذبة العالية في أجهزة المراقبة والتحكُّم، على ألا يزيد ما تحتوي عليه من الزئبق عن 20 ملغ لكل قنطرة أو مفتاح أو مرحِّل"
الصف الرابع من الجدول الوارد في الجزء الأول من المرفق ألف	"مصابيح الفلورسنت الأفقية لأغراض الإنارة العامة"	"مصابيح الفلورسنت الخطية لأغراض الإنارة العامة"
الصف السادس من الجدول الوارد في الجزء الأول من المرفق ألف	"الزئبق في مصابيح الفلورسنت ذات المهبط البارد للوحات العرض الإلكترونية"	"الزئبق في مصابيح الفلورسنت ذات المهبط البارد ومصابيح الفلورسنت ذات الإلكترود الخارجي للوحات العرض الإلكترونية"
الصف الثامن من الجدول الوارد في الجزء الأول من المرفق ألف	"مبيدات الآفات، والمبيدات الأحيائية، ومواد تطهير الجروح"	"مبيدات الآفات، والمبيدات الأحيائية، والمطهرات الموضعية للجروح"

[TEXT IN ARABIC – TEXTE EN ARABE]

مكان التغيير	*النص العربي الأصلي*	*التصويبات المقترح إدخالها على النص العربي*
المادة 1-4	"لا يسمح أي طرف، من خلال اتخاذه تدابير مناسبة، بتصنيع أو استيراد أو تصدير المنتجات المضاف إليها الزئبق المدرجة في الجزء الأول من المرفق ألف بعد انقضاء موعد الإنهاء التدريجي المحدَّد لتلك المنتجات، ..."	"لا يسمح أي طرف، من خلال اتخاذه تدابير مناسبة، بتصنيع أو استيراد أو تصدير المنتجات المضاف إليها الزئبق المُدرجة في الجزء الأول من المرفق ألف بعد انقضاء الموعد المحدَّد للتخلص التدريجي من تلك المنتجات، ..."
المادة 7-5	"يحول كل طرف دون تطوير أي مرفق يستخدِم أي عملية تصنيع أخرى يُستخدَم فيها الزئبق أو مركّبات الزئبق عن عمد ..."	"يحول كل طرف دون تطوير أي مرفق يستخدِم أي عملية تصنيع أخرى يُستخدَم فيها الزئبق أو مركّبات الزئبق عن عمد ..."
المادة 8-5	"تُشجَّع الأطراف على تبادل المعلومات بشأن التطوّرات التكنولوجية الجديدة ذات الصلة ..."	"تُشجَّع الأطراف على تبادل المعلومات بشأن التطوّرات التكنولوجية الجديدة ذات الصلة ..."
المادة 4-8	"فيما يتعلق بالمصادر الجديدة لكل طرف، يشترط الطرف استخدام أفضل التقنيات المتاحة وأفضل الممارسات البيئية لضبط الانبعاثات وتخفيضها، وحيثما أمكن، في أقرب وقت ممكن من الناحية العملية، ..."	"فيما يتعلق بالمصادر الجديدة لكل طرف، يشترط الطرف استخدام أفضل التقنيات المتاحة وأفضل الممارسات البيئية لضبط الانبعاثات، وحيثما أمكن، تخفيضها في أقرب وقت ممكن من الناحية العملية، ..."
المادة 5-8	"يدرج كل طرف، فيما يتعلق بمصادره القائمة، في أي خطة وطنية تدبيراً أو أكثر من التدابير التالية وأن ينفِّذ ما يلي، ..."	"يدرج كل طرف، فيما يتعلق بمصادره القائمة، في أي خطة وطنية تدبيراً أو أكثر من التدابير التالية وأن ينفِّذها، ..."
المادة 6-9	"يضع كل طرف قائمة جرد للإطلاقات من المصادر ذات الصلة، وذلك في غضون خمسة أعوام بعد تاريخ دخول الاتفاقية حيِّز النفاذ بالنسبة له، وأن يحتفظ بها بعد ذلك".	"يضع كل طرف قائمة جرد للإطلاقات من المصادر ذات الصلة في أقرب وقت ممكن، وذلك في غضون خمسة أعوام بعد تاريخ دخول الاتفاقية حيِّز النفاذ بالنسبة له، وأن يحتفظ بها بعد ذلك".
المادة 4-12	"تشجَّع الأطراف على التعاون في وضع استراتيجيات وتنفيذ أنشطة لتحديد المواقع الملوَّثة بالزئبق وتقييمها وتحديد أولوياتها وإدارتها والقيام، وفقاً للمقتضى، بتطهيرها".	"تشجَّع الأطراف على التعاون في وضع استراتيجيات وتنفيذ أنشطة لتحديد المواقع الملوَّثة بالزئبق وتقييمها وتحديد أولوياتها وإدارتها والقيام، وفقاً للمقتضى، بتطهيرها".

[TEXT IN CHINESE – TEXTE EN CHINOIS]

	Authentic Chinese text/Texte authentique chinois	Proposal of correction to the authentic Chinese text/ Proposition de correction du texte authentique chinois
Article 6(8)	八、尽管有第一款的规定，任何国家或区域经济一体化组织均不得在附件A或附件B中所列相关产品或工艺的淘汰日期到期后5年之后登记注册任何豁免，除非一个或多个缔约方就该产品或工艺一直享有业经登记的豁免，而且业已依照第六款的规定获准延期。在此种情形中，一国或一经济一体化组织可按第一条第一款和第二款中所给出的时间段就该产品或工艺登记某项豁免。此种豁免应当自相关的淘汰日期起10年后失效。	八、尽管有第一款的规定，任何国家或区域经济一体化组织均不得在附件A或附件B中所列相关产品或工艺的淘汰日期到期后5年之后登记注册任何豁免，除非一个或多个缔约方就该产品或工艺一直享有业经登记的豁免，而且业已依照第六款的规定获准延期。在此种情形中，一国或一**区域**经济一体化组织可按第一条第一款和第二款中所给出的时间段就该产品或工艺登记某项豁免。此种豁免应当自相关的淘汰日期起10年后失效。

[TEXT IN SPANISH – TEXTE EN ESPAGNOL]

	Authentic Spanish text/Texte authentique espagnol	Proposal of correction to the authentic Spanish text/Proposition de correction du texte authentique espagnol
Article 8 (4 and 5)	4) En lo relativo a las nuevas fuentes, cada Parte exigirá el uso de las mejores técnicas disponibles y las mejores prácticas ambientales para controlar y, cuando sea viable, reducir las emisiones lo antes posible, pero en cualquier caso antes de que transcurran cinco años desde la entrada en vigor del Convenio para esa Parte. 5) En lo relativo a las fuentes existentes, cada Parte incluirá una o más de las siguientes medidas en cualquier plan nacional, y las aplicará lo antes posible, pero en cualquier caso antes de que transcurran diez años desde la fecha de entrada en vigor del Convenio para ella, teniendo en cuenta las circunstancias nacionales y la viabilidad económica y técnica, así como la asequibilidad, de las medidas:	4) En lo relativo a las nuevas fuentes, cada Parte exigirá el uso de las mejores técnicas disponibles y las mejores prácticas ambientales para controlar y, cuando sea viable, reducir las emisiones lo antes **factible**, pero en cualquier caso antes de que transcurran cinco años desde la entrada en vigor del Convenio para esa Parte. 5) En lo relativo a las fuentes existentes, cada Parte incluirá una o más de las siguientes medidas en cualquier plan nacional, y las aplicará lo antes **factible**, pero en cualquier caso antes de que transcurran diez años desde la fecha de entrada en vigor del Convenio para ella, teniendo en cuenta las circunstancias nacionales y la viabilidad económica y técnica, así como la asequibilidad, de las medidas:
Article 19 (2)	Cuando corresponda, las Partes deberán aprovechar las redes de vigilancia y los programas de investigación existentes al realizar las actividades definidas en el párrafo 1.	Cuando corresponda, las Partes **deberían** aprovechar las redes de vigilancia y los programas de investigación existentes al realizar las actividades definidas en el párrafo 1.

PROCÈS-VERBAL OF RECTIFICATION OF THE MINAMATA CONVENTION ON MERCURY. NEW YORK, 9 APRIL 2015

PROCÈS-VERBAL DE RECTIFICATION DE LA CONVENTION DE MINAMATA SUR LE MERCURE. NEW YORK, 9 AVRIL 2015

Entry into force: 9 April 2015

Authentic text: Spanish

Registration with the Secretariat of the United Nations: ex officio, 16 August 2017

Entrée en vigueur : 9 avril 2015

Texte authentique : espagnol

Enregistrement auprès du Secrétariat de l'Organisation des Nations Unies : d'office, 16 août 2017

[TEXT IN SPANISH – TEXTE EN ESPAGNOL]

	Authentic text/Texte authentique espagnol	Proposal of correction to the authentic Spanish text/Proposition de correction du texte authentique espagnol
Article 6 (1)	Cualquier Estado u organización de integración económica regional podrá inscribirse para una o más exenciones a partir de las fechas de eliminación que figuran en el anexo A y en el anexo B, en adelante denominadas "exenciones", notificándolo por escrito a la Secretaría:	Cualquier Estado u organización de integración económica regional podrá inscribirse para una o más exenciones **del cumplimiento** de las fechas de eliminación que figuran en el anexo A y en el anexo B, en adelante denominadas "exenciones", notificándolo por escrito a la Secretaría:

PROCÈS-VERBAL OF RECTIFICATION OF THE MINAMATA CONVENTION ON MERCURY. NEW YORK, 27 APRIL 2017

PROCÈS-VERBAL DE RECTIFICATION DE LA CONVENTION DE MINAMATA SUR LE MERCURE. NEW YORK, 27 AVRIL 2017

Entry into force: 27 April 2017

Authentic text: Chinese

Registration with the Secretariat of the United Nations: ex officio, 16 August 2017

Entrée en vigueur : 27 avril 2017

Texte authentique : chinois

Enregistrement auprès du Secrétariat de l'Organisation des Nations Unies : d'office, 16 août 2017

[TEXT IN CHINESE – TEXTE EN CHINOIS]

No.	Reference / Référence	Authentic Chinese text / Texte authentique chinois	Proposal of corrections to the authentic Chinese text / Proposition de corrections au texte authentique chinois
1	Preamble	*序言* 意识到特别是在发展中国家，因人口中的脆弱群体接触汞而引发的各种健康问题，尤其是对妇女和儿童以及通过**她**们给子孙后代造成的健康问题，	*序言* 意识到特别是在发展中国家，因人口中的脆弱群体接触汞而引发的各种健康问题，尤其是对妇女和儿童以及通过**他**们给子孙后代造成的健康问题，
2	Article 3.1 (b)	*第三条第一款第二项* “汞化合物”系指…**朱砂矿石**和硫化贡。	*第三条第一款第二项* “汞化合物”系指…**朱砂**和硫化汞。
3	Article 3.8	*第三条第八款* 任何缔约方均不得允许从它将提供书面同意的非缔约方进口汞，除非该非缔约方已提供了**证书**，表明所涉及的汞并非来自第三款或第五款第二项规定不允许使用的来源。	*第三条第八款* 任何缔约方均不得允许从它将提供书面同意的非缔约方进口汞，除非该非缔约方已提供了**证明**，表明所涉及的汞并非来自第三款或第五款第二项规定不允许使用的来源。
4	Article 3.12	*第三条第十二款* 缔约方大会应当在其第一次会议上就本条文、特别是其中**第五条第一款**、第六和第八款提供进一步指导，并应确定并通过**第六条第二款**和第八款所述证明书应列明的相关内容。	*第三条第十二款* 缔约方大会应当在其第一次会议上就本条文、特别是其中**第五款第一项**、第六和第八款提供进一步指导，并应确定并通过**本条第六款第二项**和第八款所述证明书应列明的相关内容。
5	Article 4.9 (c)	*第四条第九款第三项* 缔约方**获得**在经济上和技术上均为可行的无汞替代品的**情况**，同时亦考虑到其所涉环境和人体健康风险和惠益。	*第四条第九款第三项* 缔约方在经济上和技术上均为可行的无汞替代品的**可获得性**，同时亦考虑到其所涉环境和人体健康风险和惠益。
6	Article 5.6	*第五条第六款* 每一缔约方均不得在本公约生效之日前不存在的使用附件 B 所列生产工艺的设施中使用汞或汞化合物。	*第五条第六款* 每一缔约方均不得在本公约**对其**生效之日前不存在的使用附件B所列生产工艺的设施中使用汞或汞化合物。

7	Article 6.8	*第六条第八款* …一国或一区域经济一体化组织可按**第一条第一款和第二款**中所给出的时间段就该产品或工艺登记某项豁免。	*第六条第八款* …一国或一区域经济一体化组织可按**本条第一款第一项和第二项**中所给出的时间段就该产品或工艺登记某项豁免。
8	Article 8.5	*第八条第五款* 对于现有来源而言，每一缔约方均应在**在**实际情况允许时尽快、但不迟于自本公约开始对其生效之日起10年内……同时考虑到其国家的具体国情、以及这些措施在经济和技术上的可行性及其可负担性；	*第八条第五款* 对于现有来源而言，每一缔约方均应在实际情况允许时尽快、但不迟于自本公约开始对其生效之日起10年内……同时考虑到其国家的具体国情、以及这些措施在经济和技术上的可行性及其可负担性**：**
9	Article 8.9 (a)	*第八条第九款第一项* 缔约方可依照**第二条第二款**制定的标准；	*第八条第九款第一项* 缔约方可依照**本条第二款第二项**制定的标准；
10	Article 9.2 (d)	*第九条第二款第四项* “重大改造”是指对某一相关来源进行的、导致其**排放**量大幅增加的改造，其中不包括因对其副产品进行的回收而导致的释放量的任何改变。应当由所涉缔约方认定所涉改造是否属于重大改造；	*第九条第二款第四项* “重大改造”是指对某一相关来源进行的、导致其**释放**量大幅增加的改造，其中不包括因对其副产品进行的回收而导致的释放量的任何改变。应当由所涉缔约方认定所涉改造是否属于重大改造；
11	Article 11.3 (b)	*第十一条第三款第二项* 仅为缔约方在本公约下获准的某种允许用途、或为依照**第三条第一款**进行环境无害化处置而得到回收、再循环、再生或直接再使用；	*第十一条第三款第二项* 仅为缔约方在本公约下获准的某种允许用途、或为依照**本条第三款第一项**进行环境无害化处置而得到回收、再循环、再生或直接再使用；
12	Article 11.4	*第十一条第四款* 在酌情审查和更新**第三条第一款**所述及的指导准则时，缔约方大会应寻求与《巴塞尔公约》的相关机构密切合作。	*第十一条第四款* 在酌情审查和更新**本条第三款第一项**所述及的指导准则时，缔约方大会应寻求与《巴塞尔公约》的相关机构密切合作。
13	Article 13.3	*第十三条第三款* 迫切鼓励各方通过多边、区域和双边来源**提供技术、财政**和技术援助、以及能力建设和技术转让…	*第十三条第三款* 迫切鼓励各方通过多边、区域和双边来源**提供财政**和技术援助、以及能力建设和技术转让…

14	Article 13.9	*第十三条第九款* 为了本公约之目的，**第六条第二款**中所提及的国际方案应当在缔约方大会的指导下运作并对缔约方大会负责。	*第十三条第九款* 为了本公约之目的，**本条第六款第二项**中所提及的国际方案应当在缔约方大会的指导下运作并对缔约方大会负责。
15	Article 19.1 (g)	*第十九条第一款第七项* 无汞产品和工艺技术经济可得性方面的信息与研究，以及减少和监测汞和汞化合物**释放**的最佳可得技术和最佳环境实践方面的信息与研究。	*第十九条第一款第七项* 无汞产品和工艺技术经济可得性方面的信息与研究，以及减少和监测汞和汞化合物**排放和释放**的最佳可得技术和最佳环境实践方面的信息与研究。
16	Annex A	*附件A* **开始禁止产品生产、进口或出口的时间(淘汰日期)**	*附件A* **在此淘汰日期之后不允许产品生产、进口或出口**
17	Annex E, Part I, Article 8	*附件E，第一部分，第八条* 争端各方和仲裁员均有义务保护其在仲裁庭审理案件期间秘密收到的任何资料或文件的**机密性**。	*附件E，第一部分，第八条* 争端各方和仲裁员均有义务保护其在仲裁庭审理案件期间秘密收到的任何资料或文件的**保密性**。
18	Annex E, Part I, Article 9	*附件E，第一部分，第九条* …仲裁庭的费用应由争端**所涉各方**平均分担。	*附件E，第一部分，第九条* …仲裁庭的费用应由争端**各方**平均分担。
19	Annex E, Part II, Article 7	*附件E，第二部分，第七条* …当事各方及调解委员会成员有义务**对**委员会议事期间**所**收到的**机密材料**或文件**保守机密**。	*附件E，第二部分，第七条* …当事各方及调解委员会成员有义务**保护其在**委员会议事期间**秘密**收到的**任何资料**或文件**的保密性**。